American Educational Rese
Volume 54, Number 6—Decem

The *American Educational Research Journal* (*AERJ*) is the flagship journal of the American Educational Research Association, featuring articles that advance the empirical, theoretical, and methodological understanding of education and learning. It publishes original peer-reviewed analyses that span the field of education research across all subfields and disciplines and all levels of analysis. It also encourages submissions across all levels of education throughout the life span and all forms of learning. *AERJ* welcomes submissions of the highest quality, reflecting a wide range of perspectives, topics, contexts, and methods, including interdisciplinary and multidisciplinary work.

American Educational Research Journal (ISSN 0002-8312) (J589) is published bimonthly—in February, April, June, August, October, and December—on behalf of the American Educational Research Association, 1430 K Street NW, Washington, DC 20005, by SAGE Publishing, 2455 Teller Road, Thousand Oaks, CA 91320. Periodicals postage paid at Thousand Oaks, California, and at additional mailing offices. POSTMASTER: Send address changes to AERA Membership Department, 1430 K Street NW, Washington, DC 20005.

Manuscript Submission: Authors should submit manuscripts electronically via SAGE Track: http://mc.manuscriptcentral.com/aerj. For more information regarding submission guidelines, please see the Manuscript Submission section of the *American Educational Research Journal*'s website: http://aerj.aera.net.

Member Information: American Educational Research Association (AERA) member inquiries, member renewal requests, changes of address, and membership subscription inquiries should be addressed to the AERA Membership Department, 1430 K Street NW, Washington, DC 20005; fax (202) 238-3250; phone (202) 238-3200; e-mail: members@aera.net; website: http://www.aera.net. AERA annual membership dues are $180 (Regular Members), $180 (Affiliate Members), $140 (International Affiliates), and $55 (Graduate Students and Student Affiliates). **Claims:** Claims for undelivered copies must be made no later than six months following month of publication. Beyond six months and at the request of the American Educational Research Association, the publisher will supply replacement issues when losses have been sustained in transit and when the reserve stock permits.

Subscription Information: All nonmember subscription inquiries, orders, back-issue requests, claims, and renewals should be addressed to SAGE Publishing, 2455 Teller Road, Thousand Oaks, CA 91320; telephone (800) 818-SAGE (7243) and (805) 499-0721; fax (805) 375-1700; e-mail journals@sagepub.com; http://journals.sagepub.com. **Subscription Price:** Institutions $1,154; Individuals $81. For all customers outside the Americas, please visit http://www.sagepub.co.uk/customerCare.nav for information. **Claims (nonmembers):** Claims for undelivered copies must be made no later than six months following month of publication. The publisher will supply replacement issues when losses have been sustained in transit and when the reserve stock will permit.

Copyright Permission: To request permission for republishing, reproducing, or distributing material from this journal, please visit the desired article on the SAGE Journals website (journals.sagepub.com) and click "Permissions." For additional information, please see www.sagepub.com/journalspermissions.nav.

Advertising and Reprints: Current advertising rates and specifications may be obtained by contacting the advertising coordinator in the Thousand Oaks office at (805) 410-7763 or by sending an e-mail to advertising@sagepub.com. To order reprints, please e-mail reprint@sagepub.com. Acceptance of advertising in this journal in no way implies endorsement of the advertised product or service by SAGE, the journal's affiliated society(ies), or the journal editor(s). No endorsement is intended or implied. SAGE reserves the right to reject any advertising it deems as inappropriate for this journal.

Change of Address: Six weeks' advance notice must be given when notifying of change of address. Please send the old address label along with the new address to the AERA Membership Department (address above) to ensure proper identification. Please specify name of journal.

American Educational Research Journal
December 2017, Vol. 54, No. 6, pp. 1011–1047
DOI: 10.3102/0002831217714321
© *2017 AERA. http://aerj.aera.net*

Pathways to Educational Success Among Refugees: Connecting Locally and Globally Situated Resources

Sarah Dryden-Peterson
Harvard University
Negin Dahya
University of Washington
Elizabeth Adelman
Harvard University

This study identifies pathways to educational success among refugees. Data are from an original online survey of Somali diaspora and in-depth qualitative interviews with Somali refugee students educated in the Dadaab refugee camps of Kenya. This research builds on Bronfenbrenner's ecological model to consider both the locally and globally situated nature of resources across refugees' ecosystems. Analysis examines the nature and content of student-identified supports and their perceived influence on access to and persistence in school as well as the mediating role of technology. The findings suggest consideration of both locally situated relationships and globally situated relationships as critical educational supports. Implications include leveraging naturally occurring virtual relationships to support educational success of refugees and other young people who are physically isolated from access to needed supports in their local region.

SARAH DRYDEN-PETERSON is an associate professor of education at the Harvard Graduate School of Education, 6 Appian Way, Gutman Library 457, Cambridge, MA 02138, USA; e-mail: *sarah_dryden-peterson@gse.harvard.edu*. Her research focuses on education in armed conflict and the ways in which learning, pedagogies, and relationships may alter trajectories of conflict for nation-states and individuals.

NEGIN DAHYA is an assistant professor at the Information School at the University of Washington. Her research explores how social and cultural contexts shape digital media production, social media participation, and technology use for girls and women.

ELIZABETH ADELMAN is an advanced doctoral candidate at the Harvard Graduate School of Education. Her research explores the experiences of teachers working in conflict-affected settings and how they understand their educational, social, and emotional obligations toward their refugee students.

KEYWORDS: refugee, globalization, academic support, comparative education, migration

Introduction

"It's always really difficult to move on when you can't see the light at the end of the tunnel," said Mahad,[1] in describing his trajectory through education. Mahad is a Somali refugee living in the Dadaab refugee camps, clustered in a small stretch of desert in eastern Kenya. There are not many places on earth where "the light at the end of the tunnel" is more difficult to see than in the Dadaab camps. Together, these camps have grown over the past three decades from 90,000 to 463,000 residents, almost all of whom have fled ongoing conflict in Somalia (United Nations High Commissioner for Refugees [UNHCR], 2015). As the largest refugee camp complex in the world, the Dadaab camps also represent the largest population of Somalis outside of Somalia (Hammond et al., 2011). In these camps, the net enrollment rate for secondary school is only 2.3%, and the Gender Parity Index is .38, meaning that there are only 38 girls enrolled for every 100 boys (UNHCR, 2014).

Refugees like Mahad are some of the most educationally marginalized children in the world. Indeed, more than half of the 58 million children who remain out of school globally live in conflict-affected settings (UNESCO, 2015). Refugees are defined by the 1951 Convention Relating to the Status of Refugees as individuals who have fled across an international border due to a well-founded fear of persecution (UNHCR, 2010). In 2015, the number of refugees globally was 21.3 million, the highest level since World War II; more than half were children under the age of 18 (UNHCR, 2016). Eighty-six percent of these refugees live in exile in neighboring host countries (UNHCR, 2016), usually characterized by already overstretched education systems. Only 1% of refugees are resettled to countries such as the United States and Canada (UNHCR, 2016), with highly resourced education systems.[2] Globally, about half of refugees live in cities and half in refugee camps, although the numbers vary substantially between countries (UNHCR, 2016).

The conflicts that cause individuals to become refugees are not short-lived and have far-reaching implications for education. In 2014, in 33 conflicts globally, the average length of displacement for refugees was 25 years (UNHCR & Global Monitoring Report, 2016). As a result, millions of children globally spend their entire childhoods engulfed in conflict with limited opportunities for education. Global commitments to Education for All and the Sustainable Development Goals will not be realized unless the educational needs of refugee children are met. Moreover, education for children in conflict settings is essential to ending existing conflict, rebuilding after conflict, and preventing conflict in the first place (Davies, 2004).

Mahad has lived in a setting of conflict his entire life: first in war-torn Somalia until the age of 6 and then in the Dadaab refugee camps up to the time of data collection, at the age of 22. Unlike the vast majority of his peers, Mahad was able to go to school. He completed both his primary and secondary education in the Dadaab camps, is now a secondary school math teacher, and dreams of "serving my people in the future . . . by help[ing] the community and promot[ing] education . . . to transform society." Students like Mahad, who live in conflict settings, have navigated challenges, and have been successful in their education, can provide lessons about the barriers to education in these contexts but also about the pathways to success.

In this article, we seek to identify pathways to educational success among refugees who live in the most common site of exile: neighboring host countries with fragile political, economic, and educational institutions. We do so by analyzing the educational trajectories of students who have been successful in their education, which, for the purposes of this analysis, we define as having graduated from secondary school. In this research, we find that refugee students identify multiple layers of interconnected supports that have enabled their success in education. They focus specifically on relational supports, in particular relationships with international agency staff, family, teachers, and peers. We analyze the nature and content of these supports and the ways in which the supports influence refugee access and persistence in school. Further, we explore the ways in which technology mediates refugee students' access to and experience of both locally and globally situated supports.

The contributions of this empirical work are both theoretical and practical. From the experiences of refugee children who have been successful in education, we build on Bronfenbrenner's (1979) ecological model. In particular, we present a theoretical model of globally situated, virtual relationships; their connection to locally situated relationships; and the social capital that accrues through both. The findings are relevant for policy and practice as well, particularly in the promotion of educational opportunities for refugees and other marginalized children, by United Nations or government agencies, nongovernmental organizations (NGOs), and communities, including families, teachers, and students themselves. While this work focuses on the experiences of Somali refugees, it has relevance theoretically and practically not only for children in conflict-affected nation-states but also for children experiencing more localized conflict, social instability, and lack of equal educational opportunities who similarly struggle to chart pathways to educational success.

Theoretical and Conceptual Frames: Charting Educational Pathways in Refugee Contexts

Given processes of flight, most refugees arrive in exile with limited resources. The nature of contemporary conflict, which targets civilians, means those who become refugees are among the most marginalized economically, politically, and educationally. Outside of their home communities, displaced from their national education systems, and in environments of little human and social capital, refugees generally have few resources and confront great challenges (Harrell-Bond, 1986; Zetter, 2015). In these contexts, how do refugee students chart educational pathways? To create a theoretical framework for understanding the educational pathways of refugees, we draw on concepts of social capital and local/global interactions and situate associated supports and resources within an ecological systems model.

Supports for Educational Success Among Refugees

Academic support, such as guidance, tutoring, writing support, exam preparation, and course selection, can play an important role in educational persistence and success, particularly for marginalized children and young people. These types of academic support are especially useful when they are embedded within relationships that also provide social support, which includes having people to talk to and feeling part of a group, and emotional support, which includes managing stress and feeling content, self-confident, and encouraged (Lawson & Lawson, 2013; Roorda, Koomen, Spilt, & Oort, 2011).

Locally situated relationships that could provide this academic support are limited in refugee settings, where literacy rates are low (UNHCR & Global Monitoring Report, 2016) and possibilities for contact with more educationally diverse national populations are limited given the isolation of camps. In marginalized communities, virtual support, mediated by technology, can be as effective and sustainable as face-to-face mentorship (Single & Single, 2005), provided there is frequent contact (Purcell, 2004) and the nature of that contact feels more like a relationship than a formal program (Spencer, 2007). Could virtual, globally situated supports enable educational persistence and success for refugees?

The formation of relationships—both face-to-face and virtual—that could provide educational supports to refugee students is importantly informed by literature on social capital. Social capital is the value of relationships and trust among people that enables productive activity (Bourdieu, 1986; Putnam, 2000). Bonding social capital describes social ties *within* communities that are bounded, for example, by geography or class. The resulting benefits, while tangible, are often limited in scope, especially in marginalized communities. They include, for example, small cash loans, transportation, or emergency child care. Bridging social capital, on the other hand, enables people to extend their opportunities through social ties built *across* communities, which often span differences of geography or class.

Bridging relationships that connect refugee students to individuals with higher levels of education, for example, might enable refugee students' success in school through connections to a scholarship opportunity, guidance on expectations for academic writing, extra help with complex math, or understanding the "rules of the game" for education. This kind of bridging social capital can be more fruitful than bonding social capital as it extends opportunities, but it is also much more challenging to build and maintain. Bridging relationships are more successful and sustainable when those involved share some characteristics, such as country of origin or gender, even when they also bridge differences, such as education level or class (Higgins & Kram, 2001; Putnam, 2000). In this way, relationships can be most effective when they stretch comfort zones and cross some lines of difference but contain enough commonalities to foster the development of a relationship.

Two possible, little understood sources of bridging social capital may derive from the unique situation of refugees. These sources of support are globally situated. We define global not in dichotomy to local but instead draw on Tsing's (2005) concept of "traveling." This concept focuses our inquiry on interactions and connections among ideas and resources that travel between the refugee camp and other spaces. Tsing helpfully notes that these interactions and connections are often made in fragments as individuals collect and piece together ideas and resources from a wide array of sources. She further analyzes how the origins of these traveling relationships disrupt conventional views of resource flows. They do not, she writes, begin—or end—in "imagined world centers such as New York, Tokyo, or Geneva" but instead circulate through informal networks with origins and destinations in all geographies (p. 271). We seek to understand if and how refugee students engage in "traveling" through globally situated interactions and connections and how these processes may foster access to bridging social capital. In this way, while many scholars are concerned with *institutions* of globalization, we focus here on the globalization of *relationships*.

The first opportunity for globally situated social capital is connected to international humanitarian organizations that work in refugee camp contexts. In this case, global resources travel physically to the refugee camp. The United Nations High Commissioner for Refugees is the organization mandated with the physical, political, and social protection of refugees; delivery of humanitarian assistance such as food, shelter, and water; and provision of education. In camps, UNHCR staff members work alongside staff from local and international NGOs. These UNHCR and NGO staff members are national (from the host country) and international (from outside the host country); they are usually highly educated, and their experiences, information, knowledge, and connections travel to the camp with them, bringing globally situated resources that are different from those already available in the camp. The second possible source of globally situated social capital involves refugees' connections to people from the same country of origin who have migrated elsewhere, in which case the traveling of resources is virtual. Economic and social ties between diaspora and their countries of origin are substantial (Levitt & Jaworsky, 2007), including increasingly in conflict settings (Bernal, 2006; Horst, 2006; Lindley, 2009). Yet aside from remittances to pay school fees, the traveling of educational resources, especially in the form of relationships, remains understudied.

This study explores the ways in which refugee students engage with locally and globally situated resources in charting their pathways to education. An ecological systems model, explained in the following section, provides a framework for understanding educational social capital and the ways it may travel to and from refugee camps.

Refugee Ecosystems: Locally and Globally Situated

In Bronfenbrenner's ecological model of human development, individuals operate within nested systems, including the microsystem (family, peer group, school), the mesosystem (interrelationships between microsystems, such as between parents and school), the exosystem (institutions and practices that affect the individual), the macrosystem (social and cultural norms), and the chronosystem (historical and environmental transitions over time) (Bronfenbrenner, 1979). Armed conflict disrupts an individual's ecosystem, acting as "an ecologic shock of destabilization" (Boothby, 2008, p. 502), separating families and peers; shifting institutional, social, and cultural contexts; and creating a culture of violence that generally interrupts supports for children. Research on refugee children's physical and mental health draws heavily on Bronfenbrenner's model to explain positive and negative developmental outcomes. When resources are compromised within any of the systems, the risk of poor developmental outcomes for children increases. Conversely, when resources are in place across the systems, refugee children can achieve more positive physical and mental health outcomes (see e.g., Betancourt, Meyers-Ohki, Charrow, & Tol, 2013; Porter & Haslam, 2005).

When resources are in place across the systems, refugee students may also achieve more positive outcomes in education. We posit that how refugee children and young people rebuild resources across their ecosystems in the face of the "ecological shock" of conflict, flight, and life in refugee camps may be usefully informed by their locally and globally situated positions, as described previously. This unique situatedness of refugees as related to Bronfenbrenner's model is explored in the following section and summarized in Table 1.

Bronfenbrenner (1992) describes microsystems as "a pattern of activities, roles, and interpersonal relations experienced by a developing person in a given face-to-face setting" (p. 227). These relationships are uniquely influential as the individual has agency over them and acts to contribute to their construction and maintenance. Local, face-to-face microsystem relationships in a refugee camp context may have different characteristics than in the refugee's country of origin or nearby national contexts in the host

Table 1
Refugees' Ecological Systems Framework

| System | Bronfenbrenner | Refugees | |
		Locally situated	Globally situated
Chronosystem	Historical/ environmental transitions and time, for example, displacement	Chronosystem is connected to collective memory, for example, of Somalia	Chronosystem is connected to deterritorialization, for example, collective experience of displacement, not geographically bounded
Macrosystem	Social and cultural norms, for example, right to education for boys and girls	Macrosystem is informed by country of origin and host country, for example, lack of history of girls going to school	Macrosystem is informed by global consensus norms, for example, universal right to education (Convention on the Rights of the Child)
Exosystem	Institutions and practices that affect the individual but over which individual has no control, for example, media, parental employment	Exosystem is part of a foreign nation-state, for example, laws in Kenya that isolate refugees geographically and prohibit refugee employment and freedom of movement	Exosystem is part of a global system of international humanitarian aid, for example, education governed by UNHCR standards
Mesosystem	Interrelationships between microsystems, for example, school-family relationships	Mesosystem involves an unfamiliar education system, for example, national system of Kenya	Mesosystem involves an unfamiliar education system, for example, UNHCR and NGO oversight
Microsystem	Interpersonal relationships in which individual has agency, for example, with teachers, peers, family members, other community members	Microsystem relationships mediated by geographic isolation, for example, separated from family members, lack of contact with national peers	Microsystem relationships mediated by technology and extend to global actors, for example, Somali peers in Canada via ICTs, international aid workers

Note. UNHCR = United Nations High Commissioner for Refugees; NGO = nongovernment organization; ICTs = information and communications technology.

country. For example, given that refugees are geographically isolated in camps in marginalized regions of host countries, they often have limited or no contact with nationals. On the other hand, given migration patterns and diasporic interactions (Horst, 2006), these same refugees may be globally situated to have virtual connections in other parts of the world. In this way, they may have access to traveling microsystem relationships not initially conceptualized by Bronfenbrenner. While not face-to-face, these connections can share similar characteristics of being frequent, influential, and highly personal relationships over which individuals have control (Li & Lee, 2013; Preece, 2000).

The mesosystem comprises interrelationships between an individual's microsystems. For children, the mesosystem importantly involves relationships between home, school, and community. These interrelationships for refugees may be limited. Refugees attend schools that are locally situated within the national education system of the host country, globally situated within structures of UNHCR and NGO partners, or a combination of local and global management and oversight (Dryden-Peterson, 2016). Viewed in terms of bridging social capital, refugee families may not share many characteristics on which relationships can easily be built within these unfamiliar educational systems.

The exosystem, which includes institutions and practices that affect the individual but over which the individual has no control, may be similarly bifurcated for refugees, including along locally and globally situated dimensions. By fleeing across an international border, refugees enter a foreign nation-state and are subject to its institutions and policies. For example, in Kenya, refugees live in geographically isolated settings, lack freedom of movement, and are prohibited from accessing employment outside of refugee camps (Lindley, 2011). Yet refugee education policies and practices are globally informed, with ideas and resources traveling from outside the camp through globally situated actors. The lack of resources embedded in the locally situated exosystem may lie in contrast to what could be viewed as an augmentation of resources in the globally situated exosystem of educational institutions and staff.

The macrosystem is the social and cultural norms comprised of "belief systems, resources, hazards, life styles, opportunity structures, life course options, and patterns of social interchange" (Bronfenbrenner, 1992, p. 228). For refugees, these macrosystems are informed by belief systems carried with them from countries of origin as well as prevailing attitudes and ideologies in the host country. Given the actors involved in camps, the macrosystem might also be described as globally situated, reflecting global consensus norms such as a universal right to education expressed in the Convention on the Rights of the Child (CRC). This right to education might be seen as a resource embedded within the globally situated macrosystem of refugees, although it may also come into conflict with norms in the country of origin or exile, such as non-ratification of the CRC by Somalia or a lack of strong support for girls' attendance in schools.

The chronosystem involves historical and environmental transitions and, unlike the other systems, involves the dimension of time. Bronfenbrenner (1992) argues that these transitions over time "alter the existing relation between person and environment" (p. 201). By definition, refugees have experienced a transition of environment, in this case in their displacement from Somalia to Kenya. Malkki (1992) describes the importance of the "deterritorialized nation" (p. 35), emphasizing, like Safran (1991), that similar to most diaspora, refugees "retain a collective memory, vision, or myth about their original homeland" (p. 83). Malkki also documents the re-territorialization of the nation in exile for Burundian refugees in Tanzania. The ongoing creation, and re-creation, of historical narratives of nation in an evolving environmental context may define the chronosystem for refugees and influence how relationships, both globally and locally situated, are constituted and reconstituted.

In examining how refugee students chart successful pathways through education, this study explores the locally and globally situated nature of refugee students' ecosystems. Rather than a reified nested system, our work draws attention to the ways in which refugee students engage in the kind of traveling Tsing (2005) describes, locating resources across these systems, and the kinds of social capital that accrue through resulting relationships.

Context of the Study

Somali Refugees and the Dadaab Camps of Kenya

Since the 1970s, Somalia has experienced ongoing instability, state collapse, and protracted armed conflict. The fall of Siad Barre's regime in 1991 marked the beginning of almost three decades during which Somalia has earned the label of the world's "most failed state" (Fund for Peace, 2014). Ninety percent of all schools were destroyed, and literacy rates fell to less than 38%, such that 4.5 million people were unable to read or write in any language (Barakat & Shanks, 2014). Drought and famine intensified the impact of conflict in Somalia, creating what Hyndman (2011) calls a "dual disaster."

This dual disaster in Somalia has generated one of the largest movements of refugees and internally displaced people in the last century. The total population of Somalia is 10.8 million people (World Bank, 2015). Between 1 and 1.5 million Somalis have been displaced outside of Somalia and live in diaspora around the world; an additional 1.5 million are internally displaced within the borders of Somalia (Hammond et al., 2011). The diaspora is both near and wide (Van Hear, 2009), the latter concentrated in the United Kingdom (population 95,000–250,000), the United

States (population ~100,000), and Canada (population 70,000–100,000), and the former, much larger diaspora concentrated in Kenya (population ~415,000) and Ethiopia (population ~250,000) (Hammond et al., 2011; UNHCR, 2016). Somali diasporas are, in general, very active and well connected to each other and the country of origin (Horst, 2006). Well documented among these connections are monetary remittances; the Somali diaspora sends $1.3 to $2 billion a year in private remittances and an additional $130 to $200 million (in US$) in humanitarian and development assistance (Hammond et al., 2011), amounts that exceed the annual GDP of Somalia (UN Data, 2014).

The largest population of Somalis in exile is in Kenya, where Somali refugees live in both urban areas around Nairobi and rural refugee camps. The vast majority of them—almost 350,000 at the time of writing—live in the Dadaab camps. Built in 1991 to accommodate 90,000 refugees, the Dadaab camps are among the oldest refugee camps globally and host the largest concentration of refugees in the world. The UNHCR manages the camps, hiring NGOs to implement direct services related to shelter, water, health, and education, among others. Aid flows to Dadaab are chronically insufficient, with many refugees unable to meet their daily needs. Further, the future of the camps—and of Somali refugees in Kenya—is in constant flux, with the Kenyan government expressing increased security concerns over terrorism connected to al-Shabaab, an al-Qaeda affiliate headquartered in Somalia (UNHCR, 2017).

Education and Information and Communications Technology in the Dadaab Camps

The international NGO CARE set up the first schools for refugees in the Dadaab camps in 1993, with funding from UNHCR. At that time, international actors were motivated to offer only primary education as education beyond that level was considered an incentive for refugees to avoid return to Somalia (Hyndman, 2000). By 1997, conflict conditions in Somalia made clear that return was not likely in any foreseeable future. Soon thereafter came the first possibilities for post-primary education for refugees. In 1999, 10 boys sat and passed the exam for the Kenyan Certificate of Primary Education (KCPE) and were given scholarships to a regional Kenyan secondary school outside of the camps (Marangu, Gitome, & Njogu, 2011).

Later that same year, UNHCR and CARE established three secondary schools in the camps and enrolled 215 students; refugee community members established three additional schools in 2008, at which time there were 2,077 students enrolled in secondary school (Marangu et al., 2011). In 2014, there were seven secondary schools in the Dadaab camps, yet net enrollment ratios at secondary level were only 2.3%. Higher education has been even more limited, including a few scholarships offered each year by World University Service of Canada and the Albert Einstein German Academic Refugee Initiative (DAFI) Program and the new Borderless Higher Education for Refugees (BHER), which opened 200 places in 2014 for a blended online and face-to-face program. Education in the Dadaab camps is guided by the UNHCR Global Education Strategy, 2012–2016 (UNHCR, 2012) and the Joint Strategy for Education in Dadaab, 2012–2015 (UNHCR & UNICEF, 2011).

Information and communications technologies (ICTs) are increasingly available in the Dadaab camps, and the most prominent use of ICTs in the camps is the mobile phone. Mobile phone usage in Kenya has grown exponentially over the past decade, including in Dadaab. A survey of students who completed secondary school and were currently enrolled in the BHER program (n = 89) indicated that 78% had mobile devices (Orgocka & Saita, 2014).

Methodology

In seeking to understand how refugees navigate schooling and achieve educational success, we have chosen to analyze the experiences of a group of students who have been successful. This decision was purposeful. More is understood about the factors that inhibit school success for extremely marginalized populations than is understood about strategies that enable success (Lewin, 2009). Existing research on the educational trajectories of refugees and the experiences of refugees in Dadaab and Kenya broadly focuses primarily on the failure of systems and lack of opportunities (Dryden-Peterson, 2016; Horst, 2006; Lindley, 2011; Mendenhall et al., 2015). We frame this investigation with a focus on opportunities and enabling factors with the aim of understanding why and how some students are successful. Despite the "ecological shock" of conflict and displacement, where across their ecosystems do refugee students locate and access supports, and what is the nature and content of these supports?

We use two different methods in order to generate complementary sources of data: in-depth semi-structured interviews (n = 21) and surveys (n = 248). The population of interest in both cases is Somali refugees who completed secondary education. The methods complement each other in both substance and sequence. Vis-à-vis substance, the study aims to build theory on supports for educational success among refugees. For this purpose, we worked within a constructivist paradigm, seeking to document and understand, through qualitative interviews, a complexity of views about these new phenomena (see, among many, Maxwell, 2013). Our survey allowed a degree of pragmatism in gathering data that could provide an albeit imperfect understanding of the scope of these nascent phenomena. We view this pragmatism as an ethical imperative in research in conflict settings (see also Wood, 2006). Vis-à-vis sequence, we integrated the methods (Johnson &

Onwuegbuzie, 2004) both in the design phase, in which the interviews shaped the content of the survey (sequential design), and analysis of the data, in which surveys and interviews informed each other (concurrent design) (Creswell, 2014).

Unlike most studies in this field (Burde, Kapit, Wahl, Guven, & Skarpeteig, 2017), this research is not commissioned. We relied on relationships with both UNHCR and Windle Trust Kenya, an NGO working on education in Dadaab, in order to access the militarized setting of the camps and arrange interviews and transport given restrictions on our movement, including travel in armed convoys and limited to gated and guarded compounds. We nevertheless remained independent in our research design, data collection, analysis, and funding. The research questions align with a long-term research agenda on refugee education; however, we did incorporate certain questions of interest to UNHCR and Windle Trust in our survey and interview guides with the aim of reciprocity and in line with our commitments to engaged scholarship that can usefully inform practice and policy. We were consistently aware, both in data collection and analysis, of our positions as outsiders in Dadaab, marked by the security infrastructure required, our different racial backgrounds, and our language proficiencies, among other factors. We attempted to create spaces to connect with our interview participants along lines of educational pursuits and often in our roles as teachers and explicitly invite them to challenge our assumptions and clarify our misconceptions. Our analytic processes also incorporated ongoing reflection on the ways our identities and experiences were shaping our views of the data. The research was approved by the Harvard University Institutional Review Board and what was then called the Republic of Kenya National Council for Science and Technology (now the National Commission for Science, Technology and Innovation).

Data Collection

We conducted in-depth semi-structured interviews with 21 Somali students who completed secondary school in Dadaab refugee camps, 14 males and 7 females. The interviews sought to elicit data on the general life history of the participant with a focus on educational trajectories and also asked specifically about educational supports received and given (e.g., Tell me about the people who have helped you be successful in your education.), current work (e.g., How has the support of [people and institutions] mattered to you in your education/in your current work?), transnational connections (e.g., Where geographically is the space you find best to pursue your education/do your work?), technology use (e.g., What kinds of support do you seek/provide through online/virtual connections?), identity (e.g., How does your work in Dadaab shape your life in Kenya?), and gender-based experiences (e.g., Who do girls/women turn to for educational support?),

Table 2
Characteristics of Interview Participants (*n* = 21)

	Country of Origin	Location of Primary/Secondary Education	Current Location			Highest Level of Education	
	Somalia	Dadaab	Dadaab	Nairobi	Canada	Secondary School	Some Higher Education
Male	14	14	8	3	3	8	6
Female	7	7	4	0	3	4	3

this latter category driven by well-documented inequalities for Somali refugee girls in accessing educational opportunities (Buck & Silver, 2012; UNHCR, 2014). We conducted the interviews in English after asking participants in which language they felt comfortable for the interview. We nevertheless recognize this limitation; while all interview participants had been educated through high school graduation in English and had passed English requirements to enroll in tertiary education, English was not the language spoken at home by any of our participants. All interviews were audio-recorded and lasted approximately one and a half hours. We also, with permission from the interview participants, took fieldnotes on pre- and post-interview conversations and the setting. At the time of the interviews, 12 of the participants continued to live in Dadaab, 3 had moved to Nairobi to pursue higher education, and 6 had been resettled to Canada to pursue higher education (see Table 2).

Our sample of research participants evolved through multiple networks of contact, including relationships with UNHCR and Windle Trust as well as connections with former refugee students, since resettled, and an ongoing snowball strategy. All but one of our interview participants were or had been (before resettlement) employed by an NGO, the highest level of employment in the camps for secondary school graduates. The interview participants fitted our sample of interest, being the most successful secondary school graduates, along metrics of scores on final exams and securing employment after graduation.

These in-depth interviews were complemented by an online survey aimed at determining, in a descriptive and exploratory way, patterns of educational supports for Somalis in a broader population. The survey included questions on types of support (e.g., Do you seek academic support [guidance, tutoring, writing support, exam preparation, course selection] from online/virtual connections [not in person]?), sources of that support (e.g., From whom do you seek online/virtual academic support?), global connections (e.g., Do you communicate with Somalis living in the Dadaab refugee camps of Kenya?, followed up with questions of with whom and how), and access to ICTs (e.g., How often do you access the Internet?); most of the questions were closed, and a few were open-response. We developed the survey following the process outlined by Gehlbach and Brinkworth (2011), including a comprehensive literature review, consultation with Somali university students, and two rounds of cognitive pretesting.

This survey was limited to Somalis who were over the age of 18 and had completed secondary school. We distributed the survey to every Somali-serving organization we could locate online in the United States, Canada, the United Kingdom, Sweden, Ireland, and the United Arab Emirates (n = 87); through social media, particularly Facebook groups (n = 34); on Somali-related radio broadcasts (n = 18); as well as via listservs (n = 8) and personal contacts for Somali (n = 106) and non-Somali (n = 133) individuals who do related work. Each contact was sent one initial e-mail and one reminder e-mail, with a request to share through their networks. The survey was open from February 25 to June 18, 2014. We analyze here the 248 surveys that were complete and from unique IP addresses.

Our survey reached Somalis who were geographically disbursed, primarily in the United States (35%), Canada (17%), Kenya (14%), Somalia (9%), and the United Kingdom (7%), broadly mimicking overall global patterns of Somali diaspora with secondary school education, although underrepresenting Somalis in the UK. Sixty-four percent of the respondents were male and 36% female, likely an indication of the continued gender disparity in access to education and technology even in diaspora (Buck & Silver, 2012). The vast majority of respondents were between the ages of 20 and 40 (82%). While the requirement for survey completion was secondary school graduation, 81% had at least some postsecondary education, a likely artifact of who is connected to the networks we accessed and who can easily access the Internet to complete an online survey in English. Seventy-nine percent of the respondents were born in Somalia. Just over half of the respondents had lived in a refugee camp, with 70% of those having lived in Dadaab (n = 88), allowing for a comparison among those who had and had not lived in camp settings (see Table 3).

Our survey had a target population with two characteristics recognized as being among the most challenging to reach: The population is mobile and marginalized (MacDonald, 2015; Vigneswaran & Quirk, 2012). An online survey with multiple entry points provided the advantage of reaching members of this target population who are not reachable in other more geographically circumscribed way (Crush et al., 2012) and who are connected to each other in highly networked ways (Friberg & Horst, 2014; Massey, 1999). However, the sampling frame remains ill defined. Given the limitations, we present only exploratory and descriptive analyses of the survey data, which importantly informed our in-depth qualitative data analysis.

Table 3
Basic Characteristics of Survey Respondents (*n* = 248)

Country of Birth, %		Country of Residence, %		Highest Level of Education Completed, %		Age (Years), %	
Somalia	79	Somalia	9	Secondary school	12	18–19	3
Kenya	7	Kenya	14	Some postsecondary	12	20–30	61
USA	3	USA	35	Diploma/certificate	13	31–40	21
UK	0.4	UK	7	Bachelor's degree	38	41–50	10
Canada	1	Canada	17	Master's degree+	18	+50	5
Other	11	Other	18	Other	7		

Lived in a Refugee Camp, %		Length of Residence in Camp, %		Distribution Among Camps, %	
Yes	51	1–5 years	31	Dadaab (Kenya)	70
No	49	6–10 years	14	Kakuma (Kenya)	7
		11–15 years	11	Utanga (Kenya)	4
		16–20 years	21	Liboi (Kenya)	2
		21+ years	23	Jijiga (Ethiopia)	2
				Other	15

Data Analysis

Analysis of the survey results was descriptive and conducted using the statistical software package Stata 13 in three stages. We first developed a set of summary statistics for each of the key variables. As a second step, we analyzed the data across a set of subcategories. We were particularly interested in considering differences in the survey results by sex, given existing inequalities (see also Dahya & Dryden-Peterson, 2017), and residence (or not) in a refugee camp and length of stay in a refugee camp, as connected to our questions about supports for education that refugees in camps access. Third, we considered the results based on the type of virtual support prioritized by the respondent. We looked separately at the data from respondents who indicated they received virtual academic support (*n* = 87). Participants were asked an additional series of questions depending on which type of support they prioritized (social support, emotional support, advice on family matters, career guidance, and spiritual/religious support), resulting in different sample sizes for each of these subanalyses. The survey allowed participants to skip questions they did not wish to answer, so sample sizes vary.

Analysis of the interview data was ongoing and iterative. Immediately following each interview, we listened to the audio recording and wrote notes on the participant's main ideas, including relevant verbatim quotes and our initial thinking about the ideas. Through this process, we wrote narrative profiles for each interview participant (Seidman, 2006), which allowed us to reconnect with data that were still connected to the participant's voice, examine the data from each interview participant as a separate unit of analysis, and identify initial emerging themes that informed later interviews and the survey design. After completion of all interviews, the audio recordings were transcribed verbatim; we used the qualitative data analysis software Atlas.ti to code these transcripts. We began with an initial list of etic codes generated from the literature; for example, within the code family of supports, we included peer-to-peer, scholarships, family, among others, with separate codes for face-to-face and virtual interactions. Two of the authors independently coded the same three transcripts with these etic codes, adding emic codes as necessary through this process. Emerging emic codes deepened our understanding of the nature of face-to-face and virtual relationships and included, for example, content of virtual communications, serving as a role model, and interaction with Kenyan society (individuals and institutions), among others. We then discussed each instance where there was a difference in coding to come to consensus on the code to be applied. The researchers agreed on a final codebook, which included definitions, exclusions, and examples for each code. One researcher coded the interviews from Dadaab, and one researcher coded the interviews from Nairobi and Canada. Each researcher reviewed the other's coding, and in any instance where there was a discrepancy, it was discussed until a consensus was reached (see Smagorinsky, 2008, who calls this process "collaborative coding"). We wrote analytic memos on each code as a mechanism to synthesize analysis across interview participants (George & Bennett, 2005). Through this memoing process and analysis across codes, the applicability to Bronfenbrenner's ecological systems model emerged.

Findings

In this section, we present and interpret the study's findings in three steps. First, we present a narrative of one refugee student—Abshir—focusing on the multiple supports and their ecological sources that he identified as contributing to his educational success. We begin our findings with this narrative to demonstrate holistically the locally and globally situated supports of one individual before analyzing separately these supports comparatively across the whole data set. We chose Abshir as the supports he described are illustrative of the kinds of supports that were salient to refugee students' educational success across our data set. We return to this narrative in the Discussion section to examine points where Abshir's educational trajectory might diverge in the absence of certain kinds of supports. Second, we present the results of the survey of Somali secondary school graduates to begin defining the types, sources, and channels of support that refugee students who have experienced educational success identified as important. Third, we explore the nature of these supports through interview data. Echoing Bronfenbrenner, we move purposefully from examining the role of globally situated institutions and actors to examining locally situated relationships with and among self, family, teachers, and peers. For these latter relationships, we identify and analyze the creation of globally and locally situated social capital.

Navigating for School Success: Abshir

Abshir was born in 1991 in central Somalia, just as the regime of Major General Siad Barre fell and the country was engulfed in a conflict that, as it turns out, would last his entire childhood and beyond. Through this childhood, he described having "no parent to guide" him as his parents were killed in the war. As the conflict in Somalia intensified, his older sister carried him—just a baby at the time—to Dadaab, set up just a year before their arrival. Abshir would watch the camps grow from their capacity of 90,000 refugees to reach their highest levels of more than 463,000 in 2012 (UNHCR, 2015).

Abshir began Standard 1, the first level of primary school, in Dadaab at an appropriate age for the class. "The agencies have supported us very well," he said. He described how as he got older, classrooms were constructed, distinct from the trees under which he used to learn. These classrooms were crowded, however, with not enough schools for the many refugees who continued to arrive in the camps. Abshir recalled that his classes were often filled with 70 children or more, and even still, there was not space for all children to attend, especially girls. His sister never had the chance to go to school, marginalized by what Abshir labeled as a "community belief" that "there is no need [for girls] to go to school. Even if she learns, her knowledge will be wasted . . . [as] she will just stay home, she will care for the children."

For children like Abshir who did have the chance to go to school, education was of limited quality. Abshir did not believe that his teachers could "teach you properly." He said, "We used to have only our teachers who are just like us. . . . They were not trained . . . my [social studies] teacher, he was a Standard 8 failure." Abshir was the only one in his class to pass the primary school leaving exam. By age 20, Abshir was a Form 4 graduate, holding a Kenyan Certificate of Secondary Education (KSCE). He was also a primary school teacher employed by the international NGO CARE and about to begin studying for a bachelor's degree with the BHER program in Dadaab. How did Abshir navigate this successful pathway through education?

"There was a teacher, Kablan," Abshir explained. "He used to encourage me. He used to push me all the time." This teacher had lost his parents, like Abshir, and "he used to tell me, 'Your parents have passed away. . . . So you study so . . . you have a good future. Tomorrow, you may become even a President.'" Abshir recounted that Kablan would take a loan to buy books for him, noting that he would not have been able to study without them. Kablan was since resettled to Canada, with a scholarship to pursue higher education. He remains connected to Abshir on Facebook, and this former teacher is one of Abshir's biggest supports in his education. On the day that the KCSE results were announced, Kablan picked up the phone, in Canada, and called Abshir, in Dadaab, to find out his score.

Sources of income were terribly hard to come by in Dadaab, and yet Abshir needed money for books and a uniform. Ironically, it was Abshir's sister who provided the instrumental support that enabled him to stay in school when costs became prohibitive. Abshir's sister and her husband made money by carrying goods from the market in a wheelbarrow, and they gave it to Abshir for school. Not all refugee students had this financial support. When the costs of education became prohibitive for one of Abshir's friends and former classmates, he decided to return to Somalia. In communicating through the Nimbuzz App[3] on their smartphones, the friend told Abshir, "[I do not] do anything. I just stay here . . . [while other classmates have] passed to the next degree of letters."

Even friends who were able to continue their education were often sitting around doing nothing, Abshir found. He explained that some who finished secondary school chewed *miraa*, plant leaves with an amphetamine-like effect; others would sit in local community-based film screening rooms all day. The experiences of his peers left Abshir questioning the purposes of persisting through all of the challenges to complete his education. What were the benefits? Abshir described the lack of opportunities to pursue studies beyond secondary school. "We cannot proceed our education further," he said, "cannot go to other parts of the country because [we] don't have any kind of ID." Again, Abshir's teacher, Kablan, despite his geographic distance, remained a persistent role model for Abshir in the presence of so many pathways away from school success. With this support, Abshir did not drop out. When Abshir got news of his acceptance into a bachelor's degree program, Kablan and his sister were the people he told first.

Defining Supports and Their Sources: Survey Results

In Abshir's pathway through education, a number of mechanisms of support are evident. These supports are diverse in their nature (e.g., academic, financial, emotional) and source (e.g., family members, teachers, peers, NGOs), drawing on both the locally and globally situated dimensions of his ecosystem. Through our survey of Somali secondary school graduates, we sought to understand the various types of supports that refugee students who have experienced educational success identified as important to their school success, from whom they received those supports, and through what mechanisms this support was provided. We term *virtual* any non–face-to-face forms of support.

Survey respondents (n = 248) converged around traditional academic support—such as guidance, tutoring, writing support, exam preparation, course selection—as important to their success in education. Seventy percent of respondents noted that this support was "extremely important" or "very important," true across men and women in the sample. The experience of living in a refugee camp augmented the salience of academic support when compared to the sample as a whole, with 81% of those who had lived for an extended time in refugee camps placing it in these categories of importance. Women who lived in a refugee camp prioritized academic support even more highly in their academic success, with 89% thus ranking it.

The most common sources of academic support were within the microsystem: teachers, friends, and family members. Approximately half of the survey respondents received academic support from each of these three sources, consistent across the full sample and the subsamples of respondents who had lived in refugee camps and when examining women alone. Most sources of support were locally situated, with 55% of respondents noting that they did not receive any academic support from virtual connections, relying instead on in-person academic support. Such was true for 47% who had lived in a refugee camp and 57% of women.

Of the 45% of respondents who did receive virtual academic support, 69% noted that their virtual academic support was locally situated. It came from people living in their same geographic location—"in the place where you live" rather than "in a different part of the country where you live" or outside of that country—indicating the likelihood, though not the certainty, of virtual connections building from preexisting face-to-face relationships. The local creation of this support was even further magnified for respondents who had lived in refugee camps and for women, with 75% and 81%, respectively, responding that their virtual connections were with community members who were local to their geographic location. At the same time, globally situated virtual connections outside the place where respondents lived were not unimportant. Teachers, friends, and student peers were the most common sources of this virtual academic support, more so than family members (see Table 4). E-mail and phone were the most cited channels of globally situated academic support, yet text messaging and Facebook were also important (see Table 5). The majority of respondents received this virtual academic support more than weekly.

Respondents prioritized career guidance, social support, and emotional support as the other virtual supports most critical to their educational success. Thirty percent of respondents ranked career guidance as most important, 22% ranked social support (e.g., having friends you can talk to and feeling part of a group), and 19% ranked emotional support (e.g., managing stress, feeling content, self-confidence, and encouragement); supports such as advice on family matters, spiritual guidance, and other kinds were ranked

Table 4
Sources of Virtual Support (%)

| | Academic Support (n = 87) | | | | Career Guidance (n = 53) | | | | Social Support (n = 39) | | | | Emotional Support (n = 33) | | | |
| | Full Sample | | Camp | | Full Sample | | Camp | | Full Sample | | Camp | | Full Sample | | Camp | |
	M	F	M	F	M	F	M	F	M	F	M	F	M	F	M	F
Teachers	59	43	56	44	53	46	52	50	46	27	44	33	56	13	64	25
Family	24	20	25	13	29	31	19	33	67	67	56	33	56	69	55	75
Friends	44	47	36	50	58	46	57	67	83	87	75	33	75	75	73	100
Student peers	41	60	42	69	39	31	29	50	46	40	44	67	50	19	55	25

Table 5

Mechanisms of Virtual Support (%)

| | Academic Support (n = 87) | | | | Career Guidance (n = 53) | | | | Social Support (n = 39) | | | |
| | Full Sample | | Camp | | Full Sample | | Camp | | Full Sample | | Camp | |
	M	F	M	F	M	F	M	F	M	F	M	F
E-mail	67	67	61	56	68	38	67	33	63	40	56	100
Phone	56	67	56	75	42	31	33	50	92	93	94	100
Text messaging	33	30	36	19	21	23	14	33	50	80	56	100
Facebook	30	20	25	6	37	31	33	33	63	60	63	33
Discussion boards	19	27	22	31	13	15	14	17	8	13	13	0

Table 6
Prioritizing Nonacademic Types of Support (*n* = 178) (%)

	Full Sample		Camp	
	M	F	M	F
Career guidance	35	20	31	29
Social support	22	24	24	14
Emotional support	15	25	16	19

to a far lesser extent. In the full sample, career guidance was consistently most important across both men and women who had lived in refugee camps. The relative importance of career guidance for women and men in camp settings could stem from the lack of career opportunities and especially restricted options for women. In the full sample, however, women prioritized social (24%) and emotional (25%) support more frequently over career guidance, perhaps because as some of the very few educated Somali women, they were physically isolated from well-established community supports (see Table 6).

Fifty-three percent of respondents received career guidance virtually but from locally situated people, primarily friends and teachers. Interestingly, 43% received guidance from people living in a different part of the same country in which they lived and 45% among those in refugee camps, perhaps indicating the national context-specific nature of this kind of support, which is dependent on knowledge and navigation of the exosystem. Likely reflecting gender differences in access to technology, women in the sample used virtual mechanisms for career guidance far less than men.

Sources of virtual social and emotional support were similar, with friends and family prioritized by a vast majority of all survey respondents, both men and women. Of note is that in our sample, women living in refugee camps received virtual emotional support overwhelmingly from family (75%) and friends (100%) and far less from teachers (25%) than their male peers (64%). More so than all of the other types of support, male and female respondents received virtual social and emotional support that was locally situated, from people who lived in the same geographic location as them. An overwhelming majority of respondents received virtual social and emotional support at least weekly, through a variety of mechanisms: phone (92%), text messaging, e-mail, and Facebook (62% each).

The importance of locally situated support was clear across all types of support: In-person and virtual interactions with people who live in the same geographic location as the respondent were the most common ways of receiving support for school success. The results echo research suggesting that virtual social networks often stem from and are strengthened by face-to-face connections (Ellison, Steinfeld, & Lampe, 2007). The combination of virtual and face-to-face supports we see in these survey data lends credence to the idea that types of support are not mutually exclusive but instead may be additive. Further, in a highly mobile population, locally situated supports can transform into globally situated ones. Our interview data shed light on this process—the traveling of relationships and the technology that mediates them—as well as the types of social capital these relationships can create.

Nature of Supports: In-Depth Interview Findings

Globally Situated Exo- and Macrosystems: Access to Education

Abshir was clear that the structures international agencies provided for education in Dadaab were a foundation upon which he built his pathway through education. All interview participants echoed the notion that education was a gift bestowed on them by UNHCR and its NGO partners. In this, Abshir felt himself to be globally situated; as he described it, the "world has assisted us." Abas—who also fled Somalia as a young child and pursued his entire education in Dadaab—noted that international organizations "paid for my free primary education" and "facilitated my high school education." They supplied materials needed for school that, according to Abas, made school life easier in a context when home life was very hard. Abroon chronicled his life in terms of the development of educational programs in Dadaab. First, upon his arrival in the camps, there was no infrastructure, and people were teaching and learning outside, under trees, and writing in the soil. Later, he was given limited resources, like notebooks split in half to share between children. Given this ability to continue learning, Abroon noted, "I stopped the plan of going back to Somalia, and I studied from there [Dadaab] under the trees." When a Norwegian agency came, "They built two rooms," he said, "[and] from there I completed my primary education."

The structures for refugee education created and augmented over time by UNHCR in collaboration with its NGO partners and refugee community groups provided the possibility that children in Dadaab could attend school. Yet as Abshir noted, he was the only one in his primary school class to pass the KCPE. All of the interview participants attributed part of their educational success to UNHCR and NGO staff members who helped them develop globally situated microsystems. For example, students who had been awarded scholarships felt supported by two staff members from Windle Trust, who were physically based in Dadaab and "who helped me a lot for advice," as Idris said. Relationships with these staff members were motivators for students in Dadaab, served as deterrents to dropping out, and through information and guidance, created opportunities for further study.

In Dadaab, resources embedded in macro- and exosystems made access to education possible, but it was the related locally and globally situated microsystem relationships that served as enablers to persist and·succeed in graduating from secondary school. It is to these relationships that we now turn.

Locally Situated Microsystem: Self and Family as Inspiration and "Backbone"

All of the students perceived the inspiration they found within themselves to work hard, seize every opportunity, and maintain that dedication even in the face of challenges as inextricably linked to the support of their families. Haboon, who completed her high school education in Dadaab and took up a scholarship in Canada in 2013, said, echoing the survey findings, "If your family doesn't support you . . . there is no way you can go to school." The hope and encouragement that parents, particularly mothers, provided to students were unparalleled. Said Abas,

> It was my mother alone. It was her alone. . . . It was my mother who went through a lot with me and my other siblings. . . . She did everything you will have expected a living organism to do for me, and I don't think someone in the future can try to do something like that of similar, the way she did for me.

Sacad was "mobilized" by his mother, and for Abroon, his mother gave him "courage."

Mothers played this supportive role in children's educational success despite often not accessing school themselves. Abukaar described his mother as the "backbone of my success." Yet he said, "She can't teach me anything because she's illiterate, [but] she used to encourage me to read and strive more so that I succeed." Kahaa noted similarly, "The only support [my parents] have is only to advise me, because they are ignorant. They don't have education."

Family members also provided critical financial assistance to students and undertook household duties to enable the students to focus on their schoolwork. Fourteen students described their mothers selling vegetables in the market or doing other jobs to make enough income to pay for school supplies. Mansoor's father pushed a wheelbarrow, transporting goods for others, and "the amount he gets is what we have used to improve our study, for buying for us pens, books," he said. Mansoor's father also created the conditions under which his children could be successful in school, constructing for them "another small house, far away from the homes [where they could study], because mostly we had distraction from noises of small children."

Mothers also undertook cooking and cleaning duties to enable their children to study. Abroon's mother "used to cook for me food at home. Maybe early in the morning, at 5:00 am, the food is already cooked. I go pray, I eat my food, I go to school." All of the girls, however, described having as many household duties as if they had not been studying but recognized the support of their mothers in two specific ways. Haboon said that "some mothers used to send their daughters to work for another family, get a wage . . . but . . . my mother never told me to do that." Hodon described coming home from school to cook and wash her siblings' clothes before sitting down to study "up to 12:00 am." Her mother supported her, though, by "not condemning" her if she was not able to finish the housework. Expectations for girls to complete domestic work consistently emerged from the research participants as a barrier to education, yet family members were enablers, taking on household duties, ensuring their children were fed and clothed; sometimes, especially for girls, a family enabled by not standing in the student's way (on gender roles, see also Dahya & Dryden-Peterson, 2017).

Expanding the Mesosystem: Teachers as Traveling Social Capital

Overall, 16 of the 21 interview participants identified teachers as providing support to their education. Teachers provided two main types of support: encouragement and academic help. The ability of teachers to provide this support depended on the relationships teachers and students were able to develop. These relationships reflected the locally and globally situated dynamics of the refugee camp. In particular, interview participants universally described the importance of refugee teachers from the local camp community in fostering close relationships with students, as compared to the predominantly male, Kenyan teachers from outside the camp (on the role of refugee teachers, see also Dryden-Peterson, 2017). Hodan described how she benefited from the refugee teachers, who themselves had just finished school: "If I cannot just understand from the [Kenyan] teacher, I usually go to them [the refugee teachers]." Salim explained that he trusted his refugee teachers more than his Kenyan teachers "because I can tell them everything and they will understand and the fact that they can explain to me . . . combination of Somali, English and everything, how I understand."

Harun, studying in Canada on a WUSC scholarship, recalled a very positive relationship with his teachers in Dadaab. His teachers, he said, "really motivate you, and they teach us, and then they keep saying that you guys should work hard—hard so that you just find the opportunity to get a scholarship, and then find yourself in the very good place of studying." He explained the teachers were "really a motivating factor for every student." Haboon expressed surprise that some of her teachers cared enough to notice when things were not going well for her. "When they see I'm not doing well this time, some of them used to call me, 'Haboon, what's wrong? What's the problem?'" They combined this interest with encouragement: One teacher used to say, "'Haboon, you . . . can perform better. Try it.'" Anwar described the specific encouragement his physics teacher provided:

> He always helped me, like I remember . . . I applied several times for
> this DAFI scholarship, and I was often left [not awarded the scholar-
> ship], so I used him to give me the courage—[he would say] "Anwar
> proceed, go for it. Don't just lose courage."

Anwar explained that at the time he studied in Dadaab, before he began
university courses in Nairobi in 2009, all they had were "the textbooks and
what the teacher says." The teachers were thus indispensable supports to his
education. Idil further noted the teachers were always available, and Kahaa
provided the example that teachers "give me extra classes during the week
and Saturdays and Sundays . . . like practicals [of] chemistry and biology."
When Haboon failed in mathematics, she went to a teacher for help, and
he served as a resource and tutor. Having "teachers who know me,"
Haboon noted, was essential to her academic performance: "I had to perform better because it will be shame for you when you perform poorly
when you are expected [to do well]." Mansoor described how when teachers
were "aware of the condition at home," they "sometimes provided material
support, buying materials such as books, papers, and writing materials that
were not available from the district with their own funds."

The presence of qualified and experienced teachers in Dadaab shifted
over time, with implications for the type of support teachers were able to
provide. Until 1997, students followed the Somali curriculum with Somali
refugees as their teachers. Refugee education in Kenya at that time was distant from the macro- and exosystem of the host country. After 1997, refugee
students began to follow the Kenyan curriculum and sit for the Kenyan
national exams at both primary and secondary levels, coming into more contact with Kenyan institutions and norms. This change also entailed a shift in
the language of instruction and examination, from Somali to English, which
meant that refugee students' success in school then additionally depended
on acquiring a new language (see also, Dryden-Peterson, 2015).
Concurrent with this shift was new hiring of Kenyan teachers in Dadaab
schools. All of our interview participants described the importance of trained
teachers—primarily Kenyan—in the camps. Abshir said, "Now, the teachers
are trained. We have even some teachers who have gone to university and
they have attained their degree," pointing to a form of social capital previously unavailable in the camps. Students also noted the increase in books
and supplies, part of the globally situated exosystem of international aid,
with the implication that teachers could be more effective under these
conditions.

Despite the benefits of qualified Kenyan teachers, refugee teachers, over
time, began to provide kinds of support that Kenyan teachers could not.
Relationships with refugee teachers did not end with graduation from secondary school, our participants made clear. The nature of these relationships
shifted, however, from locally situated to globally situated. All but three of

our interview participants were connected on Facebook to their former teachers, many of whom had since been resettled to study in Canada or the United States or on scholarships in Nairobi. These virtual connections built on previously existing in-person relationships to stretch across expanses of time and distance. Abas, for example, who moved to Canada, remained in contact with some of his former students. "When we see online each other," he said, "they will seek my advice to reach the WUSC [higher education] goal, to perform well. . . . I just give counseling to students who are waiting to do their final exams, something like this." In this way, social, career, and academic support melded together, as suggested by effective models of academic support. Interview participants in Dadaab universally described the WUSC students studying in Canada as their "role models" who encouraged them and showed them higher education is possible. It was in this synthesis of being a trusted role model and being available to provide concrete academic guidance that refugee teachers, who had themselves become educated under similar conditions, provided globally situated bridging social capital that extended their students' opportunities. Echoing the survey findings, being able to stay connected to these teachers virtually built on the face-to-face connections established through student-teacher relationships in Dadaab.

Expanding the Mesosystem: Peers as Traveling Social Capital

In addition to teachers, support from peers resonated across all interview participants as central to their academic success. Interestingly, students defined peers not by age or school cohort but by who had charted a similar educational pathway. In particular, peers were the students who were struggling together to pursue an education as well as those who "came before" and completed high school ahead of our interview participants. With this definition, peers included family members such as brothers, sisters, and cousins; friends and classmates; as well as some teachers. Our interview participants emphasized the ways in which these peers served as role models and provided academic guidance. Peers served these roles from a place of experience and success; they knew the challenges the students faced and understood possible strategies to overcome them. The ways in which our interview participants engaged peers as role models and for academic guidance were multiple and included informal one-on-one mentoring-like relationships with older students and teachers, the formation of study groups, and ongoing connections through social media. These relationships often involved interrelationships among groups of students and teachers, both locally situated as in face-to-face study groups and globally situated via online platforms.

Classmates and older students were role models to our interview participants in being proof that one could succeed in education as a refugee in

Dadaab and in demonstrating how to get there. Haron described the example set by students who had been selected for scholarships. When WUSC students returned to the camps from Canada, she said, "everyone is really motivated" as this student served as a "motivating factor, an agent." Salim, now a WUSC student in Canada himself, said, "In the camp what supported me most is . . . that I saw some students from the camps who made it. So it was definitely possible for me to make it." In an open-ended response on the survey, one respondent noted: "Seeing other successful role model Somalis has been a great motivation for me. . . . 'If they can do it why not me?' has been my motto." This kind of inspirational support was often coupled with concrete academic support. Kahaa described an older cousin who was one year ahead of her in school. At the point where the work was getting very challenging and Kahaa thought about dropping out, this older cousin began to come to her home every night to help her understand the concepts.

Study groups were one site of relationship building and academic guidance. Initially formed in informal ways, the study groups frequently became strong networks of students who supported each other's success. Mandeeq described the formation of a "small working group whereby we advised during night hours" with the goal that, in Mansoor's words, "when two bright students are sitting together, in fact they can benefit from one another." Aaden said, "The best thing is when you are a student you have another student, [then] when you discuss a challenge, you can have a solution." As a teacher, he encouraged his students to form study groups as he had done.

Frequently, these study groups involved recently graduated students and teachers. In these cases, the study groups were more formal, involving structured lessons or review of previous exams and the payment of tuition. All of our interview participants credited these extra classes with critical support they needed to succeed. Girls in particular noted how these study groups gave them structured opportunities to interact with male peers and teachers, which lacked in school settings. Hodan and Dahabo, for example, found the boys to be "bright" and "clever" and more open to assisting and explaining concepts in detail than their female peers, for whom the expectation was not to speak up or demonstrate knowledge in mixed-sex settings.

Study groups were not only a face-to-face mechanism of support for educational success; they were also globally situated, existing virtually through social media. All but one of the interview participants had an Internet-enabled mobile phone on which they accessed Facebook and e-mail. Each of these 20 interview participants did not identify virtual communication with agencies or family members as providing support for education, but they did identify virtual peer support as critical. Reflecting the survey findings, all of the support-building social media connections described by the participants stemmed initially from face-to-face relationships: They were with students from Dadaab who had been resettled outside of the camp, usually for further study. From their places of even greater school success, these virtual connections were embedded with globally situated social capital, and they "gave me hope," Anwar noted. He said, "It gives me the courage of people that I know that are studying in different places." Mandeeq described how she used Facebook to stay connected to her peers, now studying in Canada, who continue to provide support virtually. She said she opens Facebook every "five minutes," and she communicates with "those boys who were taken to WUSC." They "exchanged ideas," and they told her "the sky is the limit" in terms of her studies.

Via globally situated social media relationships, participants described being able to receive specific guidance relevant to their education. Abroon found Somali students who give "very good advice on Facebook" and appreciated the ability to have a conversation about that advice, not only to receive it but to engage in dialogue. Hogol described sending her essays to her peer who now studies in Canada who reads them and provides feedback virtually. In addition to these one-to-one connections, Salim described a Facebook group of 30 students from Dadaab. The purpose of the group was to share past exam papers and help each other, using the chat function. The group has become transnational, with 11 members remaining in Dadaab, 6 studying in North America, 7 in East Africa, 1 in Somalia, and the location of 5 unknown. It includes current students and current teachers. This virtual group is an example of supports for educational success within the mesosystem that span locally and globally situated resources.

Chronosystems Driven by Purpose: Paying It Forward and Rebuilding Somalia

When asked about their future aspirations, all but two of our interview participants connected the various types of support that enabled their educational trajectories to an overarching purpose of contributing to the reconstruction of Somalia (of the two that did not, one considered himself Kenyan now, and the other, resettled to Canada, saw her future work in contributing to education in Dadaab). The inspiration they found within themselves, the encouragement of their families and teachers, the academic guidance of their teachers and peers all stemmed not only from a desire to forward the life possibilities of one individual but to work toward the betterment of community and nation. "One of my educational goals is to become someone, then take part in the reconstruction of Somalia," said Abas. He continued:

> The only way we can get out of these problems [is] through education. From my primary school, with the help of my parents and how life was, I was just thinking about making a change in the family and to the society. That's how I made it to secondary school.

This sense of purpose, which synthesized locally situated and globally situated resources with an orientation toward the de-territorialized notion of "home," was a strong support for refugees' educational success.

This belief in the future possibilities of education stemmed from the locally and globally situated resources that refugee students marshalled within the refugee camps. One of the few benefits of living in a refugee camp was free education. For all of what was lost in living outside one's country of origin, education could be what was gained. This free education was perceived by our interview participants as perhaps the only upside of the destruction of livelihoods they had experienced, both individual and collective. As Haboon put it, "I myself going to school was a contribution to my community." Abroon described a common religious foundation to this way of thinking. He said,

> In Islam . . . if you dig a well and the people are still drawing water from that well, and maybe you plant a tree that is shading all the creatures and human beings, or other animals, even if you die, that river will go for you. It will be endless.

The current state of Somalia was consistently on the minds of interview participants as they pursued education along with the goal of contributing to the reconstruction of what they saw as their home. Anwar, who completed his secondary schooling in Dadaab and was sponsored for a bachelor's degree in Nairobi, expressed his thinking: "Why not . . . come back to Somalia and add a value on this tree that's growing called Somalia. It's very small and very delicate now." Idiris stated that his "burning issue is to go back to Somali country and construct that collapsed country." The belief in a possible contribution motivated continued studies for the students and in that way provided support to their academic success.

Despite the desire to contribute in Somalia, interview participants universally stated they could not return to Somalia until there was peace. Teaching was one of the only work options open to secondary school graduates in the Dadaab camps, and our interview participants described this professional opportunity as both a way to provide an income for their families and also to build toward the future while continuing to live outside of Somalia. Abroon noted that as a teacher he is "making a good contribution to society . . . because I am building [my students'] brains and their future. . . . If you run away with only your shirt *and* you have the brain, you can work somewhere else and earn a living." Sacad pointed out the direct link he saw between his teaching and the future of Somalia: "The work I am doing now is related to Somalia because if these people [my students], I teach them well, they will be going back, and they will teach there." Students who had been successful in their education in Dadaab were, bit by bit, creating the possibilities for more young people to have the kinds of traveling supports they had had to enable more current and future successes in education.

Discussion

Refugee children are some of the most educationally marginalized children in the world, facing enormous social, political, and economic challenges with few visible resources. In this context, the primary focus of research and practice in refugee education has been on barriers to pursuing education. Through examination of the educational trajectories of refugee students who have been successful in their education, which we defined as graduating from secondary school, this study has aimed to shift the deficit-oriented paradigm, identifying supports that enable refugee students to succeed. In its findings, the study counters two assumptions: first, that refugee young people are solely reliant on globally situated international humanitarian aid structures for educational success and second, that few educational supports are accessible in refugee communities, particularly in isolated camp-based settings.

Refugee students in Dadaab described as critical, but not singular, the assistance provided by UNHCR and its NGO partners, particularly in building schools, hiring and paying teachers, and providing scholarships for higher education. Within these support structures, refugee students drew on a complex web of locally and globally situated relationships, which spanned the layers of Bronfenbrenner's ecosystem. Many of these relationships enabled access to what Tsing would call traveling resources, connecting refugee students to the kinds of social capital—academic guidance, support, and encouragement—that they needed to chart pathways through education.

These locally and globally situated relationships were particularly essential in moments where students' educational trajectories might have diverged. A reexamination of Abshir's narrative in the context of these findings sheds light on how various locally and globally situated relationships mattered to his educational success. Abshir's coming of school age coincided with a shift in the globally situated exosystem in which UNHCR funded the building of classrooms to accommodate the rapidly expanding population of Dadaab, so he was able to attend school. When he did not have enough money for books, uniforms, and fees, his locally situated microsystem relationship with his sister and her husband facilitated their financial help. Abshir's relationship with one particularly supportive teacher, Kablan, was initially locally situated but transformed, through his teacher's migration, into one that was globally situated, and his mesosystem was embedded with new and different kinds of social capital. For example, as he progressed in school, Abshir began to doubt the purpose of education in a country where the exosystem prevented his freedom of movement or the right to work. Yet the virtual connection he maintained with his teacher, whose ideas traveled to Dadaab virtually from a different macrosystem, represented to Abshir expanded possibilities for his future and motivated him to persist, applying to and gaining acceptance into a higher education degree program. Abshir's experience is illustrative of the kinds of locally and globally situated relationships with international organization staff, families, teachers, and peers that mattered to refugee students' educational success across our whole data set. His experience captures the complex locally and globally situated supports that operate both face-to-face and virtually as enablers of refugee students' success.

This study contributes to the development of a theory of educational supports for refugee students that are both locally and globally situated, and it may have relevance for others who are marginalized within nation-states yet with access to traveling resources. For refugees, beyond globally situated macro- and exosystems that accompany structures of international humanitarian aid, the expansion of personal technology has enabled individuals to build micro- and mesosystem relationships virtually to find globally situated supports that were unavailable locally. The survey and interview findings suggest an extension of Bronfenbrenner's ecosystems in light of these types of locally and globally situated supports, which are both face-to-face and virtual. Following Bronfenbrenner, many of the most important educational supports for refugee students were face-to-face within micro- and mesosystems. Girls described the support of mothers in lessening the domestic work required of them to allow them to focus on schoolwork. Both girls and boys relied heavily on self-initiated networks of peers to study together and prepare for exams. Teachers were central supporters, providing encouragement, skills, and knowledge to navigate high-stakes exams and further study. Departing from Bronfenbrenner, refugee students also cultivated micro- and mesosystem relationships that were virtual, spanning geographic space and extending opportunities.

Most of these virtual relationships stemmed from initial face-to-face relationships. Through individual migration, the relationships shifted in nature, in particular in relation to the type of social capital they could provide: Refugee students accessed information and academic and social support that was not available in their locally situated ecosystem. These naturally occurring relationships reflect the principles of bonding and bridging social capital. They leverage bonding relationships, based on shared characteristics of language, history as a refugee in Dadaab, and Somali origin, as the basis on which to cultivate bridging relationships across geography and resource context to extend opportunities.

Bridging relationships are more challenging to build, what Putnam (2000) described as "the toughest to create" (p. 363). Yet when they begin from a place of connection, they are more easily fostered and sustained (Kramer, 2006). Building on bonding relationships, refugee students in Dadaab were able to bridge across certain differences, enabling them to accrue new educational supports. These differences included geographic space (e.g., Canada), type of education (e.g., higher education), gender norms (e.g., sharing household duties), information (e.g., scholarship opportunities), academic skills (e.g., essay writing), and aspirations (e.g., living in a context with the freedom of movement and the right to work). The virtual, globally situated bridging relationships, which were built on commonalities, stretched but did not break the students' capacity for negotiating these types of difference. For example, Somali women in Canada who were connected to female students in Dadaab had a shared understanding of the gender-based constraints on time and aspirations in Dadaab and were thus able to provide guidance and support that pushed the students to shift gender norms but not so far that they would be ostracized from the community.

Naturally occurring locally and globally situated virtual relationships are not *the* solution for millions of refugee children globally who struggle to chart a pathway to educational success. The survey respondents and interview participants in this study have succeeded in their education in ways that have eluded so many others with similar origins in Somalia and exile experiences in Kenya. Yet the students in this study demonstrate similar "navigational capacities" that have been documented among other marginalized young people globally, capacities to overcome obstacles in pursuit of opportunities, particularly through the building of relational supports (e.g., Rana, Qin, Bates, Luster, & Saltarelli, 2011; Swartz, Khalema, Cooper, De Lannoy, & Segal, 2012; World Bank, 2013).

Moving forward, programs in refugee settings might work to intentionally cultivate these supports that refugee students have identified as central to their success. Many of these supports are locally situated in the refugee context and could be bolstered by shifting gender norms to facilitate girls balancing schoolwork and domestic work, strengthening family livelihoods so that families can invest in uniforms and books, and facilitating peer-to-peer networks and study groups. Virtual relationships could also be intentionally developed as ways to access academic and social support that is less available in refugee settings. Technology, particularly personal mobile devices, can permeate the isolation of refugee camp contexts, connecting individual refugee students to resources that are in shorter supply in the camps. The virtual connections we document in this study highlight technologically mediated, globally situated support for refugees, who are otherwise bounded by the legal restrictions that accompany their refugee status. This study demonstrates existing involvement of Somali diaspora in these types of relationships and points to potential to expand, at low cost, that involvement through purposeful facilitation of virtual relationships.

Virtual connections can provide a mechanism for refugee students to access the locally and globally situated supports they need to see "the light at the end of the tunnel" as they pursue pathways through education. These relationships are less contingent on shifting geopolitical dynamics of international aid and security, and they can break down physical isolation to expand opportunities for education. The benefits of expanded opportunities for refugees to be successful in their education accrue not only to the individual but as collective goods. Refugee students' motivation for education is so often tied to a desire to contribute to peace-building and post-conflict reconstruction in their countries of origin. The intersection of locally and globally situated supports may enable more refugee students to chart pathways to success in education, which will benefit not only themselves and their communities but may assist in resolution of the intractable conflicts that engulf their homes.

Notes

We would like to thank many people who have contributed to this work: the young people in Dadaab, Nairobi, and Canada, for participating in this research and sharing their successes and challenges; Windle Trust and United Nations High Commissioner for Refugees for facilitating field research in Dadaab; Kenyatta University, in particular Josephine Gitome; the Borderless Higher Education for Refugees project, in particular Wenona Gilles, Don Dippo, Aida Orgocka, and Emily Antze; Bethany Mulimbi, Sameena Eidoo, Salathiel Ntakirutimana, and Shazia Khan for research assistance; and the Mowana Lab at the Harvard Graduate School of Education and our anonymous reviewers for invaluable feedback. The study was generously funded by the Weatherhead Center for International Affairs at Harvard University.

[1] All names of research participants are pseudonyms.
[2] For a detailed description of the distinctions between neighboring host countries and distant resettlement countries as well as the uniquely unfolding situation in Europe, which has characteristics of both, see Dryden-Peterson (2016).
[3] Nimbuzz is a free mobile application for calling and messaging, aggregating into one instant messaging (IM) accounts like MSN Messenger and Facebook Messenger.

References

Barakat, B., & Shanks, K. (2014). *Beyond fragility: A conflict and education analysis of the Somali context.* New York, NY: UNICEF.

Bernal, V. (2006). Diaspora, cyberspace and political imagination: The Eritrean diaspora online. *Global Networks, 6*(2), 161–179.

Betancourt, T. S., Meyers-Ohki, S. E., Charrow, A. P., & Tol, W. A. (2013). Interventions for children affected by war: An ecological perspective on psychosocial support and mental health care. *Harvard Review of Psychiatry, 21*(2), 70–91.

Boothby, N. (2008). Political violence and development: An ecologic approach to children in war zones. *Child and Adolescent Psychiatric Clinics of North America, 17*(3), 497–514.

Bourdieu, P. (1986). The forms of capital. In J. G. Richardson (Ed.), *Handbook for the theory and research for the sociology of education* (pp. 241–258). New York, NY: Greenwood.

Bronfenbrenner, U. (1979). *The ecology of human development: Experiments by nature and design.* Cambridge, MA: Harvard University Press.

Bronfenbrenner, U. (1992). Ecological systems theory. In R. Vasta (Ed.), *Six theories of child development: Revised formulations and current issues* (pp. 187–249). London: Kingsley.

Buck, P., & Silver, R. (2012). *Educated for change?: Muslim refugee women in the west.* Charlotte, NC: Information Age Publishing.

Burde, D., Kapit, A., Wahl, R. L., Guven, O., & Skarpeteig, M. I. (2017). Education in emergencies. *Review of Educational Research, 87,* 619–358.

Creswell, J. W. (2014). *Research design: Qualitative, quantitative, and mixed methods approaches* (4th ed.). Thousand Oaks, CA: SAGE Publications.

Crush, J., Eberhardt, C., Caesar, M., Chikanda, A., Pendleton, W., & Hill, A. (2012). Diasporas on the web: New networks, new methodologies. In C. Vargas-Silva (Ed.), *Handbook of research methods in migration* (pp. 345–365). Northampton, MA: Edward Elgar.

Dahya, N., & Dryden-Peterson, S. (2017). Tracing pathways to higher education for refugees: The role of virtual support networks and mobile phones for women in refugee camps. *Comparative Education, 53*, 284–301.

Davies, L. (2004). *Education and conflict: Complexity and chaos.* New York, NY: RoutledgeFalmer.

Dryden-Peterson, S. (2015). Refugee education in countries of first asylum: Breaking open the black box of pre-resettlement experiences. *Theory and Research in Education, 14*(2), 1–18.

Dryden-Peterson, S. (2016). Refugee education: The crossroads of globalization. *Educational Researcher, 45*(9), 473–482.

Dryden-Peterson, S. (2017). Refugee education: Education for an unknowable future. *Curriculum Inquiry, 47*(1), 14–24.

Ellison, N. B., Steinfeld, C., & Lampe, C. (2007). The benefits of Facebook "friends": Social capital and college students' use of online social network sites. *Journal of Computer Mediated Communication, 12*(4), 1143–1168.

Friberg, J. H., & Horst, C. (2014). RDS and the structure of migrant populations. In G. Tyldum & L. Johnston (Eds.), *Applying respondent driven sampling to migrant populations: Lessons from the field* (pp. 17–26). New York, NY: Palgrave Macmillan.

Fund for Peace. (2014). *The failed states index.* Washington, DC: Author.

Gehlbach, H., & Brinkworth, M. E. (2011). Measure twice, cut down error: A process for enhancing the validity of survey scales. *Review of General Psychology, 15*(4), 380–387.

George, A. L., & Bennett, A. (2005). *Case studies and theory development in the social sciences.* Cambridge, MA: MIT Press.

Hammond, L., Awad, M., Dagane, A. I., Hansen, P., Horst, C., Menkhaus, K., & Obare, L. (2011). *Cash and compassion: The role of the Somali diaspora in relief, development and peace-building.* New York, NY: UNDP.

Harrell-Bond, B. E. (1986). *Imposing aid: Emergency assistance to refugees.* New York, NY: Oxford University Press.

Higgins, M., & Kram, K. E. . (2001). Reconceptualizing mentoring at work: A developmental network perspective. *Academy of Management Review, 26*(2), 264–288.

Horst, C. (2006). *Transnational nomads.* Oxford, UK: Berghahn.

Hyndman, J. (2000). *Managing displacement: Refugees and the politics of humanitarianism.* Minneapolis, MN: University of Minnesota Press.

Hyndman, J. (2011). *Dual disasters: Humanitarian aid after the 2004 Tsunami.* Sterling, VA: Kumarian Press.

Johnson, R. B., & Onwuegbuzie, A. J. (2004). Mixed methods research: A research paradigm whose time has come. *Educational Researcher, 33*(7), 14–26.

Kramer, R. M. (2006). Social identity and social capital: The collective self at work. *International Public Management Journal, 9*(1), 25–45.

Lawson, M. A., & Lawson, H. A. (2013). New conceptual frameworks for student engagement research, policy, and practice. *Review of Educational Research, 83*(3), 432–479.

Levitt, P., & Jaworsky, B. N. (2007). Transnational migration studies: Past developments and future trends. *Annual Review of Sociology, 33*, 129–156.

Lewin, K. M. (2009). Access to education in sub-Saharan Africa: Patterns, problems and possibilities. *Comparative Education, 45*(2), 151–174.

Li, H., & Lee, K. C. (2013). An interpersonal relationship framework for virtual community participation psychology: From covert to overt process. *Social Science Computer Review, 31*(6), 703–724.

Lindley, A. (2009). The earlymorning phonecall: Remittances from a refugee diaspora perspective. *Journal of Ethnic and Migration Studies, 35*(8), 1315–1334.

Lindley, A. (2011). Between protracted and a crisis situation: Policy responses to Somali refugees in Kenya. *Refugee Survey Quarterly, 30*(4), 14–49.

MacDonald, A. L. (2015). *Review of selected surveys of refugee populations, 2000–2014.* Geneva: UNHCR.

Malkki, L. H. (1992). National geographic: The rooting of peoples and the territorialization of national identity among scholars and refugees. *Cultural Anthropology, 7*(1), 24–44.

Marangu, N., Gitome, J., & Njogu, I. (2011). *Background of education in Dadaab.* Paper presented at the Borderless Higher Education for Refugees Workshop, Kampala, Uganda.

Massey, D. S. (1999). International migration at the dawn of the twenty-first century: The role of the state. *Population and Development Review, 25*(2), 303–322.

Maxwell, J. A. (2013). *Qualitative research design: an interactive approach* (3rd ed.). Thousand Oaks, CA: Sage Publications.

Mendenhall, M., Dryden-Peterson, S., Bartlett, L., Ndirangu, L., Imonje, R., Gakunga, D., . . . Tangelder, M. (2015). Quality education for refugees in Kenya: Pedagogy in urban Nairobi and Kakuma refugee camp settings. *Journal on Education in Emergencies, 1*(1), 92–130.

Orgocka, A., & Saita, K. (2014). *Borderless higher education for refugees: Use of mobile devices among BHER students* (Draft report). Toronto: York University.

Porter, M., & Haslam, N. (2005). Predisplacement and postdisplacement factors associated with mental health of refugees and internally displaced persons: A meta-analysis. *JAMA: Journal of the American Medical Association, 294*(5), 602–612.

Preece, J. (2000). *Online communities: Designing usability, supporting sociability.* New York, NY: John Wiley.

Purcell, K. (2004). Making e-mentoring more effective. *American Journal of Health Systems and Pharmacy, 61,* 284–286.

Putnam, R. D. (2000). *bowling Alone: The collapse and renewal of American community.* New York, NY: Simon & Schuster.

Rana, M., Qin, D. B., Bates, L., Luster, T., & Saltarelli, A. (2011). Factors related to educational resilience among Sudanese unaccompanied minors. *Teachers College Record, 113*(9), 2080–2114.

Roorda, D. L., Koomen, H. M. Y., Spilt, J. L., & Oort, F. J. (2011). The influence of affective teacher-student relationships on students' school engagement and achievement: A meta-analytic approach. *Review of Educational Research, 81*(4), 493–529.

Safran, W. (1991). Diaspora in modern societies: Myths of homeland and return. *Diaspora: A Journal of Transnational Studies, 1*(1), 83–99.

Seidman, I. (2006). *Interviewing as qualitative research.* New York, NY: Teachers College Press.

Single, P. B., & Single, R. M. (2005). E-mentoring for social equity: Review of research to inform program development. *Mentoring and Tutoring, 13*(2), 301–320.

Smagorinsky, P. (2008). The method section as conceptual epicenter in constructing social science research reports. *Written Communication, 25*(3), 389–411.

Spencer, R. (2007). "It's not what I expected": A qualitative study of youth mentoring relationship failures. *Journal of Adolescent Research, 22*(4), 331–354.

Swartz, S., Khalema, E., Cooper, A., De Lannoy, A., & Segal, H. (2012). *Navigational capacities for youth employment: A review of research, policies, frameworks and methodologies.* Cape Town, South Africa: Human Sciences Research Council.

Tsing, A. L. (2005). *Friction: An ethnography of global connection.* Princeton, NY: Princeton University Press.

UN Data. (2014). *World statistics pocketbook: Somalia.* Retrieved from http://www.un-ilibrary.org/united-nations/world-statistics-pocketbook-2014-edition_f7ffe7d5-en;jsessionid=3j157qdmboaro.x-oecd-live-02

UNESCO. (2015). *EFA global monitoring report: Education for All 2000–2015: Achievements and Challenges.* Paris: Author.

United Nations High Commissioner for Refugees. (2010). *Convention and protocol relating to the status of refugees.* Geneva: Author.

United Nations High Commissioner for Refugees. (2012). *Education strategy 2012–2016.* Geneva: Author.

United Nations High Commissioner for Refugees. (2014). *Operations plan: Kenya.* Nairobi: Author.

United Nations High Commissioner for Refugees. (2015). *Kenya fact sheet, March 2015.* Nairobi: Author.

United Nations High Commissioner for Refugees. (2016). *Global trends: Forced displacement in 2015.* Geneva: Author.

United Nations High Commissioner for Refugees. (2017). *Refugees in the Horn of Africa: Somali displacement crisis.* Nairobi: Author.

United Nations High Commissioner for Refugees & Global Monitoring Report. (2016). *No more excuses: Provide education to all forcibly displaced people.* Paris: UNESCO.

United Nations High Commissioner for Refugees & UNICEF. (2011). *Joint strategy for education in Dadaab, 2012–2015.* Dadaab, Kenya: UNHCR.

Van Hear, N. (2009). The rise of refugee diasporas. *Current History, 108,* 180–185.

Vigneswaran, D., & Quirk, J. (2012). Quantitative methodological dilemmas in urban refugee research: A case study of Johannesburg. *Journal of Refugee Studies, 26*(1), 110–116.

Wood, E. J. (2006). The ethical challenges of field research in conflict zones. *Qualitative Sociology, 29*(3), 373–386.

World Bank. (2013). *Learning and resilience: The crucial role of social and emotional well-being in contexts of adversity.* Washington, DC: Author.

World Bank. (2015). *World DataBank.* Washington, DC: Author.

Zetter, R. (2015). *Protection in crisis: Forced migration and protection in a global era.* Washington, DC: Global Knowlegde Partnership on Migration and Development.

Manuscript received May 20, 2015

Final revision received April 7, 2017

Accepted May 8, 2017

American Educational Research Journal
December 2017, Vol. 54, No. 6, pp. 1048–1078
DOI: 10.3102/0002831217716084
© 2017 AERA. http://aerj.aera.net

Short Intervention, Sustained Effects: Promoting Students' Math Competence Beliefs, Effort, and Achievement

Brigitte Maria Brisson
University of Tübingen
Anna-Lena Dicke
University of California, Irvine
Hanna Gaspard
Isabelle Häfner
Barbara Flunger
Benjamin Nagengast
Ulrich Trautwein
University of Tübingen

The present study investigated the effectiveness of two short relevance interventions (writing a text or evaluating quotations about the utility of mathematics) using a sample of 1,916 students in 82 math classrooms in a cluster randomized controlled experiment. Short-term and sustained effects (6 weeks and 5 months after the intervention) of the two intervention conditions on students' competence beliefs (self-concept, homework self-efficacy), teacher-rated individual effort, and standardized test scores in mathematics were assessed. Hierarchical linear regression analyses showed that students' homework self-efficacy was higher in both intervention groups 6 weeks and 5 months after the intervention compared to the control condition. Students' self-concept, teacher-rated effort, and achievement in mathematics were promoted through the quotations condition, partly in the long term.

KEYWORDS: competence beliefs, effort, expectancy-value theory, math achievement, relevance intervention

How can secondary school students be supported to become more self-confident, hardworking, and successful in mathematics? To foster student motivation and performance, especially in science, technology, engineering, and mathematics (STEM) subjects, researchers and educational stakeholders promote relevance-enhanced teaching (e.g., Davis & McPartland, 2012; Osborne & Dillon, 2008). Indeed, yearlong teaching programs systematically emphasizing connections between mathematical learning material and career opportunities have been found to raise students' math grades (Woolley, Rose, Orthner, Akos, & Jones-Sanpei, 2013), and shorter interventions using writing assignments about the personal relevance of STEM subjects have been shown to improve students' perceived utility of and interest in STEM (e.g., Hulleman & Harackiewicz, 2009).

These findings are promising, but only little is known about the potential of short relevance interventions implemented in school classrooms (for an exception, see Hulleman & Harackiewicz, 2009). First, there is a need for comparative studies to investigate the relative strength of different intervention approaches. To this end, successful intervention strategies could be combined or added with new features to create various treatment conditions. Second, the majority of studies on the effects of classroom-based relevance interventions focused mainly on the focal construct (value beliefs) and achievement as outcomes. The impact of relevance interventions on students' competence beliefs and effort, however, has not yet been investigated

Brigitte Maria Brisson was a doctoral student at the Hector Research Institute of Education Sciences and Psychology at the University of Tübingen and is now a research fellow at the German Institute for International Educational Research in Frankfurt am Main, Schloßstr. 29, 60486 Frankfurt am Main, Germany; e-mail: *Brigitte.Brisson@dipf.de*. She is interested in motivation research and the design, implementation, and evaluation of educational interventions in the school context.

Anna-Lena Dicke, PhD, is a project scientist at the School of Education at the University of California, Irvine. Her research focuses on understanding the influence of the educational context on students' motivation, interests, and career pathways.

Hanna Gaspard, PhD, is a junior research group leader at the Hector Research Institute of Education Sciences and Psychology at the University of Tübingen. Her research interests include students' motivational development and interventions to foster motivation in the classroom context.

Isabelle Häfner, PhD, was a postdoctoral research fellow at the Hector Research Institute of Education Sciences and Psychology at the University of Tübingen. Her research focuses on parental influences on student motivation and the effectiveness of interventions to promote student motivation.

Barbara Flunger, PhD, was a postdoctoral research fellow at the Hector Research Institute of Education Sciences and Psychology at the University of Tübingen and is now an assistant professor of education at Utrecht University. Her research interests refer to individual differences in students' motivation and learning behavior.

Benjamin Nagengast is professor of educational psychology at the Hector Research Institute of Education Sciences and Psychology at the University of Tübingen. His research interests include quantitative methods (causal inference, latent variable models, multilevel modeling), educational effectiveness, the evaluation of educational interventions and motivation, and academic self-concept.

Ulrich Trautwein is professor of education sciences at the Hector Research Institute of Education Sciences and Psychology at the University of Tübingen. His research interests include teaching quality, educational effectiveness, and the development of student motivation, personality, academic effort, and achievement.

in school classroom settings. Concerning treatment effects on performance, students' grades or exam scores but no standardized test scores have been used as achievement measures, producing inconsistent findings (e.g., Hulleman, Godes, Hendricks, & Harackiewicz, 2010, Study 2; Woolley, Rose, Orthner, Akos, & Jones-Sanpei, 2013). Besides, no outcomes other than grades have so far represented the teachers' perspective in the evaluation of relevance interventions.

To shed light on these research gaps, we used data from the Motivation in Mathematics (MoMa) study in which two different relevance interventions (one adapted from previously used approaches and one novel one) were implemented in 82 math classrooms in Grade 9 using a cluster randomized controlled study design. Prior analyses have found these interventions to improve students' value beliefs of mathematics (Gaspard, Dicke, Flunger, Brisson, et al., 2015) and students' self-reported effort (Gaspard et al., 2016). The present study analyzed and compared the short-term and sustained effects of the same treatments on further outcomes neglected in previous classroom-based relevance experiments, namely, students' self-concept, homework self-efficacy, teacher-rated effort, and standardized test scores in mathematics.

The Importance of Perceived Utility Value in Mathematics

The Eccles et al. (1983) expectancy-value theory (EVT) is a powerful framework highlighting the importance of students' perceived utility value in determining students' achievement-related behaviors and performance (Eccles & Wigfield, 2002). According to EVT, students perceive high levels of utility value when they believe that engaging in an academic task will help them reach their personal goals. With regards to intrinsic and extrinsic motivation—two motivational concepts referring to either doing an activity for inherent satisfaction or to reach some separable outcome (self-determination theory, e.g., Ryan & Deci, 2000)—the utility value component defined in expectancy-value theory simultaneously comprises both intrinsic and extrinsic reasons for putting effort in a task (Eccles, 2005). More precisely, task completion is valued because the outcome of the task is expected to serve another end; this goal, however, may be personally meaningful to the student. Supporting students to relate the learning contents to their personal goals and to thus link intrinsic and extrinsic reasons for task engagement seems a promising approach for classroom motivational interventions (e.g., Trautwein et al., 2013).

Numerous empirical studies underline that it is beneficial for students' motivation, behavior, and performance when students perceive the learning contents to be useful (for overviews, see Roeser, Eccles, & Sameroff, 2000; Wigfield & Cambria, 2010; Wigfield, Eccles, Schiefele, Roeser, & Davis-Kean, 2006). In mathematics, students reporting high levels of utility value also show high levels of competence beliefs (for instance, self-efficacy and ability perceptions), effort, and achievement (e.g., Cole, Bergin, & Whittaker, 2008; Eccles & Wigfield, 1995; Gaspard, Häfner, Parrisius, Trautwein, & Nagengast, 2017; Husman & Hilpert, 2007). However, studies on the development of students' value beliefs demonstrate that students' utility value in mathematics is decreasing continuously throughout secondary school (e.g., Chouinard, Karsenti, & Roy, 2007; Chouinard & Roy, 2008; Jacobs, Lanza, Osgood, Eccles, & Wigfield, 2002). In line with these findings, interviews have shown that secondary school students have a hard time coming up with concrete examples for the utility of mathematical knowledge in real-life situations (Harackiewicz, Hulleman, Rozek, Katz-Wise, & Hyde, 2010).

Researchers have therefore examined how students' perceived utility value can be promoted and found relevance-enhanced teaching approaches to bear a huge potential in fostering STEM-related student outcomes in both laboratory and natural learning settings (for overviews, see Durik, Hulleman, & Harackiewicz, 2015; Lazowski & Hulleman, 2016; Rosenzweig & Wigfield, 2016; Yeager & Walton, 2011). Two types of strategies have been employed to convey the relevance of STEM subjects to students: (a) providing information about the utility of the learning material, for instance, for daily life (e.g., Durik & Harackiewicz, 2007, Study 2) and (b) having students generate arguments for the utility of the learning material themselves (e.g., Hulleman & Harackiewicz, 2009). Results concerning the effectiveness of these intervention strategies, however, vary across different types of settings (laboratory vs. classroom), outcomes, and students' prerequisites (see Durik, Hulleman, et al., 2015). In a series of lab studies (Canning & Harackiewicz, 2015, Studies 1 and 2; Durik & Harackiewicz, 2007, Study 2; Durik, Shechter, Noh, Rozek, & Harackiewicz, 2015, Study 1; Hulleman et al., 2010, Study 1; Shechter, Durik, Miyamoto, & Harackiewicz, 2011, Study 1), both strategies have been shown to raise undergraduates' perceived utility of and interest in a math multiplication technique. Furthermore, the provision of utility information promoted students' involvement, effort, competence valuation, perceived competence, and test scores when applying the same technique—in particular for high achievers. For low achievers, a combination of both strategies has been found to increase students' perceived utility of and interest in the math multiplication technique as well as test scores when applying the technique (Canning & Harackiewicz, 2015, Study 2).

Fewer studies intervened on students' utility value of STEM subjects in real-life classroom settings, but their success is compelling: Providing information about the utility of mathematical learning contents for career opportunities has been found to foster secondary school students' math grades (Woolley et al., 2013). Having students generate arguments for the relevance of specific topics in science or psychology courses promoted students' utility value, interest, success expectancies, and—partially—grades or exam scores, especially for students with low actual or perceived competence (Hulleman et al., 2010, Study 2; Hulleman & Harackiewicz, 2009; Hulleman, Kosovich, Barron, & Daniel, 2017, Study 2). An overview of the central characteristics of these classroom-based studies (setting, sample size, intervention, evaluation design, and results) is provided in Table 1. Drawing from these studies, we created two relevance interventions including new features with regards to the focus, strategies, and level of the interventions and compared their short-term and sustained effects on previously neglected outcomes, including different perspectives (students and teachers).

Characteristics of the MoMa Interventions

In previous school interventions in STEM subjects, students typically looked into the relevance of specific learning topics for their lives using numerous writing assignments or teacher-led lessons (see Table 1). However, instead of concentrating on topic-specific relevance, students in the MoMa interventions had to reflect on the personal relevance of mathematics as a broader domain, in particular for future education and career pathways. This approach aims to support students' continuous math investment over and above the topic currently dealt with in class (cf. correlational and experimental research on the importance of students' school and professional goals for their math investment, e.g., Peetsma & van der Veen, 2011; Schuitema, Peetsma, & van der Veen, 2014).

In addition, the MoMa interventions integrated previous successful intervention approaches, namely, presenting and self-generating utility arguments (e.g., Durik & Harackiewicz, 2007, Study 2; Hulleman & Harackiewicz, 2009), into one approach. Combining different interventions may have additive effects if the interventions depend on different mechanisms (Yeager & Walton, 2011). Self-generating utility arguments in individual writing assignments enables students to make personalized connections with the learning material (Hulleman et al., 2017). The personalization of the intervention message in turn has been found to be crucial for the meaningfulness and effectiveness of educational interventions (Walton, 2014; Yeager & Walton, 2011). However, as students might lack concrete examples of the utility of mathematics in real-life situations (Harackiewicz et al., 2010), generating utility arguments in individual essays without any preparation (e.g., Hulleman & Harackiewicz, 2009) might be a difficult task for them. Presenting some examples for the utility of mathematics for specific education and career pathways might help students in reflecting about their own personal relevance of mathematics in a more productive way. In addition, discussing occupations in which general math knowledge and analytic skills are needed might create a moment of sudden insight for students—in particular, when the need for mathematics is not very obvious (e.g., for studying social sciences). This might help to change the way students think about the

Table 1

Overview of Relevance Interventions in STEM Subjects in the Classroom

Study	Setting	Sample Size	Intervention				Evaluation Design	Reported Results
			Level	Instructor	Design			
Hulleman and Harackiewicz (2009)	High school, Grade 9 Subject: science (biology, integrated science, physical science)	$n = 262$ E: $n = 136$ C: $n = 126$	Student	Research assistant, teacher	8 essays in 1 semester: E: describe utility of course material to one's life C: summarize course topic		SQ before first and after last essay End-of-semester grade (1 week after last essay) No follow-up	No main effects Effects on interest in science and grades moderated through success expectations No effects on interest in science-related courses and careers No moderation through gender and race
Hulleman, Godes, Hendricks, and Harackiewicz (2010), Study 2	College Introductory psychology course	$n = 318$ E1: $n = 78$ E2: $n = 82$ C1: $n = 78$ C2: $n = 80$	Student	Research assistant	2 essays in 3 weeks: E1: describe relevance of course topic in a letter to a significant person in one's life E2: discuss relevance of media report for course topic C1: summarize course topic C2: discuss how abstract of scientific article expands on course topic		SQ before first and after second essay End-of-year grade (3 weeks after last essay) No follow-up	Main effects of E1 and E2 on situational interest Effects of E1 and E2 on utility value and maintained interest moderated through initial performance No effects on grades

(continued)

Table 1 (continued)

			Intervention				
Study	Setting	Sample Size	Level	Instructor	Design	Evaluation Design	Reported Results
Hulleman et al. (2017), Study 2	University Introductory psychology course	$n = 357$ E1: $n = 116$ E2: $n = 122$ C: $n = 119$	Student	Teacher (online)	2 essays (after first and second exam): E1, E2: relate course material to one's life (enhanced intervention): (after first exam) create implementation intentions for relating course material to one's life, (after second exam) reflect on self-regulation strategies C: summarize course topic	SQ before first and about 6 weeks after second essay Exam scores throughout the semester Final course grade	Main effects of E1 and E2 on success expectancy and grade Effects of E1 and E2 on interest and success expectancy moderated through initial performance Effects of E1 and E2 on final exam scores moderated through success expectancy and initial performance; three-way interactions with initial performance, gender No effects on utility value or cost
Woolley, Rose, Orthner, Akos, and Jones-Sanpei (2013)	Middle school, Grades 6–8 Subject: mathematics (and others)	$n = \sim6,500$ E: $n = 3,295$ C: $n = \sim3,200$	School	Teacher	E: follow 10 teacher-led math lessons per year in Grades 6–8 including career relevant examples and problems linked to the standard curriculum (class-level intervention) C: regular instruction	End-of-year grades in Grades 3–5 End-of-year grades in Grades 6–8 No follow-up	Main effects on math grades in Grades 7 and 8 No effects on math grades in Grade 6

Note. E = experimental group; C = control group; SQ = student questionnaire.

relevance of mathematics (cf. Walton, 2014). We expected that the effectiveness of the first MoMa intervention condition, namely, writing a text about the personal relevance of math (Hulleman & Harackiewicz, 2009), would benefit from a preceding input on the utility of mathematics.

Another way to possibly enhance the effectiveness of social-psychological interventions is the use of contextually appropriate anecdotes or quotations from older students about situations in which they needed mathematical knowledge (Yeager & Walton, 2011). This assumption is supported by a social cognition perspective as found in social learning theory (Bandura, 1977), possible-selves theory (Markus & Nurius, 1986), and identity-based motivation (Oyserman & Destin, 2010), which postulate that students can learn from persons they identify with. Accordingly, young adults describing the utility of mathematics in their lives could help students imagine a potential future identity and the importance of mathematical skills in developing this identity. As interview quotations provide personal and authentic utility information, they might be an effective tool to encourage students' personal reflection about the relevance of mathematics (see Harackiewicz, Rozek, Hulleman, & Hyde, 2012, who used a similar approach as part of a more comprehensive motivation intervention in STEM subjects). Having students evaluate quotations about the relevance of mathematics in the second MoMa intervention condition was thus aimed at supporting students' own valuing of math.

Compatibility with students' natural learning environment is an important precondition for the effectiveness of classroom-based interventions. Previous relevance interventions in STEM subjects were mainly conducted at the student level (see Table 1). As students are typically taught together in classes, however, intervening at the classroom level would come closer to the natural learning setting. At the same time, class-level interventions allow for students' active participation, for instance, in discussions about the relevance of mathematics. This might help in triggering personal reflection and thus increase treatment effects. As an additional advantage, between-class experimental designs allow for a more precise estimation of the intervention effects: They bear a reduced risk of diffusion effects that occur in within-class experimental designs when classmates randomized into different intervention conditions interact with each other (Craven, Marsh, Debus, & Jayasinghe, 2001).

Lastly, we also evaluated the effectiveness of the interventions more broadly than the studies presented in Table 1. More precisely, research is missing investigating direct treatment effects of classroom-based relevance interventions on motivational, behavioral, and achievement outcomes simultaneously. Findings so far considered students' grades (all studies shown in Table 1), interest (all studies by Hulleman et al.), utility value (Hulleman et al., 2010, Study 2, 2017, Study 2), and cost and success expectancy (Hulleman et al., 2017, Study 2). However, further motivational outcomes such as students' self-concept and self-efficacy, behavioral outcomes such as effort, and standardized performance measures have been neglected in previous research. Moreover, as all previous outcome measures with the exception of grades were measured using students' self-reports, the teacher's perspective has not yet been considered in the evaluation of the effectiveness of relevance interventions. Besides, the sustainability of the intervention effects through the use of a follow-up measurement has so far only been investigated for performance (Hulleman et al., 2017, Study 2; Woolley et al., 2013).

Competence Beliefs, Effort, and Test Scores: Understudied Outcomes of Classroom-Based Relevance Interventions

A closer examination of the Eccles et al. (1983) expectancy-value theory suggests a range of educational outcomes that could be affected by relevance interventions. First of all, EVT assumes students' value beliefs to be positively interrelated (Eccles & Wigfield, 2002), which implies that promoting students' utility value may also foster other value beliefs (see Gaspard, Dicke, Flunger, Brisson, et al., 2015, for the effects of the MoMa interventions on students' value beliefs). Furthermore, according to EVT, students' utility value is closely associated with students' competence beliefs and predicts achievement-related behaviors (e.g., effort) and test performance (Eccles & Wigfield, 2002; Wigfield et al., 2006)—outcomes that are understudied when analyzing the effectiveness of relevance interventions in secondary schools.

If students are aware of the utility of a subject for attaining their personal goals, they may be ready to tackle related tasks intensely and thereby discover their academic potential in a domain (see Hulleman et al., 2017). They may also be willing to put in more effort, thus positively engaging in learning (e.g., Reschly & Christenson, 2012). Hence, pondering over the relevance of the learning material could promote students' academic self-concept, self-efficacy, and effort. Students' academic self-concept is a domain-specific competence belief referring to how students evaluate their abilities in an academic domain (Eccles & Wigfield, 2002). Students' math self-concept has been found to be a strong predictor of students' interest, effort, persistence, choice of task difficulty, course choice, and performance in mathematics (e.g., Denissen, Zarrett, & Eccles, 2007; Marsh, Trautwein, Lüdtke, Köller, & Baumert, 2005; Trautwein, Lüdtke, Roberts, Schnyder, & Niggli, 2009). Students' self-efficacy is a task-specific competence belief assessing students' confidence in their ability to successfully accomplish a specific task like their math homework (Bandura, 1994). Students' math homework self-efficacy has been shown to influence students' homework-related value beliefs as well as homework effort and compliance in mathematics (Trautwein, Lüdtke, Schnyder, & Niggli, 2006)—behaviors that in turn impact math performance (e.g., Zimmerman & Kitsantas, 2005).

Supporting the assumptions made in EVT, numerous nonexperimental studies have shown positive associations of secondary school students' utility value beliefs with their self-concept or self-efficacy concerning mathematics or math homework (e.g., Chouinard et al., 2007; Eccles & Wigfield, 1995; Husman & Hilpert, 2007; Jacobs et al., 2002; Trautwein & Lüdtke, 2009) as well as effort in mathematics (e.g., Chouinard et al., 2007; Cole et al., 2008; Trautwein, Lüdtke, Kastens, & Köller, 2006; Trautwein, Lüdtke, Schnyder, et al., 2006). In addition, in lab experiments, subgroups of students (e.g., low achievers) were more confident in applying a new math technique correctly and put more effort in using the technique after reading about its utility (Durik & Harackiewicz, 2007, Study 2; Shechter et al., 2011, Study 1). Similarly, a classroom intervention during which undergraduate students collected arguments about the personal relevance of various topics in introductory psychology fostered low achievers' expectancies to succeed in the course (Hulleman et al., 2017, Study 2). However, the effects of relevance interventions conducted in secondary school classrooms on students' domain-specific self-concept, task-specific self-efficacy, and effort as well as the sustainability of such effects have not yet been investigated.

Furthermore, relevance interventions could promote students' test performance. Yet, whereas lab-based relevance experiments have been found to foster students' test scores (e.g., Canning & Harackiewicz, 2015, Studies 1 and 2; Durik & Harackiewicz, 2007, Study 2), classroom-based intervention studies have only investigated students' grades or exam results as achievement outcomes so far; these analyses yielded inconsistent results, namely, either main effects (Woolley et al., 2013), moderated effects (e.g., Hulleman & Harackiewicz, 2009; Hulleman et al., 2017, Study 2), or no effects (Hulleman et al., 2010, Study 2) on grades or exam scores. These mixed results might in part be due to teachers' subjective grading practices (e.g., McMillan, 2001). Consequently, there is a need to analyze whether classroom-based relevance interventions promote achievement measured by standardized test scores.

The Current Study

In the present study, we investigated the short-term and sustained effects of two short relevance intervention conditions (quotations, text) implemented at the classroom level on ninth-grade students' competence beliefs, teacher-rated effort, and test scores in mathematics compared to a control group. Based on previously established approaches, students were first presented arguments for the utility of mathematics and then reflected on the personal utility of mathematics in an individual writing assignment. Drawing on a social cognition perspective (Bandura, 1977; Markus & Nurius, 1986; Oyserman & Destin, 2010) and prior intervention approaches (Harackiewicz et al., 2012), students in the quotations condition commented on interview quotations by young adults about the relevance of mathematics. Adapted from a successful strategy first tested by Hulleman and Harackiewicz (2009), students in the text condition generated texts about the personal relevance of mathematics. We included a broad range of important outcomes, namely, students' self-concept, homework self-efficacy, effort, and standardized test scores in mathematics. As students' effort is observable (e.g., Fredricks, Blumenfeld, & Paris, 2004), teachers rated individual students' effort in the current study, thereby including teachers' perspective on the effectiveness of the interventions and going beyond previous investigations concerning student-reported effort (Gaspard et al., 2016). To learn about the sustainability of the intervention effects, we used a follow-up design evaluating treatment effects 6 weeks and 5 months after the interventions.

Prior analyses with the same data set showed that students' utility value was fostered through both intervention conditions for at least 5 months and that students' other value beliefs of mathematics (attainment and intrinsic value) except for cost were promoted to different degrees (Gaspard, Dicke, Flunger, Brisson, et al., 2015). Furthermore, the quotations condition had stronger effects on students' self-reported effort than the text condition (Gaspard et al., 2016). Grounded on EVT (Eccles & Wigfield, 2002) and findings from correlational (e.g., Chouinard et al., 2007; Cole et al., 2008; Trautwein, Lüdtke, Kastens, et al., 2006) and experimental research (e.g., Durik & Harackiewicz, 2007, Study 2; Hulleman et al., 2017, Study 2), we hypothesized students' self-concept, homework self-efficacy, teacher-rated effort, and test scores in mathematics to be promoted through both intervention conditions. Due to lack of empirical evidence, no hypotheses were formulated concerning the stability of the treatment effects and the comparative strength of the two intervention conditions.

Method

Sample and Data Collection

Data were gathered in the project Motivation in Mathematics in 82 ninth-grade math classrooms from 25 academic track schools (*Gymnasium*) in the German state of Baden-Württemberg. The sample size was based on a power analysis for a multisite cluster randomized trial indicating a power of $\beta = .73$ to detect an effect of $\delta = .20$ per intervention condition compared to the control condition (see Gaspard, Dicke, Flunger, Brisson, et al., 2015, for more information). In the present sample, mathematics was taught as one comprehensive subject including different domains such as algebra, geometry, or calculus during four compulsory lessons per week. There was no further tracking of students in math courses within school. Math homework assignments were common in all but one class (98.8%). A total of 1,978 students with active parental consent participated in the study, corresponding to a participation rate of 96.0%. Sixty-two students absent during the day of the intervention were excluded from the analyses, yielding a sample of 1,916 students (53.3% female; mean age at the start of the study: $M = 14.41$ years, $SD = 0.57$; mean SES/ISEI[1]: $M = 65.24$, $SD = 16.21$). The large majority of students were Caucasian, and students with an immigrant background (21.2% with at least one parent born outside Germany) came from predominantly Western countries and were Caucasian.

Data collections took place from September 2012 to March 2013 and were administered by trained researchers. Students in the intervention conditions completed questionnaires before the intervention (pretest = T1) as well as 6 weeks (posttest = T2) and 5 months (follow-up = T3) after the intervention. Students in the waiting control group completed the same questionnaires at the same time points but did not receive any intervention before T3. Students' competence beliefs and effort were measured at all three time points. Students' math achievement was measured in the beginning of the school year and at the follow-up. Students' perceived utility of mathematics was also measured at all three time points and will be reported to give an account of how it was associated with the outcome variables and affected by the interventions (see also Gaspard, Dicke, Flunger, Brisson, et al., 2015). All 82 classes fully completed all waves of data collections.

Relevance Interventions

In the beginning of the study, all 73 participating teachers and their classes[2] were randomly assigned within their schools to one of the three study conditions (quotations: 25 classes, 561 students; text: 30 classes, 720 students; waiting control group: 27 classes, 635 students[3]). Before the first data collection, teachers participated in an information session about the design and theoretical background of the study. To gain teachers' trust in the project and avoid spillover effects (Craven et al., 2001), teachers in the waiting control group were informed that their classes would also receive the intervention after the last data collection and that they were not supposed to ask their colleagues in the experimental groups about the contents of the intervention. Teachers in the experimental groups were not informed whether their classes had been assigned to the quotations or text condition.

After students in all treatment conditions had completed the pretest, students in the intervention conditions received a 90-minute standardized relevance intervention led by five trained researchers in class and followed by two short intervention reinforcements to be completed at home. To control for implementation fidelity, researchers recorded the actual procedure of each intervention in the minutes. Every researcher conducted 8 to 13 interventions with roughly equal distribution between the two intervention conditions.

The interventions were designed combining previously tested strategies, namely, the presentation and self-generation of relevance arguments (e.g., Canning & Harackiewicz, 2015, Study 2), with newly developed features.

As a result, the interventions consisted of a psychoeducational presentation and an individual writing assignment differing by condition. High initial competence beliefs have been shown to be a prerequisite for appreciating relevance information (Canning & Harackiewicz, 2015; Durik, Hulleman, et al., 2015; Durik, Shechter, Noh, Rozek, & Harackiewicz, 2015, Study 2). As a confidence reinforcement, students were informed about research results concerning the importance of effort, different interpretations of achievement-related experiences, and frame of reference effects in school classrooms (see Marsh, 2005; Wigfield et al., 2006) in the first part of the presentation. The second and main part of the presentation dealt with the utility of mathematics as a broader domain for future education, career opportunities, and leisure time activities.

After the presentation, students completed individual writing assignments differing by condition. Based on theories of social cognition that assume that students can learn from persons they identify with (e.g., Bandura, 1977; Markus & Nurius, 1986; Oyserman & Destin, 2010), students in the quotations condition were encouraged to reflect on the personal relevance of mathematics by reading six interview quotations from young adults who describe the utility of mathematics to their lives. Covering a broad range of real-life situations, the quotations stemmed from a preceding interview study in which 30 persons (ranging from college students to working adults) were asked to describe personal situations where they needed math skills. During the intervention, the students were asked to evaluate the relevance of these quotations to their own lives by responding to a set of questions (for sample quotations and questions, see Appendix in the online version of the journal). Students in the text condition were asked to collect arguments for the personal relevance of mathematics to their current and future lives and then write a coherent text detailing their notes. This task was adapted from prior relevance interventions (e.g., Hulleman & Harackiewicz, 2009) by switching the focus of the assignment from specific course topics to mathematics as a domain (for the instruction and a sample text written by a student, see Appendix in the online version of the journal).

At the end of the intervention, students received a portfolio including two short intervention reinforcements to be filled out at home 1 week and 2 weeks after the intervention session, respectively. In the first reinforcement, students were asked to summarize what they remembered from their individual writing assignments in class. The second reinforcement differed by condition and corresponded to the type of individual assignment dealt with in class (quotations: reflection on given relevance information; text: self-generation of relevance arguments). Students in the quotations condition were asked to choose one out of several arguments about the relevance of mathematics provided on a webpage (www.dukannstmathe.de) and describe why it was convincing to them. Students in the text condition were asked to explain why mathematics was useful to a person they knew.

Students in classes in the waiting control condition did not follow any presentation or do any individual writing assignments. However, they received the more successful intervention approach after the last measurement point.

Measures

Math Competence Beliefs

Students' competence beliefs in mathematics were assessed with a student questionnaire using 4-point Likert type scales ranging from 1 (*completely disagree*) to 4 (*completely agree*) that were adapted from previous studies (e.g., Baumert, Gruehn, Heyn, Köller, & Schnabel, 1997; Prenzel et al., 2006). Math self-concept was measured with five items (e.g., "I am good at math," α = .93). The math homework self-efficacy scale consisted of four items (e.g., "When I try hard, I can solve my math homework correctly," α = .76).

Math Effort

Teachers rated individual students' math effort by responding to the item "This student works thoroughly on all of his/her math tasks and homework assignments" on a 4-point Likert type scale ranging from 1 (*completely disagree*) to 4 (*completely agree*).

Math Achievement

Students' results from a curriculum-based standardized test assessing math knowledge in the state of Baden-Württemberg in the beginning of Grade 9 served as an initial measure of math performance. The test assessed students' competencies in the mathematical domains of algebra, geometry, and probability calculus with 38 math problems. The math problems focused on three aspects of math proficiency: numbers and algorithms, space and shapes, linking and modeling (38 questions; assessed by percent correct). At the follow-up, students completed a 3-minute normed speed test, which measured students' fluency of solving typical math operations (50 questions; maximum number of points = 50) (Schmidt, Ennemoser, & Krajewski, 2013). Validity studies showed that this short speed test is a very good proxy for students' achievement in longer assessments using standardized, curriculum-based math tests (Ennemoser, Krajewski, & Schmidt, 2011; Schmidt et al., 2013). The internal consistency of the test was good (Cronbach's α = .89).

Math Utility Value

Students' utility value of mathematics was measured through student ratings using a 4-point Likert type scale ranging from 1 (*completely disagree*) to

4 (*completely agree*). A comprehensive utility value scale consisting of 12 items (e.g., "I will often need math in my life") out of a newly developed value instrument was used (Gaspard, Dicke, Flunger, Schreier, et al., 2015). The scale showed good internal consistency (Cronbach's α = .84) (for more details, see Gaspard, Dicke, Flunger, Schreier, et al., 2015).

Statistical Analyses

Multilevel Regression Analyses

In order to test the treatment effects on students' competence beliefs, teacher-rated effort, and achievement, two-level linear regression analyses[4] were computed with Mplus (Version 7; Muthén & Muthén, 1998–2012) for each of the outcome variables. Separate multilevel regression analyses were carried out using students' competence beliefs and teacher-rated effort at T2 and T3 as well as students' math test scores at T3 as outcomes and two dummy variables indicating the treatment (quotations, text) as class-level predictors. Each outcome variable was regressed on the intervention conditions at the class level, the control condition being the reference group. In line with the recommended procedure to test intervention effects in cluster randomized trials (Raudenbush, 1997), initial values of the respective outcome variables were used as covariates both at the student level and class level. To account for contextual effects, all effects on the respective outcomes were freely estimated at both levels (Korendijk, Hox, Moerbeek, & Maas, 2011; Marsh et al., 2009). Covariates were added to the models using group-mean centering at the student level (Enders & Tofighi, 2007) and manifest aggregation at the class level (Marsh et al., 2009).

Effect Sizes

Before running the analyses, all continuous (but not dichotomous) variables were standardized. Consequently, the regression coefficients of the dummy variables can be directly interpreted as measures of the class-level effect sizes of the intervention conditions on the outcomes as compared to the control condition (Marsh et al., 2009; Tymms, 2004).

One-Tailed Versus Two-Tailed Tests

To evaluate the statistical significance of the treatment effects, the use of two-tailed tests is recommended, particularly if the literature does not support any directional hypotheses (e.g., Howell, 2012). Yet given our directional a priori hypotheses, the significance of the treatment effects was tested on the basis of one-tailed tests with an α level of 5%. This testing procedure additionally improves the power to detect small treatment effects at the class level (Stevens, 2012).

Missing Data

Missing data ranged from 2.3% to 19.6% for the outcome variables (see Table 2). Based on suggestions for the treatment of missing values by Graham (2009), the full information maximum likelihood method integrated in Mplus was used to deal with missing data. To make the assumption of missing at random more plausible, correlations of three auxiliary variables (students' gender; pretest cognitive ability score assessed with a figural cognitive ability test by Heller & Perleth, 2000; and end-of-year math grade in Grade 8) with the predictor variables were included in the models at both levels (Enders, 2010). The auxiliaries' and predictors' residuals were also included in the models at both levels.

Implementation Fidelity

To account for implementation fidelity, analyses were run with two types of samples: (a) including all classes participating in the interventions and (b) excluding two classes in which deviations from the intervention manual had been recorded in the minutes. Deviations occurred in two classes in the text condition: In one class, the initial presentation had to be held without any projector due to technical problems; in the other class, the researcher conducting the intervention noted that students were reluctant to participate in the intervention and in particular did not work quietly on their individual writing assignments. A comparison of the results showed no noteworthy differences, which is why all classes were included in the final analyses.

Results

Descriptive Statistics, Randomization Check, and Effects on Perceived Utility Value

Before analyzing treatment effects, the descriptive statistics (see Table 2) and the intercorrelations of all outcome variables including utility value beliefs (see Table 3) were calculated at all measurement points. As a randomization check, the differences in the pretest means for students' perceived utility value, competence beliefs, teacher-rated effort, and math achievement between the three study conditions were tested for statistical significance. No statistically significant differences between the conditions emerged, based on two-tailed Wald χ^2 tests (Bakk & Vermunt, 2016) with an α level of 5% (utility value: $\chi^2(2) = 0.79$, $p = .675$; self-concept: $\chi^2(2) = 0.88$, $p = .643$; homework self-efficacy: $\chi^2(2) = 3.73$, $p = .155$; teacher-rated effort: $\chi^2(2) = 5.01$, $p = .082$; math test score: $\chi^2(2) = 1.51$, $p = .470$). Concerning intervention effects on the focal construct, students' perceived utility of mathematics, analyses revealed a significant promotion through both the quotations

Table 2

Descriptive Statistics of the Sample Characteristics and the Study Variables per Intervention Condition

	Quotations (561 Students, 52.8% female)				Text (720 Students, 52.4% female)				Control group (635 Students, 55.6% female)			
	n	*M*	*SD*	ICC	*n*	*M*	*SD*	ICC	*n*	*M*	*SD*	ICC
Sample characteristics												
Age	561	14.61	0.45	.00	718	14.63	0.47	.00	635	14.64	0.47	.01
Cognitive ability score	519	19.96	4.01	.04	681	19.99	4.22	.05	610	19.62	4.27	.01
Math grade in Grade 8[a]	557	2.81	0.97	.04	714	2.73	0.97	.06	624	2.89	0.90	.02
Study variables[b]												
T1 Utility value	517	2.56	0.49	.05	680	2.52	0.47	.07	607	2.52	0.49	.09
Self-concept	515	2.76	0.79	.03	678	2.74	0.81	.04	606	2.67	0.81	.05
Homework self-efficacy	427	2.80	0.62	.03	599	2.72	0.62	.06	514	2.71	0.65	.04
Effort (TR)	497	3.03	0.81	.11	695	2.92	0.85	.03	601	2.84	0.94	.05
Test score	517	48.67	16.50	.08	676	49.85	18.19	.20	600	46.26	16.75	.15
T2 Utility value	530	2.64	0.50	.04	680	2.53	0.51	.08	601	2.45	0.50	.08
Self-concept	530	2.78	0.80	.03	679	2.73	0.80	.04	602	2.63	0.81	.06
Homework self-efficacy	492	2.82	0.64	.05	659	2.71	0.67	.05	586	2.67	0.65	.03
Effort (TR)	541	3.07	0.79	.10	719	2.89	0.90	.05	581	2.84	0.97	.05
T3 Utility value	516	2.60	0.49	.02	627	2.53	0.49	.11	557	2.44	0.51	.07
Self-concept	514	2.84	0.76	.03	628	2.80	0.76	.05	559	2.70	0.77	.05
Homework self-efficacy	460	2.89	0.64	.02	581	2.82	0.65	.05	523	2.71	0.69	.04
Effort (TR)	540	3.05	0.85	.09	710	2.90	0.92	.07	622	2.87	0.94	.03
Test score	516	32.59	7.51	.03	634	31.85	8.55	.04	559	30.74	8.24	.02

Note. ICC = intraclass correlation coefficient; T = time point; TR = teacher rating.
[a]In Germany, the grading system ranges from 1 (best grade) to 6 (worst grade).
[b]All study variables refer to the subject of mathematics.

Table 3
Intercorrelations of the Study Variables Within Class (Below Diagonal) and Between Class (Above Diagonal)

	(1)	(2)	(3)	(4)	(5)	(6)	(7)	(8)	(9)	(10)	(11)	(12)	(13)	(14)
T1 (1) Utility value	—	.52***	.58***	.02	.23*	.72***	.55***	.27*	-.02	.73***	.48***	.41***	-.03	.03
(2) Self-concept	.38***	—	.60***	.10	.38***	.29*	.81***	.38***	.06	.35**	.78***	.46***	.05	.14
(3) HW self-efficacy	.31***	.48***	—	.06	.34**	.36**	.60***	.66***	.14	.38***	.63***	.54***	.07	.09
(4) Effort (TR)	.16***	.28***	.13***	—	.28**	.09	.14	.03	.55***	.02	.11	.17	.50***	.43***
(5) Test score	.23***	.54***	.27***	.42***	—	.15	.44***	.25**	.24*	.12	.34**	.43***	.21*	.48***
T2 (6) Utility value	.68***	.29***	.25***	.14***	.19***	—	.44***	.29*	.12	.84***	.36**	.45***	.05	.16
(7) Self-concept	.36***	.84***	.47***	.29***	.54***	.35***	—	.44**	.12	.41***	.88***	.55***	.09	.29**
(8) HW self-efficacy	.30***	.38***	.58***	.15***	.28***	.29***	.46***	—	.21*	.25†	.46***	.48***	.19*	.14†
(9) Effort (TR)	.23***	.30***	.16***	.67***	.41***	.21***	.33***	.18***	—	.06	.07	.20*	.72***	.37***
T3 (10) Utility value	.60***	.27***	.19***	.11***	.20***	.66***	.30***	.26***	.18***	—	.36***	.47***	.12	.02
(11) Self-concept	.32***	.79***	.43***	.25***	.50***	.31***	.85***	.41***	.29***	.35***	—	.58***	.04	.26*
(12) HW self-efficacy	.29***	.41***	.52***	.10***	.27***	.30***	.48***	.59***	.16***	.33***	.51***	—	.19*	.20*
(13) Effort (TR)	.20***	.30***	.15***	.62***	.37***	.18***	.32***	.21***	.71***	.16***	.33***	.17***	—	.30**
(14) Test score	.16***	.43***	.19***	.22***	.51***	.11***	.40***	.20***	.24***	.12***	.40***	.18***	.24***	—

Note. T = time point; HW = homework; TR = teacher rating.
†p < .10. *p < .05. **p < .01. ***p < .01.

condition (posttest: β = .30, p < .000; follow-up: β = .26, p < .001) and the text condition (posttest: β = .14, p = .011; follow-up: β = .16, p = .004) (see Gaspard, Dicke, Flunger, Brisson, et al., 2015).

Treatment Effects at Posttest and Follow-Up

Treatment effects at posttest and follow-up are reported in Table 4. Concerning math self-concept, students in classes in the quotations condition reported statistically significant higher values at the posttest (β = .10, p = .019) than students in classes in the control condition, controlling for their initial values. At the follow-up, this effect was slightly smaller and missed statistical significance (β = .09, p = .062). The text condition did not show a statistically significant effect on students' math self-concept neither at the posttest (β = .03, p = .240) nor follow-up (β = .03, p = .264).

With regards to math homework self-efficacy, students in classes in the quotations condition reported statistically significant higher values than students in classes in the control condition at both the posttest (β = .16, p = .002) and follow-up (β = .20, p = .001). For students in classes in the text condition, no treatment effect on math homework self-efficacy was observed at the posttest (β = .08, p = .069). However, at the follow-up, a statistically significant positive treatment effect emerged (β = .16, p = .008), which was not significantly different from the effect of the quotations condition according to a Wald χ^2 test, $\chi_2(1)$ = 0.37, p = .544.

Concerning students' individual effort in mathematics as rated by their teachers, positive effects of the quotations condition emerged at both the posttest (β = .14, p = .029) and the follow-up (β = .12, p = .046). The text condition had no statistically significant effect on students' effort as observed by their teachers neither at the posttest (β = .01, p = .463) nor follow-up (β = −.01, p = .474).

As for math achievement, students in classes in the quotations condition had statistically significant better scores in the speed test (β = .18, p = .004) than students in classes in the control condition. Students in classes in the text condition, however, did not perform significantly better at the test (β = .06, p = .168) than students in classes in the control group.

Discussion

What can be done to help secondary school students become more self-confident, work harder, and show higher performance in mathematics? Based on the findings of the present study, a short relevance intervention (90 minutes in class, two reinforcement tasks at home) seems to be a promising support measure. In a cluster randomized controlled experiment, the effectiveness of two relevance interventions including the presentation of examples about the utility of mathematics for various life domains and individual writing assignments differing by condition was compared in math

Table 4

Effects of the Relevance Interventions on Students' Competence Beliefs, Teacher-Rated Effort, and Test-Based Achievement in Mathematics

| | Self-Concept | | | | | | Homework Self-Efficacy | | | | | | Teacher-Rated Effort | | | | | | Test Score | | |
| | T2 | | | T3 | | | T2 | | | T3 | | | T2 | | | T3 | | | T3 | | |
	β	(SE)	p	β	(SE)	p	β	(SE)	p	β	(SE)	p	β	(SE)	p	β	(SE)	p	β	(SE)	p
Student level																					
DV at T1	.84	(.02)	.000	.79	(.02)	.000	.59	(.03)	.000	.53	(.02)	.000	.67	(.03)	.000	.63	(.02)	.000	.55	(.03)	.000
Class level																					
DV at T1	.83	(.06)	.000	.80	(.06)	.000	.69	(.08)	.000	.62	(.09)	.000	.52	(.10)	.000	.46	(.09)	.000	.30	(.06)	.000
Quotations	.10	(.05)	.019	.09	(.06)	.062	.16	(.05)	.002	.20	(.06)	.002	.14	(.08)	.029	.12	(.07)	.046	.18	(.07)	.004
Text	.03	(.05)	.240	.03	(.05)	.264	.08	(.06)	.069	.16	(.06)	.008	.01	(.07)	.463	−.01	(.07)	.474	.06	(.06)	.168
Residuals																					
Student level	.27	(.01)	.000	.35	(.02)	.000	.63	(.03)	.000	.68	(.03)	.000	.51	(.03)	.000	.58	(.03)	.000	.72	(.03)	.000
Class level	.02	(.01)	.000	.02	(.01)	.001	.01	(.01)	.104	.02	(.01)	.057	.05	(.01)	.000	.05	(.01)	.000	.02	(.01)	.002

Note. Students' gender, pretest cognitive ability score, and end-of-year math grade in Grade 8 were included in the models as auxiliary variables. β = standardized regression coefficient; SE = standard error; p = one-tailed p value; DV = dependent variable; T = time point.

classrooms in Grade 9. Commenting on quotations about the relevance of mathematics fostered students' self-concept, homework self-efficacy, teacher-rated effort, and test scores in mathematics until up to 5 months after the intervention. Writing a text about the relevance of mathematics promoted students' long-term homework self-efficacy in mathematics to the same extent as the quotations condition, but no statistically significant effects were found on other outcomes under study.

New Insights Into the Effectiveness of Classroom-Based Relevance Interventions

Researchers in STEM fields acknowledge a need for relevance-enhanced teaching approaches that are highly effective and implementable by educational practitioners in real-life classroom contexts (e.g., Davis & McPartland, 2012; Osborne & Dillon, 2008). However, experimental studies testing the effectiveness of different relevance interventions under realistic and natural educational conditions are still rare. Using an adequate sample size of 82 ninth-grade classes, the effects of two class-level relevance interventions implemented in a real-life classroom setting on students' competence beliefs, teacher-rated effort, and achievement were assessed in the current study. Such a broad range of important outcomes has rarely been considered in prior motivation intervention studies (see meta-analytic and narrative reviews on motivation interventions in education by Lazowski & Hulleman, 2016; Rosenzweig & Wigfield, 2016). The direct comparison of two treatment conditions, inclusion of the teacher's perspective, and use of a follow-up measurement in the treatment evaluation constitute further innovations in classroom-based relevance intervention research.

The Quotations Condition: A Promising New Approach

The overall pattern of results found in the present study suggests that a newly developed intervention approach including the evaluation of quotations about the relevance of mathematics in young adults' lives was more effective than a strategy adapted from prior research, namely, the self-generation of arguments for the relevance of mathematics in a text (e.g., Hulleman & Harackiewicz, 2009). This finding corresponds with the results concerning the effects of the MoMa interventions on students' value beliefs (Gaspard, Dicke, Flunger, Brisson, et al., 2015) and student-rated effort (Gaspard et al., 2016) and may be explained in various ways.

First, although several examples of the utility of mathematics were discussed in the presentation preceding the writing assignment, finding and describing reasons for the relevance of mathematics as a domain in a text might have been a difficult task for the students (see Harackiewicz et al., 2010). Students in the text condition might therefore not have come up with the same number and range of relevance arguments that students read in the quotations.

Second, the writing of a text using reasoned argument—a typical task performed in diverse school subjects—might have been less engaging to students than the comparatively novel task of commenting on quotations. Compared to the text assignment, the novelty of the quotations assignment might thus have resulted in more in-depth and sustained learning about the relevance of mathematics (see Finn & Zimmer, 2012).

Third, differences in the quality of the connections made between mathematical knowledge and students' personal lives might also have contributed to the different pattern of results for the intervention conditions (e.g., Canning & Harackiewicz, 2015; Hulleman & Cordray, 2009; Hulleman et al., 2017). By getting authentic information about the utility of mathematics from young adults that ninth graders can easily connect to, students might have identified with the interviewees and realized that mathematical knowledge will be meaningful to their possible future (e.g., Markus & Nurius, 1986; Oyserman & Destin, 2010). In addition, students in the quotations condition were asked to relate the interviewees' utterances about the utility of mathematics to their personal lives by answering several questions one after the other (see Appendix in the online version of the journal). This guided step-by-step procedure might have helped students in the quotations condition to reflect on the personal relevance of mathematics more in depth than students in the text condition (see Acee & Weinstein, 2010, for another example of a successful motivation intervention using a step-by-step guidance to process persuasive messages).

Promoting Students' Competence Beliefs, Effort, and Achievement: Are the Effects Stable?

A closer look at the results of the present study suggests that students' math self-concept was promoted through the quotations condition for 6 weeks, whereas students' homework self-efficacy was fostered through both intervention conditions for 5 months. These differential treatment effects on students' competence beliefs might pertain to conceptual differences in the nature of these two outcomes (Bong & Skaalvik, 2003): Students' domain-specific self-concept seems to be more stable and less easily malleable than students' homework self-efficacy beliefs, which was also reflected in the high predictive power of students' initial math self-concept for students' subsequent math self-concept in the present study (see Table 4). The disappearance of the positive effect of the quotations condition on students' self-concept at the follow-up might have resulted from two processes taking place over time: On the one hand, students may not (yet) have perceived any actual improvement in their math achievement (compared to their previous math achievement or their performance in other domains).

An actual improvement in performance in turn has been found to be a pre-condition of a sustained promotion of students' domain-specific self-concept (see meta-analysis on self-concept interventions by O'Mara, Marsh, Craven, & Debus, 2006). On the other hand, students may have compared their own math achievement with their classmates' math performance. Such internal and external frame of reference processes (Marsh, 1986) could have led to a re-adaption to students' initial levels of math self-concepts over the course of 5 months.

Another particularly interesting finding is that teachers of classes in the quotations condition rated their students as putting more effort in their math tasks. As effects only occurred in one intervention condition and largely corresponded with findings on students' self-reported effort (Gaspard et al., 2016), it is unlikely that teachers gave a positively biased account of their students' effort due to their awareness of the class's study condition. To the contrary, it could be that the effects found on students' effort were actually underestimated due to the limited objectivity of the teacher ratings. In our sample, 57% of the teachers had already taught their students in mathematics in previous school years. Additional analyses showed that these teachers' judgments of students' effort were significantly more stable (r_{T1-T2} = .70) than those of the teachers who had not taught their classes in earlier school years (r_{T1-T2} = .63, p = .008). Preexisting evaluations of students' attitudes as well as social comparisons between the students in a class, as has been emphasized, for instance, in research on teachers' evaluations of students' achievement (e.g., McMillan, 2001; Südkamp, Kaiser, & Möller, 2012), might then have contributed to an underestimation of the intervention effects on students' effort.

Last but not least, the positive effect of the quotations condition on students' achievement 5 months after the intervention highlights the potential of this intervention approach in the longer run. The increase in both motivation and effort—factors that are particularly important for students' achievement in standardized math tests (e.g., Cole et al., 2008; Marsh et al., 2005)—might have resulted in the better test performance of students in the quotations condition.

Limitations and Suggestions for Future Research

Apart from constraints to the generalizability of the current research findings and the need for replication with other student samples—which applies to all intervention studies—there are four central limitations to the present investigation as well as resulting research suggestions. First, because in Germany students are typically not administered more than one state-based standardized achievement test (as used in the pretest) within one school year and subject, a different achievement measure had to be used in the posttest. To minimize the risk that students coping better with one of the two types of math tests would be unevenly distributed across control and experimental groups, a huge sample was used, and randomization was blocked within school. However, using achievements tests based on the same metrics would have strengthened the study even further.

Second, as this study's focus consisted of analyzing and comparing the main effects of two relevance interventions, no statements can be made about the mechanisms leading to the differences in the effects on the studied outcomes within and between the intervention conditions. More research is needed to clarify, for instance, why students' math self-concept was promoted only shortly after the intervention whereas students' homework self-efficacy was mainly affected 5 months after the intervention. Similarly, further studies are needed to explore why the quotations condition fostered all of the studied outcomes whereas the text condition only promoted homework self-efficacy. Qualitative content analyses of students' writing assignments (e.g., the range and type of relevance arguments found in the text condition, see Canning & Harackiewicz, 2015, Studies 2 and 3) and elaborate investigations on students' responsiveness (i.e., the degree to which students worked on the intervention material as intended, e.g., Hulleman & Cordray, 2009), which both are beyond the scope of the current study, might provide additional insights into these open questions. Besides, students' literacy skills might affect the quality of students' writings and thus the intervention effects. Investigating the mediating role of students' reading and writing skills in essay-based relevance interventions would be an interesting direction for future research.

Third, the unique contributions of the different elements of the relevance interventions to their effectiveness cannot be disentangled in the present study. Based on theoretical considerations made in EVT (Eccles & Wigfield, 2002) and empirical evidence from prior relevance intervention studies (e.g., Durik, Shechter, et al., 2015; Hulleman & Harackiewicz, 2009; Woolley et al., 2013), three elements were combined: First, a confidence reinforcement was implemented to avoid negative treatment effects on students who believe they cannot improve their math achievement; second, examples about the utility of mathematics were provided to facilitate working on the third element, the individual writing assignments. As students have heterogeneous motivational preconditions and needs, a combination of these different elements was chosen to address a maximum of students. Such a high fit with educational reality is an important prerequisite to enable the scaling up of educational interventions (Cohen & Loewenberg Ball, 2007). It would thus be up to future studies to investigate the importance of the three treatment elements used in the present interventions by creating different conditions with and without these respective elements (e.g., Canning & Harackiewicz, 2015; Durik, Shechter, et al., 2015).

Last but not least, the present interventions have been implemented by trained researchers who were unfamiliar with and to the classes. Future research also needs to examine the effectiveness of the present interventions when math teachers themselves carry them out in their classrooms. When teachers are responsible for implementing an intervention in their classes, there are several sources of infidelity, such as the dosage of the intervention or students' responsiveness to the treatment (e.g., Hulleman & Cordray, 2009), which could affect the treatment's effectiveness. Teachers might focus on specific elements of the interventions more strongly than others or even completely adapt the contents of the treatment based on personal and professional beliefs as well as their students' motivational features (Cohen & Loewenberg Ball, 2007). Comparing the effectiveness of teacher- and researcher-led relevance interventions with each other would thus be a crucial next step to find the most effective way of implementing the current interventions (cf. implementation science, e.g., Forman et al., 2013).

Conclusions

Despite its shortness (90 minutes in class, two short reinforcement tasks at home), the present relevance intervention program showed a sustained impact on students' competence beliefs, teacher-rated effort, and test scores in mathematics in a real-life learning setting. Integrating the presentation of utility information and a self-generation task into one approach was particularly impactful when students commented on interview quotations about the utility of mathematics in daily life situations in a writing assignment. The success of this type of relevance intervention in fostering a broad range of important educational outcomes could inspire future researchers to develop further practically relevant and even more sustained motivation interventions in STEM (e.g., by integrating different motivation theories, see Acee & Weinstein, 2010). In addition, the interventions tested in the present study could be extended by including teachers in the implementation process. By taking such further steps, the current investigation could have the potential to contribute to improving educational practice and attracting more students to STEM-related courses and occupations on a larger scale.

Notes

This research was funded in part by German Research Foundation Grant TR 553/7-1 awarded to Ulrich Trautwein, Oliver Lüdtke, and Benjamin Nagengast. Brigitte Maria Brisson, Hanna Gaspard, and Isabelle Häfner were members of the Cooperative Research Training Group of the University of Education, Ludwigsburg, and the University of Tübingen, which is supported by the Ministry of Science, Research, and the Arts in Baden-Württemberg. Hanna Gaspard and Isabelle Häfner were doctoral students of the LEAD Graduate School (GSC 1028) funded by the Excellence Initiative of the German federal and state governments. We thank Katharina Allgaier and Evelin Herbein for their help conducting this research.

[1]The ISEI is an international standard measure indicating the status of the occupation, ranging from 16 to 90.

[2]Nine of the teachers taught two classes each.

[3]Unequal class sample sizes in different conditions resulted from the fact that classes whose teachers participated with two classes were deliberately assigned to the same condition. The sample characteristics of each condition can be found in Table 2.

[4]As maximally 1.2% of the variance in the outcome variables was due to differences between schools, the school level was neglected in the analyses.

References

Acee, T. W., & Weinstein, C. E. (2010). Effects of a value-reappraisal intervention on statistics students' motivation and performance. *The Journal of Experimental Education*, *78*(4), 487–512. doi:10.1080/00220970903352753

Bakk, Z., & Vermunt, J. K. (2016). Robustness of stepwise latent class modeling with continuous distal outcomes. *Structural Equation Modeling: A Multidisciplinary Journal*, *23*(1), 20–31. doi:10.1080/10705511.2014.955104

Bandura, A. (1977). *Social learning theory*. Englewood Cliffs, NJ: Prentice-Hall.

Bandura, A. (1994). Self-efficacy. In V. S. Ramachaudran (Ed.), *Encyclopedia of human behavior* (pp. 71–81). New York, NY: Academic Press.

Baumert, J., Gruehn, S., Heyn, S., Köller, O., & Schnabel, K. U. (1997). *Bildungsverläufe und psychosoziale Entwicklung im Jugendalter (BIJU). Dokumentation – Band 1: Skalen Längsschnitt Welle 1–4* [Learning processes, educational careers, and psychosocial development in adolescence and young adulthood (BIJU). Documentation–Volume 1: Scales of Data collections 1–4]. Berlin: Max-Plank-Institut für Bildungsforschung.

Bong, M., & Skaalvik, E. M. (2003). Academic self-concept and self-efficacy: How different are they really? *Educational Psychology Review*, *15*(1), 1–40. doi:10.1023/A:1021302408382

Canning, E. A., & Harackiewicz, J. M. (2015). Teach it, don't preach it: The differential effects of directly-communicated and self-generated utility value information. *Motivation Science*, *1*(1), 47–71. doi:10.1037/mot0000015

Chouinard, R., Karsenti, T., & Roy, N. (2007). Relations among competence beliefs, utility value, achievement goals, and effort in mathematics. *British Journal of Educational Psychology*, *77*, 501–517. doi:10.1348/000709906x133589

Chouinard, R., & Roy, N. (2008). Changes in high-school students' competence beliefs, utility value and achievement goals in mathematics. *British Journal of Educational Psychology*, *78*, 31–50. doi:10.1348/000709907x197993

Cohen, D. K., & Loewenberg Ball, D. (2007). Educational innovation and the problem of scale. In B. Schneider & S.-K. McDonald (Eds.), *Scale-up in education: Ideas in principle* (Vol. 1, pp. 19–36). Plymouth, UK: Rowman & Littlefield Publishers.

Cole, J. S., Bergin, D. A., & Whittaker, T. A. (2008). Predicting student achievement for low stakes tests with effort and task value. *Contemporary Educational Psychology*, *33*(4), 609–624. doi:10.1016/j.cedpsych.2007.10.002

Craven, R. G., Marsh, H. W., Debus, R. L., & Jayasinghe, U. (2001). Diffusion effects: Control group contamination threats to the validity of teacher-administered interventions. *Journal of Educational Psychology*, *93*(3), 639–645. doi:10.1037/0022-0663.93.3.639

Davis, M. H., & McPartland, J. M. (2012). High school reform and student engagement. In S. L. Christenson, A. L. Reschly, & C. Wylie (Eds.), *Handbook of research on student engagement* (pp. 515–539). New York, NY: Springer.

Denissen, J. J., Zarrett, N. R., & Eccles, J. S. (2007). I like to do it, I'm able, and I know I am: Longitudinal couplings between domain-specific achievement, self-concept, and interest. *Child Development*, 78(2), 430–447. doi:10.1111/j.1467-8624.2007.01007.x

Durik, A. M., & Harackiewicz, J. M. (2007). Different strokes for different folks: How individual interest moderates the effects of situational factors on task interest. *Journal of Educational Psychology*, 99(3), 597–610. doi:10.1037/0022-0663.99.3.597

Durik, A. M., Hulleman, C. S., & Harackiewicz, J. M. (2015). One size fits some: Instructional enhancement to promote interest. In K. A. Renninger, M. Nieswandt, & S. Hidi (Eds.), *Interest in mathematics and science learning* (pp. 49–62). Washington, DC: American Educational Research Association.

Durik, A. M., Shechter, O. G., Noh, M., Rozek, C. S., & Harackiewicz, J. M. (2015). What if I can't? Success expectancies moderate the effects of utility value information on situational interest and performance. *Motivation and Emotion, 39*, 104–118. doi:10.1007/s11031-014-9419-0

Eccles, J. S. (2005). Subjective task values and the Eccles et al. model of achievement related choices. In A. J. Elliott & C. S. Dweck (Eds.), *Handbook of competence and motivation* (pp. 105–121). New York, NY: Guilford.

Eccles, J. S., Adler, T. F., Futterman, R., Goff, S. B., Kaczala, C. M., Meece, J. L., & Midgley, C. (1983). Expectancies, values and academic behaviors. In J. T. Spence (Ed.), *Achievement and achievement motives: Psychological and sociological approaches* (pp. 75–146). New York, NY: Freeman.

Eccles, J. S., & Wigfield, A. (1995). In the mind of the actor: The structure of adolescents' achievement task values and expectancy-related beliefs. *Personality and Social Psychology Bulletin, 21*(3), 215–225. doi:10.1177/0146167295213003

Eccles, J. S., & Wigfield, A. (2002). Motivational beliefs, values, and goals. *Annual Review of Psychology, 53*(1), 109–132. doi:10.1146/annurev.psych.53.100901.135153

Enders, C. K. (2010). *Applied missing data analysis*. New York, NY: Guilford Press.

Enders, C. K., & Tofighi, D. (2007). Centering predictor variables in cross-sectional multilevel models: A new look at an old issue. *Psychological Methods, 12*(2), 121–138. doi:10.1037/1082-989x.12.2.121

Ennemoser, M., Krajewski, K., & Schmidt, S. (2011). Entwicklung und Bedeutung von Mengen-Zahlen-Kompetenzen und eines basalen Konventions-und Regelwissens in den Klassen 5 bis 9 [Development and importance of sets and numbers competencies and of a basic knowledge of conventions and rules in classes 5 through 9]. *Zeitschrift für Entwicklungspsychologie und Pädagogische Psychologie / German Journal of Developmental and Educational Psychology, 43*(4), 228–242. doi:10.1026/0049-8637/a000055

Finn, J. D., & Zimmer, K. S. (2012). Student engagement: What is it? Why does it matter? In S. L. Christenson, A. L. Reschly, & C. Wylie (Eds.), *Handbook of research on student engagement* (pp. 97–132). New York, NY: Springer.

Forman, S. G., Shapiro, E. S., Codding, R. S., Gonzales, J. E., Reddy, L. A., Rosenfield, S. A., . . . Stoiber, K. C. (2013). Implementation science and school psychology. *School Psychology Quarterly, 28*(2), 77–100. doi:10.1037/spq0000019

Fredricks, J. A., Blumenfeld, P. C., & Paris, A. H. (2004). School engagement: Potential of the concept, state of the evidence. *Review of Educational Research, 74*(1), 59–109. doi:10.3102/00346543074001059

Gaspard, H., Dicke, A.-L., Flunger, B., Brisson, B. M., Häfner, I., Trautwein, U., & Nagengast, B. (2015). Fostering adolescents' value beliefs for mathematics with a relevance intervention in the classroom. *Developmental Psychology, 51*(9), 1226–1240. doi:10.1037/dev0000028

Gaspard, H., Dicke, A.-L., Flunger, B., Häfner, I., Brisson, B. M., Trautwein, U., & Nagengast, B. (2016). Side effects of motivational interventions? Effects of an intervention in math classrooms on motivation in verbal domains. *AERA Open*, *2*(2), 1–14. doi:10.1177/2332858416649168

Gaspard, H., Dicke, A.-L., Flunger, B., Schreier, B. M., Häfner, I., Trautwein, U., & Nagengast, B. (2015). More value through greater differentiation: Gender differences in value beliefs about math. *Journal of Educational Psychology*, *107*(3), 663–677. doi:10.1037/edu0000003

Gaspard, H., Häfner, I., Parrisius, C., Trautwein, U., & Nagengast, B. (2017). Assessing task values in five subjects during secondary school: Measurement structure and mean level differences across grade level, gender, and academic subject. *Contemporary Educational Psychology*, *48*, 67–84. doi:10.1016/j.cedpsych.20 16.09.003

Graham, J. W. (2009). Missing data analysis: Making it work in the real world. *Annual Review of Psychology*, *60*(1), 549–576. doi:10.1146/annurev.psych.58.110 405.085530

Harackiewicz, J. M., Hulleman, C. S., Rozek, C. S., Katz-Wise, S., & Hyde, J. S. (2010, March). *Parents' understanding of the utility value of STEM courses for high school students.* Paper presented at the 2010 Biennial Meeting of the Society for Research on Adolescence, Philadelphia, PA.

Harackiewicz, J. M., Rozek, C. S., Hulleman, C. S., & Hyde, J. S. (2012). Helping parents to motivate adolescents in mathematics and science: An experimental test of a utility-value intervention. *Psychological Science*, *23*(8), 899–906. doi:10.1177/0956797611435530

Heller, K. A., & Perleth, C. (2000). *Kognitiver Fähigkeitstest für 4. bis 12. Klasse* [Cognitive Ability Test for Grades 4 through 12]. Göttingen, Germany: Hogrefe.

Howell, D. C. (2012). *Statistical methods for psychology* (8th ed.). Belmont, CA: Cengage Learning.

Hulleman, C. S., & Cordray, D. S. (2009). Moving from the lab to the field: The role of fidelity and achieved relative intervention strength. *Journal of Research on Educational Effectiveness*, *2*(1), 88–110. doi:10.1080/1934574080253925

Hulleman, C. S., Godes, O., Hendricks, B. L., & Harackiewicz, J. M. (2010). Enhancing interest and performance with a utility value intervention. *Journal of Educational Psychology*, *102*(4), 880–895. doi:10.1037/A0019506

Hulleman, C. S., & Harackiewicz, J. M. (2009). Promoting interest and performance in high school science classes. *Science*, *326*(5958), 1410–1412. doi:10.1126/ science.1177067

Hulleman, C. S., Kosovich, J. J., Barron, K. E., & Daniel, D. B. (2017). Making connections: Replicating and extending the utility value intervention in the classroom. *Journal of Educational Psychology*, *109*(3), 387–404. doi:10.1037/edu0000146

Husman, J., & Hilpert, J. (2007). The intersection of students' perceptions of instrumentality, self-efficacy, and goal orientations in an online mathematics course. *Zeitschrift für Pädagogische Psychologie / German Journal of Educational Psychology*, *21*(3–4), 229–239. doi:10.1024/1010-0652.21.3.229

Jacobs, J. E., Lanza, S., Osgood, D. W., Eccles, J. S., & Wigfield, A. (2002). Changes in children's self-competence and values: Gender and domain differences across grades one through twelve. *Child Development*, *73*(2), 509–527. doi:10.1111/ 1467-8624.00421

Korendijk, E. J. H., Hox, J. J., Moerbeek, M., & Maas, C. J. M. (2011). Robustness of parameter and standard error estimates against ignoring a contextual effect of a subject-level covariate in cluster-randomized trials. *Behavior Research Methods*, *43*(4), 1003–1013. doi:10.3758/s13428-011-0094-8

Lazowski, R. A., & Hulleman, C. S. (2016). Motivation interventions in education: A meta-analytic review. *Review of Educational Research*, *86*(2), 602–640. doi:10.3102/0034654315617832

Markus, H., & Nurius, P. (1986). Possible selves. *American Psychologist*, *41*(9), 954–969. doi:10.1037/0003-066X.41.9.954

Marsh, H. W. (1986). Verbal and math self-concepts: An internal/external frame of reference model. *American Educational Research Journal*, *23*(1), 129–149. doi:10.3102/00028312023001129

Marsh, H. W. (2005). Big-fish-little-pond effect on academic self-concept. *Zeitschrift für Pädagogische Psychologie / German Journal of Educational Psychology*, *19*(3), 119–129. doi:10.1024/1010-0652.19.3.119

Marsh, H. W., Lüdtke, O., Robitzsch, A., Trautwein, U., Asparouhov, T., Muthén, B. O., & Nagengast, B. (2009). Doubly-latent models of school contextual effects: Integrating multilevel and structural equation approaches to control measurement and sampling error. *Multivariate Behavioral Research*, *44*(6), 764–802. doi:10.1080/00273170903333665

Marsh, H. W., Trautwein, U., Lüdtke, O., Köller, O., & Baumert, J. (2005). Academic self-concept, interest, grades, and standardized test scores: Reciprocal effects models of causal ordering. *Child Development*, *76*(2), 397–416. doi:10.2307/3696511

McMillan, J. H. (2001). Secondary teachers' classroom assessment and grading practices. *Educational Measurement: Issues and Practice*, *20*(1), 20–32. doi:10.1111/j.1745-3992.2001.tb00055.x

Muthén, L. K., & Muthén, B. O. (1998–2012). *Mplus user's guide* (7th ed.). Los Angeles, CA: Muthén & Muthén.

O'Mara, A. J., Marsh, H. W., Craven, R. G., & Debus, R. L. (2006). Do self-concept interventions make a difference? A synergistic blend of construct validation and meta-analysis. *Educational Psychologist*, *41*(3), 181–206. doi:10.1207/s15326985ep4103_4

Osborne, J., & Dillon, J. (2008). *Science education in Europe: Critical reflections*. London: The Nuffield Foundation.

Oyserman, D., & Destin, M. (2010). Identity-based motivation: Implications for intervention. *The Counseling Psychologist*, *38*(7), 1001–1043. doi:10.1177/0011000010374775

Peetsma, T., & van der Veen, I. (2011). Relations between the development of future time perspective in three life domains, investment in learning, and academic achievement. *Learning and Instruction*, *21*(3), 481–494. doi:10.1016/j.learnstruc.2010.08.001

Prenzel, M., Baumert, J., Blum, W., Lehmann, R., Leutner, R., Neubrand, M., . . . Schiefele, U. (2006). *Pisa 2003: Dokumentation der Erhebungsinstrumente* [Pisa 2003: Documentation of assessment instruments]. Münster: Waxmann Verlag.

Raudenbush, S. W. (1997). Statistical analysis and optimal design for cluster randomized trials. *Psychological Methods*, *2*(2), 173–185. doi:10.1037//1082-989x.2.2.173

Reschly, A. L., & Christenson, S. L. (2012). Jingle, jangle, and conceptual haziness: Evolution and future directions of the engagement construct. In S. L. Christenson, A. L. Reschly, & C. Wylie (Eds.), *Handbook of research on student engagement* (pp. 3–20). New York, NY: Springer.

Roeser, R. W., Eccles, J. S., & Sameroff, A. J. (2000). School as a context of early adolescents' academic and social-emotional development: A summary of research findings. *Elementary School Journal*, *100*(5), 443–471. doi:10.1086/499650

Rosenzweig, E. Q., & Wigfield, A. (2016). STEM motivation interventions for adolescents: A promising start, but further to go. *Educational Psychologist, 51*(2), 146–163. doi:10.1080/00461520.2016.1154792

Ryan, R. M., & Deci, E. L. (2000). Self-determination theory and the facilitation of intrinsic motivation, social development, and well-being. *American Psychologist, 55*(1), 68–78. doi:10.1037110003-066X.55.1.68

Schmidt, S., Ennemoser, M., & Krajewski, K. (Eds.). (2013). *Deutscher Mathematiktest für 9. Klassen* [German mathematics test for Grade 9]. Göttingen: Hogrefe.

Schuitema, J., Peetsma, T., & van der Veen, I. (2014). Enhancing student motivation: A longitudinal intervention study based on future time perspective theory. *The Journal of Educational Research, 107*(6), 467–481. doi:10.1080/002206 71.2013.836467

Shechter, O. G., Durik, A. M., Miyamoto, Y., & Harackiewicz, J. M. (2011). The role of utility value in achievement behavior: The importance of culture. *Personality and Social Psychology Bulletin, 37*(3), 303–317. doi:10.1177/0146167210396380

Stevens, J. P. (2012). *Applied multivariate statistics for the social sciences* (5th ed.). London: Routledge.

Südkamp, A., Kaiser, J., & Möller, J. (2012). Accuracy of teachers' judgments of students' academic achievement: A meta-analysis. *Journal of Educational Psychology, 104*(3), 743–762. doi:10.1037/a0027627

Trautwein, U., & Lüdtke, O. (2009). Predicting homework motivation and homework effort in six school subjects: The role of person and family characteristics, classroom factors, and school track. *Learning and Instruction, 19*(3), 243–258. doi:10.1016/j.learninstruc.2008.05.001

Trautwein, U., Lüdtke, O., Kastens, C., & Köller, O. (2006). Effort on homework in grades 5–9: Development, motivational antecedents, and the association with effort on classwork. *Child Development, 77*(4), 1094–1111. doi:10.1111/j.1467-8624.2006.00921.x

Trautwein, U., Lüdtke, O., Roberts, B. W., Schnyder, I., & Niggli, A. (2009). Different forces, same consequence: Conscientiousness and competence beliefs are independent predictors of academic effort and achievement. *Journal of Personality and Social Psychology, 97*(6), 1115–1128. doi:10.1037/a0017048

Trautwein, U., Lüdtke, O., Schnyder, I., & Niggli, A. (2006). Predicting homework effort: Support for a domain-specific, multilevel homework model. *Journal of Educational Psychology, 98*(2), 438–456. doi:10.1037/0022-0663.98.2.438

Trautwein, U., Nagengast, B., Marsh, H. W., Gaspard, H., Dicke, A.-L., Lüdtke, O., & Jonkmann, K. (2013). Expectancy-value theory revisited: From expectancy-value theory to expectancy-valueS theory? In D. M. McInerney, H. W. Marsh, & R. G. Craven (Eds.), *Theory driving research: New wave perspectives on self-processed and human development* (pp. 233–249). Charlotte, NC: Information Age Publishing.

Tymms, P. (2004). Effect sizes in multilevel models. In I. Schagen & K. Elliot (Eds.), *But what does it mean? The use of effect sizes in educational research* (pp. 55–66). London: National Foundation for Educational Research.

Walton, G. M. (2014). The new science of wise psychological interventions. *Current Directions in Psychological Science, 23*(1), 73–82. doi:10.1177/0963721 413512856

Wigfield, A., & Cambria, J. (2010). Students' achievement values, goal orientations, and interest: Definitions, development, and relations to achievement outcomes. *Developmental Review, 30*(1), 1–35. doi:10.1016/J.Dr.2009.12.001

Wigfield, A., Eccles, J. S., Schiefele, U., Roeser, R. W., & Davis-Kean, P. (2006). Development of achievement motivation. In N. Eisenberg (Ed.), *Handbook of child psychology* (6th ed., Vol. 3, pp. 933–1002). Hoboken, NJ: John Wiley & Sons.

Woolley, M. E., Rose, R. A., Orthner, D. K., Akos, P. T., & Jones-Sanpei, H. (2013). Advancing academic achievement through career relevance in the middle grades: A longitudinal evaluation of CareerStart. *American Educational Research Journal, 50*(6), 1309–1335. doi:10.3102/0002831213488818

Yeager, D. S., & Walton, G. M. (2011). Social-psychological interventions in education: They're not magic. *Review of Educational Research, 81*(2), 267–301. doi:10.3102/0034654311405999

Zimmerman, B. J., & Kitsantas, A. (2005). Homework practices and academic achievement: The mediating role of self-efficacy and perceived responsibility beliefs. *Contemporary Educational Psychology, 30*(4), 397–417. doi:10.1016/j.cedpsych.2005.05.003

Manuscript received March 1, 2016
Final revision received March 24, 2017
Accepted April 5, 2017

American Educational Research Journal
December 2017, Vol. 54, No. 6, pp. 1079–1116
DOI: 10.3102/0002831217716301
© 2017 AERA. http://aerj.aera.net

Strategic Staffing?
How Performance Pressures Affect the Distribution of Teachers Within Schools and Resulting Student Achievement

Jason A. Grissom
Vanderbilt University
Demetra Kalogrides
Susanna Loeb
Stanford University

School performance pressures apply disproportionately to tested grades and subjects. Using longitudinal administrative data—including achievement data from untested grades—and teacher survey data from a large urban district, we examine schools' responses to those pressures in assigning teachers to high-stakes and low-stakes classrooms. We find that teachers with more positive performance measures in both tested and untested classrooms are more likely to be placed in a tested classroom in the following year. Performance measures even more strongly predict a high-stakes teaching assignment in schools with low state accountability grades and where principals exercise more assignment influence. In elementary schools, we show that such "strategic" teacher assignment disadvantages early grades, concentrating less effective teachers in K–2 classrooms. Reassignment of ineffective upper-grades teachers to early grades systematically results in lower K–2 math and reading achievement gains. Moreover, evidence suggests that students' lower early-grades achievement persists into subsequent tested grades.

KEYWORDS: accountability, early learning, principals, student achievement, teacher placement

Evidence abounds that schools respond strategically to the pressures of high-stakes accountability systems in both productive and unproductive ways. Researchers have documented a long list of unintended responses to these pressures, including gaming the composition of the population by suspending low achievers during the testing window or reclassifying them as learning disabled (e.g., Figlio, 2006; Jacob, 2005), focusing school resources away from lower achievers toward those near proficiency cutoffs (Booher-Jennings, 2005), or cheating by altering students' responses to test items (Jacob & Levitt, 2003). More productively, accountability pressures push schools to increase instructional time, focus teacher attention on core subjects, provide supplemental educational services for struggling students, and expand time for teacher collaboration (see Dee, Jacob, & Schwartz, 2013; Hannaway & Hamilton, 2008; Jacob & Lefgren, 2004; Rouse, Hannaway, Goldhaber, & Figlio, 2007). Some recent evidence suggests that strategic behavior seeking to improve student test performance may also extend to how schools make decisions about their teacher workforce. For example, in interviews principals report engaging in strategic hiring, assignment, development, and dismissal practices with the goal of improving their schools' average test performance (Cohen-Vogel, 2011). However, research documenting these strategic talent management decisions systematically or linking them explicitly to accountability pressures or subsequent impacts is scarce.

In this article, we focus specifically on one area of strategic staffing that Cohen-Vogel (2011) identified: assignments of teachers to students and classes. While a long literature has examined the sorting of teachers across schools—and repeatedly documented the matching of better qualified teachers toward higher achieving students (e.g., Clotfelter, Ladd, & Vigdor, 2006; Lankford, Loeb, & Wyckoff, 2002)—a small literature has begun to consider teacher assignment decisions within schools as well. For example, despite research demonstrating that beginning teachers are less effective (Nye, Konstantopoulos, & Hedges, 2004; Rockoff, 2004), schools systematically assign less experienced teachers to lower performing students, though evidence also suggests that this tendency is less pronounced in high-growth schools (Grissom, Kalogrides, & Loeb, 2015; Kalogrides, Loeb, & Béteille, 2013; Loeb, Kalogrides, & Béteille, 2012). Decisions about how schools deploy existing teacher resources likely impact student achievement levels and gaps among students, given that matching a student to an effective teacher is a primary means whereby a school can affect his or her outcomes (e.g., Aaronson, Barrow, & Sander, 2007). Assignment decisions are also likely more amenable to direct influence from school leaders than some other areas of personnel management, such as teacher hiring, which may rest more heavily on factors (e.g., the quality of the applicant pool) that are beyond school leader control.[1]

JASON A. GRISSOM is an associate professor of public policy and education at Vanderbilt University's Peabody College, 230 Appleton Place, Nashville, TN 37203; e-mail: *jason.grissom@vanderbilt.edu*. His research interests include school leadership, educator labor markets, and K–12 politics and governance.

DEMETRA KALOGRIDES is a research associate at the Center for Education Policy Analysis at Stanford University. Her research interests include inequality in educational attainment and achievement, teacher and principal labor markets, school segregation, and quantitative methods.

SUSANNA LOEB is the Barnett Family Professor of Education at Stanford University. She specializes in education policy with a focus on school governance and finance and educator labor markets.

Thus, by understanding and adjusting patterns of teacher assignment across classrooms, we may be able to improve outcomes for students and reduce gaps in access to high-quality teachers.

Because accountability systems measure school performance using student achievement test scores from some grades and subjects but not others, accountability pressures are felt disproportionately in some classrooms. Under No Child Left Behind (NCLB), in most states—including Florida, the context for the present study—elementary schools were evaluated on the basis of math and reading achievement performance in Grades 3, 4, and 5, a requirement that continues under the Every Student Succeeds Act (ESSA). In Cohen-Vogel's (2011) interviews, principals reported reassigning teachers from these "high-stakes" classrooms if their students showed inadequate test score performance to "low-stakes" assignments in grades K–2. Such a strategic move may improve student performance in the tested grade (and thus *measured* school performance) in the short term, particularly if a more effective teacher is available to fill the reassigned teacher's position. Longer term effects on school performance are less clear. They could be positive if, for example, the move results in a better match of a teacher's skills to his or her students or the content, or they could be negative if that match is poor or if the move is to an assignment that is low-stakes but that has important effects on later learning, as might be the case for an ineffective third-grade teacher moved to an untested position in first grade (Claessens, Duncan, & Engel, 2009; Fuller & Ladd, 2013). Evidence on the importance of early-grades learning for later life outcomes suggests that a system that pushes schools to concentrate ineffective teachers in the earliest grades could have serious unintended consequences (Chetty et al., 2011; Schweinhart et al., 2005).

Using detailed administrative and survey data from Miami-Dade County Public Schools (M-DCPS), we begin by asking whether the test performance of a teacher's students is associated with the likelihood that a teacher remains in or is moved out of a tested grade or subject in a subsequent year and how these patterns vary by school characteristics, such as accountability grade. This analysis is a replication of analysis by Chingos and West (2011), who showed that Florida teachers with lower value-added scores were less likely to be reassigned to tested classrooms, and Fuller and Ladd (2013), who found similar results in North Carolina. We then significantly extend prior analyses in several important ways. First, we draw on data from a survey that we conducted with M-DCPS teachers to characterize class assignment policies in each school and test whether the relationship between teacher performance and where they are subsequently assigned varies by the participants that have higher perceived influence over assignments (e.g., the principal, parents). Second, we make use of a low-stakes test given in early grades in M-DCPS, the Stanford Achievement Test, Version 10 (SAT-10), to estimate value-added for early-grades teachers and test whether high performers are more likely to be moved into grades tested for accountability purposes, a pattern suggested by Fuller and Ladd's (2013) analysis of reassignment of K–2 teachers by measures of teacher qualifications (e.g., licensure exam scores). Finally, we assess whether a strategic school response to accountability pressure that moves low-performing teachers from high- to low-stakes classrooms is likely to have negative effects on student learning in grades in which the accountability pressures are weaker, focusing specifically on elementary schools. We estimate achievement gains on the SAT-10 for first and second graders taught by teachers reassigned from tested elementary grades, then further investigate whether there are indirect consequences for achievement when these students later move into grades tested under the accountability regime.

The next section reviews what we know about strategic responses to accountability pressures, including the small body of research on strategic personnel assignments. We then detail our data and methods before turning to a presentation of the results. We conclude with a discussion of the implications of the study for school and district policy and for future research.

Strategic Responses to Accountability Pressures

Test-based accountability systems, such as those imposed by NCLB and ESSA, create incentives for schools to improve student outcomes and sanctions for schools that fail to do so. Prior research has documented the effects of accountability policy on the behaviors of teachers and school leaders. The types of strategies identified by these studies can be grouped into two categories: behaviors that increase average test scores without improving productivity and those that create changes in the ways that schools deliver education that generate meaningful improvements in student achievement.

There are several examples in the literature that describe educators' attempts to "game the system" as a means of increasing average student test scores. Jacob and Levitt (2003), for example, estimate that a minimum of 4% to 5% of elementary school teachers in Chicago Public Schools cheated on state tests by systematically altering students' responses to test items. The frequency of cheating increased when the incentives to do so increased (via grade retention policies tied to minimum test score cutoffs and threats to reconstitute low-performing schools). Figlio (2006) shows that schools differentially punish low-achieving students for misbehavior, particularly during testing periods, as a way of removing them from the testing pool. He compares incidents involving more than one student that was suspended. He finds that schools always tend to assign harsher punishments to low-performing students than to high-performing students but that this gap grows during the testing period of the school year. Moreover, these patterns are only evident in tested grades. There is also evidence of schools responding to accountability pressure by differentially reclassifying low-achieving students as learning disabled to exclude their scores from the formula that determines schools' accountability ratings. Figlio and Getzler (2006), for instance, use student fixed-effects models and find increases in reclassification rates for low-income and previously low-performing students as *disabled* after the introduction of Florida's testing regime. Such behaviors were concentrated among low-income schools on the margin of failing to meet the accountability standards.

Such practices may increase schools' average test scores—all important for high-stakes accountability systems—but have little impact on actual student learning. Other studies, however, suggest that schools also respond to accountability pressures in educationally meaningful ways. Rouse et al. (2007), for example, find that student achievement increases in response to accountability pressure and that changes to school policy explain at least some of these increases. In their study, increased accountability pressure was associated with increased focus on low-performing students, increases in the amount of the school day spent on instruction, increases in the resources available to teachers, and decreases in the amount of control held by the principal. Dee et al. (2013) similarly conclude that NCLB increased the allocation of instructional time to math and language arts, which may partially account for achievement gains associated with the law (Dee & Jacob, 2011). Cohen-Vogel's (2011) study shows that school leaders engage in a variety of personnel policies in hopes of increasing student achievement, which she calls "staffing to the test." In interviews, principals reported hiring, developing, and dismissing teachers in an effort to improve their schools' average test performance. For example, principals described selecting teacher candidates in part by looking at their past student outcomes data in hopes of ensuring that they are hiring more effective teachers.

Strategic Assignment of Personnel

Principals report using student test scores when making decisions to reassign teachers within their schools (Cohen-Vogel, 2011; Goldring et al., 2014; Grissom et al., 2017). This strategic approach to human resource decisions is especially evident in lower performing schools, where some principals report moving effective teachers to tested grades (Cohen-Vogel, 2011). In keeping with the principals' reports, Chingos and West (2011) find that effective teachers are more likely to remain in grades and subjects where high-stakes testing takes place and that this relationship is strongest in schools receiving lower ratings from the state's accountability system. Similarly, Fuller and Ladd (2013), in an examination of the distribution of elementary teacher credentials across grades in North Carolina, show that NCLB pushed schools to move more qualified early-grades teachers to higher grades and less qualified upper elementary teachers to early-grades.

The strategic allocation of staff described by these prior studies aligns with the large body of literature demonstrating that there is wide variability in teacher effectiveness and that teachers are one of the most important resources available to schools to improve student learning outcomes (Aaronson et al., 2007; Kane, Rockoff, & Staiger, 2008; Nye et al., 2004; Rivkin, Hanushek, & Kain, 2005; Rockoff, 2004; Sanders & Rivers, 1996). Test-based accountability systems focus on student achievement in certain grades and subjects while placing less emphasis on others. School leaders therefore have clear incentives to keep their more effective teachers in tested grades and subjects while reassigning less effective teachers to positions that will not influence the school's accountability rating.

It is not clear, however, what effects on students or schools this type of strategic reallocation of low-performing teachers to low-stakes classrooms has over the long term, particularly if those low-stakes classrooms are in earlier grades that feed into later high-stakes classrooms. On one hand, the skills necessary to be successful in earlier grades may not be the same as those required to teach older children effectively, and reassignment may positively impact a teacher's performance if it leads to a better match with that teacher's skills. In this case, student achievement may be positively affected. On the other hand, if an ineffective teacher in later grades is also ineffective in earlier grades, such reassignment may have negative longer-run consequences for both students and the school, particularly if student learning trajectories are affected by the foundations laid in earlier grades. Certainly learning is a cumulative process, and student learning in early grades is a strong predictor of achievement in later schooling (e.g., Claessens et al., 2009; Perry, Guidubaldi, & Kehle, 1979; Watts, Duncan, Siegler, & Davis-Kean, 2014). As one principal in a high-growth school interviewed by Cohen-Vogel (2011) put it,

> You can't say you want your higher achieving teachers in grades three, four, five. If you have high achieving teachers in K, one, and two, then you are going to be okay with three, four. . . . You need strong teachers everywhere. (p. 494)[2]

Relocating an ineffective teacher to a grade prior to the onset of high-stakes testing may allow for the placement of a more effective teacher in the tested grade, but gains from that replacement may be undercut in subsequent years if there are deleterious effects on student learning in the earlier grade associated with the ineffective teacher that cannot be fully remediated. Moreover, student learning in early grades may affect post-schooling outcomes as college attendance and earnings, even if gains made in early grades do not show up in differences in achievement scores in later grades (Chetty et al., 2011).

Data

Our analysis of strategic assignment uses data from administrative files on all staff, students, and schools in the Miami-Dade County Public School district from the 2003–2004 through the 2013–2014 school years. We also use data from a web-based survey of 8,000 M-DCPS teachers we conducted in 2011.[3] M-DCPS is the largest public school district in Florida and the fourth largest in the United States, trailing only the school districts in New York City, Los Angeles, and Chicago. In 2010, M-DCPS enrolled 347,000 students, more than 225,000 of whom were Hispanic. Nearly 90% of students in the district are either Black or Hispanic, and 60% qualify for free or reduced price lunches.

Administrative data come from three different files provided by the district: test scores and basic demographic information for all students in the district, course-level data that link students to each of their teachers in each year, and a staff-level file with information on all district employees. The student-level files include student race, gender, free/reduced price lunch eligibility, number of times the student was absent that year, and the number of days the student missed school due to suspensions that year. The test score data include FCAT math and reading scores. The FCAT is given in math and reading to students in Grades 3–10. We also obtained spring SAT-10 scores for students in Grades Kindergarten, 1, and 2. The second grade SAT-10 scores are available from spring 2004 to 2014, but M-DCPS began administering the test to kindergartners and first graders later; first-grade scores are available from 2009 to 2014 and kindergarten scores from 2011 to 2014. The staff database includes demographic measures, prior experience in the district, current position, and highest degree earned for all district staff from the 2003–2004 through the 2013–2014 school years.

In our 2011 survey, we asked teachers which actors were involved in the assignment of students to their classroom that year (i.e., 2010–2011). We provided the teachers with a list of actors, including themselves, other teachers in their grade, the principal, and parents, and the respondents indicated involvement with a binary response of yes or no. Next, we presented teachers with the same set of actors and asked how much influence each one had over the assignment of students to their classroom that year. We recorded responses on a scale of 1 (*not involved/no influence*) to 5 (*a lot of influence*). We use responses to these items about the matching of students to teachers to proxy for influence in the teacher assignment process more generally. Note that not all survey respondents were asked each of these assignment influence items; to reduce respondent burden, teachers were presented with a random set of items (within a broader module on class assignments). Although we still have approximately 3,000 responses to each of these items, the individual teachers differ. Partly for this reason, in our analyses we aggregate teachers' responses to the school level.[4]

We combine the survey data with the administrative data to create a teacher-level file with aggregate survey responses, demographic information from administrative data, and characteristics of the students in teachers' courses generated by matching teachers to student course-level data. Florida schools test students in Grades 3 through 10. In K–5 elementary schools, therefore, kindergarten, first, and second grades are untested grades while third, fourth, and fifth grades are tested grades. For middle and high schools, we consider math and English/reading in Grades 6 through 10 to be tested grades/subjects. We code a teacher as teaching in a tested grade or subject if more than 50% of his or her students in a given year are in Grades 3–10 and are enrolled in math or English/reading courses with that teacher. Note that in our data, elementary school students also have course-level data, but their teacher is generally the same across most subjects.

Table 1 provides the means and standard deviations of the main variables used in our analyses. The first three columns show descriptive statistics for teachers in the administrative data, and the final three columns show descriptive statistics for teachers that responded to our survey. The characteristics of our survey sample look remarkably similar to the characteristics of the district as a whole. Survey respondents are similar to the district population of teachers in terms of race/ethnicity, gender, highest degree earned, total years of experience, and whether they teach in a tested grade or subject. Teachers average about 11 years of experience in the district, they are predominately female (80%), roughly 45% are Hispanic, 25% are Black, and nearly 40% have a master's degree or higher. The average teacher's class is 28% Black, 9% White, and includes approximately 70% of students receiving free/reduced price lunches.

Table 1 also shows basic descriptive statistics for teacher reports of stakeholder involvement in class assignments in the survey. Sixteen percent of survey respondents report that they themselves participate in the class assignment process at their school. Teachers report more involvement from principals, assistant principals, and counselors, with 51%, 64%, and 38%, respectively, reporting involvement from these three types of personnel. Seven percent of teachers also report that students and parents play some role in determining student/class assignments.

Methods

Our analysis comprises multiple components. First, we examine whether principals engage in strategic staffing when making teacher assignments to high-stakes classrooms. We do so by estimating the relationship between teacher effectiveness and assignments to tested grades and subjects. We test whether teachers in tested areas are more likely to be moved into a nontested area following a year that their students perform poorly on state tests. For teachers who teach in a tested classroom in year t, we predict

Table 1
Descriptive Statistics

	Administrative Data			Survey Data		
	M	SD	N	M	SD	N
Teacher characteristics						
Female	0.77		196,879	0.80		6,232
White	0.27		196,882	0.30		6,232
Black	0.26		196,882	0.25		6,232
Hispanic	0.45		196,882	0.43		6,232
Other race	0.02		196,882	0.02		6,232
MA or higher	0.37		196,882	0.40		6,232
Experience in the district	10.54	9.16	196,882	11.09	8.95	6,232
Teaches tested grade	0.37		182,739	0.36		5,882
Switches from tested to nontested grade next year[a]	0.14		61,241	0.16		2,104
Class characteristics						
Average prior year math achievement	−0.13	0.71	150,119	−0.11	0.71	5,260
Average prior year reading achievement	−0.14	0.72	150,878	−0.13	0.72	5,260
Proportion receiving free or reduced lunch	0.69	0.24	196,770	0.74	0.22	6,228
Proportion Black	0.28	0.32	196,770	0.29	0.33	6,228
Proportion White	0.09	0.12	196,770	0.08	0.11	6,228
Involvement in class assignments (yes/no)						
Me				0.16	0.36	6,568
Other teachers in my grade				0.12	0.32	6,568
Teachers in the grade below				0.16	0.36	6,568
Other teachers in my grade				0.11	0.32	6,568
Principal				0.51	0.50	6,568
Assistant principals				0.64	0.48	6,568
Counselors				0.38	0.48	6,568
Parents				0.07	0.26	6,568
Students				0.07	0.25	6,568

[a]Restricted to teachers in a tested grade in year $t − 1$.

whether they remain in a tested classroom in year $t + 1$ as a function of a measure of their performance and control variables:

$$\Pr \left(tested\ classroom\ at\ t + 1\right)_{it} = \beta_0 + PERFORMANCE_{it}\beta_1 + T_{it}\beta_2 + \delta_{st} + \varepsilon_{ist}. \quad (1)$$

Equation 1, which we estimate as a linear probability model, models the probability of remaining in a high-stakes classroom next year as a function of teacher performance, teacher-level characteristics T (gender, race, highest degree, years in current school), and a school by year fixed effect that isolates the association between assignment and performance to be within school and year combinations, namely, makes comparisons among teachers at the same school at the same time. These models are run at the teacher level, with standard errors clustered at the teacher level as well.

We use three measures of teacher performance: (a) the average math and reading test scores of students in a teacher's class(es) in year t, (b) the proportion of students in a teacher's class(es) scoring proficient or higher in math and reading, and (c) teacher's value-added to math and reading achievement in year t.[5] Each are entered separately. Correlations among the measures are shown in Supplementary Table S1 in the online version of the journal. The first two sets of measures capture whether principals consider the distribution of achievement of teachers' students when determining class assignments, while the third measure captures whether principals consider (adjusted) achievement gains, which is a better proxy for teacher effects. Both average test performance and test score gains are considered in Florida's accountability formula, so principals have incentives to consider both kinds of metrics in teacher placement decisions. Importantly, however, we do not argue that principals necessarily use these *particular* measures when making class assignment decisions because the measures likely are returned to schools after such decisions are made (Goldring et al., 2015). Instead, we anticipate that principals make use of a range of other information that correlates with these measures, such as benchmark assessment results or their own classroom observations, in their decision processes.

In the second stage of our analysis, we assess whether the association between student test performance and the probability that a teacher remains in a tested area varies across schools with different characteristics. This analysis of heterogeneous responses is motivated by the likelihood that schools differ in both the strength of their incentives to improve test scores and their capacity to respond to the incentives they face. In most cases, this analysis simply includes appropriate interaction terms in the estimation of Equation 1, though in the case of one characteristic, school level, we reestimate Equation 1 separately for elementary, middle, and high schools given differences in the accountability context at each school level. For example, in middle schools, all grades are tested, so in general, the only way a middle school teacher can be switched out of a tested area is if they change subjects or switch schools. In high schools, higher grades with more advanced course content are generally preferred by teachers (Neild & Farley-Ripple, 2008), so principals may feel pressured to assign their best or more experienced teachers to those (untested) grades.

We then test interactions between teacher performance and school accountability grades, which are assigned on a 5-point scale of A (5) to F (1).[6] Here, we expect that schools facing more accountability pressure—presumably, those with low grades—feel more compelled to engage in strategic staffing as a means of improving their school's performance (Chingos & West, 2011). In a third analysis, we test for an interaction with school value-added.[7] School value-added captures the average adjusted achievement gains associated with a school in a year. We hypothesize that schools with low value-added may have less organizational capacity, including capacity to behave strategically. Thus, we expect that school value-added will be a positive moderator between teacher performance and the probability of future assignment to a tested classroom.

We next include interactions of the teachers' average student achievement/proficiency level and value-added with teacher reports of who influences class assignments. We use school-average ratings of the amount of influence of the following personnel over assignments (on a scale of 1 to 5): the teacher themselves, other teachers in their grade, teachers in the grade below, other teachers, principals, assistant principals, counselors, parents, and students. In particular, if principals' strategic considerations are driving associations between teacher performance and future assignments to tested grades—as opposed to, for example, a desire of low-performing teachers to avoid high-stakes classrooms—we expect a significant positive interaction with principal influence. Although we collected these measures in 2011, when collapsing them to the school level and combining them with administrative data from other years, we treat them as a time-invariant feature of schools.

We also test whether student learning gains in early grades are affected when students are taught by a (presumably less effective) teacher reassigned from a high-stakes grade. For this analysis, we estimate student growth models separately for math and reading using student scores on the SAT-10 in those subjects in Grades 1 and 2. These models take the form:

$$A_{it} = \beta_0 + A_{it-1}\beta_1 + Upper\_to\_Lower\_Reassigned_{it}\beta_2 + Lower\_to\_Lower\_Reassigned_{it}\beta_3 + First\_Year\_Teacher_{it}\beta_4 + X_{it}\beta_5 + C_{ct}\beta_6 + \delta_{sgt} + \varepsilon_{icgt}.$$

$$(2)$$

In this model, student i's achievement at time t is a function of his or her prior-year achievement A_{t-1} (i.e., in Grades K or 1), a vector of student characteristics X (student race, gender, free lunch eligibility, and limited English proficiency status), and the aggregate of those variables to the classroom level (C), plus a school by grade by year fixed effect δ. The variable of interest in Equation 2, *Upper_to_Lower_Reassigned*, is set equal to 1 if the student's teacher at time t was reassigned from Grades 3, 4, or 5 (i.e., a high-stakes classroom) to Grades 1 or 2 at the end of the prior year. Since all teachers that are new to a grade might exhibit lower student performance, we also include *Lower_to_Lower_Reassigned*, which is set equal to 1 if the student's teacher at time t was teaching a different K–2 grade in the prior year; and *First_Year_Teacher*, which is set to 1 if the teacher is in their first year in teaching. If teachers reassigned from high- to low-stakes classrooms are associated with lower average learning gains, the coefficient β_2 will be negative and potentially larger in magnitude (i.e., more negative) than β_3 and β_4. We cluster standard errors at the teacher level.

Finally, we test whether students taught by a reassigned teacher in Grade 2 have lower achievement in Grades 3 and 4. If reassigned teachers are less effective, then students with reassigned teachers may learn less in second grade, which may contribute to lower achievement in later grades. For this analysis, we predict student achievement on the FCAT in third and fourth grades separately for math and reading. The following equation describes the model:

$$A_{ik} = \beta_0 + SAT10_{i1}\beta_1 + Upper\_to\_Lower\_Reassigned_{i2}\beta_2$$
$$+ Lower\_to\_Lower\_Reassigned_{i2}\beta_3 + First\_Year\_Teacher_{i2}\beta_4 \qquad (3)$$
$$+ X_{it}\beta_5 + C_{ct}\beta_6 + \delta_{sgt} + \varepsilon_{icgt}.$$

Similar to Equation 2, in this model, student i's achievement in Grade K = 3 or 4 is a function of his or her SAT-10 test score in Grade 1, a vector of student characteristics X (student race, gender, free lunch eligibility, and limited English proficiency status), and the aggregate of those variables to the classroom level (C), plus a school by grade by year fixed effect. The variable of interest in Equation 2, *Upper_to_Lower_Reassigned*, is set equal to 1 if the student's teacher in Grade 2 was reassigned from Grades 3, 4, or 5 (i.e., a high-stakes classroom) at the end of the year before the student was in their class. Again, since all teachers that are new to a grade might exhibit lower student performance, we also include *Lower_to_Lower_Reassigned*, which is set equal to 1 if the student's teacher in second grade was teaching Grade K or 1 in the year before the student was in their class. Finally, *First_Year_Teacher* is set to 1 if the student's second-grade teacher was in their first year when the student was in their class. If having a reassigned teacher in second grade has negative effects on third grade achievement, the coefficient β_2 will be negative and potentially larger in magnitude than β_3 and β_4. For these analyses, standard errors are clustered at the second-grade teacher level.

Results

Teacher Effectiveness and Assignment to Tested Students

We first examine the relationship between the test performance of a teacher's students and whether he or she remains in a tested area in a subsequent year. Approximately 70% of "tested" teachers in our sample remain in a tested grade/subject in the same school in the following year. Thirteen percent move within the same school to an untested classroom, while 7% move to a different school (5% to a tested classroom, 2% to an untested one). The remaining 10% exit the sample. We drop exiters from our analytic sample.

For teachers in a tested grade/subject in year t, we predict the probability that they stay in a tested grade/subject in $t + 1$ in three samples: all tested teachers, all tested teachers who remained in the same school, and all tested teachers who changed schools.[8] Comparing estimates for the second and third samples provides suggestive evidence about whether teacher performance is as important in determining assignments to tested/nontested areas for teachers that switch schools as those who do not.

Table 2 describes the results of these models.[9] The first row in each panel shows average effects across all school levels. Coefficients on covariates are omitted for brevity but shown in Supplementary Table S2 in the online version of the journal.

Across different teacher performance measures, the first model in each group shows a strong positive relationship between teacher performance and the probability that a teacher remains in a tested area. For example, Model 1 in Panel A shows that a one standard deviation increase in students' math test scores predicts an 8% increase in the probability that a teacher remains in a tested area in the following year. For reading (Model 4), the corresponding probability is 7%. Results are consistent when using the proportion of their students scoring proficient (Panel B) and teachers' value-added (Panel C) instead of class average achievement.[10] These results suggest that principals or others may consider both status measures (average test scores or proficiency rates of a teacher's students) and adjusted growth measures (teacher's value-added) when moving teachers across grades within schools. The value-added result holds despite the fact that the district only began providing value-added estimates to principals as part of teacher evaluations in the last two years of the data stream, suggesting that principals make use of other information about teachers' impacts on students, such as informal classroom observations, rather than on formal value-added estimates when making placement decisions.[11]

Interestingly, while coefficients are systematically larger in the samples of teachers who remain in their schools, the positive relationship between the performance measures and remaining in a tested grade generally holds up even among teachers who switch schools (value-added is the exception, though these models have much smaller samples). This result lines up with those from prior (qualitative) studies that find that many principals use information on the test performance of teachers' students when making hiring decisions and assigning transferring teachers (Cannata et al., 2017; Cohen-Vogel, 2011; Goldring et al., 2014).[12]

We also ran models relaxing the assumption of linearity in the association between the performance measures and the probability of remaining in a tested classroom. In particular, if a teacher in a tested classroom is performing at a very high level (and thus is likely performing significantly above his or her peers), it seems less likely that further increases in test scores or value-added would impact the likelihood of transitioning to a low-stakes

Table 2
Linear Probability Models Predicting Staying in a Tested Grade From Current Year to Next Year

Sample Is Teachers in Tested Classrooms at Time t Who	Math			Reading		
	Taught in Any School or Left the District at $t+1$	Remained in Same School at $t+1$	Moved to a Different School at $t+1$	Taught in Any School or Left the District at $t+1$	Remained in Same School at $t+1$	Moved to a Different School at $t+1$
	(1)	(2)	(3)	(4)	(5)	(6)
Panel A: Performance measure is mean achievement of current students this year						
Mean achievement scores of teachers' students	0.075***	0.079***	0.060***	0.069***	0.074***	0.041**
	(0.003)	(0.003)	(0.014)	(0.003)	(0.003)	(0.014)
N	58,373	46,201	4,068	60,384	47,032	4,141
Models estimated separately by school level						
Elementary	0.082***	0.084***	0.066***	0.078***	0.082***	0.035[+]
	(0.004)	(0.004)	(0.019)	(0.004)	(0.004)	(0.018)
Middle	0.070***	0.078***	0.053[+]	0.050***	0.055***	0.058[+]
	(0.007)	(0.008)	(0.029)	(0.007)	(0.008)	(0.031)
High	0.056***	0.064***	0.052[+]	0.055***	0.066***	0.034
	(0.009)	(0.009)	(0.031)	(0.008)	(0.009)	(0.033)
Panel B: Performance measure is proportion of teachers' current students scoring proficient or better this year						
	(7)	(8)	(9)	(10)	(11)	(12)
Proportion of students proficient or better	0.186***	0.187***	0.155***	0.180***	0.187***	0.133***
	(0.008)	(0.008)	(0.035)	(0.008)	(0.008)	(0.036)
N	58,356	46,186	4,068	60,367	47,017	4,141

(continued)

Table 2 (continued)

	Math			Reading		
Sample Is Teachers in Tested Classrooms at Time t Who	Taught in Any School or Left the District at $t + 1$	Remained in Same School at $t + 1$	Moved to a Different School at $t + 1$	Taught in Any School or Left the District at $t + 1$	Remained in Same School at $t + 1$	Moved to a Different School at $t + 1$
Models estimated separately by school level						
Elementary	0.213***	0.211***	0.189***	0.213***	0.222***	0.166***
	(0.009)	(0.009)	(0.045)	(0.009)	(0.009)	(0.044)
Middle	0.150***	0.154***	0.061	0.103***	0.104***	0.124
	(0.018)	(0.018)	(0.075)	(0.018)	(0.018)	(0.076)
High	0.129***	0.142***	0.133	0.133***	0.147***	−0.025
	(0.023)	(0.024)	(0.084)	(0.023)	(0.026)	(0.110)
Panel C: Performance measure is teacher value-added this year						
	(13)	(14)	(15)	(16)	(17)	(18)
Teacher value-added	0.049***	0.046***	0.013	0.034***	0.031***	0.015
	(0.003)	(0.003)	(0.016)	(0.003)	(0.003)	(0.015)
N	25,457	20,247	1,621	25,404	20,633	1,676
Models estimated separately by school level						
Elementary	0.052***	0.046***	0.049*	0.040***	0.035***	0.024
	(0.003)	(0.003)	(0.020)	(0.003)	(0.003)	(0.019)
Middle	0.054***	0.057***	0.020	0.007	0.006	−0.017
	(0.006)	(0.006)	(0.027)	(0.008)	(0.008)	(0.036)
High	0.028**	0.034***	−0.097*	0.037***	0.038***	0.015
	(0.009)	(0.009)	(0.038)	(0.008)	(0.008)	(0.038)

Note. All models contain teacher covariates and school by year fixed effects. Samples are restricted to teachers who teach students tested in math or reading in a given year. The outcome is a binary indicator for whether a teacher remains in a tested grade/subject at time $t + 1$. Standard errors (in parentheses) are clustered at the teacher level.

$^{+}p < .10.$ $^{*}p < .05.$ $^{**}p < .01.$ $^{***}p < .001.$

classroom. Supplementary Table S4 in the online version of the journal shows the result of including a squared term in the main models in Table 2. Consistent with expectations, this term is negative across models, suggesting that the probability of staying in a tested grade increases as student performance increases but does so at a declining rate.

Heterogeneity by School Characteristics

The secondary panels of Table 2 reestimate Equation 1 separately by school level. In general, the coefficients are similar across school levels, though somewhat smaller in magnitude, on average, in middle and high schools than elementary schools. Smaller coefficients for middle schools make sense because middle school teachers cannot be moved away from tested classrooms without switching subjects. While we do not know why the results are less strong for high school, it is possible that in high schools, teacher effectiveness data are less central in assignments decisions or that effective teachers' preferences for teaching 11th- and 12th-grade students are stronger than the desire on principals' part to keep experienced and/ or effective teachers in tested grades (9th and 10th grades). In addition, high school students take some end-of-course exams, which, while not important for NCLB-driven accountability, may factor into teacher assignment decisions. Still, patterns indicate that high-performing teachers, regardless of how performance is measured, tend to be reassigned to tested classrooms in all three school levels.

In Table 3, we examine whether the relationship between student performance and staying in a tested area varies by school accountability grade and school value-added. School grades of A and F are entered as indicators (with grades of B, C, and D omitted) to test for possible nonlinearities. We show results for all teachers and those who remained in the same school at time $t + 1$; we have little reason to expect accountability grade or school value-added of the "sending" school to moderate the performance-assignment relationship for school-switchers, so we omit that subsample.[13]

Results from Panel A provide evidence in support of the hypothesis that schools with lower grades might feel greater external accountability pressure that leads them to keep high-performing teachers in tested classrooms. Although among all teachers there is no evidence of an interaction for either subject (Models 1 and 3), when the sample is limited to teachers who do not switch schools, we see that the association between student achievement and the probability of remaining in a tested classroom is higher in F schools than other schools in both math and reading (Models 2 and 4). Results from Model 2 indicate that a 1 standard deviation increase in the mean math achievement of a teacher's students would be associated with an 11% increase in the probability of returning to a tested classroom the next year among teachers staying in a school with a grade of B, C, or D, compared

Table 3

Linear Probability Models Predicting Staying in a Tested Grade Between Years, by School Performance

	Math		Reading	
Sample Is Teachers in Tested Classrooms at Time t Who	Taught in Any School at $t+1$	Remained in Same School at $t+1$	Taught in Any School at $t+1$	Remained in Same School at $t+1$
	(1)	(2)	(3)	(4)
Panel A: Performance measure is mean achievement of current students this year				
School accountability grade interaction				
Mean achievement scores of teachers' students	0.082***	0.111***	0.066***	0.093***
	(0.009)	(0.010)	(0.010)	(0.011)
Mean Achievement Scores of Teachers' Students × A Grade	−0.000	−0.011+	0.009	−0.003
	(0.006)	(0.006)	(0.006)	(0.006)
Mean Achievement Scores of Teachers' Students × F Grade	0.003	0.064**	0.007	0.054*
	(0.021)	(0.024)	(0.023)	(0.026)
N	56,430	44,713	58,416	45,537
	(5)	(6)	(7)	(8)
School value-added interaction				
Mean achievement scores of teachers' students	0.071***	0.079***	0.067***	0.075***
	(0.004)	(0.004)	(0.004)	(0.004)
Mean Achievement Scores of Teachers' Students × School Value-Added	0.011**	0.015***	0.011**	0.016***
	(0.004)	(0.004)	(0.004)	(0.004)
N	46,079	36,092	46,729	36,622
	(9)	(10)	(11)	(12)
Panel B: Performance measure is proportion of teachers' current students scoring proficient or better this year				
School accountability grade interaction				
Proportion of students proficient or better	0.172***	0.182***	0.159***	0.181***
	(0.011)	(0.012)	(0.011)	(0.012)
Proportion of Students Proficient or Better × A Grade	0.028+	0.003	0.038*	0.010
	(0.015)	(0.016)	(0.015)	(0.016)
Proportion of Students Proficient or Better × F Grade	0.044	0.179*	0.075	0.215*
	(0.064)	(0.072)	(0.083)	(0.091)
N	58,356	46,186	60,367	47,017

(continued)

Table 3 **(continued)**

	Math		Reading	
	Taught in Any School at $t+1$	Remained in Same School at $t+1$	Taught in Any School at $t+1$	Remained in Same School at $t+1$
Sample Is Teachers in Tested Classrooms at Time t Who	(13)	(14)	(15)	(16)
School value-added interaction				
Proportion of students proficient or better	0.181***	0.192***	0.175***	0.193***
	(0.009)	(0.009)	(0.009)	(0.009)
Proportion of Students Proficient or Better × School Value-Added	0.032***	0.039***	0.036***	0.052***
	(0.009)	(0.010)	(0.009)	(0.010)
N	46065	36080	46715	36610
Panel C: Performance measure is teacher value-added this year				
School accountability grade interaction	(17)	(18)	(19)	(20)
Teacher value-added	0.050***	0.064***	0.043***	0.040***
	(0.009)	(0.009)	(0.009)	(0.009)
Teacher Value-Added × A Grade	−0.005	−0.008	−0.010$^+$	−0.011*
	(0.005)	(0.005)	(0.005)	(0.005)
Teacher Value-Added × F Grade	−0.004	0.058*	−0.022	−0.019
	(0.023)	(0.024)	(0.021)	(0.022)
N	24862	19777	24886	20247
School value-added interaction	(21)	(22)	(23)	(24)
Teacher value-added	0.050***	0.049***	0.035***	0.031***
	(0.003)	(0.003)	(0.003)	(0.003)
Teacher Value-Added × School Value-Added	0.003	0.003	0.008*	0.009**
	(0.003)	(0.003)	(0.003)	(0.003)
N	22,528	17,855	22,039	18,096

Note. All models contain teacher covariates and school by year fixed effects. Samples are restricted to teachers who teach students tested in math or reading in a given year. The outcome is a binary indicator for whether a teacher remains in a tested grade/subject at time $t + 1$. Standard errors (in parentheses) are clustered at the teacher level. p values are not adjusted for multiple comparisons.
$^+ p < .10.$ $* p < .05.$ $** p < .01.$ $*** p < .001.$

to a 10% increase in an A school and a 17% increase in an F school. Accountability grade results for proficiency in Panel B are similar to those in Panel A and suggest that each 10% of students who achieve proficiency in either math or reading is associated with an additional increase of about 2% in that teacher's probability of remaining in a tested grade in an F school beyond what is expected in other schools.

Panel C, in which the performance measure is teacher value-added, also shows evidence of differential activity in F schools, at least in math (Model 18). Here, a 1 *SD* increase in teacher value-added is associated with a 12% increase in the probability of teaching in a tested classroom next year in an F school, compared to just 6% in schools with higher grades.

Turning instead to school value-added as a moderator, Panel A shows that teachers whose students have higher achievement (in math and reading) are even more likely to remain in a tested classroom in schools with higher value-added, particularly when they remain in the same school (Models 5–8). In a school with average value-added, a 1 *SD* increase in student math performance is associated with an 8% increase in the probability of teaching in a tested classroom the following year, compared to 9.5% in schools whose value-added is 1 *SD* above the mean. Proficiency results (Panel B) are again very consistent with mean achievement results.

When the performance measure is teacher value-added (Panel C), we again find that higher school value-added moderates the association between performance and returning to a tested classroom among school-stayers in reading but not math. The reading result may indicate that higher value-added schools have greater capacity for strategic personnel action.

As shown in Table 4, we also find that the strength of the relationship between teacher performance and remaining in a tested area varies across teachers' reports of who influences teacher-student assignments.[14] In particular, the relationship consistently is magnified in schools where teachers say principals exercise more influence; in fact, principal influence is the only positive, statistically significant moderator in all six models. In some cases, it is also magnified where teachers report that other teachers—particularly those in the same grade—influence assignments. In contrast, the association between performance and likelihood of remaining in a tested classroom is attenuated in schools where other stakeholders, especially students and counselors, have more influence. The finding that principal influence moderates this association is consistent with the expectation that strategic behavior on behalf of school administrators, perhaps resulting from external accountability pressures, to improve measured school performance contributes to the propensity of high-performing teachers to stay in tested classrooms.[15]

Table 4

Linear Probability Models Predicting Staying in a Tested Grade Between Years, by Influence Over School Assignment Processes

	Mean Achievement Models		Proficiency Models		Value-Added Models	
	Mean Achievement Scores of Teachers' Students	Mean Achievement Scores of Teachers' Students × Assignment Factor	Proportion of Students Proficient or Better	Proportion of Students Proficient or Better × Assignment Factor	Teacher Value-Added	Teacher Value-Added × Assignment Factor
Panel A: Math						
Me	0.077***	−0.004	0.181***	0.015	0.051***	−0.005
	(0.005)	(0.011)	(0.013)	(0.028)	(0.004)	(0.009)
Other teachers in my grade	0.069***	0.023*	0.162***	0.088***	0.048***	0.003
	(0.004)	(0.011)	(0.011)	(0.027)	(0.004)	(0.009)
Teachers in the grade below	0.070***	0.011	0.168***	0.042*	0.050***	−0.002
	(0.005)	(0.007)	(0.012)	(0.019)	(0.004)	(0.007)
Principals	0.060***	0.009*	0.141***	0.025**	0.035***	0.008*
	(0.008)	(0.004)	(0.019)	(0.009)	(0.007)	(0.003)
Assistant principals	0.073***	0.001	0.179***	0.004	0.051***	−0.001
	(0.009)	(0.004)	(0.023)	(0.011)	(0.007)	(0.003)
Counselors	0.081***	−0.007[+]	0.208***	−0.026**	0.054***	−0.005
	(0.004)	(0.004)	(0.011)	(0.010)	(0.004)	(0.003)
Parents	0.083***	−0.050**	0.207***	−0.131**	0.053***	−0.023
	(0.004)	(0.019)	(0.011)	(0.048)	(0.004)	(0.016)
Students	0.083***	−0.072***	0.210***	−0.234***	0.054***	−0.049*
	(0.004)	(0.020)	(0.009)	(0.053)	(0.003)	(0.019)
N for all models in group	58,300		58,283		25,431	
Panel B: Reading						
Me	0.065***	0.009	0.163***	0.045	0.034***	−0.000
	(0.005)	(0.011)	(0.013)	(0.028)	(0.004)	(0.009)

(continued)

Table 4 (continued)

	Mean Achievement Models		Proficiency Models		Value-Added Models	
	Mean Achievement Scores of Teachers' Students	Mean Achievement Scores of Teachers' Students × Assignment Factor	Proportion of Students Proficient or Better	Proportion of Students Proficient or Better × Assignment Factor	Teacher Value-Added	Teacher Value-Added × Assignment Factor
Other teachers in my grade	0.059***	0.035**	0.145***	0.122***	0.032***	0.007
	(0.004)	(0.011)	(0.011)	(0.027)	(0.004)	(0.009)
Teachers in the grade below	0.061***	0.018*	0.154***	0.059**	0.029***	0.010
	(0.005)	(0.008)	(0.012)	(0.019)	(0.004)	(0.007)
Principals	0.052***	0.009*	0.130***	0.027**	0.017*	0.009**
	(0.008)	(0.004)	(0.019)	(0.009)	(0.007)	(0.003)
Assistant principals	0.065***	0.002	0.154***	0.013	0.043***	−0.005
	(0.009)	(0.004)	(0.023)	(0.010)	(0.008)	(0.004)
Counselors	0.077***	−0.009*	0.208***	−0.035***	0.039***	−0.007+
	(0.004)	(0.004)	(0.011)	(0.010)	(0.004)	(0.003)
Parents	0.073***	−0.026	0.191***	−0.074	0.030***	0.027
	(0.004)	(0.019)	(0.011)	(0.046)	(0.004)	(0.017)
Students	0.075***	−0.062**	0.200***	−0.214***	0.037***	−0.036*
	(0.004)	(0.020)	(0.009)	(0.052)	(0.003)	(0.018)
N for all models in group	60,305		60,288		25,378	

Note. Each row reflects estimates from three separate models. Teacher responses to our 2011 survey items on class assignments are aggregated to the school level and then treated as a time-invariant school characteristic. All models contain teacher covariates and school by year fixed effects. Samples are restricted to teachers who teach students tested in math or reading in a given year. The outcome is a binary indicator for whether a teacher remains in a tested grade/subject in the same school at time $t + 1$. Standard errors (in parentheses) are clustered at the teacher level.
+ $p < .10$. * $p < .05$. ** $p < .01$. *** $p < .001$.

Reassignments of Teachers Who Switch

Our next set of analyses builds on the models in Table 2 and shows descriptively how value-added for teachers in tested classrooms at time t varies by what grade and subject they teach at time $t + 1$. Samples are restricted to teachers who stay in the same school from time t to $t + 1$.

Table 5 shows the results. For elementary school teachers, we show mean math and reading value-added estimates for tested teachers (i.e., those in Grades 3–5) who move the next year to kindergarten, first grade, second grade, or another tested grade (i.e., moves from fourth to fifth grade), compared to those who stay in the same grade. The asterisks indicate the results of simple two-sided t tests of the hypothesis that the value-added of a given group is the same as that of teachers who do not switch grades. Note that the largest group of teachers who switch to an untested grade move to second grade (63%), followed by first grade (22%) and kindergarten (13%).[16]

For both reading and math, we find that teachers in tested classrooms who subsequently switch to early grades have substantially lower value-added than those who remain in the same grade. Estimates of the difference range in math from .43 *SD* (second grade) to .50 *SD* (first grade) and in reading from 0.32 *SD*. (first grade) to .45 *SD* (kindergarten). Teachers who switch among Grades 3–5 also have lower value-added than those who remain in the grade, but the differences in both subjects (.06–.14 *SD*) are much smaller than for those who switch to K–2; for reading, in fact, the difference is not statistically distinguishable from zero.

In middle schools, every grade is a tested grade, so teachers remaining within the same school can only be moved out of a tested classroom by moving to an assignment teaching an untested subject, such as social studies. Comparing mean value-added of this small group of teachers ($N = 123$) to those who stay in a tested subject in the same grade, we again find large differences, ranging from .34 *SD* in reading to .45 *SD* in math. Teachers who continue to teach middle school math or reading but who switch grades also have lower value-added than non-movers, but as with elementary schools, the differences are much smaller.

In high schools, tested teachers are primarily those who teach 9th and 10th graders. We examine teachers of math and reading courses in Grades 9 and 10 at time t who at time $t + 1$: (a) stayed in the same subject but moved to teaching Grades 11 and 12, which have few tested students; (b) moved to Grades 11 and 12 and switched subjects; (c) stayed in the same grade but switched to an untested modal subject; (d) continued to teach a tested subject but switched from primarily teaching 9th graders to primarily teaching 10th graders (or vice versa); or (e) stayed in a tested subject in the same grade (the comparison group). The vast majority (94%) of high school teachers that leave a tested grade/subject switch from teaching 9th- or 10th-grade students to teaching 11th- and 12th-grade students but remain in the same

Table 5

Mean Value-Added Among Teachers in Tested Grades in Year _t_, by Status in Year _t_ + 1

	Math Value-Added	Reading Value-Added	Percent of Those Who Move Overall		Percent of Those Who Move Out of Tested Classroom
			Percent	N	
Elementary school					
Moves to K from Grades 3–5	−0.409***	−0.429***	5	783	13
Moves to first from Grades 3–5	−0.457**	−0.293***	8	1,320	22
Moves to second from Grades 3–5	−0.393***	−0.365***	23	3,725	63
Stays in Grades 3–5 but changes grades	−0.100***	−0.037	64	10,355	
Stays in Grades 3–5, same grade (comparison group)	0.039	0.022			
Middle school					
Different subject, Grades 6–8	−0.232***	−0.198*	4	123	100
Stays in math/reading in Grades 6–8 but changes grades	−0.020***	0.035*	94	3,135	
Stays in math/reading, same grade (comparison group)	0.217	0.145			
High school					
Same subject, Grades 11–12	−0.067	−0.110***	51	1,653	94
Different subject, Grades 11–12	−0.038	−0.123	2	74	4
Different subject, Grades 9–10	−0.451⁺	−0.365	1	38	2
Stays in math/reading in Grades 9–10 but changes grade	0.009	−0.137***	46	1,482	
Stays in math/reading, same grade (comparison group)	0.019	0.115			

Note. Values shown are means. Asterisks indicate results of two-sided _t_ tests comparing value-added for teachers that switch grades/subjects to the value-added of teachers that remain in the same grade and subject in the following year. Analysis is restricted to teachers that teach in tested areas in year _t_ and that stay in the same school in year _t_ + 1.

⁺ _p_ < .10. * _p_ < .05. ** _p_ < .01. *** _p_ < .001.

subject, which is unsurprising given subject certification requirements for high school teachers. We again find that teachers who switch to untested subjects, particularly those who stay in Grades 9 and 10, have lower value-added. The estimate of the difference is similar in math and reading (approximately .47 *SD*), though given the small sample of teachers who fall into this group, the reading difference is not statistically significant, and the math difference is only significant at the .10 level. Teachers who switch to Grades 11 and 12 have similar value-added in math but somewhat lower value-added in reading; a similar pattern holds for those who stay in tested subjects but switch from one tested grade to the other.

Given the particularly stark patterns in teacher movement in elementary schools, we further investigate the within-school sorting of teachers between and among high- and low-stakes K–5 classrooms by teacher performance measures. We first use SAT-10 data to calculate average achievement in early-grades teachers' classrooms and estimate value-added for those teachers using the same modeling approach as for the high-stakes standardized tests (i.e., FCAT) in prior analyses. Next, we standardize average achievement and value-added for early-grades teachers and pool teachers in early grades and those in Grades 3 through 5. Using linear probability models, we predict where teachers work at time $t + 1$ as a function of their performance at time t (based on SAT-10 or FCAT), classifying teachers as working (a) in the same grade, (b) in a different grade but still within the same early or upper primary set (e.g., a teacher who moves from second grade to first grade), or (c) in a different grade and *not* in the same early or upper primary set (e.g., a teacher who moves from second grade to third grade). We then run three different models for math and reading, results of which are presented in Table 6. The focal variables in each model are average achievement (Panel A) or value-added (Panel B), an indicator for whether the teacher teaches in an early-grades (K–2) classroom, and the interaction between the two.

The results are generally consistent for mean achievement and value-added. Given similarities between math and reading, we focus on the math results. The first column predicts the probability of teaching in the same grade next year. On average, Model 1 suggests that mean achievement is strongly related to the probability of teaching the same grade next year and that K–2 teachers are somewhat less likely to remain in the same grade; the interaction term is not significant. The pattern is similar for value-added (Model 4 in Panel B) except that high-performing K–2 teachers are considerably *less* likely than high-performing 3–5 teachers to remain in the same grade next year. The second column makes the binary comparison between teachers who teach a different grade next year but still within the lower primary or upper primary set to teachers who either remain in the same grade or switch to the opposite grade set. Here, the average math achievement and math value-added model tell the same story, which is that high-performing

Table 6
Comparing Movement of K–2 and 3–5 Teachers by Measures of Performance

	Math			Reading		
Assignment Next Year	Same Grade	Different Grade in the Same K–2 or 3–5 Set	Different K–2 or 3–5 Set	Same Grade	Different Grade in the Same K–2 or 3–5 Set	Different K–2 or 3–5 Set
	(1)	(2)	(3)	(4)	(5)	(6)
Panel A: Performance measure is mean achievement of current students this year						
Mean achievement scores of teachers' students	0.097***	−0.021***	−0.041***	0.096***	−0.024***	−0.038***
	(0.004)	(0.003)	(0.003)	(0.004)	(0.003)	(0.003)
K–2 teacher	−0.012**	−0.066***	0.087***	−0.012**	−0.067***	0.087***
	(0.004)	(0.003)	(0.003)	(0.004)	(0.003)	(0.003)
Mean Achievement × K–2 Teacher	0.008	−0.033***	0.029***	0.011^{+}	−0.032***	0.027***
	(0.006)	(0.005)	(0.004)	(0.006)	(0.005)	(0.004)
Constant	0.357***	0.247***	0.165***	0.358***	0.246***	0.165***
	(0.006)	(0.005)	(0.005)	(0.006)	(0.005)	(0.005)
N (school by year observations)	2,412	2,412	2,412	2,412	2,412	2,412
N (total observations)	77,733	77,733	77,733	77,730	77,730	77,730
	(7)	(8)	(9)	(10)	(11)	(12)
Panel B: Performance measure is teacher value-added this year						
Teacher value-added	0.060***	−0.006*	−0.036***	0.044***	−0.003	−0.029***
	(0.004)	(0.003)	(0.002)	(0.003)	(0.003)	(0.002)
K–2 teacher	−0.056***	−0.020**	0.082***	−0.066***	−0.011	0.083***
	(0.009)	(0.007)	(0.006)	(0.009)	(0.007)	(0.006)
Teacher Value-Added × K–2 Teacher	−0.025**	−0.021**	0.044***	−0.016^{+}	−0.016*	0.032***
	(0.008)	(0.006)	(0.005)	(0.008)	(0.006)	(0.005)
Constant	0.523***	0.178***	0.091***	0.508***	0.191***	0.091***
	(0.012)	(0.009)	(0.008)	(0.013)	(0.010)	(0.009)
N (school by year observations)	2,123	2,123	2,123	2,123	2,123	2,123
N (total observations)	22,594	22,594	22,594	24,417	24,417	24,417

Note. Models include teachers that teach grades K–2 and 3–5, so Grades 3–5 teachers are the reference group. All models include the same control variables as in Table 2 and school by year fixed effects. Standard errors (in parentheses) are clustered at the teacher level.
$^{+}p < .10.$ $^{*}p < .05.$ $^{**}p < .01.$ $^{***}p < .001.$

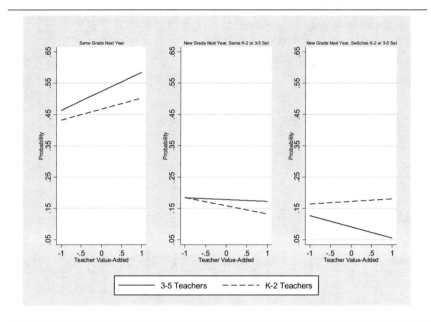

Figure 1. **Association between teacher value-added in math and probability of staying or switching grades.**

teachers—and high-performing K–2 teachers in particular—are less likely to move to other grades with the same stakes (Models 2 and 5).

The final column compares teachers who switch to the *other* primary grade set (i.e., switch from K–2 to 3–5 or vice versa) to those teachers who remain in the same set either in the same grade or a different grade. Grades 3–5 teachers are less likely to switch to K–2 as their performance increases by either measure. For K–2 teachers, the probability of switching to 3–5 slightly decreases as mean achievement increases but slightly increases as value-added increases. This latter result is illustrated graphically in Figure 1; high value-added teachers in Grades 3–5 are *less* likely to switch to Grades K–2, while high value-added K–2 teachers in fact are slightly *more* likely to switch to tested classrooms. All else held equal, a K–2 teacher with math value-added 1 *SD* below the mean has a probability of moving to Grades 3–5 of about 16%, compared to 18% for a teacher 1 *SD* above the mean; comparable values for upper-grades teachers are 13% and 5%. This pattern is consistent with schools on the margins reallocating more effective teachers from across the school into the high-stakes (later) grades, concentrating relatively less effective teachers in classrooms with the schools' youngest students.

Unintended Consequences of Strategic Staffing

Our final analysis considers the potential impact of shifting low-performing teachers to untested grades. We focus on elementary schools, where we have test score data from a low-stakes assessment that allow us to track student performance in the classrooms of tested teachers reassigned to lower grades.

Table 7 shows the result of estimating Equation 2 for SAT-10 math and reading, pooling first- and second-grade students. The primary variable of interest is whether the student's teacher switched from an upper elementary (tested) grade. Panel A of Table 7 focuses on a switch from last year to the current year. The coefficients show that in both subjects, being taught by a teacher recently reassigned from a high-stakes grade is associated with learning gains that are .06 to .07 *SD* lower than those attained by students in classrooms with teachers that were not reassigned. For comparison, we also included indicators for having a teacher who switched from another K–2 grade and for having a first-year teacher. In both subjects, point estimates suggest that the effects of having a switcher from Grades 3–5 may be slightly more negative than having a switcher from another early grade, and in reading, the effects may also be more negative than having a first-year teacher, though tests of equality among these coefficients could not reject the null hypotheses that each is the same as the one for switching from Grades 3–5.

An alternative interpretation of the results in Panel A is that the negative impact of having a teacher who switched from Grades 3–5 is transitory and simply reflects a dip in teacher performance associated with teaching a new subject. To investigate further, Panel B shows the results of adding indicators for switching from Grades 3–5 two years ago, switching from another K–2 grade two years ago, and being a second-year teacher. If the performance dip is transitory rather than reflective of lower quality of grade switchers, we might expect to see a negative coefficient for teachers who switched last year but not for those who switched two years ago and thus have had an additional year of experience in the new classroom. Results suggest some reduction of the negative association in the second year—though we cannot reject the hypothesis that the coefficients are the same—but still substantially lower achievement in those classrooms than in classrooms whose teachers taught in the same grade.

Panel C provides another look at this issue. These models are similar to those in Panel A, only with an additional covariate indicating whether the teacher ever taught Grades 3–5 in the past. The omitted group is thus K–2 teachers who did not switch grades last year and have always taught in K–2 classrooms. Coefficients demonstrate that teachers who have ever been reassigned from Grades 3–5 see substantially lower achievement growth, on average, than those who have not (approximately –.07 *SD* in

Table 7
Achievement Gains Among First- and Second-Grade Students

	Math	Reading
Panel A: Early grades performance in the year after a teacher switch		
	(1)	(2)
Student's teacher taught the same K–2 grade last year (omitted)		
Student's teacher switched from Grades 3–5 last year	−0.072***	−0.062***
	(0.014)	(0.011)
Student's teacher taught different K–2 grade last year	−0.050***	−0.051***
	(0.014)	(0.011)
Student's teacher is a first-year teacher	−0.097***	−0.045*
	(0.025)	(0.022)
N (school by year by grade cells)	2,177	2,172
N (students)	86,920	85,766
Panel B: Early grades performance multiple years after a teacher switch		
	(3)	(4)
Student's teacher taught the same K–2 grade last year (omitted)		
Student's teacher switched from Grades 3–5 last year	−0.097**	−0.090***
	(0.030)	(0.021)
Student's teacher switched from Grades 3–5 two years ago	−0.087***	−0.056***
	(0.014)	(0.011)
Student's teacher taught different K–2 grade last year	−0.086***	−0.078***
	(0.026)	(0.020)
Student's teacher taught different K–2 grade two years ago	−0.080***	−0.052***
	(0.015)	(0.011)
Student's teacher is a first-year teacher	−0.134***	−0.074***
	(0.022)	(0.020)
Student's teacher is a second-year teacher	−0.082**	−0.092***
	(0.026)	(0.020)
N (school by year by grade cells)	2,159	2,150
N (students)	83,630	82,537
Panel C: Early grades performance of switchers compared to K–2 teachers who have never taught Grades 3–5		
	(5)	(6)
Student's teacher taught the same K–2 grade last year and never taught 3–5 (omitted)		
Student's teacher ever taught Grades 3–5 (excluding last year)	−0.065***	−0.049***
	(0.014)	(0.010)
Student's teacher switched from Grades 3–5 in prior year	−0.108***	−0.083***
	(0.017)	(0.012)
Student's teacher taught different K–2 grade last year	−0.083***	−0.071***
	(0.017)	(0.013)
Student's teacher is a first-year teacher	−0.151***	−0.100***
	(0.030)	(0.026)

(continued)

Table 7 **(continued)**

	Math	Reading
N (school by year by grade Cells)	2,197	2,200
N (students)	90,005	89,916

Note. The models include first- and second-grade students with valid test scores from the prior year. The outcome is student test scores in a given year with controls for the prior year test score, student race/ethnicity, gender, free lunch eligibility, and limited English proficiency as well as the aggregate of these student-level measures at the class level. They also include school by year by grade fixed effects. The standard errors (in parentheses) are clustered at the teacher level. Asterisks indicate significant differences from the omitted category.
*$p < .05$. **$p < .01$. ***$p < .001$.

math and $-.05$ *SD* in reading), beyond the even lower effects they have in the first year following the switch.

To summarize the results across Table 7, although the analysis does not have the statistical power to distinguish well between teachers who switch from upper to early grades and either new teachers or those who switch within the early grades, switchers from Grades 3–5 are clearly less effective in the early grades than non-switchers, and these differences persist beyond their first year in the lower grades. Moreover, the direction of the point estimates suggests that switchers from 3–5 may be less effective both initially and in the long run than switchers from within early elementary grades. However, the data do not allow us to statistically disentangle the effect of negative selection of poorly performing upper grades teachers into Grades K–2 from the effect of inexperience in a grade for any teacher who switches.

Having established that having a teacher who switched from the upper primary grades is associated with lower student achievement in the lower primary grades, in our final analysis, we consider whether the apparently negative effect of being taught by a reassigned teacher in second grade is associated with lower FCAT achievement as of the end of the next two years, third grade and fourth grade, which are the first grades "counted" for accountability purposes. The results are shown in Table 8. Panel A shows third-grade achievement results first for math, then for reading. Columns 1 and 4 show results without a control for first-grade SAT-10 score. Columns 2 and 5 also omit this control but limit the models to the sample with first-grade scores, which is only about one-third as large as the full sample because the first-grade test has only been administered since 2009. Columns 3 and 6 show our preferred models, which include first-grade scores in the models as a baseline achievement measure prior to second grade.

In all six columns, there is consistent evidence of a negative effect of having a second-grade teacher who switched from Grades 3–5 in the prior

Table 8

Achievement Among Third- and Fourth-Grade Students by Status of Second-Grade Teacher

Panel A: Third-grade achievement

	Math						Reading					
	(1)	p	(2)	p	(3)	p	(4)	p	(5)	p	(6)	p
Student's second-grade teacher switched from Grades 3–5 in year prior to teaching student	−0.023**	Reference	−0.029*	Reference	−0.031**	Reference	−0.032***	Reference	−0.032**	Reference	−0.028**	Reference
	(0.008)		(0.013)		(0.011)		(0.008)		(0.011)		(0.009)	
Student's second-grade teacher taught different K–2 grade in year prior to teaching student	−0.012	0.31	0.010	0.03	−0.006	0.10	−0.018*	0.15	0.005	0.02	−0.005	0.08
	(0.009)		(0.014)		(0.012)		(0.008)		(0.013)		(0.011)	
Student's second-grade teacher was a first-year teacher	−0.037***	0.25	−0.050*	0.40	−0.027	0.83	−0.033***	0.97	−0.031	0.96	−0.015	0.50
	(0.010)		(0.023)		(0.019)		(0.009)		(0.022)		(0.018)	
N (school by year by grade cells)	2,187		1,001		1,001		2,191		1,005		1,005	
N (students)	154,332		49,918		49,918		148,779		47,438		47,438	

Panel B: Fourth-grade achievement

	Math						Reading					
	(7)	p	(8)	p	(9)	p	(10)	p	(11)	p	(12)	p
Student's second-grade teacher switched from Grades 3–5 in year prior to teaching student	−0.014+	Reference	−0.016	Reference	−0.020	Reference	−0.016*	Reference	−0.019	Reference	−0.016	Reference
	(0.008)		(0.014)		(0.013)		(0.007)		(0.012)		(0.011)	
Student's second-grade teacher taught different K–2 grade in year prior to teaching student	−0.006	0.44	0.010	0.17	−0.013	0.66	−0.013	0.76	−0.009	0.55	−0.017	0.92
	(0.009)		(0.015)		(0.014)		(0.008)		(0.014)		(0.013)	
Student's second-grade teacher was a first-year teacher	−0.042***	0.02	−0.015	0.98	−0.001	0.41	−0.043***	0.01	−0.053**	0.14	−0.039*	0.26
	(0.010)		(0.024)		(0.021)		(0.009)		(0.020)		(0.018)	
N (school by year by grade cells)	1,968		759		759		1,963		758		758	
N (students)	115,549		31,498		31,498		109,408		29,107		29,107	
Restricted to sample with first-grade scores	No		Yes		Yes		No		Yes		Yes	
Control for first-grade SAT-10 scores	No		No		Yes		No		Yes		Yes	

Note. Models are restricted to third- and fourth-grade students. Outcome is student test score in third grade (Panel A) or fourth grade (Panel B). Key predictors are characteristics of students' second-grade teachers; the omitted category is second-grade teachers who also taught second grade in the year prior to teaching the student. Models include controls for student race/ethnicity, gender, free lunch eligibility, and limited English proficiency and the aggregate of these student-level measures at the class level. They also include school by year fixed effects. Standard errors (in parentheses) are clustered at the second-grade teacher level. Values shown in the columns labeled p are p values for a test of equality between the coefficient and the coefficient on switching from Grades 3–5.

+p < .10. *p < .05. **p < .01. ***p < .001.

year, and it is of similar magnitude in math and reading. In the models that control for first-grade scores, being taught by a reassigned second-grade teacher is associated with third-grade scores that are approximately .03 *SD* lower than for students whose teacher had taught second grade in the year prior to teaching the student (both coefficients significant at the .01 level). Generally, this coefficient is much more negative than the indicator for whether the student's second-grade teacher had switched from another K–2 (i.e., low-stakes) grade the prior year (in Columns 3 and 6, equality of these coefficients can be rejected at the .10 level), suggesting that the negative effects of having a teacher reassigned from a high-stakes grade is not simply an artifact of a performance dip from any grade switch. Instead, coefficients suggest that this effect is similar to the effect of having a first-year teacher in second grade; equality of these two coefficients cannot be rejected in any model.

Panel B turns to fourth-grade achievement. With one fewer cohort of data, sample sizes are smaller. Across all six columns, coefficients are consistent with lower fourth-grade achievement among students with reassigned (from 3–5) second-grade teachers, though standard errors are large. Preferred results in Columns 9 and 12, which include controls for first-grade SAT-10 scores, suggest that having such a reassigned teacher is associated with fourth-grade scores that are about .02 *SD* lower in math (*p* = .12) and reading (*p* = .15), though these coefficients miss conventional cutoffs for statistical significance. These coefficients are smaller than those shown for third grade in Panel A, which is not surprising given research on the decay of teacher effects in future years (Jacob, Lefgren, & Sims, 2010; Rothstein, 2010). Still, overall the results in Table 8 suggest that reassignment of low-performing teachers to early grades may have longer term consequences for student learning trajectories.

Discussion and Conclusions

Consistent with prior studies (Chingos & West, 2011; Fuller & Ladd, 2013), our analysis of strategic staffing in tested and nontested classrooms in a large urban school district finds that teacher effectiveness, as proxied by different measures of student test score performance, in one year is a strong predictor of whether a teacher continues to teach tested students in a subsequent year. More specifically, higher achievement levels and proficiency rates of a teacher's students make it more likely that a teacher returns to a tested classroom, as do higher value-added estimates. Although we cannot say for sure the degree to which these patterns are driven by principal strategy versus low-performing teachers seeking to avoid high-stakes classrooms, the observation that these patterns are particularly apparent in schools with low accountability ratings (where leaders presumably face greater pressure to improve test scores) and where principals have more influence are consistent with the view that principals' strategic decisions play an important role.

We find that schools with high test score growth generally staff more strategically by this measure as well, which may indicate that concentrating effective teachers in tested classrooms may pay off if the goal is to show higher gains on standardized tests that count for external judgments of school performance. This result may also reflect greater organizational capacity for strategic response, including greater awareness of teacher performance or the larger supply of higher performing teachers available in these schools to take the place of lower performers who are reassigned. Also, the association between performance and assignment is strongest among school stayers in which principals (and others) are likely to have better performance information, though past performance often is predictive of subsequent assignment to a high-stakes classroom even among teachers that switch schools, suggesting that principals accepting teacher transfers utilize performance information in strategic placement decisions as well.

Importantly, however, gains from the strategic assignment of high-performing teachers to high-stakes grades have limits. Using data on student scores on the SAT-10, a low-stakes assessment administered in early grades, we show that reassignment of low-performing elementary teachers to early grades results in reduced student achievement gains in those classrooms in both math and reading as measured by a low-stakes assessment. This result is concerning from the perspectives of both schools and families if achievement in early grades provides a foundation for later learning. In responding to the acute pressures of the accountability system, schools may be disadvantaging students taught by these less effective reassigned teachers over the longer term, opening up the possibility that by providing incentives to increase student learning by increasing teacher effectiveness in later grades, current test-based accountability systems may also be perversely incenting reduced investment in students' earliest schooling years when returns on that investment are greatest (Heckman, 2006; Hill, Bloom, Black, & Lipsey, 2008).

Consistent with the idea that a student's achievement is influenced by the quality of his or her past teachers, we find evidence that lower performance in second grade among reassigned teachers translates into lower than expected student achievement at the end of third grade and potentially in fourth grade as well, though data limitations prevent us from making strong claims about fourth-grade outcomes. Being taught by a teacher moved from the upper elementary grades in second grade is roughly equivalent to being taught by a first-year teacher in terms of impacts on math and reading scores at the end of third grade. These results should give pause to school leaders aiming to boost school performance in the eyes of the accountability regime by focusing only on teacher effectiveness in high-stakes classrooms.

Follow-up research with additional years of K–2 achievement data linked to a longer panel of student achievement scores in tested grades may provide additional power to investigate the effects of the reassignment of low-performing teachers to lower grades on student performance later in school. Studies of the persistence of teacher effects suggest that effects of this kind of systematic reassignment on later outcomes may be substantial (Konstantopoulos & Chung, 2011). Analysis could also be extended to non-achievement outcomes, such as high school graduation or college attendance, which may be impacted by early education experiences even when test score effects fade out. In either case, if teachers at the earliest stages of a child's schooling career have a disproportionately large impact on the child's learning trajectory but policymakers have designed an accountability system that pushes schools to sort their best teachers away from those grades, the long-term consequences for student outcomes are potentially large.

It is also possible, however, that given the choice between a lower quality K–2 teacher or 3–5 teacher, a school should choose the former if more effective teachers later are better able to remediate and position a student for success in upper grades. Unfortunately, most accountability systems' focus on testing beginning in third grade further means that the kind of information on early-grades performance necessary to investigate the link between early-grades teacher quality and later performance, or optimal teacher allocation, is missing from most large-scale administrative data bases. Our results underscore the importance of education researchers bringing new data to these issues.

Our analysis faces several limitations. First, we do not have access to the same measures of teacher effectiveness principals have when making teacher assignment decisions. The kinds of performance measures we create from administrative data would not be available to principals at the time next year's assignment decisions typically are made, so principals likely instead rely on their own observations of teachers, results from interim assessments, or other information. Although principals' informal assessments of teachers tend to correlate positively with value-added and other performance measures (Grissom & Loeb, in press; Jacob & Lefgren, 2008), we would need access to a broader range of data to investigate what specific information principals consider in making assignments of teachers between tested and untested grades. The study also has concerns about generalizability. M-DCPS is a very large urban district whose school settings may be very unrepresentative of those in the typical school district. Although the accountability pressures faced by M-DCPS are similar to those faced by other Florida school districts, Florida's accountability system is among the nation's most stringent, and the pressures it applies on schools—particularly low-performing schools—may elicit particularly strong responses from schools (Rouse et al., 2007). Assessment of assignment practices both in general and the context of school accountability set in other districts or states would be useful in developing our understanding of how schools approach human capital decision making.

Future research might also consider whether the reassignment of low-performing teachers to low-stakes classrooms might have implications for student outcomes beyond those associated with moving teachers to early grades. Evidence in Table 5 suggests that high schools move many relatively low-performing teachers to nontested classrooms in Grades 11 and 12, for example, which may affect students' preparation for postsecondary opportunities. Reassignment of ineffective teachers to other kinds of untested classrooms (e.g., arts, non–core subjects) may similarly have consequences for student learning beyond math and reading.

Notes

This research was supported by a grant from the Institute of Education Sciences at the U.S. Department of Education (R305A100286). The authors thank the leadership of the Miami-Dade County Public Schools, particularly Gisela Feild, for their cooperation and assistance with data collection. Seminar participants at the University of Chicago and the 2014 meeting of the Association for Public Policy Analysis and Management provided helpful feedback. All errors are the responsibility of the authors.

[1]Of course, if a school has only been able to hire ineffective teachers, for example, the scope for strategic assignment behavior will be limited as well, though we note that studies find within-school variation in teacher quality to be substantial (e.g., Clotfelter, Ladd, & Vigdor, 2006; Hanushek, Kain, O'Brien, & Rivkin, 2005), suggesting many school leaders have room to staff classrooms strategically.

[2]To this same point, another pointed out: "If you don't teach your children to read in first and second grade, you cannot make that up in third, fourth and fifth grade. . . . So, I have always hired my strongest teachers and put them in that first and second configuration" (Cohen-Vogel, 2011, p. 494).

[3]The response rate for this survey was 38%.

[4]Teachers' perceptions of who influenced teacher-student assignments show greater within- than between-school variation for every item. The reliabilities of the school-level means of these items varies from a low of .27 (parents) to .88 (counselors), though all but two (parents and myself) are above 05, and four (teachers in the grade below, assistant principals, principals, and counselors) are above .7. We also collected data on what factors teachers perceived to be important in class assignments as part of the randomized survey module but discovered that school mean reliabilities for these items were low to support their use in the empirical models.

[5]Teacher value-added is computed by predicting student math test scores in the current year as a function of math and reading scores in the prior year-, student-, school-, and class-level control variables; grade and year indicators; and a teacher by year fixed effect. The teacher by year fixed effect, which we shrink to account for measurement error using the empirical Bayes method, is our measure of value-added.

[6]School grades are determined by a formula used by the district that weighs the percentage of students meeting high standards across various subjects tested, percentage of students making learning gains, whether adequate progress is made among the lowest 25% of students, and percentage of eligible students who are tested. For more information, see: http://schoolgrades.fldoe.org/pdf/0708/2008SchoolGradesTAP.pdf.

[7]School value-added is estimated from student FCAT scores using a model comparable to the one used to estimate teacher value-added, only replacing the teacher by year fixed effect with a school by year fixed effect.

[8]All tested teachers includes those who left the district. District leavers are excluded from the "school stayers" and "school changers" models, so the sample sizes for the second and third columns in each set do not sum to the sample size for the first model.

[9]All models employ complete case analysis. Item-level missingness in the Miami-DadeCounty Public Schools administrative data files is minimal (see Table 1), so given large sample sizes, we do not impute data. Sample sizes do vary substantially across models according to which teacher performance measure is used because value-added can only be estimated for a fraction of teachers. A version of Table 2 that limits all estimation samples to the subsample of teachers with value-added scores yielded very similar results.

[10]Because the scales for mean achievement, value-added, and proficiency are not the same, a direct comparison of the relative magnitudes of the results for the different performance metrics is difficult. The high correlation between mean achievement and proficiency rate (.9 for math and .8 for reading) suggests that if rescaled, the results likely would be quite similar.

[11]The value-added results are largely unchanged if we limit the sample to years prior to the 2011 change to teacher evaluation policies that formalized the use of value-added scores for summative evaluation purposes.

[12]The estimates in Table 2 are from linear probability models (LPMs). We also ran a version of Table 2 using logistic regression, shown as Supplementary Table S3 in the online version of the journal. Substantively, the two versions yield very similar results. We opted to report LPMs in the main text because they more easily accommodate fixed effects and are more straightforward to interpret in the context of interactions in subsequent tables.

[13]Preliminary estimates from the school-switcher subsample indeed showed no consistent evidence that school accountability or school value-added moderated this association.

[14]We also investigated how teacher reports of influence correlated with school performance measures. In general, status measures (e.g., average performance) are only weak predictors of teacher reports, with no correlation above .2, though the patterns generally suggest greater involvement of parents and teachers as achievement increases and little evidence of an association with other stakeholders. Correlations with school value-added are higher. For example, for math value-added, higher gains are associated with greater involvement by principals ($r = .33$) and other teachers (r ranges, .26–.35) and less involvement by counselors (–.47), parents (–.18), and students (–.48). Results for reading are similar.

[15]The finding that schools where teachers exercise assignment influence show this assignment pattern is somewhat unexpected. We suspect that other teachers, especially other teachers in the same grade, have a good idea about teacher performance, even when they do not directly observe test score outcomes, through their day-to-day interactions with one another. A possible explanation is that some schools give teachers influence over assignments so that that knowledge can be utilized, reflecting that those schools are more strategic about assignments in general, giving rise to this correlation.

[16]Very few teachers move to pre-kindergarten or another kind of untested classroom, so we do not show those cells in the table.

References

Aaronson, D., Barrow, L., & Sander, W. (2007). Teachers and student achievement in Chicago public high schools. *Journal of Labor Economics, 25*(1), 95–135.

Booher-Jennings, J. (2005). Below the bubble: "Educational triage" and the Texas accountability system. *American Educational Research Journal, 42*(2), 231–268.

Cannata, M., Rubin, M., Goldring, E. B., Grissom, J. A., Neumerski, C. M., Drake, T. A., & Schuermann, P. (2017). Using teacher effectiveness data for information-rich hiring. *Educational Administration Quarterly, 53*(2), 180–222.

Chetty, R., Friedman, J. N., Hilger, N., Saez, E., Schanzenbach, D. W., & Yagan, D. (2011). How does your kindergarten classroom affect your earnings? Evidence from Project STAR. *Quarterly Journal of Economics*, 126(4):1593–1660.

Chingos, M. M., & West, M. R. (2011). Promotion and reassignment in public school districts: How do schools respond to differences in teacher effectiveness? *Economics of Education Review*, 30, 419–433.

Claessens, A., Duncan, G., & Engel, M. (2009). Kindergarten skills and fifth-grade achievement: Evidence from the ECLS-K. *Economics of Education Review*, 28(4), 415–427.

Clotfelter, C. T., Ladd, H. F., & Vigdor, J. L. (2006). Teacher-student matching and the assessment of teacher effectiveness. *Journal of Human Resources*, 41(4), 778–820.

Cohen-Vogel, L. (2011). Staffing to the test: Are today's school personnel practices evidence based? *Educational Evaluation and Policy Analysis*, 33(4), 483–505.

Dee, T., & Jacob, B. (2011). The impact of No Child Left Behind on student achievement. *Journal of Policy Analysis and Management*, 30(3), 418–446.

Dee, T., Jacob, B., & Schwartz, N. (2013). The effects of NCLB on school resources and practices. *Educational Evaluation and Policy Analysis*, 35(2), 252–279.

Figlio, D. N. (2006). Testing, crime, and punishment. *Journal of Public Economics*, 90(4–5), 837–851.

Figlio, D. N., & Getzler, L. S. (2006). Accountability, ability and disability: Gaming the system? In T. J. Gronberg & D. W. Jansen (Eds.), *Improving school accountability: Advances in applied microeconomics* (Vol. 14, pp. 35–49). Bingley, UK: Emerald.

Fuller, S. C., & Ladd, H. F. (2013). School-based accountability and the distribution of teacher quality across grades in elementary school. *Education Finance and Policy*, 8(4), 528–559.

Goldring, E., Grissom, J. A., Rubin, M., Neumerski, C. M., Cannata, M., Drake, T., & Schuermann, P. (2015). Make room value added: Principals' human capital decisions and the emergence of teacher observation data. *Educational Researcher*, 44(2), 96–104.

Goldring, E., Neumerski, C. M., Cannata, M., Drake, T. A., Grissom, J. A., Rubin, M., & Schuermann, P. (2014). *Principals' use of teacher effectiveness data for talent management decisions*. Nashville, TN: Peabody College, Vanderbilt University. Retrieved from http://www.principaldatause.org/assets/files/reports/Summary-Report-201405.pdf

Grissom, J. A., Kalogrides, D., & Loeb, S. (2015). The micropolitics of educational inequality: The case of teacher-student assignments. *Peabody Journal of Education*, 90(5), 601–614.

Grissom, J. A., & Loeb, S. (in press). Assessing principals' assessments: Subjective evaluations of teacher effectiveness in low- and high stakes-environments. *Education Finance and Policy*.

Grissom, J. A., Rubin, M., Neumerski, C. M., Cannata, M., Drake, T. A., Goldring, E., & Schuermann, P. (2017). Central office supports for data-driven talent management decisions: Evidence from the implementation of new systems for measuring teacher effectiveness. *Educational Researcher*, 46(1), 21–32.

Hannaway, J., & Hamilton, L. (2008). *Performance-based accountability policies: Implications for school and classroom practices*. Washington, DC: Urban Institute and RAND Corporation.

Hanushek, E. A., Kain, J. F., O'Brien, D. M., & Rivkin, S. G. (2005). *The market for teacher quality* (No. w11154). Cambridge, MA: National Bureau of Economic Research.

Heckman, J. J. (2006). Skill formation and the economics of investing in disadvantaged children. *Science, 312*(5782), 1900–1902.

Hill, C. J., Bloom, H. S., Black, A. R., & Lipsey, M. W. (2008). Empirical benchmarks for interpreting effect sizes in research. *Child Development Perspectives, 2*(3), 172–177.

Jacob, B. A. (2005). Accountability, incentives and behavior: The impact of high-stakes testing in the Chicago Public Schools. *Journal of Public Economics, 89*(5–6), 761–796.

Jacob, B. A., & Lefgren, L. (2004). Remedial education and student achievement: A regression-discontinuity analysis. *Review of Economics and Statistics, 86*(1), 226–244.

Jacob, B. A., & Lefgren, L. (2008). Can principals identify effective teachers? Evidence on subjective performance evaluation in education. *Journal of Labor Economics, 26*(1), 101–136.

Jacob, B. A., Lefgren, L., & Sims, D. P. (2010). The persistence of teacher-induced learning. *Journal of Human Resources, 45*(4), 915–943.

Jacob, B. A., & Levitt, S. D. (2003). Rotten apples: An investigation of the prevalence and predictors of teacher cheating. *Quarterly Journal of Economics, 118*(3), 843–877.

Kalogrides, D., Loeb, S., & Béteille, T. (2013). Systematic sorting: Teacher characteristics and class assignments. *Sociology of Education, 86*(2), 103–123.

Kane, T. J., Rockoff, J. E., & Staiger, D. O. (2008). What does certification tell us about teacher effectiveness? Evidence from New York City. *Economics of Education Review, 27*(6), 615–631.

Konstantopoulos, S., & Chung, V. (2011). The persistence of teacher effects in elementary grades. *American Educational Research Journal, 48*(2), 361–386.

Lankford, H., Loeb, S., & Wyckoff, J. (2002). Teacher sorting and the plight of urban schools: A descriptive analysis. *Educational Evaluation and Policy Analysis, 24*(1), 37–62.

Loeb, S., Kalogrides, D., & Béteille, T. (2012). Effective schools: Teacher hiring, assignment, development, and retention. *Education Finance and Policy, 7*(3), 269–304.

Neild, R. C., & Farley-Ripple, E. (2008). Within-school variation in teacher quality: The case of ninth grade. *American Journal of Education, 114*, 271–305.

Nye, B., Konstantopoulos, S., & Hedges, L. V. (2004). How large are teacher effects? *Educational Evaluation and Policy Analysis, 26*(3), 237–257.

Perry, J. D., Guidubaldi, J., & Kehle, T. J. (1979). Kindergarten competencies as predictors of third-grade classroom behavior and achievement. *Journal of Educational Psychology, 71*(4), 443–450.

Rivkin, S. G., Hanushek, E. A., & Kain, J. F. (2005). Teachers, schools, and academic achievement. *Econometrica, 73*(2), 417–458.

Rockoff, J. (2004). The impact of individual teachers on student achievement: Evidence from panel data. *American Economic Review, 94*, 247–252.

Rothstein, J. (2010). Teacher quality in educational production: Tracking, decay, and student achievement. *Quarterly Journal of Economics, 125*(1), 175–214.

Rouse, C. E., Hannaway, J., Goldhaber, D., & Figlio, D. (2007). *Feeling the Florida heat? How low-performing schools respond to voucher and accountability pressure.* Cambridge, MA: National Bureau of Economic Research.

Sanders, W., & Rivers, J. (1996). *Cumulative and residual effects of teachers on future student academic achievement.* Knoxville, TN: University of Tennessee Value-Added Research and Assessment Center.

Schweinhart, L. J., Montie, J., Xiang, Z., Barnett, W. S., Belfield, C. R., & Nores, M. (2005). *Lifetime effects: The HighScope Perry Preschool Study through age 40* (Monographs of the HighScope Educational Research Foundation, 14). Ypsilanti, MI: HighScope Press.

Watts, T. W., Duncan, G. J., Siegler, R. S., & Davis-Kean, P. E. (2014). What's past is prologue: Relations between early mathematics knowledge and high school achievement. *Educational Researcher, 43*(7), 352–360.

Manuscript received March 19, 2015
Final revision received April 18, 2017
Accepted May 15, 2017

American Educational Research Journal
December 2017, Vol. 54, No. 6, pp. 1117–1153
DOI: 10.3102/0002831217716540
© *2017 AERA. http://aerj.aera.net*

Do Teacher Financial Awards Improve Teacher Retention and Student Achievement in an Urban Disadvantaged School District?

Dara Shifrer
Portland State University
Rice University
Ruth López Turley
Holly Heard
Rice University

Teacher performance pay programs are theorized to improve student achievement by incentivizing teachers, but opponents counter that teachers are not motivated by money. We used regression discontinuity techniques and data on a census of the students, teachers, and schools in a large urban minority-majority school district to show receipt of a financial award did not consistently relate to higher mean student test score gains or teachers' likelihood of retention. This study contributes to the literature by focusing on the effects of award receipt rather than award eligibility, differentiating by award amount, and using data from a large district serving predominantly disadvantaged students.

DARA SHIFRER, PhD, is an assistant professor of sociology at Portland State University, 1721 SW Broadway, Portland OR 97201; e-mail: *dshifrer@pdx.edu*. Her research focuses on the effects of inequality outside of schools on processes inside schools. Recent studies use quantitative methodologies to apply this lens to neurological disabilities (e.g., learning disabilities, autism, ADHD), the experience of teaching, youth's social psychological health, and students' math and science outcomes.

RUTH LÓPEZ TURLEY, PhD, is a professor of sociology at Rice University. She founded the Houston Education Research Consortium (HERC), a research-practice partnership between Rice and the Houston Independent School District (HISD) that aims to improve the connection between education researchers and decision makers for the purpose of closing achievement gaps and improving outcomes for students. She also helped to launch the National Network of Education Research-Practice Partnerships, which supports and develops partnerships between research institutions and education agencies throughout the country.

HOLLY HEARD, PhD, is the associate director for research operations at the Houston Education Research Consortium and was previously assistant professor in the Department of Sociology at Rice University. She directs the research management and data acquisition processes for the HERC/HISD partnership.

KEYWORDS: teachers, teacher motivation, performance pay, merit pay, achievement gaps

Teacher performance pay programs aim to improve student achievement through financial incentives for teachers (Hanushek, 2011). The theories motivating these programs align with economic and business theories related to personal motivation (Lawler, 1973; Storey, 2000). With teaching portrayed as a profession founded in a public service ethic (Serow, 1994), some argue teachers are not motivated by money and prefer an emphasis on collaboration rather than competition (Ballou, 2001). Building on recent federal emphases on accountability (Goldstein, 2014), teacher performance pay programs remain politically contentious (Aaronson, Barrow, & Sander, 2007). Previous studies on these programs found mixed evidence on their effectiveness. Nonetheless, these programs are increasingly considered by districts across the nation as a tool for reform (Podgursky & Springer, 2007). This study uses regression discontinuity techniques with data on the district's core teachers of Grades 3 through 8 from 2009–2010 and 2010–2011 as well as data on their students and schools to answer two research questions:

> *Research Question 1*: Does receiving financial awards improve teachers' likelihood of retention and mean student achievement gains?
> *Research Question 2*: Are the outcomes of teachers who receive large awards better than those of otherwise similar teachers who receive small awards?

Whereas previous studies have largely focused on the effect of award eligibility in randomly implemented pilot programs, we focus on an established program in which all teachers are eligible for an award. Research that takes a longer term perspective on teachers' motivation levels (Finnigan & Gross, 2007; Santibáñez et al., 2007) demonstrates the importance of understanding the influence of established performance pay programs. Only a handful of studies have investigated whether receiving an award has an independent effect above and beyond eligibility. This study's consideration of differences in the effect of receiving an award depending on the award amount is also an important contribution. The district's large size and predominantly socially disadvantaged student body provide an ideal context in which to explore a policy intervention aimed at reducing educational disparities (Glazerman, Chiang, Wellington, Constantine, & Player, 2011). The review of the literature that follows describes mechanisms whereby award receipt may or may not influence teachers' behaviors, relevant findings from previous studies, and the structure of the performance pay program.

Theorized Effect of Teacher Performance Pay Programs

With employee motivation a key goal of any effective organization (Lawler & Jenkins, 1992), business and economic traditions of thought emphasize motivation through financial incentives (Storey, 2000). Financial incentives include base pay, skill-based compensation systems, pay for individual performance, or pay for organizational performance (Lawler & Jenkins, 1992). Our public school system is criticized for not providing financial incentives for teachers to excel (Springer, Ballou, et al., 2010), with teachers' base pay, for one, low relative to other professional careers (Ramirez, 2011). Teachers' salaries increase on the basis of characteristics inconsistently associated with higher student achievement levels, such as postgraduate work and years of experience (West & Mykerezi, 2011). Performance pay programs build on the ideas of pay for individual and organizational performance. Teachers can be paid for individual performance on the basis of the achievement of students they actually teach and for organizational performance on the basis of the achievement of all students on the campus. Building on the long-standing idea that student academic growth is contingent on teacher effectiveness (Good, 1979; Hanushek & Woessmann, 2011), performance pay programs are theorized to improve average student achievement by boosting teacher morale and incentivizing teachers to increase their productivity (Glazerman et al., 2011). Performance pay programs may also support a culture in which teachers perceive their efforts as rewarded and their compensation as fair (Marsh et al., 2011). From these perspectives, students of teachers who received awards should experience added achievement gains.

Some argue financial awards will not motivate teachers to increase the achievement of their students. Business models are described as inapplicable to schools and teachers as not motivated by money (Morice & Murray, 2003). Psychologists find extrinsic motivators like rewards and punishments undermine intrinsic motivation and ultimately result in only short-term positive effects, if any (Benabou & Tirole, 2003). Financial incentives may actually erode morale and organizational trust (Finnigan & Gross, 2007) and diminish teachers' autonomy and professionalism (Storey, 2002). Alternatively, student achievement growth may remain unaffected by changes in teacher motivation related to award receipt because student and peer qualities explain variation in student achievement better than teacher qualities (Yuan et al., 2013). In other words, differences in academic achievement levels are more closely tied to differences across homes than differences across schools and teachers (Coleman, 1990; Hill, 2016). From these perspectives, students' achievement growth may be unaffected by their teacher's receipt of an award or even negatively affected.

Empirical Evidence on the Effect of
Teacher Performance Pay Programs

Among those focused on the United States, the vast majority of previous studies on performance pay programs explore the effect of award eligibility rather than award receipt. That is, the vast majority of previous studies compare schools or school districts with award programs to ostensibly similar schools or school districts without award programs, whereas this study compares teachers who do and do not receive awards in a district where all teachers are eligible. Average achievement gains are generally higher in schools or school districts where teachers are eligible for awards than in schools or school districts where teachers are not eligible for awards (Ladd, 1999; Solmon, White, Cohen, & Woo, 2007), but these studies' descriptive results could reflect unmeasured differences across schools other than a performance pay program. Schacter and Thum (2005), comparing treatment schools to matched control schools, find higher achievement gains in schools where teachers are eligible for financial awards. Among studies using regression modeling to better account for selection bias, positive effects (Figlio & Kenny, 2007; Springer, Ballou, & Peng, 2008; Springer, Lewis, et al., 2010) of award eligibility for achievement gains are evidenced more often than negative effects (Springer, Lewis, Podgursky, Ehlert, Taylor, et al., 2009). Findings are also mixed among studies relying on quasi-experimental designs, with propensity score matching showing higher academic performance levels in schools where teachers are eligible for awards than in the district overall (Bayonas, 2010) but regression discontinuity techniques showing no systematic difference in achievement gains between schools with and without performance pay programs (Springer, Lewis, Podgursky, Ehlert, Gronberg, et al., 2009). In studies using an experimental approach in which assignment to the treatment occurred randomly at the school or teacher level, there is no real evidence that teacher eligibility for awards improves student achievement gains (R. G. Fryer, 2011b; Glazerman & Seifullah, 2010; Goodman & Turner, 2010, 2011; Marsh et al., 2011; Springer, Ballou, et al., 2010). With internal validity potentially highest in randomized experiments (Schneider, Carnoy, Kilpatrick, Schmidt, & Shavelson, 2007), these results illustrate the importance of research design in attempts to understand the effects of performance pay programs. Whereas an experimental design suits these studies' focus on award eligibility, an experimental design is not feasible for this study's focus on award receipt as a randomized distribution of awards runs counter to the purpose of performance pay programs.

Only a handful of studies focus on award receipt rather than award eligibility. Cooper and Cohn (1997) use regression modeling to show average test score gains are higher for teachers who received awards. Imberman and Lovenheim (2012) find more positive effects of award receipt on student achievement among teachers responsible for a greater share of the students whose achievement determined the award but also use standard regression techniques. Imberman and Lovenheim also focus on teachers eligible for department level awards, whereas this study focuses on teachers eligible for individualized awards. Although the positive effects of award eligibility are less evident with quasi-experimental techniques, studies using regression discontinuity techniques find performance levels are higher on average in schools that qualified for an award for all teachers the previous year (Jinnai, 2012), just as the value-added scores of teachers are higher the subsequent year for teachers who received awards than for counterparts (Dee & Wyckoff, 2015). With the findings of these studies not generalizable beyond the programs they focus on, this study contributes an investigation of the effects of a performance pay program that has received little external evaluation.

Performance pay programs are also expected to improve the composition of the teaching workforce, namely, by improving teacher retention (Glazerman et al., 2011). More specifically, the odds of retention should be higher for higher performing teachers—teachers who receive awards— while lower performing teachers should be encouraged to attrit through their nonreceipt of an award. Teachers choose to stay or leave for a multitude of reasons, but if this program provides additional motivation to high-performing teachers to continue teaching in the district, teachers who receive awards for 2009–2010 should be more likely to be retained on average as of August 2011. Standard regression techniques show rates of teacher retention are higher in schools where teachers are eligible to receive awards than in comparable schools without a program (Springer, Lewis, Podgursky, Ehlert, Taylor, et al., 2009). Quasi-experimental techniques, respectively, propensity score matching (Bayonas, 2010) and regression discontinuity (Springer, Lewis, Podgursky, Ehlert, Gronberg, et al., 2009), also show teacher retention rates are higher in schools where teachers are eligible for awards. Similar to patterns with test score gains, studies that use an experimental research design find no positive effects of award eligibility for teacher retention (Glazerman & Seifullah, 2010; Goodman & Turner, 2010), but both of these studies focus on aggregate rather than teacher-level differences.

Among studies focused on award receipt rather than eligibility, Springer, Lewis, et al. (2010) used descriptive means to show the probability of retention is higher among teachers who receive awards than teachers who do not, but this association may be due to other unmeasured differences across teachers that covary with award status. Guarino, Brown, and Wyse (2011) use regression modeling to show turnover rates are higher for teachers in schools that do not receive awards, but this may be an artifact of other differences between schools that do and do not receive awards. The study with the most internal validity uses regression discontinuity techniques to show teachers who receive awards are more likely to be retained than teachers who do not (Dee & Wyckoff, 2015). This study also uses regression discontinuity techniques to investigate whether retention benefits are evident for this performance pay program.

This District's Performance Pay Program

This district's performance pay program is described as "the most aggressive reform to date" (citation masked to protect district confidentiality). The district contracts the Education Value-Added Assessment System (EVAAS) to produce individualized, subject-specific, value-added scores for each core teacher of Grades 3 through 8. (The district classifies math, reading, language arts, science, and social studies as core subjects.) While teachers of other grade levels in this district were eligible for departmental- or school-level awards, this study focuses on teachers of Grades 3 through 8, the only teachers eligible for individualized awards, because these awards are particularly expected to increase teacher motivation (Buck & Greene, 2011). Teachers are ranked within subject on the basis of their value-added scores. Teachers with scores between the 50th and 75th percentiles receive small awards for the subject, while teachers with scores at or above the 75th percentile receive large awards. Because the extent to which an award acts as a financial incentive may depend on its amount (Storey, 2000), we also investigate whether the outcomes of teachers who receive large awards improve more than those of teachers who receive small awards. Among teachers who received at least one award, and summing across subjects, total 2009–2010 award amounts averaged $3,801 and ranged from $350 to $7,000.

It is important to consider the possibility that the better outcomes of teachers who receive awards are attributable to qualities that led them to receive awards rather than to behaviors resulting from the receipt of awards. In other words, teachers who receive awards may have had better outcomes than other teachers even in the absence of an award program. In addition to the qualities of the students themselves, student achievement is at least partially a function of differences across teachers and schools (Coleman, 1990; Dee, 2005; Ehrenberg, Goldhaber, & Brewer, 1995; Huang & Moon, 2009; Rothstein, 2004). These differences may also relate to variation in teachers' likelihoods of receiving awards, particularly with value-added methodologies criticized for being unable to account for the nonrandom sorting of teachers across students and schools (Hill, Kapitula, & Umland, 2011). This study may actually benefit from the unreliability and imprecision of value-added scores (Schochet & Chiang, 2010) because of increased comparability among teachers with value-added scores just below and above the cutoff for an award. Moreover, regression discontinuity techniques are thought to have more internal validity, or to better account for selection bias, than regression, matching, and instrumental variable techniques (Nichols, 2007).

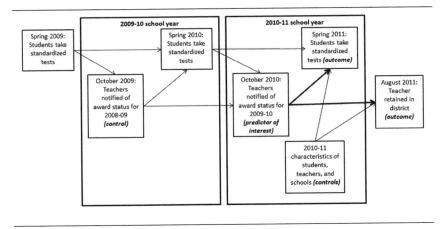

Figure 1. **Conceptual model of this study.**

Purpose of This Study

Figure 1 provides a conceptual model of the goals of this study. We first focus on whether financial awards for teachers benefit student achievement gains. Student achievement gains are measured by the difference in each student's test scores in the subject from late spring 2010 to late spring 2011. Test score gains are ostensibly less influenced by student background than test scores from one point in time (Chetty, Friedman, & Rockoff, 2014; Goldhaber, Gabele, & Walch, 2012; Goldhaber & Theobald, 2013). Teachers learn their award status in October 2010 when they receive their value-added reports for 2009–2010, giving them approximately three-quarters of the school year to exert more effort as a result of receiving an award. While all teachers are theoretically expected to exert more effort because of their eligibility for a 2010–2011 award, teachers who received 2009–2010 awards may be more motivated and confident of their ability to secure an award in the same subject for 2010–2011 than teachers who did not receive an award for the previous year. We also investigate whether teachers who receive 2009–2010 awards are more likely to be retained as of August 2011 and whether the benefits of awards for student achievement gains and teacher retention are greater when awards are large rather than small.

By focusing on programs implemented among a random selection of schools or teachers (Podgursky & Springer, 2007), the vast majority of evaluations compare changes over time between eligible and ineligible but otherwise similar teachers (Dee & Keys, 2004; J. Fryer, Levitt, List, & Sadoff, 2012; Springer, Ballou, et al., 2010; Springer et al., 2012) or otherwise similar schools (R. G. Fryer, 2011b; Glazerman & Seifullah, 2010; Goodman & Turner, 2010, 2011; Marsh et al., 2011; McCollum, 2001; Schacter & Thum,

2005; Solmon et al., 2007; Springer et al., 2008; Springer, Lewis, et al., 2010; Springer, Lewis, Podgursky, Ehlert, Taylor, et al., 2009). This performance pay program is an established program rather than a pilot, and all teachers are eligible for awards within the district. The theorized positive effects of these programs ostensibly should extend beyond the first year in which the program is implemented. In addition to considering differences by award amount, this is one of only a few studies focused on award receipt net of award eligibility.

Data and Methods

This study used data on the census of the district's core teachers of Grades 3 through 8 and their students and schools from 2009–2010 through 2010–2011. In 2010–2011, the district consisted of approximately 200,000 students, 12,000 teachers, and 300 schools. Eighty-two percent of the district students qualified for the free or reduced lunch program, 62% were Hispanic, 26% were Black, and 30% were limited English proficient (LEP). We excluded 380 teachers who received 2009–2010 value-added scores but were no longer in the district by August 2010 as they could not experience the treatment (being notified of their 2009–2010 award status in October 2010). We also excluded charter school teachers (n = 83), teachers who opted out of the award program (n = 7), and instructional specialists assigned to offices rather than schools (n = 3). We did not exclude the 68 teachers who lost eligibility for the award program through poor attendance rates because these teachers were ostensibly unaware through some part of the school year that they would eventually become ineligible, just as other teachers are unsure whether student achievement is high enough to warrant their receipt of an award. In all, retention analyses focused on 3,363 teachers.

We began achievement analyses by linking teachers to the 2009–2010 and 2010–2011 test scores of their 2010–2011 students. In all, linked students were excluded from analyses if they were tested for an ineligible grade, did not have a 2010–2011 test score for the subject, or were only linked to a teacher with fewer than seven students for the subject. Teachers who had 2009–2010 value-added scores were excluded from achievement analyses if they were linked to no 2010–2011 students in Grades 3 through 8 or no students for the subject, only linked to students without 2010–2011 test scores or students tested for an ineligible grade level, or linked to fewer than seven students with test scores (the last criterion consistent with Corcoran, Jennings, & Beveridge, 2010). Supplementary Table S1 in the online version of the journal details the numbers of students and teachers excluded for each of these reasons.

There were very few measures with missing values. In exceptions, we used multiple imputation by the MICE system of chained equations for the 5,608 students (2.4%) missing all 2009–2010 test scores, the 2,143 students

(.009%) missing both their demographic information and all 2009–2010 test scores, and the 703 students (.003%) missing only their demographic information. Supplementary Table S2 in the online version of the journal shows how students differ depending on the degree to which they were missing on variables. Students with demographic data but without 2009–2010 test scores may have started school in the district and then left as they were more likely to be White and in earlier grade levels, which fits with the patterns of White flight in the district. Students with test scores but without demographic information as well as students without test scores or demographic information had much poorer 2010–2011 test scores than students without missing information; these students' relative social disadvantage aligns with their likely mobility (entering the district midyear in 2009–2010 or at the start of 2010–2011). Generally, missing data should not influence results because of the low levels of missingness.

Analytic Plan

We used regression discontinuity techniques to examine the association between award receipt and teachers' outcomes. Regression discontinuity techniques are thought to approximate a randomized experiment by narrowing the focus on the cases closest to the cutoff for receiving the treatment, in this case, an award. Because the performance of the teachers within the window around the cutoff was likely very similar, with only very minor differences (if any at all) determining which teachers received awards and which did not, a discontinuous difference in outcomes at the award cutoff would suggest an effect of receiving an award. Regression discontinuity designs also have more mild assumptions than other quasi-experimental methods (Hahn, Todd, & Klaauw, 2001). We investigated the primary assumption that individuals did not have precise control over the assignment variables with figures (Supplementary Figures S1–S3 in the online version of the journal) showing the continuity of the distribution of teachers' value-added scores across both cutoffs, as suggested by Imbens and Lemieux (2007). This assumption is also supported by evidence that district teachers report great uncertainty as to how EVAAS estimates value-added scores (citation masked to protect district confidentiality). Finally, we tested this assumption with descriptive statistics showing the similarity of the baseline qualities of teachers who did and did not receive awards within the bandwidths around cutoffs (Supplementary Table S3 in the online version of the journal), as suggested by D. S. Lee and Lemieux (2010).

We primarily followed a regression discontinuity design suggested by D. S. Lee and Lemieux (2010). To start, we graphically showed the relationships between teachers' value-added scores and outcomes on either side of both cutoffs. While these figures increase the transparency of the regression discontinuity design, local regression models on either side of the cutoffs next provided an explicit estimate of effects and assessment of the robustness of results (Dee & Wyckoff, 2015). We used regression modeling to predict teachers' outcomes (O) with indicators of whether the teacher received a small award (T), the distance of their value-added score from the cutoff for the award (D), and an interaction between the two (TD) to allow the regression function to differ on either side of the cutoff: $O = \alpha + T + D + TD + \epsilon$. Logistic regression models predicted teacher retention, and linear regression models predicted teachers' mean student achievement gains. As suggested by Nichols (2007), we began with the optimal bandwidth produced by Stata's lpoly command, which estimates a kernel-weighted local polynomial regression of the dependent variable on the value-added score—optimal bandwidths are documented in the column headers of the results tables. Combining Nichols's suggestions for varying bandwidth sizes with model tests suggested by D. S. Lee and Lemieux, we estimated regression models within windows around the cutoff the size of the optimal bandwidth and then the optimal bandwidth divided by two, four, and eight.

Within each of these four windows, we estimated three more sets of models, respectively, adding polynomials of orders two through four to reduce estimate bias (i.e., indicators squaring, cubing, etc., the distance indicator and interaction in the first model): $O = \beta_0 + \beta_1 T + \beta_2 D + \beta_3 TD + \beta_4 D^2 + \beta_5 (TD)^2 + \epsilon$, $O = \beta_0 + \beta_1 T + \beta_2 D + \beta_3 TD + \beta_4 D^2 + \beta_5 (TD)^2 + \beta_6 D^3 + \beta_7 (TD)^3 + \epsilon$, and so on. To identify overly restrictive specifications, we next reestimated each of these 16 models with dummies added for minibins of width .01 (e.g., $O = \beta_0 + \beta_1 T + \beta_2 D + \beta_3 TD + + \beta_8 \text{minibin}_2 + \ldots + \beta_{\{[(2 \times \text{OptimalBandwidth})/.01]+6\}} \text{minibin}_{[(2 \times \text{OptimalBandwidth})/.01]} + \epsilon$).

The models passed the minibin goodness-of-fit test if a joint test indicated the dummies did not significantly contribute to the model (D. S. Lee & Lemieux, 2010), that is, the model did not over-smooth the data (Jacob, Zhu, Somers, & Bloom, 2012). We described the estimate as "from the best-fit model" if the model had the lowest Akaike Information Criterion ([AIC] which captures the relative goodness of fit of a model by capturing the bias-variance trade-off; Jacob et al., 2012) among the models that passed the minibin goodness-of-fit test (D. S. Lee & Lemieux, 2010). We also explored the sensitivity of results to the inclusion of baseline covariates, namely, all controls that measure differences in teachers and schools. If including covariates influences the estimated discontinuity, the no-manipulation assumption may not hold, invalidating the regression discontinuity design (D. S. Lee & Lemieux, 2010). We repeated these steps to investigate differences in teachers' outcomes at the cutoff for receiving a large versus small award. Sensitivity analyses relying on standard regression techniques evidenced much more consistent and larger positive effects of receiving awards, but we only show results from regression discontinuity analyses to optimize internal validity (Schneider et al., 2007).

Dependent Variables

Teacher Retained in District, August 2011

Following the lead of district research staff, we classified teachers with an August 2011 status of *active* or *leave* as retained (.002% of retained teachers were on leave) and teachers with a status of *terminated, retired,* or *death* as not retained. The district codes teachers who quit as terminated, and only a negligible number of teachers died.

Teachers' 2010–2011 Mean Student Test Score Gains

We constructed measures describing teachers' mean student gains from 2009–2010 to 2010–2011 on the State math and reading test (name masked to preserve district confidentiality) and the Stanford math, reading, language, science, and social studies tests (The Stanford Achievement Test Series). Because of the prevalence of LEP students in the district, we also used scores from the Spanish version of the State test as well as the Aprenda (a Spanish version of the Stanford tests; Pearson Education, 2014). Providing results on multiple tests, particularly some tests not used for accountability ratings (R. G. Fryer, 2011a), increases our confidence that findings are not an artifact of a certain test (Corcoran et al., 2010). Some students with mild disabilities or linguistic minorities take an "accommodated" State test (i.e., same test but with more time). Some students with more severe disabilities take a "modified" State test (different test). Pearson, responsible for developing the Stanford tests, states there are no accommodated or modified versions of Stanford tests because of these tests' lack of a time limit (K. Dwyer, personal communication, September 25, 2014). Similar to Corcoran et al. (2010) and in order to include scores on different scales in the same analyses, we standardized all test scores within each school year (2009–2010 or 2010–2011), test (State test or Stanford), subject, test version (English or Spanish), grade level, and accommodation status.

In order to include the maximum number of students in analyses, we averaged each student's standardized 2009–2010 scores across all subjects (alpha = .67). We then constructed test-specific student level gain scores by subtracting this 2009–2010 average from each 2010–2011 test score. Gain scores are a common alternative to lagged models (or predicting one year's test score with the previous year's test score) within value-added methodology (Buckley & Marion, 2011). Because students were linked to multiple teachers for the same subject, we weighted each student's test score gain by multiplying it by the instructional percentage indicator, such that a teacher responsible for 100% of the student's instruction in math is linked to the test score gain times 1, whereas a teacher responsible for 30% of the student's instruction in math is linked to the test score gain times .30. We aggregated students' gain scores to a teacher level mean for each 2010–2011 test.

Independent Variables

2009–10 Award Indicators

Performance pay program category. The district's performance pay program categories indicated the awards for which teachers were eligible and differences in award determination and potential award amounts. Core teachers of Grades 3 through 8 were classified as either self-contained or departmentalized. Because award cutoffs differed for the latter group depending on their school level, we constructed performance pay program category indicators that do the same: (a) self-contained, (b) departmentalized-elementary, and (c) departmentalized–middle school.

Value-added scores. Regression discontinuity analyses used teachers' value-added scores as the assignment variable and teachers' award receipt status as the treatment indicator. The district contracted EVAAS to calculate a value-added score for each subject core teachers of Grades 3 through 8 taught in 2009–2010. EVAAS does not release context-specific notes on its methodology but uses either multivariate longitudinal linear mixed models or univariate response models to produce the scores (Wright, White, Sanders, & Rivers, 2010). Within each subject, EVAAS actually produces different versions of value-added scores depending on teachers' performance pay program category, school level (elementary or middle), grade level(s), and total number of subjects taught. The district rewarded teachers with a value-added score in the top quartile with a large award and teachers with a value-added score in the second quartile a small award. We first standardized scores (within subject, performance pay program category, school level, and grade level) to create more similar distributions and facilitate averaging scores across subjects (Reardon & Robinson, 2012). Because the cutoffs for small and large awards were different for each value-added score version, we then recentered all value-added scores so all cutoffs for receiving a small award versus no award were at zero. Because the values of the standardized versions of value-added scores no longer corresponded with the award cutoffs specified by EVAAS, we compared unstandardized and standardized versions to determine what value the cutoffs had transformed to because of standardization. For instance, a cutoff of −.15 might be .23 after standardization. In this case, we subtracted .23 from all scores so that cases originally at −.15 were at zero on the standardized version of the score. Because it is not possible to center the same variable at two different cutoffs, we constructed a second set of value-added scores with the cutoffs for large versus small awards centered at zero. Because all award indicators were subject-specific, we averaged each teacher's value-added scores across subjects to create a single index representative of all cutoffs (consistent with suggestions from Wong, Steiner, & Cook, 2013) for analyses focused on retention.

Award receipt. We were able to determine whether teachers received no award, a small award, or a large award on the basis of their award amounts. The district standardized the amounts depending on the number of subjects each teacher taught so that teachers who taught more subjects were eligible for the same total award amount as teachers who taught fewer subjects. We also used a control for total number of subjects taught to adjust for differences in award amount sizes. Because retention analyses are not subject-specific, we estimated award status using teachers' value-added score averaged across subjects.

Teacher and School Level Controls

Measures describing differences across teachers and schools were used as controls in the final step of the regression discontinuity process. Teacher level controls described each teacher's sex, race, years of experience, performance pay program category, and whether the teacher received a new hire recruitment stipend, 2009–2010 school level awards, or any 2008–2009 individualized award. To the extent that these value-added scores validly distinguish between high- and low-quality teachers (Chetty et al., 2011), the control for a 2008–2009 award should capture unmeasured qualities of teachers related to their 2009–2010 award status and 2010–2011 outcomes. This control also accounted for the possible influence of structural factors related to award receipt, such as parents choosing to place their high-achieving student in the classroom of a teacher who received an award. It is important to note that the sorting of students into certain classrooms is unlikely to be a direct mechanism between teachers' 2009–2010 awards and 2010–2011 outcomes as award decisions occurred after the 2010–2011 school year began. School-level controls described the size of the student body and the proportions of students at the school that were Black, in poverty, in special education, or in the Gifted and Talented (GT) program. We focused on teachers' 2010–2011 schools because teachers were notified of their 2009–2010 award status in October 2010, a notification that would influence their behaviors with their 2010–2011 students. We did not include controls for teachers' educational attainment or the percent of students at the school who were linguistic minorities because the former was not correlated with outcomes, and the latter was not correlated with award receipt.

Statistical Significance

Although often misrepresented (Kline, 2013), *p* values (or statistical significance estimates) ostensibly indicate the extent to which results from sample data are relevant for the entire population. This study uses data on a census rather than a sample of district teachers, and we do not intend for these results to be generalized to other years (program guidelines are modified each year) or even other similar districts (as we did not sample the nation's majority-minority districts). In other words, the differences evidenced in results are "real" differences rather than being potentially influenced by sampling error. In addition to being inapplicable for this study, not reporting confidence intervals and significance estimates aligns with the increasing call for a shift in emphasis from statistical to substantive significance (Healy & Moody, 2014; Nuzzo, 2014; Williams, 2012). Some argue null hypothesis significance testing is logically invalid and provides little information on the actual likelihood of either the null or experimental hypothesis (Lopez, Valenzuela, Nussbaum, & Tsai, 2015; Trafimow, 2014; Trafimow & Rice, 2009). Standardized measures of test scores are prevalent in the research literature because differences in standardized scores are analogous to effect sizes and even somewhat comparable across different tests (Reardon & Galindo, 2009). We also provide effects from other studies as a base of comparison.

Results

Descriptive Statistics

In addition to providing descriptive statistics, Table 1 demonstrates the analytic relevance of this study's controls by showing how the average qualities of teachers and their schools vary depending on their award amount, retention, and mean student test score gains. (The award amount indicator streamlines these results, being the best summary of all small and large awards each teacher receives for all subjects.) Teachers who receive 2009–2010 school-level awards or 2008–2009 individualized awards, are female or Asian, receive a recruitment stipend, have fewer years of experience, and work in schools with fewer Black, poor, and special education students are more likely to receive 2009–2010 individualized awards and be retained by August 2011 and have higher average mean test score gains from 2009–2010 to 2010–2011. The average differences in teachers and their schools by award receipt status present the possibility that teachers who receive awards have better outcomes because of the characteristics that led them to receive the award rather than the award itself.

In addition to providing more detailed descriptive statistics on teachers' 2009–2010 awards, Table 2 shows baseline differences in teachers' outcomes depending on their 2009–2010 award status. As a function of the award program's design (more details in Data and Methods section), approximately a quarter of teachers eligible for an individualized award in each subject receive a small award, and a quarter receive a large award. Depending on the subject, average small awards range from $1,200 to $1,600 and average large awards from $2,500 to $3,500. The bottom half of Table 2 shows the outcomes of teachers who receive a small award are better on average than those of teachers who receive no award, just as the outcomes of

Table 1
Descriptive Statistics on Teachers, Schools, Award Amount, and Outcomes

	Means/Proportions[a]	2009–2010 Individualized Award Amount[b]	Outcomes	
			Retention, August 2011	Average Test Score Gain, 2009–2010 to 2010–11
Teacher award characteristics		Difference in mean amount for teachers with characteristic		
Received 2009–2010 school-level (value-added) award	.62	$756	.03	.03
Received 2009–2010 school-level (other) award	.97	$1,118	.11	.03
Received 2008–2009 individualized award for any subject	.60	$1,436	.04	.06
Teacher characteristics, 2010–2011				
Male	.23	–$138	–.01	–.01
Received recruitment stipend	.31	$537	.22	.01
		Mean amount for each category		
2009–2010 performance pay category				
Self-contained	.30	$2,582	.89	.04
Departmentalized–elementary	.32	$2,589	.87	.01
Departmentalized–middle school	.38	$2,642	.82	.01
Number of 2009–2010 award-eligible subjects				
One	.41	$2,674	.84	.01
Two	.20	$2,522	.85	.00
Three	.23	$2,600	.87	.05
Four	.02	$2,183	.91	.00
Five	.14	$2,610	.87	.03
Race				
White, non-Hispanic	.29	$2,681	.82	.02

(continued)

1131

Table 1 (continued)

	Means/Proportions[a]	2009–2010 Individualized Award Amount[b]	Retention, August 2011	Outcomes — Average Test Score Gain, 2009–2010 to 2010–11
Black, non-Hispanic	.38	$2,496	.86	.01
Hispanic, White	.25	$2,630	.89	.03
Asian	.05	$3,024	.90	.05
Other race	.04	$2,494	.84	.02
			Correlations	
Years of experience	12.31 (9.33)	–.01	.00	–.03
School characteristics, 2010–2011				
Size of student body	810.61 (338.31)	.10	.06	–.01
Proportion students Black	.25 (.26)	–.06	–.04	–.05
Proportion students in poverty	.32 (.13)	–.10	–.09	–.05
Proportion students in Gifted and Talented program	.15 (.13)	.08	.09	.03
Proportion students in special education	.08 (.05)	–.09	–.10	–.03

Note. Estimates based on the largest pool of teachers used in analyses (retention analyses, $n = 3,363$).
[a]Standard deviations below means in parentheses.
[b]This table uses total individualized award amount to streamline results related to subject-specific small and large award receiving—this measure is highly correlated with the number of large awards teachers received.

Table 2
Descriptive Statistics on 2009–2010 Awards and 2010–2011 Outcomes

	Teachers With 2009–2010 Value-Added Scores	Proportion Teachers Received		Average Award Amount for Teachers Who Received:	
		Small Award	Large Award	Small Award	Large Award
Math	1,747	.26	.25	$1,638	$3,533
Reading	1,755	.24	.25	$1,275	$2,519
Language arts	1,895	.24	.25	$1,224	$2,702
Science	1,127	.23	.26	$1,569	$3,379
Social studies	1,169	.25	.25	$1,177	$2,979

	Teachers Included in Analyses	Average Level on Outcome		
		Received No Award	Received Small Award	Received Large Award
Retention, August 2011[a]	3,363	.83	.87	.91
Average test score gains, 2009–2010 to 2010–2011				
Math-State	1,447	-.08	.04	.16
Math-Stanford	1,448	-.03	.07	.17
Reading-State	1,414	-.05	.00	.07
Reading-Stanford	1,415	-.01	.04	.09
Language arts-Stanford	1,525	-.01	.04	.11
Science-Stanford	908	-.02	.02	.12
Social studies-Stanford	926	-.02	.03	.17

[a]For retention analyses, award receipt status was estimated through teachers' average value-added score across subjects.

1133

teachers who receive a large award are better on average than those of teachers who receive a small award. More specifically, 83% of teachers who receive no award are retained in August 2011 in contrast to 91% of teachers who receive a large award. In another example, the average mean student gain on the State math test of teachers who receive no award is −.08 in contrast to .16 for teachers who receive a large award. Rather than the effect of receiving an award, these differences may reflect average differences across teachers, students, and schools related to award receipt status. We next use regression discontinuity techniques to narrow the focus on teachers with very similar value-added scores, that is, teachers who should be very similar with the exception of the awards they receive.

Regression Discontinuity Analyses

Figures 2 through 5 provide a visual inspection of relationships between award receipt and teachers' outcomes. With teachers within the windows around award cutoffs likely very similar, with only very minor differences (if any at all) determining award receipt, discontinuities or nonlinear changes at award cutoffs suggest an effect of receiving the award. For instance, if teachers respond positively to receiving a small award, there should be a discontinuous or nonlinear increase in teachers' outcomes at the cutoff between no award and a small award (zero along x-axes). Similarly, if teachers' outcomes benefit more from a large than a small award, there should be a discontinuous or nonlinear increase in teachers' outcomes at the cutoff between a small and large award (the second vertical line).

In a first example, the top panel in Figure 2 shows no real discontinuity at the cutoff for a small versus no award but a slight discontinuous decrease at the cutoff between a small and large award. This suggests no positive effect of receiving a small award and a slightly positive effect of receiving a large award on teachers' mean student gains on the State math test. In all, preliminary graphical evidence suggests a positive effect of receiving a small award for teachers' mean student gains on the State reading test (Figure 3) and Stanford language arts test (Figure 4) as well as teachers' probability of retention (Figure 5). Receiving a small award appears to have no effect on teachers' mean student gains on the State math test (Figure 2) and Stanford social studies test (Figure 5) and a negative effect on teachers' mean gains on the Stanford math test (Figure 2), Stanford reading test (Figure 3), and Stanford science test (Figure 4). Moving from small to large awards, graphical evidence suggests a positive effect of receiving a large versus small award for teachers' mean student gains on the State math test (Figure 2), State reading test (Figure 3), and Stanford language arts test (Figure 4) and a negative effect on teachers' mean gains on the Stanford math test (Figure 2), Stanford reading test (Figure 3), and

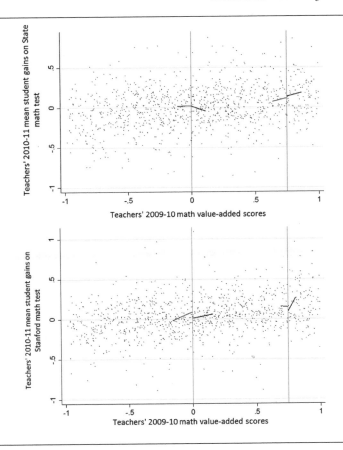

Figure 2. **Regression lines of teacher's 2010–2011 mean student gains on math tests relative to 2009–2010 cutoffs for small and large awards.**

Note. First vertical line represents cutoff between small and no award, and second represents cutoff between large and small award. Value-added scores centered at cutoff for small versus no award.

Stanford science test (Figure 4) as well as teachers' probability of retention (Figure 5).

We next use a series of analytic steps established by D. S. Lee and Lemieux (2010) to assess result robustness and produce more explicit estimates of the effect of receiving awards. Tables 3 through 6 show estimates from 16 models for each cutoff of each outcome, exploring a range of bandwidths and polynomial orders. Shaded cells show estimates from models that failed the minibin goodness-of-fit test, namely, that overfit the data. Bolded text represents the estimate from the best-fit model, as based on

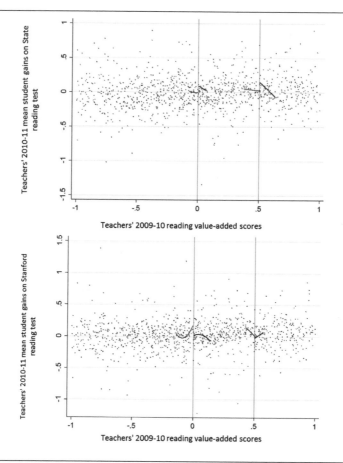

Figure 3. **Regression lines of teacher's 2010–2011 mean student gains on reading tests relative to 2009–2010 cutoffs for small and large awards.**

Note. First vertical line represents cutoff between small and no award, and second represents cutoff between large and small award. Value-added scores centered at cutoff for small versus no award.

AICs, among the models that did not fail the minibin goodness-of-fit test. Starting with results related to teachers' mean student gains on the State math test as a specific example (Table 3a), typical estimates range from −.12 to −.05. Although estimates from models with higher-order polynomials are less precise, the negative direction (if not the magnitude) of the effect of a small award on teachers' mean gains on the State math test is robust to different polynomial orders. Similarly, findings are robust to the inclusion of covariates (bottom row) with the estimate from the best-fit model only

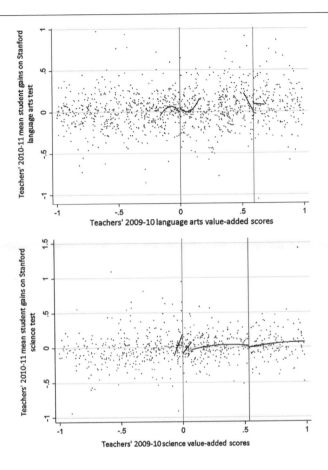

Figure 4. **Regression lines of teacher's 2010–2011 mean student gains on Stanford language arts and science tests relative to 2009–2010 cutoffs for small and large awards.**
Note. First vertical line represents cutoff between small and no award, and second represents cutoff between large and small award. Value-added scores centered at cutoff for small versus no award.

reduced from −.05 to −.04, suggesting the assumptions of the regression discontinuity design were met (D. S. Lee & Lemieux, 2010). Receiving a small award also negatively relates to teachers' mean student gains on the Stanford math test (Table 3c). Estimates become less precise with larger bandwidths but are robust to different bandwidths, polynomial orders, and the inclusion of covariates, with typical estimates ranging from −.48 to

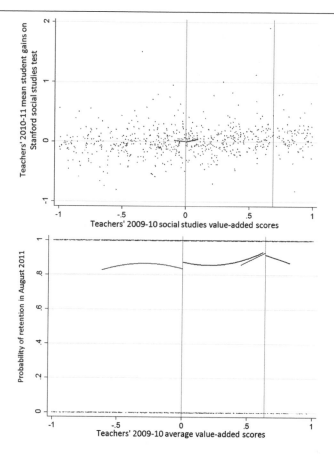

Figure 5. **Regression lines of teacher's 2010–2011 mean student gains on social studies tests and teacher's August 2011 retention relative to 2009–2010 cutoffs for small and large awards.**

Note. First vertical line represents cutoff between small and no award, and second represents cutoff between large and small award. Value-added scores centered at cutoff for small versus no award.

.00 and the estimate from the best-fit model at −.06. The Stanford math test estimate aligns with graphical evidence, but graphical evidence indicated no effect of small award receipt on State math test gains (Figure 2). Although D. S. Lee and Lemieux caution analysts that graphs are only preliminary evidence requiring verification by more rigorous statistical investigation, this inconsistency also points to the small size of this effect.

Table 3

Regression Discontinuity Estimates for Teachers' Average Test Score Gains on Math Tests

| | State Math Test | | | | | | | | Stanford Math Test | | | | | | | |
| | 3a: Cutoff Between Small and No Award (OB = .45) | | | | 3b: Cutoff Between Large and Small Award (OB = .46) | | | | 3c: Cutoff Between Small and No Award (OB = .45) | | | | 3d: Cutoff Between Large and Small Award (OB = .45) | | | |
PO	RD	SE	AIC	GOF	RD	SE	AIC	GOF	RD	SE	AIC	GOF	RD	SE	AIC	GOF
OB																
1	0.02	(0.04)	0.087	[0.000]	0.06	(0.05)	0.131	[0.000]	-0.01	(0.04)	-0.084	[0.000]	0.04	(0.04)	-0.116	[0.000]
2	-0.06	(0.06)	0.089	[0.000]	0.00	(0.07)	0.136	[0.000]	-0.03	(0.05)	-0.078	[0.000]	0.02	(0.07)	-0.118	[0.000]
3	-0.15	(0.08)	0.091	[0.000]	-0.01	(0.09)	0.143	[0.000]	-0.14	(0.07)	-0.079	[0.000]	-0.02	(0.08)	-0.114	[0.000]
4	-0.13	(0.10)	0.097	[0.000]	0.01	(0.11)	0.148	[0.000]	-0.09	(0.09)	-0.074	[0.000]	-0.01	(0.11)	-0.110	[0.000]
	n = 580 (40.1%)				n = 466 (32.2%)				n = 580 (40.1%)				n = 463 (32.0%)			
OB divided by 2																
1	-0.08	(0.06)	0.033	[0.019]	0.02	(0.07)	0.210	[0.009]	-0.06	**(0.05)**	-0.187	[0.053]	0.00	(0.06)	-0.118	[0.000]
2	-0.13	(0.09)	0.043	[0.004]	-0.05	(0.10)	0.220	[0.010]	-0.12	(0.08)	-0.176	[0.000]	-0.04	(0.09)	-0.102	[0.000]
3	0.00	(0.12)	0.044	[0.009]	0.12	(0.13)	0.225	[0.002]	0.00	(0.10)	-0.175	[0.215]	-0.02	(0.12)	-0.085	[0.000]
4	-0.10	(0.15)	0.050	[0.018]	0.05	(0.15)	0.237	[0.002]	-0.10	(0.10)	-0.168	[0.069]	-0.18	(0.13)	-0.080	[0.000]
	n = 283 (19.6%)				n = 218 (15.1%)				n = 283 (19.5%)				n = 215 (14.8%)			
OB divided by 4																
1	**-0.05**	**(0.08)**	-0.029	[0.440]	**0.05**	**(0.10)**	**0.270**	**[0.057]**	-0.09	(0.08)	-0.026	[0.717]	0.00	(0.08)	-0.031	[0.002]
2	-0.09	(0.13)	-0.003	[0.141]	0.05	(0.13)	0.305	[0.028]	-0.01	(0.10)	-0.004	[0.399]	-0.08	(0.12)	-0.002	[0.000]
3	-0.19	(0.17)	-0.013	[0.426]	0.05	(0.17)	0.339	[0.017]	-0.14	(0.12)	0.012	[0.303]	-0.22	(0.15)	0.014	[0.000]
4	-0.12	(0.25)	0.004	[0.354]	-0.19	(0.29)	0.362	[0.002]	-0.31	(0.13)	0.026	[0.259]	-0.40	(0.23)	0.038	[0.000]
	n = 140 (9.7%)				n = 115 (7.9%)				n = 140 (9.7%)				n = 113 (7.8%)			
OB divided by 8																
1	-0.08	(0.11)	0.047	[0.014]	0.01	(0.13)	0.193	[0.005]	-0.03	(0.10)	0.025	[0.100]	**-0.10**	**(0.11)**	**0.010**	**[0.870]**
2	-0.14	(0.18)	0.057	[0.026]	0.00	(0.20)	0.263	[0.015]	-0.19	(0.12)	0.055	[0.074]	-0.34	(0.19)	0.016	[0.962]
3	-0.29	(0.27)	0.079	[0.019]	0.20	(0.29)	0.170	[0.003]	-0.29	(0.16)	0.100	[0.070]	0.00	(0.22)	0.013	[0.000]
4	-0.35	(0.39)	0.132	[0.048]	1.25	(0.69)	0.179	[0.001]	-0.48	(0.22)	0.146	[0.075]	-0.03	(0.99)	0.083	[0.000]
	n = 71 (4.9%)				n = 57 (3.9%)				n = 71 (4.9%)				n = 57 (3.9%)			
	RD	SE	AIC		RD	SE	AIC		RD	SE	AIC		RD	SE	AIC	
Best Model With Covariates	-0.04	(0.09)	0.078		0.00	(0.10)	0.396		-0.06	(0.05)	-0.159		-0.18	(0.15)	0.266	

Note. Shaded cells show estimates from models that failed the minibin goodness-of-fit test, namely, that overfit the data. Bolded estimate has the lowest AIC among those not rejected by the minibin test. OB = optimal bandwidth; PO = polynomial of order; RD = regression discontinuity estimate; SE = standard error; AIC = Akaike Information Criterion; GOF = p value from minibin goodness-of-fit test.

Fitting the data around the cutoff for a large versus small math award was more difficult, with most models failing the minibin goodness-of-fit test (Table 3b, 3d). Per estimates from the best-fit models, mean score gains on the State math test are .05 *SD*s higher on average for teachers who received a large rather than small award (Table 3b), while large award recipients' mean score gains on the Stanford math test are −.10 *SD*s lower (Table 3d). In models including covariates, the State math test estimate decreases from .05 to .00, and the Stanford math test estimate decreases from −.10 to −.18. This suggests average differences in teachers just below and above this cutoff artificially inflate the actual effect of receiving a large award for math instruction. Math value-added scores may be manipulable around the large award cutoff, potentially invalidating the regression discontinuity design for this case. Rather than intentional manipulation, a structural difference may relate to an increased likelihood of being scored just above this cutoff and also covary with this study's measured qualities of teachers. For instance, the proportion of math teachers who are middle school teachers was higher among large award recipients than small award recipients (.32 vs. .14), even within a small window around the award cutoff (Supplementary Table S3 in the online version of the journal). The graphical evidence in Figure 2 aligns better with the unadjusted estimates than the adjusted estimates, but we are generally less certain about the magnitude of these effects.

Estimates for the effect of receiving a small award on teachers' mean student gains on the State reading test range from −.09 to .67, with estimates typically positive and .06 the estimate from the best-fit model (Table 4a). Estimates for the effect of receiving a small award on teachers' mean student gains on the Stanford reading test ranged from −.76 to .13, with estimates typically negative and −.22 the estimate from the best-fit model (Table 4c). Both best-fit estimates are substantially altered through the inclusion of covariates, with the State reading test estimate increasing from .06 to .18 and the Stanford reading test estimate increasing from −.22 to −.10, presenting the possibility that average differences in teachers just below and above the cutoff suppressed the actual effect of receiving a small award. Reading value-added scores may be manipulable around the small award cutoff, potentially invalidating the regression discontinuity design for this case. For instance, within a small window around the cutoff for a small award, recipients of a small award for reading worked at schools with an average of 18% students qualifying as GT, whereas teachers who received no award worked at schools with an average of 14% of students qualifying as GT (Supplementary Table S3 in the online version of the journal). The adjusted estimates align better with the graphical evidence in Figure 3 than the unadjusted estimates, but we generally have less certainty on the magnitude of the effect of small awards for reading test score gains.

Estimates of the effect of receiving a large award on teachers' mean student gains on the State reading test range from −.07 to .56, with .01 the

Table 4
Regression Discontinuity Estimates for Teachers' Average Test Score Gains on Reading Tests

| | | State Reading Test | | | | | | | | Stanford Reading Test | | | | | | | |
| | | 4a: Cutoff Between Small and No Award (OB = 0.52) | | | | 4b: Cutoff Between Large and Small Award (OB = 0.50) | | | | 4c: Cutoff Between Small and No Award (OB = 0.55) | | | | 4d: Cutoff Between Large and Small Award (OB = 0.56) | | | |
	PO	RD	SE	AIC	GOF	RD	SE	AIC	GOF	RD	SE	AIC	GOF	RD	SE	AIC	GOF
OB	1	−0.09	(0.03)	−0.074	[0.000]	−0.03	(0.04)	0.023	[0.001]	−0.02	(0.04)	−0.025	[0.000]	−0.02	(0.04)	0.011	[0.000]
	2	−0.09	(0.04)	−0.069	[0.000]	0.02	(0.07)	0.028	[0.012]	−0.04	(0.04)	−0.022	[0.000]	−0.03	(0.05)	0.018	[0.000]
	3	−0.08	(0.05)	−0.064	[0.000]	0.04	(0.08)	0.036	[0.008]	0.00	(0.06)	−0.019	[0.000]	0.03	(0.07)	0.022	[0.000]
	4	−0.05	(0.07)	−0.060	[0.000]	0.05	(0.11)	0.044	[0.004]	−0.05	(0.08)	−0.016	[0.000]	−0.04	(0.07)	0.019	[0.000]
		n = 638 (45.1%)				*n* = 490 (34.7%)				*n* = 665 (47.0%)				*n* = 544 (38.4%)			
OB divided by 2	1	−0.06	(0.05)	−0.097	[0.000]	0.06	(0.06)	−0.111	[0.423]	−0.04	(0.05)	−0.018	[0.020]	0.01	(0.05)	−0.205	[0.000]
	2	0.00	(0.07)	−0.090	[0.059]	−0.02	(0.09)	−0.101	[0.415]	−0.03	(0.08)	−0.007	[0.003]	−0.03	(0.07)	−0.192	[0.001]
	3	−0.04	(0.08)	−0.079	[0.001]	0.04	(0.12)	−0.089	[0.254]	−0.16	(0.08)	−0.005	[0.035]	−0.01	(0.08)	−0.189	[0.001]
	4	0.01	(0.10)	−0.069	[0.000]	−0.07	(0.15)	−0.078	[0.183]	−0.20	(0.10)	0.006	[0.037]	0.09	(0.09)	−0.190	[0.000]
		n = 342 (24.2%)				*n* = 248 (17.5%)				*n* = 360 (25.4%)				*n* = 274 (19.4%)			
OB divided by 4	1	−0.09	(0.07)	−0.089	[0.341]	0.01	(0.08)	−0.118	[0.231]	−0.03	(0.07)	0.055	[0.030]	−0.02	(0.06)	−0.178	[0.004]
	2	0.08	(0.08)	−0.082	[0.332]	0.00	(0.13)	−0.089	[0.596]	−0.22	(0.09)	0.057	[0.068]	0.04	(0.08)	−0.192	[0.046]
	3	0.01	(0.11)	−0.072	[0.246]	−0.04	(0.17)	−0.060	[0.271]	−0.07	(0.10)	0.071	[0.000]	0.13	(0.11)	−0.174	[0.005]
	4	0.05	(0.12)	−0.048	[0.204]	−0.03	(0.20)	−0.027	[0.019]	−0.10	(0.10)	0.093	[0.000]	−0.07	(0.15)	−0.157	[0.006]
		n = 166 (11.7%)				*n* = 116 (8.2%)				*n* = 184 (13.0%)				*n* = 129 (9.1%)			
OB divided by 8	1	0.06	(0.08)	−0.102	[0.917]	−0.01	(0.12)	0.031	[0.534]	−0.08	(0.11)	0.295	[0.589]	0.00	(0.07)	−0.155	[0.669]
	2	−0.03	(0.10)	−0.069	[0.885]	−0.06	(0.17)	0.092	[0.116]	−0.17	(0.14)	0.336	[0.589]	0.04	(0.10)	−0.101	[0.700]
	3	0.09	(0.15)	−0.026	[0.949]	0.02	(0.24)	0.149	[0.038]	0.13	(0.22)	0.320	[0.270]	0.22	(0.16)	−0.086	[0.048]
	4	0.67	(0.30)	−0.005	[0.904]	0.56	(0.30)	0.166	[0.134]	−0.76	(0.39)	0.314	[0.071]	−0.15	(0.28)	−0.058	[0.026]
		n = 83 (5.9%)				*n* = 64 (4.5%)				*n* = 88 (6.2%)				*n* = 71 (5.1%)			
		RD	SE	AIC		RD	SE	AIC		RD	SE	AIC		RD	SE	AIC	
Best Model With Covariates		0.18	(0.11)	0.031		−0.04	(0.09)	−0.047		−0.10	(0.08)	0.076		−0.01	(0.11)	−0.119	

Note. Shaded cells show estimates from models that failed the minibin goodness-of-fit test, namely, that overfit the data. Bolded estimate has the lowest AIC among those not rejected by the minibin test. OB = optimal bandwidth; PO = polynomial of order; RD = regression discontinuity estimate; *SE* = standard error; AIC = Akaike Information Criterion; GOF = *p* value from minibin goodness-of-fit test.

estimate from the best-fit model (Table 4b). Whereas most estimates from different specifications vary in magnitude but not direction, these estimates vary in both. In addition to this lack of reliability, this estimate is reduced through the inclusion of covariates and is quite inconsistent with graphical evidence. With the models predicting teachers' mean student gains on the Stanford reading test more difficult to fit, the estimate from the best-fit model was .00. This estimate is robust to inclusion of covariates and consistent with graphical evidence. Overall, there is no clear evidence to support higher mean student gains on reading tests for teachers who receive large rather than small awards.

Mean gains on the Stanford language arts tests for teachers who received a small award are .07 higher on average than those for teachers who received no award (Table 5a). Mean student gains on the Stanford language arts test for large award recipients are estimated to be .13 higher than those for small award recipients, with estimates ranging from .03 to .48 (Table 5b). Estimates of the effect of receiving a small award on teachers' mean student gains on the Stanford science test ranged from −.45 to −.26, with −.26 the estimate from the best-fit model (Table 5c). Mean student gains on the Stanford science test were estimated to be .10 lower for teachers who received a large award (Table 5d). All estimates focused on language arts and science were robust to the inclusion of covariates and consistent with graphical evidence (Figure 4).

Mean gains on the Stanford social studies test are .02 higher for teachers who received a small award (Table 6a). All models focused on large awards are overfit (Table 6b). Moreover, the .02 estimate is not robust to the inclusion of covariates (increases to .10) or consistent with graphical evidence (Figure 5). The regression discontinuity design may not be valid for social studies value-added scores; fitting the data within small bandwidths may have been complicated by the relatively smaller number of social studies teachers. Social studies teachers who received small awards worked in schools with an average of 15% of the student body Black, whereas teachers who received no award worked in schools with an average of 21% of the students Black, even within a small window around the cutoff for a small award (Supplementary Table S3 in the online version of the journal). In another indicator that the social studies value-added scores do not meet the assumptions for a regression discontinuity design, the proportion of social studies teachers working in a school that received a school level award is much higher than the proportion of social studies teachers who received a small award (.77 vs. .59) (Supplementary Table S3 in the online version of the journal).

Estimates of the effect of receiving a small award on teacher retention range from 0.87 (odds 13% lower) to 2.12 (odds 212% higher) with all but one estimate positive and 1.79 the estimate from the best-fit model. This estimate is generally robust to the inclusion of covariates and consistent with

Table 5

Regression Discontinuity Estimates for Teachers' Average Test Score Gains on Language Arts and Science Tests

| | Stanford Language Arts Test | | | | | | | | Stanford Science Test | | | | | | | |
| | 5a: Cutoff Between Small and No Award (OB = 0.64) | | | | 5b: Cutoff Between Large and Small Award (OB = 0.63) | | | | 5c: Cutoff Between Small and No Award (OB = 0.58) | | | | 5d: Cutoff Between Large and Small Award (OB = 0.56) | | | |
PO	RD	SE	AIC	GOF	RD	SE	AIC	GOF	RD	SE	AIC	GOF	RD	SE	AIC	GOF
OB																
1	−0.05	(0.03)	−0.214	[0.000]	0.02	(0.03)	−0.118	[0.000]	−0.05	(0.04)	−0.218	[0.000]	−0.03	(0.04)	−0.244	[0.261]
2	−0.03	(0.04)	−0.214	[0.000]	0.04	(0.05)	−0.117	[0.000]	−0.09	(0.04)	−0.221	[0.000]	0.03	(0.05)	−0.244	[0.254]
3	0.00	(0.05)	−0.213	[0.000]	0.05	(0.07)	−0.117	[0.000]	−0.10	(0.05)	−0.214	[0.000]	−0.10	(0.06)	−0.249	[0.260]
4	−0.06	(0.06)	−0.211	[0.000]	0.13	(0.08)	−0.119	[0.000]	−0.09	(0.07)	−0.206	[0.000]	−0.06	(0.07)	−0.241	[0.312]
	n = 792 (51.9%)				n = 631 (41.4%)				n = 461 (50.8%)				n = 443 (48.8%)			
OB divided by 2																
1	−0.02	(0.04)	−0.288	[0.025]	0.03	(0.04)	0.024	[0.462]	−0.09	(0.05)	−0.284	[0.000]	−0.02	(0.04)	−0.543	[0.000]
2	−0.02	(0.05)	−0.285	[0.017]	0.10	(0.07)	0.024	[0.511]	−0.12	(0.07)	−0.276	[0.000]	−0.08	(0.06)	−0.534	[0.000]
3	−0.02	(0.07)	−0.276	[0.030]	0.08	(0.10)	0.034	[0.512]	−0.17	(0.09)	−0.268	[0.000]	0.03	(0.09)	−0.530	[0.000]
4	0.03	(0.09)	−0.272	[0.043]	0.23	(0.11)	0.035	[0.416]	−0.38	(0.12)	−0.307	[0.000]	−0.05	(0.10)	−0.533	[0.000]
	n = 410 (26.9%)				n = 357 (23.4%)				n = 303 (33.4%)				n = 224 (24.7%)			
OB divided by 4																
1	−0.06	(0.05)	−0.340	[0.046]	0.04	(0.07)	−0.005	[0.194]	−0.09	(0.07)	−0.107	[0.043]	0.00	(0.06)	−0.604	[0.000]
2	0.05	(0.07)	−0.338	[0.000]	0.18	(0.10)	−0.001	[0.440]	−0.29	(0.10)	−0.154	[0.144]	−0.09	(0.09)	−0.586	[0.000]
3	0.11	(0.10)	−0.323	[0.039]	0.16	(0.13)	0.017	[0.395]	−0.34	(0.13)	−0.133	[0.106]	0.06	(0.13)	−0.569	[0.000]
4	**0.07**	**(0.13)**	**−0.308**	**[0.052]**	0.28	(0.16)	0.031	[0.318]	−0.45	(0.17)	−0.139	[0.053]	−0.08	(0.24)	−0.548	[0.000]
	n = 217 (14.2%)				n = 177 (11.6%)				n = 157 (17.3%)				n = 112 (12.3%)			
OB divided by 8																
1	0.05	(0.07)	−0.487	[0.041]	**0.13**	**(0.09)**	**−0.107**	**[0.183]**	−0.26	(0.11)	−0.172	[0.327]	−0.26	(0.11)	−0.172	[0.327]
2	0.03	(0.11)	−0.469	[0.031]	0.18	(0.14)	−0.071	[0.099]	−0.45	(0.14)	−0.241	[0.001]	−0.45	(0.14)	−0.241	[0.001]
3	0.16	(0.15)	−0.447	[0.019]	0.48	(0.15)	−0.078	[0.057]	−0.30	(0.17)	−0.224	[0.007]	−0.30	(0.17)	−0.224	[0.007]
4	−0.05	(0.17)	−0.431	[0.022]	0.57	(0.26)	−0.048	[0.039]	−0.28	(0.25)	−0.207	[0.016]	−0.28	(0.25)	−0.207	[0.016]
	n = 112 (7.3%)				n = 105 (6.9%)				n = 99 (10.9%)				n = 99 (10.9%)			
	RD	SE	AIC		RD	SE	AIC		RD	SE	AIC		RD	SE	AIC	
Best Model With Covariates	0.05	(0.12)	−0.222		0.11	(0.09)	−0.045		−0.26	(0.13)	0.124		−0.09	(0.06)	−0.189	

Note. Shaded cells show estimates from models that failed the minibin goodness-of-fit test, namely, that overfit the data. Bolded estimate has the lowest AIC among those not rejected by the minibin test. OB = optimal bandwidth; PO = polynomial of order; RD = regression discontinuity estimate; SE = standard error; AIC = Akaike Information Criterion; GOF = *p* value from minibin goodness-of-fit test.

Table 6

Regression Discontinuity Estimates for Teachers' Average Test Score Gains on Stanford Social Studies Test (Linear Coefficient) and Teachers' Retention by August 2011 (Odds Ratios)

| | Stanford Social Studies Test | | | | | | | | Teacher Retention | | | | | | | |
| | 6a: Cutoff Between Small and No Award (OB = 0.75) | | | | 6b: Cutoff Between Large and Small Award (OB = 0.75) | | | | 6c: Cutoff Between Small and No Award (OB = 0.72) | | | | 6d: Cutoff Between Large and Small Award (OB = 0.77) | | | |
PO	RD	SE	AIC	GOF	RD	SE	AIC	GOF	RD	SE	AIC	GOF	RD	SE	AIC	GOF
OB																
1	−0.07	(0.03)	0.104	[0.000]	0.05	(0.05)	0.058	[0.000]	0.87	(0.17)	0.803	[0.213]	1.11	(0.41)	0.713	[0.000]
2	−0.02	(0.04)	0.107	[0.000]	0.00	(0.09)	0.052	[0.000]	1.01	(0.27)	0.804	[0.308]	0.51	(0.20)	0.711	[0.000]
3	0.02	(0.05)	0.111	[0.000]	−0.02	(0.10)	0.059	[0.000]	1.79	(0.66)	**0.802**	[0.434]	0.43	(0.15)	0.712	[0.000]
4	0.03	(0.05)	0.116	[0.000]	−0.05	(0.12)	0.066	[0.000]	1.54	(0.75)	0.803	[0.355]	0.42	(0.15)	0.714	[0.000]
	n = 563 (60.8%)				*n* = 509 (55.0%)				*n* = 2,178 (64.8%)				*n* = 1,900 (56.5%)			
OB divided by 2																
1	−0.03	(0.05)	0.078	[0.001]	0.03	(0.08)	0.110	[0.001]	1.22	(0.35)	0.823	[0.092]	0.54	(0.21)	0.673	[0.087]
2	−0.01	(0.07)	0.067	[0.000]	−0.05	(0.11)	0.118	[0.000]	1.29	(0.59)	0.826	[0.093]	0.43	(0.15)	0.675	[0.000]
3	0.06	(0.11)	0.075	[0.005]	−0.07	(0.15)	0.133	[0.005]	2.06	(1.27)	0.828	[0.056]	0.39	(0.16)	0.674	[0.065]
4	0.02	(0.13)	0.082	[0.007]	−0.17	(0.19)	0.126	[0.007]	1.47	(1.05)	0.830	[0.007]	—			
	n = 333 (36.0%)				*n* = 265 (28.6%)				*n* = 1,274 (37.9%)				*n* = 981 (29.2%)			
OB divided by 4																
1	0.00	(0.07)	−0.118	[0.011]	0.02	(0.11)	0.222	[0.011]	1.39	(0.57)	0.818	[0.935]	0.37	(0.14)	**0.649**	[0.248]
2	0.06	(0.11)	−0.101	[0.009]	−0.12	(0.15)	0.213	[0.009]	1.76	(1.05)	0.823	[0.945]	0.34	(0.14)	0.653	[0.351]
3	−0.01	(0.15)	−0.079	[0.038]	−0.27	(0.22)	0.227	[0.038]	1.59	(1.35)	0.829	[0.712]	0.20	(0.11)	0.655	[0.057]
4	−0.07	(0.23)	−0.059	[0.012]	−0.42	(0.34)	0.237	[0.012]	2.12	(2.35)	0.835	[0.507]	—			
	n = 171 (18.5%)				*n* = 128 (13.8%)				*n* = 682 (20.3%)				*n* = 378 (11.2%)			
OB divided by 8																
1	0.02	(0.10)	−0.232	[0.071]	−0.09	(0.15)	0.683	[0.000]	1.36	(0.76)	0.819	[0.796]	0.23	(0.10)	0.698	[0.887]
2	−0.06	(0.17)	−0.192	[0.043]	−0.34	(0.26)	0.686	[0.000]	1.99	(1.90)	0.828	[0.694]	0.24	(0.16)	0.713	[0.634]
3	0.13	(0.30)	−0.167	[0.001]	−0.58	(0.45)	0.720	[0.000]	—				—			
4	0.24	(0.46)	−0.166	[0.000]	−0.18	(0.70)	0.690	[0.000]	—				—			
	n = 91 (9.8%)				*n* = 63 (6.8%)				*n* = 495 (14.7%)				*n* = 256 (7.6%)			
	RD	SE	AIC		RD	SE	AIC		RD	SE	AIC		RD	SE	AIC	
Best Model With Covariates	0.10	(0.10)	−0.120		0.00	(0.10)	0.396		1.65	(0.63)	0.778		0.36	(0.15)	0.651	

Note. In retention analyses, the control for receiving a recruitment stipend was excluded from the model with covariates to facilitate convergence; the dichotomous outcome limited the extent to which models with higher order polynomials would converge. Shaded cells show estimates from models that failed the minibin goodness-of-fit test, namely, that overfit the data. Bolded estimate has the lowest AIC among those not rejected by the minibin test. OB = optimal bandwidth; PO = polynomial order; RD = regression discontinuity estimate; *SE* = standard error; AIC = Akaike Information Criterion; GOF = *p* value from minibin goodness-of-fit test.

graphical evidence (Figure 5, keeping in mind the table presents odds ratios and the figure presents predicted probabilities). Typical estimates of receiving a large award on teacher retention range from 0.20 to 0.54 (Table 6d), with the estimate from the best-fit model, 0.37, robust to the inclusion of covariates and consistent with graphical evidence (Figure 5).

Conclusion

Building on theories that performance pay programs increase teacher motivation and effort, this study investigates whether teachers in a large urban majority-minority district who receive financial awards achieve higher student achievement gains and are more likely to be retained the following school year. The previous literature largely focuses on pilot programs implemented randomly for the purpose of evaluation, leaving the effects of an established performance pay program like this one less clear. Random implementation is not a common characteristic of enduring educational interventions. This study's findings largely fail to support consistent positive effects of financial awards for teachers in this district. The effect of receiving a small award was negative for both math tests, just as the effect of receiving a large versus small award was negative for the Stanford science test and teacher retention. Other estimated effects were either of negligible magnitude or based on award cutoffs that appeared to covary with other differences across teachers and schools, invalidating the regression discontinuity design. In the few exceptions, the likelihood of retention was slightly higher for teachers who received a small award rather than no award. Achievement gains on the Stanford language arts test were also slightly higher for teachers who received a small versus no award and teachers who received a large rather than small award.

This study's largely null findings are inconsistent with previous studies that used quasi-experimental techniques to focus on the effect of award receipt on achievement gains (Dee & Wyckoff, 2015; Jinnai, 2012). Just as this study's results may not generalize to other contexts, neither of these studies were focused on the program of interest in this study. For instance, the awards in the Jinnai (2012) study were schoolwide rather than individualized. Dee and Wyckoff (2015) used program-generated performance scores rather than test score gains as a dependent variable. Moreover, even estimates from regression discontinuity analyses can be affected by bias. It is unclear why this study only finds positive effects for language arts test score gains. These effects are still small relative to effect size benchmarks established in previous studies (e.g., Briggs & Domingue, 2011; R. G. Fryer, 2011a; J. Lee, Finn, & Liu, 2012).

The indications in this study that the assumptions of the regression discontinuity design are not met along several award cutoffs suggest that both award receipt and subsequent achievement gains are influenced by differences across schools and teachers that should not be reflected in value-added scores (e.g., school level [elementary, middle], proportion of students in GT, proportion of students Black). Future research should more directly investigate the validity and reliability of these value-added scores, that is, whether EVAAS value-added scores accurately distinguish high-performing teachers from low-performing teachers. In 14% to 30% of schools (depending on the subject), either all or no teachers received an individualized award for the subject. While this may indicate high-performing teachers are clustered in certain schools, it also presents the possibility that EVAAS methodology does not sufficiently account for differences across schools that influence achievement but are not within teachers' control. This study's exploratory analyses also show the characteristics of teachers' students relate to their award status, which may indicate EVAAS's value-added methodology does not sufficiently account for the bias introduced by the nonrandom sorting of students across teachers (Newton, Darling-Hammond, Haertel, & Thomas, 2010).

This is the first study to our knowledge to evaluate whether the effect of receiving an award varies depending on its amount. Inconsistent with theorized predictions (Storey, 2000), we find little evidence to support larger benefits for the outcomes of teachers who receive large rather than small awards. Although focused on a specific context, these results may run counter to previous studies that attributed the lack of effect from financial awards to the size of the award (R. G. Fryer, 2011b; Goodman & Turner, 2010; Marsh et al., 2011; Springer, Lewis, Podgursky, Ehlert, Gronberg, et al., 2009). Importantly, to facilitate the regression discontinuity design, this study compared large award recipients to small award recipients rather than comparing teachers who received large awards to teachers who received no award. Results from sensitivity analyses using standard regression techniques evidenced larger effect sizes for large award recipients, but these results lack internal validity. Future research is needed to ascertain the degree to which award size affects the efficacy of performance pay programs.

The evidence relating award receipt to teacher retention the following year was mixed. To the extent that higher value-added scores validly identify higher-performing teachers, the positive effects of a small award on teacher retention may support the potential of performance pay programs to improve the quality of the teaching workforce. Although focused on a different program and context, Dee and Wyckoff (2015) also used quasi-experimental techniques to show award receipt improved teacher retention. While it is not surprising that teachers might be motivated both by the nature of their work and the compensation and recognition they receive for it, these results are difficult to interpret in light of the fact that this study also found teachers who received a large award were less likely than teachers who received a small award to be retained in the district. Perhaps a large award convinces teachers they have the talent to work in an industry more profitable than teaching. Qualitative data from teachers and principals might clarify the specific mechanisms producing these results (Hoogeveen & Gutkin, 1986).

Some limitations of this study merit mention. First, the few positive effects identified in this study may be an artifact of unmeasured factors. In other words, it remains possible teachers who receive awards experience better outcomes because of the qualities that led them to receive the award rather than behaviors resulting from award receipt. Any award benefits evidenced could also be indicative of the durability of high-performing teachers. Regression discontinuity is the best known method for addressing selection bias, short of a randomized experiment (Nichols, 2007). Nonetheless, regression discontinuity techniques focus on a subpopulation (those closest to the cutoff), making it unclear whether findings are generalizable to teachers with value-added scores further from the cutoff for an award (Imbens & Lemieux, 2007). It is also possible teachers who receive awards only appear to have more improved outcomes because of negative effects for teachers who did not receive awards, as EVAAS's value-added scores and achievement gains are measured relative to other teachers within the district.

Our study is also limited by excluded cases. First, these results are not generalizable to district charter school teachers. Second, 380 teachers who received a 2009–2010 value-added score left the district by August 2010, before they were aware of their award status. These teachers were generally much less likely to receive awards (Supplementary Table S4 in the online version of the journal), making their exit from the district consistent with our finding that non–award-receiving teachers are also more likely to attrit by August 2011. Teachers excluded from achievement analyses are less likely to have received awards, more likely to be self-contained rather than departmentalized, more likely to be Black or Hispanic, and less likely to have received a recruitment stipend. Excluded teachers also work in 2010–2011 schools serving proportionally more Black students and poor students. These qualities are all associated with a lower likelihood of receiving awards, and it may be these teachers' lower value-added scores made them more likely to experience a change in teaching assignment between 2009–2010 and 2010–2011 (the seemingly largest contributor to exclusion from the achievement analyses). Our study may also be limited by biased measures. The psychometric properties of vertically scaled test scores are questioned (Meyer & Dokumaci, 2010). Moreover, standardized scores may not represent similar levels of achievement at different points in time. Higher test scores may be an artifact of test-taking skills rather than actual gains in academic knowledge, particularly on higher-stake tests (Corcoran et al., 2010). These are issues faced by most studies using standardized test scores.

Despite these limitations, this study contributes to the body of knowledge focused on understanding the effects of performance pay programs, particularly by focusing on an under-evaluated program in which all teachers are eligible for awards. This study's evidence that teacher awards inconsistently link to student achievement gains may align with research that finds factors outside of teachers' control substantially contribute to student achievement, including inequities across neighborhoods and homes and the clustering of socially disadvantaged students in the same schools (Noguera, 2003; Rothstein, 2004). Nonetheless, our societal emphasis on teachers' public service ethic may amount to a public education system structured to depend on the goodwill of its employees. The wages of teachers relative to other college graduates have fallen steadily since 1940 (Hanushek & Rivkin, 2007). At the same time, pressures related to accountability have increased, with teachers and schools vilified in the media (Valli & Buese, 2007). Teachers' financial compensation should reflect the value we ostensibly hold for education and the possibility of social mobility, potentially through higher salaries for teachers working with students who begin school at an academic disadvantage.

Note

This project benefitted from support from the Houston Education Research Consortium (HERC). HERC is directed by Dr. Ruth López Turley and funded by the Laura and John Arnold Foundation and the Houston Endowment Inc. This project also benefitted from the assistance of research staff from the school district and advice from Rose Medeiros, Steven Glazerman, Scott Imberman, Adam Gamoran, John Robert Warren, Joseph Paul Robinson-Cimpian, Justin McCrary, Matias D. Cattaneo, Sebastian Calonico, anonymous reviewers, and HERC colleagues.

References

Aaronson, D., Barrow, L., & Sander, W. (2007). Teachers and student achievement in the Chicago public high schools. *Journal of Labor Economics, 25*, 95–135.

Ballou, D. (2001). Pay for performance in public and private schools. *Economics of Education Review, 20*, 51–61. doi:10.1016/s0272-7757(99)00060-6.

Bayonas, H. (2010). *Guilford County Schools Mission Possible Program: Year 3 (2008–09) external evaluation report.* Greensboro, NC: The SERVE Center, University of North Carolina at Greensboro.

Benabou, R., & Tirole, J. (2003). Intrinsic and extrinsic motivation. *Review of Economic Studies, 70*, 489–520. doi:10.1111/1467-937x.00253.

Briggs, D., & Domingue, B. (2011). *A review of the value-added analysis underlying the effectiveness rankings of Los Angeles Unified School District teachers by the* Los Angeles Times. Boulder, CO: National Education Policy Center.

Buck, S., & Greene, J. P. (2011). Blocked, diluted, and co-opted. *Education Next, 11*(2), 26–31.

Buckley, K., & Marion, S. (2011). *A survey of approaches used to evaluate educators in non-tested grades and subjects.* Dover, NH: National Center for the Improvement of Educational Assessment.

Chetty, R., Friedman, J. N., & Rockoff, J. E. (2011). *The Long-term impacts of teachers: Teacher value-added and student outcomes in adulthood* (Working Paper 17699). Cambridge, MA: National Bureau of Economic Research.

Chetty, R., Friedman, J. N., & Rockoff, J. E. (2014). Measuring the impacts of teachers I: Evaluating bias in teacher value-added estimates. *American Economic Review, 104,* 2593–2632.

Coleman, J. S. (1990). *Equality and achievement in education.* Boulder, CO: Westview Press.

Cooper, S. T., & Cohn, E. (1997). Estimation of a frontier production function for the South Carolina educational process. *Economics of Education Review, 16,* 313–327.

Corcoran, S. P., Jennings, J. L., & Beveridge, A. A. (2010). *Teacher effectiveness on high- and low-stakes tests* (Working Paper). New York, NY: New York University.

Dee, T. S. (2005). A teacher like me: Does race, ethnicity, or gender matter? *American Economic Review, 95,* 158–165.

Dee, T. S., & Keys, B. J. (2004). Does merit pay reward good teachers? Evidence from a randomized experiment. *Journal of Policy Analysis and Management, 23,* 471–488. doi:10.1002/pam.20022.

Dee, T. S., & Wyckoff, J. (2015). Incentives, selection, and teacher performance: Evidence from IMPACT. *Journal of Policy Analysis and Management, 34,* 267–297.

Ehrenberg, R. G., Goldhaber, D. D., & Brewer, D. J. (1995). Do teachers' race, gender, and ethnicity matter? Evidence from the National Educational Longitudinal Study of 1988. *Industrial and Labor Relations Review, 48,* 547–561.

Figlio, D. N., & Kenny, L. W. (2007). Individual teacher incentives and student performance. *Journal of Public Economics, 91,* 901–914. doi:10.1016/j.jpubeco.2006.10.001.

Finnigan, K. S., & Gross, B. (2007). Do accountability policy sanctions influence teacher motivation? Lessons from Chicago's low-performing schools. *American Educational Research Journal, 44,* 594–629.

Fryer, R. G. (2011a). *Injecting successful charter school strategies into traditional public schools: Early results from an experiment in Houston* (NBER Working Paper 17494). Cambridge, MA: The National Bureau of Economic Research.

Fryer, R. G. (2011b). *Teacher incentives and student achievement: Evidence from New York City public schools.* Cambridge, MA: National Bureau of Economic Research.

Fryer, J., Ronald, G., Levitt, S. D., List, J., & Sadoff, S. (2012). *Enhancing the efficacy of teacher incentives through loss aversion: A field experiment* (Working Paper 18237). Cambridge, MA: National Bureau of Economic Research.

Glazerman, S., Chiang, H., Wellington, A. J., Constantine, J. M., & Player, D. (2011). *Impacts of performance pay under the teacher incentive fund: Study design report.* Washington, DC: Mathematica Policy Research.

Glazerman, S., & Seifullah, A. (2010). *An evaluation of the teacher Advancement Program (TAP) in Chicago: Year two impact report.* Washington, DC: Mathematica Policy Research, Inc.

Goldhaber, D., Gabele, B., & Walch, J. (2012). *Does the model matter? Exploring the relationship between different achievement-based teacher assessments* (CEDR Working Paper 2012-6). Seattle, WA: University of Washington.

Goldhaber, D., & Theobald, R. (2013). *Do different value-added models tell us the same things?* (Working paper). Retrieved from http://www.carnegieknowledge network.org/briefs/value-added/different-growth-models/

Goldstein, D. (2014). *The teacher wars: A history of America's most embattled profession.* New York, NY: Doubleday.

Good, T. L. (1979). Teacher effectiveness in the elementary school. *Journal of Teacher Education, 30,* 52–64.

Goodman, S. F., & Turner, L. J. (2010). *Teacher incentive pay and educational outcomes: Evidence from the New York City bonus program.* New York, NY: Columbia University.

Goodman, S. F., & Turner, L. (2011). Does whole-school performance pay improve student learning? Evidence from the New York City schools. *Education Next, 11*, 67–71.

Guarino, C. M., Brown, A. B., & Wyse, A. E. (2011). Can districts keep good teachers in the schools that need them most? *Economics of Education Review, 30*, 962–979.

Hahn, J., Todd, P., & Klaauw, W. V. D. (2001). Identification and estimation of treatment effects with a regression-discontinuity design. *Econometrica, 69*, 201–209.

Hanushek, E. A. (2011). The economic value of higher teacher quality. *Economics of Education Review, 30*, 466–479. doi:10.1016/j.econedurev.2010.12.006.

Hanushek, E. A., & Rivkin, S. G. (2007). Pay, working conditions, and teacher quality. *The Future of Children, 17*, 69–86.

Hanushek, E. A., & Woessmann, L. (2011). Overview of the Symposium on Performance Pay for Teachers. *Economics of Education Review, 30*, 391–393. doi:10.1016/j.econedurev.2010.12.005.

Healy, K., & Moody, J. (2014). Data visualization in sociology. *Annual Review of Sociology, 40*, 105–128.

Hill, H. C. (2016). 50 years ago, one report introduced Americans to the Black-White achievement gap. Here's what we've learned since. *Chalkbeat*. Retrieved from http://www.chalkbeat.org/posts/us/2016/07/13/50-years-ago-the-coleman-report-revealed-the-black-white-achievement-gap-in-america-heres-what-weve-learned-since/

Hill, H. C., Kapitula, L., & Umland, K. (2011). A validity argument approach to evaluating teacher value-added scores. *American Educational Research Journal, 48*, 794–831.

Hoogeveen, K., & Gutkin, T. B. (1986). Collegial ratings among school personnel: An empirical examination of the merit pay concept. *American Educational Research Journal, 23*, 375–381.

Huang, F. L., & Moon, T. R. (2009). Is experience the best teacher? A multilevel analysis of teacher characteristics and student achievement in low performing schools. *Educational Assessment Evaluation and Accountability, 21*, 209–234.

Imbens, G., & Lemieux, T. (2007). Regression discontinuity designs: A guide to practice. *Journal of Econometrics, 142*, 615–635.

Imberman, S. A., & Lovenheim, M. F. (2012). *Incentive strength and teacher productivity: Evidence from a group-based teacher incentive pay system* (NBER Working Paper No. 18439). Cambridge, MA: National Bureau of Economic Research.

Jacob, R., Zhu, P., Somers, M.-A., & Bloom, H. (2012). *A practical guide to regression discontinuity.* New York, NY: MDRC.

Jinnai, Y. (2012). *The impact of teacher performance pay on student achievement: A regression discontinuity approach.* Unpublished working paper.

Kline, R. B. (2013). *Beyond significance testing: Statistics reform in the behavioral sciences* (2nd ed.). Washington, DC: American Psychological Association.

Ladd, H. F. (1999). The Dallas school accountability and incentive program: An evaluation of its impacts on student outcomes. *Economics of Education Review, 18*, 1–16.

Lawler, E. E., III. (1973). *Motivation in work organizations.* Monterey, CA: Brooks/Cole.

Lawler, E. E., III, & Jenkins, G. D. (1992). *Strategic reward systems* (CEO Publication G 92-2 (205)). Los Angeles, CA: Center for Effective Organizations, Marshall School of Business, University of Southern California.

Lee, D. S., & Lemieux, T. (2010). Regression discontinuity designs in economics. *Journal of Economic Literature, 48*, 281–355.

Lee, J., Finn, J., & Liu, X. (2012). *Time-indexed effect size for P–12 reading and math program evaluation.* Paper presented at the Society for Research on Educational Effectiveness.

Lopez, X., Valenzuela, J., Nussbaum, M., & Tsai, C.-C. (2015). Editorial: Some Recommendations for the reporting of quantitative studies. *Computers & Education, 91,* 106–110.

Marsh, J. A., Springer, M. G., McCaffrey, D. F., Yuan, K., Epstein, S., Koppich, J., . . . Peng, A. X. (2011). *A Big apple for educators: New York City's experiment with schoolwide performance bonuses—Final evaluation report.* Santa Monica, CA: The RAND Corporation.

McCollum, S. (2001). How merit pay improves education. *Educational Leadership, 58,* 21–24.

Meyer, R. H., & Dokumaci, E. (2010). *Value-added models and the next generation of assessments.* Lawrence Township, NJ: Educational Testing Service, Center for K–12 Assessment & Performance.

Morice, L. C., & Murray, J. E. (2003). Compensation and teacher retention: A success story. *Educational Leadership, 60,* 40–43.

Newton, X. A., Darling-Hammond, L., Haertel, E., & Thomas, E. (2010). Value-added modeling of teacher effectiveness: An exploration of stability across models and contexts. *Education Policy Analysis Archives, 18,* 2–27.

Nichols, A. (2007). Casual inference with observational data. *The Stata Journal, 7,* 507–541.

Noguera, P. (2003). *City schools and the American dream: Reclaiming the promise of public education.* New York, NY: Teachers College Press.

Nuzzo, R. (2014). Scientific method: Statistic errors. *Nature, 506,* 150–152.

Pearson Education, I. (2014). Aprenda 3 (Aprenda®: La Prueba de Logros en Espanol, Tercera Edicion). *Learning Assessments.* Retrieved from http://www.pearsonassessments.com/learningassessments/products/100000585/aprenda-3-aprenda-la-prueba-de-logros-en-espanol-tercera-edicion.html

Podgursky, M. J., & Springer, M. G. (2007). Teacher performance pay: A review. *Journal of Policy Analysis and Management, 26,* 909–949. doi:10.1002/pam.20292.

Ramirez, A. (2011). Merit pay misfires. *Educational Leadership, 68,* 55–58.

Reardon, S. F., & Galindo, C. (2009). The Hispanic-White achievement gap in math and reading in the elementary grades. *American Educational Research Journal, 46,* 853–891.

Reardon, S. F., & Robinson, J. P. (2012). Regression discontinuity designs with multiple rating-score variables. *Journal of Research on Educational Effectiveness, 5,* 83–104.

Rothstein, R. (2004). *Class and schools: Using social, economic, and educational reform to close the Black-White Achievement gap.* New York, NY: Teachers College Press.

Santibáñez, L., Martínez, J. F., Datar, A., McEwan, P. J., Setodji, C. M., & Basurto-Dávila, R. (2007). *Breaking ground: Analysis of the assessment system and impact of Mexico's teacher incentive program "Carrera Magisterial."* Santa Monica, CA: RAND Education, RAND Corporation.

Schacter, J., & Thum, Y. M. (2005). TAPping into high quality teachers: Preliminary results from the Teacher Advancement Program comprehensive school reform. *School Effectiveness and School Improvement, 16,* 327–353.

Schneider, B., Carnoy, M., Kilpatrick, J., Schmidt, W. H., & Shavelson, R. J. (2007). *Estimating causal effects: Using experimental and observational designs.* Washington, DC: American Educational Research Association.

Schochet, P. Z., & Chiang, H. S. (2010). *Error rates in measuring teacher and school performance based on student test score gains* (NCEE 2010-4004). Washington, DC: National Center for Education Evaluation and Regional Assistance, U.S. Department of Education.

Serow, R. C. (1994). "I want to see some kind of growth out of them": What the service ethic means to teacher-education students. *American Educational Research Journal, 31,* 27–48.

Solmon, L. C., White, J. T., Cohen, D., & Woo, D. (2007). *The effectiveness of the Teacher Advancement Program.* Santa Monica, CA: National Institute for Excellence in Teaching.

Springer, M. G., Ballou, D., Hamilton, L., Le, V.-N., Lockwood, J. R., McCaffrey, D. F., . . . Stecher, B. M. (2010). *Teacher pay for performance: Experimental evidence from the project on incentives in teaching.* Nashville, TN: National Center on Performance Incentives at Vanderbilt University.

Springer, M. G., Ballou, D., & Peng, A. X. (2008). *Impact of the Teacher Advancement Program on student test score gains: Findings from an independent appraisal.* Nashville, TN: National Center on Performance Incentives.

Springer, M. G., Lewis, J. L., Ehlert, M. W., Podgursky, M. J., Crader, G. D., Taylor, L. L., . . . Stuit, D. A. (2010). *District Awards for Teacher Excellence (D.A.T.E.) program: Final evaluation report.* Nashville, TN: National Center for Performance Incentives.

Springer, M. G., Lewis, J. L., Podgursky, M. J., Ehlert, M. W., Gronberg, T. J., Hamilton, L. S., . . . Peng, A. X. (2009). *Texas Educator Excellence Grant (TEEG) program: Year three evaluation report.* Nashville, TN: National Center on Performance Incentives.

Springer, M. G., Lewis, J. L., Podgursky, M. J., Ehlert, M. W., Taylor, L. L., Lopez, O. S., & Peng, A. X. (2009). *Governor's Educator Excellence Grant (GEEG) program: Year three evaluation report.* Nashville, TN: National Center on Performance Incentives.

Springer, M. G., Pane, J. F., Le, V.-N., McCaffrey, D. F., Burns, S. F., Hamilton, L. S., & Stecher, B. (2012). Team pay for performance: Experimental evidence from the Round Rock pilot project on team incentives. *Educational Evaluation and Policy Analysis, 34,* 367–390.

Storey, A. (2000). A leap of faith? Performance pay for teachers. *Journal of Education Policy, 15,* 509–523. doi:10.1080/026809300750001667.

Storey, A. (2002). Performance management in schools: Could the balanced scorecard help? *School Leadership & Management, 22,* 321–338.

Trafimow, D. (2014). Editorial. *Basic and Applied Social Psychology, 36,* 1–2.

Trafimow, D., & Rice, S. (2009). A test of the null hypothesis significance testing procedure correlation argument. *The Journal of General Psychology, 136,* 261–269.

Valli, L., & Buese, D. (2007). The changing roles of teachers in an era of high-stakes accountability. *American Educational Research Journal, 44,* 519–558.

West, K. L., & Mykerezi, E. (2011). Teachers' unions and compensation: The impact of collective bargaining on salary schedules and performance pay schemes. *Economics of Education Review, 30,* 99–108.

Williams, R. (2012). Using the margins command to estimate and interpret adjusted predictions and marginal effects. *The Stata Journal, 12,* 308–331.

Wong, V. C., Steiner, P. M., & Cook, T. D. (2013). Analyzing regression-discontinuity designs with multiple assignment variables: A comparative study of four estimation methods. *Journal of Educational and Behavioral Statistics, 38,* 107–141.

Wright, S. P., White, J. T., Sanders, W. L., & Rivers, J. C. (2010). *SAS EVAAS statistical models.* Cary, NC: SAS Institute Inc. World Headquarters.

Yuan, K., Le, V.-N., McCaffrey, D. F., Marsh, J. A., Hamilton, L. S., Stecher, B. M., & Springer, M. G. (2013). Incentive pay programs do not affect teacher motivation or reported practices: Results from three randomized studies. *Educational Evaluation and Policy Analysis, 35*, 3–22.

Manuscript received March 11, 2014
Final revision received December 18, 2016
Accepted May 19, 2017

American Educational Research Journal
December 2017, Vol. 54, No. 6, pp. 1154–1186
DOI: 10.3102/0002831217716767
© 2017 AERA. http://aerj.aera.net

Asked More Often:
Gender Differences in Faculty Workload in Research Universities and the Work Interactions That Shape Them

KerryAnn O'Meara
Alexandra Kuvaeva
Gudrun Nyunt
University of Maryland
Chelsea Waugaman
Clemson University
Rose Jackson
The Universities at Shady Grove

Guided by research on gendered organizations and faculty careers, we examined gender differences in how research university faculty spend their work time. We used time-diary methods to understand faculty work activities at a microlevel of detail, as recorded by faculty themselves over 4 weeks. We also explored workplace interactions that shape faculty workload. Similar to past studies, we found women faculty spending more time on campus service, student advising, and teaching-related activities and men spending more time on research. We also found that women received more new work requests than men and that men and women received different kinds of work requests. We consider implications for future research and the career advancement of women faculty in research universities.

KEYWORDS: gender differences, faculty, workload, time diary, workplace interactions

Scholars have gained important insights into how organizational workplaces, including research universities, reflect and maintain gendered inequalities (Acker, 1990, 2006; Avent-Holt & Tomaskovic-Devey, 2012; Britton, 2000; Dinovitzer, Reichman, & Sterling, 2009). Such scholars begin from the premise that orientations to and decisions about discretionary work activity, such as campus service, teaching and mentoring, and research, are neither stable nor biologically determined (Acker, 1990; Smith, 1990). Rather, gendered roles and practices stem from historical patterns related to the division of labor in organizations, and socialization toward gender norms and expectations (Smith, 1990). Specifically, Acker's (1990, 2006) theory of gendered organizations highlights the ways in which divisions of labor and workload maintain and perpetuate gender inequality through role models, recognition systems, and routine interactions between individuals within the organization. The purpose of this study was to examine gender differences in higher education faculty workloads in research universities and the everyday workplace interactions that produce differences, with a particular emphasis on campus service.

Research on faculty workload found conflicting results regarding gender differences. Many studies indicate that factors associated with the amount of time faculty spend on different work activities include individual attributes and work contexts such as gender (Acker & Armenti, 2004; Winslow,

---

KERRYANN O'MEARA is professor of higher education, director of the ADVANCE Program for Inclusive Excellence, and affiliate faculty in women's studies at the University of Maryland, College Park, 3112-C Benjamin Building, MD 20742; e-mail: *komeara@umd.edu*. She received her BA in English literature from Loyola University in Maryland, her MA in higher education from The Ohio State University, and her PhD in education policy from the University of Maryland. Her research focuses on organizational practices that facilitate the full participation of diverse faculty and the legitimacy of diverse scholarship in the academy. She studies organizational policies, practices, and cultures with an eye toward changing them to be more inclusive, equitable, and agency-enhancing for all faculty.

ALEXANDRA KUVAEVA is a doctoral candidate in international education policy and research assistant at the University of Maryland. She received her MA in international education policy from the University of Maryland. Her research interests include gender, education policies, and impact of globalization on higher education.

GUDRUN NYUNT is a doctoral candidate in the student affairs concentration and serves as a faculty specialist for the ADVANCE Program for Inclusive Excellence at the University of Maryland, College Park. She received her BA in journalism from the State University of New York at New Paltz and her master's in higher education and student affairs from the University of Connecticut. Her research interests focus on educational initiatives that prepare students for engaged participation in a global society, and she currently serves as chair of ACPA's Commission for the Global Dimensions of Student Development.

CHELSEA WAUGAMAN is a doctoral candidate in the educational leadership–higher education program at Clemson University. She earned her MA in higher education administration from The University of Maryland and her BA in English from Baldwin Wallace University. Her research interests center on the academic profession, specifically on promotion and tenure, faculty career trajectories and development, college teaching and learning, and student learning assessment.

ROSE JACKSON is the research and data coordinator for the Universities at Shady Grove. She earned her master's in higher education administration from the University of Maryland and her BS in business administration from Frostburg State University. Her research interests include the intersectionality of gender and faculty/staff development, student learning assessment, and college access and choice.

2010), race/ethnicity (Baez, 2000; Griffin, Pifer, Humphrey, & Hazelwood, 2011), the intersection of race/ethnicity and gender (Griffin & Reddick, 2011), career stage (Misra, Lundquist, Holmes, & Agiomavritis, 2011; Neumann & Terosky, 2007), and institutional type (Tierney & Minor, 2004). Specifically, the vast majority of studies found that female faculty and faculty of color engage in more campus service than their White male colleagues and that this difference becomes more pronounced as faculty move along in their careers and focus more on teaching and teaching-related activities (Acker & Armenti, 2004; Carrigan, Quinn, & Riskin, 2011; Clark & Corcoran, 1986; Link, Swan, & Bozemann, 2008; Misra et al., 2011; Park, 1996; Winslow, 2010). Moreover, the kinds of campus service that women engage in are often less prestigious, more time-consuming, or "token" (Misra et al., 2011; Mitchell & Hesli, 2013; Porter, 2007; Twale & Shannon, 1996). Several studies, however, contradict these findings by showing that only a few gender differences in workload remain significant after controlling for variables such as rank, discipline, career stage, and institutional type (see Mitchell & Hesli, 2013; Porter, 2007; Singell, Lillydahl, & Singell, 1996). Conflicting findings seem to stem from scholars using different methods, controlling for different sets of variables, and not accurately accounting for all kinds of academic labor.

There are in fact important weaknesses of past studies of faculty workload. First, most faculty workload studies do not count "smaller" work activities such as writing letters of recommendation, mentoring a faculty member in one's department, and ad hoc requests by campus colleagues favoring instead reports of courses taught and publications completed. Second, most workload studies limit reporting to a single snapshot assessment, such as a one-time accounting of a past year's activity the day the survey or interview is conducted. Requiring faculty to estimate their activities retrospectively over a long period of time increases the likelihood of slippage and inaccuracy in accounting. Third, most studies of faculty workload leave out the processes by which workload is produced such as workplace interactions where faculty volunteer, are asked to engage in work activities, and make responses to requests. Although it has been well-argued that faculty are increasingly "managed professionals" (Rhoades, 1998, p. 4) with fewer choices about how they spend work time, it is also true that there is much discretion and choice built into the organization of tenure-track faculty workloads in research universities (Blackburn & Lawrence, 1995; Tierney & Bensimon, 1996). Given this, it is critical to understand workplace interactions that shape faculty workload.

In this study, we examined gender differences in how research university faculty spend their work time. We aimed to understand faculty work activities at a microlevel of detail, as recorded by faculty themselves over 4 weeks. We also explored the kinds of work requests made of faculty and who was making the requests. We studied faculty responses to work requests and faculty reasons for those responses. Our examination of workload and processes shaping it was guided by research on gendered organizations and faculty careers.

Guiding Perspectives

We were guided by research on faculty careers within U.S. research universities and factors that influence how faculty spend their time (Blackburn & Lawrence, 1995; Fairweather, 1996; Tierney & Bensimon, 1996). Acker's theory of gendered organizations and gendered divisions of labor (Acker, 1990, 2006), Bird's (2011) view of academic institutions as cases of gendered bureaucracy, and Smith's (2005) conception of ruling relations helped us further contextualize ways in which men and women faculty might find themselves spending different amounts of time on various work activities despite operating in similar reward systems.

Although it is beyond the scope of this study, we further recognize that faculty workloads are influenced by social and institutional forces shaping higher education institutions, among other organizations (Ylijoki, 2013). Some of these forces include globalization, technology, and neoliberal ideologies. Such aspects of modern academic life speed up and intensify work in today's university and the ways in which academics work across sites in the United States and around the world (Grummell, Devine, & Lynch, 2009). Some examples are new automated advising and admissions programs or requirements for annual posttenure and graduate outcome assessments. Such new requirements take over faculty time that was previously dedicated to other tasks or add to the amount of time faculty work (Grummell et al., 2009). These new demands can come from external mandates for greater accountability, institutional efforts to mimic aspirational peers, or cost-cutting measures. Regardless of the source, an acceleration of academic work can lead to an overextension of faculty and the dissolution of work-life balance (Gill, 2014; Ylijoki, 2013).

Demographic and Structural Influences on Workload

Among the many predictors of faculty workload and time allocation are institutional type, discipline, gender, critical mass of women in a work environment, race, and rank (Blackburn & Lawrence, 1995; Carrigan et al., 2011; Link et al., 2008; Winslow, 2010). These factors are not independent from the gendered nature of higher education organizations but are embedded within and are shaping the power relations and decision-making of these gendered bureaucracies (Bird, 2011). For the purpose of this study, we focus on structural influences of gender and rank. Although we were not able to examine race in this study, many studies have shown the disproportionate amount of service completed by faculty of color based on service to student groups of the same background, a desire to have diverse faculty on committees, and because of faculty commitments to student development and mentoring (Antonio, 2002; Baez, 2000; Griffin & Reddick, 2011; Umbach, 2006). Intersectionality is important to consider as well, as women of color may be involved in more campus service based on the intersection of gender and race (Griffin & Reddick, 2011).

Gender is argued to be "embedded in the structure of academic careers" (Winslow, 2010, p. 786). Faculty decide how they will allocate time based on gender socialization, perceived expectations, preferences, commitments, and everyday work interactions within gendered department contexts (Acker & Dillabough, 2007; Blackburn & Lawrence, 1995; Winslow, 2010). Therefore, gender has long been a predictor of faculty allocation of time to different work activities (Bellas & Toutkoushian, 1999; Carrigan et al., 2011; Link et al., 2008).

Rank also plays a key role in predicting faculty workload because expectations change from one faculty rank to another (Tierney & Bensimon, 1996). Assistant professors in research universities are generally expected to do less campus service and teaching, so they can focus on research, which counts most for tenure in research university reward systems (Trower, 2012; Ward, 2003). It is important to note though that this is often not the case for faculty of color for reasons previously mentioned. Associate professors, on the other hand, tend to have the heaviest campus service and teaching workload (Misra et al., 2011; Modern Language Association of America, 2009; Neumann, 2009; Neumann & Terosky, 2007; Stout, Staiger, & Jennings, 2007; Valian, 1998). Rank also influences the opportunities that faculty have to serve on certain committees. Full professors may have access to high profile and more valued service roles than assistant and associate professors (Tierney & Bensimon, 1996). There is, however, a relationship between gender and rank (Xu, 2012). Male faculty hold a higher percentage of highly ranked positions and women are more likely than men to leave academic positions before reaching higher ranks (Xu, 2012). Therefore, to understand gendered divisions of labor in time devoted to teaching and service versus research, it is important to examine rank and gender side by side.

Work Interactions That Shape Workload

In the previous section, we outlined demographic and structural factors that shape workload. In other words, being a woman or being an associate professor has been found to predict faculty time allocation to different roles. Another important consideration is how and why such factors shape the way faculty spend work time. This is where Acker's (1990, 2006) work on gendered organizations and Smith's (2005) work on "ruling relations" are helpful.

Acker's (1990, 2006) theory of gendered organizations posits that all contemporary organizations, including research universities, are gendered, meaning they are organized in ways that create and reproduce inequality for women when compared to men. This occurs in many ways, but for the purposes of this study, we focus on how work is assigned or taken up by workers and valued by the organization. In gendered organizations, men are positioned in locations of greater organizational power and women in more vulnerable, peripheral, or undervalued positions (Kanter, 1977). This takes place through hierarchy and titles but also through the nature of work employees do and whether that work is considered skilled or unskilled (Acker, 1990). For example, in many organizations, women managers are more often responsible for tasks that are widely defined as organizational housekeeping, while men are more often tasked with problem-solving, visioning, and strategic planning (Acker & Dillabough, 2007; Ely & Meyerson, 2000). In these cases, a division of labor wherein women are engaged in unskilled labor and men in skilled tasks reproduces gendered assumptions about their value and capabilities as workers. Likewise, many feminist scholars have observed that academic reward systems do not value institutional housekeeping and campus service activities, which have become defined as "women's work" (Acker & Armenti, 2004; Clark & Corcoran, 1986; Park, 1996). Research and work in professional societies and for journals, often considered "cosmopolitan" faculty activity, are likely to add to one's prestige in a field as well as the institution's, whereas teaching and service are considered "local" contributions, less likely to add to the stature of individual faculty (Rhoades, Kiyama, McCormick, & Quiroz, 2008). Thus, gendered organizations place greater value on work more often taken up by men and less value on work more often taken up by women.

However, in turning to how work is "taken up," it is important to note that both women and men faculty have agency and make choices (Baez, 2000; Neumann, 2009). Most faculty in public research universities negotiate their workload from agreed upon parameters within their departments for course load, expected external grant funding, and general service expectations. However, experiences differ beyond this common template, which explains differences in workload. Feminist standpoint theorist Dorothy Smith (2005) offers a concept helpful to framing how workplace interactions might differ for women and men in a gendered university. Smith (2005) observes that men and women are subject to different "ruling relations," or the organization of people by hierarchies and privilege into work experiences (p. 13). Ruling relations in this context could include campus policies and practices requiring that a woman or person of color serve on search committees but not necessarily on campus APT committees. Such arrangements make it more likely for women and faculty of color to be invited to serve on search committees than male White peers as there are generally more White male faculty to invite. Ruling relations can be general sets of expectations about what is possible and legitimate (e.g., membership in campus APT committees being only full professors), social interactions embedded with power (e.g., a department chair asking an associate professor who wants to advance to lead the department's accreditation review), and the way in which certain groups, like women, are expected to play certain roles (e.g., academic mother) (Smith, 2005). All three kinds of ruling relations could lead to cumulative disadvantage (Merton, 1968) for women's careers. In sum, there are formal and visible aspects of research university cultures and organization as well as informal norms and expectations that shape workplace interactions likely to result in gender differences in workload. This could play out in at least three ways.

First, women faculty may choose to engage in more teaching and service than men. Most research studies exploring gender inequality in faculty workload begin from the premise that women are assigned more campus service and advising than men, as opposed to women faculty seeking out certain activities to impact issues and groups they value. Yet this is often the case. Being involved in teaching and campus service may be a form of agency to influence their programs and diversity issues in ways that are important to women (Baez, 2000; Griffin, Bennett, & Harris, 2013; Griffin & Reddick, 2011; Stanley, 2006; Turner, 2002; Umbach, 2006). Acker and Feuerverger (1996) found that women faculty strongly believed in improving their academic programs, supporting colleagues and students, and being good citizens of their department, though they felt disappointed in male colleagues' lack of passion for these activities. Likewise, studies of women of color have found a personal commitment to mentoring and diversity work that might explain work choices (Griffin & Reddick, 2011; Griffin et al., 2011; Stanley, 2006; Turner, 2002). Determining whether women faculty choose to engage in this work out of personal interest is difficult, as they are influenced by gendered organizational practices and cultures. Tierney and Bensimon (1996) noted that engagement in teaching and service activities may help women feel less isolated and invisible in an environment where they are underrepresented and experience sexism. Therefore, differences in workload may occur by women volunteering for more teaching and service and men choosing to spend more time on research, but these "choices" occur within the context of and are shaped by existing hierarchies, power relations, and internalized gender roles.

Second, administrators and colleagues may invite women faculty more often than men to become involved in teaching and campus service. Research found that women are asked more often because administrators and colleagues want to add diversity to a committee, anticipate that women will say yes, perceive women as being good at teaching and service, and know that many women are deeply committed to the activities being pursued (Padilla, 1994; Tierney & Bensimon, 1996; Turner, 2002). Pyke (2015) highlighted that women may also be typecast as critical to caretaking and institutional housekeeping tasks and therefore asked more often to engage in teaching, advising, mentoring, and campus service. Social role theory indicates that the historical division of labor between women, whose responsibilities revolved around the home, and men, who worked outside the home, has led to expectancies for male and female behaviors, which continue to be transmitted to future generations through socialization (Eagly, 1987). Gender stereotypes describe women as more concerned with the welfare of others, willing to accept other's directions, interdependent, and collective in their thinking, while men are seen as being more individualistic, self-reliant, and assertive (Cross & Madson, 1997). Society at large embraces these stereotypes and different expectations of women and men. Individuals, consciously and unconsciously, reinforce such expectations through micro-interactions with others. For example, students expect women faculty more than men to be helpful, approachable, available, and warm (Anderson, 2010; Basow, 2000). Women faculty may actually reinforce these expectations themselves as they report devoting more time than men to teaching-related involvements and to using student-centered pedagogies (Eagan & Garvey, 2015). When individuals do not live up to these gender stereotypes, they are often perceived in a negative light (Heilman, Wallen, Fuchs, & Tamkins, 2004; Rudman, 1998). For example, women, who are successful at traditional male tasks or embrace typically male traits and behaviors, are perceived as less likeable and may face personal derogation (Heilman et al., 2004). Because of social role expectations (Eagly, 1987), unconscious bias (Williams, 2003), and gender schema prevalent in society and higher education institutions (Valian, 1998), women may be asked more often than men to participate in teaching, advising, and academic house keeping and recognize they will suffer greater consequences for saying no.

Third, when asked to engage in new work activities, women may say yes more often than men for many reasons. For example, faculty may feel vulnerable in saying no to requests because they are of a lesser rank than the colleague asking them. Given women are underrepresented in higher ranks, many times the person asking women faculty to take on additional non-research-related work are men of higher rank. As noted earlier, women saying "no" to work requests may violate the requestor's gender stereotypes, causing the woman faculty member to be perceived as cold, selfish, and not a team player (Moss-Racusin & Rudman, 2010). Also, men and women differ in approaches to negotiation: Women tend to prefer job environments with set rules or understandings for compensation and resources for various activities over environments where compensation for various activities is ambiguous (Leibbrandt & List, 2012). In environments where such rules exist, there are few gender differences; in environments with ambiguity, men negotiate more. Many teaching and service tasks occur in ambiguous environments where it is not clear what rewards or penalties are associated with the decision to say yes or no. Even when women and men both say "yes," men may ask for more resources than women to support the additional work. One of the only studies to look at whether women are volunteering more for non-research-related work or are being asked more was Mitchell and Hesli's

(2013) cross-sectional survey of political science faculty. They found women faculty were asked to engage in service and said yes to requests more often, but women did not volunteer more often.

In sum, research on faculty careers and the gendered nature of universities indicates that gender, rank, and workplace interactions influence faculty work time. We wanted to explore how these factors impact faculty work time but enhance the literature by using time-diary methods. Also, we sought to understand whether, and if so how, new work requests were gendered.

Methods

We employed a modified time-diary approach to understand whether gender differences exist among associate and full professors in 13 universities that are members of the Big 10 Conference, the oldest Division I collegiate athletic conference in the United States, and the Association of American Universities. We specifically looked at (a) the amount of time faculty were spending on different work activities, (b) the number and kinds of new work requests faculty received each week, (c) who was making those requests, (d) faculty responses to work requests each week, and (e) the reasons faculty provided for their responses to work requests. Participants were first asked to complete an in-take survey that provided a general sense of their semester workload. Then, participants were asked to report time spent on weekly activities in an open write-in format. After collecting faculty responses, we coded the reported activities into categories of research, teaching, student and faculty advising, campus and professional service, and institutional housekeeping. At the end of the time-diary instrument for each week, we asked about work requests that the participants received. In this section, we describe our modified time-diary approach, sample and participants, analysis, and limitations.

Modified Time-Diary Approach and Instrument

Time-diary approaches have a long history in social science research to understand events that occur in a specific period of time and participant meaning-making about those events, in real time (Hofferth & Sandberg, 2001; Juster & Stafford, 1985). The time-diary method has been used reliably to study diverse topics such as how often parents read to children (Hofferth, 2006), the amount of leisure time of people living in poverty (Merz & Rathjen, 2014), and the relative amount of housework men and women complete (Bianchi, Sayer, Milkie, & Robinson, 2012). However, time diaries have not been a popular method in studies of faculty workload and time use. Most of these studies come from cross-sectional national surveys such as the National Study of Postsecondary Faculty (NSOPF), the Higher Education Research Institute's (HERI) Faculty Survey, and the Collaborative on Academic Careers in Higher Education's (COACHE) survey. Participants are asked on a single occasion to estimate their workload allocation in broad categories over the last year or semester. This means that faculty participants are estimating their workloads up to 11 months from when work was done, and in broad brush strokes rather than in detail. In contrast, this study is one of the few illuminating work activities that participants are involved in throughout a 24-hour period. The time-diary approach used in this study has been gaining popularity over recall estimate (*stylized*) measures, because it provides more complete, systematic, rich, contextual, and less biased description of daily behavior (Juster, Ono, & Stafford, 2003; Robinson, Martin, Glorieux, & Minnen, 2011). Juster and Stafford (1985) first recognized that this 24-hour format provides the most precise and accurate time-use estimates. It allows faculty to record their work activities in their own language in real time as the activities are happening. Therefore, a time-diary approach offers a more comprehensive way of understanding gender differences in faculty time allocation and workload, because it allows us to study faculty work activities at a microlevel or in fine-grain detail, so that we can see whether differences exist in the kinds of work activities that women and men faculty are completing within each area of teaching, research, campus service, and professional service.

Our time-diary instrument asked participants to record their work activities in 5-minute increments. We also asked participants to avoid recording being on email alone as a task but to note the kind of task they were completing on email. Other than these two modifications, our instrument followed the typical time-diary form of asking participants to record their activities in their own language, chronologically, throughout or at the end of each day using 5-minute increments for 4 consecutive weeks.

Prior to completing the time diary, all participants completed an in-take survey, which included questions about background demographics (tenure status, discipline, marital status, and partner's employment status, whether they had dependents and how many) and work activities for the current academic semester (Spring 2014). Specifically, we asked about teaching (number of courses and advisees, dissertations, master's theses, and undergraduate capstone projects chaired), research and grant activity (numbers of articles, book chapters, conference papers submitted, presentations, manuscripts reviewed for journals, editorial positions, grants directed and submitted), on- and off-campus service activities (ongoing campus leadership roles, mentoring other faculty, number and kind of campus committees), and whether participants felt that overall the distribution of service work in their department was fair.

The in-take and weekly time-diary instruments were pilot tested with 10 research university faculty who served on an advisory board for this project. Feedback was received by email and conference calls, and minor revisions were made to instruments before they were approved by the authors' Institutional Review Board.

Participant Selection

We chose to study gender differences among associate and full professors, and exclude assistant professors, for several reasons. Many assistant professors, when looking at faculty as a whole and not focusing on faculty of color specifically, are protected from campus service assignments pretenure and have smaller course loads (Ponjuan, Conley, & Trower, 2011; Trower, 2012). This makes assistant professors different in some distinct ways from their posttenure colleagues as they can focus more time on research. Requests for many kinds of work activities (e.g., campus service, editorial positions, requests to present research) are likely to increase as one advances in career, and requests were a focus of our study. A recent study of time allocation in a research university environment found gender differences the greatest among tenured associate professors (Misra et al., 2011). Finally, several studies have noted gender differences in career advancement from associate to full professor with women faculty taking longer. These studies suggest gender differences in work time allocation may help explain time to advancement differences (Modern Language Association of America, 2009; Neumann & Terosky, 2007; Stout et al., 2007). For each of these reasons, we chose to study associate and full professors only.

We chose 13 Big 10 research universities as our setting because research universities are an institutional type with significant underrepresentation of women in higher ranks, where time spent on research and external funding matters most to advancement and career success (Curtis, 2011; Glazer-Raymo, 1999; Massachusetts Institute of Technology, 1999). The Big 10 institutions embodied within the Committee on Institutional Cooperation offered a subset of research universities that have similar public missions, external research funding, large faculties, and research and funding expectations for promotion and tenure (see http://www.cic.net).

Initially, we hoped to analyze faculty time allocation and critical mass of women in a discipline, using Xu's (2012) research design. Xu (2012) used National Research Council (NRC), National Science Foundation (NSF), and National Center for Education Statistics (NCES) data to create four categories of disciplines based on gender representation: those with 1%–25% of women faculty, 26%–50% of women faculty, 51%–75% of women faculty, and 76%–100% of women faculty (four disciplines chosen for each group). Thus, we invited men and women faculty from 16 different disciplines, hoping to have responses from disciplines where there tend to be more women, fewer women, and disciplines in between these extremes. Unfortunately, the final group of participants was not big enough to conduct this analysis but nonetheless represents faculty from 16 disciplines (see Tables 1 and 2 for the list of participant disciplines).

Table 1
Demographics, by Rank

		Associate Professors, % (*n* = 62)	Full Professors, % (*n* = 49)
Gender	Male	29.0**	59.2**
	Female	71.0**	40.8**
Disciplines	STEM total	24.2*	42.9*
	Engineering	14.5	20.4
	Mathematics	3.2	8.2
	Physics	1.6	6.1
	Biology	1.6	6.1
	Geology	3.2	2.0
	Non-STEM total	75.8*	57.1*
	Sociology	12.9	6.1
	Nursing sciences	8.1	6.1
	Special education	8.1	4.1
	Psychology	9.7	2.0
	Communication	6.5	6.1
	Foreign languages	6.5	4.1
	Speech-language pathology and audiology	4.8	4.1
	Teacher education	4.8	2.0
	Business administration	1.6	2.0
	Economics	0	2.0
	American literature	1.6	0
	Other	11.3	18.4
Race	Asian American	6.5	10.2
	Black/African American	1.6	4.1
	Hispanic	6.5	2.0
	White/non-Hispanic	85.5	83.7
Marital status	Married	87.1	87.8
	Divorced	4.8	6.1
	Separated	1.6	0
	Widowed	0	2.0
	Single	6.5	4.1
Spouse's employment	Works full-time at their institution	29.0	24.5
	Employed full-time elsewhere	30.6	14.3
	Works part-time at their institution	9.7	10.2
	Works part-time elsewhere	8.1	10.2
	Unemployed but looking for work	0	2.0
	Unemployed but not looking for work	9.7	16.3
	Student	0	2.0
	Retired	1.6	8.2
	Not applicable (no spouse)	11.3	12.2

*$p < .05$. **$p < .01$,

O'Meara et al.

		Women, % (n = 64)	Men, % (n = 47)
Rank	Tenured associate professor	68.8**	38.3**
	Tenured full professor	31.2**	61.7**
Disciplines	STEM total	25.0	42.6
	Engineering	14.1	21.3
	Mathematics	3.1	8.5
	Physics	3.1	4.3
	Biology	3.1	4.3
	Geology	1.6	4.3
	Non-STEM total	75.0	57.4
	Sociology	10.9	8.5
	Nursing sciences	12.5	0
	Special education	7.8	4.3
	Psychology	6.3	6.4
	Communication	0	10.6
	Foreign languages	4.7	6.4
	Speech-language pathology and audiology	6.3	2.1
	Teacher education	4.7	2.1
	Business administration	1.6	2.1
	Economics	0	2.1
	American literature	1.6	0
	Other	15.6	12.8
Race	Asian American	3.1	14.9
	Black/African American	1.6	4.3
	Hispanic	4.7	4.3
	White/non-Hispanic	90.6*	76.6*
Marital status	Married	82.8	93.6
	Divorced	7.8	2.1
	Separated	0	2.1
	Widowed	1.6	0
	Single	7.8	2.1
Spouse's employment	Works full-time at their institution	23.4	31.9
	Employed full-time elsewhere	34.4**	8.5**
	Works part-time at their institution	6.3	14.9
	Works part-time elsewhere	6.3	12.8
	Unemployed but looking for work	0	2.1
	Unemployed but not looking for work	6.3**	21.3**
	Student	1.6	0
	Retired	4.7	4.3
	Not applicable (do not have a spouse)	17.2**	4.3**

Table 2
Demographics, by Gender

*p < .05. **p < .01.

Table 3
Invited Faculty and Participants by Gender, Rank, and Race

		Invited Faculty (*N* = 6,438)		Participants (*N* = 111)	
Gender	Male	4,713	73.2%	47	42.3%
	Female	1,712	26.6%	64	57.7%
	Gender not indicated	13	0.2%	—	—
Rank	Associate	2,402	37.3%	62	55.9%
	Full	4,036	62.7%	49	44.1%
Race	White faculty	5,138	79.8%	94	84.7%
	Faculty of color	1,170	18.2%	17	15.3%
	Race not decipherable	130	2.0%	—	—

Data Collection

We began data collection using a stratified sampling technique of randomly selecting a pool of 1,200 faculty balanced by gender, rank, and discipline with the goal of having a final sample of at least 300 participants. A sample of this size would enable us to control for gender, rank, and discipline in one model and to see significant differences, if present, along with a minimum detectable effect size. We chose to invite such a large number of participants because we knew under normal circumstances faculty responses to national surveys are typically around 25%–35% (Eagan & Garvey, 2015), but to complete a time diary for 4 consecutive weeks during a regular academic semester was a significant investment of time and energy and required an incentive. The length of the time diary significantly decreases the response rate: from over 50%–80% in a 1-day diary to 20%–25% in a 7-day diary, with the 7-day diary being the longest period for nationally representative time diaries ever collected (Fisher & Gershuny, 2015). Due to an initially low response rate, we had to increase the number of invitations up to 6,438 faculty (our entire original database). The demographics of those invited to participate are provided in Table 3. The demographics of the invited faculty are generally comparable to nationwide statistics of Research Universities with Very High Research Activity (RU/HV): In 2012, of all the tenure-track/tenured faculty at 108 RU/HVs, 68% were male and 32% female; 23% were assistant, 27% associate, and 50% full professors; and 70% were White faculty (Integrated Postsecondary Education Data System).

We sent faculty an email invitation with a link to participate in the Faculty Time Study. Participants were offered a $50.00 Amazon gift card if they completed an in-take survey and four weekly online time-diary surveys through Qualtrics. Our in-take survey acted as a screening device for participation in the weekly time-diary study. We asked participants if this was a typical semester for them or unusual work-wise, such as being on sabbatical, being about to retire, being interim department chair, or on parental or sick leave. Out of 6,438 faculty who were invited to participate, 185 completed the in-take survey, but only 143 with a typical semester were eligible to participate further. Out of the 143 faculty, 15 participants completed 1 week of the time diary, 10 completed 2 weeks, 7 completed 3 weeks, and 111 completed all 4 weeks. In this paper, we report results from the 111 faculty participants who had a typical semester and completed both the in-take survey and 4 weeks of time diaries (for demographics, see Table 3).

Additional background characteristics can be found in Tables 1 and 2.

Data Analysis

First, descriptive statistics were calculated to determine the overall numbers and percentages of faculty involved in various work activities, work requests, and responses. Chi-squared statistics were calculated to determine whether the breakdown differed by gender or rank. One-way ANOVA analyses were conducted to determine whether there were significant differences in time spent on each type of weekly work activity based on gender and rank. To control for differences in time spent on reported activities depending on the week (when they spent less time on certain categories due to conference travel, exam week, etc.), we calculated the mean number of minutes and hours spent on each activity for all 4 weeks.

Then, controlling for gender and rank in the models, a regression analysis was conducted to determine significant differences in the main areas of work: research, teaching, student advising, faculty advising, professional service, campus service, institutional housekeeping, and total work hours. Interaction effects (Gender × Rank) were entered into the regression model for each work activity to test for significant interactions between the factors. When significant interactions were found, separate regression models were run by each group. Finally, regression analyses were conducted to estimate the effects of gender and rank on the number and kinds of work activity requests reported by faculty during the 4 weeks as well as the types of requestors and participants' responses to the requests.

Limitations

There were limitations to this research design. First, and most obviously, the selection of participants was not fully randomized due to the low response rate. Thus, when interpreting the results, one should keep in mind the demographic differences between the invited population and the final sample. Compared to the population of the invited faculty (n = 6,438), in the final sample (n = 111) women and associate professors were overrepresented, suggesting that faculty with higher service and/or teaching loads were more willing to participate. The final group was representative of the population by race/ethnicity. As a result of the small final sample, we could not analyze findings by more than gender and rank. Additional contexts such as race and disciplinary categories are important contexts shown to influence faculty time allocation and should be analyzed in future research with a larger sample.

We acknowledge a possible existence of nonresponse bias in the study. Faculty participated on a voluntary basis, and we could only examine those who agreed to participate. We therefore do not know if the rest of the invited faculty declined to participate due to them being busier than the respondents or for other reasons. It is challenging to solicit research participation from email requests. This challenge was further compounded by the fact that we were soliciting participants who likely have significant demands placed on them (as tenured faculty in high-level research universities) and by the fact that the demands of the study (recording 5-minute intervals) were time-consuming.

Nonresponse bias is a function not only of the response rate but also of the differences between respondents and nonrespondents (Jowell, Roberts, Fitzgerald, & Eva, 2007). In fact, the response rate does not determine the level of nonresponse bias: A study with a very high response rate can still be subject to response bias if nonrespondents differ significantly from respondents, and vice versa (Menachemi, 2011). Although many factors, such as demographics, time, and willingness to participate, may contribute to nonparticipation, they do not all necessarily lead to response bias (Menachemi, 2011). Nevertheless, it is commonly accepted that a high response rate reduces response bias (Armstrong & Overton, 1977; Gore-Felton, Koopman, Bridges, Thoresen, & Spiegel, 2002; Leece et al., 2004).

Comparing demographics of respondents versus nonrespondents is the most common approach to test response bias (Armstrong & Overton, 1977; Etter & Perneger, 1997). Another approach involves comparing answers of participants who responded to different waves ("reminders") of the survey (Hikmet & Chen, 2003; Montori, Leung, Walter, & Guyatt, 2005). Our study design did not make comparing waves of participants possible, but the study design allowed us to compare demographics to infer about potential response bias.

Surveys requiring participant involvement over an extended period of time tend to suffer from a high nonresponse and attrition rate (Deng, Hillygus, Reiter, Si, & Zheng, 2013; Goldstein, 2009). We expected that recording every work activity in 5-minute increments over 4 weeks would present a challenge for faculty during the busy time of the year. However, we intentionally did not implement our time diary in the summer because faculty schedules may differ significantly from their typical work during a regular semester. Furthermore, we wanted faculty to record their work activities over a long enough time to control for differences in their schedules due to "unusual" weeks of travelling, conferences, etc. As such, the length of the study was intentional but likely decreased the response rate. However, we also believe it helped to increase the accuracy of the reported workload. Analysis of reliability and validity of the time-diary method in several studies, even with small and unrepresentative samples, showed consistent, positive results about the basic generalizability of the data (Robinson, 1999). Thus, the time-diary approach is more comprehensive in recording work activities than methods used in past studies. Also, while the sample is not fully representative of a larger population of faculty, the data allow us to consider how gender may shape workplace interactions. The arguments developed in the paper can be further tested with more random samples in future research.

Despite these limitations, these data provide a comprehensive and unique portrait of the daily workload experiences of research university faculty to be built upon in future studies. To our knowledge, the only other studies to come close to this kind of inside view of faculty work are those done as structured observations where the sample was less random and the sample size much smaller (e.g., Colbeck, 2006, had 13 participants; Ziker et al., 2014, 30 participants). Thus, this study makes a novel and important contribution to the way faculty workload is studied.

Key Findings

Here we present findings regarding how our research university faculty spent their work time. Specifically, we present (a) how faculty allocated their time to teaching, research, and service; (b) the kinds of requests faculty received for new work activities and who the requestors were; and (c) the responses faculty gave to requests and their reasons for responses. As a reminder, we collected semester-long, ongoing workload data via an in-take survey and work time data, on a microlevel of detail, including (b) and (c) through weekly time diaries.

Faculty Time Allocated to Teaching, Research, and Service

In this section, we report statistically significant findings.

By gender. The in-take survey results showed statistically significant gender differences in many teaching, research, and service activities. For example, women were more likely than men to chair master's theses, comps papers, or undergraduate capstone projects in the current semester and to have submitted or to be planning to submit grants that semester. Men were more likely than women to serve as editor or associate/deputy editor of a journal and to have one or more submissions of journal articles that semester (Table 4).

Table 4
In-Take Survey Gender Differences in Teaching, Research, and Service

	M (*SD*) or %	
Activity	Women (*n* = 64)	Men (*n* = 47)
Teaching		
Master's theses, comps papers, or undergraduate projects chaired*	3.03 (4.55)	1.34 (1.68)
Professional service		
Faculty serving as a journal editor or associate/ deputy editor**	35.9%	68.1%
Research		
Faculty who had one or more submission(s) of this type of publication:		
Journal articles*	85.9%	97.9%
Faculty having or planning on submitting one or more grant(s)*	73.4%	51.1%

Note. Chi-square and ANOVA tests were conducted to determine statistical significance. All data refer to activities performed in a given semester.
*$p < .05$. **$p < .01$.

    In their weekly activities, women reported more hours per week spent on reading dissertations, master's theses, capstone projects, and comps papers than men, while men reported spending more hours per week on lab, field work, and general research preparation than women, and total research activities. Men also reported spending almost twice as much time as women in professional conversations with colleagues (Table 5). We considered whether the intersection of gender and discipline influenced time spent on conversation with colleagues. Indeed, there were differences between the number of women (25%) in STEM vs. men in STEM (42.6%), however they were not significant. Therefore, we do not have enough evidence to find a correlation between the number of women in STEM, the time spent in labs with other colleagues vs. on their own, and professional discussion. There are women in STEM in our sample, and they were as likely to be based in a lab as men in STEM. Furthermore, while time spent in lab and professional communication may be correlated, these activities happened at different times. The activities coded in our study are unique to one category, such that the time reported being spent on professional conversations was not reported at the same time as (or as a part of) lab work but outside the lab activities.

    A pattern of the in-take survey showing women spending more time teaching and advising students (Table 4) continued throughout the weekly survey (Table 5).

Table 5
Gender Differences in Time Spent on Weekly Work Activities, in Hours

Work Activity	M (SD)	
	Male	Female
Research		
Total research time**	16.13 (11.26)	10.21 (7.25)
Lab/fieldwork/general research preparation**	5.20 (5.69)	2.72 (3.15)
Teaching		
Reading dissertations/theses/capstone projects/ comps papers*	0.51 (0.84)	1.17 (1.93)
Faculty advising		
Professional conversations*	1.01 (1.10)	0.59 (0.63)

*$p < .05$. **$p < .01$.

By rank. The in-take survey results showed some statistically significant rank differences in teaching, research, and service workload. Full professors were more likely than associates to consider themselves a primary mentor for faculty at their institution, to serve as editor or associate/deputy editor of a journal, to serve as PI of active grants, and to make off-campus professional presentations. Overall, associate professors were less satisfied with the fairness of service work distribution in their department (Table 6).

In their weekly activities, full professors reported more total work hours than associate professors. Full professors spent more time than associate professors on research activities: manuscript preparation; lab, fieldwork, and general research preparation; research group meetings; and their research overall. Associate professors reported spending more time on teaching and advising than full professors: course administration and advising undergraduate students (Table 7).

Gender and rank together. In the overall regression models, gender was a significant negative predictor of time spent on research, controlling for rank, and rank was a significant negative predictor of time spent on research and total weekly work activities, controlling for gender. On average, women reported spending 355 minutes, or 5.92 hours, per week fewer than men on research (*Beta* = −.232, adjusted R^2 = .134, $p < .05$). Associate professors reported spending 367 minutes, or 6.11 hours, per week fewer than full professors on research (*Beta* = −.248, adjusted R^2 = .134, $p < .05$), and 323 minutes, or 5.38 hours, fewer on all types of work activities combined (*Beta* = −.243, adjusted R^2 = .047, $p < .05$).

While regression analysis showed statistically significant gender differences only in time spent on research, women reported spending more time on all other categories except for faculty advising. Particularly, we

Table 6
In-Take Survey Rank Differences in Teaching, Research, and Service

	M (SD)	
Activity	Associate Professors (n = 62)	Full Professors (n = 49)
Campus service		
Number of faculty at their institution that they consider themselves the primary mentor for*	1.21 (1.19)	1.84 (1.53)
Faculty who believe that the distribution of service work in their department is fair*	43.5%	67.3%
Professional service		
Faculty serving as a journal editor or associate/ deputy editor*	40.3%	61.2%
Research		
Grants as PI*	0.87 (1.17)	1.47 (1.94)
Off-campus professional presentation this semester**	1.73 (1.5)	2.73 (2.3)

Note. Chi-square and ANOVA tests were conducted to determine statistical significance. All data refer to activities performed in a given semester.
*$p < .05$. **$p < .01$.

Table 7
Rank Differences in Time Spent on Weekly Work Activities, in Hours

	M (SD)	
Work Activity	Associate Professor	Full Professor
Total work hours**	40.37 (10.06)	45.76 (10.76)
Research		
Total research time**	10.02 (6.71)	16.13 (11.49)
Manuscript preparation*	2.55 (3.02)	3.82 (3.60)
Lab, field work, general research preparation*	2.99 (3.30)	4.75 (5.65)
Research group meetings*	0.98 (1.27)	1.72 (2.13)
Teaching		
Course administration*	0.36 (0.61)	0.16 (0.47)
Student advising		
Advising undergraduate students*	0.29 (0.55)	0.13 (0.25)

*$p < .05$. **$p < .01$.

found that campus service, student advising, and institutional housekeeping categories had the largest positive standardized regression coefficients, which may be an indicator of the time spent on these categories eating up the time that would otherwise be spent on research. However, the differences on each of these categories separately were not big enough to stand out as significant within the sample size. Yet when categories of campus service and student advising were combined, regression analysis showed statistically significant gender differences, specifically women spending 142 minutes, or 2.37 hours, more than men on these two categories together (*Beta* = .189), $F(1, 109) = 4.036$, $p = .047$.

The interaction of gender and rank was significant for time spent on research: The relationship between gender and time spent on research activities differed for associate and full professors. The model accounted for 14.5% of the variance (adjusted R^2) in time spent on research, $F(3, 107) = 7.236$, $p < .001$. There were no other significant interactions between gender and rank with regard to time spent on work activities. Based on the results of the interaction effect tests, separate regression models were run for associate and full professors on time spent on research. The results showed that gender was a significant, negative predictor for full professors but not significant for associate professors. The regression model for full professors accounted for 8.2% of the variance in time spent on research, $F(1, 47) = 5.275$, $p = .026$. Female full professors reported spending on average 441 minutes, or 7.3 hours, per week less on research activities than male full professors (*Beta* = −.318), $t(47) = -2.297$, $p = .026$.

Requests for New Work Activities: Kinds of Requests and Requestors

Number of requests. Women reported a total of 378 and men reported a total of 118 new work activity requests during the 4 weeks. Across all 4 weeks, women consistently received a significantly higher number of work activity requests than men, on average 3.4 requests more than men in 4 weeks combined. Associate professors reported a total of 294 and full professors reported a total of 202 new work activity requests during the 4 weeks.

Controlling for gender and rank, the overall regression models showed that gender was a significant positive predictor of the total number of new work activity requests (*Beta* = .271), $t(108) = -2.784$, $p = .006$, while rank was not found to be a significant predictor. The model accounted for 5.2% of the variance (adjusted R^2) in the number of requests, $F(2, 108) = 4.008$, $p = .021$. The gender differences persisted both for associate and full professors: Female associate professors ($M = 5.98$, $SD = 8.95$) were more likely than male associate professors ($M = 1.72$, $SD = 1.78$) to receive work activity requests, $F(1, 60) = 3.969$, $p = .004$; female full professors ($M = 5.75$, $SD = 5.29$) were more likely than male full professors ($M = 3.00$, $SD = 2.89$) to receive work activity requests, $F(1, 47) = 5.494$, $p = .044$.

Kinds of requests. Of the total 496 work activity requests reported by participants, over half of them were related to professional service (27.8%) and campus service (29%), followed by student advising (20.7%), faculty advising (10%), teaching (7.7%), and research (4.8%).

Table 8
Percent of Received Work Activity Requests, by Kind

Request Category	Male	Female	Associate	Full
Research	8.0%	3.8%	3.5%	6.6%
Teaching	6.3%	8.1%	8.1%	7.1%
Student advising	17.9%	21.6%	22.8%	17.8%
Faculty advising	8.9%	10.3%	11.6%	7.6%
Professional service	29.5%	27.3%	21.8%	36.5%
Campus service	29.5%	28.9%	32.3%	24.4%

Note. The percent is based on the group total: e.g., 8% of all work activity requests received by men over the 4 weeks are research-related.

Controlling for gender, rank, and total number of work activity requests, the overall regression models showed that associate professors received fewer requests than full professors in professional service (*Beta* = −.181), $t(107)$ = −2.809, p = .006. The regression model for professional service requests accounted for 58.5% of the variance, $F(3, 107)$ = 52.609, $p < .001$. Descriptive statistics of the kinds of requests by gender and rank are reported in Table 8.

Requestors. Students and former students of the participants (23.4%) and off-campus colleagues in the participants' field (23.6%) were the primary categories of requestors, followed by another administrator at their university (13.5%), a peer colleague on campus (11.9%), their department chair (7.8%), a senior colleague on campus (5.1%), and a junior colleague on campus (3.1%). Controlling for gender, rank, and total number of work activity requests, the overall regression models did not show significant differences in the categories of requestors by gender and rank of the participants.

Over the 4 weeks, men received most work activity requests from male requestors (61.3% of all requests received by male faculty came from men), while women received most requests from female requestors (56.8% of all requests received by female faculty came from women). Controlling for gender, rank, and the total number of work activity requests, the overall regression models showed that the differences were significant. The regression model for a female requestor accounted for an impressive 87.9% of the variance, $F(3, 107)$ = 266.847, $p < .001$. Female faculty were more likely than men to receive requests from women (*Beta* = .072), $t(107)$ = −2.809, p = .006. The regression model for a male requestor accounted for a large 83.7% of the variance, $F(3, 107)$ = 189.658, $p < .001$, showing that female faculty are less likely than men to receive requests from men (*Beta* = −.096), $t(107)$ = −2.307, p = .023.

Table 9
Reasons for Saying "Yes"

	Percentage of Study Participants
Reasons for saying "yes"[1]	
This will allow me to support an issue, group, or person I care about	28.4
There are professional benefits for me	18.9
I wanted to show I am a good citizen or team player	16.7
I did not want to disappoint or cause conflict with the person who asked	9.8
No one else, or no one else good, will volunteer to do it	6.3
I felt uncomfortable saying no	5.1
There could be negative repercussions for me if I said no	2.5
I have no idea why I said yes, I just did	0.4
Primary reason for saying "yes"[2]	
This would allow me to support an issue, group, or person I care about	41.7
There are professional benefits for me	13.3
I wanted to show I am a good citizen or team player	10.6
No one else, or no one else good, will volunteer to do it	4.7
I did not want to disappoint or cause conflict with the person who asked	4.4
I felt uncomfortable saying no	4.2
There could be negative repercussions for me if I said no	1.4
I have no idea why I said yes, I just did	0.8

[1]Participants were asked to select all reasons for saying yes to a new work request.
[2]Participants were asked to select the primary reason for saying yes to a new work request.

Faculty responses to requests and reasons for responses. Controlling for gender, rank, and total number of work activity requests, the overall regression models did not show statistically significant gender or rank differences in the number of times the participants chose the suggested reasons for saying "yes." However, we have provided descriptive statistics on the most popular reasons for responses to work activity requests in Table 9 (e.g., supporting important issues, professional benefits, being a good citizen).

Discussion and Implications

We examined how 111 research university associate and full professors spent their work time using time-diary methods. We found women faculty spending more time than men on campus service, student advising, and teaching-related activities and male faculty spending more time on research-related activities. Interestingly men spent almost twice as much time as women in professional conversations with colleagues in their field. Men also spent more time than women in editor and associate editor roles and noted more article submissions that semester. Similar to previous studies (Modern Language Association of America, 2009; Stout et al., 2007), we found that associate professors, who were less likely to feel the distribution of work in their department was fair, were engaged in more teaching and advising, course administration, and advising of undergraduates than full professors. Although there were also work activity areas where we did not find significant differences, these differences should be read as further evidence, through a different research method and lens, of gendered divisions of labor in research universities as well as evidence of workload constraints faced by women and associate professors (Misra et al., 2011; Winslow, 2010).

However, this study's most important contribution relates to gendered workplace interactions shaping workload. We examined several kinds of workplace interactions that could have been associated with gender differences in workload. Two of these interactions—the number of work requests and the kinds of work requests women received—are particularly important findings. Across all 4 weeks, women consistently received higher numbers of work activity requests than men. Over 4 weeks, women received 3.4 more requests for new work activities than men. Gender was a significant positive predictor of requests, with women receiving more requests, for both associate and full professors. It should be noted that these additional requests per week for women (4.26 more requests to women associate professors than male associate professors; 2.75 more requests to women full professors than male full professors) occurred during a semester when women faculty already reported spending more time engaged in teaching-related activities, while men reported spending more time in research-related activities. Receiving new requests would perhaps not be so harmful for women, if those requests were primarily to become more engaged in research activities or to pull women more into research conversations and communities. However, they were not as men were more likely to receive new research-related requests.

The kinds of new work requests women and men faculty received were different. Women received more requests to be engaged in teaching, student advising, and professional service than men. Thus, women began with more time allocated to non-research-related activities and then received more requests to be engaged in even more of this work. This finding of receiving more requests for service is consistent with Mitchell and Hesli's (2013) study of political science faculty wherein women were asked to serve in campus service roles more often than men.

A third workplace interaction we examined was who was asking for faculty to complete new work activities. Though little research has been done in this area, many scholars working to improve gender equity assume a key problem is male faculty and administrators, who are more senior in rank, asking women to become engaged in teaching and campus service in greater numbers than men. In this scenario, women feel vulnerable and must say yes or put their career standing in jeopardy. Given there are fewer women full professors in research universities, we also thought it likely new work requests, especially for campus service, might come from male department chairs and colleagues. Yet we found that most requests for new work activities, for men and women, came from students or former students and off-campus colleagues in the participants' field. Consistent with previous studies of homophily in social network analysis that show gender patterns in mentoring, scholarly conversations, and publications (Feinberg, Watnick, & Sacks, 2009; Griffin & Reddick, 2011), we found women received more work activity requests from women and men more requests from men.

Returning to Smith's (2005) notion of different ways in which workplace interactions might reflect "ruling relations" that contribute to gendered organizations (Acker 1990), we see less evidence in our findings that unequal requests and kinds of requests are due to social interactions embedded with power (men with more power asking women to do more work requests). Instead, there seems to be more suggestion of workload inequity ordered, disciplined, and otherwise organized by sets of expectations, commitments, and roles enacted between women. This makes sense in at least two ways. First, those most involved in activities such as teaching, mentoring, and campus service are likely to be among the individuals asking others to become involved. Second, research recognizes women as well as men hold implicit biases toward other women as helpful and communal and hold expectations that women will play organizational housekeeping roles (Cross & Madson, 1997; Heilman et al., 2004; Rudman, 1998). Therefore, it should not be a surprise that women are gendering their organizations through workload requests to other women even as they are burdened by such requests in their own careers.

A final workplace interaction we examined was whether women were saying yes more often to new work requests. Although we found that women were slightly more likely than men to say "yes" to a new request, less likely to say "no," and less likely to delay their response, none of the differences were found to be significant. Women were not necessarily saying yes more often than men, nor were their reasons for saying yes or no that different; they simply had more requests and different kinds of requests. This differs from Mitchell and Hesli's (2013) study that found women said yes more often when asked, although the methods of the two studies were very different (cross-sectional survey versus time diary).

Our findings shed light on how workplace interactions within gendered organizations such as research universities reproduce inequality (Acker, 1990; Bird, 2011). Time is one of the most valuable resources faculty have to achieve career goals (Winslow, 2010). We found faculty time use was being shaped by a number of factors that fostered cumulative disadvantage for women faculty careers (Merton, 1968). Integrating our findings with previous research allows us to see the disadvantages accrued through the structures and workplace interactions embedded in academic careers. Women and men faculty begin their academic labor within a gendered research university wherein organizational logic values research over teaching and service (Acker, 1990; Ely & Meyerson, 2000). Before the female faculty member even begins her work week, she is scheduled to be involved in more teaching-related activities than her male colleagues, whereas her male colleague is signed up to be involved as an editor, in preparing publications, and in professional conversations about research with colleagues. Now the work week begins, and she receives more new work requests than he does, and for teaching- and service-related activities. Research suggests she is likely to be committed to teaching and campus service in particular ways (O'Meara, 2016; Umbach, 2006; Winslow, 2010), and students have expectations that she is more available to them than her male colleagues (Anderson, 2010). She does not say yes or no more than her colleague; in fact, both she and her male colleague say yes about three-fourths of the time (women said yes to 72% of the requests received; men said yes to 82% of the requests received); however, she has to consider and come up with more responses. Also, more of the male faculty members' requests will be from off-campus colleagues who can advance his career and involve him in more research activities; more of the female faculty members' requests will be related to teaching and campus service, which, though these activities may be fulfilling, will not count much toward career advancement in her institution or field. Furthermore, more of her requests will be from other women who she recognizes expect her kinship and communal behavior (O'Meara, 2016). By the time these two faculty have reached midcareer, one has accumulated more of the social capital necessary to advance. They did not start as equals, but what happened in the organizing of work along the way, or what Smith (2005) refers to as "ruling relations," further enhanced the male faculty members' career advantage, reproducing a gendered organization.

Although our study examined work time and not family care, it is also important to consider the cumulative career effects of women faculty spending less time on research *and* more time than men faculty on family care, as many studies of academic parents found (Acker & Dillabough, 2007; Misra, Lundquist, & Templar, 2012). In this study, we found women full professors engaged in 7.3 less hours per week on research than male full professors, which is significant. Imagine that the same female professor is also spending 3 hours more per week on family care and housework than male peers. Martell, Lane, and Emrich (1996) showed that a gender difference in performance evaluations favoring men but accounting for only 1% of the variability in scores can produce an organizational structure over time in which only 35% of the highest level positions are filled by women. They make the point that "male-female differences are best determined not by the magnitude of the effect but its consequences in natural settings" (p. 158). Thus, if researchers find even a 30-minute per week difference in research time, long-term consequences need to be considered.

Turning to implications for further research, we observe that our study was not able to determine cause and effect between workplace interactions (such as women receiving more requests for teaching-related work and service) and actual workload (such as women spending more work time on teaching-related work and service). The relationships between workplace interactions and workload seem intuitive, but there are other factors shaping workload as well. This research makes an important contribution by pointing to some key kinds of workplace interactions likely to shape faculty time allocation. However, future research with a larger sample might try to understand which workplace interactions have the greatest direct impact on gender differences in workload and if this differs by race, discipline, and critical mass of women.

Also, associate professors were less likely than full professors to perceive the distribution of work in their department as fair. Although rank and gender are connected, both because gendered logics advance faculty for certain work activities and not others and because only about 28% of full professors (or less) in research universities are likely to be women (Curtis, 2011), it is important to tease apart what aspects of workload here are considered within these departments as earned privileges. For example, being able to make one's own office hours in many law firms is a privilege earned through becoming a partner. To what degree is spending a preferred amount of time on research considered to be an earned privilege of full professorship within these organizations? And if this is indeed a cultural norm, why are women associate professors finding it harder than male associate professors to make it through the "earning years" to this position? We found that even among full professors, women were engaged in less research each week, suggesting other factors, such as work-life demands and social networks, may be influencing research productivity and workload.

In terms of implications for practice, these findings provide a more complex picture of the individual, institutional, and field interventions needed to improve workload equity. For example, one of the traditional remedies for gender inequality in workload is to provide workshops for women that encourage them to be more strategic about agreeing to additional teaching and service requests (Pyke, 2015). These workshops include strategies for saying no to activities that will not advance one's career and yes to opportunities that can. Likewise, there are many career advice articles and book chapters that advise women on how to be more strategic about their work choices (Hogan, 2010; Rockquemore, 2015). This has been heavily critiqued as a "fix the woman" deficit approach, most recently by Pyke (2015), who compares these interventions to the "just say no to drugs" campaign that puts "the burden on individuals, rather than complex bureaucratic structures" (p. 83–84). This is an appropriate critique of "just say no" service workshops, particularly if they are done in isolation or exclusively to address workload inequity without structural interventions. No one has initiated "just say yes" workshops for men, and so the likelihood that men will spontaneously begin to pick up the work that women will begin to say no to is doubtful. Also, such workshops focus on only one work interaction in the process—what to do when requests come in, which in this study was not found to be the most unequal part of the system per say. From this perspective, it is much more important to improve faculty (men and women) and department chair awareness of the social science research on implicit bias. Implicit bias workshops can provide strategies to reduce the likelihood that women are asked more often than men to play institutional care-taking and housekeeping roles (Mitchneck, Smith, & Latimer, 2016).

On the other hand, the fact that women received more work requests than men, and that they were more likely to receive them from other women, suggests the importance of helping women navigate requests. Research has shown that stress, emotional exhaustion, and burnout are associated with teaching-related faculty work, which was a primary area of requests for women (Watts & Robertson, 2011). Student and colleague expectations for women may create different demands on their time. Until universities engage in organizational practices that produce equitable situations related to these requests, professional development can play an important role in helping women navigate workload decisions in gendered organizations.

At the institutional level, it is critical that campuses create greater awareness of workload inequity by collecting data on it and sharing it widely. Creating campus dashboards of minimum, average, and high teaching, advising, and campus service workloads can increase faculty awareness of inequality and then spur action toward change in organizational practices (O'Meara, 2016). Examples of possible interventions that might be put in place are required rotations for time-intensive service roles, fair distribution of advising loads, and credit for faculty who take on more than their fair share through merit review processes.

In regard to field implications, one asset-based approach to workload equity in research universities may be to pull women further into research networks. Drennan, Clarke, Hyde, and Politis (2013) found that involvement in the wider research community through editorial positions and peer reviewing was a predictor of research productivity. Thus, disciplinary associations might work with programs like NSF-funded ADVANCE programs by trying to claim a bigger portion of the work week in which female associate professors engage with colleagues on research work. Another strategy would be for women in research universities to work together to monitor the requests made to other women, especially for less valued faculty roles. Just as feminist scholars have worked together to create vehicles for increasing awareness and reforming gendered language in letters of recommendation (The University of Arizona Commission on the Status of Women, n.d.) and for ensuring women's representation on panels at professional conferences (GenderAvenger, n.d.), women faculty might devise ways to increase awareness about differential requests, workloads, and types of work to change behavior toward more equitable outcomes.

Notes

This research was supported by NSF ADVANCE Grant HRD1008117 UM ADVANCE - Toward an Institution for Inclusive Excellence (UM = T12E).

References

Acker, J. (1990). Hierarchies, jobs, bodies: A theory of gendered organizations. *Gender and Society, 4*(2), 139–158.

Acker, J. (2006). Inequality regimes: Gender, class, and race in organizations. *Gender and Society, 20*(4), 441–464.

Acker, S., & Armenti, C. (2004). Sleepless in academia. *Gender and Education, 16*(1), 3–24.

Acker, S., & Dillabough, J.- A. (2007). Women "learning to labour" in the "male emporium": Exploring gendered work in teacher education. *Gender and Education, 19*(3), 297–316.

Acker, S., & Feuerverger, G. (1996). Doing good and feeling bad: The work of women university teachers. *Cambridge Journal of Education, 26*(3), 401–422.

Anderson, K. J. (2010). Students' stereotypes of professors: An exploration of the double violations of ethnicity and gender. *Social Psychology of Education, 13*, 459–472.

Antonio, A. L. (2002). Faculty of color reconsidered: Reassessing contributions to scholarship. *Journal of Higher Education, 73*(5), 482–602.

Armstrong, J., & Overton, T. (1977). Estimating nonresponse bias in mail surveys. *Journal of Marketing Research, 14*(3), 396–402.

Avent-Holt, D., & Tomaskovic-Devey, D. (2012). Relational inequality: Gender earnings inequality in U.S. and Japanese manufacturing plants in the early 1980s. *Social Forces, 91*(1), 157–180.

Baez, B. (2000). Race-related service and faculty of color: Conceptualizing critical agency in academe. *Higher Education, 39*(3), 363–391.

Basow, S. A. (2000). Best and worst professors: Gender patterns in students' choices. *Sex Roles, 43*(5/6), 407–417.

Bellas, M., & Toutkoushian, R. K. (1999). Faculty time allocations and research productivity: Gender, race, and family effects. *Review of Higher Education, 22*(4), 367–390.

Bianchi, S. M., Sayer, L. C., Milkie, M. A., & Robinson, J. P. (2012). Housework: Who did, does, or will do it and how much does it matter? *Social Forces, 91*, 55–63.

Bird, S. (2011). Unsettling universities' incongruous, gendered bureaucratic structures: A case-study approach. *Gender, Work and Organization, 18*(2), 202–230.

Blackburn, R. T., & Lawrence, J. H. (1995). *Faculty at work: Motivation, expectation, satisfaction*. Baltimore, MD: Johns Hopkins University Press.

Britton, D. M. (2000). The epistemology of the gendered organization. *Gender and Society, 14*(3), 418–434.

Carrigan, C., Quinn, K., & Riskin, E. A. (2011). The gendered division of labor among STEM faculty and the effects of the critical mass. *Journal of Diversity in Higher Education, 4*(3), 131–146.

Clark, S. M., & Corcoran, M. (1986). Perspectives on the professional socialization of women faculty: A case of accumulative disadvantage? *Journal of Higher Education, 57*(1), 20–43.

Colbeck, C. L. (2006). How female and male faculty with families manage work and personal roles. In S. J. Bracken, J. K. Allen, & D. R. Dean (Eds.), *The balancing act: Gendered perspectives in faculty roles and work lives* (pp. 31–50). Sterling, VA: Stylus.

Cross, S. E., & Madson, L. (1997). Models of the self: Self construals and gender. *Psychological Bulletin, 122*(1), 5–37.

Curtis, J. W. (2011). *Persistent inequity: Gender and academic employment.* A report prepared for the American Association of University Professors. Retrieved from http://www.aaup.org/NR/rdonlyres/08E023AB-E6D8-4DBD-99A0-24E5EB73A7 60/0/persistent_inequity.pdf

Deng, Y., Hillygus, D. S., Reiter, J. P., Si, Y., & Zheng, S. (2013). Handling attrition in longitudinal studies: The case for refreshment samples. *Statistical Science, 28*(2), 238–256.

Dinovitzer, R., Reichman, N., & Sterling, J. (2009). The differential valuation of women's work: A new look at the gender gap in lawyers' incomes. *Social Forces, 88*(2), 819–864.

Drennan, J., Clarke, M., Hyde, A., & Politis, Y. (2013). The research function of the academic profession in Europe. In U. Teichler & E. A. Höhle (Eds.), *The work situation of the academic profession in Europe: Findings of a survey in twelve countries* (pp. 109–136). London, UK: Springer.

Eagan, M. K., Jr., & Garvey, J. C. (2015). Stressing out: Connecting race, gender, and stress with faculty productivity. *The Journal of Higher Education, 86*(6), 923–954.

Eagly, A. H. (1987). *Sex differences in social behavior: A social-role interpretation.* Hillsdale, NJ: Erlbaum.

Ely, R. J., & Meyerson, D. E. (2000). Theories of gender in organizations: A new approach to organizational analysis and change. *Research in Organizational Behavior, 22*, 103–151.

Etter, J. F., & Perneger, T. V. (1997). Analysis of non-response bias in a mailed health survey. *Journal of Clinical Epidemiology, 50*(10), 1123–1128.

Fairweather, J. S. (1996). *Faculty work and public trust: Restoring the value of teaching and service in American academic life.* Boston, MA: Allyn & Bacon.

Feinberg, G., Watnick, B., & Sacks, A. (2009). Solo vs. collaborative research in the social sciences and higher education: Unraveling the realities of male-female research publication patterns in the context of gender politics and social justice issues. *Journal of Multidisciplinary Research, 3*(3), 47–63.

Fisher, K., & Gershuny, J. (2015, June 11). *Multinational time use study user's guide and documentation* (Version 7). Oxford, UK: University of Oxford, Centre for Time Use Research.

GenderAvenger. (n.d.). *GA Gender Avenger! Take the GenderAvenger pledge.* Retrieved from http://www.genderavenger.com/the-pledge/

Gill, R. (2014). Academics, cultural workers and critical labour studies. *Journal of Cultural Economy, 7*(1), 12–30.

Glazer-Raymo, J. (1999). Taking stock: Perspectives on women and leadership in higher education in the UK and the US. *Society for Research into Higher Education News, 41*, 8–10.

Goldstein, H. (2009). Handling attrition and non-response in longitudinal data. *Longitudinal and Life Course Studies, 1*(1), 63–72.

Gore-Felton, C., Koopman, C., Bridges, E., Thoresen, C., & Spiegel, D. (2002). An example of maximizing survey return rates: Methodological issues for health professionals. *Evaluation & the Health Professions, 25*(2), 152–168.

Griffin, K. A., Bennett, J. C., & Harris, J. (2013). Marginalizing merit? An analysis of gender differences in Black faculty D/discourses on tenure, advancement, and professional success. *The Review of Higher Education, 36*(4), 489–512.

Griffin, K. A., Pifer, M. T., Humphrey, J. R., & Hazelwood, A. M. (2011). (Re)Defining departure: Exploring black professors' experiences with and responses to racism and racial climate. *American Journal of Education, 117*(4), 495–526.

Griffin, K. A., & Reddick, R. J. (2011). Surveillance and sacrifice: Gender differences in the mentoring patterns of black professors at predominantly white research universities. *American Educational Research Journal, 48*(5), 1032–1057.

Grummell, B., Devine, D., & Lynch, K. (2009). The care-less manager: Gender, care and new managerialism in higher education. *Gender and Education, 21*(2), 191–208.

Heilman, M. E., Wallen, A. S., Fuchs, D., & Tamkins, M. M. (2004). Penalties for success: Reactions to women who succeed at male gender-typed tasks. *Journal of Applied Psychology, 89*(3), 416–427.

Hikmet, N., & Chen, S. K. (2003). An investigation into low mail survey response rates of information technology users in health care organizations. *International Journal of Medical Informatics, 72*(13), 29–34.

Hofferth, S. L. (2006). Response bias in a popular indicator of reading to children. *Sociological Methodology, 36*(1), 301–315.

Hofferth, S. L., & Sandberg, J. F. (2001). How American children spend their time. *Journal of Marriage and Family, 63*(2), 295–308.

Hogan, K. (2010, January 8). Managing service duties. *Inside Higher Ed: Career Advice*. Retrieved from https://www.insidehighered.com/advice/2010/01/08/hogan

Jowell, R., Roberts, C., Fitzgerald, R., & Eva, G. (2007). *Measuring attitudes cross-nationally: Lessons from the European Social Survey*. London, UK: Sage.

Juster, F. T., Ono, H., & Stafford, F. P. (2003). An assessment of alternative measures of time use. *Sociological Methodology, 33*, 19–54.

Juster, F. T., & Stafford, F. P. (Eds.). (1985). *Time, goods and well-being*. Ann Arbor, MI: Institute for Social Research, The University of Michigan.

Kanter, R. M. (1977). *Men and women of the corporation*. New York, NY: Basic Books.

Leece, P., Bhandari, M., Sprague, S., Swiontkowski, M. F., Schemitsch, E. H., Tornetta, P., Devereaux, P. J., & Guyatt, G. H. (2004). Internet versus mailed questionnaires: A controlled comparison (2). *Journal of Medical Internet Research, 6*(4), e30.

Leibbrandt, A., & List, J. A. (2012, November). *Do women avoid salary negotiations? Evidence from a large-scale natural field experiment* (NBER Working Paper No. w18511). Cambridge, MA: National Bureau of Economic Research. Retrieved from http://www.offnews.info/downloads/w18511.pdf

Link, A. N., Swan, C. A., & Bozeman, B. (2008). A time allocation study of university faculty. *Economics of Education Review, 27*(4), 363–374.

Martell, R. F., Lane, D. M., & Emrich, C. (1996). Male-female differences: A computer simulation. *American Psychologist, 51*(2), 157–158.

Massachusetts Institute of Technology. (1999). *A study of the status of women faculty in science at MIT*. Retrieved from http://web.mit.edu/fnl/women/women.pdf

Menachemi, N. N. (2011). Assessing response bias in a web survey at a university faculty. *Evaluation & Research in Education, 24*(1), 5–15.

Merton, R. K. (1968). The Matthew effect in science. *Science, 159*, 56–63.

Merz, J., & Rathjen, T. (2014). Time and income poverty: An interdependent multidimensional poverty approach with German time use diary data. *Review of Income and Wealth, 60*(3), 450–479.

Misra, J., Lundquist, J. H., Holmes, E. D., & Agiomavritis, S. (2011). The ivory ceiling of service work. *Academe, 97*, 2–6.

Misra, J., Lundquist, J. H., & Templer, A. (2012, June). Gender, work time, and care responsibilities among faculty. *Sociological Forum, 27*(2), 300–323.

Mitchell, S. M., & Hesli, V. L. (2013). Women don't ask? Women don't say no? Bargaining and service in the political science profession. *Political Science and Politics, 46*(2), 355–369.

Mitchneck, B., Smith, J., & Latimer, M. (2016). A recipe for change: Creating a more inclusive academy. *Insights, 352*(6282), 148–149.

Modern Language Association of America (MLA). (2009, April 27). *Standing still: The associate professor survey. Report of the Committee on the Status of Women in the profession.* Retrieved from http://www.mla.org/ pdf/cswp_final042909.pdf

Montori, V. M., Leung, T. W., Walter, S. D., & Guyatt, G. H. (2005). Procedures that assess inconsistency in meta-analyses can assess the likelihood of response bias in multiwave surveys. *Journal of Clinical Epidemiology, 58*(8), 856–858.

Moss-Racusin, C. A., & Rudman, L. A. (2010). Disruptions in women's self-promotion: The backlash avoidance model. *Psychology of Women Quarterly, 34*(2), 186–202.

Neumann, A. (2009). *Professing to learn: Creating tenured lives and careers in the American research university.* Baltimore, MD: Johns Hopkins University Press.

Neumann, A., & Terosky, A. L. (2007). To give and to receive: Recently tenured professors' experiences of service in major research universities. *Journal of Higher Education, 78*(3), 282–310.

O'Meara, K. (2016). Whose problem is it? Gender differences in faculty thinking about campus service. *Teachers College Record, 118*(8), 1–38.

Padilla, A. M. (1994). Ethnic minority scholars, research, and mentoring: Current and future issues. *Educational Researcher, 1994,* 24–27.

Park, S. M. (1996). Research, teaching, service: Why shouldn't women's work count? *Journal of Higher Education, 67*(1), 46–84.

Ponjuan, L., Conley, V. M., & Trower, C. (2011). Career stage differences in pre-tenure track faculty perceptions of professional and personal relationships with colleagues. *The Journal of Higher Education, 82*(3), 319–346.

Porter, S. (2007). A closer look at faculty service: What affects participation on committees? *Journal of Higher Education, 78*(5), 523–541.

Pyke, K. (2015). Faculty gender inequity and the "just say no to service" fairy tale. In K. De Welde & A. Stepnick (Eds.), *Disrupting the culture of silence* (pp. 83–95). Sterling, VA: Stylus.

Rhoades, G. (1998). *Managed professionals: Unionized faculty and restructuring academic labor.* Albany, NY: State University of New York Press.

Rhoades, G., Kiyama, J. M., McCormick, R., & Quiroz, M. (2008). Local cosmopolitans and cosmopolitan locals: New models of professionals in the academy. *The Review of Higher Education, 31*(2), 209–235.

Robinson, J. P. (1999). The time-diary method: Structure and uses. In W. E. Pentland, A. S. Harvey, M. P. Lawton, & M. A. McColl (Eds.), *Time use research in the social sciences* (pp. 47–89). New York, NY: Kluwer Academic/Plenum.

Robinson, J. P., Martin, S., Glorieux, I., & Minnen, J. (2011). The overestimated workweek revisited. *Monthly Labor Review, 134*(6), 43–53.

Rockquemore, K. A. (2015, April 8). Evaluating opportunities. *Inside Higher Ed: Career Advice.* Retrieved from https://www.insidehighered.com/advice/2015/ 04/08/essay-how-evaluate-opportunities-may-or-may-not-help-you-win-tenure

Rudman, L. A. (1998). Self-promotion as a risk factor for women: The costs and benefits of counter stereotypical impression management. *Journal of Personality and Social Psychology, 74*(3), 629–645.

Singell, L. D., Jr., Lillydahl, J. H., & Singell, L. D., Sr. (1996). Will changing times change the allocation of faculty time? *Journal of Human Resources, 31*(2), 429–449.

Smith, D. E. (1990). *The conceptual practices of power: A feminist sociology of knowledge.* Toronto, Ontario, Canada: University of Toronto Press.

Smith, D. E. (2005). *Institutional ethnography: A sociology for people.* New York, NY: AltaMira Press.

Stanley, C. A. (2006). Coloring the academic landscape: Faculty of color breaking the silence in predominantly white colleges and universities. *American Educational Research Journal, 43*(4), 701–736.

Stout, P. A., Staiger, J., & Jennings, N. A. (2007). Affective stories: Understanding the lack of progress of women faculty. *NWSA Journal, 19*(3), 124–144.

The University of Arizona Commission on the Status of Women. (n.d.). *Avoiding gender bias in reference writing.* Retrieved from http://www.csw.arizona.edu/sites/default/files/csw_2015-10-20_lorbias_pdf_0.pdf

Tierney, W. G., & Bensimon, E. (1996). *(En)gender(ING) socialization: In promotion and tenure: Community and socialization in academe.* Albany, NY: State University of New York Press.

Tierney, W. G., & Minor, J. T. (2004). A cultural perspective on communication and governance. *New Directions for Higher Education, 2004*(127), 85–94.

Trower, C. A. (2012). *Success on the tenure track: Five keys to faculty job satisfaction.* Baltimore, MD: Johns Hopkins University Press.

Turner, C. S. V. (2002). Women of color in academe: Living with multiple marginality. *Journal of Higher Education, 73*(1), 74–93.

Twale, D. J., & Shannon, D. M. (1996). Professional service involvement of leadership faculty: An assessment of gender, role, and satisfaction. *Sex Roles, 34*(1/2), 117–126.

Umbach, P. D. (2006). The contribution of faculty of color to undergraduate education. *Research in Higher Education, 47*(3), 317–345.

Valian, V. (1998). Sex, schemas, and success: What's keeping women back? *Academe, 84*(5), 50–55.

Ward, K. (2003). *Faculty service roles and the scholarship of engagement.* Hoboken, NJ: Jossey-Bass.

Watts, J., & Robertson, N. (2011). Burnout in university teaching staff: A systematic literature review. *Educational Research, 53*(1), 33–50.

Williams, J. C. (2003). Litigating the glass ceiling and the maternal wall: Using stereotyping and cognitive bias evidence to prove gender discrimination. *Employee Rights & Employment Policy Journal, 7,* 401–547.

Winslow, S. (2010). Gender inequality and time allocations among academic faculty. *Gender and Society, 24*(6), 769–793.

Xu, Y. J. (2012). Lessons from the past and directions for the future. *New Directions for Institutional Research, 2012*(155), 99–104.

Ylijoki, O. H. (2013). Boundary-work between work and life in the high-speed university. *Studies in Higher Education, 38*(2), 242–255.

Ziker, J. P., Wintermote, A., Nolin, D., Demps, K., Genuchi, M., & Meinhardt, K. (2014, April 21). *Time distribution of faculty workload at Boise State University.* Poster presented at the 2014 Undergraduate Research and Scholarship Conference at Boise State University, Boise, ID. Retrieved from http://scholarworks.boisestate.edu/cgi/viewcontent.cgi?article=1022&context=sspa_14

Manuscript received April 23, 2015

Final revision received February 1, 2017

Accepted May 23, 2017

American Educational Research Journal
December 2017, Vol. 54, No. 6, pp. 1187–1220
DOI: 10.3102/0002831217717692
© 2017 AERA. http://aerj.aera.net

Scaffolding Fidelity and Adaptation in Educational Program Implementation: Experimental Evidence From a Literacy Intervention

David M. Quinn
University of Southern California
James S. Kim
Harvard University

In a common approach for scaling up effective educational practice, schools adopt evidence-based programs to be implemented with fidelity. An alternative approach assumes that programs should be adapted to local contexts. In this randomized trial of a reading intervention, we study a scaffolded sequence of implementation in which schools first develop proficiency by implementing the program with fidelity before implementing structured adaptations. We find evidence supporting the scaffolded sequence: A fidelity-focused approach promoted learning and instructional change more so for teachers inexperienced with the intervention, while a structured adaptive approach was more effective for teachers experienced with the intervention. Students benefited more from the structured adaptive approach but only when their teacher had prior experience with the fidelity-focused version.

KEYWORDS: cluster-randomized trial, fidelity of implementation, flexible implementation, scale-up

An important and enduring question in education is that of how research-based instructional practices can be brought to scale (Coburn, 2003; Elmore, 1996). In one common model for scaling up education interventions,

---

DAVID M. QUINN *is an assistant professor of education at the Rossier School of Education, University of Southern California, 3470 Trousdale Parkway, Los Angeles, CA 90089; e-mail: quinnd@usc.edu. His research focuses on measuring and explaining inequalities in educational outcomes by race/ethnicity and socioeconomic status; he is particularly interested in the role that teachers can play in closing achievement gaps and improving student outcomes.*

JAMES S. KIM *is a professor at Harvard University. His research examines the effectiveness of literacy reforms and interventions in improving student outcomes.*

schools adopt evidence-based programs, and administrators do their best to ensure that teachers implement those programs with fidelity (the "fidelity-focused" approach). Scholars have argued, however, that consistently achieving positive results across the dynamic and varied settings of schools requires a different model, in which teachers adapt a program's instructional practices to better fit their context while adhering to core program principles (McDonald, Keesler, Kauffman, & Schneider, 2006). While this approach of "structured adaptive" implementation has the potential to improve the fit between instructional practices and local conditions, adaptation also introduces the possibility that teachers will alter practices in ways that make them less effective (McLaughlin & Mitra, 2002). A third model for managing program implementation combines the fidelity-focused and structured adaptive approaches into a "scaffolded sequence" designed to prepare teachers to make effective rather than counterproductive adaptations (McMaster et al., 2014; Slavin, Madden, & Datnow, 2007). In this scaffolded sequence, teachers first internalize a program's theory and become proficient with its procedures by implementing the program with fidelity. After mastering the program as designed, teachers transition into an adaptive phase of program implementation during which structures guide their tailoring of the program to their context. However, little empirical work has been done to test the effects of such a scaffolded sequence of program implementation on teacher and student outcomes.

In this study, we investigate the effectiveness of the scaffolded sequence of program implementation in the context of a randomized trial of READS for Summer Learning, a summer literacy intervention for elementary school students that includes school- and home-based components. We randomly assigned 27 schools to one of two conditions: (a) a *core fidelity-focused condition* (Core READS), in which teachers were expected to faithfully implement program procedures used in previous experiments, or (b) a *core treatment plus structured teacher adaptations condition* (Adaptive READS), in which teachers were afforded opportunities to adapt program components so as to better meet the needs of their students (without contradicting core program principles). In other work, we found a positive main effect on student reading comprehension of Adaptive READS compared to Core READS (Kim et al., 2017). This left open the question, however, of what effect a scaffolded sequence of program implementation might have on teachers' and students' learning. The present study addresses this question.

At baseline for this study, some teachers had already participated in Core READS due to a within-school random assignment experiment in the previous year in which teachers were assigned to Core READS or a business-as-usual control group. Consequently, a subset of teachers in the present study followed the scaffolded sequence of a fidelity-focused implementation approach in the first year (Core READS), followed by a structured adaptive approach the next year (Adaptive READS). As we describe in more detail below, this feature allows us to examine the effectiveness of the scaffolded sequence by testing whether the effects of the structured adaptive condition (vs. the fidelity-focused condition) depended on whether the teacher had prior experience with the fidelity-focused version of the program.

We begin by describing the fidelity-focused and structured adaptive approaches and how the approaches differ in their underlying assumptions and the demands they place on implementers. We then discuss theory suggesting that the optimal approach to scaling up educational programs may be the scaffolded sequence of program implementation in which schools first develop proficiency in implementing an evidence-based program with fidelity and then implement structured adaptations to fit their local contexts. After describing how we test the scaffolded hypothesis in this study, we present our results and end by discussing the implications of our findings.

Background

Bringing an educational program to scale involves implementing that program in numerous and varied contexts. While randomized controlled trials have helped the field to identify programs that can work for some students in some circumstances, we have much to learn about the complicated process of scaling up programs and sustaining them over time, a process that involves engaging teachers in deep learning, changing instructional practice, and shifting ownership over educational programs from developers to teachers (Bryk, Gomez, Grunow, & LeMahieu, 2015; Coburn, 2003). The fidelity-focused and structured adaptive approaches to implementation represent two schools of thought for how programs should be scaled up.

The Linear Model of Research and Fidelity of Program Implementation

A common approach for bridging the research-practice gap at scale is that of the "linear model" of scientific research (Coburn & Stein, 2010). As applied to education, the linear model describes a sequence that begins with basic research conducted in the social science disciplines, followed by applied research motivated by problems of educational practice, which eventually leads to the codification of professional knowledge and the dissemination of best practices. Often, these practices take the form of educational programs, or "set[s] of replicable instructional events" (Popham, 1967, p. 402). The programs that are shown through research to have positive effects for students become candidates for scale-up (O'Donnell, 2008). This has been the model championed by the Institute of Education Sciences since 2002 (Coburn & Stein, 2010).

A key concept related to the linear model in education research is that of program implementation fidelity. In the applied research phase, it is only meaningful to measure the effect of an educational treatment if that treatment is well defined and administered faithfully (Dane & Schneider, 1998;

Dusenbury, Brannigan, Falco, & Hansen, 2003; Murnane & Nelson, 2007). When studies indicate that a program has positive effects for students, practitioners are encouraged to implement the program with fidelity because it was under this condition that the positive effects were observed (Dusenbury et al., 2003; LaChausse, Clark, & Chapple, 2014). Bolstering the argument for implementation fidelity is research showing that lower fidelity predicts lower effectiveness and that fidelity is lower in field experiments than in the lab (Hulleman & Cordray, 2009).

Scholars have conceptualized fidelity in various ways (for reviews, see Dane & Schneider, 1998; Mowbray, Holter, Teague, & Bybee, 2003; O'Donnell, 2008), but in its most basic sense, fidelity can be thought of as "the degree to which teachers and other program providers implement programs as intended by the program developers" (Dusenbury et al., 2003, p. 240). Some researchers argue that any change to the original program procedures represents a departure from fidelity regardless of the extent to which the change adheres to foundational program principles (Domitrovich et al., 2009; Sherin & Drake, 2009). However, others accept some program adaptations within the bounds of fidelity as long as the changes are not so drastic as to compromise the program's integrity or effectiveness (Hall & Loucks, 1978 as cited in O'Donnell, 2008). In this study, we adopt the former conception of fidelity (i.e., strict adherence to researcher-designed program procedures) as a contrast to the structured adaptive implementation approach described in the next section.

However important treatment fidelity may be to program evaluation, success stories from the fidelity-focused approach to scale-up are somewhat rare as programs that show promise during initial efficacy trials often (but not always) fail to replicate positive effects in large-scale effectiveness studies (Coalition for Evidence-based Policy, 2013). This may happen for a variety of reasons. First, counterfactuals vary across contexts, and any given intervention may not be superior to all business-as-usual practices. Second, the instructional practices that comprise a program may only be effective for students with certain characteristics or in certain contexts, or perhaps only certain teachers in certain contexts are able to effectively implement these programs (Slavin, 2002).

The Structured Adaptive Approach to Program Implementation

As an alternative to the fidelity-focused approach to instructional scale-up, some scholars argue that educational treatments need not be thought of as recipes to be strictly followed; rather, bringing a program to scale may be more a process of instituting practices across schools that bear a "family resemblance" with one another (Elmore, 1996). In this conception, scaling up educational treatments requires balancing program fidelity with program adaptation (Castro, Barrera, & Martinez, 2004; Dane & Schneider, 1998;

Ferrer-Wreder, Adamson, Kumpfer, & Eichas, 2012; McDonald et al., 2006; McLaughlin, 1990; U.S. Department of Health and Human Services, 2002). According to this line of thinking, programs may have the best chance of improving educational outcomes at scale if the "core components" of the program are kept intact while practitioners adapt the intervention so as to make it more compatible with their context (e.g., more responsive to the particular needs or interests of students or teachers) (Castro et al., 2004; Ferrer-Wreder et al., 2012; McDonald et al., 2006; McLaughlin, 1990). This requires that we consider practitioners' depth of learning, change in practice, and ownership over the program as important elements of scale-up beyond the count of schools that are "doing" the program (Coburn, 2003).

Effective structured adaptive program implementation likely requires more than simply giving teachers permission to depart from fidelity. Rather, teachers are likely to be better positioned to make effective adaptations if they are supported in doing so through program management structures (Sailors et al., 2014). While research on such structures is rare, one recent article (Lemons, Fuchs, Gilbert, & Fuchs, 2014) reported an evaluation of the effectiveness of structured autonomy compared to a fidelity focus for teachers implementing Peer-Assisted Learning Strategies in Reading (PALS), an evidence-based peer-tutoring program for reading. The structure came through researchers' classification of program activities as "core," meaning teachers could not adapt them, and "noncore," meaning teachers could omit or adapt them. This study showed promising results for the effect of the structured adaptive approach to program implementation; however, teachers self-selected into the fidelity-focused and structured adaptive conditions, precluding causal inference. Additionally, it was not possible to test the scaffolded hypothesis, that structured adaptive management is more effective when preceded by fidelity-focused management.

Fidelity Versus Structured Adaptation: Contrasting Assumptions and Demands

The fidelity-focused and the structured adaptive approaches to program implementation make different assumptions and different demands on the practitioners implementing any given program. In the fidelity-focused approach, the teacher's job is to achieve the program ideal envisioned by the program developers, in other words, to follow the instructional recipe as closely as possible. Teachers are not expected to diagnose, prescribe, design, or innovate. This approach lends itself well to what has been called the "control" approach to instructional management (Rowan, 1990), in which the teacher's instructional tasks are predetermined and well defined and the school administrator's role is to ensure that the teachers execute those tasks. Given that job tasks are prescribed, there is little need for teachers to share innovations with one another or engage in group problem solving or decision making. Consequently, this approach typically lacks work structures or learning experiences that are collaborative in nature. Under a fidelity-focused approach, the types of learning experiences that support teachers' implementation more often follow the traditional workshop model of professional development, in which the goal is for teachers to learn program-specific procedures and the importance of implementing them faithfully (LaChausse et al., 2014). The approach assumes that the linear model of scientific research will optimize student learning, that is, that research will uncover what works in education and if we can just get teachers to follow these effective practices, students will learn more.

In contrast, teachers under the structured adaptive approach to program implementation must be able to recognize what is working and what is not working about an intervention. When a program isn't working, teachers must diagnose the problem by integrating their general instructional knowledge with specific knowledge about their context and their students, then devise solutions, test those solutions, and repeat the process as needed. As such, the adaptive approach assumes that teachers have the knowledge and skill necessary to plan and execute program adaptations that will improve intervention outcomes, as opposed to adapting the program in ways that will render it less effective. This requires more from the teacher in terms of critical thinking and knowledge about the instructional theory of the program. Without deep knowledge of the program, teachers cannot make adaptations that are consistent with the program theory, so they are unlikely to improve the program (Penuel, Gallagher, & Moorthy, 2011). In the worst case, teachers' adaptations may even be harmful (McLaughlin & Mitra, 2002).

The adaptive approach also calls for more teacher autonomy over instructional practice (as opposed to administrator control) and for collaborative work structures, given the increased potential payoff of exchanging information about innovations and engaging in group problem-solving (Elmore, 1996). As such, learning experiences built around peer collaboration and experimentation may be more useful for teachers under the structured adaptive approach compared to the fidelity-focused approach. One implication of the adaptive model including collaborative work structures is that the experiences of individual teachers will depend on the colleagues with whom they are collaborating. Teachers may learn more and improve their implementation more when they are collaborating with expert colleagues (Frank, Zhao, Penuel, Ellefson, & Porter, 2011).

The Scaffolded Sequence of Program Implementation

The distinct demands made of teachers by the fidelity-focused and structured adaptive approaches to program implementation, and the contrasting work structures that support teachers in meeting those demands, suggest that these approaches may be better-suited for different sets of circumstances, where their respective assumptions are met (Berman, 1980). Teachers with less curricular knowledge may perform better under a stricter fidelity approach, while more experienced or effective teachers may be capable of improving the program under the freedom offered by an adaptive approach. Furthermore, skilled teachers who are used to making instructional decisions can sometimes feel frustrated by rigid implementation requirements, making the fidelity-focused approach a poor fit (Meyer, Miller, & Herman, 1993; Murnane & Nelson, 2007; Rowan, 1990).

A Vygotskyan perspective (Vygotsky, 1978) suggests that organizing these approaches to program implementation into a scaffolded sequence may optimize structured results. That is, rather than choosing between a fidelity-focused versus adaptive approach when adopting a new program, a school might begin with a fidelity-focused phase of program implementation, followed by a structured adaptive phase. In other words, the scaffolded sequence may be thought of as a structure for chronologically organizing the fidelity-focused and adaptive approaches. The logic behind this scaffolding is that implementing a program with fidelity enables teachers new to the program to understand how the various components work together as designed and to execute them proficiently. After mastering the program as designed through this period of fidelity, teachers are prepared to make structured adaptations that may enhance program effectiveness because they possess the foundational knowledge and skills necessary for designing and executing effective adaptations (McMaster et al., 2014; Slavin et al., 2007). While the theory behind this scaffolded sequence is sound, no experimental studies have directly tested this approach.

Scaffolded Learning for Teachers

Frank and colleagues (2011) devised the mnemonic *focus, fiddle, friends* to describe a learning process for teachers that aligns well with the scaffolded sequence outlined above. According to Frank et al.'s (2011) progression, teachers who are unfamiliar with a particular educational approach first learn about the approach through *focused* professional development and direct instruction. This enables teachers to develop an understanding of an educational program and its theory of action and achieve a basic level of implementation. Teachers then *fiddle* with these techniques by experimenting with variations on the techniques to determine what works best for them and their students. Through this process, teachers develop specific and high-level questions, requiring them to receive expert assistance from experienced *friends* (colleagues). Such discussions with colleagues also help to spread useful innovations and keep the program alive.

Frank et al. (2011) tested this conceptual model using data from schools in which teachers were being encouraged to incorporate computer technology into their classroom instruction. Consistent with the model, the

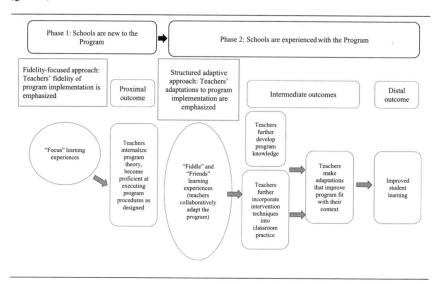

Figure 1. **Conceptual model for the scaffolded sequence of program implementation.**

researchers found that teachers who were initially infrequently using computer technology experienced greater implementation gains when they received focused professional development on technology use. Teachers who were initially at medium levels of implementation benefitted most from having opportunities to experiment with the technology, while teachers initially at a high level of implementation benefitted from interacting with colleagues about computers (though the highest-level implementers experienced implementation gains from all types of learning experiences). The authors suspected that fiddle experiences may be more effective when they followed focus learning experiences but were unable to empirically test this.

Differentiated Learning and The Scaffolded Sequence

The results of the Frank et al. (2011) study suggest that teachers may learn the most, and improve implementation the most, when approaches to program implementation are differentiated according to teachers' intervention-related experience or knowledge. Such differentiation fits well with the model of fidelity-focused and structured adaptive program implementation as a scaffolded sequence. In Figure 1, we merge these ideas into a graphical conceptual model. We test this approach in the present study through the methods described later.

As seen under the Phase 1 heading of Figure 1, when schools initially adopt an intervention, teachers experience a period of fidelity-focused program implementation in which their primary intervention-related learning comes through explicit instruction on how to implement the program faithfully. These *focused* learning experiences enable new teachers to internalize the program theory and achieve basic proficiency with the instructional procedures as designed by the program developers (the Phase 1 proximal outcome).

According to this conceptual framework, after teachers develop sufficient mastery of the program, they are ready for the second phase, which emphasizes teachers' structured adaptations to program implementation. In this phase, teachers collaboratively (i.e., with friends) design adaptations (fiddle) that they believe will make the program more effective for their students. Through these fiddle and friends learning experiences, teachers acquire a deeper understanding of the program and how its active ingredients interact with their context, which enables teachers to more successfully incorporate the program techniques into their classroom practice (intermediate outcomes).

During Phase 2, one source of teacher learning may be peer effects facilitated through the collaborative implementation structures. That is, individual teachers may have greater success with the program when their collaborators are more expert with the program (Jackson & Bruegmann, 2009) because more expert teachers are more likely to accurately diagnose program difficulties, design effective solutions they can share with colleagues, and provide colleagues with high-quality feedback.

Finally, teachers' experimentation with program adaptations leads to an enacted program that fits better with their context. The improved tailoring of the program to the context then leads to the distal outcome of improved student learning.

The Present Study and Research Questions

In this study, we test the scaffolded sequence of program implementation by analyzing data from a randomized trial of READS for Summer Learning, an evidence-based literacy program for elementary school students. In the year prior to the present study, teachers were randomly assigned within schools to either implement a fidelity-focused version of READS or a business-as-usual control condition. In the next year—the year we focus on in this article—we employed school-level random assignment with a subset of these schools. Specifically, we randomly assigned schools to either implement READS under the same fidelity-focused approach as year 1 (Core READS) or implement the program under a structured adaptive approach (Adaptive READS). In other work, we have shown Core READS to be more effective, compared to business as usual, at improving students' reading comprehension (Kim et al., 2016). We have also shown a positive main effect of Adaptive versus Core READS on student outcomes (and some teacher outcomes not examined here; Kim et al., 2017). The present study makes a unique contribution to the literature beyond these prior studies by offering an empirical test of the scaffolded sequence of program implementation.

Our primary objective in the present study is to test the hypothesis that a scaffolded sequence of program implementation optimizes teacher learning, changes in practice, and ultimately, student learning. We do this by exploiting baseline variation in teachers' prior participation in Core READS. Specifically, we test the scaffolded hypothesis by examining whether the effects of the adaptive condition (vs. the core, or fidelity-focused, condition) differ depending on whether the teacher had prior experience with Core READS (i.e., we compare the Adaptive effect for teachers with prior Core experience to the Adaptive effect for teachers without prior Core experience). According to the scaffolded hypothesis (as outlined previously), the Adaptive condition will be more effective for teachers who had prior experience implementing the intervention with fidelity, while the Core (fidelity-focused) condition will be more effective for teachers who did not have prior intervention experience. To be clear, we did not begin this study by randomly assigning a set of teachers to a "scaffolded" experimental condition; rather, in the present study, we have a fidelity-focused condition (Core READS) and a structured adaptive condition (Adaptive READS), and we test the scaffolded hypothesis by testing whether an interaction exists between condition and teacher prior experience with (Core) READS. Additionally, as an exploratory question, we seek to understand whether, as suggested previously, peer effects facilitated teacher learning under the collaborative program implementation activities of the Adaptive approach. Understanding how contrasting program implementation structures may interact with characteristics of teachers and schools will help education researchers, decision makers, and practitioners design effective adoption processes for school improvement efforts.

In this study, we ask the following research questions:

Research Question 1 (RQ1; main effects of implementation approach): In the second year of program implementation, does Adaptive READS (i.e., the structured adaptive approach), as compared to Core READS (i.e., the fidelity-focused approach), affect teachers' intervention-related learning and incorporation of intervention techniques into regular classroom practice?

Research Question 2 (RQ2; scaffolded hypothesis/interaction effects): In the second year of program implementation, do the effects of Adaptive READS (i.e., the structured adaptive approach) versus Core READS (i.e., the fidelity-focused approach) on teacher outcomes depend on teachers' prior experience with Core READS (RQ2a) or on teachers' peers' prior experience with Core READS (RQ2b)?

Research Question 3 (RQ3; scaffolded hypothesis/interaction effects): In the second year of program implementation, do the effects of Adaptive READS (i.e., the structured adaptive approach) versus Core READS (i.e., the fidelity-focused approach) on student reading comprehension depend on the teacher's prior experience with Core READS?

Methods

Procedures

READS for Summer Learning

READS for Summer Learning is a program designed to narrow income-based reading skill gaps among elementary school students. In this study, we compare two versions of READS executed over the 2014–2015 school year and summer of 2015: Core READS and Adaptive READS. Core READS is an evidence-based program (Kim et al., 2016; White, Kim, Kingston, & Foster, 2014) representing a fidelity-focused approach to management in which teachers receive training and resources to support their adherence to researcher-designed program procedures. Adaptive READS takes a structured adaptive approach by having teachers work collaboratively with their grade-level teams, with guidance from researchers, to adapt READS in ways they believe will increase its effectiveness for their students.

Core READS. Students in Core READS receive eight books in the mail over summer vacation that are matched to their reading level and interests. Each book includes a trifold (or paper folded into thirds) that leads students through the "READS reading routine." This routine, which is designed to engage students and scaffold their reading, includes a pre-reading activity, which focuses students' attention on important text structures, and a post-reading comprehension check. Students are expected to mail back completed trifolds (with postage prepaid).

Core READS teachers attended a two-hour training during which they learned how to implement six scripted lessons at the end of the school year that prepare students for the summer activities. During the training, teachers received an overview of the program procedures and materials, watched video clips of teachers implementing key lesson components, and practiced delivering the lessons. To bridge the home and the school, students and their families are invited to a READS Family Night (RFN) in the spring. At this event, parents learn about READS and the trifolds. Also in the spring, students complete a reading comprehension assessment and reading interest survey; this information is used in an algorithm to match books to students. Prior to summer break, students receive copies of the two books used in the end-of-year lessons. Over the summer, the families of students who do not return trifolds receive phone calls with reminders and inquiries about additional support they may need to complete the trifold activities.

Adaptive READS. In keeping with previous research suggesting that teachers must understand a program's theory in order to make productive adaptations (Penuel et al., 2011), teachers at schools assigned to Adaptive READS attended an orientation session in November 2014 in which they learned the underlying research-based principles of READS. Teachers received school-specific data from a previous year of (Core) READS implementation (e.g., data on trifold return rates and RFN attendance) and examined these data with their grade-level teams to develop hypotheses about ways the program may be improved in their school. After this initial meeting, teachers could elect to earn district professional development credit by completing six online modules in December designed to teach them more about the research-based principles underlying READS (81% of teachers surveyed in the spring participated in the modules). Teachers then attended two additional formal meetings—one in January and one in February—to finalize a plan, based on the data and the research-based principles, for how they would adapt READS. Each school submitted their adaptation plan, allowing us to code the types of adaptations that teachers made. At a majority of Adaptive schools, teachers modified program components so as to improve student and family engagement with the program. For example, a common adaptation included locally developed plans to improve outreach to parents and increase attendance at the family literacy event. A majority of schools also organized a new fall READS event. Additionally, a majority of Adaptive schools modified READS lessons through extensions and/or substitutions, and a majority of Adaptive teachers made changes to their students' summer book lists. See Kim et al. (2017) for detail on these and other adaptations.

Teachers in Adaptive READS received a $600 stipend for participating; teachers in Core READS received $300. See Table 1 for a comparison of Core and Adaptive READS.

Setting, Design, and Participants

In Figure 2, we present a graphic illustrating this study's random assignment procedures. In the school year prior to the present study (the 2013–2014 school year), teachers were randomly assigned within participating elementary schools to a treatment group that implemented Core READS or to a business-as-usual control condition. From this set of schools, 27 high-poverty schools from seven North Carolina school districts were determined eligible and were successfully recruited to participate in the present study over the next school year (to be eligible, schools needed to be 75% or more free or reduced-price lunch, due to prior research showing that READS was effective with this population). Consenting schools were then matched within district based on school poverty level and performance on the state standardized test (in one case, due to the odd number of schools, a triad was formed). Within each matched pair (or triad), one randomly selected school was assigned to Adaptive READS for the 2014–2015 school year; the other schools were assigned to Core READS.

Given that teachers in the previous year were randomly assigned within schools, some teachers had prior experience with Core READS at baseline of

Table 1

Operationalization of READS Core Components in Core and Adaptive READS

Core Component	Operationalization in Core READS	Operationalization in Adaptive READS	Potential for Acceptable Adaptation
Lessons and summer materials: Students learn a comprehension routine (READS Reading Routine) to use with summer books	• Teachers must deliver 6 scripted lessons over 6 consecutive school days	• Teachers must teach at least 6 READS lessons (scripts are optional) • Teachers must prepare students to use the routine independently over the summer	• Make procedural changes to facilitate lesson implementation • Make content changes to address student engagement in or understanding of the routine
Family engagement activities: Families learn about READS and how they can encourage their children to participate	• Teachers must distribute fliers to recruit families to the event • Teachers must attend the event • A trained facilitator demonstrates the routine and describes how families can encourage participation over the summer	• Each school must host at least 1 family event where parents learn about READS • Teachers must recruit families to the event; they may distribute fliers and/or use other strategies • Teachers must attend the event; they may take on additional responsibilities at the event(s)	• Use knowledge of families to increase attendance • Make procedural changes to facilitate implementation • Make content changes to address student and family engagement in or understanding of READS

(continued)

Table 1 (continued)

Core Component	Operationalization in Core READS	Operationalization in Adaptive READS	Potential for Acceptable Adaptation
Summer books:Students receive 10 free books over the summer that are matched to their reading level and interests	• Teachers play no role in this component • Student reading level is measured using Lexile framework • Students complete a reading preferences survey • A computer algorithm matches books to students (20 books matched; 8 matched books and 2 lesson books sent over the summer) • Books are distributed over the summer	• Student reading level and preferences are measured as in core, and a computer algorithm matches books to students • Teachers may move student Lexile bands up/down by 100 points, generating new book lists • Teachers may rearrange ordering of books, making matches more or less likely • Teachers may opt to send students additional matched books rather than the 2 lesson books • Teachers may opt to have some books delivered at the end of the school year	• Address measurement error in reading test and/or survey by using knowledge of students to improve computer book matches • Increase the chances that students receive their books over the summer
Summer nudges:Students and families receive nudges (reminders, incentives) over the summer to encourage participation in READS	• Teachers play no role in this component • Families receive tips and reminders via text or phone calls (sent by research team) • Students receive prizes for turning in trifolds (sent by research team)	• Families receive tips and reminders via text or phone calls; teachers can personalize the tips • Students receive prizes for turning in trifolds • Teachers can create additional nudges to remind and/or incentivize students over the summer	• Capitalize on personal relationships with students to encourage participation • Devise "nudges" that more successfully engage students and families in READS over the summer

Source. Adapted from Kim et al. (2017).

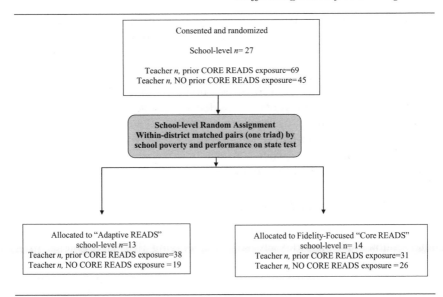

Figure 2. **School-level randomization to Adaptive versus Core READS.**

the present study, while others did not (in the first year, teachers were not aware of the future possibility of participating in a structured adaptive version of READS). Consequently, the present study includes four types of teachers: (a) teachers who did not participate in Core READS in the past but participated in Core READS for this study; (b) teachers who did not participate in Core READS in past and participated in Adaptive READS for this study; (c) teachers who had previously participated in Core READS, followed by a second year of Core READS in this study; (d) teachers who had previously participated in Core READS, followed by Adaptive READS for this study. This last group participated in the full scaffolded sequence. According to the scaffolded hypothesis described earlier, Adaptive READS will be more effective (compared to Core) among teachers who had previous (Core) READS experience, and Core READS will be more effective (compared to Adaptive) among teachers who had no prior exposure to READS. As described in more detail below, we can therefore test the scaffolded hypothesis by testing whether the effect of Adaptive READS (compared to Core READS) on select outcomes differed depending on whether the teacher had previous experience with Core READS.

In both conditions for this study, all teachers (regardless of prior experience) were required to participate in their condition's learning structures (i.e., all Core teachers participated in lesson training for the present study, regardless of whether they had previously participated in Core READS; all

Adaptive teachers participated in the working group meetings, regardless of whether they had previously participated in Core READS).

Measures

Teachers completed a web-based survey in the spring of 2015 with questions about their intervention experiences. The survey included original items and items adapted from previously validated surveys. In developing the survey, we went through several rounds of review with external experts and piloted items with teacher consultants (for text from selected survey items, see Appendix A in the online version of the journal).

Teachers' Literacy-Related Learning

We measured teachers' literacy-related learning in areas related to the intervention with an index created by averaging five survey items (α = .84) and standardizing those averages to a mean of 0 and standard deviation of 1. Items comprising the index were presented to teachers following the introduction, "In this set of questions, we'd like you to think about your literacy-related learning this school year. This learning could have taken place in any setting." Teachers were then asked several questions with the stem "How much did you learn this school year about each of the following?" The areas teachers were asked about were areas related to the READS components: "matching books to students for independent reading," "teaching students a reading comprehension routine," "engaging students' families in student literacy," "supporting students' independent reading," and "increasing students' engagement in reading." Answer choices were *nothing, very little, some, quite a bit,* and *a tremendous amount,* which were scaled from 0 (*nothing*) to 4 (*a tremendous amount*). A principal components analysis (PCA) revealed only one component with an eigenvalue above 1, which positively weighted all items. For interpretive clarity, we present the results using the mean-based index, but results replicate with a PCA-derived index (see Appendix B in the online version of the journal).

READS-Related Literacy Activities in Teachers' Regular Classroom Practice

We created a scale to measure changes in teachers' literacy practices by averaging teachers' responses on five relevant survey items (α = .85) and standardizing the index to a mean of 0 and standard deviation of 1. Teachers were asked a series of questions about the extent to which they incorporated new literacy strategies or followed READS-based principles in their regular classroom instruction (i.e., outside of READS). The areas asked about were the same five areas described previously for teachers' literacy-related learning, and READS was not explicitly referenced as a source of the change in practice. For example, one question asked, "This school year, to what extent did you incorporate new strategies for supporting students' independent reading into your regular classroom practice (i.e., outside of your planned READS activities)?" Answer choices were *not at all, very little, some, quite a bit,* and *a tremendous amount,* again with scores ranging from 0 (*not at all*) to 4 (*a tremendous amount*). A principal component analysis revealed only one component with an eigenvalue over 1, which positively weighted all items. Again, we present analyses using the mean-based index, but results replicate with the PCA-derived index (see Appendix B in the online version of the journal).

We inquired about teachers' literacy practices outside of READS, as opposed to their practices as part of READS, for two primary reasons. First, our interest is in the broad impact of the scaffolded approach on teachers' instruction. Compared to teachers' behaviors during READS, teachers' incorporation of READS-related principles into their instruction outside of READS is a better indicator of the spread of instructional principles, which is an important dimension of scale-up (Coburn, 2003). Second, because teachers in neither the Core nor Adaptive condition were encouraged to incorporate READS-inspired practices into their regular classroom instruction, teachers' practices outside of READS provide an "apples to apples" comparison, unlike teachers' practices during READS (given that Core teachers were required to implement the program with fidelity while Adaptive teachers were encouraged to adapt).

Student Reading Comprehension

Students took the reading comprehension section of the Iowa Test of Basic Skills (ITBS), Level 10, Form C in fall of 2015 as a posttest. The ITBS is a reliable assessment with reported KR-20 coefficients above .93 (Hoover et al., 2003). We use the ITBS developmental standard score metric, standardized to a sample mean of 0 and standard deviation of 1, to allow the treatment effect coefficient to be interpreted as an effect size.

Analytic Plan

RQ1: Main Effects of Program Implementation Approach on Teacher Outcomes

To test for Adaptive-Core differences on teachers' literacy-related learning and classroom literacy practices, we fit ordinary least squares (OLS) regression models of the form:

$$Y_{is} = \beta_1 ADAPTIVE_s + \beta_2 EXP_{is} + \sum \beta_k x_s + \varepsilon_{is}, \tag{1}$$

where Y_{is} is the standardized index score for teacher i in school s on either the learning index or the classroom practices index, *ADAPTIVE* is a binary indicator variable expressing whether school s was randomly assigned to the Adaptive READS condition, *EXP* is a binary indicator expressing whether teacher i had prior experience implementing (Core) READS, and x_s is a set of dummy variables indicating to which randomization bloc (i.e., within-district pair or triad) school s belonged. We use cluster-robust standard errors to account for residual dependence within schools.[1]

RQ2 and RQ3: Interaction Effects Between Teacher Intervention Experience and Program Implementation Approach (Scaffolded Hypothesis)

RQ2a and RQ2b: Teacher outcomes. To test whether the effect of Adaptive READS differed for teachers with and without prior READS experience (RQ2a), we added an interaction term to Model 1:

$$Y_{is} = \beta_1 ADAPTIVE_s + \beta_2 EXP_{is} + \beta_3 \left(ADAPTIVE_s \times EXP_{is}\right) + \sum \beta_k x_s + \varepsilon_{is}, \quad (2)$$

where all other terms are as defined previously.[2] To test whether the effect of Adaptive differed depending on the extent to which teachers' peers were experienced with the intervention (RQ2b), we added to Model 1 the interaction between *ADAPTIVE* and the number of teacher i's READS team colleagues who had prior experience with READS, the main effect of the number of other teachers with READS experience, and the main effect of the total number of teachers on the READS team in school s.

RQ3: Student Reading Comprehension

As noted previously, in other work, we report a significant positive main effect of Adaptive READS (compared to Core READS) on student reading comprehension (Kim et al., 2017). In the present study, our interest is in testing the scaffolded hypothesis by examining whether the effect of Adaptive READS on student reading comprehension differed depending on teachers' prior experience with Core READS. We use OLS regression to model the fall ITBS posttest score of student i in teacher t's classroom in school s as:

$$ITBS_{its}^{(fall)} = \beta_1 ADAPTIVE_s + \beta_2 EXP_{ts} + \beta_3 (ADAPTIVE_s \times EXP_{ts})$$
$$+ \beta_4 PRETEST_{its} + \sum \beta_k x_s + \varepsilon_{its}, \quad (3)$$

where *PRETEST* is a pre-randomization pretest covariate (student score on spring 2014 state reading test) included to improve precision, other variables are as defined earlier, and standard errors are clustered by school.

We also present models showing the main effect of Adaptive READS on student reading comprehension overall and the main effect of Adaptive READS separately for the subgroups of students whose teachers were new to READS and those whose teachers had READS experience. Because the outcome is standardized to a mean 0 and *SD* of 1, the coefficients on *ADAPTIVE* in these models can be interpreted as effect sizes.

Results

Descriptive Statistics

In Table 2, we present descriptive statistics by condition for school-, teacher-, and student-level baseline characteristics (top panel) and outcome variables (bottom panel). As seen, random assignment was successful in creating groups of schools that were similar in terms of student percent free or reduced-price lunch and mean reading achievement. Teachers in both conditions were similar in terms of experience in the field of education and master's degree attainment. A slightly higher proportion of teachers in the Adaptive condition had prior experience with READS, and Adaptive READS teachers were slightly more likely to be Black or female relative to Core READS teachers (some demographic information was collected through a fall survey; note incomplete sample sizes). All active teachers at the time of spring survey administration submitted a survey. Among students in the analytic sample, pretest reading scores did not differ by condition. Additionally, among students with pretest scores, attrition did not differ significantly by condition (19.31% for Core READS, 17.32% for Adaptive READS).

Teacher Outcomes

Literacy-related learning

Main effect of program implementation approach (RQ1). In Table 3, we present models predicting teachers' standardized scores on the literacy learning index. In the first column, we see that condition did not have a significant main effect on teachers' self-reported learning (with a nonsignificant advantage for Adaptive READS of .17 *SD*). Unsurprisingly, teachers across conditions with READS experience reported learning less than teachers who were new to READS (effect size [ES] = −.59 *SD*).

Interaction between intervention experience and program implementation approach (RQ2a, scaffolded hypothesis). In the second column, we find that the effect of Adaptive READS differed significantly depending on whether teachers had past experience with READS. While the effect of Adaptive READS was negatively-signed and not significant for teachers new to READS, the effect of Adaptive READS was positive for teachers with past READS experience (ES = −.29 + .75 = .46 *SD, p* = .052). These results are consistent with the theory behind the scaffolded model as they show that the management structures were not equally effective for teachers with different levels of experience with the intervention. Specifically, the structures and activities of Adaptive READS—as compared to the structures

Table 2
Descriptive Statistics by Condition

	Core READS (Control)			Adaptive READS (Treatment)			Adjusted T-C Difference	p Value
	Mean	SD	N	Mean	SD	N		
Background characteristics								
School-level variables								
School percent free or reduced-price lunch	84.61	10.39	14	85.81	6.5	13	1.38	.54
Average score on fourth-grade state reading test	441.72	3.08	14	442.08	3.18	13	0.12	.87
Percent of fourth graders scoring proficient or above on state reading test	41.84	14.61	14	43.66	13.34	13	0.79	.84
Teacher-level variables								
Number years working in field of education	9.74	7.76	53	10.46	6.71	54	1.19	.14
Number of years teaching in current grade level (Grade 4)	4.41	4.96	54	4.08	4.03	53	-0.3	.52
Number of years working at current school	4.61	5.73	54	4.81	5.42	54	0.26	.65
Worked with READS before this school year? (1 = yes, 0 = no)	0.55		56	0.68		56	0.13	.05
Have or working toward master's degree? (1 = yes, 0 = no)	0.54		54	0.56		54	0.02	.67
Female (1 = yes, 0 = no)	0.88		56	0.96		56	0.08	.05
Black (1 = yes, 0 = no)	0.2		54	0.31		54	0.12	.19
White (1 = yes, 0 = no)	0.67		54	0.57		54	-0.1	.23
Student-level variables								
Student end of grade pretest scores	435.34	10.34	518	435.55	10.1	611	-0.07	.92
Outcomes								
Literacy Learning Index (standardized)	-0.04	1.09	56	0.01	0.96	56	0.09	.65
How much did you learn this school year about: matching books to students for independent reading?	3.3	0.87	56	3.59	0.89	56	0.32	.01
How much did you learn this school year about: teaching students a reading comprehension routine?	3.61	0.97	56	3.59	0.87	56	0.01	.97
How much did you learn this school year about: engaging students' families in student literacy?	3.54	0.76	56	3.5	0.85	56	-0.01	.95
How much did you learn this school year about: supporting students' independent reading?	3.66	0.94	56	3.56	0.83	55	-0.08	.62
How much did you learn this school year about: increasing students' engagement in reading?	3.66	0.86	56	3.7	0.85	56	0.07	.67

(continued)

Table 2 (continued)

	Core READS (Control)			Adaptive READS (Treatment)			Adjusted T-C Difference	p Value
	Mean	SD	N	Mean	SD	N		
READS-related Literacy Practices Index (standardized)	−0.06	1.14	56	0.12	0.91	56	0.18	.43
Over the past 2 months, to what extent did you guide students in selecting books for independent reading?	3.27	0.94	56	3.39	0.97	56	0.16	.41
This school year, to what extent did you incorporate new strategies for teaching reading comprehension into your regular classroom practice?	3.48	0.99	56	3.71	0.82	56	0.2	.29
Over the past 2 months, how much emphasis did you place on engaging students' families in student literacy?	3.16	0.91	56	3.21	0.85	56	0.1	.49
This school year, to what extent did you incorporate new strategies for supporting students' independent reading?	3.48	1.03	56	3.62	0.85	55	0.11	.65
This school year, to what extent did you incorporate new strategies for engaging students in independent reading?	3.48	1	54	3.55	0.81	56	0.08	.68

Note. Means and *SD* are unadjusted. *p* value is for test of the null hypotheses that T-C = 0 (standard errors clustered at the school level). Variables listed under indices in "Outcomes" panel represent index components (measured at posttest). Adj. T-C Diff = difference estimated from regression that controls for fixed effects of randomization blocs.

Table 3
Regression Models Predicting Teachers' Literacy-Related Learning

	(1) Literacy Learning Index (Standardized)	(2) Literacy Learning Index (Standardized)	(3) Literacy Learning Index (Standardized)
Adaptive READS	0.171	−0.288	−0.497
	(0.199)	(0.270)	(0.479)
READS experience	−0.587***	−0.945***	−0.622**
	(0.148)	(0.180)	(0.179)
Adaptive READS × READS Experience		0.750*	
		(0.307)	
Adaptive READS × Number of Other Experienced Teachers on Team			0.285
			(0.181)
Number of other experienced teachers on team			−0.230
			(0.123)
Number of teachers on team			0.189*
			(0.0756)
N	112	112	112
R^2	0.250	0.278	0.283

Note. Cluster-robust standard errors in parentheses. All models control for fixed effects of randomization blocs. School-level $n = 27$.
*$p < .05$. **$p < .01$. ***$p < .001$.

and activities of Core READS—were more beneficial for teachers who had previously participated in Core READS.

We present this interaction graphically in Figure 3. The y-axis represents the original (unstandardized) teacher literacy learning index, with teachers' expected values reported on the original index scale for interpretive purposes. The x-axis contrasts teachers in the Core condition to teachers in the Adaptive condition. The dashed line connects expected values for teachers with no prior READS experience, while the solid line connects expected values for teachers with prior READS experience (expected values derived holding values for bloc dummy variables constant at their means). As can be seen, all subgroups of teachers have predicted values falling between 2 and 3, which represent "some learning" and "quite a bit of learning," respectively. Examining the dashed line, we see that among teachers with no READS experience, the Core condition promoted more learning (though not by a statistically significant amount). The solid line shows that among

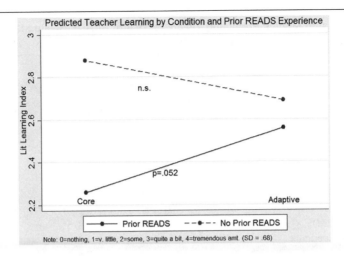

Figure 3. **Interaction between treatment condition and teacher experience predicting intervention-related teacher learning. Difference in slopes is statistically significant at *p* < .05.**

teachers with prior READS experience, the Adaptive condition promoted more learning (*p* = .052). Again, the difference-in-differences, which tests the scaffolded hypothesis, is statistically significant.

Peer effects (RQ2b). In the third column of Table 3, we test whether Adaptive READS was more effective at promoting learning for teachers in schools in which a greater number of other teachers had experience with READS. The interaction was not statistically significant.

READS-Related Literacy Activities Outside of READS

Main effect of program implementation approach (RQ1). In Table 4, we present models predicting the extent to which teachers incorporated READS-related principles and practices into their regular classroom instruction. As seen in Column 1, the Adaptive condition had no significant main effect on this outcome (with a coefficient of .23 *SD*), and teachers' prior experience with READS also did not significantly predict their READS-related literacy practices outside of READS (−.33 *SD*).

Interaction between intervention experience and program implementation approach (RQ2a, scaffolded hypothesis). In Column 2, we again see that the effect of Adaptive READS differed significantly depending on whether the teacher had prior READS experience. The effect of Adaptive was

Table 4
Regression Models Predicting Teachers' Use of READS-Related Literacy Activities Outside of READS

	(1) READS-Related Literacy Practices Index (Standardized)	(2) READS-Related Literacy Practices Index (Standardized)	(3) READS-Related Literacy Practices Index (Standardized)
Adaptive READS	0.227	−0.309	−0.456
	(0.227)	(0.272)	(0.663)
READS experience	−0.330	−0.748**	−0.346
	(0.199)	(0.260)	(0.219)
Adaptive READS × READS Experience		0.875*	
		(0.363)	
Adaptive READS × Number of Other Experienced Teachers on Team			0.319
			(0.275)
Number of other experienced teachers on team			−0.206
			(0.157)
Number of teachers on team			0.0942
			(0.172)
N	112	112	112
R^2	0.111	0.149	0.131

Note. Cluster-robust standard errors in parentheses. All models control for fixed effects of randomization blocs. School-level $n = 27$.
*$p < .05$. **$p < .01$.

negatively signed and statistically zero for teachers new to READS and was positive and marginally significant for teachers with READS experience (ES = −.309 + .875 = .57 SD, $p = .054$).

In Figure 4, we present this interaction graphically, again using model-predicted values on the original (unstandardized) survey scale (and again, holding values for bloc dummy variables constant at their means). All groups' predicted values fall between 2 and 3 ("some" and "quite a bit" of use of the READS-related practices during regular classroom instruction). From the dashed line, we see that among teachers with no prior READS experience, Core READS teachers used more READS practices (though the difference is not statistically significant). The solid line illustrates that among teachers with READS experience, the Adaptive condition promoted more incorporation of READS practices into regular instruction ($p = .054$). Again,

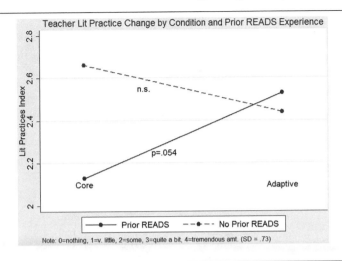

Note: 0=nothing, 1=v. little, 2=some, 3=quite a bit, 4=tremendous amt. (SD = .73)

Figure 4. **Interaction between treatment condition and teacher experience predicting teachers' changes in literacy practices. Difference in slopes is statistically significant at *p* < .05.**

the difference-in-differences, which tests the scaffolded hypothesis, is statistically significant.

Peer effects (RQ2b). In the third column of Table 4, we find that the effect of Adaptive READS on individuals' literacy practices did not differ depending on the number of a teacher's colleagues who had READS experience.

Student Reading Comprehension

In Table 5, we present models predicting student fall reading comprehension. As reported elsewhere (Kim et al., 2017), Adaptive READS had a significant main effect on students' fall reading comprehension posttest compared to Core READS (Column 1).[3] The results in Columns 2 through 4 show that this main effect was driven by the subgroup of students whose teachers had READS experience.

Interaction Between Teachers' Intervention Experience and Program Implementation Approach (RQ3, Scaffolded Hypothesis)

In Columns 2 and 3, we present the Adaptive effects for the subgroups of students taught by teachers who were new to READS and those taught by teachers who had previous READS experience, respectively. The effect of Adaptive READS for students taught by inexperienced READS teachers

Table 5
Regression Models Predicting Student Reading Comprehension Posttest Scores.

	(1) All Teachers	(2) Teachers New to READS	(3) Teachers With READS Experience	(4) Interaction
Adaptive READS	0.114*	−0.0557	0.226***	−0.0425
	(0.0460)	(0.0679)	(0.0397)	(0.0700)
Teacher READS experience	0.0465			−0.105
	(0.0532)			(0.0683)
Adaptive READS × Teacher READS Experience				0.281***
				(0.0718)
N	1,129	470	659	1,129
R^2	0.534	0.569	0.531	0.538

Note. Cluster-robust standard errors in parentheses. All models control for student pretest and fixed effects of randomization blocs. Teacher-level n = 91; school-level n = 27.
*$p < .05$. ***$p < .001$.

was not significant (ES = −.06; Column 2), while the effect size for students taught by teachers with READS experience was large and statistically significant (ES = .23). Furthermore, as indicated in Column 4 through the interaction between adaptive and teacher READS experience, the Adaptive effects were statistically different for students whose teachers did and did not have READS experience. These results are consistent with the hypothesis that the benefits of the Adaptive condition for experienced teachers reported earlier translate into more effective instructional experiences for students.

Discussion

In this study, we tested the hypothesis that a scaffolded sequence of educational program implementation would improve intervention outcomes for teachers and students. In the scaffolded sequence, practitioners new to a program first experience a phase of fidelity-focused implementation, the intention of which is for them to internalize the program theory and procedures by implementing the program as designed by the researchers. After developing proficiency with the program in this way, practitioners transition into a structured adaptive approach to program implementation, during which they make changes that they believe will improve the fit of the program with their context (without compromising core program principles). We found evidence in favor of our hypothesis that a fidelity-focused approach to implementing READS (i.e., Core READS) would lead to more learning and changes in practice for teachers new to READS, while a structured adaptive approach (i.e., Adaptive READS) would be more effective for teachers who had previously experienced the fidelity-focused version of READS. We also found evidence that these effects for teachers mattered for students, such that the Adaptive condition had positive effects on student reading comprehension only when those students were taught by teachers with prior READS experience. As discussed below, the extent to which these results might generalize to other types of interventions is unclear; however, collectively our findings are consistent with the scaffolded hypothesis.

The Scaffolded Sequence

This study adds experimental evidence to the small set of nonexperimental studies bringing evidence to bear on the effectiveness of a scaffolded sequence of program implementation. Our findings are consistent with Lemons et al. (2014), who found (in a nonexperimental setting) that after implementing a fidelity-focused version PALS, teachers who self-selected into an adaptive PALS condition demonstrated better outcomes compared to teachers who continued in the fidelity-focused condition. Our findings also suggest that the differentiation of teacher learning activities suggested by Frank et al.'s (2011) focus, fiddle, friends framework is well aligned with the stages of the scaffolded sequence. In their observational study, Frank et al. found that teachers who were inexperienced with classroom technology reforms improved their implementation most when their learning experiences centered around information delivery (focus), while teachers who had already reached a basic level of implementation improved most when they experimented with adaptations to the techniques (fiddle) and consulted with colleagues (friends). Accordingly, the professional learning component of Core READS focused on basic information delivery and practice implementing the scripted lessons, while the learning component of Adaptive READS consisted of experimentation and collaboration. Our pattern of results, showing that the effects of these conditions depended on teachers' prior experience with (Core) READS, offers experimental evidence in favor of fusing the focus, fiddle, friends differentiated learning concepts with the scaffolded sequence of program implementation.

Contrary to expectation, we did not find that Adaptive READS teachers learned more or improved their implementation more when more of their grade-level peers had prior experience with Core READS. The interaction coefficients were signed in the expected direction, however, and the null effects could simply be a matter of statistical power. Alternatively, it could be that the extent to which teachers benefit from the collaborative adaptive structures depends more on their own prior knowledge than their peers' knowledge. Relatedly, perhaps Adaptive READS teachers need to have established mastery of the program through prior experience with Core

READS before they are able to benefit from the expertise of their peers. While this three-way interaction (between Adaptive READS, READS experience, and number of other experienced teachers on team) was not significant (models not shown), power to detect this three-way interaction is low, and the direction of the effects was in the expected direction. In short, future research is needed to replicate this null effect and further probe potential explanations.

The Value of the Scaffolded Sequence

Even in cases in which teachers are expected to implement a program with fidelity, program adaptation may be inevitable (Berman & McLaughlin, 1976; Datnow & Castellano, 2000). Consequently, it is important that teachers' adaptations do not compromise the effectiveness of the program. This requires that teachers have deep enough knowledge of the program theory to avoid detrimental adaptations. The scaffolded implementation sequence is a promising way to help teachers develop this knowledge, and the approach to program implementation could be designed with this pedagogical purpose in mind. Teachers' internalization of the program theory is likely to be improved if the fidelity phase is framed as an opportunity for teachers to learn the program before adapting it, as opposed to being framed as the end goal, where teachers' value comes primarily from the fact that they are executing the program designer's vision. In other words, given that teachers' instincts seem to be to adapt programs, the scaffolded approach can be a way of harnessing and focusing that instinct in a way that maximizes the potential for the adaptations to be productive.

Some scholars argue that implementers may be more likely to sustain programs over time when they adapt them to their context (Dearing, 2008). If a particular program has positive effects on student achievement, then sustainability is desirable. Consequently, program adaptation may serve the important goal of sustainability even if the adaptations do not lead to measurable improvements in short-term intervention effects for students. Furthermore, there is potential for adaptation to lead to cascading effects. If teacher involvement in program decision-making leads to higher teacher morale and improved school culture, this may indirectly improve student outcomes (Lee, Dedrick, & Smith, 1991; Lee & Smith, 1996). Of course, adaptations that sustain a program while rendering it ineffective would be counterproductive. Again, this speaks to the value of providing scaffolds that prepare teachers for making effective adaptations.

Local Capacity and Will

Successful implementation of educational policies depends on both the capacity and the will of the implementers (McLaughlin, 1987). The scaffolded sequence discussed here primarily concerns capacity. Although it is not easy for policymakers to influence local capacity, it may be easier than building will, given that training and consultation can be provided to improve capacity (McLaughlin, 1987). While more explicit research is needed on what, if any, effect the scaffolded sequence may have on teachers' will to implement programs, theory suggests that positive feedback loops affecting teachers' will may arise. To begin with, will and capacity are related because teachers tend to be more willing to implement a program when they believe the program is effective (Kearns et al., 2010); building teachers' capacity to effectively implement a program may therefore also indirectly build their will to implement the program. Second, skillful teachers can be resentful of being asked to follow a program with fidelity, and involving teachers in the decision-making process is one way of earning teacher buy-in (Berman, 1980; Blakely et al., 1987). By framing the fidelity phase as a temporary scaffold that helps teachers acquire the knowledge and skill necessary for teacher-led adaptation, school leaders provide teachers with additional motivation for learning the program at a deeper level and may therefore improve the effectiveness of the scaffolded approach.

Limitations and Future Research

Continuous Versus Binary Constructs

Throughout this article, we have used binary constructs—fidelity-focused versus structured adaptive program implementation approaches and teachers experienced versus inexperienced with a program. Applying simplifying heuristics is useful when developing and testing theory, but in practice, these concepts may exist as continua rather than binaries (Berman, 1980). It is possible that the process of transitioning from a fidelity-focused to structured adaptive approach may be improved with intermediary scaffolds, such that implementers' authority and decision making increase gradually, perhaps beginning with simple decisions before building up to the full structured adaptive approach. Some researchers have suggested that programs should include built-in adaptation suggestions (Webster-Stratton, Reinke, Herman, & Newcomer, 2011), which could serve as adaptation scaffolds. Similarly, suggestions for alternative learning experiences could be built into training materials so as to enable differentiated scaffolding when preparing teacher implementers (Harn, Parisi, & Stoolmiller, 2013). In short, the scaffolded sequence might be scaffolded differently across settings depending on local needs, and future research is needed to experiment with such variations.

While we have focused on teachers' experience with a particular set of instructional procedures, other dimensions of teacher experience or expertise are likely to be relevant to teachers' success at implementing a program under each of the management approaches. Some teachers who are particularly skilled in general teaching practice may require less time in the fidelity-focused phase or may indeed be capable of bypassing that phase to immediately begin making program adaptations. Other teachers may need a longer fidelity period to gain the skill necessary for effective adaptations. Relatedly, the effect of the structured adaptive approach on student outcomes may differ depending on teachers' overall level of effectiveness in addition to their experience with the particular intervention. We leave this hypothesis to future study.

Interventions Beyond READS

One way in which READS for Summer Learning differs from many other educational interventions is that it consists of both home- and school-based student learning experiences. While teachers play an important role in preparing students for successful program participation over the summer, the key learning experiences for students (i.e., reading the summer books) take place outside of teacher guidance or supervision. It is therefore unclear how the principles underlying the findings in this study might play out in a program that is entirely school-based or primarily teacher-led. On the one hand, we might expect some of the patterns seen in this study to be even more pronounced for interventions in which teachers play a more central role. For example, in a curricular intervention in which student learning relies entirely on teacher-led instruction, effects on student learning may be more sensitive to teachers' learning, instructional practice, and adaptations. On the other hand, adaptations to such a program may need to be more substantial for the adapted intervention to be sufficiently distinct from the intervention as originally designed. Relatedly, teachers may need more program-specific knowledge or general expertise to effectively adapt more complex programs. Finally, the demands made on teachers when collaboratively adapting a year-long curricular intervention may be more taxing compared to what occurred in READS. If teachers oppose frequent collaborative meetings and a more demanding adaptation process, teacher investment in the program may be negatively impacted. Given all of these complexities, future research is needed to build an understanding of how fidelity-focused versus structured adaptive approaches play out with other types of educational interventions across various settings.

Methodological Limitations

One methodological limitation is the self-report nature of the teacher outcomes. This concern is less about whether the effects observed here are trustworthy; randomization reassures us that causal inferences regarding the program effects within each teacher subgroup are warranted, and it seems unlikely that these interaction effects would be seen on teachers' perceptions of their learning and behaviors but not on their actual learning and behaviors. Given that teachers were blind to our hypothesized interaction between experience and condition, it also seems unlikely that social desirability bias could be driving results. Finally, the student outcomes provide additional support for the conclusion that teachers' actual learning and behaviors were affected. Instead, the limitation here is that we cannot know exactly how these measures of teachers' perceptions might relate to observable behavior change. The precise content of teachers' learning is unknown, and we cannot draw conclusions about whether certain teacher learning is relevant to changing practice and whether certain practices are relevant to improving student outcomes. Relatedly, we do not have measures of teachers' mastery of the program theory, which is hypothesized to enable teachers to make more effective adaptations. To obtain a finer-grained picture of this process, further study will be needed.

Conclusion

By understanding the circumstances under which a fidelity-focused approach versus a structured adaptive approach to educational program management will generally lead to improved outcomes, practitioners will be better positioned to tailor school improvement efforts to their contexts. The findings in this study provide empirical support for the notion that fidelity-focused and structured adaptive approaches can form an effective scaffolded sequence of program implementation, and point toward new areas of exploration that can inform teacher-implemented instructional programs and educational programs more broadly.

Notes

This study was made possible by an Investing in Innovation Fund (i3) grant from the U.S. Department of Education (PR/Award No. U396B100195). However, the contents of this article do not represent the policy of the U.S. Department of Education, and the content is solely the responsibility of the authors. David Quinn received support from the Dean's Summer Fellowship at the Harvard Graduate School of Education. We are grateful to Heather Hill, Ebony Bridwell-Mitchell, Andrew Volkert, Margaret Troyer, Celia Gomez, Rebecca Unterman, Ann Mantil, and Beth Schuler for feedback on earlier drafts. Helen Chen Kingston, Mary Burkhauser, and Kirsten Aleman contributed to the design of Adaptive READS. Communities in Schools-North Carolina were crucial to implementation efforts. Any errors or omissions are our own.

[1]We also fit multilevel models with random intercepts for schools as sensitivity analyses; all conclusions are unchanged (see Appendix C in the online version of the journal).

[2]We include only teachers who were in these schools prior to randomization for the present study. Some teachers joined these schools prior to this study's randomization but after the previous year's randomization. For these teachers, prior READS experience is considered a baseline characteristic but not random. Models that include only teachers for whom experience was randomly assigned largely replicate the results presented here, as do models using the analytic sample and fit separately for teachers with and without prior READS experience or models that fully interact experience with all covariates (including bloc).

[3]These models differ slightly from those reported in Kim et al. (2017). In Kim et al. (2017), we fit multilevel models with random effects for schools and use school-mean imputation for pretest controls, leading to different sample sizes across articles. Conclusions from Table 5 in this article replicate when using pretest imputation.

References

Berman, P. (1980). Thinking about programmed and adaptive implementation: Matching strategies to situations. In H. M. Ingram & D. E. Mann (Eds.), *Why policies succeed or fail* (pp 205–227). Beverly Hills, CA: Sage Publications.

Berman, P., & McLaughlin, M. W. (1976). Implementation of educational innovation. *The Educational Forum, 40*(3), 345–370. doi:10.1080/00131727609336469

Blakely, C. R., Mayer, J. P., Gottschalk, R. G., Schmitt, N., Davidson, W. S., Roitman, D. B., & Emshoff, J. G. (1987). The fidelity-adaptation debate: Implications for the implementation of public sector social programs. *American Journal of Community Psychology, 15*(3), 253–268.

Bryk, A. S., Gomez, L. M., Grunow, A., & LeMahieu, P. G. (2015). *Learning to improve: How America's schools can get better at getting better.* Cambridge, MA: Harvard Education Press.

Castro, F. G., Barrera, M., & Martinez, C. R. (2004). The cultural adaptation of prevention interventions: Resolving tensions between fidelity and fit. *Prevention Science, 5*(1), 41–45.

Coalition for Evidence-based Policy. (2013). *Randomized controlled trials commissioned by the Institute of Education Sciences since 2002: How many found positive versus weak or no effects.* Retrieved from http://coalition4evidence.org/wp-content/uploads/2013/06/IES-Commissioned-RCTs-positive-vs-weak-or-null-findings-7-2013.pdf

Coburn, C. E. (2003). Rethinking scale: Moving beyond numbers to deep and lasting change. *Educational Researcher, 32*(6), 3–12.

Coburn, C. E., & Stein, M. K. (2010). *Research and practice in education: Building alliances, bridging the divide.* Blue Ridge Summit, PA: Rowman & Littlefield Publishers, Inc.

Dane, A. V., & Schneider, B. H. (1998). Program integrity in primary and early secondary prevention: Are implementation effects out of control? *Clinical Psychology Review, 18*(1), 23–45.

Datnow, A., & Castellano, M. (2000). Teachers' responses to Success for All: How beliefs, experiences, and adaptations shape implementation. *American Educational Research Journal, 37,* 775–799.

Dearing, J. W. (2008). Evolution of diffusion and dissemination theory. *Journal of Public Health Management and Practice, 14*(2), 99–108.

Domitrovich, C. E., Gest, S. D., Jones, D., Gill, S., & DeRousie, R. M. S. (2010). Implementation quality: Lessons learned in the context of the Head Start REDI trial. *Early Childhood Research Quarterly, 25*(3), 284–298.

Dusenbury, L., Brannigan, R., Falco, M., & Hansen, W. B. (2003). A review of research on fidelity of implementation: Implications for drug abuse prevention in school settings. *Health Education Research, 18*(2), 237–256.

Elmore, R. F. (1996). Getting to scale with good educational practice. *Harvard Educational Review, 66*(1), 1–26.

Ferrer-Wreder, L., Adamson, L., Kumpfer, K. L., & Eichas, K. (2012). Advancing intervention science through effectiveness research: A global perspective. *Child Youth Care Forum, 41,* 109–117. doi:10.1007/s10566-012-9173-y

Frank, K. A., Zhao, Y., Penuel, W. R., Ellefson, N., & Porter, S. (2011). Focus, fiddle, and friends: Experiences that transform knowledge for the implementation of innovations. *Sociology of Education, 84*(2), 138–156.

Harn, B., Parisi, D., & Stoolmiller, M. (2013). Balancing fidelity with flexibility and fit: What do we really know about fidelity of implementation in schools? *Exceptional Children, 79*(2), 181–193.

Hoover, H., Dunbar, S., Frisbie, D., Oberley, K., Ordman, V., Naylor, R., & Shannon, G. (2003). *Iowa Test of Basic Skills guide to research and development*. Itasca, IL: The Riverside Publishing Company.

Hulleman, C. S., & Cordray, D. S. (2009). Moving from the lab to the field: The role of fidelity and achieved relative intervention strength. *Journal of Research on Educational Effectiveness*, *2*, 88–110. doi:10.1080/19345740802539325

Jackson, K. C., & Bruegmann, E. (2009). Teaching students and teaching each other: The importance of peer learning for teachers. *American Economic Journal: Applied Economics*, *1*(4), 85–108.

Kearns, D. M., Fuchs, D., McMaster, K. L., Saenz, L., Fuchs, L. S., Yen, L., . . . Smith, T. (2010). Factors contributing to teachers' sustained use of kindergarten peer-assisted learning strategies. *Journal of Research on Educational Effectiveness*, *3*, 315–342. doi:10.1080/19345747.2010.491151

Kim, J. S., Burkhauser, M. A., Quinn, D. M., Guryan, J., Kingston, H. C., & Aleman, A. (2017). Effectiveness of structured teacher adaptations to an evidence-based summer literacy program. *Reading Research Quarterly*. Advance online publication. doi:10.1002/rrq.178

Kim, J. S., Guryan, J., White, T. G., Quinn, D. M., Capotosto, L., & Kingston, H. C. (2016). Delayed effects of a low-cost and large-scale summer reading intervention on elementary school children's reading comprehension. *Journal of Research on Educational Effectiveness*, *9*(Suppl. 1), 1–22. doi:10.1080/19345747.2016.1164780

LaChausse, R. G., Clark, K. R., & Chapple, S. (2014). Beyond teacher training: The critical role of professional development in maintaining curriculum fidelity. *Journal of Adolescent Health*, *54*, S53–S58.

Lee, V. E., Dedrick, R. F., & Smith, J. B. (1991). The effect of the social organization of schools on teachers' efficacy and satisfaction. *Sociology of Education*, *64*, 190–208.

Lee, V. E., & Smith, J. B. (1996). Collective responsibility for learning and its effects on gains in achievement for early secondary school students. *American Journal of Education*, *104*(2), 103–147.

Lemons, C. J., Fuchs, D., Gilbert, J. K., & Fuchs, L. S. (2014). Evidence-based practices in a changing world reconsidering the counterfactual in education research. *Educational Researcher*, *43*, 242–252.

McDonald, S., Keesler, V. A., Kauffman, N. J., & Schneider, B. (2006). Scaling-up exemplary interventions. *Educational Researcher*, *35*(3), 15–24.

McLaughlin, M. W. (1987). Learning from experience: Lessons from policy implementation. *Educational Evaluation and Policy Analysis*, *9*(2), 171–178.

McLaughlin, M. W. (1990). The RAND change agent study revisited: Macro perspectives and micro realities. *Educational Researcher*, *19*(9), 11–16.

McLaughlin, M. W., & Mitra, D. (2002). Theory-based change and change-based theory: Going deeper, going broader. *Journal of Educational Change*, *2*, 301–322.

McMaster, K. L., Jung, P., Brandes, D., Pinto, V., Fuchs, D., Kearns, D., . . . Yen, L. (2014). Customizing a research-based reading practice: Balancing the importance of implementation fidelity with professional judgment. *The Reading Teacher*, *68*(3), 173–183. doi:10.1002/trtr.1301

Meyer, A., Miller, S., & Herman, M. (1993). Balancing the priorities of evaluation with the priorities of the setting: A focus on positive youth development programs in school settings. *The Journal of Primary Prevention*, *14*(2), 95–113.

Mowbray, C. T., Holter, M. C., Teague, G. B., & Bybee, D. (2003). Fidelity criteria: Development, measurement, and validation. *American Journal of Evaluation*, *24*(3), 315–340.

Murnane, R. J., & Nelson, R. R. (2007). Improving the performance of the education sector: The valuable, challenging, and limited role of random assignment evaluations. *Economics of Innovation & New Technology, 16*(5), 307–322.

O'Donnell, C. L. (2008). Defining, conceptualizing, and measuring fidelity of implementation and its relationship to outcomes in k–12 curriculum intervention research. *Review of Educational Research, 78*(1), 33–84.

Penuel, W. R., Gallagher, L. P., & Moorthy, S. (2011). Preparing teachers to design sequences of instruction in earth systems science: A comparison of three professional development systems. *American Educational Research Journal, 48*, 996–1025. doi:10.3102/0002831211410864

Popham, J. W. (1967). Instructional product development: Two approaches to training. *AV Communication Review, 15*, 402–411.

Rowan, B. (1990). Commitment and control: Alternative strategies for the organizational design of schools. *Review of Research in Education, 16*, 353–389.

Sailors, M., Hoffman, J. V., Pearson, P. D., McClung, N., Shin, J., Phiri, L. M., & Saka, T. (2014). Supporting change in literacy instruction in malawi. *Reading Research Quarterly, 49*(2), 209–231. doi:10.1002/rrq.70

Sherin, M. G., & Drake, C. (2009). Curriculum strategy framework: Investigating patterns in teachers' use of a reform-based elementary mathematics curriculum. *Journal of Curriculum Studies, 41*(4), 467–500.

Slavin, R. E. (2002). Evidence-based education policies: Transforming educational practice and research. *Educational Researcher, 31*(7), 15–21.

Slavin, R. E., Madden, N. A., & Datnow, A. (2007). Research in, research out: The role of research in the development and scale-up of Success for All. In D. K. Cohen, S. H. Fuhrman, & F. Mosher (Eds.), *The state of education policy research* (pp. 261–280). Mahwah, NJ: Lawrence Erlbaum Associates.

U.S. Department of Health and Human Services. (2002). *Finding the balance: Program fidelity and adaptation in substance abuse prevention.* Washington, DC: Author.

Vygotsky, L. S. (1978). *Mind in society: The development of higher psychological processes.* Cambridge, MA: Harvard University Press.

Webster-Stratton, C., Reinke, W. M., Herman, K. C., & Newcomer, L. L. (2011). The Incredible Years teacher classroom management training: The methods and principles that support fidelity of training delivery. *School Psychology Review, 40*(4), 509–529.

White, T. G., Kim, J. S., Kingston, H. C., & Foster, L. (2014). Replicating the effects of a teacher-scaffolded voluntary summer reading program: The role of poverty. *Reading Research Quarterly, 49*(1), 5–30. doi:10.1002/rrq.62

Manuscript received June 3, 2016
Final revision received May 27, 2017
Accepted June 5, 2017

American Educational Research Journal
December 2017, Vol. 54, No. 6, pp. 1221–1255
DOI: 10.3102/0002831217771815
© 2017 AERA. http://aerj.aera.net

Them That's Got: How Tie Formation in Partnership Networks Gives High Schools Differential Access to Social Capital

E. N. Bridwell-Mitchell
Harvard University

School partnerships are important sources of school social capital. Schools may have unequal access to social capital due to the pattern of relationships in the school-partner network. Using data on school resource needs, socio-metric measures, and a set of multilevel logit models, the results of a study of 211 New York City public high schools and 1,098 partner organizations from 1999 to 2005 suggest that high schools have unequal access to partner resources. Already well-endowed schools, in terms of having many experienced teachers or being embedded in dense networks, are most likely to partner. Disadvantaged schools, in terms of having many low socioeconomic status students or being in high-competition network positions, are least likely to partner. So, some policies promoting school partnerships may unintentionally reinforce existing structural inequalities among schools.

KEYWORDS: school partnerships, social capital, high school networks

Educational partnerships surfaced as a major educational policy issue in the United States following the 1983 *Nation at Risk Report*, which highlighted the threat to the nation's position in the global economy. Five years after the report's release, the 100th U.S. Congress passed the Educational Partnerships Act (1988). The described purpose of the act was

> to encourage the creation of alliances between public elementary and secondary schools or institutions of higher education and representatives of the private sector in order to apply the resources of the private and nonprofit sectors of the community to the needs of the elementary and secondary schools.

EBONY N. BRIDWELL-MITCHELL is an associate professor of education at the Harvard Graduate School of Education, Harvard University, Monroe C. Gutman Building, 6 Appian Way, Cambridge, MA 02138; e-mail: *ebony_bridwell-mitchell@gse.harvard.edu*. Her research builds on three areas of study in public policy, organization management, and education to examine the social and cognitive factors that constrain and enable institutional changes, such as U.S. public school reform.

Since this time, private and nonprofit organizations have come to play an increasingly pervasive role in the education sector as intermediary organizations (Honig, 2004).

Schools' relationships with partners are a critical source of *social capital*, meaning the potential and actual set of cognitive, social, and material resources made available through direct and indirect relationships with others (Bourdieu, 1986; Coleman, 1988; Lin, 2001). Whereas much educational research focuses on individuals' social capital, social capital also accrues to "corporate actors" or organizations (Coleman, 1988, p. S98). So, for example, schools' relationships with other schools can confer cognitive resources, such as information that may help schools innovate or solve difficult problems (Bridwell-Mitchell & Lant, 2014; Hite, Williams, & Baugh, 2005). Relationships with high-profile foundations or political groups can confer social resources, such as legitimacy (Dacin, Oliver, & Roy, 2007). Cognitive and social resources in turn can confer material resources, such as financial support from donors, volunteered labor, special services, materials and supplies, or the use of facilities (Feuerstein, 2001; Galaskiewicz, 1985). In the current work, *school social capital* refers to these kinds of resources, which schools receive through their ties or relationships to other organizations (Tsang, 2009).

The important resources that social capital confers raises at least two important questions. One is a question about whether schools involved in partnerships have better outcomes than schools not involved in partnerships (Byrd & Maloy, 1988; Sanders, 2006). Indeed, the conventional focus of social capital research is on its effects or outcomes (Coleman, 1988; Dika & Singh, 2002; Frank, Zhao, & Borman, 2004; Granovetter, 1973; Holme & Rangel, 2012; Leana & Pil, 2006). Increasingly, however, researchers are recognizing that taking access to social capital for granted and then determining its effects may be putting the proverbial cart before the horse (Gulati & Gargiulo, 1999; Oliver, 1990). In other words, it is not only important to ask what the outcomes of school partnerships are, it is also important to ask how schools gain access to partner resources in the first place. In the current research, I focus on this second question by examining what factors predict whether schools have partnership ties, where having a relational tie is the axiomatic necessary condition for access to social capital (Coleman, 1988). By answering this question, it is possible to better understand not only why different patterns of partner relationships result in different school outcomes but, more essentially, why different patterns of partner relationships exist to begin with.[1]

One approach to answering the above question is to examine how individuals inside schools, such as principals, community-school coordinators, or other school-based personnel, exercise agency to solicit and manage partnerships (Sanders, 2014). Planning and outreach activities play an important role in how schools access partner resources. However, these activities are only one part of the story. Individuals who work to establish partnerships do not have access to the universe of all possible partnerships. The partnerships entered into depend on opportunities for establishing partnerships. Therefore, in the current work, I examine one important factor that determines opportunities for establishing partnerships and accessing social capital—the overall structure or pattern of relationships between schools and other organizations in the school-partner network.

The pattern of relationships between schools and other organizations in the school-partner network is important because a classic and persistent finding of social capital research is that access to social capital depends on the structure or pattern of relationships between actors. This structure includes how well connected actors are to every other actor or the extent to which there are gaps in the connections between actors (Burt, 1992; Coleman, 1988; Granovetter, 1973). Schools' access to social capital may be similarly constrained or enabled by network structure. This means partnerships might provide schools with access to the cognitive, social, and material resources needed to enhance school operations and improve educational opportunities for students (Koka & Prescott, 2002). However, the structure of the school-partner network may mean not all schools have equal access to resources, and there may be resultant disparities in the educational opportunities schools can offer to their students.

The U.S. School Partnership Movement

In the K–12 school context, the organizational field is constituted by a variety of informal and formal organizations linked together by their involvement in schooling and education as institutions (DiMaggio & Powell, 1983; Meyer, 1977). Historically, this set of organizations has expanded from including only the family, as an informal organization, and formal governing bodies, such as local, state, and federal education agencies, to also include universities, nonprofits, businesses, community groups, and other K–12 schools (Byrd & Maloy, 1988; Sanders, 2006). The diverse types of relationships schools have with such organizations tend to be broadly characterized as partnerships—namely, school-family partnerships, school-community partnerships, school-university partnerships, and school-industry or -business partnerships.

Following the Educational Partnership Act of 1988, the partnership movement was renewed in 2001 with the authorization of the No Child Left Behind Act (NCLB). The law's strict accountability stipulations highlighted partnerships as a means of helping schools achieve Annual Yearly Progress by relying on the private sector to provide academic support. In 2002, the U.S. Department of Education began to fund 21st Century Community Learning Centers grants, which would provide afterschool enrichment and family support activities through partnerships. These activities included youth development, tutorial services, drug and violence prevention programs, counseling programs, art, music, and recreation programs, technology education programs, character education programs; and offering families educational development opportunities (James-Burdumy et al., 2005).

The history of educational partnerships in New York City, which is the focal context of the current work, predates national trends. School partnerships in New York City can be traced back as far as 1945 to the founding of the New York City Youth Board, which was designed to formalize the link between the city's public schools and private and public organizations. Throughout the 1970s and 1980s, the New York City School Community Education Program required relationships with numerous external service providers to support school programming, such as student tutoring, teacher training, arts programs, early childhood literacy, and bilingual education (The City of New York, 2013). More recently, the New York Network for School Renewal—a collaboration among nonprofit organizations, foundations, and the New York City Department of Education—spearheaded a movement to forge "partnerships with parents, teachers, community-based agencies, civic groups, and representatives of the business sector" (Kane, 2000, p. 69).

Studies of school partnerships often focus on the quality of these relationships, meaning their longevity, management, or impact on school outcomes (Jones & Maloy, 1988; Sanders, 2006; Smith &Wohlstetter, 2006).[2] In contrast, research on partnerships or alliances outside of the education sector often focuses on the formation of relationships because this influences which organizations can gain access to the social capital resources of the field (Chung, Singh, & Lee, 2000; Galaskiewicz, 1985; Gulati & Gargiulo, 1999; Mitsuhashi & Greve, 2009; Oliver, 1990). Consider, for example, the starting premise of some research on community involvement in schools: "There is an array of community partners and opportunities for community partnerships available to schools" (Sanders, 2003, p. 174). Yet, opportunities for community partnerships may not be equally available to all schools. The set of partners to which schools have access—and thus the ultimate payoff of partnerships—may depend on particular features of the partnership formation process.

Partnership Formation and Access to School Social Capital

School Resource Needs

A number of inputs or resources are important for core school operations and for providing enrichment opportunities. Most controversial among these resources has been monetary or financial resources, typically measured by per-pupil dollars (Hanushek, 1997). A number of other school-level factors related to teacher and instructional quality, such as teacher education, certification, experience, and salary, have also been described as important school inputs (Berne, 1994; Butler & McNertney, 1991; Ehrenberg & Brewer, 1994; Figlio, 1999; Hanushek, 1997; Schwartz & Stiefel, 2004). Factors such as school enrollment, curriculum, instructional time, materials and technology, facilities, maintenance and operations, and administrative capacity have been argued to be important resources for educational outcomes, as well (Berne, 1994; Butler & McNertney, 1991; Caldas, 1993; Calvo, Picus, Smith, & Guthrie, 2000; Figlio, 1999; Greenwald, Hedges, & Laine, 1996; Hanushek, 1996).

In addition to the aforementioned resources related to school characteristics, schools also have resource needs driven by the background characteristics of their student bodies. For example, the degree to which students are English proficient, their socioeconomic status, as well as their parents' educational and occupational backgrounds may determine students' initial levels and future rates of learning (Butler & McNertney, 1991; Calvo et al., 2000; Glasman & Biniamov, 1981; Schwartz & Stiefel, 2004; Tuckman, 1971). Thus, student background factors determine the resources schools will need to invest in academic and nonacademic supports. Such supports might include extensions to the core curriculum and instruction, health and social services, recreational activities, or additional exposure to vocational experiences and careers.

The aforementioned resource needs, determined by school and student characteristics, may be important drivers of partnership formation, just as resource needs are a fundamental driver of interorganizational relations in other sectors (Galaskiewicz, 1985). Resource needs may be particularly strong drivers of partnerships for schools because school budgets are often constrained both in terms of the amount of funding needed and the extent to which funds can be distributed discretionarily to different activities (Ouchi, 2003). If schools need to provide students with supports that exceed budget constraints, then external resources are necessary. One way to obtain external resources is by forming partnerships with other organizations. This suggests that schools with greater resource needs might pursue partnerships more vigorously. Because the mission of many organizations in the education sector is to provide services and support to schools, schools with greater resource needs may also be more attractive to potential partners (Jones & Maloy, 1988).

> *Hypothesis 1:* The probability of a partnership between schools and other organizations increases with the level of schools' resource needs.

The potential effect of schools' resource needs on partnership formation suggests a rational choice model of schools forming partnerships to maximize needed resources. However, the rational choices actors make are often determined by social factors, which enable and constrain choice (Giddens, 1979). More specifically, the immediate set of relationships in which actors are embedded can impact their interests, decisions, and actions by determining their opportunities and access to resources (Granovetter, 1985). In other words, the immediate set of relationships in which schools are embedded may play an important role in partnership formation.

School-Partner Network Structure

Relationships between schools and other organizations in the field result in a social network of actors, meaning a structured pattern of relationships emerging from actors' direct and indirect ties to one another. Classic studies of social networks have demonstrated that the strength or weakness of ties between actors determines how information flows between actors and determines who adopts certain practices (Coleman, Katz, & Menzel, 1957; Granovetter, 1973). Closure in ties among actors, meaning the extent to which every actor has a relationship with every other actor, not only facilitates knowledge transfer and the acquisition of human capital but is also a source of strong norms, reciprocal exchange, and trust (Coleman, 1988). When actors have a unique set of ties to others, such as bridging or brokering connections between otherwise disparate groups, these uniquely positioned actors have exclusive access to resources; meanwhile, actors without unique ties may have to compete for access to resources (Burt, 1992).

Research on social capital *inside* schools has demonstrated the previously described structural effects. For example, the position of teachers in their school's social network has been associated with teachers' access to expertise, advice, and resources (Penuel, Riel, Krause, & Frank, 2009). Similarly, the position of principals in their schools' advice network is associated with critical social resources, such as influence, legitimacy, trust, and obligation, which allow principals to coordinate and control school activities, which, in turn, is associated with school performance (Friedkin & Slater, 1994). The overall pattern or configuration of internal network relationships is also associated with the development of norms for instructional reform and raising student achievement (Atteberry & Bryk, 2010; Leana & Pil, 2006). In the same way that the structure of social networks among actors inside or internal to schools is associated with social capital, the structure of social networks among actors outside or external to schools also is associated with social capital. For instance, Finnigan and Daly (2010) demonstrate that principals' ties to district leaders influence access to the resources needed to improve school performance.

A broad body of sociological research on social capital demonstrates that network structure and an actor's position in the network can have a greater effect on social capital than an actor's individual characteristics (Burt, 1992; Coleman, 1988; Granovetter, 1973). This finding holds at both the individual and organizational levels since, as noted by Brass, Galaskiewicz, Greve, and Tsai (2004), "many of the variables that explain the formation of interpersonal and interunit networks explain the creation of inter-organizational networks as well" (p. 802) Thus, the structure of the school-partner network may have a greater effect on school social capital than school-specific characteristics related to resource needs.[3]

> *Hypothesis 2:* The structural features of the school-partner network have a greater effect on the probability of a partnership between a school and other organizations than the effect of schools' resource needs.

One structural network feature that may be particularly important for partnership formation is the strength of the relationship between schools and partners. More specifically, social network research suggests the frequency of interaction among actors is associated with the strength of their relationship because of increasingly shared understandings, feelings of attachment, and sense of predictability or trust in the others' motives and actions (Granovetter, 1973). For example, because actors tend to prefer certain or known outcomes to unknown outcomes, this suggests partnerships would be more likely between schools and organizations that have partnered in previous years (e.g., Kahneman, Slovic, & Tversky, 1982). Likewise, repeated interactions between individuals who orchestrate partnerships, such as the principal of a school and a liaison at the partner organization, may also result in a sense of attachment between the two individuals. Also, the longer a school and a partner organization have a relationship, the more similar the two organizations might become, such as developing a common understanding of local contexts or viewing their missions as intertwined (Gulati & Gargiulo, 1999). A preference for certainty, attachment between agents, and increasing similarity suggest that schools without preexisting ties or with weak ties to partners would be disadvantaged in forming partnerships. The converse would also hold.

> *Hypothesis 3:* The probability of a partnership between schools and other organizations increases with the strength of their preexisting relationship.

The strength of a relationship describes a dyadic or one-to-one relationship between schools and partners. Global features that describe the broader pattern of relationships between schools and partners, as well as schools' position in that broader pattern, may also be important for access to social capital. For example, consider a simple network structure comprised of one actor who is a hub with ties to four other actors arranged at the tips of the spokes around the hub (i.e., a letter *X*, with one actor at the center point and the other four actors arrayed at the tips of the two crossing strokes). In this simple network structure, the actor at the hub occupies the most central position because this actor has the greatest number of ties to the other actors and because this actor can interact with every other actor directly while all other actors must go through the central actor

(Freeman, 1979). For schools, a central position in the school-partner network can have similar benefits because schools would have direct access to partners. Also, to the extent a central school is a go-between for other schools to access partners, a central position might result in *quid pro quo* opportunities to form new relationships with the partners of the schools for which they are a go-between.

Hypothesis 4: The probability of a partnership between schools and other organizations increases with a school's centrality in the school-partner network.

Another important position a school might occupy in the school-partner network is being in a position that is structurally similar or equivalent to other schools (Burt, 1992). Being in a structurally equivalent position means two actors have to go through the same intermediaries to reach a third party and as a result must compete for access to the third party. Consider, for example, that sometimes the best way for a school to form a new partnership is to rely on a relationship the school has with another school already tied to that partner (i.e., like making friends with the friend of a friend). If two schools attempt to rely on the same third school as an intermediary to connect with a potential partner, then the two schools are in structurally equivalent positions because they are connected to the partner through the same intermediary school. Being in a structurally equivalent position can be disadvantageous because the school acting as an intermediary may not be able to connect both of the two other schools to the partner. Thus, the two schools are essentially in competition for access to the partner's resources, and one of the schools may lose out. As a result, schools in structurally equivalent positions may have greater difficulty forming partnerships and gaining access to partner resources.

Hypothesis 5: The probability of a partnership between schools and other organizations decreases with a school's structural equivalence to other schools in the school-partner network.

Finally, the density of the school-partner network, meaning the overall proportion of possible relationships between schools and partners that have been realized, also might affect schools' access to social capital. Schools embedded in dense local networks might have greater direct and indirect access to partners (i.e., a school with connections to five partners has more avenues to build relationships with their partners' partners compared to a school with connections to two partners). Schools in dense local networks might also gain unique skills for soliciting and managing partnerships and thus be more advantaged in terms of partnership formation. On the other hand, being embedded in a dense local network could have negative effects because access to too many partnerships could dilute the time and attention needed to solicit and manage these relationships. In other words, there may be declining marginal benefits to network density.

Hypothesis 6a: The probability of a partnership between schools and other organizations increases with the density of the local school-partner network.

Hypothesis 6b: The probability of a partnership between schools and other organizations decreases with the increasing density of the local school-partner network.

Research Methods

Sample and Data Collection

The sample for the current study is the set of relationships between 211 New York City high schools and 1,098 organizations between the 1999–2000 and 2004–2005 school years. The schools in the study were identified from the New York City Department of Education's (NYC DOE) school contact roster. Because a school's designation as a high school can be fluid, in the current study I define high school as any school with either an entry grade of 9 or an exit grade of 12. During the study period, some schools opened, merged, or closed, resulting in the 211 unique schools in the sample.

The sample of partner organizations is identified from each school's annual report to the NYC DOE, which asks schools to provide a listing of "community support." To determine whether the listed organizations provided resources to schools that were consistent with the definition of partnership in this study, I contacted an informant at the NYC DOE, who indicated that the listed organizations were in fact considered educational partnerships. Thus, the 1,098 unique organizations listed—which include a variety of community organizations, nonprofits, businesses, universities, and other public schools—comprise the sample of partners in the current study. For illustrative purposes, Figure 1 provides a sociogram of the full school-partner network in the first year of the study, 1999–2000. Figure 2 is an inset map providing a more detailed view of the 1999–2000 school-partner network for one of the more densely populated regions of the sociogram where some of the most central actors are located.[4]

The main strength of this data set is that in contrast to partnership research that takes a case study approach, the large scale makes it possible to draw more robust and generalizable inferences about patterns in partnership formation. The longitudinal data also make some causal inference possible. However, a limitation of this large-scale archival data is that it cannot provide rich, fine-grained detail about how schools form partnerships, as might be provided by case study research. This also means that while the identified measures might be considered strong because of their reliability across many organizations, some might consider the measures weak because

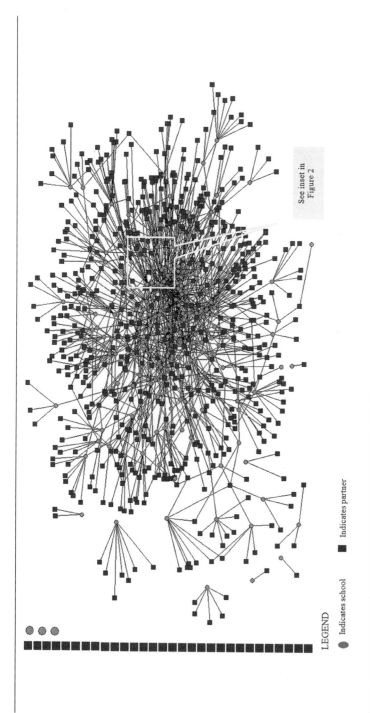

See inset in
Figure 2

LEGEND

● Indicates school   ■ Indicates partner

Figure 1. School-partner network in 1999–2000 school year. The size of isolated nodes on the left indicates that nodes represents approximately 17 other nodes. Thus, there are 514 potential partners and 48 schools not involved in partnerships in the 1999–2000 school year. This may be because the school or organization did not exist in the year or the school reported no partnerships. The sociogram was produced with UCINET's Netdraw function using multidimensional scaling (MDS), which positions nodes by geodesic distance, taking edge-length into account (Borgatti, 2002).

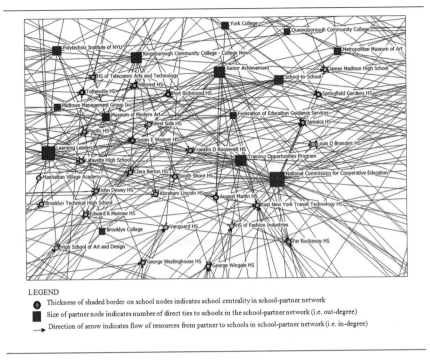

LEGEND

⬤ Thickness of shaded border on school nodes indicates school centrality in school-partner network

■ Size of partner node indicates number of direct ties to schools in the school-partner network (i.e. out-degree)

➝ Direction of arrow indicates flow of resources from partner to schools in school-partner network (i.e. in-degree)

Figure 2. **School-partner network in 1999–2000 school year (inset from Figure 1).**

more context-specific and nuanced measures might provide a more valid representation of the underlying constructs. Finally, it is important to note that consistent with the intended scope of this research, the data only indicate whether partnerships exist and do not include indicators of partnership quality or effectiveness, both of which are arguably important moderators of social capital. Examining how access to partners and partnership quality interact to affect school outcomes is an important avenue for future research.

A second limitation of the data is that the sample may not include all possible partners. Between 2% and 5% of schools did not submit an annual school report in one or more years of the study, so any partners these schools might have listed could be missing from the data set if no other school reported a relationship with the partners.[5] A nonresponse analysis for schools that did and did not list partners indicates that schools are significantly more likely to report partnerships in Period 2 ($\hat{\beta}$ = 3.86 $p \leq$ .01) and Period 3 ($\hat{\beta}$ = 3.63 $p \leq$. 01) of the study compared to Period 1. Additionally, schools in the specially designated Chancellor's district, which assembled persistently underperforming schools, are significantly less likely to report having partners ($\hat{\beta}$ = −8.45 $p \leq$ .001) compared to schools in the Manhattan Superintendency District. Thus, the partnership patterns reported should be interpreted in light of the possibility that the results may differ for the very lowest performing schools and for schools closer to the start of the study period. The results of the study should also be interpreted in light of the geographic and organizational boundary conditions for sampled schools, namely, high schools in New York City. Results may differ for elementary or middle schools, which differ in size and structure from high schools. The results may also be different for high schools in smaller, less urban locales.

Data for the measures on schools were collected from three sources: (a) I used NYC DOE annual school reports to collect data on schools' student bodies, teacher and administrative characteristics, expenditures, and performance. (b) I used New York City Department of City Planning reports to collect data on schools' community characteristics, such as the availability of health and social services in school communities. (c) I used U.S. census data to collect data on school community characteristics, such as income, educational attainment, and industry diversity in a school's census tract. For partner data, I used the U.S. census North American Industry Classification System (NAICS) to identify partners' industry as a proxy for the activities in which partners are involved and thus the resources they might provide to schools.

Measures

Dependent Variable

The outcome of interest is whether a partnership tie exists between school i and partner j in a given school year, t. I examine this outcome with three different measures. First, I examine current partnership ties, which is measured as the 0–1 categorical variable P_{ijt} indicating that a tie exists (1) or does not exist (0) in the current observation period, t. If partner j appears on school i's list of community support organizations for the current year, then P_{ijt} is set to 1; if the partner does not appear on the list, P_{ijt} is set to 0.

While the existence of a tie indicates that schools and partners have formed a relationship, some might argue that a more conceptually valid measure of formation is the initial appearance or emergence of a tie. Therefore, as a second measure of tie formation, I examine the emergence of a partnership tie, $P_{ijt=0}$, which is set to 1 if it is the first period that a tie exists between school i and organization j and 0 otherwise (e.g., Gulati & Gargiulo, 1999).[6] Third, I examine future partnership ties, P_{ijt+1}, which measures whether a tie between school i and organization j exists in the year subsequent to the current observation period ($P_{ijt+1} = 1$) or does not exist ($P_{ijt+1} = 0$).

Independent variables: School resource needs (Hypotheses 1 and 2). One set of independent variables measures schools' resource needs, which were first determined by reviewing the existing literature to identify key school inputs or resources. Specifically, three raters reviewed the 25 most relevant articles returned from a keyword search of the phrases *school inputs* or *school resources* in the largest existing educational research database. After independently listing inputs described in the articles, the raters conferred and came to consensus about six convergent categories for the identified inputs. The six categories were (a) teacher characteristics, (b) student-body endowment, (c) neighborhood characteristics, (d) nonacademic supports, (e) curriculum, and (f) facilities and noninstructional supplies.

I measured schools' resource needs related to teacher characteristics as the percent of teachers at a school who have been teaching for more than five years, as indicated in the NYC DOE Annual School Reports. I consider schools with a greater proportion of experienced teachers to have fewer resource needs related to teacher experience. I measured the endowments of the student body as the percent of students receiving free and reduced lunch, as reported in the NYC DOE Annual School Reports. This measure is taken as an indicator of socioeconomic status (SES), where I consider lower SES schools to have greater resource needs. I measured schools' neighborhood characteristics using U.S. census bureau data to determine the median family income in a school's census tract. This measure was then log-transformed to correct the non-normal distribution of the raw measure.

I measured school resource needs for nonacademic supports in three ways: (a) the log-transformed mean distance to any one of three major recreational facilities (YMCAs, JCCs, and NYC recreational centers) within five miles as identified from a listing of each facility's address;[7] (b) the log-transformed mean distance to all identified health and social service facilities in the school's NYC community district, as listed in the NYC Department of City Planning Reports; and (c) a quasi–Herfindahl-Hirshman index—a commonly accepted measure of concentration—for the level of occupational diversity in a school's census tract (Rosenbluth, 1955). I consider occupational diversity a proxy for how much exposure students at a school might have to different careers and vocational opportunities. In this case, I argue that exposure to a less diverse set of occupations indicates a school has greater resource needs in terms of exposing students to vocations and careers. The index was calculated as $\sum_{i=1}^{N} s_i^2$, where s is the percent of total workers in the census tract working in industry I, and the N industries are those identified by the U.S. Bureau of the Census. I measured characteristics of schools' curriculum as the percent of students passing the New York State regents diploma exam in English language arts.[8] I measured resources for facilities and noninstructional supplies as the percent of schools' budgets spent on building services, as reported in NYC DOE Annual School Reports.[9]

Independent variables: School-partner network features (Hypotheses 3– 6). A second set of independent variables measures the structural characteristics of the school-partner network. I constructed school-partner network measures for each of the six time periods. To construct the sociometric measures for each period, I began with a two-mode square matrix, where all schools, i, and partners, j, in a given period appear on both the rows and columns of the matrix; the cells indicate whether a relationship existed (1/ 0) between i and j in that time period. Because there is one matrix for each of the six time periods, all together, there are six sociometric matrices, which I use to construct sociometric measures for each time period.

The strength of a relationship between schools and partners is a count of the number of *prior* years school i has been partnered with organization j, $\sum_{t=1}^{6} P_{ijt-1}$. Thus, for a partnership that existed in all six periods, tie strength in Period 6 has a value of five. In addition to measuring tie strength, this variable also serves as a control for prior behavior on the outcome (i.e., partnering), which is an important model identification strategy and addresses some potential issues of selection bias (Pohl, Steiner, Eisermann, Soellner, & Cook, 2009; Steiner, Cook, Shadish, & Clark, 2010).

Preliminary analyses indicated that for tie strength equal to four years or five years, there were zero observations of $P_{ij} = 0$. In other words, if a partnership exists for more than three years, it continues to exist, which is to say, tie strength greater than three is a perfect predictor of having a partner. While this is an important substantive lesson about partnerships, it is also problematic from an empirical standpoint. As explained in comprehensive discussions on modeling categorical outcomes, "[Maximum likelihood] estimation is not possible when the dependent variable does not vary within one of the categories of the independent variable" (Long & Freese, 2003, p. 140). I address this problem in two ways. For the main analyses, I dichotomize the measure so that the strength of a partnership is indicated by whether the partnership existed in at least one year prior to the year of observation, which is coded as 1 and coded 0 otherwise. Then, because the construction of this variable introduces an artificial variance structure, I check the robustness of the results by conducting follow-up analyses using the subset of data for which ties exist for three or fewer years. These results are discussed in the findings section.

I constructed the density measure using Borgatti, Everett, and Freeman's (2002) common metric available in the social network analysis software UCINET. Density is the actual number of partner ties a school has in its local network divided by the total possible ties in the network. This is to say, density is the proportion of possible ties that have been realized in the network: $\sum_{i}^{j} l/n(n-1)/2$, where l is an existing tie between organization i and organization j, and n is the total number of organizations in the network (Wasserman & Faust, 1994).[10] Note also that some of the models also include the square of the density measure to capture the potentially nonlinear effects of density on partnership formation to indicate potentially declining marginal benefits to density.

Schools' network centrality is measured as reach centrality, meaning the path distance in direct and indirect ties between school i and all other schools and partners in the network. The measure, constructed in UCINET, is the count of paths or steps between school i and all other schools and partners and then normed by the total number of schools and partners in the network (Borgatti et al., 2002). The maximum score is achieved when all schools and partners are one step or path distance from school i. This measure is reverse scored for interpretability; thus, high values represent more central schools, and low values represent less central schools.

I calculated structural equivalence as a Jaccard similarity index (Goodall, 1966). The index measures the size of the overlap or intersection between two sets of observations and is divided by the size or union of the two sets $\frac{A \cap B}{A \cup B}$. In other words, structural equivalence, constructed in UCINET, is the count of overlapping partners between school i and all other schools given all partners in the network at a given time period (Borgatti et al., 2002).

Independent variables: Covariates. The additional variables in the analysis are controls for factors that may influence baseline propensity for partnership formation. Since proximity has been demonstrated as a reliable predictor of tie formation in other research, one covariate is the geodesic distance, in miles, between school i and partner j (Reagans, 2010; Spillane, Shirrell, & Sweet, 2017). The second covariate is the number of enrolled students as a control for school size since larger schools may not only have greater resource needs but also more staff to seek out partnerships. Because partners' activities, services, or products offered may influence partnership formation, I include covariates for partner industry. Partner industry was assigned by comparing partner names and activities to industry descriptions for the 2012 two-digit NAICS. Specifically, I constructed five dummy variables, one for each of the four most frequent industries and one for all other industries (see Table 1 in the Results section for the distribution of industries). All analyses are conducted with respect to the educational services industry.

Analysis

Data Structure

In the data set for the analysis, the observations are school-partner pairs, ij, or partnerships across six time periods, where the longitudinal nature of the data is accommodated by stacking the observations for each year on the rows. Thus, each school, i, repeats on the row t times, where t is the number of years the school appears in the data; each school also repeats on the rows n times, where n is the number of partner organizations in a given year, t. So, for example, if a school exists for five years in the data and there are 100 potential partners each year, then the school would repeat on the rows 500 times. Likewise, because the observations are school-partner pairs, each partner, j, repeats on the rows m times, where m is the number of schools and repeats t times, where t is the number years the partner appears in the data set. Thus, the rows are repeated observations of school-partner pairs, ij, or partnerships. The variables of interest for each partnership appear on the columns of the data matrix. This data structure is identical to the structure of data in social network studies in which the unit of analysis is the tie, or relationship, between i and j rather than the individual actor i or j (Wasserman & Faust, 1994).[11]

Including all possible 1,390,068 resulting observations in the data set is an approach taken in some other studies of tie formation (Gulati, 1995). However, because the great majority of school-partner pairs do not have a partnership ($P_{ijt} = 0$), including all possible observations introduces a preponderance of zeros into the data set; this inflates standard errors, making the results and their statistical significance difficult to interpret (Sorenson & Stuart, 2001). In previous studies, researchers have addressed this problem by randomly sampling a subset of the observations that are equal to zero (Mitsuhashi & Greve, 2009; Powell, White, Koput, & Owen-Smith, 2005). I follow the same random sampling approach.

I include all realized partnerships ($P_{ijt} = 1$) in the data set. Then, for each realized partnership, I randomly sample a fixed number of the observations where a partnership is unrealized ($P_{ijt} = 0$) for a given school-partner pair (Mitsuhashi & Greve, 2009).[12] I selected 7 as the fixed number because it is the mean number of partners for schools in the study. Thus, the data matrix used to estimate the models is a 72,009 by 20 matrix of sampled partnership observations on the rows and variables for school, partner, and network characteristics on the columns.[13]

Model Estimation

The previously described data have a nested structure in which partners $j-z$ are nested in a given school, i. However, partners are not fully nested in schools because partner j may appear as a realized or unrealized partnership for more than one school, which means that partners are cross-classified by schools (Raudenbush & Bryk, 2002). Additionally, there are repeated observations of schools over the six time periods, it, and repeated observations of partners over the six time periods, jt. Thus, the data have a two-level, cross-classified structure.

As specified in more detail in the following equation, the Level 1 observations are the unique observations for each school-partner pair, ijt; this includes the dependent variable, tie strength, and distance. The Level 2 observations include the unique observations for schools, it, including schools' resource needs, network structure, and size. The Level 2 observations also include the unique observations for partners, jt, namely, partner industry. Because the dependent variable is categorical—the existence of a partnership (0/1)—I formulated a logistic cross-classified model using xtmelogit in Stata 13.0 (Rabe-Hesketh & Skrondal, 2008): The mixed-model notation for the conceptual form is:

$$\text{logitPr}\left(P_{ij[t]}=1 \mid X_{ijt}W_{it}Z_{jt}\right)=\theta_{000}+\beta_{00}+\gamma_{00}+\pi_1(\text{tie strength})_{ijt}+\pi_2(\text{distance})_{ijt}$$
$$+\beta_{1-8}(\text{school resource needs})_{it}+\beta_9(\text{school size})_{it}$$
$$+\beta_{10-12}(\text{school network features})_{it}$$
$$+\gamma_{1-4}(\text{partner industry})_{jt}+r_{it}+r_{jt}+e_{ijt}$$

where the Level 1 components are:

$P_{ij[t]}$, the probability that a partnership exists between school i and organization j at one of three time points, [t]: the current observation period t; the subsequent observation period, $t + 1$; and the observation period in which the tie first emerged, $t = 0$;

θ_{000}, the overall model intercept when all explanatory variables are set to zero;

π_{pijt}, the effects for X_{ijt}, the variables for the unique observation of school i and partner j at time t, namely, tie strength and geodesic distance;

e_{ijt}, the random variance component for the unique observation of school i and partner j at time t;

and where the Level 2 components are:

β_{pit}, the effects for W_{it}, the vector of variables for the unique observations of school i at time t, including the main effect for school (β_{00}), the eight measures for school resource needs, and the measure for school size;

γ_{pjt}, the effects for Z_{jt}, the vector of variables for the unique observations of partner j at time t, including the main effect for partner (γ_{00}) and the four indicators for partner industry;

r_{it} and r_{jt}, the random variance components for schools i and partners j, including cell-specific random effects for the interaction of school i and partner j.

There are two ways this modeling strategy addresses the nonindependence of observations, meaning the repeated observations of partners by schools as well as repeated observations of schools and partners over time.[14] First, the model allows for random intercepts for schools and partners across time periods (i.e., because each school and partner may have unique main effect across the six periods). Second, the model estimates the random variance components for schools and partners across time periods (i.e., because of the remaining deviation each school and partner observation may have from average school and partner effects across time periods). It is important to note that while the modeling strategy does not estimate changes in the overall network structure, as might be done with an exponential random graph model (ERGM), the modeling strategy does take into account the formation of partnerships over time. This is accomplished by predicting the probability of a partnership given potential differences across time in both school characteristics and network features. I also examine the formation of partnerships over time by testing the effects of the variables of interest on future existence of partnerships, P_{ijt+1}, and on the first-time existence or emergence of partnerships, $P_{ijt=0}$.

Results

In the current work, I am interested in schools' access to social capital given their partner ties. First, it is interesting to note that the number of organizations involved in partnerships with schools increased by 40% over the study period, with the most dramatic increase in the 2001–2002 school year. This was the first year of the No Child Left Behind Act, which may have encouraged both increased demand for and supply of organizations providing resources to schools. The descriptive statistics for partner industry in Table 1 illustrate that the majority of organizations partnering with schools are, as one would expect, in the educational service industry (30.64%). These partners are organizations such as colleges and universities, including New York University and Columbia University Teachers College, as well as organizations providing academic services, including other schools, the East Harlem Tutorial, Facing History and Ourselves, and the Princeton Review. In addition to these more expected educational services partnerships, a large proportion of partners are organizations that provide "other kinds of services" (21%). This includes churches, foundations, local business development groups, and community organizations, such as El Puente and the Kiwanis Club. Organizations providing arts, entertainment, and recreation, such as the Mark Morris Dance Company, the Village Vanguard Jazz Orchestra, Chelsea Piers, and the Bronx Zoo, comprise the smallest proportion of partner organizations (11.25%).

The characteristics of schools in the study are also illustrated in Table 1. While there is some variation across years, on average, 55.62% of teachers working at the schools have five or more years of teaching experience, and there is an average of 1,578 students enrolled at the schools, but with wide variation across schools (SD = 1,242.42). Of enrolled students, the measure of student SES indicates that on average, 58.02% received free or reduced-price lunch and 45.03% of students received a passing score on the statewide English regents exam. In contrast to costs directly related to classroom instruction, schools spent an average of 10.8% of their budgets on school facilities and noninstructional supplies. The neighborhood characteristics of schools in the study, where neighborhood is proxied by census tract, indicate that median family income is $38,019 (i.e., the base 10 antilog of the mean for median family income: $10^{4.58}$). Average occupational diversity, given the variety of occupations and employed workers in the census tract, is 36%. Finally,

Table 1
Descriptive Statistics

	Mean N (Schools)	Mean N (Partners)	Mean	SD	Minimum	Maximum	1	2	3	4	5	6	7	8	9	10	11	12	13	14
1. Percentage teachers with 5+ years	189.33	1,098	55.62	15.22	4.8	100	1													
2. Percentage receiving free or reduced lunch	189.33	1,098	58.02	24.49	2.9	100	-0.059***	1												
3. Percentage passing English Regents exam	189.33	1,098	45.03	22.73	0	100	0.019***	0.079***	1											
4. Percentage budget spent on building	189.33	1,098	10.80	6.8	0.3	57	-0.001	-0.016***	-0.088***	1										
5. School enrollment	189.33	1,098	1,577.83	1242.42	4	4,769	-0.189***	0.009**	-0.03***	0.016***	1									
6. Median family income (log)	189.33	1,098	4.58	0.59	0	5.3	0	-0.001	0.002	-0.007	-0.001	1								
7. Mean distance to recreational facilities	189.33	1,098	1.35	0.08	1.13	1.54	-0.001	0.003	0.001	-0.002	0.002	-0.116***	1							
8. Mean distance to health facilities	189.33	1,098	1.36	0.07	1.13	1.59	0.001	0	0.001	-0.004	0	0.151***	0.491***	1						
9. Occupational diversity	189.33	1,098	0.36	0.17	0.16	0.87	0.003	-0.001	-0.001	0.003	0.001	-0.185***	0.117***	0.046***	1					
10. School centrality	189.33	1,098	0.52	0.08	0.18	0.69	-0.039***	0.114***	0.172***	-0.253***	-0.01**	-0.023***	0.02***	-0.001	0.014***	1				
11. School density	189.33	1,098	50.23	19.21	0	100	0.108***	-0.074***	-0.114***	0.123***	0.061***	-0.003	0.005	0.001	0.006	-0.189***	1			
12. School density squared	189.33	1,098	2,892.39	2056.12	0	10,000	0.088***	-0.085***	-0.132***	0.131***	0.052***	-0.001	0.002	0	0.004	-0.273***	0.954***	1		
13. Structural equivalence	189.33	1,098	0.03	0.02	0.01	0.33	0.005	-0.017***	-0.081***	0.129***	-0.032***	-0.005	-0.002	-0.003	0.001	-0.419***	-0.221***	-0.183***	1	
14. Geodistance	189.33	1,098	2.17	0.96	0	3.92	-0.001	0.003	0.002		0.005	0	0	0	0	-0.001	0.002	0.002	-0.005	1
15. Previous tie†	189.33	1,098	0.09	—	—	—	—	—	—	—	—	—	—	—	—	—	—	—	—	—
16. Partnership exists[a]	189.33	1,098	0.12	—	—	—	—	—	—	—	—	—	—	—	—	—	—	—	—	—
17. Partnership emerges[a]	189.33	1,098	0.03	—	—	—	—	—	—	—	—	—	—	—	—	—	—	—	—	—
18. Educational services	189.33	1,098	0.30	—	—	—	—	—	—	—	—	—	—	—	—	—	—	—	—	—
19. Health care and social assistance	189.33	1,098	0.17	—	—	—	—	—	—	—	—	—	—	—	—	—	—	—	—	—
20. Arts, entertainment, and recreation	189.33	1,098	0.11	—	—	—	—	—	—	—	—	—	—	—	—	—	—	—	—	—
21. Other services	189.33	1,098	0.21	—	—	—	—	—	—	—	—	—	—	—	—	—	—	—	—	—
22. All other industries	189.33	1,098	0.21	—	—	—	—	—	—	—	—	—	—	—	—	—	—	—	—	—

Note. Correlations are constructed from mean deviation of the measures to minimize the effects of autocorrelation from repeated observations; all other statistics use raw measures.

[a]Categorical variable means indicate frequency.

**$p < .01$. ***$p < .001$.

the average school in the study is 1.35 miles away from the closest YMCA, JCC, or NYC department of recreation facility. The average school is 1.36 miles away from the nearest health or social service facility.

In the current work, I argued that the aforementioned school characteristics were an indicator of schools' resource needs. Hypotheses 1 posited that the probability of a partnership between schools and other organizations increased with the level of schools' resource needs. This hypothesis is tested in Model 1 of Table 2, which presents the logit coefficients for the results. The results of Model 1 indicate that only a school's need for facilities and noninstructional supplies is associated with the likelihood of a partnership. One might expect that schools spending a greater proportion of their budgets on facilities and noninstructional supplies would have a greater need for partnerships and thus be more likely to partner to reallocate funds to instruction. On the contrary, the results suggest schools that arguably have greater needs for facilities and noninstructional supplies are less likely to have partners ($\hat{\beta} = -.0056$; $p \leq .05$). What these results mean for a real school can be better understood with an example of how the odds of a partnership change for schools with specific characteristics. Consider, for instance, a school spending 10% more than another school on its budget for facilities. If the two schools are the same in all other respects, then for the school spending 10% more on its facilities budget, the odds of a partnership decrease by approximately 5.45%.[15]

Another way to examine how schools' resource needs are related to partnering is to examine the effects of schools' neighborhood characteristics, which reflect schools' needs to provide students with nonacademic supports. Model 2 in Table 2 shows that if a school is one mile closer to a YMCA, JCC, or NYC Department of Recreation facility, this is associated with a 186.1% significant increase in the odds of a partnership ($\hat{\beta} = 1.015$; $p \leq .001$). Another nonacademic support schools may need to provide is exposure to careers and vocations. Schools in neighborhoods with greater occupational diversity might enroll students with greater prior exposure to a diversity of careers and vocations. Thus, these schools may have fewer resource needs with respect to exposing students to different occupations and so be less likely to have certain partnerships. However, the results suggest that a 1% increase in occupational diversity is associated with a 93.4% increase in the odds of a partnership by ($\hat{\beta} = 0.6966$; $p \leq .001$). Overall, the results in Model 1 and Model 2 for the effects of schools' resource needs on partnerships seem to provide limited support for Hypothesis 1.

Hypothesis 2 argued that the structural features of the school-partner network have a greater effect on the probability of a partnership between schools and other organizations than the effect of schools' resource needs. This hypothesis is tested in Model 3 in Table 2. Note first that once the features of the school-partner network are accounted for, all four school-specific characteristics become significant. This suggests that some of the

Table 2
Logit Coefficients for Multilevel Cross-Classified Logistic Regression of School, Partner, and Network Characteristics on Partnership Formation

	Model 1 (P_{ijt}) β (SE)	Model 2 (P_{ijt}) β (SE)	Model 3 (P_{ijt}) β (SE)	Model 4 ($P_{ijt\sim o}$) β (SE)	Model 5 (P_{ijt+1}) β (SE)
Percentage teachers with 5+ years experience	0.0007 (0.001)	0.0017 (0.001)	0.0066** (0.002)	0.0064** (0.002)	0.0070 (0.004)
Percentage students receiving free/reduced lunch	−0.0010 (0.001)	−0.0009 (0.001)	−0.0049*** (0.001)	−0.0048** (0.001)	−0.0095*** (0.003)
Percentage students passing English regents exam	−0.0009 (0.001)	−0.0005 (0.001)	−0.0086*** (0.001)	−0.0094*** (0.002)	−0.0095*** (0.003)
Percentage school budget spent on building expenses	−0.0056* (0.003)	−0.0036 (0.002)	0.0199*** (0.004)	0.0228*** (0.005)	0.0186* (0.008)
Number of enrolled students	0.0000 (0.000)	0.0000 (0.000)	0.0000 (0.000)	0.0001 (0.000)	0.0000 (0.000)
Median family income in neighborhood (log)	—	−0.0320 (0.029)	0.0227 (0.053)	0.0184 (0.056)	0.0237 (0.103)
Mean distance to recreational facilities	—	1.0511*** (0.233)	0.0891 (0.437)	−0.2727 (0.455)	−1.4755 (0.833)
Mean distance to health/social service facilities	—	−0.2543 (0.284)	0.1156 (0.536)	0.1646 (0.557)	0.7405 (0.980)
Occupational diversity in neighborhood	—	0.6596*** (0.109)	0.5553** (0.202)	0.4552* (0.210)	−0.1248 (0.381)
School centrality in school-partner network	—	—	8.4321*** (0.631)	9.2729*** (0.655)	12.8352*** (1.016)
Strength of school-partner relationship	—	—	11.1126*** (0.227)	—	8.5773*** (0.370)
Density of school's partner network	—	—	0.0242*** (0.005)	0.0265*** (0.005)	0.0239** (0.009)
Density of school's partner network (squared)	—	—	−0.0002*** (0.000)	−0.0002*** (0.000)	−0.0001 (0.000)
School's equivalence in school-partner network	—	—	−6.7710*** (1.636)	−7.0763*** (1.652)	−4.4555 (3.298)
Distance (in miles) between school and partner	−0.9271*** (0.021)	−0.9275*** (0.021)	−0.8217*** (0.036)	−0.6990*** (0.034)	−0.6740*** (0.052)
Health care and social assistance industry	−0.4935*** (0.055)	−0.4943*** (0.055)	−0.5147*** (0.102)	−0.4325*** (0.099)	−0.8058*** (0.139)
Arts, entertainment, and recreation industry	−0.6696*** (0.065)	−0.6689*** (0.065)	−0.5333*** (0.116)	−0.4586*** (0.114)	−0.7673*** (0.164)
Other service industries	−0.6484*** (0.054)	−0.6453*** (0.054)	−0.5928*** (0.098)	−0.5173*** (0.096)	−0.8583*** (0.134)
All other industries	−0.4524*** (0.054)	−0.4496*** (0.054)	−0.4847*** (0.098)	−0.3901*** (0.096)	−0.6916*** (0.134)
Constant	−0.0718 (0.119)	−1.2716** (0.434)	0.6162 (0.857)	1.0518 (0.893)	7.5618*** (1.614)
Random effects (variance)					
School	0.182	0.130	0.226	0.259	0.475
Partner (by period)	0.983	0.986	1.526	1.451	1.243
Log likelihood	−23,820.999	−23,790.662	−8,428.471	−8,513.926	−2,726.116
Observations	72,009.000	72,009.000	71,276.000	71,276.000	9,647.000

Note. Log likelihood ratio test comparing Model 2 and Model 1: $\chi^2(14) = 58.68$; $p < .001$. Log likelihood ratio test comparing Model 3 and Model 2: $\chi^2(19) = 30,724.38$; $p < .001$.

*$p < .05$. **$p < .01$. ***$p < .001$.

variation in school characteristics is associated with variation in the structure of the school-partner network and that the apparent parameter instability in Models 1 and 2 resulted from the bias of omitting important network variables (i.e., Hansen, 1992). Once variation in the school-partner network structure is controlled, the unique effect of school-specific characteristics becomes more apparent. Indeed, as reported in Table 2, the log-likelihood ratio test comparing Models 2 and 3 indicates that Model 3 has greater explanatory power than Model 2.

While having a high proportion of disadvantaged students suggests that schools would have greater resource needs and thus would be more likely to have partnerships, Model 3 indicates that a school having a larger proportion of students receiving free and reduced lunch is associated with being less likely to have partnerships ($\hat{\beta}$ = −0.0049; $p \leq .001$). This effect means, for example, that a school having 10% more low SES students than an otherwise similar school would decrease its odds of having a partnership by 4.78%. In contrast, a school having 10% more teachers with five or more years of experience compared to an otherwise similar school is associated with 6.82% increase in the odds of a having a partnership ($\hat{\beta}$ = 0.0066; $p \leq .001$). This result is inconsistent with Hypothesis 1, which asserted that schools with more experienced teachers would have less need of partnerships.

More consistent with Hypothesis 1 is the result for schools with fewer curriculum needs. The results indicate that a school having 10% more students performing well on the English regents exam is associated with an 8.24% decrease in the odds of having a partnership compared to similar schools ($\hat{\beta}$ = −0.0086; $p \leq .001$). The positive and significant effects for the percent of the school budget spent on facilities and noninstructional supplies in Model 3 also are consistent with Hypothesis 1 ($\hat{\beta}$ = 0.0199; $p \leq .001$). For example, schools that are spending 10% more of their budgets on facilities are more budget constrained than similar schools and thus are in greater need of partnerships. The results from Model 3 suggest that this level of spending significantly increases the school's odds of having a partnership by 22.02%. So, in contrast to the conclusions drawn from Model 1, the results for Model 3 provide partial support for Hypothesis 1 and strong support for Hypothesis 2.

A comparison of school and neighborhood characteristics with school-partner network features in Model 3 reveals that the effects of four of the five network characteristics—school centrality, strength of relationship, density, and equivalence—are greater than the effects for all school or neighborhood characteristics, excluding occupational diversity. The network feature with the largest effect on the probability of a partnership is the strength of the partnership, measured as an indicator variable for whether a school has had a previous relationship with an organization in at least one prior year ($\hat{\beta}$ = 11.1326; $p \leq .001$). This significant effect means that all else being equal—in other words, among schools with the same resource needs, with partners in the same industry, and with the same network density, centrality, and structural equivalence—schools that have previously partnered with an organization are much more likely to have a partner compared to schools that have had no previous relationship with a partner.

Indeed, as previewed in the methods section, schools having had a partner at least three years are essentially guaranteed to have the partner in subsequent years. Given this, I conducted a follow-up analysis of the subgroup of schools that had partners for three years or less and examined the effects for total tie duration (i.e., 0, 1, 2, 3 years). The results of the follow-up analysis support the main results. Namely, the odds of having a partnership are almost 10,000 times greater for each additional year of having a tie with a partner, all else being equal ($\hat{\beta}$ = 9.1838; $p \leq$ .01). Thus, based on the results of the main analyses and follow-up analyses, there is strong support for Hypothesis 3, which argued that the probability of a partnership between schools and other organizations increases with the strength of their relationship.

Still, because having a previous relationship has such a large effect on the existence of a partnership, one might ask why partner ties emerge in the first place. This question can be partially answered by examining what predicts a partnership in its initial year ($P_{ijt=0}$ = 1). The results of this analysis are presented in Model 4. Consistent with the size and direction of effects in Model 3, the results of Model 4 indicate that the odds of partnership emergence increase with the percentage of experienced teachers and the percentage of spending on facilities and noninstructional supplies. The odds of partnership emergence decrease with the percentage of students receiving free and reduced lunch and with the percentage of students passing the English regents exam. Still, as in Model 3, the size of the effects in Model 4 indicates that structural features of the school-partner network have a much greater effect on partnership emergence than almost all school resource needs.

Hypothesis 4 asserted that the probability of a partnership increases with a school's centrality in the school-partner network because increased centrality would make it easier for schools to gain access to partners. The results of Model 3 indicate that school centrality in the school-partner network has a large, positive, significant effect on partnership formation. This means that when a school is in a network position allowing it to reach partners in one fewer steps or paths—in other words, through one less set of intermediaries—this is associated with the odds of partnership being more than 4,637 times greater than otherwise similar schools that are less central ($\hat{\beta}$ = 8.4321; $p \leq$ .001). Thus, there is strong support for Hypothesis 4.

One network feature that makes it less likely for schools to either have or initially form partnerships is structural equivalence. As seen in Model 3, schools that share many partners in common with other schools are less likely to have partnerships ($\hat{\beta}$ = −6.7710; $p \leq$ .001). So, each additional partner a school shares with another school is associated with a 99.89% decrease in the odds of having a partner. Likewise, the results of Model 4 indicate that each additional partner a school shares with another school is associated with a 99.92% decrease in the odds that a partnership will initially emerge ($\hat{\beta}$ = −.0763; $p \leq$ .001). These results provide strong support for Hypothesis 5.

Hypothesis 6a argued that the probability of partnership increases with the density of the school-partner network. It was also argued in Hypothesis 6b that the probability of a partnership between schools and other organizations decreases with the *increasing* density of the school-partner network because being embedded in an overly dense network might dilute the time and attention needed to solicit and manage these relationships. The results in Models 3 and 4 provide support for both Hypotheses 6a and 6b. In Model 3, the coefficient for network density is positive and significant ($\hat{\beta}$ = .0242; $p \leq$ .001) and suggests that a 10% increase in the density or relative proportion of network ties realized by a school significantly increases the odds of partnering by 27.13%. Yet, there is a negative coefficient for the squared measure for density ($\hat{\beta}$ = −0.0002; $p \leq$ .001), which captures the diminishing effects of density. This means that after a certain point, each additional 10% increase in density decreases the odds of partnering by .20%. In other words, there is a slight cost to being in an overly dense network. The results in Model 4 confirm this pattern for the initial emergence of partnerships; schools in dense networks are more likely to have partnerships emerge ($\hat{\beta}$ = .0265; $p \leq$ .001), but this positive effect on emergence diminishes the more dense the network becomes ($\hat{\beta}$ = −0.0002; $p \leq$ .001).

One important final question to ask about the results is whether they appropriately capture the direction of causation in patterns of partnership formation. Consider, for example, that density in the school-partner network may make a school more likely to have a partnership. Alternatively, some set of unobserved features that makes schools more likely to have partnerships might be responsible for schools being embedded in more dense networks in the first place. One way to disentangle the direction of causality is to examine how school resource needs and network features are associated with *future* partnerships (P_{ijt+1}). Model 5 in Table 2 presents the results of this analysis.[16]

The results of Model 5 are largely consistent with the results of Model 3 and Model 4 in terms of the effects of school-partner network features relative to school resource needs. However, the results of Model 5 show that the occupational diversity of schools' neighborhoods has no effect on future partnerships; the percentage of teachers with five or more years of experience has only marginally significant effects ($\hat{\beta}$ = 0.007; $p \leq$ .1). Model 5 also shows that while future partnerships—like the existence and emergence of partnerships—are positively affected by network centrality, there are no significant effects for the number of overlapping partnerships shared with other schools (i.e., structural equivalence). Taken together, the results of Model 5 raise important questions about how having experienced teachers and having to compete with other schools affects partnership formation. I examine these questions and the other findings in more detail in the discussion section.

Discussion

High Needs High Schools and Access to Social Capital

The main question in the current research has been how school social capital is distributed among New York City high schools given their partnerships with other organizations. The results suggest that social capital is unequally distributed because some schools are less likely to have partnerships than other schools. Differences in partnership formation might be appropriate if schools with the least resource needs were least likely to have partnerships. However, this is not always the case. Schools with a greater proportion of lower income students arguably have greater needs. Yet, in this study, these schools are less likely to have partnerships compared to schools with wealthier students. In contrast, schools with arguably fewer resource needs, such as schools with more experienced teachers and schools in neighborhoods that expose students to more diverse occupations, are more likely to have partnerships.

One explanation for schools with fewer needs being more likely to have partnerships is that these schools have better opportunities for forming partnerships. For example, in their study of schools' social capital, Holme and Rangel (2012) suggest that schools benefit from being located in particular geographic areas. The current work supports the benefits of geographic location for schools' social capital since schools in neighborhoods with greater occupational diversity are more likely to have partnerships. Holme and Rangel also demonstrate that stability among the administrators and teachers results in staff with more experience, which generates greater social capital—a finding that is also consistent with the current work.

Specifically, schools with more experienced teachers are more likely to form partnerships; one conclusion to be drawn is that teachers who have been teaching longer have more relationships with a diversity of actors in the field and more expertise for reaching out to these actors. It is important to note, however, that the marginally significant effect for teacher experience on *future* partnerships may be evidence that teachers with greater experience do not necessarily help schools obtain more partnerships. Instead, schools that are more likely to have partnerships may be the same schools that also attract more experienced teachers. Alternatively, these results might also indicate that schools with existing partnerships have already reaped the benefits of teacher experience. This same logic may explain the nonsignificant effects of neighborhood occupational diversity on future partnerships.

School-Partner Network Structure and Access to Social Capital

While potential disparities in schools' access to partnerships given their resource needs may be striking, what may be more striking is that such effects are outweighed by effects for school-partner network structure. Ultimately, the network feature with the largest positive effect on a school having a partnership is whether the school has partnered with an organization in the past (i.e., Ouellette & Wood, 1998). A similar pattern holds for the effects of school centrality and density. Schools that are easily reached by potential partners or have a dense network of partner ties are more likely to have partnerships.

One of the largest negative effects on schools partnering with other organizations is the extent to which schools share many partners in common with other schools and so are effectively competing for the same sets of partners (Burt, 1992). In such a competition, some schools win and gain access to much needed resources. Yet, the current findings suggest that this kind of competition leads, on average, to schools losing out. And while these effects for competition do not hold for the future likelihood of partnerships, this might be expected given the possible tournament model underlying schools' competition for partners. This is to say that schools with more established partnerships are most likely the winners of previous rounds of competition and hold on to those partners, which is also suggested by the large positive effects of partnership strength in this study.

One limitation of the current work is that the strength of a partnership is the number of prior years a partnership has existed. While this measure captures some dimensions of partnership strength (i.e., frequency of interactions, which is a conventional measure of tie strength in the network literature), one might argue that a more valid measure would take into account the actual activities occurring in a partnership. For example, a partner might appear on the annual school report for multiple years but in fact provide few resources to a school. Meanwhile, a partner appearing for only one year may be deeply engaged with the work of the school, such as providing ongoing training for teachers or substantive academic and nonacademic support for students. Thus, the latter partnership might be said to be stronger even though it is shorter in duration. The fact that this study does not identify actual partnership activities also limits conclusions that can be drawn about schools' social capital. Using the existence of ties between schools and partners to measure access to partner resources and thus to social capital assumes that schools that have partner ties also have more access to resources than schools without ties. Because partnership activities may moderate the resources a school receives through partnership ties, it is not possible to draw conclusions from the current work about exactly how much social capital results from schools' partner ties—only how much access results.

The current findings also do not reveal the mechanisms by which schools form partnerships. For example, one important mechanism for partnership formation may be how much initiative principals take in soliciting partnerships and what kind of expertise they have for doing so (Sanders, 2014). I cannot directly examine this mechanism in the current study. Still, because the annual school reports list each principal's name, it is possible to construct an indicator variable for principal turnover to test whether new principals, who arguably may be more motivated to solicit partners, or continuing principals, who arguably may have more expertise for soliciting partners, have a greater effect on partnership formation.

If the listed name for the principal is the same from $t = n$ to $t = n + 1$, I set the turnover variable to 0; if the listed name is different from $t = n$ to $t = n + 1$, then I set the variable to 1. The previous results of Model 3 with the principal turnover variable included indicate that while the pattern of results for all other parameters is the same, a school having a new principal is associated with a 27.33% increase in the odds of partnership ($\hat{\beta} = .2416; p \leq .01$). The odds of a new partnership emerging (i.e. Model 4) increase 33.24% with a new principal ($\hat{\beta} = .2870; p \leq .001$). Having a new principal is one of the largest effects for school characteristics on partnership formation and suggests that one mechanism for partnership formation may be principal initiative. If so, this is consistent with research that describes how outreach by school-based personnel, including the principal, is critical for partnerships (Auerbach, 2012; Sanders, 2014). Having a new principal does not have a significant effect on future partnership. Thus, while having a motivated new principal may initially mitigate some disadvantages of network structure, there may be few additional benefits once initial benefits are reaped.

Lessons for Future Research, Policy, and Practice

Based on the current findings, future research interested in school social capital would benefit from more fine-grained data not only on the mechanisms of partnership formation, such as the role school staff play, but also on the partnering strategies used by different schools. For example, it might be particularly instructive to conduct qualitative research examining whether there are differences in the way schools with different resource needs and in different network positions solicit and secure partnerships. It might also be instructive to learn whether certain strategies can increase schools' probability of partnering even if they are otherwise disadvantaged. For example, perhaps the negative effects of competition among structurally equivalent schools could be lessened if schools attempted to partner with a smaller, more targeted subset of organizations with resource offerings that best matched schools' resource needs. A large-scale study examining this question could also examine whether different partnering strategies lead to more effective partnerships, which would be especially instructive since I do not examine partnership effectiveness in the current research.

The findings in the current research have important implications for policy and practice. One lesson is that simply encouraging schools to seek partnerships will not necessarily have the intended effect of helping schools gain access to resources. In fact, the underlying features of school-partner networks suggest that existing inequalities between schools may persist and perhaps deepen unless some schools are provided special support in the partnership formation process. Consider, for example, that some states and districts have begun providing schools with a vetted list of potential partners with the aim of encouraging effective partnerships. While this is a step in the right direction, the current work suggests this step may not be enough.

Many schools may select appropriate partners—from a vetted list, from local organizations, or from a larger pool—by relying on advice from informal contacts, including teachers, parents, colleagues at other schools, or existing partner liaisons. Schools that have well-connected teachers and parents, many good relationships with colleagues at other schools, or an extensive set of supportive liaisons will have more information and opportunities for securing partners. So, when advocating partnerships as a solution to school resource needs, state and district officials will need to provide special support to the neediest schools.

One way to identify such schools would be to map schools' positions in the current school-partner network or simply identify schools with the fewest partners, as a proxy for structural disadvantage. One way to help these schools form partnerships would be to provide personnel, training, or funding for partner outreach (Auerbach, 2012; Sanders, 2014). Likewise, districts might organize venues in which representatives from disadvantaged schools could meet with colleagues from schools that already have established partnerships. In this case, the goal would not only be for disadvantaged schools to receive advice about securing partnerships but to ultimately extend and strengthen their schools' network relationships—both with other schools and, indirectly, with potential partners. To accomplish this goal, it will be especially important to structure interactions in such venues so that competition that might arise between schools seeking partnerships is minimized.

Conclusion

Existing research on social capital in school contexts mainly focuses on students' relationships or relationships among teachers and administrators inside schools and districts (Bridwell-Mitchell & Cooc, 2016; Dika & Singh, 2002; Holme & Rangel, 2012; Leana & Pil, 2006; Spillane, Kim, & Frank, 2012). The current work extends existing understanding about social capital in schools by illuminating the dynamics of external social capital. And in contrast to a focus on external ties to actors, such as parents, principals, or district administrators, the current work extends existing research by examining schools' ties to a diversity of other actors in the organizational field (Bridwell-Mitchell & Lant, 2014; Finnigan & Daly, 2010; Hite et al., 2005; Wohlstetter, Malloy, Chau, & Polhemus, 2003).

The main conclusion to be drawn from the current work is that schools that are already well endowed in terms of partnership opportunities are most likely to have partnerships and schools that are already disadvantaged are least likely to have partnerships. Sociologist Robert Merton referred to this type of rich-get-richer phenomenon as the Matthew effect, referring to the Matthew 25:29 bible verse: "For unto every one that hath shall be given, and he shall have abundance: but from him that hath not shall be taken even that which he hath" (Merton, 1968). Iconic jazz songstress Billy Holiday popularized the same phenomenon with the memorable refrain, "Them that's got shall have; them that's not shall lose" (Herzog & Holiday, 1942). More recently, Brian Arthur (1990) has noted that these kinds of increasing returns from early investment manifest in many sectors across the economy, not only education. One important implication of these findings is that educational inequalities among students may be further institutionalized in inequalities among schools and their access to school social capital. Thus, while policymakers may advocate partnerships as a way to provide additional resources to schools and potentially equalize existing disparities in educational opportunities, this admirable goal may often be unrealized.

Notes

This work was supported by a National Science Foundation grant for the study of human and social dynamics (SES-0433280). I gratefully acknowledge this support, the research assistance of Nicholas Vockerodt, and the feedback of colleagues who provided thoughtful comments on earlier drafts of this manuscript, including Alan Daly and Jim Spillane. I am solely responsible for any errors.

[1]In addition to their antecedents and consequences, another important question to be asked about school partnerships is why they end (i.e., tie dissolution). While being an important topic and one addressed in other studies (i.e., Baker, Faulkner, & Fisher, 1998; Polidoro, Ahuja, & Mitchell, 2011), examining tie dissolution is outside the scope of the current research.

[2]The quality or nature of schools' relationships with other organizations has been a source of debate about what kind of arrangements should be specifically termed *partnerships* (Galaskiewicz, 1985; Oliver, 1990). In the current work, I use the term *partnership* in the broadest sense to refer to a variety of interorganizational arrangements through which schools might receive resources from other organizations whether this is through reciprocal exchange, one-way procurement, or cooperative agreements to jointly acquire new resources. However, the distinctions between these different types of arrangements are an important area of investigation in other types of research (e.g., Coburn & Stein, 2010).

[3]Supplementary Table S1 in the online version of the journal provides an overview of the sociometric constructs.

[4]Supplementary Table S2 in the online version of the journal lists some of the major schools and partners in the 1999–2000 school-partner network, given measures for centrality, density, and structural equivalence.

[5]It is also important to note that another reason the sample does not include all possible partner organizations is because schools can conceivably partner with any organization in the New York City metro area, the United States, or even the world. Indeed, one school listed a partnership with a university in Puerto Rico. This means the list of all possible partner organizations could conceivably include every organization in New York City or even the world. However, for pragmatic and analytical purposes, the sample includes only organizations listed as having a partnership with at least one school during the study period. All other organizations are considered outside the specified boundary of the network (cf. Laumann, Marsden, & Prensky, 1983). The sociometric measures and the analyses do not account for possible ties outside the network boundary.

[6]It is not possible to determine when partnerships that exit in the 1999-2000 school year first emerged. So, if a partnership exists in this period, I assume it is the period of emergence, $P_{ijt=1}=1$. In other words, in Period 1, $P_{ijt=0}$ is set to 0 only for partnerships that do not yet exist in1999–2000. This is an imperfect measure, which is why I also employ two alternative measures of tie formation. A sensitivity analysis for results using only observations from Periods 2 through 6 shows a pattern of results that are substantively the same as the results for Periods 1 through 6 except that teacher quality, budgetary spending, and occupational diversity are not significant; the effects for network structure and all other variables are unchanged.

[7]I selected the 5-mile cutoff based on an estimate of the distance/time an average school might regularly bus students for recreational activities during the school day. I conducted sensitivity analyses with 1-mile and 10-mile cutoffs but these had no significant effects, which I attribute to there being too few facilities within 1 mile and so many within 10 miles that there was little variation by school. Empirically, 5 miles captures most of the accessible recreational facilities for schools since the maximum distance to facilities is 1.54 miles (see Table 1). Five miles is also conveniently the cut-point between the 1-mile and 10-mile poles.

[8]The percentage of students passing the New York State regents diploma exam in mathematics was also available as a measure. Preliminary analyses indicated that the mathematics and English language arts measures were highly correlated and had the same predictive effects in the models. Thus, only one of the measures was needed in the model. Rather than take the mean, which would make direct interpretation of the coefficients difficult, I selected the English language arts over the mathematics measure by flipping a coin.

[9]I explored a factor-analytic solution for the six resource measures, which suggested the factor approach was not appropriate. There was no clear conceptual underpinning for the identified factors (Child, 2006). Some identified factors captured variations in measurement error since items from different data sources loaded on the same factor even when the measures were conceptually distinct (Yang, 2005). The proportion of variance in each measure explained by the factors was low on average but had wide variation (.238 < communalities < .804), and the reliability for the scale suggested by each factor was low (.008 < Cronbach's α < .671). Thus, I determined individual measures were more appropriate.

[10]So, for example, in the 1999–2000 school year, Brooklyn's Freedom Academy High School had eight partners, which tied Freedom Academy indirectly to 16 other schools, resulting in a local school-partner network of 24 organizations. The density of Freedom Academy's local network is the proportion of ties among all 276 possible pairs (i.e., 24(24 − 1) / 2 = 276) that have been realized, in this case, 225 ties or a density of 81.52%, thus making Freedom Academy the school with the 25th densest network in the 1999–2000 school year (see Supplementary Table S1 in the online version of the journal).

[11]This matrix used for the final analysis is different from the matrices used to calculate the sociometric measures in UCINET but does include the sociometric measures as column variables.

[12]This approach results in the same proportional number of unobserved partnerships across schools, mitigating the need for sampling weights. One limitation of the approach is that it is equivalent to assuming that the base rate for unobserved partnerships is equal

across schools, which may be unrealistic. An alternative approach is to sample a fixed proportion of unrealized partnerships, such as 25% (e.g., Powell, White, Koput, & Owen-Smith, 2005). One drawback of this alternative approach is that schools with more partnerships will have fewer zeros such that the effect of having a partnership is amplified. My sensitivity analyses using a sample of 1, 4, and 10 unobserved partnerships as well as 1%, 5%, and 10% unobserved partnerships indicate the pattern of results is substantively the same for all approaches.

[13]Even though the sample size is reduced from its full possible size, the number of observations still might raise concerns about the power of the analyses, especially because standard methods for power analysis are less suitable for models with random effects and noncontinuous measures as dependent variables (i.e., Johnson, Barry, Ferguson, & Muller, 2015). Thus, with a large sample size, the analyses may be "over-powered," meaning that relatively small substantive effects would still have a high likelihood of achieving statistical significance. This is why in the results section, I not only report effects but also substantive interpretations for the effects.

[14]Empirically, the partner measures are time invariant because the only partner variable is industry, which is constant across time. The distance between partners and schools is also time invariant.

[15]The percentage change in the odds can be calculated using the logit coefficients in Table 2. In this instance the calculation is $e^{\wedge} - .0056 \times 10 = 0.9455$; $0.9455 - 1 = -.0545$ or -5.45%. As explained by Long and Freese (2003, p. 180), the interpretations is, as stated previously, that for an additional 10% of budget spending on facilities, the odds of a partnership decrease by 5.45%, holding all other variables constant. It is important to note that this result is an *instantaneous* effect, meaning the result gives the percentage change in the odds at a specific point on the regression line, which is to say at a specific value of the independent variable (Roncek & Swatt, 2006). In the current example, the value is 10 for the additional budget spending on facilities, the unit of measure for which also happens to be a percentage. More generally, for multinomial logits, "the exponential value of a coefficient represents the change in the risk-ratio (for that outcome) for a one unit change in a determining variable" (Borooah, 2002, p. 52). In a binary model, such as the one in this study (i.e., partnership 1/0), the risk-ratio is equivalent to the odds ratio. The logit coefficient is the log of these odds; thus, using Long and Freese's (2003) formula—$100\{\exp(\beta_k \times \delta) - 1\}$, where β_k is the logit coefficient and δ is the number of units of change—the logit coefficient can be transformed to indicate the percentage change in the odds.

[16]Because this analysis can only include partnerships that have existed for more than one period and excludes all partnerships in the first period of the study (i.e., because there are no prior observations), the sample size for this analysis is much smaller than the main analysis ($n = 9,647$).

References

Arthur, W. B. (1990, February). Positive feedbacks in the economy. *Scientific American*, 92–99.

Atteberry, A., & Bryk, A. S. (2010). Centrality, connection, and commitment: The role of social networks in a school-based literacy initiative. In A. J. Daly (Ed.), *Social network theory and educational change* (pp. 51–76). Cambridge, MA: Harvard Education Press.

Auerbach, S. (Ed.). (2012). *School leadership for authentic family and community partnerships: Research perspectives for transforming practice*. New York, NY: Taylor and Francis.

Baker, W. E., Faulkner, R. R., & Fisher, G. A. (1998). Hazards of the market: The continuity and dissolution of interorganizational market relationships. *American Sociological Review*, *63*, 147–177.

Berne, R. (1994). Educational input and outcome inequities in New York State. In R. Berne & L. Picus (Eds.), *Outcome equity in education* (pp. 191–223). Thousand Oaks, CA: Corwin Press Inc.

Borgatti, S. P., Everett, M. G., & Freeman, L. C. (2002). *UCINET for Windows: Software for social network analysis* (Version 6.0). Harvard, MA: Analytic Technologies.

Borooah, V. K. (2002). *Logit and probit: Ordered multinomial models* (Vol. 138). Thousand Oaks, CA: Sage.

Bourdieu, P. (1986). The forms of capital. In J. G. Richardson (Ed.), *Handbook of theory and research for the sociology of education* (pp. 241–258). New York, NY: Greenwood Press.

Brass, D. J., Galaskiewicz, J., Greve, H. R., & Tsai, W. (2004). Taking stock of networks and organizations: A multilevel perspective. *Academy of Management Journal, 47*(6), 795–817.

Bridwell-Mitchell, E. N., & Cooc, N. (2016). The Ties that bind: How social capital is forged and forfeited in teacher communities. *Educational Researcher, 45*(1), 7–17.

Bridwell-Mitchell, E. N., & Lant, T. K. (2014). Be careful what you wish for: The effects of issue interpretation on social choices in professional networks. *Organization Science, 25*(2), 401–419.

Burt, R. (1992). *Structural holes: The social structure of competition*. Cambridge, MA: Harvard University Press.

Butler, M., & McNertney, E. (1991). Estimating educational production functions: The problem of multicollinearity. *Social Science Journal, 28*(4), 489–499.

Byrd, B., & Maloy, R. (1988). *Partnerships for improving schools*. New York, NY: Greenwood Press.

Caldas, S. J. (1993). Reexamination of input and process factor effects on academic achievement. *Journal of Educational Research, 86,* 206–214.

Calvo, N., Picus, L. O., Smith, J. R., & Guthrie, J. W. (2000). *A review of the Oregon quality education model*. Davis, CA: Management Analysis & Planning.

Child, D. (2006). *Essentials of factor analysis*. New York, NY: Continuum.

Chung, S., Singh, H., & Lee, K. (2000). Complementarity, status similarity and social capital as drivers of alliance formation. *Strategic Management Journal, 21,* 1–22.

The City of New York. (2013). *NYC department of youth & community development: Seventy years of serving New York City youth and communities*. Retrieved from http://www.nyc.gov/html/dycd/html/about/history.shtml

Coburn, C. E., & Stein, M. K. (Eds.). (2010). *Research and practice in education: Building alliances, bridging the divide*. Lanham, MD: Rowman and Littlefield.

Coleman, J. (1988). Social capital and the creation of human capital. *American Journal of Sociology, 94,* S95–S120.

Coleman, J., Katz, E., & Menzel, H. (1957). The diffusion of innovation among physicians. *Sociometry, 20*(4), 253–270.

Dacin, T., Oliver, C., & Roy, J. P. (2007). The legitimacy of strategic alliances: An institutional perspective. *Strategic Management Journal, 28,* 169–187.

Dika, S. L., & Singh, K. (2002). Applications of social capital in educational literature: A critical synthesis. *Review of Educational Research, 72*(1), 31–60.

DiMaggio, P., & Powell, W. (1983). The iron cage revisited: Institutional isomorphism and collective rationality in organizational fields. *American Sociological Review, 48,* 147–160.

Educational Partnership Act of 1988, P.L. 100-418 Congress, 20 U.S.C. 5031-5039 Cong. Rec. § Title VI, Subtitle A, Chapter 5 (1988).

Ehrenberg, R. G., & Brewer, D. J. (1994). Do school and teacher characteristics matter? Evidence from high school and beyond. *Economics of Education Review, 13*(1), 1–17.

Feuerstein, A. (2001). Selling our school? Principals' views on schoolhouse commercialism and school-business interactions. *Educational Administration Quarterly, 37*(3), 322–371.

Figlio, D. N. (1999). Functional form and the estimated effects of school resources. *Economics of Education Review, 18*(2), 242–252.

Finnigan, K., & Daly, A. (2010). Learning at a system level: Ties between principals of low-performing schools and central office leaders. In A. Daly (Ed.), *Social network theory and educational change* (pp. 179–196). Cambridge, MA: Harvard Education Press.

Frank, K. A., Zhao, Y., & Borman, K. (2004). Social capital and the diffusion of innovations with organizations: The case of computer technology in schools. *Sociology of Education, 77,* 148–171.

Freeman, L. C. (1979). Centrality in social networks: Conceptual clarification. *Social Networks, 1,* 215–239.

Friedkin, N. E., & Slater, M. (1994). School leadership and performance: A social network approach. *Sociology of Education, 67,* 139–157.

Galaskiewicz, J. (1985). Interorganizational relations. *Annual Review of Sociology, 11,* 281–304.

Giddens, A. (1979). *Central problems in social theory: Action, structure and contradiction in social analysis.* Berkeley, CA: University of California Press.

Glasman, N., & Biniamov, I. (1981). Input-output analyses of schools. *Review of Educational Research, 51*(4), 509–539.

Goodall, D. W. (1966). A new similarity index based on probability. *Biometrics, 22*(4), 882–907.

Granovetter, M. (1973). The strength of weak ties. *American Journal of Sociology, 778*(6), 1360–1380.

Granovetter, M. (1985). Economic action and social structure: The problem of embeddedness. *American Journal of Sociology, 91*(3), 481–510.

Greenwald, R., Hedges, L. V., & Laine, R. D. (1996). The effect of school resources on student achievement. *Review of Educational Research, 66*(3), 361–396.

Gulati, R. (1995). Social structure and alliance formation patterns: A longitudinal analysis. *Administrative Science Quarterly, 40,* 619–652.

Gulati, R., & Gargiulo, M. (1999). Where do interorganizational networks come from? *American Journal of Sociology, 104*(5), 473–506.

Hansen, B. E. (1992). Testing for parameter instability in linear models. *Journal of Policy Modeling, 14*(4), 517–533.

Hanushek, E. (1996). School resources and student performance. In G. Burtless (Ed.), *Does money matter? The effect of school resources on student achievement and adult success* (pp. 43–73). Washington, DC: Brookings Institution Press.

Hanushek, E. (1997). Assessing the effects of school resources on student performance: An update. *Educational Evaluation and Policy Analysis, 19*(2), 141–164.

Herzog, A., & Holiday, B. (1942). God bless the child. New York, NY: Okeh Records.

Hite, J. M., Williams, E. J., & Baugh, S. C. (2005). Multiple networks of public school administrators: An analysis of network content and structure. *International Journal of Leadership in Education, 8*(2), 91–122.

Holme, J. J., & Rangel, V. S. (2012). Social capital, and school performance putting school reform in its place: Social geography, organizational. *American Educational Research Journal, 49*(2), 257–283.

Honig, M. I. (2004). The new middle management: Intermediary organizations in education policy implementation. *Educational Evaluation and Policy Analysis, 26*(1), 65–87.

James-Burdumy, S., Dynarski, M., Moore, M., Deke, J., Mansfield, W., Pistorino, C., & Warner, E. (2005). *When schools stay open late: The national evaluation of the 21st century community learning centers program final report.* Retrieved from https://www2.ed.gov/rschstat/eval/other/cclcfinalreport/index.html.

Johnson, P. C. D., Barry, S. J. E., Ferguson, H. M., & Muller, P. (2015). Power analysis for generalized linear mixed models in ecology and evolution. *Methods in Ecology and Evolution, 6*, 133–142.

Jones, B., & Maloy, R. (1988). *Partnerships for improving schools*. New York, NY: Greenwood Press.

Kahneman, D., Slovic, P., & Tversky, A. (1982). *Judgments under uncertainty. Heuristics and biases*. Cambridge, UK: Cambridge University Press.

Kane, P. R. (Ed.). (2000). *The difference between charter schools and charter like schools*. Baltimore, MD: John Hopkins University Press.

Koka, B., & Prescott, J. (2002). Strategic alliances as social capital: A multidimensional view. *Strategic Management Journal, 23*, 795–816.

Laumann, E. O., Marsden, P. V., & Prensky, D. (1983). The boundary specification problem in network analysis. In R. S. Burt & M. J. Minor (Eds.), *Applied network analysis: A methodological introduction* (pp. 195–222). Beverly Hills, CA: Sage.

Leana, C. R., & Pil, F. K. (2006). Social capital and organizational performance: Evidence from urban public schools. *Organization Science, 17*(3), 353–366.

Lin, N. (2001). *Social capital: A theory of social structure and action*. Cambridge, UK: Cambridge University Press.

Long, J. S., & Freese, J. (2003). *Regression models for categorical dependent variables using STATA*. College Station, TX: STATA.

Merton, R. K. (1968). The Matthew effect in science. *Science, 159*(3810), 56–63.

Meyer, J. W. (1977). The effects of education as an institution. *American Journal of Sociology, 83*(1), 55–77.

Mitsuhashi, H., & Greve, H. R. (2009). A matching theory of alliance formation and organizational success: Complementarity and compatibility. *Academy of Management Journal, 52*(5), 975–995.

Oliver, C. (1990). Determinants of interorganizational relationships: Integration and future directions. *The Academy of Management Review, 15*(2), 241–265.

Ouchi, W. (2003). *Making schools work: A revolutionary plan to get your children the education they need*. New York, NY: Simon & Schuster.

Ouellette, J. A., & Wood, W. (1998). Habit and intention in everyday life: The multiple processes by which past behavior predicts future behavior. *Psychological Bulletin, 124*(1), 54–74.

Penuel, W. R., Riel, M., Krause, A. E., & Frank, K. A. (2009). Analyzing teachers' professional interactions in a school as social capital: A social network approach. *Teachers College Record, 111*(1), 124–163.

Pohl, S., Steiner, P. M., Eisermann, J., Soellner, R., & Cook, T. D. (2009). Unbiased causal inference from an observational study: Results of a within-study comparison. *Educational Evaluation and Policy Analysis, 31*(4), 463–479.

Polidoro, F., Ahuja, G., & Mitchell, W. (2011). When the social structure overshadows competitive incentives: The effects of network embeddedness on joint venture dissolution. *Academy of Management Journal, 54*(1), 203–223.

Powell, W. W., White, D. R., Koput, K. W., & Owen-Smith, J. (2005). Network dynamics and field evolution: The growth of interorganizational collaboration in the life sciences. *American Journal of Sociology, 110*(4), 1132–1205.

Rabe-Hesketh, S., & Skrondal, A. (2008). *Multilevel and longitudinal modeling using Stata* (2nd ed.). College Station, TX: Stata Press.

Raudenbush, S. W., & Bryk, A. S. (2002). *Hierarchical linear models: Applications and data analysis methods*. Thousand Oaks, CA: Sage.

Reagans, R. (2010). Close encounters: Analyzing how social similarity and propinquity contribute to strong network connections. *Organization Science, 22*(4), 835–849.

Roncek, D. W., & Swatt, M. L. (2006). For those who like odds: A direct interpretation of the logit coefficient for continuous variables. *Social Science Quarterly, 87*(3), 731–738.

Rosenbluth, G. (1955). Measures of concentration. In National Bureau of Economic Research (Ed.), *Business concentration and price policy* (pp. 57–59). Princeton, NJ: Princeton University Press.

Sanders, M. G. (2003). Community involvement in schools. *Education and Urban Society, 35*(2), 161–180.

Sanders, M. G. (2006). *Building school-community partnerships: Collaboration for student success.* Thousand Oaks, CA: Corwin Press, Inc.

Sanders, M. G. (2014). Principal leadership for school, family, and community partnerships: The role of a systems approach to reform implementation. *American Journal of Education, 120*(2), 233–255.

Schwartz, A., & Stiefel, L. (2004). Immigrants and the distribution of resources in an urban school district. *Educational Evaluation and Policy Analysis, 26*(4), 303–327.

Smith, J., & Wohlstetter, P. (2006). Understanding the different faces of partnering: A typology of public-private partnerships. *School Leadership and Management, 26*(3), 249–268.

Sorenson, O., & Stuart, T. E. (2001). Syndication networks and the spatial distribution of venture capital investments. *American Journal of Sociology, 106*(6), 1546–1588.

Spillane, J. P., Kim, C. M., & Frank, K. A. (2012). Instructional advice and information seeking behavior in elementary schools: Exploring tie formation as a building block in social capital development. *American Educational Research Journal, 49*(6), 1112–1145.

Spillane, J. P., Shirrell, M., & Sweet, T. M. (2017). The elephant in the schoolhouse: The role of propinquity in school staff interactions about teaching. *Sociology of Education, 90,* 149–171.

Steiner, P. M., Cook, T. D., Shadish, W. R., & Clark, M. H. (2010). The importance of covariate selection in controlling for selection bias in observational studies. *Psychological Methods, 15*(3), 250–267.

Tsang, K.-K. (2009). School social capital and school effectiveness. *Education Journal, 37*(1–2), 119–136.

Tuckman, H. P. (1971). High school inputs and their contribution to school performance. *Journal of Human Resources, 6*(4), 490–509.

Wasserman, S., & Faust, K. (1994). *Social network analysis: Methods and applications.* New York, NY: Cambridge University Press.

Wohlstetter, P., Malloy, C. L., Chau, D., & Polhemus, J. L. (2003). Improving schools through networks: A new approach to urban school reform. *Educational Policy, 17*(4), 399–430.

Yang, B. (2005). Factor analysis methods. In R. A. Swanson & E. F. Holton, III (Eds.), *Research in organizations: Foundations and methods of inquiry* (pp. 181–200). San Francisco, CA: Berrett-Koehler.

Manuscript received January 23, 2015
Final revision received March 21, 2017
Accepted May 15, 2017

American Educational Research Journal
December 2017, Vol. 54, No. 6, pp. 1256–1287
DOI: 10.3102/0002831217717949
© 2017 AERA. http://aerj.aera.net

Cognitive Validity:
Can Multiple-Choice Items Tap
Historical Thinking Processes?

Mark D. Smith
Stanford University

Cognitive validity examines the relationship between what an assessment aims to measure and what it actually elicits from test takers. The present study examined whether multiple-choice items from the National Assessment of Educational Progress (NAEP) grade 12 U.S. history exam elicited the historical thinking processes they were designed to measure. Think-aloud data from 27 accomplished high school students revealed that in no instances did students engage in the intended processes. Rather, the items typically elicited three construct-irrelevant processes: factual recall/recognition, reading comprehension, and test-taking strategies. Further, findings revealed that although the items often prompted students to engage in factual recall, they were often not sound indicators of student knowledge. Implications for history testing and alternative forms of assessment are discussed.

KEYWORDS: assessment, historical thinking, validity

Introduction

The history testing landscape in the United States is dominated by a single testing format: the discrete multiple-choice item. Each of the 24 states that mandate history exams for K–12 students uses multiple-choice items for a significant portion of the exam, and 13 of these states use *only* multiple-choice items (Martin, Maldonado, Schneider, & Smith, 2011). Standardized tests that transcend state borders, like the National Assessment of Educational Progress (NAEP) U.S. history exam and Advanced Placement (AP) history tests, also rely heavily on multiple-choice items to sample student achievement nationwide.

MARK D. SMITH is the director of assessment for the Stanford History Education Group, Stanford Graduate School of Education, 485 Lasuen Mall, Stanford, CA 94305; e-mail: *msmith4@stanford.edu*. His research focuses on history/social studies curriculum and assessment.

Multiple-choice items are commonly used to assess student achievement in a wide range of knowledge and processes in history, including higher order disciplinary processes known as *historical thinking*. There is no universally agreed on definition of historical thinking, but there is broad consensus among history educators that it comprises the complex cognitive processes used by historians to reason about the past, like evaluating the reliability of historical documents, using evidence to formulate historical arguments, and thinking about historical documents as products of the context in which they were created (cf. Holt, 1990; Kelly, 2013; Lévesque, 2008; Nokes, 2013; Seixas, Morton, Colyer, & Fornazzari, 2013; VanSledright, 2004; Wineburg, 2001). These processes are distinct from traditional approaches to history teaching and learning that stress the recall of declarative knowledge about the past (e.g., names, dates, events). Although historians may draw on declarative knowledge of the past when engaged in historical thinking, recall alone is not considered a historical thinking process (Immerwahr, 2008; Lévesque, 2008; VanSledright, 2004; Wineburg, 2001). Recalling that Abraham Lincoln ran against Stephen Douglas in the 1858 Illinois Senate race is very different than reasoning about how the political context of the time may have shaped Lincoln's words on race in the Lincoln-Douglas debates or mounting an evidence-based argument about how and why Lincoln's views on race changed over time. Just as remembering the freezing point of water does not indicate proficiency in the scientific method, recalling facts about the past is not considered to be a hallmark of historical thinking.

Historical thinking is also distinct from more generalized academic skills like basic reading comprehension and writing fluency. Basic literacy skills are clearly required for any textual analysis or written argument, but the disciplinary literacy skills employed by historians when engaged in historical thinking are history-specific and distinct from basic reading and writing abilities as well as the processes employed by experts in other academic domains (like science and mathematics; Gottlieb & Wineburg, 2012; C. Shanahan, Shanahan, & Misischia, 2011; T. Shanahan & Shanahan, 2008).

A seminal study by Wineburg (1991) illustrated how historical thinking differs from more generalized reading comprehension. Wineburg asked both professional historians and accomplished high school students to evaluate the trustworthiness of eight historical documents about the Battle of Lexington prior to the start of the American Revolution. The talented high school students had no trouble understanding the literal meaning of the text and, fresh from completing a course in AP U.S. history, sometimes knew more factual information about the American Revolution than did the historians who had specialized in other areas of history. The historians, however, engaged the documents very differently. Rather than simply read the texts to understand what the author was saying, they interrogated them as historical evidence. For example, when presented with a 1775 diary entry from a British officer (named Barker) that described the events he had witnessed at the Battle of Lexington, all of the historians (but none of the students) questioned the trustworthiness of the account. One historian responded:

> I want to stop and see where it came from. . . . My guess is that this probably wasn't written until that night or probably not until the next day. He is going to be too busy marching around to stop and write in his diary, so he's had some time to stop and think . . . and having time to think and knowing that with what happened there was going to be possibly some kind of inquest or something . . . he probably would be very careful about what he was going to write. (Wineburg, 1994, p. 104)

Rather than simply read the document to decode what Barker was saying, the historian engaged in processes central to historical thinking. The historian has considered who wrote the document, when it was written, and for what purpose—and then used these factors to call the trustworthiness of the document into question. The historian questioned whether Barker may have felt the need to alter his account to protect himself from later prosecution for his role in provoking "the shot heard round the world." All of the high school students masterfully decoded the words in the diary but failed to question whether the source was good historical evidence. This illustrates a key difference between historical thinking and basic reading comprehension. Historical thinking assumes some basic literacy but goes beyond decoding text for literal meaning to interrogate it as evidence of past events and their causes (Gottlieb & Wineburg, 2012; Leinhardt & Young, 1996; C. Shanahan et al., 2011; T. Shanahan & Shanahan, 2008).

Examples of tests that use multiple-choice items to assess students in historical thinking processes abound. The National Assessment Governing Board (NAGB), for example, uses multiple-choice items on the NAEP grade 12 U.S. history test to draw inferences about student ability to engage in "Historical Analysis and Interpretation," which includes the ability to "explain points of view, biases, and value statements in historical sources"; "determine the significance of people, events and historical sources"; and "develop sound generalizations and defend these generalizations with persuasive arguments" (NAGB, 2011, pp. 42–43). The Texas Education Agency relies solely on multiple-choice items to evaluate high school students' mastery of its state history standards. The Texas standards call for students to be able to "understand how historians interpret the past (historiography) and how their interpretations of history may change over time" and "evaluate the validity of a source based on language, corroboration with other sources, and information about the author, including points of view, frames of reference, and historical context" (Texas Education Agency, 2011, p. 10). These ambitious standards are a departure from traditional teacher-centered history instruction in the United States in which students are expected to memorize and recite factual information about the past (Scheurman & Reynolds, 2010). They call for students to engage in the analytical processes that are at the heart of authentic historical inquiry.

Although multiple-choice items are commonly used to measure aspects of historical thinking, little research has been done to determine whether these measures are sound. In modern measurement theory, validity is widely understood as a logical argument about the uses and interpretations of a measure (Cronbach, 1988; Kane, 2006, 2013). To evaluate the validity of a history assessment is to evaluate whether the inferences drawn from the exam are sound. Unfortunately, little evidence exists to support inferences about student historical thinking from extant multiple-choice tests.

Of particular need is research that investigates aspects of *cognitive validity*, which explores whether assessments elicit the knowledge, skills, and cognitive processes they are designed to measure (Pellegrino, Chudowsky, & Glaser, 2001; Ruiz-Primo, Shavelson, Li, & Schultz, 2001). Few researchers (or test publishers) have sought empirical evidence about what students actually do when taking history tests and whether the tests tap the kind of thinking they claim to measure. Most cognitive validity studies that have examined history tests have relied solely on theoretical analysis by subject matter experts about what test items will elicit when in the hands of students (e.g., Grant & Horn, 2006; Karras, 1991). But expert judgments about what test items will elicit are prone to error, and without empirical evidence of student thinking, these judgments can amount to little more than educated guesses.

A study by Haney and Scott (1987) illustrated how expectations about how test items function can be wrong. Data from think-aloud interviews showed that students found items from selected standardized tests to be ambiguous and that test items did not always tap what they purported to measure. One powerful example from the study illustrated how the multiple-choice format could lead to false conclusions about student achievement. An item from the Stanford Achievment Test asked students which of three plants required the least amount of water: a flower, cabbage, or a cactus (see Figure 1). For test developers, the keyed answer was clear: The desert cactus required the least water. However, one student selected the cabbage because it had already been picked and needed water "only when you clean it." The other two plants, the child reasoned, needed more water because they were still growing in pots. But under normal test conditions, this sophisticaed reasoning would be masked behind a darkened bubble, and educators would be left to mistakenly conclude that this student did not possess basic knowledge about plants' use of water.

Two studies by Reich (2009, 2013) are rare examples of research that elicited empirical evidence about the cognitive demands of items from a published history test. Reich employed think-aloud methods to elicit the

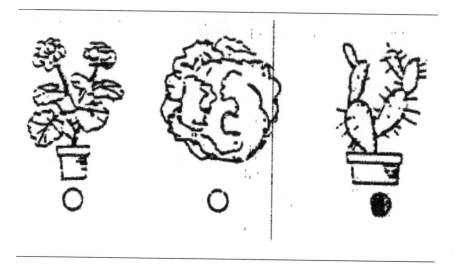

Figure 1. **Sample multiple-choice question from Haney and Scott's (1987) study.**

cognitive processes used by 10th-grade history students in New York when solving selected multiple-choice items from the New York Global History and Geography Regents Examination. Reich published two separate analyses of these data. In the first, he found that Regents multiple-choice items tapped student mastery of history content, basic literacy, and test-wiseness—but did not elicit clear evidence of the higher order cognitive processes identified in the New York state curriculum (Reich, 2009). In the second, Reich (2013) coded the verbal protocols on the degree to which the questions reflected student mastery of New York content standards. He concluded that student answers did not reliably reflect student knowledge of the historical information listed in the standards. Students were commonly able to arrive at the correct answer without exhibiting mastery of the declarative knowledge that the question was designed to measure.

Ercikan, Seixas, Lyons-Thomas, and Gibson (2015) also conducted think-aloud interviews with 35 high school juniors to examine the cognitive demands of an unpublished test of historical thinking that the authors had designed to measure student achievement in three aspects of historical thinking: (a) using primary source evidence, (b) taking historical perspectives, and (c) understanding the ethical dimension of historical interpretation. The test comprised a combination of six multiple-choice and five constructed-response tasks. Protocol analysis revealed that both the multiple-choice items and constructed-response items evoked the targeted historical thinking constructs, and researchers concluded that there were no discernable differences in rates of historical thinking elicited based on item format. An analysis of the written responses, however, revealed that the scoring of the constructed-response answers better reflected whether students had engaged in the targeted processes. This study, along with Reich's two analyses, were welcome steps in building a body of research on the cognitive validity of history tests, but these studies were modest in scale, and more research is needed to better understand the cognitive demands of multiple-choice items from standardized history exams.

Research on testing from other academic domains suggests that multiple-choice items tend to measure little more than factual recall (Frederiksen, 1984; Martinez, 1999). Some measurement specialists believe that multiple-choice items are poorly equipped to measure complex cognitive abilities like historical thinking. One reason is that multiple-choice items exhibit low *fidelity*—a term used by Fitzpatrick and Morrison (1971) and Haladyna (1997, 2004) to describe the match between the demands of a criterion measure (e.g., a state history exam) and the criterion domain (e.g., historical thinking). Fidelity of multiple-choice items to complex domains is low because the cognitive demands of multiple-choice items represent only a small portion of the demands of many complex domains (cf. Martinez, 1999; Resnick & Resnick, 1992). The range of demands of a complex domain like writing, for example, may be poorly represented by a multiple-choice item. Choosing the correct verb conjugation from a list of possible answers is a poor approximation for the ability to write a convincing essay.

The cognitive demands of multiple-choice items may indeed be wholly incompatible with the demands of a complex domain like history. Some critics argue that multiple-choice items demand what Guilford (1959) termed *convergent thinking*. Multiple-choice items require test takers to converge on one correct answer from a bounded list of choices, which is a process unfamiliar to many complex domains. The multiple-choice format may even preclude cognitive processes central to some academic domains— like the generation of new ideas and *divergent thinking* (Martinez, 1999; Ward, Frederiksen, & Carlson, 1980). The misalignment between the discipline of history and the testing instrument is problematic. If the cognitive demands of multiple-choice items underrepresent or even conflict with the cognitive demands of the domain, then inferences drawn from performance on a multiple-choice test about proficiency in historical thinking are undermined (Kane, 2006, 2013).

The validity of multiple-choice items for measuring complex domains is also threatened by *construct-irrelevant variance*, a term used to describe factors unrelated to the intended construct of measurement that affect test performance (cf. Haladyna & Downing, 2004; Kane, 2006; Messick, 1995). Performance on multiple-choice items may be affected by student proficiency in construct-irrelevant processes that arise from item format, like response elimination (Haladyna, 2004; Skakun, Maguire, & Cook, 1994) and working backwards from response options to the prompt (Hamilton,

1994). There is also evidence from testing in other domains that format-specific strategies affect cognitive processes employed by students when solving multiple-choice problems. Farr, Pritchard, and Smitten (1990) showed that students taking a reading comprehension test spent more time searching reading passages for answers than reading for understanding. Similarly, Kazemi (2002) showed that primary school students reported in retrospective interviews that they tended to evaluate possible answer choices rather than engage in the intended mathematics problem-solving processes.

Although some research suggests that multiple-choice items are poorly equipped for measuring complex domains, other research provides evidence that this characterization may be premature. Research in several domains suggests that multiple-choice items can be used to measure some aspects of higher-order reasoning (Aiken, 1982; Haladyna, 2004; Martinez, 1991, 1999). Hamilton, Nussbaum, and Snow (1997), for example, used think-aloud protocols to show that multiple-choice items from the science portion of the NELS:88 exam elicited higher order scientific reasoning better than constructed-response items intended to measure the same content and skills. Hibbinson (1991) also used think-alouds to detect the cognitive processes used by college freshmen when taking a 40-item multiple-choice English composition test. He found that the items elicited 27 types of inferences that could be attributed to higher order metacognitive, cognitive, and affective processes (cf. Haladyna, 2004).

Questions about whether multiple-choice items can be used to measure aspects of higher order processes are timely. New learning standards, like the Common Core State Standards, address complex cognitive processes—including key aspects of historical thinking (National Governors Association & Council of Chief State School Officers, 2010). State departments of education and school districts are currently attempting to revise their assessment practices in light of these new learning standards. Because federal legislation and initiatives like No Child Left Behind and Race to the Top have focused primarily on assessment of mathematics and English/language arts, efforts to reformulate assessments in the United States have focused disproportionately on those subjects. However, efforts to rethink history/social studies tests are also underway in states, districts, and education agencies across the country. California, for example, is planning to revamp its statewide history/social studies testing program to align with the Common Core (Hill, 2013). The College Board is also engaged in an ongoing process to revise its AP U.S. history exam to measure student achievement in historical thinking (Charap, 2015; College Board, 2014).

Research that explores whether multiple-choice items can be used to measure achievement in historical thinking is worth pursuing. There are considerable advantages to using multiple-choice items if they can be shown to tap historical thinking. Multiple-choice tests are far less expensive to administer and score than constructed-response items and do not suffer from problems of low statistical reliability and generalizability that can hinder more complex performance assessments (Lane & Stone, 2006). Furthermore, because multiple-choice items can be administered in less time than many constructed-response alternatives, they could be useful in constructing tests that sample a broader range of historical thinking processes in less time than tests comprising constructed-response items. Using tests that sample student thinking in a broader range of historical thinking constructs could bolster confidence that student test performance accurately reflects proficiency in the domain of historical thinking. So, it is possible that tests employing multiple-choice items could be used to measure student proficiency in historical thinking more effectively than tests comprising a small number of constructed-response items alone.

The use of multiple-choice items to measure historical thinking would also provide an expedient policy solution for states and agencies looking to measure higher order skills in history. States and testing agencies could maintain their heavy reliance on multiple-choices items and efficiently address demands for tests of higher order skills without an expensive overhaul of established testing technology. But the use of multiple-choice items to measure historical thinking skills is only a reasonable and defensible proposition if empirical evidence supports the conclusion that multiple-choice items are capable of measuring these skills.

The present study helps to address the need for empirical research about the use of multiple-choice items for measuring complex cognitive processes in history. It employed think-aloud protocols to uncover the processes used by high school students to solve selected multiple-choice items from an established standardized history test. In doing so, it elicited evidence relevant to a discussion about the validity of the use of multiple-choice items to evaluate student achievement in historical thinking.

Research Questions

This investigation explored whether mutliple-choice items from a highly regarded American standardized history test, the NAEP 2010 grade 12 U.S. history exam, tap the higher order disciplinary constructs that they were designed to measure. The study was designed to shed light on the cognitive processes that students use to solve multiple-choice items that were written to elicit complex cognitive processes. It also sought to elicit evidence about whether multiple-choice items in general can capture complex disciplinary skills in history. More specifically, it addressed the following question:

Research Question: Do selected multiple-choice items from an established standardized history test tap the aspects of historical thinking they were designed to measure?

Method

Data and Procedures

This study used *concurrent* and *retrospective* think-aloud protocols to collect evidence about the cognitive demands of selected multiple-choice items (Ericsson & Simon, 1993; Taylor & Dionne, 2000). A great deal of research has shown that think-aloud protocols are an effective means for revealing the cognitive processes used by individuals when completing tasks and solving problems in complex academic domains and that the process of verbalizing thinking has minimal effect on the types of cognitive processes that participants use to solve problems (e.g., Ericsson & Simon, 1993; Kuusela & Pallab, 2000; Leighton, 2004). Think-alouds are also a recommended method for eliciting evidence about whether test items tap aspects of a targeted domain and are a widely accepted tool for evaluating the validity of test score interpretations (American Educational Research Association, American Psychological Association, & National Council on Measurement in Education, 2014; Kane, 2006, 2013).

The efficacy of think-aloud methods depends in part on the difficulty of the tasks that participants are asked to complete. If tasks are too complex or challenging, then participants may struggle to verbalize the processes they are using to solve them. Conversely, overly simple tasks may prompt processes that are implicit or too fleeting to report (Ericsson & Simon, 1993; Leighton, 2004). Although researchers must be vigilant about these threats, think-alouds have a strong track record for eliciting complex historical thinking processes used by experts and novices when working through history problems (e.g., Gottlieb & Wineburg, 2012; Reich, 2009; T. Shanahan & Shanahan, 2008; Wineburg, 1991, 1998). They have also been used extensively to successfully uncover the cognitive processes used by secondary students when solving standardized test items across a range of academic subjects (e.g., Farr et al., 1990; Hamilton et al., 1997; Katz, Bennett, & Berger, 2000; Ruiz-Primo et al., 2000) and have been embraced by history education scholars as an indispensable tool for examining the cognitive demands of assessments that aim to measure historical thinking among secondary students (e.g., Ercikan et al., 2015; Kaliski, Smith, & Huff, 2015). So although think-alouds may not be an effective tool for revealing cognitive processes in all circumstances, it is reasonable to expect that they can be used to elicit the processes high school students use to solve items from a standardized history test designed to measure aspects of historical thinking.

The research protocol was based around individual interviews with high school history students. Each student ($n = 27$) was interviewed by one of three researchers trained in the research protocol. Students were first introduced to the protocol procedures and completed a series of practice items to bolster their confidence and provide researchers an opportunity to ensure that students were proficient in reporting cognitive processes (Ericsson & Simon, 1993; Pressley & Afflerbach, 1995; Taylor & Dionne, 2000). Students then thought aloud as they completed four multiple-choice items. For the concurrent protocol, students were asked to think aloud without interruption while solving each item. After students completed each item, they were then asked retrospective questions to probe their thinking and clarify information elicited during the concurrent report. Researchers asked a set of structured questions during retrospective questioning but were allowed to vary from the script as needed to elicit information about student thinking. The analysis that follows focuses primarily on concurrent interview data. Retrospective data were only used to clarify statements made by students during the concurrent portion of the interview (Desimone & Le Floch, 2004; Taylor & Dionne, 2000).

Materials

The protocol included four released multiple-choice items from the NAEP 2010 grade 12 U.S. history exam. The NAEP exam was chosen for several reasons. First, the grade 12 U.S. history exam expressly targets aspects of historical thinking. The NAGB, who developed the test, followed best practice in assessment development by clearly specifying the constructs that each item was intended to measure. Their diligence in specifying the constructs targeted by each question allowed for a more precise cognitive validity investigation. Rather than evaluating whether NAEP items tap vague notions of historical thinking, it was possible to evaluate alignment between the cognitive processes elicited by test items and the precise constructs that test developers were targeting when constructing the items.

Each item on the grade 12 U.S. history exam was expressly designed to measure one of two broad "ways of knowing and thinking about U.S. history." Thirty percent of the items were designed to measure "Historical Knowledge and Perspective," which encompasses traditional aspects of history learning like "knowing and understanding people, events, concepts" and "developing a general conceptualization of history" (NAGB, 2011, p. 40). Seventy percent of the items were designed to tap "Historical Analysis and Interpretation," which includes key facets of historical thinking. According to the NAGB (2011), the items aligned to this construct "should ensure that the assessment tasks will address the whole range of historical thinking" (p. 42). Included in this broad range are the abilities to:

- explain points of view, biases, and value statements in historical sources;
- determine the significance of people, events, and historical sources;
- weigh and judge different views of the past as advanced by historical figures themselves, historians, and present-day commentators and public figures;

- demonstrate that the interpretation and meaning of the past are open to change as new information and perspectives emerge;
- develop sound generalizations and defend these generalizations with persuasive arguments (National Assessment Governing Board, 2011, pp. 42–43).

(See Appendix A for a complete enumeration of all aspects of the construct.) Because each item tied to historical analysis and interpretation was expressly designed to measure some aspect of historical thinking, the four items included in the protocol were tied to this construct.

In addition to providing clarity about the constructs targeted by each item, the NAEP exam was selected because it is held in high regard by educators, researchers, and policymakers. Furthermore, the 2010 NAEP U.S. history exam has been used to draw broad conclusions about national student achievement in historical thinking (e.g., National Center for Educational Statistics, 2011; Robelen, 2011). Thus, the NAEP exam provided an opportunity to examine items from a trusted exam that has been central to discussions about student proficiency in historical thinking in recent years.

The present study focused on whether established multiple-choice items *can* tap aspects of historical thinking rather than the properties of the average NAEP item. So rather than select NAEP items at random, items were chosen strategically. Three expert history educators conducted a *logical analysis* (cf. Li, Ruiz-Primo, & Shavelson, 2006) of the 20 released items and selected items that were deemed likely to tap aspects of historical thinking. It is important to note that the nonrandom selection of items was not designed to support inferences about how the items function within the context of the broader NAEP exam or the validity of interpretations drawn from composite scores from the NAEP grade 12 U.S. history exam. The NAEP exam includes a range of item formats, and the analysis of 4 items out of the context of the overall exam does not reflect the overall effectiveness of the NAEP exam as a measure of historical thinking. It does, however, represent a purposeful sample of those items that researchers believed most likely to elicit such performances.

Participants

Participants included a strategic sample of 27 high school students (26 seniors, 1 junior) from three comprehensive high schools in an urban public school district in the Midwest of the United States. Each student selected had completed a one-year AP U.S. history course and had scored a three or better out of five on the national exam, which would have earned the students college credit at two of the three public universities in their home state. These parameters ensured that students had the opportunity to learn the material tested and had demonstrated proficiency in the subject matter on a rigorous standardized exam. The AP U.S. history curriculum also calls for students to engage in historical thinking, so a passing score on the AP exam increased

Table 1
**Average Scores on National Assessment of Educational Progress (NAEP)
Protocol Items**

NAEP Item	National Sample (%)	Participant Sample (%)
Item 1: Dust Bowl	56	89
Item 2: Shays' Rebellion	59	93
Item 3: *Brown v. Board*	51	96
Item 4: 14th Amendment	78	93
Overall average	61	93

confidence that students had the ability to engage in aspects of historical thinking if prompted. Further, because the AP U.S. history course and exam are designed for students who read at a university level, these parameters also ensured that the literacy demands of the mulitple-choice items would not impose barriers to students engaging in historical thinking processes. Student answers to the selected NAEP items supported these assumptions. Participants performed well on the selected items relative to a national sample of high school seniors. Table 1 compares the percentage of study participants who recorded correct answers to the percentage of students who answered correctly from a national sample of NAEP examinees (National Center for Educational Statistics, n.d.).

Although this strategic sample offered theoretical advantages, it also had inherent limitations. The performance of high-achieving students tells us little about how these items might function in the hands of students at the lower ends of the achievement spectrum. Further, the small sample size—common in this type of time-intensive analysis—limits the generalizability of the findings, even among highly accomplished students. It is possible that these four items would elicit different responses when administered to a broader sample of high school students.

Protocol Analysis

Interview data were audio recorded and transcribed verbatim (Afflerbach & Johnston, 1984; Taylor & Dionne, 2000). The principal investigator coded the transcripts on three dimensions. First, items were coded iteratively to identify the cognitive processes used by students to answer each question. During the initial iterative phase, transcripts were coded line by line to identify all processes used by students to arrive at an answer. The NAGB definition of historical analysis and interpretation formed the basis of the coding scheme to start. (See Appendix A for the definition.) Any instances of student thinking that matched these processes were coded as historical analysis and interpretation. So, if a student explained points of view, biases, and value statements in a historical source, then the student response would have been coded as historical analysis and interpretation because the student engaged in a relevant aspect of the construct as defined by NAEP. Other codes were added to the coding scheme as they emerged from the data. So, if students engaged in processes not enumerated in the NAGB's definition of historical analysis and interpretation—like guessing or simple factual recall—then a new code was generated. After the iterative coding phase, the transcript for each item received a single code that identified the primary cognitive process students used to arrive at an answer. Appendix B lists the codes that emerged from transcript analysis on Dimension 1 and provides a brief definition of each.

For the second dimension, the student transcript for each item was assigned a binary code based on whether the student engaged aspects of the construct historical analysis and interpretation identified by the NAGB. If the item elicited an aspect of the construct, the item was coded as *construct-relevant process*. For example, if a student were to explain points of view, biases, and value statements in historical sources—an aspect of historical analysis and interpretation—then the item would be coded as construct-relevant process. If the item failed to elicit an aspect of this broader construct, then the student response was coded as *construct-irrelevant process*. So, if a student guessed the correct answer, then the transcript would be coded as construct-irrelevant process.

The second dimension represents researcher interpretations of the match between the description of the construct provided by the test developer and the cognitive processes evoked by the items when students answer them. A validity argument for the use of an assessment depends in part on the alignment between the processes targeted by test developers and those that test takers use to solve the problems. A high degree of alignment supports an argument that the assessment is a sound measure of the intended constructs. However, if students do not engage in the intended processes, then inferences about student proficiency in the targeted processes are undermined.

A third coding dimension emerged from the data. Coding on the first two dimensions revealed that students frequently engaged in factual recall, but the first two coding dimensions did not evaluate whether the items were a good reflection of student knowledge. Dimension 3 directly examined whether items that had elicited factual recall were in fact sound indicators of student proficiency in the historical topics covered by each item. Items that had been coded as factual recall/recognition on Dimension 1 were then coded on Dimension 3. Answers were coded as *proficiency match* at the item level if a student: (a) revealed knowledge of the past and selected the correct answer or (b) made a significant error in historical knowledge and selected an incorrect answer. Responses were coded as *proficiency mismatch* if a student: (a) made a significant historical error or revealed lack of knowledge about the past but still selected the correct answer or (b) demonstrated knowledge but selected an incorrect answer. Coding on Dimension 3 elicited evidence relevant to a validity argument about whether student answers supported valid inferences about student proficiency in historical knowledge.

Appendix C provides an example of a transcript coded at the item level on all three dimensions. In this transcript, the student was responding to a NAEP item about the Dust Bowl (see Figure 2 to view the item). The student drew on his knowledge of *The Grapes of Wrath* to select an answer, so the item was coded as factual recall/recognition on Dimension 1. Because the student primarily engaged in factual recall/recognition, which is not included in the NAGB definition of historical analysis and interpretation, the transcript was coded as construct-irrelevant process on Dimension 2. Finally, because the student engaged in factual recall/recognition on Dimension 1, it was selected for coding on Dimension 3. The student demonstrated basic knowledge of *The Grapes of Wrath* and used that knowledge to select the correct answer, so the transcript was coded as proficiency match on Dimension 3.

A second rater coded a random sample of 32 transcripts for each of the three dimensions, and Cohen's kappa was used to estimate interrater agreement. Estimates were high for all three dimensions (kappa = 0.88 for Dimension 1; kappa = 1.0 for Dimension 2; and kappa = 0.93 for Dimension 3).

Results

Finding 1

Protocol analysis suggested that the NAEP multiple-choice items did not evoke the aspects of historical analysis and interpretation targeted by the NAGB. *None* of the student responses were coded as historical analysis and interpretation for *any* of the four multiple-choice items. Instead of historical thinking, coding revealed that the items elicited three construct-irrelevant processes: factual recall/recognition, reading comprehension, and test-taking strategies.

The most frequent construct-irrelevant process elicited was factual recall/recognition. It was the primary cognitive process elicited in 84 of the 108 responses (27 students × 4 items). Students who engaged in recall/recognition used declarative knowledge to select the answer choice that fit best with their understanding of the past. Although teaching students facts about the past is a central component of history education, the recall of factual historical information alone is not among the processes that historians consider to constitute historical thinking (cf. Calder, 2006; Díaz, Middendorf, Pace, & Shopkow, 2008; Hynd, Holschuh, & Hubbard, 2004; Nokes, 2013; Pace, 2004; Wineburg, 1991). Processes like evaluating the reliability of information or reasoning about historical evidence as a product of

Q. Which is a famous book about conditions like those in the picture?
   a. *The Great Gatsby,* F. Scott Fitzgerald
   b. *The Scarlet Letter,* Nathaniel Hawthorne
   c. *The Grapes of Wrath,* John Steinbeck
   d. *For Whom the Bell Tolls,* Ernest Hemingway

NOTE: This item is from the 2010 NAEP *Grade 12 US History* test. NAEP identified its "Cognitive Level" as "Historical Analysis and Interpretation" (National Center for Educational Statistics, n.d.).

Figure 2. **Sample National Assessment of Educational Progress (NAEP) item related to the Dust Bowl.**

its time are more complex than recalling facts. Moreover, the NAEP items targeted for analysis were precisely those that test designers claimed go beyond factual knowledge to tap complex processes, like defending generalizations with persuasive arguments and weighing different views of the past. (See Appendix A for what processes were targeted.) Further, the NAGB identifies factual recall as an aspect of a separate construct, historical knowledge and perspective, which asks students to "name, recognize, list, identify, and give examples of people, places, events, concepts, and movements" (NAGB, 2011, p. 42). So, although NAGB aimed to measure factual recall on the exam, factual recall was not included among the higher order processes that comprise the construct to which the item was aligned. Thus, factual recall responses to these items were coded as construct irrelevant.

A response from a 17-year-old senior provides an example of how a NAEP item classified as historical analysis and interpretation elicited factual recall. The item presents a scene from the Dust Bowl. The photograph depicts a large dust cloud looming behind three modest bungalows (see Figure 2). Students are asked, "Which famous book is about conditions like those in the picture?" Students must then choose one answer from a list of four books with the corresponding authors. This student, like every other in the sample, quickly recognized the photograph: "Well, it's a picture of lots of dust and two houses. Probably the Dust Bowl." He then addressed the question:

> *Which is a famous book about conditions like those in the picture?* I would definitely, have to go with answer (C), *The Grapes of Wrath*. I definitely know this book. *The Grapes of Wrath* is about that time frame in history. So, I have to go with (C).

This student drew on his knowledge of the content of the book and selected the correct answer. However, rather than engaging in the type of analysis and interpretation outlined by NAEP, he identified the correct answer because he knew that *The Grapes of Wrath* was associated with the Dust Bowl. This process of selecting a single answer that fits with acquired declarative knowledge is distinct from the types of analysis and interpretation defined by the NAGB.

While this student confidently selected an answer based on his knowledge of the past, other students engaged in factual recall/recognition in a subtly different way. Rather than identify a single answer as correct from the outset, some students read the prompt and then searched the answers to find which one fit best with their (often limited) knowledge of the past. A second student, for example, evaluated each answer to find the best fit for the prompt:

> The picture shows a bunch of houses. You know it's a dust storm. The options are:
>
> (A) *The Great Gatsby* by F. Scott Fitzgerald, which I have to admit I've never read;
> (B) *The Scarlet Letter* by Nathaniel Hawthorne, which I know is a book about cheating—I have actually not yet read any of these—so, that one can be eliminated off the bat.
> (C) *The Grapes of Wrath* by John Steinbeck, and;
> (D) *For Whom the Bell Tolls*, which I've never even heard of.
>
> I just know *Grapes of Wrath* because it was something we talked about in history. This is almost a rote memory question.

In a moment of metacognition, this student recognized that she was simply drawing on "rote memory" to answer the question. But her strategy revealed more than that. She exhibited a cognitive process rare in complex domains like history but common among participants solving the NAEP multiple-choice items. She used declarative knowledge to evaluate each answer choice for its *relative goodness of fit*—or how well it fit with the prompt vis-à-vis other answers. This process is not included in the NAGB's definition of historical analysis and interpretation. Furthermore, it is alien to the discipline of history. Real-world historical questions are not

---

This question refers to the excerpt below from the Fourteenth Amendment to the Constitution.

All persons born or naturalized in the United States . . . are citizens of the United States and of the State wherein they reside. No State shall make or enforce any law which shall abridge the privileges or immunities of citizens of the United States; nor shall any State deprive any person of life, liberty, or property, without due process of law; nor deny to any person . . . equal protection of the laws.

Q. This amendment has been most important in protecting the
   a. right of communities to control what goes on in their schools
   b. rights of foreigners living in the United States
   c. rights of individual citizens of the United States
   d. right of the government to keep secrets for reasons of national security

NOTE: This item is from the 2010 NAEP *Grade 12 US History* test. NAEP identified its "Cognitive Level" as "Historical Analysis and Interpretation" (National Center for Educational Statistics, n.d.).

Figure 3. **National Assessment of Educational Progress (NAEP) item on the 14th Amendment to the U.S. Constitution.**

solved through an evaluation of a discrete list of choices and circling the letter of an answer that fits better with the question than other choices.

A second construct-irrelevant process revealed by transcript analysis was *reading comprehension*, which involved reading a passage and selecting the one answer that fits best with its content. This process was especially prevalent on an item about the 14th Amendment (see Figure 3), with 20 of 27 students (74%) engaging in this strategy to arrive at the correct answer. The item presents students with an excerpt from the 14th Amendment to the U.S. Constitution. Students are then asked to identify one of four "rights" that the amendment has been "most important" in protecting. For some, this item primarily required factual recall. Seven students were familiar with the 14th Amendment and were able to select the correct answer without drawing on the content of the passage. Students simply knew that the 14th Amendment had been crucial in protecting the "rights of individual citizens." For example, one student read the passage and replied, "I know this has to do with . . . Yeah, because the Thirteenth Amendment was abolishing slavery and the Fourteenth was giving African-Americans citizenship rights. So, it has to do with the individual rights of individual citizens of the United States." The student quickly alighted on the correct answer. While 7 students were able to answer the item from memory, 20 of the 27 participants were able to circumvent the process of retrieving factual information from memory. Instead, they inferred an answer from the content of the passage. Thus, students were not evaluating the impact of the 14th Amendment on the rights of Americans across time, but rather, they were evaluating which answer best matched the content of the passage.

A response from a student named Jonathan provided an example how a student deployed a reading comprehension strategy to arrive at an answer:

> Well, in the text of the Fourteenth Amendment it talks about persons born or naturalized in the United States, and they're talking about their rights, so (b) is pretty clearly not right because that talks about foreigners—which would apply to somebody who is visiting and probably not naturalized. So that's sort of the opposite. And then (a) and (d) are talking about either communities controlling their schools or government keeping secrets for national security. Those things just aren't really even addressed in the text at all. And then (c) is the last one left, and rights of individual citizens is definitely hit on in this, so that one makes the most sense.

Rather than engage in analysis of the historical impact of the 14th Amendment, Jonathan read the passage and then deduced which answer best fit the literal meaning of the text. He understood that the passage addressed the rights of citizens, so he eliminated the choice (answer b) that included noncitizens. He then eliminated the two remaining distractors because they included groups or topics that were not mentioned in the passage. Finally, he selected the correct answer because the keywords in the answer choice matched the content of the passage. In a retrospective report, Jonathan succinctly reflected on his strategy:

> Having [the passage] in there allows you to do a little more "process of elimination" and just sort of "logic it out" from the things you're given instead of actually having to know what the Fourteenth Amendment is. You can just read these general statements.

Jonathan's strategy, although effective in answering the item, is a far cry from the aspects of historical analysis and interpretation outlined by the NAGB (see Appendix A).

A third construct-irrelevant process elicited by the NAEP multiple-choice items was *test-taking strategies*. These were processes unrelated to historical thinking that were a function of the multiple-choice item format. The selected NAEP items elicited two distinct test-taking strategies: *guessing* and *process of elimination*. Only in rare instances did students simply guess an answer (4 of the 108 item responses). When answering the Dust Bowl item, for example, one student first reflected on her own familiarity with each of the books, and with little knowledge to draw from, guessed one of the titles that she recognized:

> I have only read one of the books, and it's *The Great Gatsby*. With this one, it's going to be kind of a guess just because, I mean, the picture is kind of rural, a few houses. I've heard of *The Grapes of Wrath*, so I'm just going to guess that.

The multiple-choice format allowed this student to circumvent historical reasoning by guessing a book that she recognized.

More commonly, the multiple-choice items prompted students to engage in process of elimination. Students used the fact that each item included a single correct answer to narrow the problem space and then converge on a single answer. In 66% of the responses, students attempted to eliminate one or more choices that they believed were implausible in order to direct more attention to answers that might be correct. Although an effective heuristic for solving multiple-choice items, this sort of thinking is rarely seen in complex disciplines like history. Legitimate historical problems are not solved by categorically eliminating discrete facts as false in order to increase the odds of selecting a correct fact. Furthermore, eliminating factual information to alight on a single answer is not a process identified by the NAGB as a facet of historical analysis and interpretation (see Appendix A).

Finding 2

Protocol analysis on Dimension 3—which examined whether student answers reflected mastery of historical knowledge—revealed that although the NAEP items disproportionately elicited factual recall/recognition, student answers were often fallible indicators of proficiency in this area. Students who engaged in factual recall or recognition rarely exhibited a sophisticated understanding of the historical topics covered by the item. In fact, in many cases, student answers revealed a lack of proficiency in these areas of knowledge. Out of the 81 correct responses in which students engaged in factual recall, 21 included statements that indicated a limited or flawed understanding of the topics covered. In such instances, students either declared their lack of knowledge about the topic central to the item or made statements that revealed significant misconceptions about a topic related to the item.

Jenna provided an example of a student who arrived at a correct answer with limited historical knowledge. The item asked students to identify why Shays' Rebellion was important and then lists four possible effects of the rebellion (see Figure 4). The few students with strong knowledge of the event were able to recall that the armed rebellion of credit-strapped farmers against the government of Massachusetts led many Americans to believe that the U.S. government needed to be strengthened. These students then correctly identified (a) "it led many people to believe that the central government was too weak" as the correct answer. Jenna, however, lacked this sort of command of the event and its effects. Jenna reasoned:

> Shays' Rebellion, I get mixed up with Bacon's Rebellion. I think it's
> either about slavery or about the government. I think it's either (A)
> or (D). I think it was to stop slavery because the slaves were the peo-
> ple like trying to stop it. So, I don't think it's to expand slavery

---

Q. Shays' Rebellion (1786) was important because it

    a. led many people to believe that the central government was too weak
    b. led to the end of public support for the First Bank of the United States
    c. made many people fear the tyranny of the President more than the tyranny of England
    d. convinced many people in the North that slavery should be expanded to new territories

NOTE: This item is from the 2010 NAEP *Grade 12 US History* test. NAEP identified its "Cognitive Level" as "Historical Analysis and Interpretation" (National Center for Educational Statistics, n.d.).

Figure 4. **Sample National Assessment of Educational Progress (NAEP) item on Shays' Rebellion.**

> (answer D). So not (C) or (D). I think it's either (A) or (B), but I don't remember much about the First Bank of the United States. I don't think it was very popular. I know that the South didn't have a good central government. So, maybe, yeah, I think it's (A).

Although she landed on the keyed answer, Jenna's knowledge of the event was limited. She had difficulty distinguishing Shays' Rebellion from Bacon's Rebellion (the two events were separated by 110 years and were profoundly different in their causes and effects), and she saw Southern slavery as the central issue. In the retrospective report, she elaborated on her knowledge of the event.

> I think [Shays' Rebellion] was about the slaves. And I remember that, in the Civil War, the North won because the South didn't have any central government. So, if Shays' Rebellion was in the South, then it would make sense that the central government was too weak and couldn't control them because they had a weak central government.

It is clear that Jenna mistakenly believed that Shays' Rebellion was about slavery and occurred in the South. Further, she falsely saw the event as an issue of weak government in the South and makes an imaginative (but implausible) connection between Shays' Rebellion and the strength of the Confederate government during the Civil War. Although Jenna engaged in historical recall, her correct response hardly supports a valid inference about her understanding of the historical topics under consideration. From her circled response, educators would be left to infer that Jenna had some understanding of this pivotal event in U.S. history. The fact is she did not.

    Other students missed items even though they demonstrated a better understanding of the topics than students who selected the correct answer. Among the incorrect responses observed across the four items, four of the nine showed significant understanding of the topics covered. For example, a student named Brian correctly placed the photo in the Dust Bowl item (see Figure 2) and then reasoned:

> *The Grapes of Wrath*, it was about the Great Depression. The first chapter was all about the dust. So maybe the Dust Bowl? I don't know. I mean, they had to leave their houses but it wasn't *really* about the dust. So, I'm going to say *For Whom the Bell Tolls*.

The concurrent think-aloud revealed that Brian was familiar with *The Grapes of Wrath* and knew that the book included scenes from the Dust Bowl. But Brian discounted the keyed answer because the picture, in his mind, didn't capture the themes of the book. In retrospective reporting, Brian shed further light on his thinking. When asked to explain why he chose *For Whom the Bell Tolls*, he responded:

> Because it was my only other option. I've read *The Grapes of Wrath* and I've watched movies about *The Scarlet Letter.* My brother told me about *The Great Gatsby* and I'm pretty sure it wasn't about the Dust Bowl. *The Grapes of Wrath* fits kind of, but then it doesn't. *The Grapes of Wrath* is more about the Depression and them like moving to find jobs, not really about the Dust Bowl.

Ironically, the depth of Brian's knowledge led to his undoing. Unlike other students, Brian was familiar with three of four books. He had actually read *The Grapes of Wrath* and knew its themes. But rather than associate the book to the Dust Bowl, as did many students who selected the correct answer, Brian went deeper and discounted the keyed answer because the photo did not truly reflect what he thought were the book's central themes. He ended up choosing an answer about a book that he knew nothing about because it was the only choice he could not eliminate.

It could be argued that Brian's conclusions about the centrality of the Dust Bowl to the story are incorrect and that his answer reflects a misunderstanding about the book (and obviously a lack of knowledge about *For Whom the Bell Tolls*). The problem with this argument is the fact that the depth of Brian's knowledge about the book exceeded every other student who recorded the correct answer. Nearly half of the students (11 of 24) who selected *The Grapes of Wrath* indicated that they had not in fact read the book. Six students made statements about the book that indicated superficial knowledge of its content or of the historical context of the photograph. A student named Matthew, who had not read the book, arrived at the correct answer by the way of the following reasoning: "I think that it is *The Grapes of Wrath*. I just feel like I have an intuition that it's *The Grapes of Wrath*. I can't exactly say why." The think-aloud interviews revealed that Brian had a better understanding of the themes of the book and how they related to the Great Depression than Matthew, but the circled answers on the multiple-choice item support the opposite inference. In this instance, the evidence of student knowledge provided by the multiple-choice item would leave educators with a distorted picture of student knowledge about this topic.

Discussion

This study examined whether selected multiple-choice items from a highly regarded standardized test tapped the historical thinking skills that they were designed to measure. The results presented here provide evidence that they did not in the hands of talented high school seniors. Protocol analysis did not uncover clear evidence that students engaged in processes included in the NAGB's definition of historical analysis and interpretation (see Appendix A). These results have implications for a validity argument about the use of these items to gauge student achievement in historical thinking. If no evidence exists that the items evoked the targeted cognitive processes and if students arrived at the correct answers without engaging in the targeted constructs in the vast majority of instances (100 out of 108), then inferences drawn from student performance on the items about student proficiency in historical analysis and interpretation are undermined.

History educators may be surprised that the NAEP items did not elicit clear evidence of historical thinking. Not only did these items appear on a well-regarded exam, but they also have a degree of face validity. At first glance, the items appear to be more sophisticated than the most basic factual recall questions. The NAEP items seem to require more complex reasoning than the much maligned rote recall items that simply ask students questions like "Who wrote the Declaration of Independence?" or "In what year was the Magna Carta signed?" Further, three of the items feature primary sources, which are often regarded as a hallmark of a historical thinking activity (Wineburg, Martin, & Monte-Sano, 2011). This analysis suggests that the inclusion of primary documents alone is insufficient for eliciting historical thinking, and it points to the need for more research into the types of items that might tap these higher order constructs in the discipline of history.

Protocol analysis revealed that instead of historical thinking, students disproportionately engaged in factual recall/recognition when answering these items. Even if these items do not adequately capture historical analysis and interpretation, it may be tempting to take solace in the assumption that they are sound indicators of historical knowledge and that at the very least these items provide useful information about what students know about the American past. However, the analysis on Dimension 3, which looked at whether items reflected student proficiency in historical knowledge, provides additional evidence of the need to be cautious. Data suggested that the NAEP items selected for this study were also imprecise indicators of historical knowledge among this sample of students. Many students arrived at correct answers with little knowledge of the topic, and some students showed considerable understanding of a topic but still missed the item.

We cannot unquestionably assume that even when multiple-choice items miss the mark on historical thinking that they are still a valid reflection of a student knowledge of the past.

The findings raise issues to consider beyond this modest sample of NAEP items. The results of this single study certainly do not warrant a broad indictment of the use of multiple-choice items for measuring historical thinking. Well-designed multiple-choice items may tap historical thinking, and it is possible that tests comprising multiple-choice items can reflect student proficiency in these disciplinary processes. However, the fact that items from a highly regarded national exam did not evoke clear evidence of historical thinking when in the hands of students underscores the need for more research into the limitations and possibilities of this item format for measuring these complex disciplinary processes. Many unanswered questions remain in this line of inquiry. Do multiple-choice items from other standardized exams (or from the NAEP exam itself) elicit different cognitive processes than did the items in this study? Are multiple-choice items more likely to elicit historical thinking among different populations of students? Are some types of multiple-choice questions more likely to elicit historical thinking than others? Little is known about how best to use this ubiquitous testing technology to meet the growing demands for history tests that gauge student proficiency in historical thinking, and further investigation into the cognitive demands of multiple-choice items is needed.

History education scholars have recognized the need for research in recent years and have posited ideas for further lines of inquiry. VanSledright (2013, 2015), for example, has suggested that using weighted multiple-choice (WMC) items may offer advantages over more traditional multiple-choice questions for measuring aspects of historical thinking. WMCs are formatted like traditional multiple-choice items but present students with three correct answer choices and only one answer choice that is completely incorrect. The correct answer choices, however, vary in quality. Students receive full credit for selecting the best answer and partial credit for selecting other correct (but less compelling) answer choices. VanSledright argues that WMCs are better equipped to reflect the contested and indeterminate nature of the discipline of history than traditional multiple-choice items that present students with only one correct answer. Although VanSeldright has articulated a vision for better multiple-choice items, additional research is needed to better test the proposition that WMCs offer advantages over more traditional multiple-choice items.

History educators have also called for research that explores alternatives to multiple-choice questions for measuring historical thinking (e.g., Bain & Shreiner, 2005; Ercikan & Seixas, 2015; Paxton, 2003; Shenkman, 2009). The Stanford History Education Group (SHEG) has responded by developing short, constructed-response items called History Assessments of Thinking (HATs). Each item presents students with a historical document and asks them a question that requires a short (two to three sentences) written response (Wineburg, Smith, & Breakstone, 2012). Validity studies suggest that HATs show promise in their ability to engage students in historical thinking processes (Breakstone, 2014; Smith & Breakstone, 2015).

One HAT, for example, was designed to assess students' ability to engage in *sourcing*—the ability to think about how the origins of a document affect it as evidence of the past (Holt, 1990; Paxton, 1999; Wineburg, 1991). The item presents students with a 20th-century painting that depicts the First Thanksgiving and asks how useful the document would be to historians trying to understand what happened at the original event in 1621. Piloting and validity studies revealed that the item reflected a range of proficiency in the ability to source a document (Breakstone, 2014; Smith & Breakstone, 2015). One 11th-grade student, for example, adeptly responded, "This painting was drawn 311 years after the actual event happened. There is no evidence of historical accuracy, as we do not know if the artist did research before painting this, or if he just drew what is a stereotypical Pilgrim and Indian painting" (Wineburg et al., 2012, p. 292). The HAT provided evidence that the student was proficient in a key aspect of sourcing—the ability to reason about how the gap in time between when a source was created and the event depicted affects the status of the document as evidence of the past. Other students' answers revealed less proficiency in this aspect of historical thinking; many students either viewed the painting as a direct window into the past or evaluated it based on how well it matched their preconceived understanding of the past—both key fallacies in historical reasoning. These assessments appear to hold some promise, but at the same time, more research is needed to investigate their effectiveness as measures of historical thinking. Further, HATs are just one idea for moving the field of history assessment forward. History education would benefit from additional efforts to explore the best practices for assessing historical thinking.

Limitations

Although the findings of this study raise important issues for continued inquiry, they should be considered with some limitations in mind. First, although the items were selected from the NAEP grade 12 U.S. history exam, this investigation was not designed to support inferences about the exam as a whole, and these findings should not be interpreted as an indicator of how the NAEP exam functioned as a measure of student historical thinking. The items selected were a small, nonrandom sample of the NAEP multiple-choice items from the 2010 exam, and the present analysis does not account for how the selected items may have functioned in conjunction with other test items to elicit student historical thinking. Further, the items selected for this investigation do not represent the full spectrum of item formats that appeared on the exam. The NAEP U.S. history test comprises a variety of item formats, including short and extended constructed-response items. So, although the NAEP multiple-choice items did not tap the skills they were designed to measure in this investigation, it is possible that the NAEP exam as a whole is an effective indicator of student proficiency in these constructs. Research that examines how the entire range of NAEP item formats function as measures of historical thinking is worth pursuing. Little is known about the effects of item format on student historical thinking, and a better understanding of how different item formats on the NAEP exam affect student thinking would be useful.

A second limitation arises from the selection of participants. The deliberate choice to include students who had demonstrated high achievement in AP U.S. history affects the generalizability of the findings. A sample of students from a broader range of abilities and achievement might have yielded different results. It is possible that these items could have elicited more instances of historical thinking among less accomplished students. The AP students in this sample disproportionately drew on their historical knowledge to arrive at correct answers. Less accomplished history students, who lack the same depth of knowledge, might have approached the items differently. For example, they might have been more likely to engage in aspects of historical thinking when presented with an item on an unfamiliar topic. Conversely, it is also possible that construct-irrelevant processes would have been even more prevalent among a more representative sample of students. Faced with an unfamiliar topic, students might be more likely than AP students, for example, to randomly guess answers or focus on irrelevant features of the item to arrive at an answer.

Conclusion

The adoption of new learning standards that emphasize historical thinking has prompted interest in assessments that measure these complex processes. The standardized tests that currently aim to assess these processes rely heavily on multiple-choice items. To date, few systematic studies have sought to gather evidence about cognitive validity, and little is known about whether these items actually tap the knowledge and skills they are commonly used to measure. The present study helped to address the need for research in this area. The results do not support broad conclusions about whether historical thinking *could* be measured with multiple-choice items. However, they do point to the need for further investigation into whether the types of multiple-choice items currently used are in fact sound measures of these complex processes. More studies that explore the cognitive demands of extant multiple-choice items would provide a clearer picture of the current state of history testing and provide insight into the strengths and limitations of our current testing practices. Further research might also provide evidence about whether particular types of multiple-choice questions are better suited for gauging aspects of historical thinking than others.

Validity research that explores the cognitive demands of other item formats is also worth pursuing. Currently, there are few proven alternatives to traditional multiple-choice items for measuring student achievement in history. The most established alternatives to multiple-choice in the United States are extended free-response essays and document-based questions made famous by the AP history tests. Both formats require students to write extended essays in response to broad prompts, which makes them time-consuming to administer and expensive to score. Because of these practical limitations, it is likely that states and agencies will be reluctant to adopt these measures as the primary tool for assessing student learning. Further, even if states were inclined to adopt broad essay prompts, there is little research to support the notion that these formats are in fact superior measures of historical thinking. History education would benefit from research that explores the cognitive demands of a wide variety of assessment formats and from efforts to develop innovative forms of history assessments designed to support inferences about student achievement in historical thinking.

Appendix

Appendix A: The National Assessment Governing Board's Definition of Historical Analysis and Interpretation

Exercises assessing **Historical Analysis and Interpretation** will examine students' ability to distinguish value judgments in historical information, weigh evidence, synthesize information, apply knowledge, make judgments, formulate generalizations, and draw conclusions. Therefore, these exercises should ensure that the assessment tasks will address the whole range of historical thinking. These exercises will probe students' ability to:

- Specify and explain cause-and-effect relationships and connect contemporary events to their origins in the past.
- Categorize information and develop strategies for organizing a large body of facts.
- Examine multiple causes of historical developments.
- Explain points of view, biases, and value statements in historical sources.
- Determine the significance of people, events, and historical sources.
- Weigh and judge different views of the past as advanced by historical figures themselves, historians, and present-day commentators and public figures.
- Demonstrate that the interpretation and meaning of the past are open to change as new information and perspectives emerge.
- Develop sound generalizations and defend these generalizations with persuasive arguments.
- Make comparisons and recognize the limitations of generalizations.

- Apply knowledge, draw conclusions, and support those conclusions with convincing evidence.

This is the National Assessment Governing Board's definition of "Historical Analysis and Interpretation" (National Assessment Governing Board, 2011, pp. 42–43). Each of the four items selected for analysis in this study were designed to measure student achievement in these processes.

Appendix B
Codes That Emerged From Analysis on Dimension 1

Code	Brief Description
Historical analysis/interpretation	Student engages in an aspect of "Historical Analysis and Interpretation" as identified by the National Assessment Governing Board (see Appendix A) (cf. National Assessment Governing Board, 2011, pp. 42–43)
Factual recall/recognition	Student draws on declarative knowledge to generate an answer, identify an answer choice, or evaluate the plausibility of an answer choice
Reading comprehension	Student uses understanding of a written passage to evaluate answer choices or select an answer choice
Test-taking strategy	Student uses a construct irrelevant process that arises from working within a particular item format
Guessing	Student randomly guesses between two or more answer choices
Process of elimination	The student narrows the problem space by eliminating one or more answer choices from consideration

Appendix C. Sample Student Transcript Coded on all Three Dimensions at the Item Level

Student 11 – NAEP Dust Bowl Item (AP 3) Form 1, Day 1

Which is a famous book about conditions like those in the picture? Well, looking at it, it looks like a dust storm in a rural area. **I just read *The Grapes of Wrath* and it was all about the Dust Bowl and the family moving west.** [D1 Code: Factual Recall/Recognition] I'm going to see that as my best choice right now. Personally, I haven't read any of these other books or really heard what they're about. **Knowing *The Grapes of Wrath* being more about a rural area, I probably have to say [answer]** C. [D1 Code: Factual recall/recognition]

    Coding Dimension 1 - Factual recall/recognition
    Coding Dimension 2 – Construct-irrelevant process
    Coding Dimension 3 – Proficiency match

Note

This research was supported by the Bill & Melinda Gates Foundation, Contract No. 19308, Sam Wineburg, principal investigator. The content is solely the responsibility of the author and does not necessarily represent the views of the Bill & Melinda Gates Foundation.

References

Afflerbach, P., & Johnston, P. (1984). On the use of verbal reports in reading research. *Journal of Literacy Research, 16*(4), 307–322.

Aiken, L. R. (1982). Writing multiple-choice items to measure higher-order educational objectives. *Educational and Psychological Measurement, 42*(3), 803–806.

American Educational Research Association, American Psychological Association, & National Council on Measurement in Education. (2014). *Standards for educational and psychological testing.* Washington, DC: American Educational Research Association.

Bain, R. B., & Shreiner, T. L. (2005). Issues and options in creating a national assessment in world history. *The History Teacher, 38*(2), 241–271.

Breakstone, J. (2014). Try, try, try again: The process of designing new history assessments. *Theory & Research in Social Education, 42*(4), 453–485.

Calder, L. (2006). Uncoverage: Toward a signature pedagogy for the history survey. *The Journal of American History, 92*(4), 1358–1370.

Charap, L. G. (2015). Assessing historical thinking in the redesigned Advanced Placement United States history course and exam. In K. Ercikan & P. Seixas (Eds.), *New directions in assessing historical thinking* (pp. 159–170). New York, NY: Routledge.

College Board. (2014). *AP United States history: Course and exam description.* Retrieved from http://media.collegeboard.com/digitalServices/pdf/ap/ap-course-exam-descriptions/ap-us-history-course-and-exam-description.pdf

Cronbach, L. J. (1988). Five perspectives on validity argument. In H. Wainer & H. I. Braun (Eds.), *Test validity* (pp. 3–17). Hillsdale, NJ: Erlbaum.

Desimone, L. M., & Le Floch, K. C. (2004). Are we asking the right questions? Using cognitive interviews to improve surveys in education research. *Educational Evaluation and Policy Analysis, 26*(1), 1–22.

Díaz, A., Middendorf, J., Pace, D., & Shopkow, L. (2008). The history learning project: A department "decodes" its students. *The Journal of American History, 94*(4), 1211–1224.

Ercikan, K., & Seixas, P. (2015). (Eds.). *New directions in assessing historical thinking.* New York, NY: Routledge.

Ercikan, K., Seixas, P., Lyons-Thomas, J., & Gibson, L. (2015). Cognitive validity evidence for validating assessments of historical thinking. In K. Ercikan & P. Seixas (Eds.), *New directions in assessing historical thinking* (pp. 206–220). New York, NY: Routledge.

Ericsson, K. A., & Simon, H. A. (1993). *Protocol analysis: Verbal reports as data.* Cambridge, MA: MIT Press.

Farr, R., Pritchard, R., & Smitten, B. (1990). A description of what happens when an examinee takes a multiple-choice reading comprehension test. *Journal of Educational Measurement, 27*(3), 209–226. doi:10.1111/j.1745-3984.1990.tb00744.x

Fitzpatrick, R., & Morrison, E. J. (1971). Performance and product evaluation. In R. L. Thorndike (Ed.), *Educational measurement* (2nd ed., pp. 237–270). Washington, DC: American Council on Education.

Frederiksen, N. (1984). The real test bias: Influences of testing on teaching and learning. *American Psychologist, 39*(3), 193–202.

Gottlieb, E., & Wineburg, S. (2012). Between *veritas* and *communitas:* Epistemic switching in the reading of academic and sacred history. *Journal of Learning Sciences, 21*(1), 84–129.

Grant, S. G., & Horn, C. (2006). The state of state-level history tests. In S. G. Grant (Ed.), *Measuring history: Cases of state-level testing across the United States* (pp. 9–27). Greenwich, CT: Information Age.

Guilford, J. P. (1959). Three faces of intellect. *American Psychologist, 14*(8), 469–479.

Haladyna, T. M. (1997). *Writing test items to evaluate higher order thinking.* Boston, MA: Allyn & Bacon.

Haladyna, T. M. (2004). *Developing and validating multiple-choice test items* (3rd ed.). London: Lawrence Erlbaum Associates.

Haladyna, T. M., & Downing, S. M. (2004). Construct-irrelevant variance in high-stakes testing. *Educational Measurement: Issues and Practice, 23*(1), 17–27.

Hamilton, L. S. (1994). *An investigation of students' affective responses to alternative assessment formats.* Paper presented at the Annual Meeting of the National Council on Measurement in Education, New Orleans, LA.

Hamilton, L. S., Nussbaum, E. M., & Snow, R. E. (1997). Interview procedures for validating science assessments. *Applied Measurement in Education, 10*(2), 181–200.

Haney, W., & Scott, L. (1987). Talking with children about tests: An exploratory study of test ambiguity. In R. O. Freedle (Ed.), *Cognitive and linguistic analysis of test performance* (pp. 298–368). Norwood, NJ: Ablex Publishing.

Hibbinson, E. P. (1991). The ideal multiple choice question: A protocol analysis. *Forum for Reading, 22*(2), 36–41.

Hill, J. (2013). The case for assessment reform for California schools. *California Council for the Social Studies Occasional Papers, 2*(1), 1–15.

Holt, T. (1990). *Thinking historically: Narrative, imagination, and understanding.* New York, NY: College Entrance Examination Board.

Hynd, C., Holschuh, J. P., & Hubbard, B. P. (2004). Thinking like a historian: College students' reading of multiple historical documents. *Journal of Literacy Research, 36*(2), 141–176.

Immerwahr, D. (2008). The fact/narrative distinction and student examinations in history. *The History Teacher, 41*(2), 199–205.

Kaliski, P., Smith, K., & Huff, K. (2015). The importance of construct validity evidence in history assessment: What is often overlooked or misunderstood? In K. Ercikan & P. Seixas (Eds.), *New directions in assessing historical thinking* (pp. 195–205). New York, NY: Routledge.

Kane, M. T. (2006). Validation. In R. L. Brennan (Ed.), *Educational measurement* (4th ed., pp. 17–64). Westport, CT: Praeger.

Kane, M. T. (2013). Validating the interpretations and uses of test scores. *Journal of Educational Measurement, 50*(1), 1–73.

Karras, R. W. (1991). Let's improve multiple-choice tests. *OAH Magazine of History, 6*(1), 8–43.

Katz, I. R., Bennett, R. E., & Berger, A. E. (2000). Effects of response format on difficulty of SAT-mathematics items: It's not the strategy. *Journal of Educational Measurement, 37*(1), 39–57.

Kazemi, E. (2002). Exploring test performance in mathematics: The questions children's answers raise. *The Journal of Mathematical Behavior, 21*(2), 203–224. doi:10.1016/S0732-3123(02)00118-9

Kelly, T. M. (2013). *Teaching history in the digital age*. Ann Arbor, MI: University of Michigan Press.

Kuusela, H., & Pallab, P. (2000). A comparison of concurrent and retrospective verbal protocol analysis. *The American Journal of Psychology, 113*(3), 387–404.

Lane, S., & Stone, C. A. (2006). Performance assessments. In R. L. Brennan (Ed.), *Educational measurement* (4th ed., pp. 387–431). Westport, CT: Praeger.

Leighton, J. P. (2004). Avoiding misconception, misuse, and missed opportunities: The collection of verbal reports in educational achievement testing. *Educational Measurement: Issues and Practice, 23*(4), 6–15.

Leinhardt, G., & Young, K. M. (1996). Two texts, three readers: Distance and expertise in reading history. *Cognition and Instruction, 14*, 441–486.

Lévesque, S. (2008). *Thinking historically: Educating students for the twenty-first century*. Toronto: University of Toronto Press.

Li, M., Ruiz-Primo, M., & Shavelson, R. (2006). Towards a science achievement framework: The case of TIMSS 1999. In S. Howie & T. Plomp (Eds.), *Contexts of learning mathematics and science: Lessons learned from TIMSS* (pp. 291–311). London: Routledge.

Martin, D., Maldonado, S. I., Schneider, J., & Smith, M. (2011). *A report on the state of history education: State policies and national programs*. Retrieved from http://teachinghistory.org/system/files/teachinghistory_special_report_2011.pdf

Martinez, M. E. (1991). A comparison of multiple-choice and constructed figural response items. *Journal of Educational Measurement, 28*(2), 131–145. doi:10.1111/j.1745-3984.1991.tb00349.x

Martinez, M. E. (1999). Cognition and the question of test item format. *Educational Psychologist, 34*(4), 207–218.

Messick, S. (1995). Validity of psychological assessment: Validation of inferences from persons' responses and performances as scientific inquiry into score meaning. *American Psychologist, 50*(9), 741–749. doi:10.1037/0003-066X.50.9.741

National Assessment Governing Board. (2011). *U.S. history framework for the 2010 National Assessment of Educational Progress*. Retrieved from http://www.nagb.org/publications/frameworks/historyframework.pdf

National Center for Educational Statistics. (n.d.). *NAEP questions tool*. Retrieved from http://nces.ed.gov/nationsreportcard/itmrlsx/search.aspx?subject=history

National Center for Educational Statistics. (2011). *The nation's report card: U. S. history 2010*. Retrieved from http://nces.ed.gov/nationsreportcard/pdf/main2010/2011468.pdf

National Governors Association & Council of Chief State School Officers. (2010). *Common Core State Standards for English language arts & literacy in history/social studies, science, and technical subjects*. Retrieved from http://www.corestandards.org/assets/CCSSI_ELA%20Standards.pdf

Nokes, J. D. (2013). *Building students' historical literacies: Learning to read and reason with historical evidence*. New York, NY: Routledge.

Pace, D. (2004). Decoding the reading of history: An example of the process. *New Directions for Teaching and Learning, 2004*(98), 13–21.

Paxton, R. J. (1999). A deafening silence: History textbooks and the students who read them. *Review of Educational Research, 69*(3), 315–339.

Paxton, R. J. (2003). Don't know much about history—never did. *Phi Delta Kappan, 85*(4), 264–273.

Pellegrino, J. W., Chudowsky, N., & Glaser, R. (Eds.). (2001). *Knowing what students know*. Washington, DC: National Academy Press.

Pressley, M., & Afflerbach, P. (1995). *Verbal protocols of reading: The nature of constructively responsive reading*. Hillsdale, NJ: Erlbaum.

Reich, G. A. (2009). Testing historical knowledge: Standards, multiple-choice questions and student reasoning. *Theory and Research in Social Education, 37*(3), 325–360.

Reich, G. A. (2013). Imperfect models, imperfect conclusions: An exploratory study of multiple-choice tests and historical knowledge. *The Journal of Social Studies Research, 37*(1), 3–16.

Resnick, L. B., & Resnick, D. P. (1992). Assessing the thinking curriculum: New tools for educational reform. In B. R. Gifford & M. C. O'Connor (Eds.), *Changing assessments: Alternative views of aptitude, achievement and instruction* (pp. 37–75). Boston, MA: Kluwer Academic Publishers.

Robelen, E. (2011, February 4). What to expect from the revised AP U.S. history program. *Education Week*. Retrieved from http://blogs.edweek.org/edweek/curriculum/2011/02/what_to_expect_from_the_revise.html

Ruiz-Primo, M. A., Shavelson, R. J., Li, M., & Schultz, S. E. (2001). On the validity of cognitive interpretations of scores from alternative mapping techniques. *Educational Assessment, 7*(2), 99–141.

Scheurman, G., & Reynolds, K. (2010). The "history problem" in curricular reform: A warning to constructivists from the new social studies. In B. Slater Stern (Ed.), *The new social studies: People, projects, and perspectives* (pp. 341–360). Charlotte, NC: Information Age Publishing.

Seixas, P., Morton, T., Colyer, J., & Fornazzari, S. (2013). *The big six: Historical thinking concepts*. Toronto: Nelson Education.

Shanahan, C., Shanahan, T., & Misischia, C. (2011). Analysis of expert readers in three disciplines: History, mathematics, and chemistry. *Journal of Literacy Research, 43*(4), 393–429.

Shanahan, T., & Shanahan, C. (2008). Teaching disciplinary literacy to adolescents: Rethinking content-area literacy. *Harvard Educational Review, 78*(1), 40–59.

Shenkman, R. (2009). Sam Wineburg dares to ask if the Teaching American History program is a boondoggle. *History News Network*. Retrieved from http://historynewsnetwork.org/article/76806

Skakun, E. N., Maguire, T. O., & Cook, D. A. (1994). Strategy choices in multiple-choice items. *Academic Medicine, 69*(10). Retrieved from http://journals.lww.com/academicmedicine/Fulltext/1994/10000/Strategy_choices_in_multiple_choice_items.25.aspx

Smith, M., & Breakstone, J. (2015). History Assessments of Thinking: An investigation of cognitive validity. In K. Ercikan & P. Seixas (Eds.), *New directions in assessing historical thinking* (pp. 233–245). New York, NY: Routledge.

Taylor, K. L., & Dionne, J. P. (2000). Accessing problem-solving strategy knowledge: The complementary use of concurrent verbal protocols and retrospective debriefing. *Journal of Educational Psychology, 92*(3), 413–425. doi:10.1037/0022-0663.92.3.413

Texas Education Agency. (2011). *Chapter 113. Texas Essential Knowledge and Skills for Social Studies: Subchapter C. High school*. Retrieved from http://ritter.tea.state.tx.us/rules/tac/chapter113/ch113c.pdf

VanSledright, B. A. (2004). What does it mean to think historically . . . and how do you teach it? *Social Education, 68*(3), 230–233.

VanSledright, B. A. (2013). *Assessing historical thinking and understanding: Innovative designs for new standards*. New York, NY: Taylor & Francis.

VanSledright, B. A. (2015). Assessing learning in the history classroom. In K. Ercikan & P. Seixas (Eds.), *New directions in assessing historical thinking* (pp. 75–88). New York, NY: Routledge.

Ward, W. C., Frederiksen, N., & Carlson, S. B. (1980). Construct validity of free-response and machine-scorable forms of a test. *Journal of Educational Measurement, 17*(1), 11–29.

Wineburg, S. (1991). Historical problem solving: A study of the cognitive processes used in the evaluation of documentary and pictorial evidence. *Journal of Educational Psychology, 83*(1), 73–87. doi:10.1037/0022-0663.83.1.7

Wineburg, S. (1994). Cognitive representation of historical texts. In G. Leinhardt, I. L. Beck, & C. Stainton (Eds.), *Teaching and learning history* (pp. 85–136). New York, NY: Routledge.

Wineburg, S. (1998). Reading Abraham Lincoln: An expert/expert study in the interpretation of historical texts. *Cognitive Science, 22*(3), 319–346. doi:10.1016/S0364-0213(99)80043-3

Wineburg, S. (2001). *Historical thinking and other unnatural acts: Charting the future of teaching the past.* Philadelphia, PA: Temple.

Wineburg, S., Martin, D., & Monte-Sano, C. (2011). *Reading like a historian: Teaching literacy in middle and high school history classrooms.* New York, NY: Teachers College Press.

Wineburg, S., Smith, M., & Breakstone, J. (2012). New directions in assessment: Using Library of Congress sources to assess historical understanding. *Social Education, 76*(6), 290–293.

Manuscript received September 29, 2015
Final revision received May 9, 2017
Accepted May 25, 2017

American Educational Research Journal
December 2017, Vol. 54, No. 6, pp. 1288–1315
DOI: 10.3102/0002831217718164
© 2017 AERA. http://aerj.aera.net

Accommodating Change:
Relating Fidelity of Implementation to
Program Fit in Educational Reforms

Eleanor R. Anderson
Northwestern University

Asking practitioners to make larger changes to their practice is often thought to lead to lower fidelity of implementation. However, salient differences between ambitious new reforms and teachers' existing practices may also facilitate processes of conceptual change and correspondingly increase fidelity of implementation. I use survey data on the implementation of two Comprehensive School Reform programs to investigate this puzzle, presenting a series of descriptive multivariate regressions that—contrary to conventional wisdom—predominantly support a positive association between larger changes and higher fidelity. I also address alternative explanations for this finding and discuss the conceptual and empirical strengths and weaknesses, implications for future research, and potential utility for practice of each interpretation.

KEYWORDS: comprehensive school reform, conceptual change, fidelity of implementation, magnitude of change, organizational change

L eaders seeking to make change in their schools often do so through the adoption of evidence-based interventions intended to establish high-quality pedagogical practices in schools and classrooms (Desimone, 2002). Evaluations of such programs in practice, however, have shown uneven implementation of their recommendations (Corcoran, Hoppe, Luhm, & Supovitz, 2000; Desimone, 2002; Sherin & Drake, 2009; Spillane, 2004). Like the frontline workers in other sectors—arguably even more so—teachers often exert wide discretion in interpreting and carrying out the elements of a reform adopted by their school or district (Berends, 2000; Lipsky, 1980;

ELEANOR R. ANDERSON is a postdoctoral fellow in the School of Education and Social Policy at Northwestern University, 2120 Campus Drive, Annenberg Hall 238, Evanston, IL 60208; e-mail: *eanderson@u.northwestern.edu*. Her research interests include the implementation and institutionalization of educational reforms and the cognitive, social, organizational, and political processes that facilitate and undermine high-quality educational practice.

Scott & Meyer, 1983). Given strongly entrenched ideas about the nature of teaching and learning, not to mention substantial constraints of time, resources, and organizational support, at times this can result in "new" practices that are only superficially different from old ones (Coburn, 2004; D. K. Cohen, 1988; Mehta, 2015; Spillane, 2004).

It is not enough then to simply design or select a program whose goals align with a particular vision for teaching and learning practices. Those seeking to bring their vision to life must also ask to what degree enactment in a given context is likely to match the program's goals. While the benefits of pursuing strict adherence to a program's designed elements may need to be weighed against other considerations (McLaughlin, 1987), for those decisions to be well informed, leaders and policymakers need good information about the dynamics that affect fidelity of implementation.

It is taken for granted, in most cases, that in adopting new programs, schools are asking teachers to make changes to their practice. However, the scope and scale of those changes may vary dramatically from case to case. The magnitude of change a new program asks of teachers is a reflection of its fit with existing practices, that is, it depends both on the specifications of the program itself and also on the practices teachers were engaging in previously (Coburn, 2004).

Put together, these issues present researchers, policy designers, and school leaders with a puzzle: Is high-fidelity implementation more likely in cases where a new program is similar to teachers' existing practices, minimizing the change they are asked to enact? Or is fidelity increased when newly specified practices are very different from existing practices, signaling to practitioners that real change has arrived? That is, how is program fit related to fidelity of implementation?

Conventional accounts of policy implementation and organizational change have postulated that practitioners asked to make bigger changes generally implement those changes with lesser fidelity (D. K. Cohen & Moffitt, 2009; W. M. Cohen & Levinthal, 1990; Guskey, 1991; Mazmanian & Sabatier, 1983; Van Meter & Van Horn, 1975). In this paper, I challenge that assumption, offering evidence that the opposite may often be true: Practitioners asked to make bigger changes may actually implement those changes with *greater* fidelity. Drawing on literature in teacher learning and conceptual change, I demonstrate that a cognitive account of implementation suggests plausible mechanisms for both possibilities. Using survey data on the implementation of two Comprehensive School Reform (CSR) programs, I present a series of descriptive multivariate regressions that predominantly support the latter relationship—an association between larger change and higher fidelity. I conclude by addressing a number of possible explanations for the empirical finding, discussing their conceptual and empirical strengths and weaknesses, implications for future research, and potential utility for practice.

Conceptual Framework

Terminology

In this paper, I am explicitly theorizing about organizational-level educational reforms, that is, programs adopted at the school level that specify aspects of the work of individuals within the school. I consider such programs to be school-level policies, and thus for the purposes of this paper I use the terms *program* and *policy* interchangeably.

Fidelity of Implementation

For years, social and behavioral researchers have called for increased attention to the fidelity with which programs and policies are implemented (Century, Rudnick, & Freeman, 2010; Dane & Schneider, 1998; Fullan, 1983). Scholars have taken a variety of conceptual and methodological approaches to measuring fidelity of implementation, corresponding to varying research questions.

For studies intended to measure the efficacy or effectiveness of a particular program or policy, knowing how much of an intervention was actually administered is critical to understanding its impact. Even under experimental conditions, without information about fidelity, mixed or limited results could be the result of the inherent (in)efficacy of a program or of inadequate implementation (Desimone, 2002; Dusenbury, Brannigan, Falco, & Hansen, 2003; Flay, 1986; Linder & Peters, 1987; Shadish, Cook, & Campbell, 2002). Large-scale experimental or quasi-experimental designs often use relatively coarse measures of fidelity of implementation. At the most basic level, this may simply take the form of a binary compliance variable or a dosage threshold to differentiate intent-to-treat from treatment-on-treated samples. In other cases, researchers may use a measure of dosage to estimate of the effect of increasing exposure to the intervention (Cordray & Pion, 2006; Lipsey & Cordray, 2000).

Other studies are designed to investigate the processes through which program and policy implementation occur. For example, they may seek to describe processes of sensemaking and interpretation (e.g., Coburn, 2004; Spillane, 2004), how teachers adapt a program to fit their local needs (e.g., Datnow & Castellano, 2000a), or how qualitatively different forms of the same policy take hold and interact with different organizational cultures (e.g., Lin, 2002). In these cases, a one-dimensional measure of fidelity is often wholly inadequate (Century & Cassata, 2016). Rather, these studies often use ethnographic observation in one or a small number of schools to provide rich descriptions of the many different forms enacted policy can take.

A third class of studies seeks to describe relationships between various aspects of implementation as a process and an outcome. Such studies might include investigations of the importance of teacher buy-in to program sustainability (Berends, 2000), the relationship between program type and styles of management (Rowan, Camburn, & Barnes, 2004), or the role of teacher knowledge in program efficacy (Phelps & Schilling, 2004). It is in this spirit that I use the construct of fidelity to intervention prescriptions— not as normative requirement but as an important factor in the dynamics of implementation. While this approach cannot capture the rich variation across different cases of implementation, its simplicity makes it well suited for operationalization across a large number of observations, offering a different type of potency.

Among the limitations of the construct of fidelity across all these uses is that it assumes a program that offers specific, observable prescriptions. Many programs and policies are not of this character at all, being much more ambiguous, and in these cases, fidelity is largely undefined (D. K. Cohen & Moffitt, 2009; Majone & Wildavsky, 1979; Matland, 1995). Organizational scholars have noted that innovations transform over time as they diffuse among organizations, a process also obscured by traditional definitions of fidelity (Ansari, Fiss, & Zajac, 2010). Other objections are more philosophical: The term often carries a normative valence that seems to suggest that practitioners *should* implement programs exactly as they are designed, in spite of the fact that teachers and other frontline workers often have information about local settings that developers don't (McLaughlin, 1987).

I agree that these limitations point to the need for better constructs in this area (Century & Cassata, 2016); however, that endeavor is not one I take up in this paper. Rather, I define fidelity of implementation as the similarity between enacted practice and the benchmark of program designers' specifications (Dane & Schneider, 1998; Lewis & Seibold, 1993). I consider the constraints this imposes on which programs I am able to explore empirically to represent boundary conditions of the analysis.

Implementation and Conceptual Change

Frontline workers shape the way new programs and policies are implemented in a host of ways. Programs cannot specify literally everything a teacher is to do. Therefore, teachers must fill in the blanks of the moment-to-moment specifics of how they will implement a program (Coburn & Stein, 2010). In addition, teachers can and often do choose to make adaptations to what is written or prescribed (Corcoran et al., 2000; Datnow & Castellano, 2000b). As a rule, what makes adaptations problematic is when they undermine some important principle underlying the reform's effect (Datnow & Castellano, 2000a; Spillane, 2004; Supovitz, Poglinco, & Bach, 2002). This means that teachers' degree of understanding of key principles (as well as their willingness and ability to follow them) is critical to fidelity of implementation (Gregoire, 2003; Spillane, 2004; Spillane, Reiser, & Reimer, 2002).

Constructivist theories of learning indicate that people's understandings of new ideas are based on and built from their existing conceptions (Rumelhart, 1980; Schank & Abelson, 1977). Everyday learning means making minor changes in the organization of existing conceptions or integrating new ideas into existing cognitive structures (Carey, 1988; Fosnot, 1996; Posner, Strike, Hewson, & Gertzog, 1982; Rumelhart, 1980). However, cognitive scientists have long observed that some ideas are more difficult to learn than others. A number of examples of such challenges have been documented in science education, including the concept of force (DiSessa, 1993), processes of natural selection (Brumby, 1984), and diffusion (Chi, 2005).

Scholars of program and policy implementation have noted similar patterns with regard to changes in educational philosophy. For example, Cohen's (1990) classic study of "Mrs. Oublier" illustrated a teacher who felt that she had made significant changes to her instructional practice based on California's mathematics reform. However, in observing her teaching, Cohen found that her practices adhered to some of the reform's more superficial prescriptions but deviated significantly from other, more philosophically unfamiliar ones. Even with enthusiastic effort, reforms can be challenging to wrap one's mind around.

Several streams of thought exist as to how and under what circumstances teachers are able to make significant shifts in their understanding (Gregoire, 2003). One set of approaches draws a distinction between small and large changes in cognitive structure, often referred to as *assimilation* and *accommodation*, respectively (Carey, 1988; Fosnot, 1996; Piaget, 1977; Posner et al., 1982; Strike & Posner, 1992). When new ideas are dramatically different from existing conceptions, making only small changes in cognitive structures through the processes of assimilation will typically lead to misconceptions. Other theories emphasize differences in the type of cognitive processing, distinguishing between heuristic and systematic processing. Heuristic processing is faster but more shallow and rarely leads to lasting transformations in understanding (Eagly & Chaiken, 1993; Gregoire, 2003).

Scholars have also offered varying explanations for what prompts these different cognitive processes. For example, among other factors, Posner et al. (1982) indicate that for cognitive accommodation to occur, a learner must experience dissatisfaction with his or her existing conceptions. In the attempt to interpret new information, a conflict must become apparent between existing conceptions and the new idea that is salient enough to prompt a rethinking and ultimately reorganization of existing understandings.

Other scholars have critiqued this approach for being excessively rational and have offered models that foreground affect, motives, and goals above and beyond the rationalistic inclination for consistency (Strike & Posner, 1992). For example, Gregoire (2003) provides an integrated model beginning with teachers' assessments of whether a reform message implicates their own practices and beliefs. Only if teachers both perceive implications for themselves and have sufficient motivation and ability will they engage with the reform's ideas through systematic processing that may lead to more substantial changes in belief.

Program Fit

This study's central question concerns a new program's fit with existing practices and thus the magnitude of change it asks teachers to enact. Many researchers have noted variation in this factor from one implementation case to the next. Policy implementation literature has often taken a macrolevel perspective, treating the ambitiousness of a reform as a feature of the policy itself (D. K. Cohen & Moffitt, 2009; Mazmanian & Sabatier, 1983; Van Meter & Van Horn, 1975). Some organizational researchers have taken a more meso-level perspective, noting that heterogeneity in implementing contexts means that the same program or innovation may have differing degrees of fit and misfit in different organizations, thus entailing changes of differing scope (Ansari et al., 2010; W. M. Cohen & Levinthal, 1990). In the context of educational reforms, even an organizational-level analysis may not be fine-grained enough as fit with a new program may vary from individual to individual even with a single school (Coburn, 2004; Sherin & Drake, 2009). Thus, for this paper, I define the magnitude of change as the degree of difference between a new program's specifications and an individual teacher's existing practices.

Relating Fit and Fidelity

Most existing policy implementation research, both in educational settings and more broadly, suggests that—other things being equal—asking practitioners to make larger changes tends to reduce fidelity of implementation (D. K. Cohen & Moffitt, 2009; W. M. Cohen & Levinthal, 1990; Guskey, 1991; Mazmanian & Sabatier, 1983; Van Meter & Van Horn, 1975). As Guskey (1991) puts it, "if there is one truism in the vast research literature on change it is that the magnitude of change persons are asked to make is inversely related to their likelihood of making it" (p. 241).

Constraints on material resources are perhaps the most straightforward obstacle to implementation. For example, money and support provided by the policy itself may or may not be adequate to the implementation task (D. K. Cohen, Moffitt, & Goldin, 2007; Van Meter & Van Horn, 1975). In the education sector, structural opportunities for enforcing accountability may be especially limited by the highly autonomous and uncertain nature of the work itself (D. K. Cohen, 1988; Lipsky, 1980; Scott & Meyer, 1983), although recent research has suggested this may be changing (Hallett, 2010; Spillane & Burch, 2006). To the extent that larger changes require greater resources or more supervision, this suggests they will be implemented with less fidelity.

Theories of conceptual change offer some evidence for a connection between larger changes and lower fidelity as well. Programs designed for educational reform are frequently built around conceptions of subject matter, teaching, and/or learning that differ substantially from those held by many practitioners (indeed, this is what marks them as reforms). Thus, differences between educators' existing ideas and those espoused by a new program are unlikely to be very small but rather may range from moderate to quite large. New ideas that do not align with people's existing conceptions are more challenging to recognize and understand (Carey, 1988; Gregoire, 2003; Posner et al., 1982; Strike & Posner, 1992). Thus, one might argue that larger changes would be increasingly likely to prompt adaptations during implementation that undercut the principles of the reform, therefore being associated with lower fidelity.

One important source of empirical evidence supporting this prediction comes from Cynthia Coburn's (2004) in-depth case comparison of three California teachers' responses to conflicting messages about literacy instruction. Using extensive shadowing, oral histories, and document analysis, Coburn identified several categories of response to policy messages including either minor or major changes to practice.[1] She also identified several message characteristics that seemed to consistently prompt different responses, including the degree of "congruence" between a new message and teachers' existing practices and beliefs. Coburn found teachers incorporated high congruence messages by making minor changes in their practice relatively frequently. When message congruence was low, teachers were much more likely to reject those messages outright and not incorporate them at all.

Yet, a few studies have suggested that this may not be the full picture (Huberman & Miles, 1984). For example, Correnti and Rowan (2007) point out that several examples of school reforms that have been successful in bringing about substantial changes in teaching practice did so using programs that were "ambitious and represent a marked change in existing practices" (p. 302).

Indeed, theories of conceptual change also support this competing prediction. For programs representing at least a moderate change from existing approaches, the bigger the difference, the more salient and problematic it may become for practitioners and the more clearly it may implicate their own practice—making it increasingly likely that it will be interpreted through accommodation or systematic processing. This provides a substantial theoretical reason to predict that larger changes might be understood better and thus implemented with greater fidelity. Spillane et al. (2002) make a similar point, emphasizing the importance of this type of cognitive conflict: "It is key to create a sense of dissonance in which agents see the issues in their current practice rather than seeing the new ideas as achieved within their current practice" (p. 418).

Indeed, Coburn's (2004) study offers empirical evidence toward this point as well. Coburn found that when teachers did incorporate low congruence messages into their classroom practice, they were much more likely to do so "in ways that pushed their thinking or caused them to reorganize their practice in more substantial ways" (p. 228). That is, when taken up at all, these larger asks were more likely to result in substantial changes to practice, aligned to the principles of the new approach.

Coburn's (2004) analysis drew on the responses of only three teachers. However, her findings underscore the potential significance of the magnitude of change a program asks in the process of policy implementation. The notion that large policy changes might frequently be implemented with higher fidelity than smaller ones is quite contrary to the conventional wisdom of policy implementation. Strong evidence of such a relationship would have significant implications for policy design, selection, implementation, and analysis and set an important agenda for future research in the area. To examine this possibility empirically with a large sample of teachers, I turn to the case of Comprehensive School Reform programs.

Empirical Analyses

Setting: Comprehensive School Reform

Schoolwide reform models experienced a meteoric rise in prominence and funding during the 1990s and 2000s. To qualify as a CSR, a program must be comprehensive, addressing the need for change systemically at the whole school level rather than only one subject or grade level or classroom at a time and also specify practices that are evidence-based, supported by research demonstrating their effectiveness (Borman, Hewes, Overman, & Brown, 2003; Comprehensive School Reform Quality Center, 2005; Orland, Hoffman, & Vaughn, 2010).

I focus on two CSR programs: America's Choice (Corcoran et al., 2000; Glazer, 2009; Poglinco et al., 2003; Supovitz et al., 2002; Supovitz, Poglinco, & Snyder, 2001) and Success for All (Datnow & Castellano, 2000b; Slavin et al., 1996; Slavin & Madden, 1999, 2000). Both programs are well specified, making them appropriate for an analysis of fidelity. Both programs also were designed around conceptions of achievement that differ substantially from the norm in many schools, making them appropriate for examining mechanisms related to conceptual change.

America's Choice (AC) was developed by the National Center on Education and the Economy and first implemented in a cohort of schools in 1998 (Corcoran et al., 2000; Glazer, 2009; Supovitz et al., 2001). The program came out of the standards movement and is built around a set of internationally benchmarked standards (National Center on Education and the Economy & University of Pittsburgh, 1997), which teachers are expected to use to develop their instructional strategies. The central philosophy is to hold all students to high expectations rather than comparing them to one another. Success for All (SFA) was developed by researchers at Johns Hopkins University and first implemented in 1987 (Slavin et al., 1996). The program's central philosophy is that "every child can and must succeed in the early grades, no matter what it takes" (Slavin et al., 1996, p. 43). Teachers and administrators are to identify difficulties as early as possible and intervene intensively, working "relentlessly" to ensure that every child learns to read (Slavin et al., 1996; Slavin & Madden, 2000).

Both programs offer prescriptions for staffing, professional development, materials, assessment, and other schoolwide practices. However, because the current study is concerned with teachers' role in the implementation process, for this analysis, I focus specifically on each program's specifications for classroom practice. Differences in the ways the two programs are structured means that high-fidelity implementation has different requirements for teachers implementing each CSR.

America's Choice offers clear recommendations for how teachers should spend their time in literacy instruction, with each day including a 2- to 2.5-hour block including an hour of Readers Workshop and an hour of Writers Workshop. While the program includes training in a range of instructional strategies for implementing these workshops, teachers do not have a script to follow, nor are all materials provided. A study of the implementation of AC found substantial variation in teachers' literacy lessons, ranging from high-quality readers and writers workshops, to workshops lacking in important elements, to no discernable workshop structure at all (Supovitz et al., 2002). Thus, high-fidelity implementation of AC involves understanding the purpose of these different elements well enough to tie them together coherently and make use of the strategies and resources that America's Choice recommends.

Success for All is a much more highly regimented literacy program in which teachers are expected to follow detailed 90-minute daily lesson plans using SFA-provided materials. A study of the implementation of SFA found that despite the clarity and specificity of instructions, most teachers made modifications in their implementation of SFA lessons (Datnow & Castellano, 2000a, 2000b). Some were relatively minor or seen by developers as appropriate adaptations to variations in student population. However, many included significant deviations from the design of the program. The most common adaptations involved spending extra time on certain areas of the lesson and eliminating or making substitutions for others. Contrary to prior research on other reforms, the inclination toward adaptation did not seem closely linked with teacher characteristics, including level of experience, gender, race, or even belief in the program's efficacy. Thus, high-fidelity implementation of SFA involves using the program-provided curriculum with minimal adaptation, even when it contradicts one's own preferences as a teacher.

Data and Measures

The data used for this study are drawn from those collected by University of Michigan researchers as part of the Study for Instructional Improvement (SII). SII was a nationwide, quasi-experimental study designed to measure the effects of comprehensive school reform programs in high-poverty elementary schools (Correnti & Rowan, 2007; Rowan, Correnti, Miller, & Camburn, 2009). The data I use were collected between 2000 and 2004, at 61 schools, each of which had adopted either SFA or AC starting in 1998, 1999, or 2000.[2] For each of the three years each school participated in the study, every teacher was administered a Teacher Questionnaire that included questions about teaching practices, perceptions of the school improvement program, educational background, teaching experience, and demographic information. Data about teaching practices were also collected in the form of Language Arts Logs.[3] Logs were designed to capture the daily instruction experienced by two cohorts of focal students in each school as they progressed from Grades K–2 or 3–5; teachers completed logs only if and when they were responsible for the language arts instruction of one or more of the focal students on the assigned log day. The response rate ranged from 84% to 77% over the course of the study (Rowan et al., 2009). To measure fidelity using the Log data, I take the annual average of each teacher's fidelity score from each log he or she completed, resulting in one fidelity score per respondent per year of available data.

The sample represented in these data is shown in Table 1. A total of 556 teachers filled out both at least one log and enough of the teacher questionnaire to be usable for this analysis. Spread over the four years of the study, this corresponds to 1,267 observations. This comprises the subsample to which all subsequent analyses will refer. This subsample is similar in composition to the complete sample with respect to teacher experience, education, demographics, and employment category. The one area in which it differs dramatically is in the relative representation of America's Choice and Success for All. While in the complete sample, these are represented nearly equally, in the subsample, there are more than twice as many SFA observations as AC observations. For this reason, in addition to differences between the programs themselves, all analyses are presented separately for AC and SFA teachers.

CSR Program Fit

As discussed previously, I conceptualize program fit as the magnitude of difference between teachers' existing practices and those specified by the program. No external measure of teachers' practices prior to program implementation exists in the SII data. Therefore, I use a teacher self-report of whether or not "The school improvement program in this school requires me to make major changes in my classroom practice." The question allowed four answers: *strongly disagree, disagree, agree,* or *strongly agree* (Study of

Table 1
Study Samples

	Complete Sample	Subsample
Total		
Observations (1/teacher/year)	4,844	1,267
Unique teachers	2,815	556
Teachers with multiple years of data	1,123	295
Intervention (%)		
America's Choice	53.39	31.81
Success for All	46.61	68.19
Teacher		
Mean experience (years)	12.85	11.93
Teacher education (%)		
Holding undergraduate degree	95.50	98.50
Holding graduate degree	68.67	71.98
Teacher demographics (%)		
Female	86.61	87.92
Non-White	48.98	46.17
Employment category (%)		
Full-time	89.24	95.66
Permanent/standard certification	77.62	81.53

Instructional Improvement, 2001, 2002, 2003, 2004). I take teachers' response to this question as a measure of the magnitude of change the program asks of them, with those who strongly disagreed experiencing the smallest changes and those who strongly agreed experiencing the largest changes.

Figure 1 shows the average reported program fit for teachers who answered the survey at least twice. It shows that on average, AC teachers report that their CSR program requires a larger change than SFA teachers do. In the full sample, both AC and SFA teachers report program misfit as progressively smaller each time that they answer the survey. The same pattern holds in the study sample for SFA teachers and AC teachers who answered the survey more than twice.

Because I use this measure to approximate the magnitude of the prescribed change at the time of the program's initial adoption, rather than the way the magnitude of a remaining change affects fidelity over time, I use individuals' earliest recorded response to this question for all subsequent analyses.

Figure 2 is a histogram representing the distribution of teachers' first reports of their CSR program's fit with existing practices. Each bar represents the proportion of teachers who strongly disagree (SD), disagree (D), agree (A), and strongly agree (SA) that their school improvement program requires major changes to their classroom practice for AC and SFA, respectively.

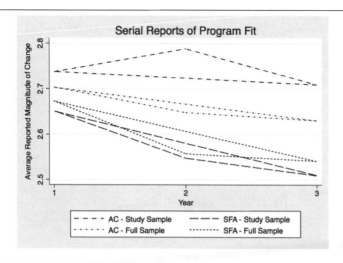

Figure 1. **Average CSR program fit reported by teachers who responded to the annual Teacher Questionnaire at least twice. Magnitude of prescribed change measured by responses to "The school improvement program in this school requires me to make major changes in my classroom practice" with *strongly disagree* = 1, *disagree* = 2, *agree* = 3, *strongly agree* = 4.**

Comparing across programs, slightly more AC teachers (58%) agree or strongly agree that AC requires major changes than the proportion of SFA teachers agreeing or strongly agreeing that SFA requires major changes (53%). Comparing within each program, for both AC and SFA, teachers' reports of the magnitude of change the program asks of them vary widely. Among teachers implementing America's Choice, 5% report that they strongly disagree and 37% that they disagree that the program requires major changes to their classroom practice, while 45% agree and 14% strongly agree that it does. Similarly, among teachers implementing Success for All, 4% report that they strongly disagree and 43% that they disagree that the program requires major changes to their classroom practice, while 38% agree and 14% strongly agree that it does. These data indicate that teachers implementing the same program differ in how large a change they experience.

To confirm the proper level at which to examine this variation, I looked for evidence that the variation in program fit shown in Figure 2 might be driven by school-level differences in preexisting teacher practices. Tables 2 and 3 show numerically how much of the variation in magnitude of change occurs among teachers within schools as compared with the variation between schools.

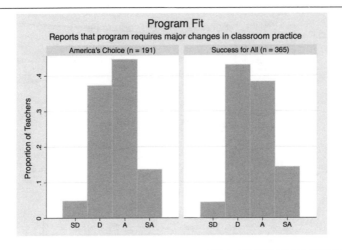

Figure 2. **Proportion of unique teachers reporting they strongly disagree (SD), disagree (D), agree (A), or strongly agree (SA) that "The school improvement program in this school requires me to make major changes in my classroom practice" in their first Teacher Questionnaire.**

Table 2
Variation in Magnitude of Change: America's Choice

Variable		Mean	SD	Minimum	Maximum	Observations
Major change	Total	2.695	0.775	1	4	$N = 403$
	Between		0.300	2.250	3.545	$n = 30$
	Within		0.720	0.775	4.401	$T = 13.433$

Table 3
Variation in Magnitude of Change: Success for All

Variable		Mean	SD	Minimum	Maximum	Observations
Major change	Total	2.624	0.778	1	4	$N = 864$
	Between		0.276	2.227	3.375	$n = 28$
	Within		0.740	0.249	4.374	$T = 30.857$

Both Table 2 and Table 3 illustrate more than twice as much variation within schools as between schools in the magnitude of change teachers report: 72% and 74% in America's Choice and Success for All, respectively.

Table 4
Fidelity of Implementation

Comprehensive School Reform	Observations	Mean	*SD*	Minimum	Maximum
America's Choice	403	0.3753	0.1511	0	0.8472
Success for All	864	0.4655	0.1729	0	1

This underscores the importance of taking the individual as the unit of analysis rather than assuming consistency within schools.

Fidelity of CSR Implementation

For each program, I constructed measures of fidelity that capture variation in teachers' implementation of its prescriptions (see Appendix A). I measured fidelity using responses to the log questions asking: "To what extent were the following topics a focus of your work with the target student in reading/language arts today?" Four check boxes were provided for each content topic listed, corresponding to answers ranging from *a major focus* to *not taught today* (Study of Instructional Improvement, 2000).

SFA and AC ask teachers to cover slightly different content and also emphasize the content areas they cover differently. Fidelity to these specifications was scored in the following way: Content that the program asked be a central component of each day's instruction was given a score of 1 if marked a major focus. Elements that the program indicated were important but not necessarily a major focus of each day's lesson were scored as 1 if marked touched on briefly or a minor focus and 0.5 if marked a major focus. Each of those elements was scored as zero if teachers reported teaching it with less emphasis than prescribed or if they did not mark a box corresponding to that content area. A weighted average of these measures was then taken, weighting daily prescriptions twice as much as the less central ones.

Summary statistics reflecting the distribution of fidelity of implementation in the sample are shown in Table 4.

Methods

To investigate the relationship between the magnitude of change teachers are asked to enact and the fidelity with which they enact that change, I used the data described previously to conduct a series of multiple regression analyses. Each one estimates the relationship between teachers' reports of the extent to which AC or SFA required major changes in their classroom practice and the fidelity with which they enacted AC or SFA's classroom-level prescriptions for literacy instruction. Each year of Log data for each teacher is treated as a separate observation (although observations of the same individual over multiple years will share the same magnitude of change value). The estimating equation is as follows:

$$y_{ist} = \beta X_{is} + \gamma A_{st} + \delta E_{ist} + \theta D_{is} + \alpha_s + u_{ist}.$$

The outcome of interest, y_{ist}, is the fidelity of implementation of individual i in school s at time since school CSR adoption t. The X_{is} term represents a set of binary variables corresponding to each possible answer to the magnitude of change self-report. The coefficients on each of these variables, represented collectively by β, are the focus of this analysis.

Recognizing that other characteristics of schools and teachers might be correlated with both program fit and fidelity of implementation and thus might obscure this central relationship, most specifications also include a series of control variables intended to reduce these confounding effects.

To account for school characteristics that might affect the relationship between program fit and fidelity of implementation, some specifications include school fixed effects, with individual school-level intercepts represented by α_s. In effect, these specifications compare teachers to other teachers within the same school while controlling for observed and unobserved differences between the schools, including district-level differences. I also control separately for the number of years passed since the school first adopted the program (range, 1–6) using a set of dummy variables, represented by γA_{st}.

Some specifications also include controls for teacher-level characteristics, consisting of both time-varying characteristics, represented by δE_{ist}, and fixed characteristics, represented by θD_{is}. These include teacher experience, teacher education, employment category (certification and full- vs. part-time), and teacher demographics, including gender and race. They also represent some variables intended to more closely capture individuals' relationship toward their school's CSR. These include a dummy variable for whether teachers worked at the school before the CSR was implemented and responses to a series of questions that address various facets of teachers' attitudes toward the CSR: "I am capable of making the kinds of changes called for by the school improvement program," "The kinds of changes called for by the school improvement program are helping my students reach higher levels of achievement," and "I strongly value the kinds of changes called for by the school improvement program" (Study of Instructional Improvement, 2001, 2002, 2003, 2004).

Results

The results of these regression analyses are represented in Tables 5 and 6. Each column represents a separate regression with different combinations of control variables indicated with Xs. (For tables including coefficients for all control variables, please see Appendix B in the online version of the journal.) The coefficients shown in Tables 5 and 6 reflect the increase in fidelity,

Table 5
Estimated Effects on Fidelity of Implementation: America's Choice

	(1)	(2)	(3)	(4)	(5)	(6)	(7)
CSR requires major change							
Strongly disagree	−0.003	0.027	−0.005	−0.009	−0.008	0.008	0.040
	(0.034)	(0.032)	(0.035)	(0.035)	(0.033)	(0.034)	(0.031)
Disagree	(omitted, reference category)						
Agree	0.016	0.023	0.021	0.023	0.026	0.027	0.020
	(0.019)	(0.017)	(0.020)	(0.021)	(0.021)	(0.021)	(0.020)
Strongly agree	0.077**	0.061*	0.081**	0.082**	0.081**	0.069*	0.039
	(0.027)	(0.028)	(0.027)	(0.026)	(0.026)	(0.026)	(0.028)
Controls							
School							
Fixed effects		X					
Years since adoption		X	X	X	X	X	X
Teacher							
Experience				X	X	X	X
Education				X	X	X	X
Employment category				X	X	X	X
Demographics					X	X	X
Present before CSR?						X	X
Attitudes toward CSR						X	X
Observations	403	403	403	403	403	403	403
R^2	0.027	0.025	0.055	0.066	0.082	0.109	0.083
Number of schools		30					30

Note. Robust standard errors in parentheses. CSR = Comprehensive School Reform.
*$p < .05$. **$p < .01$.

Table 6
Estimated Effects on Fidelity of Implementation: Success for All

	(1)	(2)	(3)	(4)	(5)	(6)	(7)
CSR requires major change							
Strongly disagree	−0.022	−0.024	−0.023	−0.028	−0.038	−0.038	−0.038
	(0.026)	(0.033)	(0.030)	(0.029)	(0.024)	(0.023)	(0.024)
Disagree	(omitted, reference category)						
Agree	−0.003	0.005	−0.007	−0.009	−0.007	−0.006	0.006
	(0.014)	(0.013)	(0.014)	(0.014)	(0.014)	(0.014)	(0.012)
Strongly Agree	0.032	0.037*	0.026	0.026	0.032$^+$	0.031$^+$	0.034*
	(0.023)	(0.018)	(0.021)	(0.021)	(0.018)	(0.018)	(0.015)
Controls							
School							
Fixed effects		X				X	X
Years since adoption		X	X	X	X	X	X
Teacher							
Experience			X	X	X	X	X
Education				X	X	X	X
Employment category				X	X	X	X
Demographics					X	X	X
Present before CSR?						X	X
Attitudes toward CSR						X	X
Observations	864	864	864	864	864	864	864
R^2	0.006	0.013	0.012	0.018	0.049	0.063	0.046
Number of schools		28					28

Note. Robust standard errors in parentheses. CSR = Comprehensive School Reform.
$^+p < .10.$ $^*p < .05.$

on a scale from 0 to 1, associated with a response of strongly disagree, agree, or strongly agree compared to a response of disagree. If teachers who are asked to make larger changes implement programs with lower fidelity, we should expect to see that the more strongly teachers agree that a CSR requires them to make major changes to their classroom practice, the smaller the coefficient associated with their fidelity of implementation. If teachers who are asked to make larger changes implement programs with greater fidelity, we should expect to see that the more strongly teachers agree that a CSR requires them to make major changes to their classroom practice, the larger the coefficient associated with their fidelity of implementation.

The results for teachers implementing America's Choice are shown in Table 5. Looking across the different specifications, the estimates are not identical, but some patterns emerge. First, the coefficient on the strongly agree response is positive and statistically significant at the .05 level or less in all but one specification, indicating that those who perceived the largest changes also implemented with the greatest fidelity. In addition, even among the coefficients not reaching statistical significance, Models 1, 3, 4, and 5 all show a similar pattern, where the point estimates indicate that fidelity increases monotonically with increasing recognition of a major change.

In Models 2, 6, and 7 the point estimates on strongly disagree are higher than in the other models and higher than for those who disagree or agree (although they still remain statistically insignificant). This could be interpreted as weak support for the prediction that teachers reporting greater changes implement programs with lesser fidelity (although it still remains statistically insignificant). However, even in these specifications, there remains a consistent pattern of increase from disagree through strongly agree, which is statistically significant at the .05 level for strongly agree in Models 2 and 6.

Table 6 presents the same set of relationships for Success for All.

In Table 6, most of the coefficients are not statistically significant. However, as in the America's Choice analysis, there are several positive and statistically significant estimates on the strongly agree response. In Models 2 and 7, the difference between individuals who disagreed (and strongly disagreed) from those who strongly agreed is statistically significant at the .05 level. In Models 5 and 6, this effect is marginally significant at the .1 level.

In addition, although the other coefficients do not reach statistical significance, the point estimates do display a consistent pattern: Those who strongly disagree implement SFA with the lowest fidelity, those who disagree or agree are about the same, and those who strongly agree implement the program with the highest fidelity. In other words, overall, there is a pattern of greater fidelity among those who agree more strongly that the CSR they are asked to implement requires them to make major changes to their classroom practice. Thus, although inconsistent in their precision, the regression coefficients offer modest evidence of a positive relationship between the magnitude of change asked and fidelity of implementation.

Discussion

Overall, the results for America's Choice are stronger than those for Success for All. However, both programs show similar trends. Across all specifications, in both AC and SFA, support for the dominant prediction that teachers asked to make larger changes would implement them with lower fidelity ranged from minimal to none at all. In no case was agreeing more strongly that a CSR required major changes in classroom practice associated with a statistically significant drop in fidelity of implementation. This indicates that traditional policy implementation accounts predicting lower fidelity in cases of greater change are inadequate.

On the contrary, in both programs, several specifications showed statistically significant positive effects for those who strongly agreed that the CSR required major changes compared with those who disagreed with that statement. Across both programs, the coefficient on strongly agree was always positive and reached statistical significance at the .1 level or below for 10 out of the 14 specifications presented. Coefficients on the other responses did not reach statistical significance. However, across both programs, they did indicate a fairly consistent trend toward a positive relationship between magnitude of change and fidelity of implementation. In other words, although the lack of statistical significance suggests that the analysis may have been underpowered, the results suggest that in these cases, practitioners asked to make larger changes generally did so with relatively greater fidelity.

These data would be difficult to interpret under traditional policy implementation accounts focusing on material resources or practitioner resistance as the causes of low fidelity implementation. By contrast, the theories discussed previously linking implementation to processes of conceptual change offer a more plausible explanatory mechanism. Still, the results of this study do not foreclose other possible explanations. Therefore, in the spirit of better understanding the relationship between educational reforms' fit with existing practices and the fidelity with which teachers implement such reforms, it is worth considering multiple explanations for the results presented here.

Conceptual Change

Theories of conceptual change indicate that the conditions under which people are introduced to ambitious new ideas make a difference in whether they are able to overcome the challenge of substantially changing their understandings. Teachers who do not experience a change as sufficiently salient or perceive its implications for their own practice are unlikely to engage with that idea in a transformative way (Gregoire, 2003). As prior studies of implementation have demonstrated, a lack of deep understanding of ambitious reforms can lead to lowered fidelity (e.g., Spillane, 2004). If the magnitude of change the CSR posed for some of the teachers in this study was too small to provoke cognitive accommodation, we might well expect to see lowered fidelity for teachers experiencing smaller changes and correspondingly higher fidelity for teachers experiencing larger changes. This is exactly the pattern this analysis revealed. Moreover, we would expect to see this effect most strongly in settings where deep conceptual understanding was especially important to high-fidelity implementation. For example, for a program relying more heavily on teachers' own planning, judgment, and discretion, fidelity of implementation would likely show more sensitivity to a teacher's depth of understanding of the reform and in turn more sensitivity to the magnitude or salience of the change teachers experience. Again, this is exactly the pattern found in these data as America's Choice showed a stronger positive relationship between magnitude of change and fidelity than that found in Success for All. If this explanation is correct, it suggests that districts and schools might do well to choose boldly in selecting potential new programs and policies as larger changes might help teachers implement new practices with greater fidelity.

At the same time, it is important to weigh the possibility of increased fidelity against the other contextual factors influencing implementation, which years of research have demonstrated are manifold (Bryk, Sebring, Allensworth, Easton, & Luppescu, 2010; Honig, 2006; Huberman & Miles, 1984). For example, both AC and SFA were well-specified, well-funded programs; individual teachers' fidelity of implementation as measured here took place within a larger school context that included substantial training and hiring of additional support staff. Future research might do well to examine the external validity of this finding, in particular considering these external factors, by looking across a wider range of programs.

Perception

An alternative explanation, also plausible, turns the direction of causality described previously on its head. Given that the data used to measure the magnitude of change being asked of teachers are drawn from self-reports, one might argue that they primarily reflect teachers' perceptions or understanding of the magnitude of change a program requires rather than the "true" magnitude or degree of difference between teachers' prior practices and those espoused by the program. If the measure of fit I use is mostly capturing perception and understanding, it might be that the type of teacher who more accurately perceives how ambitious a program is is also more likely to implement it with high fidelity. Or, the measurement may even be capturing the *effects* of conceptual change rather than its causes. Especially for a CSR like SFA that provides very detailed prescriptions, it might be relatively straightforward to implement the program with high fidelity even without a deep conceptual understanding of the distinctions between new and old practices. In this case, a positive statistical relationship could appear not because asking for larger changes leads to higher fidelity but because high fidelity retrospectively leads people to recognize the magnitude of change they have enacted. If true, this would mean that these analyses don't tell us much about the relationship between "true" program fit and fidelity of implementation.

Without an experimental research design, this ambiguity can't be clarified with certainty. If it were the case that big changes in practice subsequently lead to the perception of large changes having been asked, we would expect that individuals' perceptions of the magnitude of change asked of them would increase after implementation. In general, however, when the same individual answered the Teacher Questionnaire in more than one year, their report of the magnitude of change tended to fall over time (see Figure 1).

Still, future research might address the possibility that features relating to the framing or salience of changes—how perceptible they are or how clearly they implicate teachers' existing practice independent of "true" magnitude—might be especially important in predicting fidelity of implementation. If true, this would have meaningful implications for practice as it suggests that manipulating relatively superficial characteristics might be a disproportionately powerful lever. While school leaders may or may not be able to choose which policies their schools must abide by, they have greater discretion about how new policies are framed in relation to existing practices.

In addition, future research and theorizing on this issue might explore the notion that the relationship between perceived magnitude of change and fidelity of implementation may not be strictly unidirectional. Perceiving and enacting larger changes may go hand in hand, mutually reinforcing one another. Longitudinal research designs using repeated interviews of the same individuals over time would help to uncover such a pattern.

Other Explanations

A third type of explanation is that the statistical relationship between constructs may be real but driven by a different mechanism than the one I have theorized. That is, there may be a real predictive positive relationship between the magnitude of change AC or SFA requires of a teacher and the fidelity with which he or she implements the program, but it may not be driven by processes of conceptual change. For example, perhaps there is something about the kind of teacher who initially teaches very differently from AC or SFA that nonetheless makes him or her more likely to fully implement a new program. Or, perhaps the relationship between measures of magnitude of change and fidelity are largely incidental and dwarfed by an independent trend in how fidelity changes over time.[4] If true, these explanations leave unclear whether magnitude of change is a useful feature to consider in program selection or not.

Without an experimental design, it is impossible to know for certain whether unobserved differences between teachers might be driving the observed effects. Many of the specifications I used include a large number of teacher-level control variables. However, as Datnow and Castellano (2000a) found, differences in implementation are not always correlated with readily measurable teacher characteristics but rather may stem from differences in pedagogical philosophy or other harder to capture facets. Most specifications also include control variables for each year of program implementation. These coefficients actually indicate that fidelity of implementation tended to rise over time for America's Choice teachers while falling for Success for All teachers (see Appendix B in the online version of the journal). This suggest that the relationship between magnitude of change and fidelity is insensitive to the difference between increasing and decreasing time trends in overall fidelity. Still, the best approach to establishing the robustness of this relationship is in future research testing for its presence in a variety of settings.

Conclusions

As schools and districts continue to explore additional models of reform, it is important for leaders and policymakers to be well informed about factors that are likely to affect the fidelity with which such reforms are implemented. A long history of implementation research has pointed to the importance of frontline workers in enacting such reforms. One important factor that has not received sufficient attention to date is how the amount of change that those frontline workers are asked to undertake is related to how fully and faithfully they implement the program. In this paper, I demonstrate that traditional policy implementation accounts suggesting that larger changes will be implemented with lesser fidelity are too simple. Instead, I argue that for reforms that ask teachers to think about their work in significantly different ways, the salience of very large changes may actually help teachers shift their thinking in ways that promote high-fidelity implementation. More moderate changes may be easier to implement in some senses but not necessarily with high fidelity as they may be more readily subsumed into existing ideas, leading to "new" practices that are only superficially different from the old. This account is supported by data on the implementation of comprehensive school reform programs, where by and large, those teachers who reported being required to make larger changes also implemented the reforms with higher fidelity, especially in the program that requires more interpretation to implement.

From a practical standpoint, it is important to acknowledge that processes of conceptual change operate alongside a whole host of other factors that are likely to affect fidelity. I do not wish to claim that resource allocation or individuals' resistance, for example, play no role at all in how programs and policies are implemented. However, I argue that the significance of cognitive mechanisms has been underestimated. This analysis offers a step forward in building theory in this area and points toward important areas of future research.

Appendix A

I calculated fidelity of implementation each year for each teacher by comparing the elements of literacy instruction that they reported using, with those recommended by their Comprehensive School Reform (CSR).

Teachers were asked about their literacy instruction in the teacher log using the prompt shown in Figure A1.

Both Success for All and America's Choice recommend slightly different program elements for younger and older students, so each teacher's reported practice was compared to the program prescriptions corresponding to their CSR and students' grade level.

To calculate fidelity, each content element received a score of 1 if the teacher reported focusing on it to a degree that aligned with their CSR program's recommendations as reflected in Table A1, a score of .5 if they reported a greater focus than called for, and a score of 0 otherwise, including for missing values. Fidelity scores ranged from 0 to 1 as a weighted average of the scores for each content element. Elements that the CSR emphasized (i.e., where the program asked for a "major" focus) were weighted more heavily. Instruction in content elements not included in the prescriptions for a given teacher's program and grade level did not affect that teacher's fidelity score.

Table A1
Measures of Fidelity

	Success for All		America's Choice	
	Grades K–1 (Reading Roots)	Grades 2–5 (Reading Wings)	Grades K–3	Grades 4–5
Comprehension	Major	Major	Major	Major
Writing		Minor/brief	Major	Major
Word analysis	Major		Minor/brief	
Concepts of print	Minor/brief			
Reading fluency	Minor/brief	Minor/brief	Minor/brief	Minor/brief
Vocabulary		Minor/brief	Minor/brief	Minor/brief
Grammar				
Spelling				
Research strategies				

4. To what extent were the following topics a focus of your work with the target student in reading/language arts today? *(Place an "X" in one of the boxes for each item.)*

	A major focus	A minor focus	Touched on briefly	Not taught today
a. Comprehension..........	☐	☐	☐	☐
b. Writing.........................	☐	☐	☐	☐
c. Word analysis.............	☐	☐	☐	☐
d. Concepts of print........	☐	☐	☐	☐
e. Reading fluency..........	☐	☐	☐	☐
f. Vocabulary..................	☐	☐	☐	☐
g. Grammar.....................	☐	☐	☐	☐
h. Spelling.......................	☐	☐	☐	☐
i. Research strategies....	☐	☐	☐	☐

Figure A1. **Language Arts Log item used to capture teachers' degree of focus on each element of literacy instruction.**

Notes

Many thanks to Jonathan Guryan and Jeannette Colyvas for their extensive support and assistance throughout the development of this manuscript. Thank you as well to Jim Spillane, Cynthia Coburn, and four anonymous reviewers who each provided feedback on earlier drafts. Earlier formulations of this paper were also presented at the Annual Meeting of the American Educational Research Association and the Structuring Work in and around Organizations Workshop. This research was supported in part by the Institute of Education Sciences, U.S. Department of Education, through Grant R305B080027 to Northwestern University. The opinions expressed are those of the author's and do not represent views of the Institute or the U.S. Department of Education. Finally, thanks to Deborah Ball, David Cohen, and Brian Rowan, who made data from the Study for Instructional Improvement publicly available, making these analyses possible.

[1]Coburn actually uses the terms *assimilation* and *accommodation* (among others) to characterize the changes teachers make to their classroom practices. These terms directly reference processes of cognitive change, underscoring the importance of teacher thinking in implementation processes. Nonetheless, since for the remainder of the article, I use the terms *assimilation* and *accommodation* to refer exclusively to cognitive processes, for the sake of clarity I use the simplified language of *minor* and *major* changes to characterize Coburn's categories of practice change here instead of her original terms.

[2]The Study for Instructional Improvement also includes data on a third Comprehensive School Reform, Accelerated Schools Project; however, the program specifications for this model were not sufficiently concrete to measure fidelity.

[3]Mathematics Logs were also administered, but these were not used in the current analysis.

[4]Thanks to Anonymous Reviewer 1 for this point.

References

Ansari, S. M., Fiss, P. C., & Zajac, E. J. (2010). Made to fit: How practices vary as they diffuse. *Academy of Management Review, 35*(1), 67–92.

Berends, M. (2000). Teacher-reported effects of New American School designs: Exploring relationships to teacher background and school context. *Educational Evaluation and Policy Analysis, 22*(1), 65–82.

Borman, G. D., Hewes, G. M., Overman, L. T., & Brown, S. (2003). Comprehensive School Reform and achievement: A meta-analysis. *Review of Educational Research, 73*(2), 125–230. doi:10.3102/00346543073002125

Brumby, M. N. (1984). Misconceptions about the concept of natural selection by medical biology students. *Science Education, 68*(4), 493–503.

Bryk, A. S., Sebring, P. B., Allensworth, E., Easton, J. Q., & Luppescu, S. (2010). *Organizing schools for improvement: Lessons from Chicago.* Chicago, IL: University of Chicago Press.

Carey, S. (1988). Reorganization of knowledge in the course of acquisition. *Ontogeny, Phylogeny, and Historical Development, 2*, 1.

Century, J., & Cassata, A. (2016). Implementation research: Finding common ground on what, how, why, where, and who. *Review of Research in Education, 40*(1), 169–215.

Century, J., Rudnick, M., & Freeman, C. (2010). A framework for measuring fidelity of implementation: A foundation for shared language and accumulation of knowledge. *American Journal of Evaluation, 31*(2), 199–218. doi:10.1177/1098214 010366173

Chi, M. T. H. (2005). Commonsense conceptions of emergent processes: Why some misconceptions are robust. *Journal of the Learning Sciences, 14*(2), 161–199.

Coburn, C. E. (2004). Beyond decoupling: Rethinking the relationship between the institutional environment and the classroom. *Sociology of Education, 77*(3), 211–244.

Coburn, C. E., & Stein, M. K. (2010). Key lessons about the relationship between research and practice. In C. E. Coburn & M. K. Stein (Eds.), *Research and practice in education: Building alliances, bridging the divide* (pp. 201–226). Lanham, MD: Rowman & Littlefield.

Cohen, D. K. (1988). *Teaching practice: Plus ça change.* Ann Arbor, MI: Institute for Research on Teaching, College of Education, Michigan State University.

Cohen, D. K. (1990). A revolution in one classroom: The case of Mrs. Oublier. *Educational Evaluation and Policy Analysis, 12*(3), 311–329.

Cohen, D. K., & Moffitt, S. L. (2009). *The ordeal of equality: Did federal regulation fix the schools?* Cambridge, MA: Harvard University Pres.

Cohen, D. K., Moffitt, S. L., & Goldin, S. (2007). Policy and practice: The dilemma. *American Journal of Education, 113*(4), 515–548. doi:10.1086/518487

Cohen, W. M., & Levinthal, D. A. (1990). Absorptive capacity: A new perspective on learning and innovation. *Administrative Science Quarterly, 35*, 128–152.

Comprehensive School Reform Quality Center. (2005). *CSRQ Center report on elementary school comprehensive school reform models.* Washington, DC: Author.

Corcoran, T., Hoppe, M., Luhm, T., & Supovitz, J. A. (2000). *America's Choice comprehensive school reform design first-year implementation evaluation summary.* Philadelphia, PA: Consortium for Policy Research in Education.

Cordray, D. S., & Pion, G. M. (2006). Treatment strength and integrity: Models and methods. In R. R. Bootzin & P. E. McKnight (Eds.), *Strengthening research methodology: Psychological measurement and evaluation* (pp. 103–124). Washington, DC: American Psychological Association.

Correnti, R., & Rowan, B. (2007). Opening up the black box: Literacy instruction in schools participating in three Comprehensive School Reform programs. *American Educational Research Journal, 44*(2), 298–339. doi:10.3102/000283 1207302501

Dane, A. V., & Schneider, B. H. (1998). Program integrity in primary and early secondary prevention: Are implementation effects out of control? *Clinical Psychology Review, 18*(1), 23–45.

Datnow, A., & Castellano, M. (2000a). *An "inside" look at Success for All: A qualitative study of implementation and teaching and learning.* Retrieved from http://www.jhucsos.com/wp-content/uploads/2016/04/Report45.pdf

Datnow, A., & Castellano, M. (2000b). Teachers' responses to Success for All: How beliefs, experiences, and adaptations shape implementation. *American Educational Research Journal, 37*(3), 775–799. doi:10.2307/1163489

Desimone, L. (2002). How can Comprehensive School Reform models be successfully implemented? *Review of Educational Research, 72*(3), 433–479.

DiSessa, A. A. (1993). Toward an epistemology of physics. *Cognition and Instruction, 10*(2/3), 105–225.

Dusenbury, L., Brannigan, R., Falco, M., & Hansen, W. B. (2003). A review of research on fidelity of implementation: Implications for drug abuse prevention in school settings. *Health Education Research, 18*(2), 237–256.

Eagly, A. H., & Chaiken, S. (1993). *The psychology of attitudes.* New York, NY: Harcourt Brace Jovanovich College Publishers.

Flay, B. R. (1986). Efficacy and effectiveness trials (and other phases of research) in the development of health promotion programs. *Preventive Medicine, 15*(5), 451–474. doi:10.1016/0091-7435(86)90024-1

Fosnot, C. T. (1996). *Constructivism: Theory, perspectives, and practice.* New York, NY: Teachers College Press.

Fullan, M. (1983). Evaluating program implementation: What can be learned from follow through. *Curriculum Inquiry, 13*(2), 215–227.

Glazer, J. L. (2009). How external interveners leverage large-scale change: The case of America's Choice, 1998-2003. *Educational Evaluation and Policy Analysis, 31*(3), 269–297. doi:10.3102/0162373709336745

Gregoire, M. (2003). Is it a challenge or a threat? A dual-process model of teachers' cognition and appraisal processes during conceptual change. *Educational Psychology Review, 15*(2), 147–179.

Guskey, T. R. (1991). Enhancing the effectiveness of professional development programs. *Journal of Educational & Psychological Consultation, 2*(3), 239–247.

Hallett, T. (2010). The myth incarnate: Recoupling processes, turmoil, and inhabited institutions in an urban elementary school. *American Sociological Review, 75*(1), 52–74.

Honig, M. I. (2006). Complexity and policy implementation: Challenge and opportunities for the field. In M. I. Honig (Ed.), *New directions in education policy implementation: Confronting complexity* (pp. 1–25). Albany, NY: SUNY Press.

Huberman, A. M., & Miles, M. B. (1984). *Innovation up close: How school improvement works.* New York, NY: Plenum Press.

Lewis, L. K., & Seibold, D. R. (1993). Innovation modification during intraorganizational adoption. *Academy of Management Review, 18*, 322–354.

Lin, A. C. (2002). *Reform in the making: The implementation of social policy in prison.* Princeton, NJ: Princeton University Press.

Linder, S. H., & Peters, B. G. (1987). A design perspective on policy implementation: The fallacies of misplaced prescription. *Review of Policy Research, 6*(3), 459–475. doi:10.1111/j.1541-1338.1987.tb00761.x

Lipsey, M. W., & Cordray, D. S. (2000). Evaluation methods for social intervention. *Annual Review of Psychology, 51*(1), 345–375.

Lipsky, M. (1980). *Street-level bureaucracy: Dilemmas of the individual in public services.* New York, NY: Russell Sage Foundation Publications.

Majone, G., & Wildavsky, A. (1979). Implementation as evolution. In J. L. Pressman & A. Wildavsky (Eds.), *Implementation* (3rd ed., pp. 163–180). Berkeley, CA: University of California Press.

Matland, R. E. (1995). Synthesizing the implementation literature: The ambiguity-conflict model of policy implementation. *Journal of Public Administration Research and Theory, 5*(2), 145–174.

Mazmanian, D. A., & Sabatier, P. A. (1983). *Implementation and public policy.* Glenview, IL: Scott Foresman.

McLaughlin, M. W. (1987). Learning from experience: Lessons from policy implementation. *Educational Evaluation and Policy Analysis, 9*(2), 171–178.

Mehta, J. (2015). *The allure of order: High hopes, dashed expectations, and the troubled quest to remake American schooling.* Oxford, UK: Oxford University Press.

National Center on Education and the Economy, & University of Pittsburgh. (1997). *New standards performance standards* (Vol. 1). Washington, DC: Author.

Orland, M., Hoffman, A., & Vaughn, E. S. (2010). *Evaluation of the Comprehensive School Reform program implementation and outcomes: Fifth-year report.* Washington, DC: U.S. Department of Education Office of Planning, Evaluation and Policy Development Policy and Program Studies Service.

Phelps, G., & Schilling, S. (2004). Developing measures of content knowledge for teaching reading. *The Elementary School Journal, 105*(1), 31–48. doi:10.1086/428764

Piaget, J. (1977). *The essential Piaget.* New York, NY: Basic Books.

Poglinco, S. M., Bach, A. J., Hovde, K., Rosenblum, S., Saunders, M., & Supovitz, J. A. (2003). *The heart of the matter: The coaching model in America's Choice schools.* Philadelphia, PA: Consortium for Policy Research in Education, University of Pennsylvania.

Posner, G. J., Strike, K. A., Hewson, P. W., & Gertzog, W. A. (1982). Accommodation of a scientific conception: Toward a theory of conceptual change. *Science Education, 66*(2), 211–227.

Rowan, B., Camburn, E., & Barnes, C. (2004). Benefiting from comprehensive school reform: A review of research on CSR implementation. In C. T. Cross (Ed.), *Putting the pieces together: Lessons from comprehensive school reform research* (pp. 1–52). Washington, DC: National Clearinghouse for Comprehensive School Reform.

Rowan, B., Correnti, R., Miller, R. J., & Camburn, E. M. (2009). *School improvement by design: Lessons from a study of Comprehensive School Reform programs.* Philadelphia, PA: Consortium for Policy Research in Education.

Rumelhart, D. E. (1980). Schemata: The building blocks of cognition. *Theoretical Issues in Reading Comprehension, 1,* 33–58.

Schank, R. C., & Abelson, R. P. (1977). *Scripts, plans, goals and understanding: An inquiry into human knowledge structures* (Vol. 2). Hillsdale, NJ: Lawrence Erlbaum Associates.

Scott, W. R., & Meyer, J. W. (1983). *The organization of societal sectors.* London: Elsevier.

Shadish, W. R., Cook, T. D., & Campbell, D. T. (2002). *Experimental and quasi-experimental designs for generalized causal inference.* Boston, MA: Wadsworth.

Sherin, M. G., & Drake, C. (2009). Curriculum strategy framework: Investigating patterns in teachers' use of a reform-based elementary mathematics curriculum. *Journal of Curriculum Studies, 41*(4), 467–500.

Slavin, R. E., & Madden, N. (1999). *Disseminating Success for All: Lessons for policy and practice* (No. 30). Baltimore, MD: Center for Research on the Education of Students Placed at Risk.

Slavin, R. E., & Madden, N. A. (2000). *One million children: Success for All.* Thousand Oaks, CA: Corwin Press.

Slavin, R. E., Madden, N. A., Dolan, L. J., Wasik, B. A., Ross, S., Smith, L., & Dianda, M. (1996). Success for All: A summary of research. *Journal of Education for Students Placed at Risk, 1*(1), 41–76.

Spillane, J. P. (2004). *Standards deviation: How schools misunderstand education policy* (Vol. 43). Cambridge, MA: Harvard University Press.

Spillane, J. P., & Burch, P. (2006). The institutional environment and instructional practice: Changing patterns of guidance and control in public education. In H.-D. Meyer & B. Rowan (Eds.), *The new institutionalism in education* (pp. 87–102). Albany, NY: SUNY Press.

Spillane, J. P., Reiser, B. J., & Reimer, T. (2002). Policy implementation and cognition: Reframing and refocusing implementation research. *Review of Educational Research, 72*(3), 387–431.

Strike, K. A., & Posner, G. J. (1992). A revisionist theory of conceptual change. In R. A. Duschl & R. J. Hamilton (Eds.), *Philosophy of science, cognitive psychology, and educational theory and practice* (pp. 147–176). Albany, NY: SUNY Press.

Study of Instructional Improvement. (2000). *Language Arts Log.* Retrieved from http://www.sii.soe.umich.edu/data/

Study of Instructional Improvement. (2001). *Teacher Questionnaire 2000–2001.* Retrieved from http://www.sii.soe.umich.edu/data/

Study of Instructional Improvement. (2002). *Teacher Questionnaire 2001–2002.* Retrieved from http://www.sii.soe.umich.edu/data/

Study of Instructional Improvement. (2003). *Teacher Questionnaire 2002–2003.* Retrieved from http://www.sii.soe.umich.edu/data/

Study of Instructional Improvement. (2004). *Teacher Questionnaire 2003–2004.* Retrieved from http://www.sii.soe.umich.edu/data/

Supovitz, J. A., Poglinco, S. M., & Bach, A. (2002). *Implementation of the America's Choice literacy workshops.* Philadelphia, PA: Consortium for Policy Research in Education.

Supovitz, J. A., Poglinco, S. M., & Snyder, B. A. (2001). *Moving mountains: Successes and challenges of the America's Choice comprehensive school reform design.* Philadelphia, PA: Consortium for Policy Research in Education.

Van Meter, D. S., & Van Horn, C. E. (1975). The policy implementation process. *Administration & Society, 6*(4), 445–488. doi:10.1177/009539977500600404

Manuscript received October 5, 2015
Final revision received May 7, 2017
Accepted May 10, 2017

American Educational Research Journal
December 2017, Vol. 54, No. 6, pp. 1316–1344
DOI: 10.3102/0002831217722120
© 2017 AERA. http://aerj.aera.net

The Psychological and Academic Costs of School-Based Racial and Ethnic Microaggressions

Micere Keels
University of Chicago
Myles Durkee
University of Michigan
Elan Hope
North Carolina State University

Research examining links between racial-ethnic microaggressions and educational and psychological outcomes can be improved with the development of brief and reliable measurement tools. Our brief School-Based Racial and Ethnic Microaggressions Scale addresses this gap. First, we examined the prevalence of school-based microaggressions among an analytic sample of 462 Black and Latinx students attending five historically White universities in the Midwest. Then, we examined the association between school-based microaggressions and depressive symptoms and academic achievement. An exploratory principal components analysis of Wave 1 data and a confirmatory factor analysis of Wave 3 data validated a three-factor model: (a) Academic Inferiority, (b) Expectations of Aggression, and (c) Stereotypical Misrepresentations. Students' exposure to microaggressions and its effects were conditional on individual and school characteristics.

MICERE KEELS is an associate professor in the Department of Comparative Human Development at the University of Chicago, Rosenwald Hall, 1101 58th St. Chicago, IL 60637; e-mail: *micere@uchicago.edu*. Her principal research interests are in understanding how race-ethnicity and poverty structure children and youth exposures to developmental inputs and contextual challenges and supports.

MYLES DURKEE is an assistant professor in the Department of Psychology at the University of Michigan. Dr. Durkee's research examines how youth and emerging adults navigate racial experiences within educational contexts.

ELAN HOPE is an assistant professor in the Department of Psychology at North Carolina State University and director of the Hope Lab. In the Hope Lab, Dr. Hope and her team take an assets-based approach to investigate factors that promote well-being for emerging adults who face racism and racial discrimination with an emphasis on both individual differences and contextual variation.

KEYWORDS: academic achievement, mental health, microaggressions, school climate

We are in a period of U.S. history where the vast majority of Americans avoid overt acts of racism and exhibit politically correct behaviors (Sue, 2010). The uncommonness of overt racism is more than political correctness as most people self-report that they are not racist and declare egalitarian values (Gaertner & Dovidio, 2005). However, as studies of implicit bias indicate, people who appear nonprejudiced on self-report measures display lingering negative biases when spontaneous response tasks are used to measure attitudes (Dovidio, Kawakami, Smoak, & Gaertner, 2009). The consensus is that thoughtful and deliberate behaviors are guided by egalitarian beliefs but subconscious negative feelings toward groups emerge when engaging in more spontaneous behaviors (Stanley, Sokol-Hessner, Banaji, & Phelps, 2011).

Theories of aversive racism account for the persistence of prejudice despite the "near universal endorsement of the principles of racial equality as a core cultural value" (Pearson, Dovidio, & Gaertner, 2009, p. 314). Aversive racists sympathize with minority groups and endorse principles of racial equality while simultaneously holding often nonconscious feelings of superiority, discomfort, anxiety, and/or fear. Aversive racism can manifest as microaggressions—"brief and commonplace daily verbal, behavioral, and environmental indignities, whether intentional or unintentional, that communicate hostile, derogatory, or negative racial slights and insults to the target person or group" (Sue et al., 2007, p. 272). Despite numerous studies substantiating the existence of implicit bias and aversive racism, recent disputes among academics, policymakers, and in the popular press have raised questions about whether minority college students are indiscriminately seeing microaggressions everywhere (McWhorter, 2014; Vega, 2014). This dismissal of people of color's experiences of racial-ethnic discrimination is one aspect of aversive racism and is evidenced in the gulf between Whites' and Blacks' perceptions of the persistence of discrimination: 69% of White Americans believe that Blacks are now treated the same as Whites, but 59% of Black Americans believe that Blacks continue to be treated worse than Whites (Dovidio & Gaertner, 2004).

Although qualitative evidence detailing the negative effects of microaggressions on racial-ethnic minority students attending historically White colleges and universities is compelling, there is a need for longitudinal quantitative studies to test and extend the generalizability of existing evidence (R. S. Harris, 2008). First, quantitative studies allow us to test the strength of the effect of exposure to microaggressions on educational and psychological outcomes. Second, quantitative studies also allow us to estimate the unique implications of microaggressions beyond the effect of the racial-ethnic composition of the school itself. The very experience of being in the demographic minority can have negative effects on one's perception of the institution's racial-ethnic climate (Carter, 2007). Finally, because existing research does not track students as they transition from one educational context to another, it remains unclear whether students distinguish changes in racial-ethnic climate between educational contexts. The high level of K–12 school segregation means that most Black and Latinx students transitioning to historically White colleges and universities attended high schools where their group was in the majority (Massey & Fischer, 2002). Consequently, for many Black and Latinx students, the transition to college is likely marked with an increase in exposure to racial-ethnic microaggressions within educational contexts.

The present study extends existing research by first developing and validating a scale that measures students' experiences of school-based racial and ethnic microaggressions (SB-REMA). We then examined stability and change in Black and Latinx students' reports of SB-REMA as they transitioned from high school to college. Lastly, we examined the associations between SB-REMA and educational and psychological outcomes, controlling for the racial-ethnic composition of the student body. We focus on Black and Latinx students to examine differences between and within two minority groups that have a history of experiencing racial and ethnic discrimination in educational contexts (Benner & Graham, 2011; Farkas, 2003).

Defining and Describing Microaggressions

The term *microaggressions* was first used by Pierce, Carew, Pierce-Gonzalez, and Willsand (1977) but laid dormant until Sue and colleagues (2007) completed the seminal work on which almost all contemporary research on microaggressions is based. Sue and colleagues identified three major classes of microaggressions. The first class of microaggressions is *micro-assaults*, which are explicit racial derogations characterized primarily by verbal and nonverbal behaviors meant to hurt the intended victim through name calling, blatant isolation of the individual, or purposeful discriminatory actions. The second class is *microinsults*, which are characterized by more indirect verbal and nonverbal behaviors that convey stereotypical beliefs. Microinsults can also be rudeness and insensitivity regarding a person's racial-ethnic heritage or identity. The third class is *microinvalidations*, which are characterized by communications that exclude, negate, or nullify the thoughts, feelings, or experiential reality of a racial-ethnic minority individual. Researchers have identified approximately 11 thematic categories that describe the content of microaggressions: alien in one's own land, ascription of intelligence, color blindness, assumption of criminality, denial of individual racism, myth of meritocracy, pathologizing cultural values and styles, second-class status, environmental invalidation, simultaneous invisibility and hypervisibility, and exoticization and objectification (Sue et al., 2007; Wong, Derthick, David, Saw, & Okazaki, 2014).

Though most of the research has been conducted with samples of Black Americans (Donovan, Galban, Grace, Bennett, & Felicié, 2013; Gómez, 2015; Solórzano, Ceja, & Yosso, 2000; Sue et al., 2007; Wong et al., 2014), several studies have shown that a range of racial-ethnic minority groups experience microaggressions: Asian Americans (Noh, Kaspar, & Wickrama, 2007; Ong, Burrow, Fuller-Rowell, Ja, & Sue, 2013), indigenous peoples (Hill, Suah, & Chantea, 2010), Latinx Americans (Rivera, Forquer, & Rangel, 2010), and multiracial individuals (Johnston & Nadal, 2010; Nadal, Wong, et al., 2011). Additionally, microaggressions appear to permeate a myriad of contextual settings across the life span, including elementary schools (Allen, 2010; Henfield, 2011), high schools (Benner & Graham, 2011; Huynh, 2012), college campuses (Sue, Lin, Torino, Capodilupo, & Rivera, 2009; Yosso, Smith, Ceja, & Solórzano, 2009), and work environments (Alabi, 2015; DeCuir-Gunby & Gunby, 2016).

Published Racial-Ethnic Microaggressions Scales

Strong quantitative scales enable researchers to respond to the critique that much of the racial microaggression literature has depended on small sample, qualitative studies (R. S. Harris, 2008). Rigorous scales are needed to examine the associations of microaggressions with various outcomes because, as noted previously, many researchers and many in the public question the "reality" and consequences of microaggressions. There is also a need for brief scales that can be included in large representative surveys that have enough racial-ethnic diversity to enable examination of subgroup differences. Brief scales would also facilitate their inclusion in large studies examining a broad range of outcomes. We focused on developing a microaggressions scale that would be ideal for survey studies focused on educational contexts and potentially provide a better understanding of how race-ethnicity is associated with differential educational experiences and how those differential experiences affect educational and psychological outcomes.

Mercer, Zeigler-Hill, Wallace, and Hayes (2011) developed the Inventory of Microaggressions Against Black Individuals (IMABI). The IMABI is a 14-item unidimensional measure of racial microaggressions that captures both microinsults and microinvalidations. The IMABI was developed to measure four types of microinsults (assumptions concerning the intellectual inferiority of Black individuals, inferior status or second-class citizenship of Black individuals, assumed criminality of Black individuals, and superiority of White cultural values), and three types of microinvalidations (assumed universality of Black experiences, denial of individual racism or color-blindness, and the myth of meritocracy). Their sample included 385 undergraduates who identified as Black or African American from two universities, one Southern institution and one Southwestern institution. Their findings support the IMABI as a reliable and valid measure of racial microaggressions, and it was associated with other stressors including racial rejection sensitivity, race-related stress, general distress, and perceived stress. Though the IMABI offers a sound measurement tool for racial microaggressions, because most of the items are nonspecific to school contexts, it does not provide contextual specificity regarding school-based microaggressions. Additionally, the IMABI does not capture microaggressions that are likely to occur in classroom environments for racial-ethnic minority students.

Nadal (2011) developed the Racial and Ethnic Microaggressions (REMA) scale to measure the microaggressions that racial-ethnic minorities experience in their everyday lives. His study included a racially ethnically and educationally diverse sample of individuals recruited from a university context and over the Internet (443 participants for the exploratory factor analysis and 218 for the confirmatory factor analysis). The REMA is a 45-item scale with six subscales: assumptions of inferiority, second-class citizen and assumptions of criminality, microinvalidations, exoticization/assumptions of similarity, environmental microaggressions, and workplace and school microaggressions. It was found to be a valid measure of racial microaggressions and reliable across four racial-ethnic groups, specifically, Asian Americans, Latinx Americans, Black Americans, and multiracial Americans. The REMA is a comprehensive scale with a wide range of items, and though none of its subscales focus on educational settings, several items assessed school-based microaggressions. These items were helpful in the development of our scale.

Torres-Harding, Andrade, and Romero Diaz (2012) developed the Racial Microaggressions Scale (RMAS) to measure the themes and categories of racial-ethnic microinsults and microinvalidations reported in the literature. The sample was racially, ethnically, and educationally diverse and was recruited from a university (N = 175) and a community (N = 202) setting. The RMAS is a 45-item scale with six subscales: invisibility, criminality, low achieving/undesirable culture, sexualization, foreigner/not belonging, and environmental invalidations. Their findings indicated that the subscales should be examined separately, as opposed to an overall measure of racial-ethnic microaggressions. The RMAS was found to be a reliable and valid measure for individuals from diverse racial-ethnic backgrounds. However, they also found different patterns of mean subscale scores indicating that some subscales were more salient for particular racial-ethnic groups than others. The RMAS offers a rigorous scale, but similar to the REMA, it does not focus specifically on racial microaggressions encountered in educational settings. We utilized items from this scale that were particularly relevant for educational contexts in the initial pool of items used to develop our scale.

People navigate numerous contexts over the course of a given period of time, and although there is often a substantial amount of similarly across contexts, exposure to racial-ethnic microaggressions is likely to differ substantially based on the racial-ethnic composition of residential contexts, community contexts (e.g., churches), and institutional contexts (e.g., schools). Therefore, it is important for research investigating the effects of a specific context, such as ours focused on the effects of educational contexts, to utilize microaggression items that are situationally specific rather than generalized items assessing aggregate exposure.

Consequences of Microaggressions

The subtlety of microaggressions and the belief that they are a normative aspect of cross race-ethnicity interactions has led to the popular misperception that microaggressions may offend but cause no real harm to one's well-being (Campbell & Manning, 2015; Marcus, 2015; Thomas, 2008). Research shows, however, that microaggressions affect individuals even when they do not consciously recognize that it has occurred; research also suggests that subtle microaggressions may have the strongest effects (Cheryan & Monin, 2005; Nguyen & Ryan, 2008). As Yosso and colleagues (2009) noted,

> The stress of one racial microaggression can last long after the assault because the victim often continues to spend time with the microaggressor while considering whether the assailant intended harm, and whether or how they must launch a sufficient response. (p. 670)

There is substantial evidence showing that microaggressions have negative associations with many aspects of well-being: anxiety and depression (Huynh, 2012; Hwang & Goto, 2008; Lambert, Herman, Bynum, & Ialongo, 2009; Smith, Allen, & Danley, 2007), substance abuse (Blume, Lovato, Thyken, & Denny, 2012; Wei, Alvarez, Ku, Russell, & Bonett, 2010), posttraumatic stress symptoms (Flores, Tschann, Dimas, Pasch, & de Groat, 2010; Pieterse, Carter, Evans, & Walter, 2010; Wei, Wang, Heppner, & Du, 2012), high blood pressure (Harrell, Hall, & Taliaferro, 2003; Steffen & Bowden, 2006), and educational performance (Reynolds, Sneva, & Beehler, 2010; Solórzano et al., 2000; Yosso et al., 2009). Because of the wide-ranging effects of microaggressions, it is important to have brief scales that can be included in large survey studies.

Though there is a substantial body of research documenting the harmful effects of overt racism on mental health across several racial-ethnic groups (Paradies, 2006), fewer studies have tested the effects of more subtle microaggressions. Four studies that explicitly tested the link found that microaggressions were positively associated with depressive symptoms (Huynh, 2012; Lambert et al., 2009; Nadal, Griffin, Wong, Hamit, & Rasmus, 2014; Torres, Driscoll, & Burrow, 2010). The general finding across these studies is that microaggressions evoke powerful emotional reactions and an increase in perceived stress, which is detrimental to depressive symptoms and mental health in general. Two proposed mechanisms that may link microaggressions to depressive symptoms are perceptions of lack of control over one's outcomes and internalization of others' negative opinion (Lambert et al., 2009).

Role of Racial-Ethnic Identity in Coping With Microaggressions

We expect that exposure to microaggressions will have direct and indirect effects on depressive symptoms and will be mediated in part by racial-ethnic identity. Racial-ethnic identity beliefs are cognitions and attitudes regarding the importance and meanings of racial-ethnic group membership (Sellers, Chavous, & Cooke, 1998). Racial-ethnic identity is a fundamental aspect of human development that facilitates the process by which individuals perceive, interpret, and cope with racial-ethnic experiences in their daily lives (Spencer, 2006; Williams, Tolan, Durkee, Francois, & Anderson, 2012). Racial-ethnic regard represents the affective dimension of racial-ethnic identity and captures positive and negative feelings about one's racial-ethnic group. Private regard represents an individual's attitudes toward their own racial-ethnic group and feelings about their racial-ethnic group membership. Public regard represents an individual's perceptions of how others view their racial-ethnic group. Research suggests that positive feelings about one's racial-ethnic group (high private regard) and recognition of negative societal perceptions of one's racial-ethnic group (low public regard) may protect Black and Latinx college students from the negative mental health repercussions of experiencing racial-ethnic discrimination (Sellers et al., 1998). Empirical evidence suggests that public regard captures a great deal of variability in one's sensitivity to detect racial-ethnic discrimination, particularly subtle or ambiguous events, and explains affective and physiological responses to racial-ethnic discrimination (Hoggard, Jones, & Sellers, 2017; Neblett & Roberts, 2013). Private regard is more closely associated with the internalization of discrimination and is linked to outcomes such as depressive symptoms (Neblett, Cooper, Banks, & Smalls-Glover, 2013; Seaton, Yip, & Sellers, 2009). The present study is one of the first to examine the mediating roles of public and private regard across multiple contexts, specifically, Black and Latinx students transitioning from high school to college, many of whom transitioned from segregated, minority-serving high schools to predominantly White universities.

We hypothesized that microaggressions experienced during high school would be associated with greater depressive symptoms at the start of college and have a longitudinal influence on depressive symptoms at the end of their first year. We also predicted that prior academic achievement (high school GPA) and racial-ethnic identity (public and private racial-ethnic regard) would mediate the relationship between microaggressions and depressive symptoms. Based on previous evidence, we expected that microaggressions experienced during high school would have a negative association with high school GPA and racial-ethnic identity, which would then be associated with greater depressive symptoms at the start of college and carry a lasting effect through the end of first-year (Rivas-Drake et al., 2014; Sellers & Shelton, 2003). Greater exposure to microaggressions during high school may stunt students' academic, emotional, and identity development, leading them to enter college less prepared for both academic and social adjustments. It is important to note an alternative hypothesis: Greater exposure to microaggressions during high school may be positively associated with first-year GPA and negatively associated with depressive symptoms. This could occur if experiencing microaggressions in high school prepares minority youth for navigating college contexts that are not always welcoming and supportive of racial-ethnic minority students.

Method

Participants and Procedures

Data come from the Minority College Cohort Study, a longitudinal investigation of Black (N = 221) and Latinx (N = 312) students who began college in fall 2013. Students were recruited from five historically White universities in the Midwest: 24% recruited from two urban private institutions that were 8% and 4% Black and 17% and 13% Hispanic, 35% recruited from an urban public institution that was 8% Black and 26% Hispanic, 28% recruited from a rural public institution that was 16% Black and 14% Hispanic, and 13% recruited from a suburban public institution that was 5% Black and 9% Hispanic. Administrators at each of the five universities distributed an e-mail containing a description of the research study and a link to the online survey during September of the 2013–2014 academic year. Students then went to the online survey, provided informed consent, and completed a screening questionnaire. To qualify, students had to be enrolled as a full-time and first-time first-year student and primarily identify as African American/Black or Hispanic/Latinx (including multiracial students who primarily identify as either Black or Latinx). Across each institution, we recruited approximately 11% to 35% of all eligible students.

Participants graduated from 255 different high schools, including 203 public high schools (86% of the sample). Approximately 75% of Black and 57% of Latinx participants were women; this is reflective of the gender imbalance in college enrollment in the United States (Snyder & Dillow, 2015). Only 8% of the sample was foreign-born: 6% of Black and 10% of Latinx students. However, 57% of the sample had at least one foreign-born parent: 25% of Black and 81% of Latinx students. The mean age of the sample at recruitment was 18.2 years old (SD = 0.45). Forty-eight percent of Black students and 69% of Latinx students were first-generation college students.

Six waves of data collection took place during the first two years after enrollment: Waves 1 and 4 occurred during the initial months of the fall term, Waves 2 and 5 occurred shortly after winter break, and Waves 3 and

6

occurred at the close of each academic year. For each wave of data collection, participants were e-mailed an individualized link to the online survey. The fall and spring waves of data collection took approximately 45 minutes to complete, and participants were compensated with a $25 electronic gift card. The winter waves of data collection took approximately 15 minutes to complete, and participants were compensated with a $15 electronic gift card. Data collection was managed using REDCap software tools hosted at the University of Chicago (P. A. Harris et al., 2009). Participant retention for each wave of data collection was above 90%. Participants remained in the study and were surveyed regardless of changes in college enrollment. The host institution's Institutional Review Board approved all study procedures. This article focuses on data from Wave 1 (fall of first year) and Wave 3 (just after the end of first year, 92% retention rate).

Measures

School-Based Racial and Ethnic Microaggressions

The SB-REMA scale was developed to capture racial-ethnic microaggressions within educational settings, including microinvalidations ("People on campus acted as if all of the people of my race/ethnicity are alike"), microinsults ("I have been made to feel like the way I speak is inferior in the classroom because of my race/ethnicity"), and microassaults ("I was singled out by police or security people because of my race/ethnicity"). The initial pool of items was based on the RMAS (Torres-Harding et al., 2012) and an unpublished measure used as part of a qualitative and quantitative examination of racial microaggressions at a large historically White university (Harwood, Huntt, Mendenhall, & Lewis, 2012). Harwood and colleagues' (2012) survey items were developed from a qualitative examination of a diverse sample of 81 racial-ethnic minority students using a semistructured interview protocol adapted from Sue et al. (2007). We selected items from these two scales based on high factor loadings and strong face validity. When the two scales had overlapping items, we retained the item with the strongest face validity. Items from these scales that did not focus on the school context, such as "I receive poorer treatment in restaurants and stores because of my race," were dropped. For Black students, "because of your race" was used, and for Latinx students, "because of your ethnicity" was used. The final list of 15 items was randomized and included, as a block, in the larger survey of over 150 items.

At Wave 1, participants were asked to indicate "how often the following things occurred during high school," and at Wave 3, they were asked to report "how often the following things occurred over first-year." A 4-point Likert scale was utilized (1 = *never,* 2 = *rarely,* 3 = *sometimes/a moderate amount,* 4 = *often/frequently,* and "refuse"). More than 60% of all participants reported that they never experienced 10 of the 15 items, and a very low proportion experienced the items often/frequently. Therefore, responses were recoded and dichotomized to indicate whether each microaggression was experienced at all (1) or never experienced (0),during the specified period. Previous racial-ethnic microaggression scales have similarly found that participants reported low frequencies, necessitating the creation of ordered categorical variables or other transformations to best reflect the observed response distribution (Mercer et al., 2011; Torres-Harding et al., 2012).

Race-Ethnicity

Participants were asked to select "all that apply" from a list of over 20 racial-ethnic groups, including the option to write in their own response. Of the participants who self-identified as Black in the screening questionnaire, we excluded 14 who selected a response such as "Filipino" or "Native Hawaiian" and did not select a Black racial-ethnic group/country of origin (African American, Caribbean, etc.) or refused to provide this information. Of the participants who self-identified as Latinx in the screening question-naire, we excluded 57 who selected a response such as "Japanese" or "European American" and did not select a Latinx racial-ethnic group/country of origin (Mexican, Puerto Rican, etc.) or refused to provide this information. Due to the limited sample size within each reported ethnic group, participants from similar racial-ethnic origins were collapsed together and grouped as either Black or Latinx in all analyses.

High School GPA

Cumulative high school GPA was self-reported at Wave 1. Ten students reported a GPA that was slightly higher than 4.0, and their responses were recoded to 4.0. The range of high school GPA was 2.0 to 4.0 with a mean of 3.55 (SD = .39).

First-Year GPA

Academic performance was collected at Waves 2 and 3, and a small por-tion of the sample with missing data provided this information at Wave 4 (n = 36). At each time point, participants were asked, "Please list all of the courses that you were enrolled in this last academic term and your final grade, even if you dropped a course." The mean and median number of completed courses after each academic term was approximately 4. For each course that was listed, participants indicated whether they dropped the course, received an incomplete grade, received a pass or fail grade, or received a final letter grade ranging from 1 (A+) to 13 (F). Responses from each course with a final letter grade were reverse coded and trans-formed to a GPA scale ranging from 0 to 4; all course grades were averaged together to create a cumulative first-year GPA that ranged from .31 to 4.0 with a mean of 3.12 (*SD* = .62).

Depressive Symptoms

Depressive symptoms were measured using the Harvard Department of Psychiatry/National Depression Screening Day Scale (HANDS; Baer et al., 2000). The HANDS was developed as a brief 10-item screening scale for depression. Participants indicated frequency of depressive symptoms over the past 2 weeks using 9 items of the HANDS scale. A question regarding suicidality was omitted given the sensitive nature of the question. Items used a 4-point scale that ranged from *none or a little bit of the time* to *all of the time*. Sample items include "had poor appetite" and "been feeling hopeless about the future." Items indicated high internal reliability at both Wave 1 (Black students α = .92; Latinx students α = .91) and Wave 3 (Black students α = .93; Latinx students α = .94).

Racial-Ethnic Identity

Public and private regard were measured using two subscales from the Multidimensional Inventory of Black Identity–Short (MIBI-S; Martin, Wout, Nguyen, Gonzalez, & Sellers, 2013). Items used a 7-point scale that ranged from *strongly disagree* to *strongly agree*. The private regard subscale consists of three items measuring the extent to which respondents assess their own racial-ethnic group positively or negatively, such as "I am happy that I am Black/Latino." Items indicated high internal reliability at both Wave 1 (Black students α = .81; Latinx students α = .88) and Wave 3 (Black students α = .85; Latinx students α = .90). The public regard subscale consisted of four items measuring the extent to which respondents believed that society viewed their racial-ethnic group positively or negatively, such as "in general, others respect Black/Latino people." Items indicated high internal reliability at both Wave 1 (Black students α = .92; Latinx students α = .91) and Wave 3 (Black students α = .92; Latinx students α = .92).

High School Percent White

At Wave 1, participants provided the name and location of the high school from which they graduated. This information was used to obtain high school composition data from the National Center for Education Statistics Common Core of Data. These data contain detailed demographic information on public and private secondary schools within the United States. Demographic data were obtained from the 2012–2013 school year (when participants were high school seniors). A total of 255 high schools were represented in the sample, and demographic data were available and obtained for 250 high schools.

Gender

Participants self-reported their gender as male, female, or transgender. Two students who identified as transgender were excluded from analysis.

First-Generation Student Status

Students with non–college educated parents were identified as first-generation college students (1), and students with at least one college-educated parent were identified as not first-generation college students (0).

Financial Distress

Previous analyses of these data revealed the importance of controlling for financial distress when examining GPA and depressive symptoms (Keels, 2015). Three questions were used to measure students' level of financial distress: (1) "How much difficulty, if any, are you having paying your bills," (2) "how upset or worried are you because you do not have enough money to pay for things," and (3) "how concerned do your current financial conditions make you about the chances you can afford to complete your college degree." Items used a 5-point scale that ranged from *no difficulty at all/ not upset or worried at all/not at all concerned* at one end of the scale to *tremendous amount of difficulty/extremely upset or worried/extremely concerned* at the other end of the scale. Items indicated good internal reliability at both Wave 1 (Black students α = .78; Latinx students α = .80) and Wave 3 (Black students α = .82; Latinx students α = .82).

Results

Scale Development

Exploratory Factor Analysis

Exploratory factor analysis (EFA) using principal component analysis with a promax rotation was used with the Wave 1 data. The percentage of students that reported experiencing each microaggression is shown in Supplementary Table S1 in the online version of the journal. Because items were bivariate and not normally distributed, the EFA was estimated in STATA 14 using a polychoric correlation matrix and promax rotation (Holgado-Tello, Chacón-Moscoso, Barbero-García, & Vila-Abad, 2009). Items with factor loadings of .45 or greater were included (Tabachnick & Fidell, 2007), and items with cross-loadings of .50 or above on more than one component were removed (Osborne & Costello, 2005). These analyses resulted in a three-factor solution (we tested up to a five-factor solution, and the strongest factor loadings with no cross-loadings occurred with the three-factor solution). One item ("People asked where I am from suggesting that I don't belong")

Table 1

Factor Loadings From Exploratory Factor Analysis

	Wave 1		
Variable	Academic Inferiority	Expectations of Aggression	Stereotypical Misrepresentations
Discouragement	**.918**	.060	−.003
Intellectually	**.900**	.092	−.022
Excluded	**.889**	.173	−.111
Minimized	**.874**	.124	.038
Speak	**.838**	.057	.142
Isolation	**.892**	−.009	.081
Segregated	**.758**	−.161	.282
Scared	.030	**.908**	.051
Aggressive	.093	**.839**	.097
Police/security	.125	**.592**	.233
Alike	.047	.402	**.541**
Obstacles	.128	.289	**.561**
Exotic	.059	.023	**.794**
Sexual	.037	.074	**.830**

Note. Bold numbers indicate the items that comprise each subscale.

was removed from the three-factor solution because its highest factor loading was only .31. The factor loadings are shown in Table 1.

The three-factor solution explained 24.1% of the scale's variance, and each of the three factors explained 9.2%, 7.7%, and 7.2% of the total variance, respectively. The first factor, named Academic Inferiority, measured experiences of discouragement at school, being made to feel intellectually inferior, feeling that one's classroom contributions were minimized, and feeling isolated at school because of one's race-ethnicity. The second factor, named Expectations of Aggression, measured others acting as if scared, assumptions that they would behave aggressively, and being singled out by police or security because of one's race-ethnicity. The third factor, named Stereotypical Misrepresentations, measured denial of individuality, denial of racial obstacles, and being exoticized because of one's race-ethnicity. At each wave, all factors were significantly positively correlated with each other, and the intercorrelations increased from Waves 1 to 3 (Wave 1: r = .54–.64; Wave 3: r = .64–.70).

Confirmatory factor analysis. The three-factor solution resulting from the EFA with Wave 1 data was entered into a confirmatory factor analysis (CFA) using Wave 3 data. Model fit statistics indicated that the three-factor solution fit the data well at Wave 3, $\chi^2(68) = 137$, $p < .001$, root mean square error of approximation (RMSEA) = .050, 90% CI [.038, .062]. A RMSEA value less than .08 suggests that the model is a close fit to the data (Hu & Bentler, 1999). Three fit indices were also examined and demonstrated good model fit: Comparative Fit Index (CFI) = .981, Tucker-Lewis Index (TLI) = .974, and standardized root mean square residual (SRMR) = .027. Generally, CFI and TLI values closer to 1.00 and SRMR values closer to zero suggest good model fit (Hu & Bentler, 1999; Steiger, 2007).

Factor structure across demographic subgroups. The final step in sub-scale development was to test the factor structure separately for Black and Latinx students and separately for men and women to assess whether the factors were comparable for each group. The goodness of fit for the three-factor model for Black students was good with Wave 3 data, $\chi^2(68)$ = 96, p = .014, RMSEA = .047, 90% CI [.022, .068], and the fit indices also indicated a good level of fit (CFI = .982, TLI = .976, SRMR = .039). Model fit statistics for Latinx students were also good with Wave 3 data, $\chi^2(68)$ = 142, p < .001, RMSEA = .070, 90% CI [.053, .086], and the fit indices indicated a good level of fit as well (CFI = .962, TLI = .949, SRMR = .036).

The goodness of fit for the three-factor model for women was good with Wave 3 data, $\chi^2(68)$ = 116, p < .001, RMSEA = .052, 90% CI [.035, .068], and the fit indices indicated a good level of fit (CFI = .978, TLI = .970, SRMR = .033). Model fit statistics for men were adequate with Wave 3 data, $\chi^2(68)$ = 144, p < .001, RMSEA = .089, 90% CI [.069, .109], and the fit indices indicated an acceptable level of fit (CFI = .951, TLI = .935, SRMR = .035). Due to sample size limitations, we did not test the factor structure separately for each race-ethnicity by gender subgroup; Black men were our smallest group (n = 56).

Internal consistency. Academic Inferiority items indicated high internal reliability at both Wave 1 (Black students α = .92; Latinx students α = .92) and Wave 3 (Black students α = .92; Latinx students α = .92). Expectations of Aggression items indicated strong internal reliability at both Wave 1 (Black students α = .80; Latinx students α = .82) and Wave 3 (Black students α = .78; Latinx students α = .88). Stereotypical Misrepresentations items indicated moderate internal reliability at both Wave 1 (Black students α = .78; Latinx students α = .77) and Wave 3 (Black students α = .71; Latinx students α = .74). Descriptive statistics for each subscale are shown in Table 2.

Differential Exposure to SB-REMA

Hypothesis 1: Reports of exposure to microaggressions would differ by students' race-ethnicity, high school racial-ethnic composition, and the interaction between these two factors.

Table 2
Descriptive Statistics for Each Subscale

Subscale	Black		Latinx		Range
	Mean	SD	Mean	SD	
			Wave 1		
Academic Inferiority	2.41	2.72	1.65	2.39	0–7
Expectations of Aggression	1.72	1.23	0.81	1.14	0–3
Stereotypical Misrepresentations	2.41	1.42	1.96	1.48	0–4
			Wave 3		
Academic Inferiority	2.95	2.79	2.05	2.61	0–7
Expectations of Aggression	1.49	1.22	0.75	1.16	0–3
Stereotypical Misrepresentations	2.39	1.34	2.06	1.43	0–4

Racial-ethnic group and school-level differences for Academic Inferiority and Expectations of Aggression microaggressions are shown in the figures and discussed in the text; Stereotypical Misrepresentation microaggressions are shown in the supplementary figures in the online version of the journal. Academic Inferiority and Expectations of Aggression had the strongest reliability, validity, and associations with racial-ethnic attitudes, GPA, and depressive symptoms. As shown in Figure 1 (Panels A and C), there was a main effect of race-ethnicity in high school. Black students reported significantly higher levels of microaggressions than Latinx students (Academic Inferiority: 2.4 vs. 1.7, p = .002; Expectations of Aggression: 1.7 vs. 0.8, p < .001). There was an interaction between student race-ethnicity and high school percent White. Black students reported significantly different levels of microaggressions based on school percent White, whereas Latinx students' reports of microaggressions did not differ by school percent White. The mean level of Academic Inferiority microaggressions for Black students in predominantly White, diverse, and predominantly non-White schools was 4.1, 3.0, and 1.9, respectively (p = .002); the mean level for Latinx students in predominantly White, diverse, and predominantly non-White schools was 1.9, 1.7, and 1.5, respectively (p = .689).

Black students reported significantly higher levels of Academic Inferiority microaggressions than Latinx students in mostly White and diverse high schools. However, in mostly non-White high schools, there was no significant difference between Black and Latinx students. In contrast, the Black-Latinx gap was always significant for Expectations of Aggression microaggressions, regardless of school composition. The Black and Latinx averages for Academic Inferiority microaggressions in mostly non-White high schools was 1.9 versus 1.5 (p = .412); the averages for Expectations of Aggression was 1.5 versus 0.9 (p = .001).

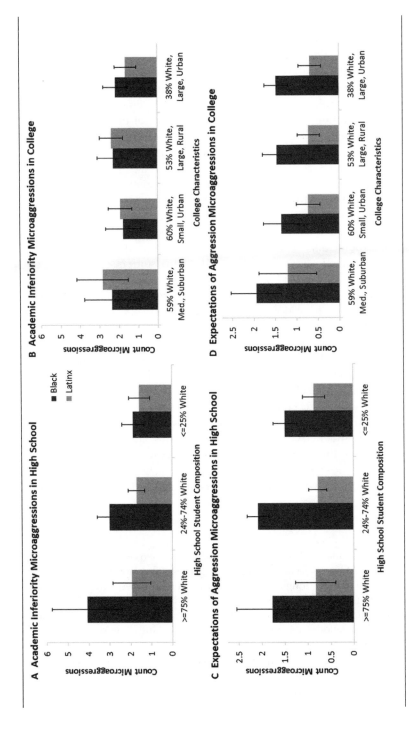

Figure 1. **Exposure to microaggressions, by race–ethnicity and school percent White.**

Note. Error bars represent 95% confidence interval.

Figure 1 (Panels B and D) shows that students' reports of microaggressions over the first year were context dependent. For both Black and Latinx students, the highest levels of Academic Inferiority and Expectations of Aggression microaggressions were reported by those attending a predominantly White, medium-sized university in a predominantly White suburban city. Reports from students at all other universities were not significantly different from each other. There was also a main effect of race-ethnicity, with higher levels of microaggressions reported by Black students compared to Latinx students (Academic Inferiority: 3.0 vs. 2.1, p = .001; Expectations of Aggression: 1.5 vs. 0.8, p < .001).

Figure 2 (Panel A) shows that students discriminated changes in their exposure to SB-REMA as they transitioned from high school to college, in accordance with the racial-ethnic composition of their schools. Students who attended predominantly non-White high schools reported a significant increase in academic inferiority microaggressions when they transitioned to college (Black students: 2.0 vs. 3.0, p < .001; Latinx students: 1.6 vs. 2.3, p = .019). Interestingly, Black students who attended predominantly White high schools reported an insignificant decrease in academic inferiority microaggressions when they transitioned to college (4.0 vs. 3.5, p = .491). More data are needed to accurately estimate this difference; only 14 Black students attended predominantly White high schools. Latinx students who attended predominantly White high schools reported no change in microaggressions when they transitioned to college. Both Black and Latinx students who attended diverse high schools reported no change in microaggressions when they transitioned to college.

Figure 2 (Panel B) shows that for Expectations of Aggression microaggressions, only Black students who attended diverse high schools reported a significant change when they transitioned to college. These students reported the highest level of these microaggressions in high school and a significant decrease in exposure over the first year of college (2.1 vs. 1.5, p < .001).

Path Analysis

Hypothesis 2: Academic Inferiority microaggressions experienced during high school would be associated with greater depressive symptoms at the start of college and have a longitudinal influence on depressive symptoms at the end of the first year of college.

Hypothesis 3: Racial-ethnic identity (public and private racial-ethnic regard) would mediate the relationship between microaggressions and depressive symptoms.

We used structural equation models (SEM) in Stata 14 to test our study hypothesis regarding the direct and indirect effects of exposure to microaggressions on academic achievement and mental health. We conducted all analyses using maximum likelihood with missing values, also known as

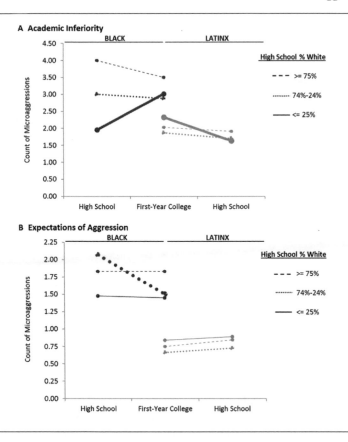

Figure 2. **High school to first-year of college change in exposure to microaggressions, by race-ethnicity.**

Note. Bold lines indicate significant difference at $p < .05$.

full information maximum likelihood estimations, to avoid listwise deletion and retain all possible data points. Analysis used robust standard error adjustments to account for the clustering of students at the five universities. We then examined goodness-of-fit statistics to determine acceptability of model fit, including chi-square (χ^2), RMSEA, CFI, and TLI (Kline, 2015).

We focused on Academic Inferiority microaggressions for modeling the effects of microaggressions because it measures issues that are most germane to educational settings. Additionally, Expectations of Aggression microaggressions did not yield an effect above and beyond Academic Inferiority microaggressions and were thus excluded from final models. The lack of significant correlations between microaggressions and GPA meant that only the mediated effects of microaggressions on depressive

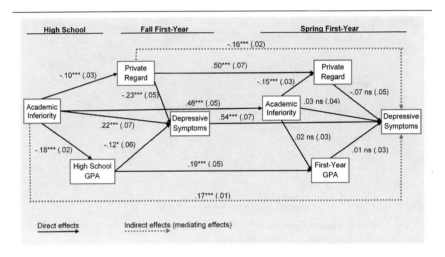

Figure 3. **Path model showing direct and indirect effects, Black Students.**
Note. Standardized coefficients are shown, and standard errors are in parentheses.
*$p < .05$. **$p < .01$. ***$p < .001$.

symptoms were modeled. Intercorrelations between all study variables are shown in Supplementary Table S2 in the online version of the journal. We used path analysis to examine mediating factors and longitudinal implications (Kline, 2015). Models controlled for high school percent White, gender, first-generation college status, financial distress, and on-campus residence.

Figure 3 shows the model for Black students. The model fit the data well, $\chi^2(39) = 42.66$, $p = .317$, RMSEA = .021, 90% CI [.000, .054], CFI = .988, TLI = .980. This model accounted for 31% and 34% of the variance in depressive symptoms at the start of college and at the end of first-year, respectively. Academic Inferiority microaggressions during high school were linked to greater depressive symptoms at the start of college (β = .22, p = .001), which resulted in a significant indirect effect on depressive symptoms at the end of first-year (β = .17, p < .001). High school GPA and racial-ethnic private regard partially mediated the relationship between Academic Inferiority microaggressions and depressive symptoms at the start of college, and this indirect effect was significant (β = .04, p = .005). Academic Inferiority microaggressions during high school were associated with lower high school GPA (β = −.18, p < .001) and less racial-ethnic private regard (β = −.10, p < .001). In return, high school GPA and racial-ethnic private regard were associated with less depressive symptoms at the start of college (β = −.12, p = .047 and β = −.23, p < .001, respectively). Racial-ethnic private regard at the start of college also yielded an indirect effect on

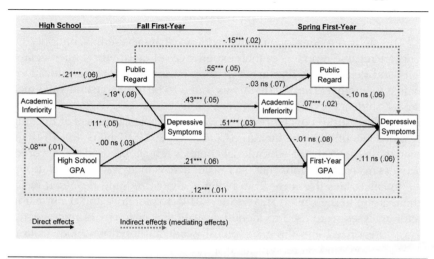

Figure 4. **Path model showing direct and indirect effects, Latinx students.**
Note. Standardized coefficients are shown, and standard errors are in parentheses.
*p < .05. **p < .01. ***p < .001.

depressive symptoms at the end of first-year (β = −.16, p < .001). Academic Inferiority microaggressions experienced during first-year were not associated with depressive symptoms at the end of first-year.

Figure 4 shows the model for Latinx students. The model fit the data well, $\chi^2(42)$ = 53.49, p = .110, RMSEA = .033, 90% CI [.000, .057], CFI = .966, TLI = .948. This model accounted for 18% and 32% of the variance in depressive symptoms at the start of college and at the end of first-year, respectively. Academic Inferiority microaggressions during high school were linked to greater depressive symptoms at the start of college (β = .11, p = .014), which influenced depressive symptoms at the end of first-year through a significant indirect effect (β = .12, p = .001). Racial-ethnic public regard partially mediated the relationship between Academic Inferiority microaggressions and depressive symptoms at the start of college. Academic Inferiority microaggressions during high school were associated with lower racial-ethnic public regard (β = −.21, p < .001), which was in turn associated with less depressive symptoms at the start of college (β = −.19, p = .019). Racial-ethnic public regard at the start of college also yielded an indirect effect on depressive symptoms at the end of first-year (β = −.15, p < .001). Academic Inferiority microaggressions experienced during first-year were associated with depressive symptoms at the end of first-year (β = .07, p < .001); however, mediation effects through public regard and GPA did not occur during first-year.

Discussion

This study provides longitudinal evidence that racial-ethnic minority students are reliable reporters of their experiences of racial-ethnic microaggressions and detect shifts in climate as they transition from one educational context to another. The SB-REMA was found to be a reliable and valid measure of students' experiences of racial and ethnic microaggressions. The items and subscales cover a broad range of thematic categories of microaggressions identified in the literature (Sue et al., 2007; Wong et al., 2014) and relate these categories to educational contexts. The items used were worded to assess microaggressions that may occur across many racial-ethnic groups due to similarities that arise from being a stigmatized and devalued racial-ethnic group in the United States (Sue, 2010). Exploratory and confirmatory factor analyses were used to identify a scale that included 14 microaggressions, categorized into three subscales: Academic Inferiority, Expectations of Aggression, and Stereotypical Misrepresentations. The intercorrelations among the subscales show that they are related yet distinct enough to be examined separately.

The factor structure of the SB-REMA was consistent across Blacks and Latinxs and across men and women, suggesting that the subscales are reliable across several demographic subgroups within the sample. As with other scales measuring racism and discrimination, the pattern of mean differences varied across race-ethnicity, indicating that exposure to microaggressions and specific themes of microaggressions are more salient for some racial-ethnic groups than for others (Torres-Harding et al., 2012). Unexamined in the existing literature is the extent to which exposure to microaggressions is associated with contextual demographics. We found that minority students' exposure to microaggressions is contingent on both race-ethnicity and demographic context. Overall, Black students reported a higher likelihood of experiencing microaggressions, across each subscale, compared to Latinx students. However, the main effect of race-ethnicity was conditioned by the demographic characteristics of the student body and the subscale examined. For example, Black but not Latinx students reported higher levels of microaggressions as the percent of the student body that was White increased.

Through our longitudinal analyses, we were able to show that minority students' exposure to microaggressions changes as they move from one demographic context to another. For example, students transitioning to college from mostly non-White high schools reported an increase in exposure to Academic Inferiority microaggressions; correspondingly, students transitioning from mostly White high schools reported no change in exposure. This indicates that students are able to discriminate changes in microaggressions across contexts. This longitudinal examination provides an important addition to the literature because existing research has either examined youth in high school or college; we are unaware of microaggression literature that has followed students as they transitioned from one educational context to another (Huynh, 2012; Hwang & Goto, 2008).

Most important, the path analyses showed that racially ethnically hostile educational contexts are detrimental for students' academic achievement and mental health. Though much of the current attention is on microaggressions in college contexts, our findings suggest that more attention should be focused on racial stressors in primary and secondary schools (Benner & Graham, 2011; Farkas, 2003; Hope, Skoog, & Jagers, 2015). Perhaps college students' greater autonomy in structuring their exposure to campus and increased efficacy to call out microaggressive experiences blunt its negative effects. This is in contrast to the argument that minority students' increasing public reporting of microaggressions is an unnecessarily oversensitive response to incidents that should be overlooked, silently pardoned, and quickly forgiven (Campbell & Manning, 2015). Research suggests that minority students' insistence on calling out each act of microaggression may be exactly what American society needs to move past the current post–Civil Rights stalemate (Kawakami, Dunn, Karmali, & Dovidio, 2009). For microaggressions to decrease, minority students need to self-disclose their experiences of microaggressions in ways that elicit individuation and build empathy—in effect, personalize majority individuals' understanding of microaggressions (Ensari, Christian, Kuriyama, & Miller, 2012; Zembylas, 2012). This must be accompanied by support from allied bystanders: "Although people anticipate feeling upset and taking action upon witnessing a racist act against an out-group, they actually respond with indifference" (Kawakami et al., 2009, p. 278).

Racial-ethnic private and public regard at the beginning of college partially mediated the detrimental consequences of academic inferiority microaggressions during high school and were associated with less depressive symptoms. We were surprised to find that these aspects of racial-ethnic identity functioned differently for Black and Latinx students. This is contrary to meta-analytic research that has found no racial-ethnic differences in the association between positive racial-ethnic affect and psychological adjustment, including depressive symptoms (see Rivas-Drake et al., 2014). Consistent with previous research examining the mediating role of private regard among Black college students (Neblett et al., 2013), we found private regard, an internally sponsored affective response, to be an important identity asset that helped blunt the negative effects of microaggressions on depressive symptoms. For Latinx students, it was public regard, an externally sponsored affective response, that helped blunt the negative effects of microaggressions on depressive symptoms. It is important to note that Latinx students reported higher public regard than Black students, indicating that they were more optimistic about how others viewed their racial-ethnic group.

Limitations and Future Research

Some limitations should be considered when interpreting our findings. Because the study only assessed self-reported experiences with microaggressions, we have no externally validated measure of the frequency of micro- versus macroaggressive insults within school contexts (Nadal, 2011). There is no easy solution to this problem; however, future validation efforts with this scale can assess its correlation with other scales measuring racial-ethnic discrimination. The regional nature of our sample limits the generalizability of the findings. The Midwest has its own history of racial-ethnic discrimination and segregation that may not generalize to the experiences of students in other regions (Torres-Harding et al., 2012).

Additionally, though the Academic Inferiority subscale was the strongest factor and aligns with the issues that are most germane to educational settings, there is an open question regarding the applicability of this subscale to Asian Americans, who are more likely to experience educational stereotypes associated with ascriptions of intelligence (Sue et al., 2009). In this regard, it is important to highlight that non-racial-ethnic–based microaggressions are also prevalent in educational settings, such as those based on gender (Capodilupo et al., 2010; Nadal, 2010), sexual orientation (Mccabe, Dragowski, & Rubinson, 2013; Nadal, Issa, et al., 2011; Platt & Lenzen, 2013; Shelton & Delgado-Romero, 2011), immigration status (Keels & Rusin, 2016; Nadal, Mazzula, Rivera, & Fujii-Doe, 2014), disability (Keller & Galgay, 2010), and religious affiliation (Nadal, Issa, Griffin, Hamit, & Lyons, 2010), to name a few. This indicates the need for the development of a diverse set of survey instruments.

Despite these limitations, our finding that students differentiate between more versus less racially ethnically hostile contexts has implications for practice. Educators can use the SB-REMA scale to assess the extent to which students of various racial-ethnic groups experience the school climate as hostile. This could be useful for producing actionable data at both the classroom and school levels. The SB-REMA could also be a tool to assist school counselors in facilitating discussions of distressing racial-ethnic experiences with minority students (Pieterse et al., 2010).

Note

The research reported in this article was supported by a Scholar's award from the William T. Grant Foundation to the first author (Grant 180804). We gratefully acknowledge the support of several graduate and undergraduate students at the University of Chicago who engaged with us on this work. We would also like to thank the anonymous reviewers of this manuscript, whose feedback strengthened the clarity of our arguments.

References

Alabi, J. (2015). Racial microaggressions in academic libraries: Results of a survey of minority and non-minority librarians. *Journal of Academic Librarianship, 41*(1), 47–53. doi:10.1016/j.acalib.2014.10.008

Allen, Q. (2010). Racial microaggressions: The schooling experiences of Black middle-class males in Arizona's secondary schools. *Journal of African American Males in Education, 1*, 125–143.

Baer, L., Jacobs, D. G., Meszler-Reizes, J., Blais, M., Fava, M., Kessler, R., . . . O'Laughlen, J. (2000). Development of a brief screening instrument: The HANDS. *Psychotherapy and Psychosomatics, 69*(1), 35–41. doi:10.1159/000012364

Benner, A. D., & Graham, S. (2011). Latino adolescents' experiences of discrimination across the first two years of high school: Correlates and influences on educational outcomes. *Child Development, 82*(2), 508–519. doi:10.1111/j.1467-8624.2010.01524.x

Blume, A. W., Lovato, L. V., Thyken, B. N., & Denny, N. (2012). The relationship of microaggressions with alcohol use and anxiety among ethnic minority college students in a historically White institution. *Cultural Diversity and Ethnic Minority Psychology, 18*(1), 45–54. doi:10.1037/a0025457

Campbell, B., & Manning, J. (2015). Microaggression and changing moral cultures. *Chronicle of Higher Education, 61*(41), A25–A26.

Capodilupo, C. M., Nadal, K. L., Corman, L., Hamit, S., Lyons, O., & Weinberg, A. (2010). The manifestation of gender microaggressions. In D. W. Sue (Ed.), *Microaggressions and marginality: Manifestation, dynamics, and impact* (pp. 193–216). Hoboken, NJ: Wiley.

Carter, D. J. (2007). Why the Black kids sit together at the stairs: The role of identity-affirming counter-spaces in a predominantly White high school. *Journal of Negro Education, 76*(4), 542–554.

Cheryan, S., & Monin, B. (2005). "Where are you really from?": Asian Americans and identity denial. *Journal of Personality and Social Psychology, 89*(5), 717–730. doi:10.1037/0022-3514.89.5.717

DeCuir-Gunby, J. T., & Gunby, N. W. (2016). Racial microaggressions in the workplace: A critical race analysis of the experiences of African American educators. *Urban Education, 51*(4), 390–414. doi:10.1177/0042085916628610

Donovan, R. A., Galban, D. J., Grace, R. K., Bennett, J. K., & Felicié, S. Z. (2013). Impact of racial macro- and microaggressions in Black women's lives: A preliminary analysis. *Journal of Black Psychology, 39*(2), 185–196. doi:10.1177/0095798412443259

Dovidio, J. F., & Gaertner, S. L. (2004). Aversive racism. In M. P. Zanna (Ed.), *Advances in experimental social psychology* (Vol. 36, pp. 1–52). San Diego, CA: Academic Presss. doi:10.1016/S0065-2601(04)36001-6

Dovidio, J. F., Kawakami, K., Smoak, N., & Gaertner, S. L. (2009). The nature of contemporary racial prejudice: Insights from implicit and explicit measures of attitudes. In R. E. Petty, R. H. Fazio, & P. Brinol (Eds.), *Attitudes: Insights from the new implicit measures* (pp. 165–192). New York, NY: Psychology Press.

Ensari, N., Christian, J., Kuriyama, D. M., & Miller, N. (2012). The personalization model revisited: An experimental investigation of the role of five personalization-based strategies on prejudice reduction. *Group Processes & Intergroup Relations, 15*(4), 503–522. doi:10.1177/1368430211434576

Farkas, G. (2003). Racial disparities and discrimination in education: What do we know, how do we know it, and what do we need to know? *Teachers College Record, 105*(6), 1119–1146.

Flores, E., Tschann, J. M., Dimas, J. M., Pasch, L. A., & de Groat, C. L. (2010). Perceived racial/ethnic discrimination, posttraumatic stress symptoms, and health risk behaviors among Mexican American adolescents. *Journal of Counseling Psychology, 57*(3), 264–273. doi:10.1037/a0020026

Gaertner, S. L., & Dovidio, J. F. (2005). Understanding and addressing contemporary racism: From aversive racism to the common ingroup identity model. *Journal of Social Issues, 61*(3), 615–639. doi:10.1111/j.1540-4560.2005.00424.x

Gómez, J. M. (2015). Microaggressions and the enduring mental health disparity: Black Americans at risk for institutional betrayal. *Journal of Black Psychology, 41*(2), 121–143. doi:10.1177/0095798413514608

Harrell, J. P., Hall, S., & Taliaferro, J. (2003). Physiological responses to racism and discrimination: An assessment of the evidence. *American Journal of Public Health, 93*(2), 243–248.

Harris, P. A., Taylor, R., Thielke, R., Payne, J., Gonzalez, N., & Conde, J. G. (2009). Research electronic data capture (REDCap)—A metadata-driven methodology and workflow process for providing translational research informatics support. *Journal of Biomedical Informatics, 42*(2), 377–381. doi:10.1016/j.jbi.2008.08.010

Harris, R. S., Jr. (2008). Racial microaggression? How do you know? *American Psychologist, 63*(4), 275–276. doi: 10.1037/0003-066X.63.4.275

Harwood, S. A., Huntt, M. B., Mendenhall, R., & Lewis, J. A. (2012). Racial microaggressions in the residence halls: Experiences of students of color at a predominantly White university. *Journal of Diversity in Higher Education, 5*(3), 159–173. doi:10.1037/a0028956

Henfield, M. S. (2011). Black male adolescents navigating microaggressions in a traditionally White middle school: A qualitative study. *Journal of Multicultural Counseling and Development, 39*(3), 141–155.

Hill, J. S., Suah, K., & Chantea, W. (2010). The context of racial microaggressions against indigenous peoples: Same old racism or something new? In D. W. Sue (Ed.), *Microaggressions and marginality: Manifestation, dynamics, and impact* (pp. 105–122). Hoboken, NJ: Wiley.

Hoggard, L. S., Jones, S. C., & Sellers, R. M. (2017). Racial cues and racial identity implications for how African Americans experience and respond to racial discrimination. *Journal of Black Psychology, 43,* 409–432. doi:10.1177/00957 98416651033

Holgado-Tello, F. P., Chacón-Moscoso, S., Barbero-García, I., & Vila-Abad, E. (2009). Polychoric versus Pearson correlations in exploratory and confirmatory factor analysis of ordinal variables. *Quality and Quantity, 44*(1), 153–166. doi: 10.1007/s11135-008-9190-y

Hope, E. C., Skoog, A. B., & Jagers, R. J. (2015). "It'll never be the White kids, it'll always be us": Black high school students' evolving critical analysis of racial discrimination and inequity in schools. *Journal of Adolescent Research, 30*(1), 83–112. doi:10.1177/0743558414550688

Hu, L. T., & Bentler, P. M. (1999). Cutoff criteria for fit indexes in covariance structure analysis: Conventional criteria versus new alternatives. *Structural Equation Modeling: A Multidisciplinary Journal, 6*(1), 1–55. doi:10.1080/1070551990 9540118

Huynh, V. W. (2012). Ethnic microaggressions and the depressive and somatic symptoms of Latino and Asian American adolescents. *Journal of Youth and Adolescence, 41*(7), 831–846. doi:10.1007/s10964-012-9756-9

Hwang, W. C., & Goto, S. (2008). The impact of perceived racial discrimination on the mental health of Asian American and Latino college students. *Cultural Diversity and Ethnic Minority Psychology, 14*(4), 326–335. doi:10.1037/1099-9809.14.4.326

Johnston, M. P., & Nadal, K. L. (2010). Multiracial microaggressions: Exposing monoracism in everyday life and clinical practice. In D. W. Sue (Ed.), *Microaggressions and marginality: Manifestation, dynamics, and impact* (pp. 123–144). Hoboken, NJ: Wiley.

Kawakami, K., Dunn, E., Karmali, F., & Dovidio, J. F. (2009). Mispredicting affective and behavioral responses to racism. *Science, 323*(5911), 276–278. doi:10.1126/science.1164951

Keels, M. (2015). *Financial distress at the start of college* (Minority College Cohort Study Policy Report). Chicago, IL: University of Chicago.

Keels, M., & Rusin, S. (2016). Perceptions may matter most: A comparative examination of teachers' perceptions of "undocumented" Latino students in two high schools. In B. A. Jones & A. Rolle (Eds.), *Leading schools in challenging times: Eye to the future* (pp. 181–202). Charlotte, NC: Information Age Publishing.

Keller, R. M., & Galgay, C. E. (2010). Microaggressions experienced by people with disabilities in US society. In D. W. Sue (Ed.), *Microaggressions and marginality: Manifestation, dynamics, and impact* (pp. 241–268). Hoboken, NJ: Wiley.

Kline, R. B. (2015). *Principles and practice of structural equation modeling* (4th ed.). New York, NY: Guilford Press.

Lambert, S. F., Herman, K. C., Bynum, M. S., & Ialongo, N. S. (2009). Perceptions of racism and depressive symptoms in African American adolescents: The role of perceived academic and social control. *Journal of Youth and Adolescence, 38*(4), 519–531. doi:10.1007/s10964-009-9393-0

Marcus, R. (2015, November 10). College is not for coddling. *The Washington Post.*

Martin, P., Wout, D., Nguyen, H. X., Gonzalez, R., & Sellers, R. M. (2013). *The Multidimensional Inventory of Black Identity–Short.* Unpublished manuscript.

Massey, D. S., & Fischer, M. J. (2002). The long-term consequences of segregation: Minority performance at selective academic institutions. *Ethnic and Racial Studies, 29*, 1–26.

Mccabe, P. C., Dragowski, E. A., & Rubinson, F. (2013). What is homophobic bias anyway? Defining and recognizing microaggressions and harassment of LGBTQ youth. *Journal of School Violence, 12*(1), 7–26.

McWhorter, J. (2014, March 21). "Microaggression" is the new racism on campus. *Time.* Retrieved from http://time.com/32618/microaggression-is-the-new-racism-on-campus/

Mercer, S. H., Zeigler-Hill, V., Wallace, M., & Hayes, D. M. (2011). Development and initial validation of the inventory of microaggressions against black individuals. *Journal of Counseling Psychology, 58*(4), 457–469. doi:10.1037/a0024937

Nadal, K. L. (2010). Gender microaggressions and women: Implications for mental health. In M. A. Paludi (Ed.), *Feminism and women's rights worldwide, Volume 2: Mental and physical health* (pp. 155–175). Santa Barbara, CA: Praeger.

Nadal, K. L. (2011). The Racial and ethnic Microaggressions Scale (REMS): Construction, reliability, and validity. *Journal of Counseling Psychology, 58*(4), 470–480. doi:10.1037/a0025193

Nadal, K. L., Griffin, K. E., Wong, Y., Hamit, S., & Rasmus, M. (2014). The impact of racial microaggressions on mental health: Counseling implications for clients of color. *Journal of Counseling and Development, 92*(1), 57–66. doi:10.1002/j.1556-6676.2014.00130.x

Nadal, K. L., Issa, M. A., Griffin, K., Hamit, S., & Lyons, O. (2010). Religious microaggressions in the United States: Mental health implications for religious minority

Keels et al.

groups. In D. W. Sue (Ed.), *Microaggressions and marginality: Manifestation, dynamics, and impact* (pp. 287–312). Hoboken, NJ: Wiley.

Nadal, K. L., Issa, M. A., Leon, J., Meterko, V., Wideman, M., & Wong, Y. (2011). Sexual orientation microaggressions: "Death by a thousand cuts" for lesbian, gay, and bisexual youth. *Journal of LGBT Youth, 8*(3), 234–259. doi:10.1080/19361653.2011.584204

Nadal, K. L., Mazzula, S. L., Rivera, D. P., & Fujii-Doe, W. (2014). Microaggressions and Latina/o Americans: An analysis of nativity, gender, and ethnicity. *Journal of Latina/o Psychology, 2*(2), 67–78. doi:10.1037/lat0000013

Nadal, K. L., Wong, Y., Griffin, K., Sriken, J., Vargas, V., Wideman, M., & Kolawole, A. (2011). Microaggressions and the multiracial experience. *International Journal of Humanities and Social Sciences, 1*, 36–44.

Neblett, E. W., Cooper, S. M., Banks, K. H., & Smalls-Glover, C. (2013). Racial identity mediates the association between ethnic-racial socialization and depressive symptoms. *Cultural Diversity and Ethnic Minority Psychology, 19*(2), 200–207. doi:10.1037/a0032205

Neblett, E. W., & Roberts, S. O. (2013). Racial identity and autonomic responses to racial discrimination. *Psychophysiology, 50*(10), 943–953. doi:10.1111/psyp.12087

Nguyen, H. H. D., & Ryan, A. M. (2008). Does stereotype threat affect test performance of minorities and women? A meta-analysis of experimental evidence *Journal of Applied Psychology, 93*(6), 1314–1334. doi:10.1037/a0012702

Noh, S., Kaspar, V., & Wickrama, K. A. S. (2007). Overt and subtle racial discrimination and mental health: Preliminary findings for Korean immigrants. *American Journal of Public Health, 97*(7), 1269–1274. doi:10.2105/AJPH.2005.085316

Ong, A. D., Burrow, A. L., Fuller-Rowell, T. E., Ja, N. M., & Sue, D. W. (2013). Racial microaggressions and daily well-being among Asian Americans. *Journal of Counseling Psychology, 60*(2), 188–199. doi:10.1037/a0031736

Osborne, J. W., & Costello, A. B. (2005). Best practices in exploratory factor analysis: Four recommendations for getting the most from your analysis. *Pan-Pacific Management Review, 10*(7), 131–146.

Paradies, Y. (2006). A systematic review of empirical research on self-reported racism and health. *International Journal of Epidemiology, 35*(4), 888–901. doi:10.1093/ije/dyl056

Pearson, A. R., Dovidio, J. F., & Gaertner, S. L. (2009). The nature of contemporary prejudice: Insights from aversive racism. *Social and Personality Psychology Compass, 3*(3), 314–338.

Pierce, C. M., Carew, J. V., Pierce-Gonzalez, D., & Wills, D. (1977). An experiment in racism: TV commercials. *Television and Education, 10*(1), 61–87. doi:10.1177/001312457701000105

Pieterse, A. L., Carter, R. T., Evans, S. A., & Walter, R. A. (2010). An exploratory examination of the associations among racial and ethnic discrimination, racial climate, and trauma-related symptoms in a college student population. *Journal of Counseling Psychology, 57*(3), 255–263. doi:10.1037/a0020040

Platt, L. F., & Lenzen, A. L. (2013). Sexual orientation microaggressions and the experience of sexual minorities. *Journal of Homosexuality, 60*(7), 1011–1034. doi:10.1080/00918369.2013.774878

Reynolds, A. L., Sneva, J. N., & Beehler, G. P. (2010). The influence of racism-related stress on the academic motivation of Black and Latino/a students. *Journal of College Studnt Development, 51*(2), 135–149.

Rivas-Drake, D., Seaton, E. K., Markstrom, C., Quintana, S., Syed, M., Lee, R. M., . . . Sellers, R. M. (2014). Ethnic and racial identity in adolescence: Implications for psychosocial, academic, and health outcomes. *Child Development, 85*(1), 40–57. doi:10.1111/cdev.12200

Rivera, D. P., Forquer, E. E., & Rangel, R. (2010). Microaggressions and the life experience of Latina/o Americans. In D. W. Sue (Ed.), *Microaggressions and marginality: Manifestation, dynamics, and impact* (pp. 59–83). Hoboken, NJ: Wiley.

Seaton, E. K., Yip, T., & Sellers, R. M. (2009). A longitudinal examination of racial identity and racial discrimination among African American adolescents. *Child Development, 80*(2), 406–417. doi:10.1111/j.1467-8624.2009.01268.x

Sellers, R. M., Chavous, T. M., & Cooke, D. Y. (1998). Racial ideology and racial centrality as predictors of African American college students' academic performance. *Journal of Black Psychology, 24*(1), 8–27.

Sellers, R. M., & Shelton, J. N. (2003). The role of racial identity in perceived racial discrimination. *Journal of Personality and Social Psychology, 84*(5), 1079–1092. doi:10.1037/0022-3514.84.5.1079

Shelton, K., & Delgado-Romero, E. A. (2011). Sexual orientation microaggressions: The experience of lesbian, gay, bisexual, and queer clients in psychotherapy. *Journal of Counseling Psychology, 58*(2), 210–221. doi:10.1037/a0022251

Smith, W. A., Allen, W. R., & Danley, L. L. (2007). "Assume the position . . . you fit the description": Psychosocial experiences and racial battle fatigue among African American male college students. *American Behavioral Scientist, 51*(4), 551–578. doi:10.1177/0002764207307742

Snyder, T. D., & Dillow, S. A. (2015). *Digest of education statistics 2013* (NCES 2015-011). Washington, DC: National Center for Education Statistics.

Solórzano, D., Ceja, M., & Yosso, T. (2000). Critical race theory, racial microaggressions, and campus racial climate: The experiences of African American college students. *Journal of Negro Education, 69*, 60–73.

Spencer, M. B. (2006). Phenomenology and ecological systems theory: Development of diverse groups. In R. M. Lerner & W. Damon (Eds.), *Handbook of child psychology* (pp. 829–893). Hoboken, NJ: John Wiley & Sons.

Stanley, D. A., Sokol-Hessner, P., Banaji, M. R., & Phelps, E. A. (2011). Implicit race attitudes predict trustworthiness judgments and economic trust decisions. *Proceedings of the National Academy of Sciences, 108*(19), 7710–7715. doi:10.1073/pnas.1014345108

Steffen, P. R., & Bowden, M. (2006). Sleep disturbance mediates the relationship between perceived racism and depressive symptoms. *Ethnicity & Disease, 16*(1), 16–21.

Steiger, J. H. (2007). Understanding the limitations of global fit assessment in structural equation modeling. *Personality and Individual Differences, 42*(5), 893–898. doi:10.1016/j.paid.2006.09.017

Sue, D. W. (Ed.). (2010). *Microaggressions and marginality: Manifestation, dynamics, and impact.* Hoboken, NJ: Wiley.

Sue, D. W., Capodilupo, C. M., Torino, G. C., Bucceri, J. M., Holder, A. M. B., Nadal, K. L., & Esquilin, M. (2007). Racial microaggressions in everyday life: Implications for clinical practice. *American Psychologist, 62*(4), 271–286. doi:10.1037/0003-066X.62.4.271

Sue, D. W., Lin, A. I., Torino, G. C., Capodilupo, C. M., & Rivera, D. P. (2009). Racial microaggressions and difficult dialogues on race in the classroom. *Cultural Diversity and Ethnic Minority Psychology, 15*(2), 183–190. doi:10.1037/a0014191

Tabachnick, B. G., & Fidell, L. S. (2007). *Using multivariate statistics* (5th ed.). Boston, MA: Pearson/Allyn & Bacon.

Thomas, K. R. (2008). Macrononsense in multiculturalism. *American Psychologist, 63*(4), 274–275. doi:10.1037/0003-066X.63.4.274

Torres, L., Driscoll, M. W., & Burrow, A. L. (2010). Racial microaggressions and psychological functioning among highly achieving African-Americans: A mixed-methods approach. *Journal of Social and Clinical Psychology, 29*(10), 1074–1099. doi:10.1521/jscp.2010.29.10.1074

Torres-Harding, S. R., Andrade, A. L., & Romero Diaz, C. E. (2012). The Racial Microaggressions Scale (RMAS): A new scale to measure experiences of racial microaggressions in people of color. *Cultural Diversity & Ethnic Minority Psychology, 18*(2), 153–164. doi:10.1037/a0027658

Vega, T. (2014, March 21). Students see many slights as racial "microaggressions." *The New York Times.*

Wei, M., Alvarez, A. N., Ku, T. Y., Russell, D. W., & Bonett, D. G. (2010). Development and validation of a coping with discrimination scale: Factor structure, reliability, and validity. *Journal of Counseling Psychology, 57*(3), 328–344. doi:10.1037/a0019969

Wei, M., Wang, K. T., Heppner, P. P., & Du, Y. (2012). Brief report ethnic and mainstream social connectedness, perceived racial discrimination, and posttraumatic stress symptoms. *Journal of Counseling Psychology, 59*(3), 486–493. doi:10.1037/a0028000

Williams, J. L., Tolan, P. H., Durkee, M. I., Francois, A. G., & Anderson, R. E. (2012). Integrating racial and ethnic identity research into developmental understanding of adolescents. *Child Development Perspectives, 6*(3), 304–311. doi:10.1111/j.1750-8606.2012.00235.x

Wong, G., Derthick, A. O., David, E. J. R., Saw, A., & Okazaki, S. (2014). The what, the why, and the how: A review of racial microaggressions research in psychology. *Race and Social Problems, 6*(2), 181–200. doi:10.1007/s12552-013-9107-9

Yosso, T. J., Smith, W. A., Ceja, M., & Solórzano, D. G. (2009). Critical race theory, racial microaggressions, and campus racial climate for latina/o undergraduates. *Harvard Educational Review, 79*(4), 659–690.

Zembylas, M. (2012). Pedagogies of strategic empathy: Navigating through the emotional complexities of anti-racism in higher education. *Teaching in Higher Education, 17*(2), 113–125. doi:10.1080/13562517.2011.611869

Manuscript received August 26, 2016
Final revision received May 26, 2017
Accepted June 18, 2017

American Educational Research Journal
December 2017, Vol. 54, No. 6, pp. 1345–1377
DOI: 10.3102/0002831217724116
© *2017 AERA. http://aerj.aera.net*

Shaping Income Segregation in Schools: The Role of School Attendance Zone Geography

Salvatore Saporito
College of William & Mary

This study investigates how much the geographic shapes of school attendance zones contributes to their levels of income segregation while holding constant levels of income segregation across residential areas. Income segregation across attendance zones is measured with the rank ordered information theory index. Income segregation across residential areas is measured using a spatial variant of segregation (newly developed to predict income segregation in school attendance zones). Findings indicate income segregation across residential areas is highly correlated with income segregation across attendance zones. Still, school districts with the most irregularly shaped zones have less income segregation than school districts with compact zones—net of residential income segregation.

KEYWORDS: gerrymandering, income segregation, school attendance zones

Recent research (Orfield, 2015; Richards, 2014; Richards & Stroub, 2015) indicates that school districts exacerbate income segregation in schools by delineating irregularly shaped attendance zones. The popular press has echoed these conclusions and, based on interviews with Meredith Richards, makes two claims: First, the evidence "shows fairly clearly" that school districts "*typically* gerrymander to segregate" children by income and race (Hannah-Jones, 2014; Yuhas, 2015). Second, the gerrymandering[1] of attendance zoned is "getting worse over time." If school districts manipulate their zones to segregate children, such machinations cry out for both legal and policy actions that prohibit school districts from engaging in this nefarious activity. Before any policy remedies are contemplated, it is important to more fully explore whether irregularly shaped school attendance

---

SALVATORE SAPORITO *is an associate professor of sociology at the College of William & Mary, 211 Morton Hall, 100 Ukrop Way, Williamsburg, VA 23187; e-mail: sjsapo@ wm.edu. He researches the causes of racial and economic segregation in political geographies such as school attendance zones and legislative districts.*

zones are in fact associated with higher levels of income segregation within a school district. I take up this task here.

My unique contribution is predicting income segregation across a school district's attendance zones based on the geographic shapes of these zone— while accounting for income segregation across the residential areas of school districts. I find that on average, school districts with irregularly shaped attendance zones have *lower levels* of income segregation, net of income segregation within districts' residential areas. These findings completely contradict claims that school districts "typically" draw irregularly shaped attendance zones to exacerbate income segregation. Contrary for a call to identify school districts with irregularly shaped attendance zones, I suggest that focus should shift to comparing income segregation in schools with income segregation in residential areas.

School Attendance Zones in an Era of Rising Income Segregation

While relatively few school districts contain irregularly shaped attendance zones (Saporito, in press; Saporito & Van Riper, 2015), this does not mean that school zones are irrelevant. In fact, school zones—especially those that appear benign since they are compact—contribute to educational inequality since they are inseparable from three social trends. First, income segregation across residential areas has increased steadily since the 1970s (Jargowsky, 1996; Mayer, 2001; Reardon & Bischoff, 2011; Watson, 2009), and almost all of the increase in income segregation is driven by families with children (Owens, 2016). Second, income inequality has risen steeply since the 1970s (Piketty, 2014; Saez & Zucman, 2016), and this rise is correlated with the growth in income segregation (Reardon & Bischoff, 2011). Finally, the last half of the twentieth century has witnessed a growing disparity in standardized tests scores between lower and higher income students (Reardon, 2011). For example, many studies find that increases in shares of lower income students in schools are associated with declines in the academic outcomes of lower income students net of their personal characteristics (Caldas & Bankston, 1997, 1999; Pong, 1998; Rumberger & Palardy, 2005; Ryabov & Van Hook, 2007). It is reasonable to theorize that some of the growing disparity in test scores may be due to increases in income segregation in neighborhoods and the school zones that serve them. Compact school attendance zones are consequential since they draw children from neighborhoods immediately surrounding a school. Whether drawn that way intentionally or not, compact zones reflect the income segregation within a school district's neighborhoods, and for that reason, compact attendance zones contribute to educational inequality.

Attendance Zone Shape and Income Segregation

A number of scholars observe that compact attendance zones may result in segregated schools (Farley, 1975; Goldring, Cohen-Vogel, Smrekar, & Taylor, 2006). This argument is straightforward: Since local residential areas tend to be comprised of people with similar income, compact attendance zones encompassing residential areas in close proximity to a school will have little economic diversity. It follows that one way to reduce income segregation in schools is to delineate irregularly shaped school attendance zones. Districts that seek diversity in their schools—whether by income, race, ethnicity, or academic achievement—must delineate at least some irregularly shaped attendance zones to draw students from far-flung residential areas. By contrast, school districts whose constituents prefer compact zones or whose administrators want to reduce transportation costs often create compact, "neighborhood school" attendance zones. Theoretically, compact attendance zones reproduce the income segregation that already exists in residential areas.

Despite these theoretical arguments, two recent papers find that "gerrymandering of attendance zones generally exacerbates segregation" (Richards, 2014, p. 1119) and serves "primarily as a means of excluding non-white and poor students from whiter and more affluent schools" (Richards & Stroub, 2015, p. 1). These findings are echoed by other scholars who make similar claims based on case studies of individual school districts (Frankenberg & Orfield, 2012; Leigh, 1997; Orfield, 2015; Orfield & Luce, 2009; Orfield, Gumus-Dawes, Luce, & Geneva, 2010; Siegel-Hawley, 2013).

The existing literature is inconsistent. On the one hand, theorists argue that irregularly shaped attendance zones are associated with less income segregation. On the other hand, empirical literature concludes that irregularly shaped attendance zones are associated with more income segregation. I try to reconcile the gulf between theory and evidence by exploring two questions: How strong is the correlation between income segregation across residential areas and income segregation across school attendance zones? As a school district's attendance zones become increasingly irregular, does income segregation across districts' attendance zones increase or decrease (net of income segregation in residential areas)? Here, irregularly shaped zones consist of multiple parts (known as multipart polygons by geographers) or are highly concave. Examples of concave shapes include crescents and sea stars. By contrast, compact attendance zones consist of a single-part polygon and generally resemble a square or other polygon in which all interior angles are less than 180°. In this study, compactness is scale invariant such that, for example, a square with an area of two square miles has the same compactness as one much larger or smaller.

Importantly, I account for two factors that may influence the relationship between zone shape and zone income segregation. The first potentially confounding factor accounts for topographic features within a school district that heavily influence the shapes of attendance zones; these topographic features include water bodies (e.g., lakes and rivers), mountains, golf courses, parks, highways, and the like. It is possible that the presence of lakes, highways, and other topographic features requires a school district to split many of its attendance zones into multiple parts. Such irregularly shaped zones could conceivably draw from economically diverse areas (e.g., lower income people could live on one side of a lake while higher income people live on the other) and account for income integration.

The second factor to consider is income segregation across residential areas. I modify spatial segregation indices (Reardon & O'Sullivan, 2004; White, 1983) so that they are suitable for predicting segregation in zonal systems that contain (roughly) equal populations. Previous scholarship measures spatial segregation based on the distances between people up to some *fixed area* (Reardon & Bischoff, 2011; Reardon & O'Sullivan, 2004). I modify this approach so that spatial segregation is based on *fixed population*. Scholarship shows that spatial measures of segregation based on fixed populations are a much better predictor of segregation in attendance zones than are spatial segregation measures based on fixed area (Saporito, in press).

While the primary issue addressed in this paper is how much income segregation in attendance zones is correlated with their shapes, the measure of spatial segregation I develop to answer this question has practical uses for school district administrators (and members of the public to whom school districts are accountable). Until now, methods of measuring income segregation were based on administrative geographies (e.g., census blocks) or spatial measures based on area—neither of which accurately predict segregation in attendance zones. By developing a method to measure segregation across residential areas that can predict segregation in equi-populous zonal systems, school districts can address public inquiries regarding how much a proposed set of attendance zones exacerbates or ameliorates segregation. To the extent that a school district wants to ensure that a proposed set of school attendance zones is no more segregated than the residential area it serves, my variant of measuring spatial segregation serves as a baseline against which to compare attendance zone segregation.

Study Overview

This paper proceeds as follows. I rely on basic principles developed in geography to explain why it makes sense for compact attendance zones to have greater income segregation than irregularly shaped zones (net of income segregation in residential areas). After providing a theoretical basis for understanding the relationship between attendance zone shape and income segregation, I review literature exploring the relationship between attendance zone shapes and segregation; this literature concludes that school attendance zones generally exacerbate income (and racial) segregation (Richards, 2014; Richards & Stroub, 2015).

This review is followed by an empirical analysis consisting of three parts. First, I regress income segregation in school districts' attendance zones against income segregation residential areas and the geographic shapes of school attendance zones—while holding constant a battery of school district characteristics that might influence income segregation in districts' attendance zones. Regression is then used to identify school districts with greater or lesser than expected levels of income segregation. Results of this analysis show that several school districts have far less income segregation in their attendance zones than expected given income segregation in their residential areas; importantly, no school district has far more income segregation in their zones than expected. The third analysis presents maps of attendance zones in some of these highly unusual school districts. These maps depict many sprawling attendance zones that appear to "reach out" to distance pockets of lower and higher income families. While maps alone cannot prove that a given school district intended to integrate students by income, the maps are highly suggestive since many of the attendance zones depicted in these maps are both highly irregular and economically balanced.

The paper includes a methodological Appendix that describes how to measure income segregation across residential areas using the spatial methods I employ in the body of the paper. When constructed appropriately, spatial measures of residential segregation serve as a baseline against which to compare attendance zone segregation. As discussed in the methodological appendix, school districts can acquire publicly accessible data to measure how much segregation exists in its residential areas. The Appendix provides guidelines allowing school districts to assess whether a set of attendance zones has an "unusually" high level of income integration or segregation given segregation across its residential areas.

Literature Review

Following previous scholars (Ong & Rickles, 2004; Rickles, Ong, & Houston, 2002), I argue that segregation in school attendance zones is driven primarily by segregation in residential areas. This argument can be understood with Tobler's (1970) First Law, which can be paraphrased as *nearby things are more similar than distant things* (Goodchild, 2008). With respect to the distribution of income groups within school districts, Tobler's First Law suggests that the income of a householder is more similar to his or her closest neighbors than the income of his or her neighbors down the street. Similarly, the income composition of two adjacent city blocks is likely more similar than the income composition of two city blocks located farther apart.

Saporito

In most school districts, most school attendance zones are relatively compact—a condition in which locations within attendance zones are near to one another, as in a circle, pentagon, or square (Saporito & Van Riper, 2015). The assumption of zone compactness is reasonable on theoretical grounds since "overcoming space requires expenditure of energy and resources, something that nature and humans try to minimize (although not exclusively, of course)" (Miller, 2004, p. 284). As applied to attendance zones, it is economical to delineate compact attendance zones, primarily to minimize transportation costs. If zones are compact, many school districts will have economically segregated attendance zones given that lower income children are more likely to live nearer to other lower income children than higher income children—a condition consistent with Tobler's First Law that closer things are more similar than distant things.

Despite the fact that no study has measured income segregation in attendance zones, one scholarly work purports to find empirical evidence that is "consistent with the argument that gerrymandered attendance zones may serve primarily as a means of excluding non-white and poor students from whiter and more affluent schools" (Richards & Stroub, 2015, p. 21). This claim warrants scrutiny on two grounds. First, existing scholarship does not measure income segregation across school attendance zones or residential areas. Second, despite a lack of evidence that the geographic shapes of attendance zones are correlated with segregation across attendance zones, the authors recommend that state or federal agencies identify school attendance zones that "fail to meet a minimum standard of compactness" (Richards & Stroub, 2015, p. 27). This policy recommendation assumes that irregularly shaped attendance zones are positively correlated with income segregation across attendance zones. A similar study by Richards (2014) claims that attendance zones generally segregate children.

Like the two quantitative studies of attendance zone segregation, only a few qualitative studies explore the relationship between attendance zone shape and attendance zone segregation. For example, Orfield and Luce (2009) depict two attendance zones in a single school district and note the racial composition inside and immediately surrounding the zone. Since these zones contain White students and appear to bypass areas containing children of color, these scholars make the case that school districts may, in general, use attendance zones to segregate children. Similarly, Siegel-Hawley (2013) examined the school rezoning process in a single school district. The original zones in that district—as well as those that were proposed and eventually adopted—were reasonably compact, and almost all of them were racially homogenous. Based on a thorough review of the rezoning process, Siegel-Hawley showed that this district did not contemplate a proposed set of zones that would have integrated children by race. While insightful, none of this small body of literature compares attendance zone segregation with residential segregation; nor does the literature

1350

examine the association between attendance zone shape and attendance zone income segregation while accounting for factors such as income segregation in residential areas and the topography of a school district.

Data and Measures

The primary data source for this study is the School Attendance Boundary Information System (SABINS) (College of William & Mary & Minnesota Population Center, 2011). SABINS consists of geographic information system (GIS) files containing thousands of school attendance zones for the 2009–2010 school year. I analyze first-grade attendance zones since they closely approximate what most people think of as an elementary school attendance zone. It is reasonable to use a lower grade given the much larger size of attendance zones at the higher grades. In many school districts, attendance zones for Grade 7 and higher are so large that they coincide with the school district in which they are located.

Attendance zones in the 2009–2010 school year SABINS database are available for most of the largest 350 school districts in the United States. Of these 350 districts, 329 are relevant to this study. (Eleven are irrelevant because they have an open enrollment policy in which any child in a district can attend any school. The remaining irrelevant districts serve high school students only.) As shown on the SABINS project's webpage, the research team requested maps of attendance zone from all of the 329 relevant districts; 304 districts complied, resulting in a 92% response rate. It is not possible to know if the zoning practices of responding districts are different from nonresponding districts. Still, a 92% response rate is high for social science research, suggesting that the results of this study are not compromised by nonresponse bias. It is important to emphasize that results apply only to the largest school districts—and not all school districts across the country. Nevertheless, over a third of public school students are enrolled in the 304 school districts I analyze.

Dependent Variable

To measure income segregation across attendance zones, I use the 2008–2012 American Community Survey Data describing the distribution of annual family income within each school attendance zone. The 2008–2012 income data describe the number of families in a block group who fall into 1 of 16 income categories (e.g., \$0–\$9,999; \$10,000–\$14,999; \$15,000–\$19,999; etc., with the last category greater than \$199,999).[2] I convert these family income categories into income percentiles and, as described in the Appendix, use these percentiles to calculate income segregation.

Income segregation among families is measured using the *rank-order information theory index* (H^R), which compares the distribution of income percentiles within each areal unit within a school district (i.e., attendance zone) with the distribution of income percentiles in the entire district (Reardon, Firebaugh, O'Sullivan, & Matthews, 2006). When the income distribution within each attendance zone is the same as a district's income distribution, H^R_{Zones} is equal to zero and no income segregation exists across a school district's attendance zones. When every attendance zone completely lacks income variation (i.e., every family within each zone is in the same income percentile), H^R_{Zones} equals one and a district is completely segregated. Formulas appear in the methodological appendix.

Independent Variables

This study creates two important sets of independent variables: The first set measures residential income segregation. The second set of measures quantify the shapes of school attendance zones with two measures.

The Spatial Rank-Order Information Theory Index ($\tilde{H}^R$) of Income Segregation

In this study, residential income segregation both predicts income segregation in school attendance zones and serves as a control variable in considering the impact of attendance zone geography on attendance zone income segregation. Most scholarship measures residential segregation across census tracts. This approach is inadequate for predicting school attendance zone segregation since census tracts typically have smaller populations than attendance zones. Since income segregation is more intense at smaller than larger scales, the smaller size of tracts makes them an inadequate geography against which to compare attendance zones.

Rather than relying on a proxy geography such as tracts, I devise and implement a spatial variant of income segregation called the spatial rank-order information theory index (hereinafter, $\tilde{H}^R$) (Reardon & O'Sullivan, 2004). Most studies using spatial measures of segregation determine the characteristics of people who live within a fixed distance around each child (hereinafter called a focal child) within a larger region (Lee et al., 2008). While this approach is entirely reasonable, it cannot be used for the current study since the number of children surrounding each focal child varies (within and between school districts). Think of school districts such as Anchorage, Alaska, and Chicago, Illinois. Anchorage has a much lower population density than Chicago, and on average, Anchorage's attendance zones are much larger geographically. Since the previous example suggests that school attendance zones are more apt to be of uniform population size than uniform geographic size, it is not ideal to use fixed radii around each focal child as the basis for predicting segregation in school attendance zones.[3]

My approach essentially builds a compact school attendance zone of equal population size around each focal child in a school district. Specifically, I determine the *N nearest* children to each child in a school district. I call this operationalization of each focal child's local environment the *proximity-based population threshold*. So far as I am aware, a spatial income segregation measure based on local areas defined by proximity-based population thresholds has never been used. In this paper, I use a threshold of 2,000 children ($\tilde{H}^R_{2,000}$) since this is about the average number of children within a typical school attendance zone included this study.[4] Like H^R for school zones, $\tilde{H}^R$ compares income diversity in local environments with the income diversity of the larger region in which they are located. In practice, values of $\tilde{H}^R$ generally range from zero to one (although it is possible to obtain values less than zero). Values of zero represent complete integration, and values of one represent complete segregation. Formulas and calculation details appear in the Appendix.

Income Segregation Across Maximally Compact, Hypothetical School Zones

To ensure that my analyses are robust across alternative measures, I also measure income segregation across residential areas by building maximally compact, hypothetic school attendance zones. I do this by building a hypothetical attendance zone around each school location. Each hypothetical attendance zone contains residential areas nearer to the school than any other school location in the district—an approach first adopted by Rickles et al. (2002). (These hypothetical zones are called Thiessen polygons by geographers.) Figure 1 shows hypothetical zones for Rialto, California, School District.

Since I build maximally compact, hypothetical zones around each school location, a measure of residential income segregation based on them can provide insight into how much school location matters when explaining income segregation across school attendance zones. If residential segregation based on maximally compact, hypothetical attendance zones are able to predict school attendance zone segregation better than residential segregation based on proximity-based population thresholds, than school location is relevant in determining levels of income segregation. I abbreviate income segregation across hypothetical zones as $H^R_{H\_Zones}$ (where H_Zones represents hypothetical zones).

Measuring Irregularly Shaped Attendance Zones

There are numerous ways to measure shape, and most are highly correlated (Niemi, Grofman, Carlucci, & Hofeller, 1990). Given these high correlations, I use two measures that capture different dimensions of attendance zone shape. The first is called concavity (Chambers & Miller, 2010). To describe concavity (or CV), it is helpful to first describe convexity. Perfectly convex shapes (e.g., circles, triangles, and rectangles) are those in which the approximate residential locations of every unique pair of children within an attendance zone can be connected by a straight line that *does*

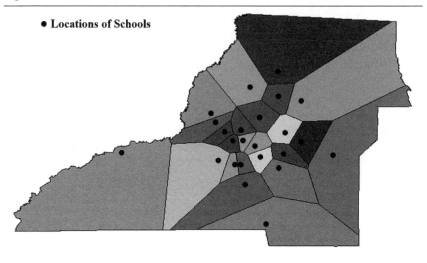

• **Locations of Schools**

Figure 1. **Thiessen polygons encompassing schools in Rialto, California, School District.**

not pass through the zone's boundary.[5] In such cases, CV is zero and a zone is completely compact. In contrast, concave shapes have at least one straight line (connecting a unique pair of children within it) passing through the boundary of an attendance zone. The greater the proportion of lines that pass through the boundary of the zone, the more concave (i.e., irregularly shaped) it is. Crescents, sea stars, or other shapes with indentations are examples of zones that may be highly concave (assuming the children within them are dispersed evenly). Since the unit of analyses in this study is a school district, I calculate the mean CV score of attendance zones for each school district.

The second measure is based on convex hulls (or CH) created around each school attendance zone. Convex hulls are convex polygons of the smallest possible area surrounding each attendance zone. One can visualize a convex hull by imagining a rubber band stretched around a polygon. (I remove any portion of a convex hull that does not lie within the school district in which a school is located.) I determine the number of school-age children inside each convex hull (who do not reside within the school attendance zone it encompasses) and divide it by the total number of children inside the convex hull. If all of the children in the convex hull are also inside the school zone, the school zone is maximally compact (and the value for CH is zero). If a very high proportion of children inside the convex hull do not reside within the school zone, the value of CH approaches one and the school zone is highly irregular. I refer to CV and CH with the generic term *irregularly shaped*.

Control Variables

The shapes of attendance zones are influenced by topographic features. In some school districts, these topographic features are convoluted (e.g., water bodies, mountains, highways, and city parks), and attendance zones abutting them may be shaped irregularly. It is plausible that school districts divided by major lakes and highways also contain many irregularly shaped attendance zones—and it is also plausible that the irregular shapes of these zone result in income integration. In other school districts, the landscape is flat, lacks water features, and in many Western states is governed by the Public Land Survey System. In these school districts, roadways form a square grid, and when school attendance zones follow these roadways, they are likely compact. I control for the influence of topography by measuring the mean values of CV and CH across census tracts within school districts. (I eliminate any portion of a tract that lies outside a school district.) If a district's topography influences the shapes of its census tracts, it likely influences the shapes of its attendance zones. More importantly, if convoluted topography leads to income integration across census tracts, then controlling for topography will reduce any statistical relationship between the shapes of school attendance zones and their levels of income segregation.

It may be that income segregation across residential areas is positively correlated with racial segregation across residential areas. It follows that some income segregation in schools results from the manipulation of attendances zones to ensure racial segregation. In this study, I control for racial segregation (among children who are non-Hispanic Black, non-Hispanic White, and all other racial categories) using a spatial measure of racial residential segregation based on proximity-based population thresholds.

Indicators That a School District Designs Zones for Income Integration

Administrators in some school districts attempt to achieve some income balance in their schools by considering economic integration when designing attendance zones. For example, the webpage for the Fayette, Kentucky, school district states that the criteria used for creating attendance zones includes "using student socio-economic status as a *primary consideration* [italics added] in the assignment of neighborhoods to schools so as to balance the economic diversity of students in every school" ("New School Attendance Zones," n.d.). Similarly, the webpage for Riverside, California, states that the "socio-economic demographics and student makeup of each boundary area will be given consideration to offer balance" ("Elementary/Middle School Boundary Presentation," n.d.). A comprehensive database describing the zoning practices of school districts is available on the SABINS webpage. To determine whether school districts' policies were correlated with income segregation in schools, I use the SABINS data to construct a dummy variable indicating whether a district's webpage (or other public documents) considered economic balance when drawing its zones. Values of one indicate that a district considered economic balance when it delineated its zones (and zero otherwise).

I also constructed a second dummy variable indicating that a school district was under a court desegregation order during the 2009–2010 school year (Logan & Oakley, 2004; Reardon et al., 2012) or reached a voluntarily agreement with the U.S. Department of Education to integrate its schools (Qui & Hannah-Jones, 2014). Values of one indicate that the district operated under a racial desegregate mandate (and zero otherwise). It may be that a racial desegregation mandate may lead some school districts to draw racially balanced—and thus economically balanced—attendance zones.

Income Inequality

Income inequality within a school district may be correlated with residential income segregation or income segregation in school attendance zones. To account for this possibility, I measure income inequality within each school district using the Gini index. Gini measures how much the actual income distribution within a school district deviates from a hypothetical distribution in which everyone earns an identical share of income. A Gini value of zero indicates perfect income equality (i.e., each person earns an equal share of total income), and one indicates perfect inequality (i.e., one person earns all income and everyone else earns no income).

Analyses

Table 1 provides summary statistics of the variables used in these analyses. Findings indicate that attendance zones are shaped more irregularly than census tracts (which are almost completely compact). In fact, attendance zones are three times more irregularly shaped than tracts. But this does not mean attendance zones are in some absolute sense irregularly shaped.

Figure 2 shows attendance zones for a school district with a mean irregularity score that for the 2009–2010 school year is .162. As shown in the figure, 9 of the 16 attendance zones have CV values below .10, and these 9 zones are, by any reasonably standard, highly compact. To be sure, several zones are shaped irregularly. In particular, Zones 1, 8, and 9 have concavity values over .40, and many people would agree that at least some zones in this district are shaped irregularly. But on the whole, the mean irregularity score of zones within this district is low. Since the school district in Figure 2 is representative of the average school district, I think it reasonable to argue that most school districts contain relatively compact attendance zones. Still, there are a handful of districts with many irregularly shaped attendance zones (e.g., Wake County, NC).

Table 1
Summary Statistics of School Districts

	Mean	Median	σ	Minimum	Maximum
Attendance zone income segregation (H^R)	.055	.05	.03	.01	.14
Residential income segregation ($\bar{H}^R_{2,000}$)	.058	.06	.02	.01	.15
Residential income segregation ($H^R_{H\_Zones}$)	.054	.05	.02	.01	.14
Attendance zones: Irregularity (CV)	.162	.15	.07	.04	.45
Attendance zones: Irregularity (CH)	.23	.22	.07	.06	.56
Census tracts: Irregularity (CV)	.047	.04	.03	.01	.14
Census tracts: Irregularity (CH)	.12	.12	.04	.02	.28
Zones drawn for income integration (0 = no, 1 = yes)	.10	—	—	.00	1.00
Desegregation mandate (0 = no, 1 = yes)	.12	—	—	.00	1.00
Residential racial segregation	.123	.10	.09	−.07	.53
Income inequality (Gini)	.471	.47	.05	.36	.64
Proportion of families in poverty	.263	.26	.10	.04	.70
Proportion of children African American	.173	.12	.17	.01	.82
Proportion of Children White	.434	.45	.23	.01	.88
Population density (in 1,000s)	.352	.24	.40	.01	2.69
Median square miles of attendance zones	8.036	3.70	11.822	.46	102.227

Note. N = 304. CV = concavity; CH = convex hull.

1357

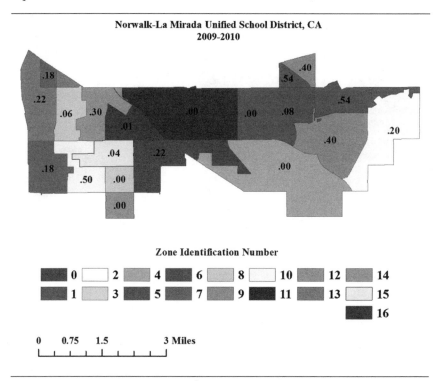

Norwalk-La Mirada Unified School District, CA
2009-2010

Figure 2. **Irregularity scores (concavity values) for attendance zones in the typical school district. Values in each zone show the proportion of unique pairs of children who are connected by a straight line that does not pass through the boundary of the zone in which they live.**

Perhaps more importantly, differences in income segregation across residential areas and attendance are negligible (about one-twentieth of a standard deviation). Specifically, income segregation across attendance zones is .003 points lower than income segregation across residential areas (as measured by $\tilde{H}^R_{2000}$), and it is .001 points higher than income segregation than $H^R_{H\_Zones}$. If the typical school district delineated attendance zones to ameliorate or exacerbate income segregation, larger differences would have emerged. Still, this findings does not eliminate the possibility that some districts have much lower (or higher) income segregation in their schools than their residential areas. I turn to this question in the following.

Predicting Income Segregation Across School Attendance Zones

I use ordinary least squares (OLS) regression to determine the correlation between the shapes of attendance zones and their levels of income segregation—while holding constant income segregation across residential areas. I run two sets of models—the first predicts school zone segregation with a spatial approach (i.e., $\tilde{H}^R_{2,000}$) and the second with hypothetical zones (i.e., $H^R_{H\_Zones}$).

Results in Table 2 that are labeled *Model 1* are straightforward—and powerful. As anticipated, income segregation across residential areas is highly correlated with income segregation across first-grade attendance zones. Specifically, for every 1 point increase in $\tilde{H}^R_{2000}$ and $H^R_{H\_Zones}$, income segregation in attendance zones increases by .97 and 1.01 points, respectively. This nearly one-to-one correspondence suggests that on average, income segregation in attendance zones and residential areas is the same. Moreover, R^2 values for models-based $\tilde{H}^R_{2,000}$ and $H^R_{H\_Zones}$ are .89 and .95, respectively. Finally, when a battery of control variables are included in the models, the correlation coefficients between residential and attendance zone income segregation barely change.

Still, there is a subtle difference between the model based on a spatial measures of residential income segregation (i.e., $\tilde{H}^R_{2,000}$) and the model based on hypothetical zones (i.e., $H^R_{H\_Zones}$). The models relying on hypothetical zones to measure residential segregation have higher R^2 values than those based on spatial measures of segregation. Recall that hypothetical zones are drawn *around each school location*—while the spatial measure of income segregation is based on compact attendance zones drawn around the residential locations of all children. It seems that a measure of income segregation that takes into consideration school location is important in predicting attendance zone segregation. This implies that school location is related to attendance zone segregation; it may be that attendance zone segregation in any particular school district could be a bit higher or bit lower if schools were located in other places.[6] (This finding should not be interpreted to mean that school locations are associated with greater or less income segregation on average.) As Table 1 shows, in the typical school district, income segregation in attendance zones is nearly the same as income segregation across hypothetical zones. The high correlation between hypothetical and actual attendance zones also implies that attendance zones in most school districts are reasonably compact. Elsewise, the correlations would be considerably lower since many attendance zones would encompass income groups that are different from those immediately surrounding each school.

The Effect of Attendance Zone Geography

The previous analyses clearly show that income segregation across residential areas almost completely accounts for income segregation across attendance zones (whether or not school location is taken into account). Yet, there have been relatively strong claims that irregularly shaped

Table 2
Ordinary Least Squares Regression Models Predicting Income Segregation Across School Attendance Zones

| | Models for $\tilde{H}_{2,000}^R$ | | | | Models for $H_{Thiessen}^R$ | | | |
| | Model 1 | | Model 2 | | Model 1 | | Model 2 | |
	b	SE b	b	SE b	b	SE	b	SE b
Residential income segregation ($\tilde{H}_{2,000}^R$)	.968***	.019	.945***	.020				
Residential income segregation ($H_{H\_Zones}^R$)					1.012***	.014	.998***	.015
Attendance zones: Irregularity (CV)			−.025*	.010			−.021**	.007
Attendance zones: Irregularity (CH)			−.036***	.010			−.018*	.008
Census tracts: Irregularity (CV)			−.003	.023			.039	.017
Census tracts: Irregularity (CH)			.014	.015			−.011	.011
Designs zones for income integration			−.005***	.001			−.004***	.001
Active racial desegregation order			−.002	.001			−.002	.001
Residential racial segregation ($H_{2,000}$)			−.005	.007			−.001	.005
Income inequality (Gini)			.020	.010			.015*	.007
Proportion of families that are poor			.011*	.005			−.006	.004
Proportion of children who are Black			.004	.003			−.001	.002
Proportion of children who are White			.007*	.003			−.002	.002
Population density (in 1,000s)			−.001	.001			−.003***	.001
Median square miles of attendance zones			−.000***	.000			.0001	.0001
Constant	−.001	.001	−.002	.005	.000	.001	.006	.004
R^2	.894		.925		.946		.959	

Note. All models contain 304 observations. CV = concavity; CH = convex hull.

*$p < .05$. **$p < .01$. ***$p < .001$.

attendance zones contribute to income segregation in school zones (Orfield, 2015; Orfield et al., 2010; Orfield & Luce, 2009; Richards, 2014; Richards & Stroub, 2015; Siegel-Hawley, 2013). I find the opposite: Irregularly shaped attendance zones are associated with lower levels of income segregation in attendance zones. Put another way, since residential areas are segregated by income, compact attendance zones will mirror that segregation.

The results shown in Table 2 are consistent with this argument. School districts in which the typical attendance zone is shaped irregularly have less income segregation in their attendance zones than comparable districts with compact zones—even while accounting for the influence of income segregation across school districts' residential areas, their topography features, the levels of racial and residential segregation, and the income inequality within the district. Two details indicate the robustness of these results. First, both measures of attendance zone irregularity (i.e., CV and CH) are associated with less income segregation. Second, the relationship between attendance zone geography and attendance zone income segregation is consistent whether I measure residential segregation using a spatial approach (i.e., $\tilde{H}^R_{2,000}$) or hypothetical zones (i.e., $H^R_{H\_Zones}$). Specifically, the relationship between attendance zone irregularity values (for both CV and CH) are negative in both models. While it is not possible to identify which school districts—if any—intentionally delineate irregularly shaped attendance zones to integrate students by income, the balance of the evidence suggests that the typical school district does not exacerbate residential segregation by delineating irregularly shaped attendance zones.

The Influence of Zoning Policies and Desegregation Orders

Roughly 10% of school districts publish statements in which they claim to consider the economic balance of attendance zones when they create new zones. The regression models examine whether school districts issuing such public statements have less income segregation than districts that do not. School districts purporting to consider income integration in their zoning practices do in fact have less income segregation in their attendance zones compared with school districts that do not make such claims public. Although these differences are statistically meaningful, they are substantively small. This suggests that some school districts that consider income integration may give priority to other factors (e.g., minimizing transportation costs). Still, districts such as Wake County, North Carolina, are very successful in delineating economically integrated attendance zones.

Identifying Exceptionally Integrated Districts

The prior section demonstrated that on average, attendance zones have slightly less income segregation than their corresponding residential areas—and that school districts with many irregularly shaped attendance zones have less income segregation than districts with compact zones (net of residential/income segregation). I explore two additional questions to provide greater insight into the correlations shown in the regression analyses: (a) How many school districts have greater than expected (and less than expected) income integration in their zones given levels of residential segregation in their residential areas? (b) Can maps of school districts with economically integrated and highly irregular attendance zones indicate that such occurrences are not likely accidental?

To answer the first question, I identify school districts with higher and lower than expected levels of integration and illustrate the results on a scatterplot. To identify school districts with greater (or lower) integration in their attendance zones than their residential areas, I run two regression models—the first regresses attendance zone income segregation against income segregation across hypothetical zones; the second regresses attendance zone segregation against segregation across residential areas based on $\tilde{H}^R_{2000}$. Both models include all variables in the second models shown in Table 2 (except the shapes of attendance zones). After running these models, I calculate the studentized residuals for each. For each model, I identify any school district in which income segregation in attendance zones is either (a) 1.5 to 2.0 or (b) more than 2.0 standard deviations above or below income segregation in attendance areas. If a school district has much less (or greater) income segregation across zones than residential areas (in both models), this suggests that the district is statistically unusual and warrants closer scrutiny.

Figure 3 plots expected levels of income segregation (the y-axis) against actual levels of income segregation in attendance zones. (Values for expected income segregation represent the mean expected values of income segregation produced from the two regression models.) Any point that is labeled identifies a school district that has consistently less or more segregation in attendance zones than in residential areas. For example, the expected value of income segregation in Fayette County's (KY) attendance zones is .084. That value is much higher than actual income segregation Fayette's attendance zones (which is .058). Fayette County and other labeled school districts above the regression line have appreciably less income segregation in their zones than should be expected given income segregation across their residential areas. Moreover, school districts symbolized with squares have levels of income segregation in their attendance zones that are at least 2.0 standard deviations higher or lower than one would expect given income segregation in residential areas. I identify districts that are 2.0 standard deviations as having "far more" or "far less" segregation in their zones. Districts symbolized with triangles are between 1.5 and 2.0 standard deviations from expected.

Figure 3 shows nine school districts with less income segregation in their zones than one would expect given income segregation in their residential areas; indeed, five of these school districts (marked with squares) have far less income segregation in their zones than residential areas. (These are

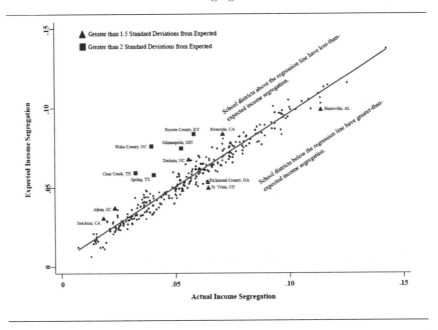

Figure 3. **School districts with lower and higher than excepted income segregation.**

Wake County, NC; Minneapolis, MN; Fayette County, KY; Clear Creek, TX; and Spring, GA.) Many of these school districts have irregularly shaped zones, and as I depict in a series of maps, these zones encompass lower and higher income families who often live in far-flung residential areas.

In contrast to the nine school districts with less than expected levels of attendance zone segregation, only three school districts have greater than expected income segregation in their attendance zones. All three of these districts have attendance zones that have irregularity values at or well below average—indicating that that these districts did not delineate highly irregular attendance zones to achieve income segregation. Importantly, no school district has far more segregation (i.e., greater than two standard deviations than expected) in attendance zones than residential areas.

Depicting School Districts With High Levels of Income Integration

Given the fact that five districts have far less segregation in attendance zones than one would expect given residential segregation (and other factors), it is helpful to depict attendance zones within economically integrated school districts. To this end, I show maps of Fayette, Kentucky; Clear Creek, Texas; and Spring, Texas (Figures 4, 5, and 6, respectively).[7] Each figure shows select attendance zones that are representative of attendance zones

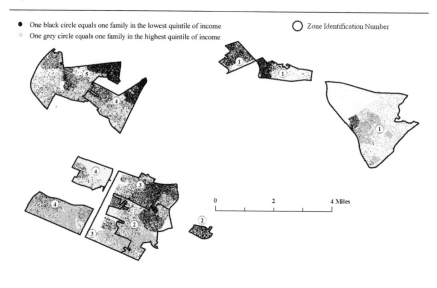

• One black circle equals one family in the lowest quintile of income
One grey circle equals one family in the highest quintile of income

○ Zone Identification Number

Figure 4. Distribution of lower and upper income people across select attendance zones within Fayette County, Kentucky.

within a given school district. (These districts contain dozens of zones—many of them highly irregular—that are difficult to depict on a single map.) Many of the zones within each of these districts contain multiple parts (as in a series of islands) that stretch across several miles and contain roughly equal proportions of lower and upper income families. For the sake of concision, I describe one or two attendance zones per school district.

Zone 1 in Figure 4 consists of a three parts—with the west and central parts containing families primarily in the lowest quintile of income while the eastern part contains a large share of families in the upper quintile of income. Similarly, Zone 4 of Figure 4 also consists of three parts, with the southernmost part with very high shares of higher income families and the northernmost part dominated by lower income families. Figure 5 depicts a selection of zones in Clear Creek, Texas. In general, higher income families live to the north and lower income families to the south. Most of the attendance zones in Clear Creek stretch north to south as well. For example, Zone 5 is shaped like an hour glass, with the northern portion containing higher income families and the southern portion containing lower income families. Similarly, Zones 3 and 7 contain multiple parts; each part tends to be economically homogenous (but the entire zone is economically heterogeneous). Finally, the school district of Spring, Texas, (Figure 6) contains many zones that have multiple, noncontiguous parts. For example, Zones

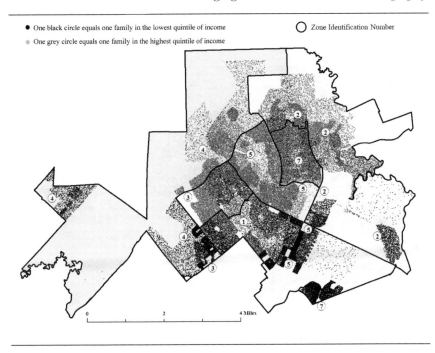

Figure 5. **Distribution of lower and upper income people across select attendance zones within Clear Creek, Texas.**

4 and 6 in Figure 6 contain higher income families in their northernmost parts, and lower income families are clustered in their southernmost parts.

There are other geographic patterns that are noteworthy in all three maps. For example, all three maps have attendance zones that "stretch around" other zones (like an ameba engorging food). These ameba-like zones stretch around other zones and "reach out" to distant clusters of lower and high-income families. Such zones can be seen in Figure 4, Zone 3; Figure 5, Zone 2; and Figure 6, Zone 1.

It may be that these irregularly shaped and economically diverse zones are "accidental." Absent extensive interviews with GIS consultants, district demographers, and school board members, it is not possible to claim that these irregularly shaped zones were drawn that way to integrate children. Yet, none of the multipart zones (or those with ameba-like shapes) depicted in Figures 4, 5, and 6 result from topographic features such as rivers, lakes, and mountains. Many of them could be consolidated to create greater income homogeneity within them. And some evidence suggests that these zones may be drawn to integrate students by income. The written policy of Fayette, Kentucky, states: "Student socio-economic status is a *primary*

● One black circle equals one family in the lowest quintile of income

◉ One grey circle equals one family in the highest quintile of income

○ Zone Identification Number

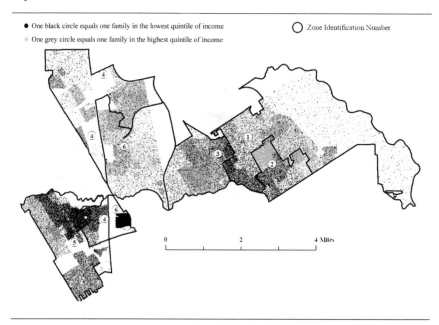

Figure 6. **Distribution of lower and upper income people across select attendance zones within Spring, Texas.**

consideration in the assignment of neighborhoods to schools so as to balance the economic diversity of students in every school" ("New School Attendance Zones," n.d.). While some school districts with exceptionally integrated zones (e.g., Clear Creek and Spring in Texas) have no written policy, their irregularly shaped and economically balanced zones suggest that somebody in these districts may have considered income integration in the zoning process.

Findings and Discussion

Findings show that the average school district does not increase income segregation by creating irregularly shaped school attendance zones. Several facts support this claim. On average, income segregation across school zones is lower than income segregation across residential areas. More importantly, the more irregularly shaped a school district's attendance zones are, the lower its level of income segregation is likely to be—and the attenuation of income segregation associated with irregular attendance zones nets out neighborhood income segregation and the topography within school districts. Maps of exceptionally integrated districts show how irregularly shaped school attendance zones are economically balanced. These zones often draw children from far-flung residential areas; some of these distant neighborhoods contain lower income families while others contain higher income families. Moreover, 10% of school districts have public documents indicating that they consider economic integration when drawing their zones; analyses show that these school districts have less income segregation in their zones than comparable school districts that lack a publicly available, written policy. All of these findings serve as clues that the average school district does not exacerbate income segregation by delineating irregularly shaped attendance zones. In fact, the opposite is more likely to be the case—irregularly shaped attendance zones are correlated with income integration. To be sure, this quantitative evidence should not be interpreted as causal evidence that some school districts intentionally draw irregularly shaped attendance zones to integrate children. Still, the evidence undermines previous claims that school districts generally delineate irregularly shaped attendance zones to increase income segregation in schools (Orfield, 2015; Richards, 2014; Richards & Stroub, 2015).

The absence of school districts with irregularly shaped and economically segregated school zones is "good news"; so is the presence of a few school districts with irregularly shaped and economically integrated zones. But the broader patterns revealed in this paper are worrisome. Most attendance zones in most school districts are relatively compact, a fact demonstrated in this paper and emphasized elsewhere (Saporito, in press; Saporito & Van Riper, 2015). The seemingly benign nature of compact school attendance zones means that the increasing economic segregation of American families—particularly those families with children—is replicated in school attendance zones. Indeed, research indicates that income segregation in schools has increased (Owens, Reardon, & Jencks, 2016). Since (compact) attendance zones are the primary mechanism of sorting children of different economic circumstances into public schools, compact attendance zones (intentionally or not) serve to separate lower income children from their high-income peers. The tight link between school zones and economically segregated schools has implications for inequality in students' access to resources that bear on academic achievement.

Given that most attendance zones in most school districts are compact, it would not be fruitful for federal or state agencies to identify school districts with irregularly shaped attendance zones—a policy recommendation made by Richards and Stroub (2015). This recommendation assumes that irregularly shaped zones are, to borrow the refrain used in recent literature, "gerrymandered" to segregate children (Richards, 2014; Siegel-Hawley, 2013). The findings in this paper suggest that in the context of rising economic segregation among American families with children, school districts can create compact attendance zones and still preserve the spatial and economic advantages of higher income families. Rather than focusing on the shapes of attendance zones as prima facie evidence that school districts segregate children by "gerrymandering" their zones, a more productive approach is to determine how much income segregation exists in a school district's residential areas (as described in the methodological Appendix). During the school rezoning process, levels of residential segregation can then be compared to segregation to proposed sets of attendance zones, and school districts, parents, and advocacy groups can use this comparison to guide their decision to adopt a final set of attendance zones.

Appendix

This appendix covers four topics. First, I describe how to prepare school attendance zones for use in studies of segregation. Second, the calculation of income segregation developed by Reardon, Firebaugh, O'Sullivan, and Matthews (2006) is explained. Third, I describe the geographic information system (GIS) procedures required to calculate spatial segregation measures based on proximity-based population thresholds such as $\tilde{H}^R$. Finally, I provide a correlation matrix containing all of the measures used throughout my study.

Preparing Attendance Zones for Measuring Segregation

The relationships between school attendance zones and the schools that serve them are counterintuitive. For example, a single school might serve two different geographic areas (i.e., attendance zones) at different grade levels. The Los Angeles School District has several dozen schools that serve one zone for grades K to 5 and different zone for Grades 6 to 8. There are variations of this basic relationship at all grade levels across hundreds of school districts in the School Attendance Boundary Information System (SABINS) data. This necessitates using a single grade when constructing a database of attendance zones.

Another important characteristic of attendance zone is that many attendance zones "overlap," as in a Venn diagram. While children who live in the nonoverlapping portion of an attendance zone are served by a single school, children who live in the overlapping portion may be enrolled in one of several schools that serve it. It is necessary to avoid counting the children in overlapping geographic areas multiple times when calculating segregation indices. It is a standard premise of many segregation indices (such as H) that complete integration is reached when every geographic area within a school district has the same racial composition as the entire district. This requires that the population count of the district—and the sums of each income category across all of its attendance zones—is tallied accurately. To achieve this, the number of children in each subarea of an attendance zone is divided by the number of schools that serve that subarea. These weighted counts are summed to each school. This procedure preserves the population totals for school attendance zones in a district.

Allocating Income Data From Census Geography to Attendance Zones

Since the geographies of block groups and attendance zones overlap, it is necessary to estimate the number of families within each block group who reside within a given school attendance zone. The estimation is as follows: for Each block-group, I calculate the proportion of families in each income bracket. I multiply the proportion of families in each income bracket by the total number of families in each census block (using 2010 block-level complete-count data) contained within each block group. This product results in the estimated number of families in each block who are in each income bracket. These block-level estimates are then summed to each school attendance zone. While this procedure is reasonably accurate, some error is introduced in the allocation process—but, as described in the SABINS project documentation, this error is likely small.

I use a similar allocation procedure estimate the number of families by income who live within maximally compact, hypothetical school attendance zones. I estimate the number of families in each income category within each hypothetical attendance zone using areal weighted interpolation (Goodchild & Lam, 1980). This technique allocates the population characteristics of census blocks to maximally compact, hypothetical school attendance zones.[8] This is accomplished by determining the proportion of the area of each census block that lies within each maximally compact, hypothetical school attendance zones and multiplying that proportion by a given population characteristic. For example, if a third of a block's area lies within a particular maximally compact, hypothetical school attendance zones, areal weighted interpolation allocates a third of families in that block to the maximally compact, hypothetical school attendance zone.

Despite the intuitive appeal of creating maximally compact, hypothetical school attendance zones, they may be unrealistic. A maximally compact, hypothetical school attendance zone may contain many more or fewer children than the seating capacity of its corresponding school and some. Some maximally compact, hypothetical school attendance zones cross major topological features (e.g., rivers and highways) that serve as transportation barriers to a given school. Despite these limitations, measuring income segregation across maximally compact, hypothetical school attendance zones provides a second way of measuring income segregation across residential areas. If predictions of attendance zone segregation are consistent for both proximity-based population thresholds and maximally compact, hypothetical attendance zones, then overall findings are more robust.

Measuring Income Segregation Using The Rank-Order Information Theory Index (H_R)

Implementation of the rank-order information theory index of income segregation (H_R) is derived from Reardon et al. (2006). The first basic step in estimating H_R of income segregation (using census data) is to create income entropy—or $E(p)$—between census-defined income thresholds for the entire school district—where (p) designates the proportion of population below each income threshold. (The 2010 census has 16 household income thresholds, beginning at less than \$10,000; \$10,000–\$14,999; \$15,000–\$19,999, etc.) Given that the census has 16 income categories, $E(p)$ is calculated 15 times, as follows:

$$E_{(p)}=p log_2 \frac{1}{p}+(1-p)log_2 \frac{1}{1-p}. \tag{1}$$

For those familiar with entropy between pairs of racial groups (e.g., entropy between White people and non-White people), Formula 1 should be recognizable since it is entropy for households at or below a given income threshold and households above a given income threshold. Once $E(p)$ is calculated for each census-defined threshold in the entire district, $E(p)$ must be calculated for each areal unit (e.g., attendance zone), and it is designated as $E_j(p)$.

Once entropy for the entire school district and each areal unit within it is calculated, $H(p)$ for each census-defined household income threshold is calculated:

$$H_{(p)}=\sum_{j=1}^{j} \frac{t_j}{TE_{(p)}} \left(E(p)-E_j(p) \right). \tag{2}$$

Where and t_j is the population in unit j, and T is the total population in a school district.[9]

Following Reardon et al. (2006), once $H(p)$ is calculated for each of the income thresholds, an Nth-order polynomial regression model (in the paper, I run a seventh-order polynomial) where values of $H(p)$ for each income threshold are regressed on corresponding values of (p) for each income threshold. I weight each point by the square of $E(p)$:

$$H_{(p)}=B_o+B_1+B_2 p^2+B_3 p^3+B_4 p^4 \ldots .+B_7 p^7. \tag{3}$$

I then run a seventh-order polynomial to estimate values of H_R:

$$H_R=\hat{B}_o+\frac{1}{2}\hat{B}_1+\frac{11}{36}\hat{B}_2+\frac{5}{24}\hat{B}_3+\frac{137}{900}\hat{B}_4+\frac{7}{60}\hat{B}_5+\frac{363}{3290}\hat{B}_6+\frac{761}{10080}\hat{B}_7. \tag{4}$$

Details of how the weights for the coefficients were derived can be found in the appendix of Reardon and Bischoff (2011).

Values of H_R range from 0 to 1, where values of zero represent complete integration—a condition in which the share of households at each income is the same for each areal unit j (and thus the school district as a whole). Values of one are obtained when household income in each areal unit j are exactly the same.

Building Local Environments Based on Proximity-Based Population Thresholds

The previous calculations can be used to create spatial income segregation for the rank-order information theory index by exchanging areal units (i.e., Thiessen polygons and attendance zones) with local environments surrounding each child. Local environments are typically defined with areas of fixed radii surrounding around each child (Reardon & O'Sullivan, 2004). For this research, I reconceptualize local environments so that each contains a fixed population.

In this study, I assume that each child lives in the center of their census block. Block centroids are roughly the center of a census block (and I use block centroids created by the U.S. Census Bureau since they are more realistic than those created by commercial software). It is reasonable to use blocks since most of them analyzed in this study are relatively small in geographic area and population size. The median number of children per populated block is 12, and the median area of populated blocks is about nine acres (I use the median since the distributions for these variables is highly skewed). Other than the definition of local environments, this is the only other major difference between my approach and that developed by Reardon and his colleagues.

To construct local environments based on proximity-based population thresholds, I create a "near table" in GIS software that measures the distance between each census block centroid (c) and all other points (hereafter $\acute{c}$), in the district. Then, for each c, I use statistical software to create a running sum of the population characteristics (in this case, for each racial group) in the area immediately surrounding each c, beginning with the population characteristics in c, the nearest $\acute{c}$, the next nearest $\acute{c}$, and so on until the running sum reaches a predetermined population threshold.

Once the population characteristics of each c are calculated, the entropy for each income percentile is calculated for each local environment (as calculated in Equation 1) and then substituted into Equation 2 in lieu of entropy within each areal unit. Since multiple children live within each block point, c, all equations must be weighted accordingly.

Spatial measures of racial and income segregation based on proximity-based population thresholds are of practical use to school districts that must undertake school rezoning to accommodate population change within their borders. Rezoning is as an extensive process that has at least two important steps: considering several school zoning plans and public school board meetings in which parents comment on a proposed set of school zones. During both steps, a question that people will consider and debate is whether a proposed set of attendance zones "increases" segregation. The only way to answer this question is to have a baseline against which to compare an "increase." An easy way to generate this baseline is to create a spatial measure of income segregation using publicly available census data. Based on the results shown in this paper, a general rule of thumb is that a set of zones that is more than .04 points above or below the level of income segregation in residential areas is unusual. A set of proposed zones that have .04 points more income segregation in its zones than its attendance areas is "highly segregated" and may consider another proposal. A school district that is trying to achieve income integration can know if a proposed set of attendance zones is exceptionally successful.

Correlation Coefficients for Variables

Table A1 shows correlation coefficients of all of the variables used in this study. Readers might speculate that: (a) the topography of a school district drives the shapes of districts' school attendance zones and (b) school districts with irregularly shaped topography (as measured by census tract shape) have less income segregation than districts containing compact neighborhoods. This logic suggests that income integration is an "accident of geography." The correlation coefficients in Table A1 do not support this proposition. The irregularity values of census tracts are, at most, modestly correlated with the irregularity values of attendance zones, suggesting that district topography does not drive attendance zone shape. While it is the case that residential income segregation is weakly correlated with attendance zone income segregation, this relationship is spurious (as shown in the regression models).

Table A1
Correlation Coefficients Among Variables Used in the Main Analyses

		A	B	C	D	E	F	G	H	I	J	K	L	M	N	O
Attend. zone segregation (H_{Zones}^R)	A	1.00														
Residential income segregation ($\tilde{H}_{2,000}^R$)	B	.95	1.00													
Residential income segregation ($H_{Thiessen}^R$)	C	.97	.97	1.00												
Attendance zones (CV)	D	-.19	-.05	-.11	1.00											
Attendance zones (CH)	E	-.15	.01	-.06	.80	1.00										
Census tracts (CV)	F	-.23	-.20	-.24	.35	.30	1.00									
Census tracts (CH)	G	-.19	-.14	-.18	.35	.43	.70	1.00								
Zoning for income integration (1 = yes)	H	.01	.07	.04	.07	.11	-.01	.00	1.00							
Desegregation mandate (1 = yes)	I	.03	.07	.07	.12	.09	.05	.08	-.06	1.00						
Racial segregation	J	.41	.41	.43	-.13	-.15	-.16	-.22	.00	.19	1.00					
Income inequality (Gini)	K	.43	.44	.44	-.04	-.01	-.05	-.13	.14	.09	.52	1.00				
Percentage poor children	L	.03	-.02	.03	-.24	-.22	-.18	-.26	-.05	.11	.39	.19	1.00			
Percentage Black children	M	.19	.19	.21	.07	-.01	-.02	.04	-.01	.15	.62	.21	.28	1.00		
Percentage White children	N	-.18	-.14	-.16	.35	.36	.27	.33	.08	.04	-.41	-.15	-.58	-.26	1.00	
Population density (in 1,000s)	O	.03	-.03	.03	-.37	-.44	-.32	-.45	-.06	-.03	.25	.08	.30	.02	-.56	1.00
Median square mile of zones	P	-.35	-.30	-.34	.21	.21	.33	.44	-.01	.13	-.20	-.14	-.09	-.01	.42	-.38

Note. CV = concavity; CH = convex hull.

Notes

George Reed Ruddy and Thomas Crocket wrote and installed computer code on William & Mary's High Performance Computing Cluster to help me calculate values of concavity. Hannah Ferster provided numerous editorial suggestions. Any errors are mine.

[1] I do not use the word *gerrymandering* to describe the shapes of attendance zones (even when attendance zones are shaped irregularly). *Gerrymandering* implies that school districts intentionally manipulate their attendance zones to achieve segregation—and the current literature, including this study, cannot make such causal claims given the limitation of available data. Throughout this paper, the term *irregular* refers to attendance zones consisting of multiple parts that are highly concave. Examples of concave shapes include crescents and sea stars. In contrast to irregularly shaped zones, compact attendance zones generally consist of a single, contiguous polygon that resembles a square or other polygon in which all interior angles are less than 180°.

[2] I would have preferred to use income for families with children, but these data are not available at the block group level.

[3] The mean square miles of attendance zones in Anchorage is 135 (with a minimum and maximum of 1.4 and 2,416 square miles, respectively). By contrast, in Chicago, the mean square miles of attendance zones is 1.1 (with a minimum and maximum of .06 and 20.9 square miles, respectively). Yet, school attendance zones in both school districts contain roughly equal numbers of children. The number of children per attendance zone is 1,430 and 1,595 for Anchorage and Chicago, respectively.

[4] Prior research (Saporito, in press) measured racial segregation using based on equal-area and equi-populous local environments and found that a spatial segregation index based on the equi-populous approach was a much better predictor of racial segregation in school attendance zones than one based on equal area.

[5] The advantage of concavity is that it leverages information about the geographic distribution of populations within attendance zones. This is critical. As Clark (1987) notes, the boundaries of some irregularly shaped attendance zones are created by nonresidential land use (e.g., city parks). What matters is the residential locations of children within a zone—not only its boundary.

[6] This finding does not mean that school districts locate schools in places that lead to income segregation; it is possible that parents move to neighborhoods next to schools and that part of their decision making is driven by the income composition of the area immediately surrounding the school. It is not possible to disentangle this causal ordering using cross-sectional data.

[7] Two other school districts have far more income integration than one would anticipate based on income segregation across residential areas. These are Wake County, North Carolina, and Minneapolis, Minnesota. I do not depict Wake County. It is a well-known example of a district that achieves intentional income integration by delineating irregular attendances zones; in fact, its zones are shaped so irregularly that they are difficult to depict on a map. Minneapolis achieves income integration by delineating large attendance zones (each served by multiple schools) that contain roughly equal proportions of lower and upper income families—and these "overlapping" zones are virtually impossible to map.

[8] Since the median area of populated census blocks used in this study is only nine square acres, the vast majority of census blocks nest entirely within Thiessen polygons. Thus, any interpolation error is bound to be minimal.

[9] It is possible to calculate the *ordinal information theory index* (i.e., H_O) by summing $H(p)$ for each income threshold and dividing that sum by $1 - K$ (where K is the number of income categories). I do not use H_O since I compare income segregation in different school districts. Since H_R uses information on the rank order of income in a school district, it is independent of the income distribution, making it possible to compare income segregation in different districts (Reardon & Bischoff 2011).

References

Caldas, S., & Bankston, C. (1997). Effect of school population socioeconomic status on individual academic achievement. *The Journal of Educational Research, 90*(5), 269–277.

Caldas, S., & Bankston, C. (1999). Multilevel examination of student, school, and district-level effects on academic achievement. *The Journal of Educational Research, 93*(2), 91–100.

Chambers, C., & Miller, A. (2010). A measure of bizarreness. *Quarterly Journal of Political Science, 5*(1), 27–44.

Clark, W. A. V. (1987). Demographic change, attendance area adjustment and school system impacts. *Population Research and Policy Review, 6*(3),199–222.

College of William & Mary & the Minnesota Population Center. 2011. *School Attendance Boundary Information System (SABINS): Version 1.0.* Minneapolis, MN: University of Minnesota.

Elementary/middle school boundary presentation. n.d. Retrieved from slideplayer. com/slide/9626113/.

Farley, R. (1975). Residential segregation and its implications for school integration. *Law and Contemporary Problems, 39*(1), 164–193.

Frankenberg, E., & G. Orfield. (2012). *The resegregation of suburban schools: A hidden crisis in American education.* Cambridge, MA: Harvard Education Press.

Goldring, E., Cohen-Vogel, L., Smrekar, C., & Taylor, C. (2006). Schooling closer to home: Desegregation policy and neighborhood contexts. *American Journal of Education, 112*(3), 335–362.

Goodchild, M. (2008). GISci as an empirical discipline. In K. Kemp (Ed.), *Encyclopedia of geographic information science.* Los Angeles, CA: Sage.

Goodchild, M., & Lam, N. (1980). Areal interpolation: A variant of the traditional spatial problem. *Geo-Processing, 1,* 297–312.

Hannah-Jones, N. (2014). Segregation now . . . sixty years after *Brown v. Board of Education,* the Schools in Tuscaloosa, Alabama, show how separate and unequal education is coming back. *The Atlantic.* Retrieved from https://www.theatlantic.com/magazine/archive/2014/05/segregation-now/359813/

Jargowsky, P. (1996). Take the money and run: Economic segregation in U.S. metropolitan areas. *American Sociological Review, 61*(6), 984–998.

Lee, B., Firebaugh, G., Matthews, S., Reardon, S., Farrell, C., & O'Sullivan, D. (2008). Beyond the census tract: Patterns and determinants of racial segregation at multiple geographic scales. *American Sociological Review, 73*(5), 766–791.

Leigh, P. (1997). Segregation by gerrymander: The creation of the Lincoln Heights (Ohio) School District. *The Journal of Negro Education, 66*(2), 121–136.

Logan, J., & Oakley, D., (2004) *The continuing legacy of the Brown decision: court action and school segregation, 1960-2000.* Albany, NY: Lewis Mumford Center for Comparative Urban and Regional Research, SUNY Albany.

Mayer, S. (2001). *How the growth in income inequality increased economic segregation* (Russell Sage Foundation working paper series). Retrieved from http://www.russellsage.org/research/reports/growth-inequality.

Miller, H. (2004). Tobler's first law and spatial analysis. *Annals of the Association of American Geographers, 94*(2), 284–289.

New school attendance zones. (n.d.). Retrieved from fcps.net/zones.

Niemi, R., Grofman, B., Carlucci, C., & Hofeller, T. (1990). Measuring compactness and the role of a compactness standard in a test for partisan and racial gerrymandering. *The Journal of Politics, 52*(4), 1155–1181.

Ong, P., & Rickles, J. (2004). The continued nexus between school and residential segregation. *Berkeley Journal of African-American Law & Policy*, *6*(2), 54–70.

Orfield, M. (2015). *Milliken, Meredith*, and metropolitan segregation. *UCLA Law Review*, *62*(2), 364–462.

Orfield, M., Gumus-Dawes, B., Luce, T., & Geneva, G. (2010). Neighborhoods and school segregation. In M. Orfield & T. Luce (Eds.), *Region: Planning the future of the Twin Cities* (pp. 85–174). Minneapolis, MN: University of Minnesota Press.

Orfield, M., & Luce, T. (Eds.). (2009). *Region: Planning the future of the Twin Cities*. Minneapolis, MN: University of Minnesota Press.

Owens, A. (2016). Inequality in children's contexts: Income segregation of households with and without children. *American Sociological Review*, *81*(3), 549–574.

Owens, A., Reardon, S., & Jencks, C. (2016). Income segregation between schools and school districts. *American Educational Research Journal*, *53*(4), 1159–1197.

Piketty, T. (2014). *Capital in the twenty-first century*. Cambridge, MA: The Belknap Press of Harvard University Press.

Pong, S. (1998). The school compositional effect of single parenthood on 10th-grade achievement. *Sociology of Education*, *71*(1), 23–42.

Qui, Y. & Hannah-Jones, N. (2014) "A national survey of school desegregation orders." *ProPublica*, December 23, 2014. Retrieved from http://projects.propublica.org/graphics/desegregation-orders

Reardon, S. (2011). The widening academic achievement gap between the rich and the poor: New evidence and possible explanations. In G. J. Duncan & R. J. Murnane (Eds.), *Whither opportunity? Rising inequality, schools, and children's life chances* (pp. 91–116). New York, NY: Russell Sage Foundation.

Reardon, S., & Bischoff, K. (2011). Income inequality and income segregation. *American Journal of Sociology*, *116*(4), 1092–1153.

Reardon, S., Firebaugh, G., O'Sullivan, D., & Matthews, S. (2006, August). *A new approach to measuring socio-spatial economic segregation*. Paper presented at the 29th General Conference of the International Association for Research in Income and Wealth, Joensuu, Finland.

Reardon, S., Grewal, E., Kalogrides, D., & Greenberg, E. (2012) Brown fades: the end of court-ordered school desegregation and the resegregation of American public schools. *Journal of Policy Analysis and Management*. *31*(4), 876–904.

Reardon, S., & O'Sullivan, D. (2004). Measures of spatial segregation. *Sociological Methodology*, *34*(1), 121–162.

Richards, M. (2014). The gerrymandering of school attendance zones and the segregation of public schools: A geospatial analysis. *American Educational Research Journal*, *51*(6), 1119–1157.

Richards, M., & Stroub, K. (2015). An accident of geography? Assessing the gerrymandering of school attendance zones. *Teachers College Record*, *117*(7), 1–32.

Rickles, J., Ong, P., & Houston, D. (2002). *The integrating (and segregating) effect of charter, magnet and traditional elementary schools: The case of five California metropolitan areas* (Working Paper No. 41, UCLA, School of Public Policy and Social Research). Retrieved from http://files.eric.ed.gov/fulltext/ED473461.pdf

Rumberger, R., & Palardy, G. (2005). Does segregation still matter? The impact of student composition on academic achievement in high school. *Teachers College Record*, *107*(9), 1999–2045.

Ryabov, I., & Van Hook, J. (2007). School segregation and academic achievement among Hispanic children. *Social Science Research*, *36*(2), 767–788.

Saez, E., & Zucman, G. (2016). Wealth inequality in the United States since 1913: Evidence from capitalized income tax data. *Quarterly Journal of Economics, 131*(2), 519–578.

Saporito, S. (in press). Irregularly-shaped school attendance zones and racial integration. *Social Science Research.*

Saporito, S., & Van Riper, D. (2015). Do irregularly-shaped school attendance zones contribute to racial segregation or integration? *Social Currents, 3*(1), 64–83.

Siegel-Hawley, G. (2013). Educational gerrymandering? Race and attendance boundaries in a demographically changing suburb. *Harvard Educational Review, 83*(4), 580–612.

Tobler, W. (1970). A computer movie simulating urban growth in the Detroit region. *Economic Geography, 46*(2), 234–240.

Watson, T. (2009). Inequality and the measurement of residential segregation by income in American neighborhoods. *Review of Income and Wealth, 55*(3), 820–843.

White, M. (1983). The measurement of spatial segregation. *American Journal of Sociology, 88*(5), 1008–1018.

Yuhas, A. (2015, September 7). *Students' return to school is marred by renewed segregation across US.* Retrieved from https://www.theguardian.com/education/2015/sep/07/school-segregation-black-latino-students-race

Manuscript received June 16, 2016
Final revision received May 9, 2017
Accepted June 6, 2017

American Educational Research Journal
December 2017, Vol. 54, No. 6, pp. 1378–1413
DOI: 10.3102/0002831217726522
© 2017 AERA. http://aerj.aera.net

Validating a Fidelity Scale to Understand Intervention Effects in Classroom-Based Studies

Pamela Buckley
University of Colorado Boulder
Brooke Moore
Fort Hays State University
Alison G. Boardman
University of Colorado Boulder
Diana J. Arya
Andrew Maul
University of California, Santa Barbara

K–12 intervention studies often include fidelity of implementation (FOI) as a mediating variable, though most do not report the validity of fidelity measures. This article discusses the critical need for validated FOI scales. To illustrate our point, we describe the development and validation of the

PAMELA BUCKLEY, PhD, is a research associate with the Institute of Behavioral Sciences, Blueprints for Healthy Youth Development and Crime Prevention at the University of Colorado Boulder, 483 UCB, Boulder, CO 80309; e-mail: *Pamela.Buckley@colorado.edu*. Her expertise includes intervention research, research design, program evaluation and quantitative data analysis.

BROOKE MOORE, PhD, is an assistant professor of special education at Fort Hays State University. Her research focuses on helping educators create equitable and inclusive learning environments for all students.

ALISON G. BOARDMAN, PhD, is an associate professor of Education at the University of Colorado Boulder. Her research focuses on effective professional development models, reading comprehension instruction, and project-based learning in classrooms with emergent bilingual learners and students with disabilities.

DIANA J. ARYA, PhD, is an assistant professor of Education at the University of California, Santa Barbara. Her research interests focus on language and literacy practices of K–12 and postsecondary populations within science and engineering contexts.

ANDREW MAUL, PhD, is an assistant professor of Education at the University of California, Santa Barbara. His scholarship broadly focuses on research methods and the philosophy of social science, and in particular on the theory and practice of educational and psychological measurement.

Implementation Validity Checklist (IVC-R), an observation tool for measuring FOI of a research-based instructional reading approach, Collaborative Strategic Reading. Following Kane (2006), Wilson (2004), and the guidelines of the Standards for Educational and Psychological Testing (Standards: AERA, APA, & NCME, 2014), findings suggest the IVC-R is a valid instrument for measuring fidelity to CSR. We hope this process will provide an informative model for the validation of FOI observation tools in future classroom-based efficacy studies.

Keywords: Fidelity, Fidelity of implementation, Measurement of program fidelity, Observation protocols, Program integrity

Introduction

An important purpose of education research is to evaluate whether programs are effective in supporting student learning and improving achievement, though intervention effects cannot be fully explained without evidence of implementation success or failure (Munter, Wilhelm, Cobb, & Cordray, 2014). Examining fidelity of implementation (FOI), or the degree to which an intervention is implemented as intended (Dane & Schneider, 1998; O'Donnell, 2008), is necessary for understanding the relationship between components of an intervention and program outcomes (Munter et al., 2014). While the randomized controlled trial (RCT) is widely regarded as a valuable method for estimating average treatment effects of educational interventions (Rosenbaum, 1995), such RCTs cannot account for differences between the design of an intervention and its actual implementation, thus resulting in a lack of clarity about the effectiveness of the intervention model (Hulleman & Cordray, 2009). Understanding variance in implementation, however, is not the only reason to measure FOI. Cordray & Pion (2006) contend that assessing FOI also helps with: "(a) specifying the amount or 'magnitude' of the treatment to be delivered, (b) understanding the coherence of the intervention or treatment, (c) enhancing the validity of inference that can be derived from studies of treatment effectiveness, and (d) optimizing the use of the results to guide interventions" (p. 105). Results drawn from valid measures of FOI can therefore give researchers assurance in attributing outcomes to the intervention and practitioners' confidence in implementing the chosen intervention as it was intended. Accurate measurement of FOI also reveals important considerations for the field regarding how to translate evidence-based findings into practice.

Though the importance of rigorous measurement of implementation fidelity is well documented in the literature, most educational intervention studies nevertheless provide limited information on their FOI measures and implementation results (Nelson, 2013; O'Donnell, 2008). Lack of time and financial resources to develop and describe sound FOI measurement practices is likely a driving force. Indeed, we are unable to locate any education intervention studies (to date) that include a full account of the development and validation of fidelity measures. We therefore sought guidance from the instrument development literature on creating high-quality educational measures (e.g., Kane, 2006; Wilson, 2004) in adapting the validation process for a new domain—fidelity. This application is necessary in that it provides a model for developing valid FOI measures that should make the process more efficient, less costly, and thus more feasible, which ultimately will improve understanding of treatment effectiveness.

While there are multiple means for collecting fidelity data (e.g., surveys, interviews, focus groups, analysis of student artifacts), Heck, Steigelbauer, Hall, & Loucks (1981) argue that classroom observation best captures the interactive process of teacher-student exchanges and thus sharpens the picture of the actual implementation practices used by teachers. In the present study, we describe the development and validation of a revised version of the Implementation Validity Checklist (IVC) classroom observation tool designed to measure the FOI of a research-based model of reading strategies instruction, Collaborative Strategic Reading (CSR; Klingner, Vaughn, Boardman, & Swanson, 2012). We discuss the IVC to provide a case study illustrating how the validation can be applied to the development of sound FOI observation measures. We do this by first briefly reviewing contemporary scholarship on the validation of measures (AERA, APA, NCME, 2014; Kane, 2006). Next we list the criteria for measuring FOI frequently cited across different disciplines and how these criteria relate to classroom-based K–12 intervention studies in general, and our case study in particular. We then describe the lack of research in the area of FOI measurement—particularly in the education literature—and the difficulties in validating fidelity assessments that may explain this shortcoming, followed by examples of FOI measurement from the implementation science literature that offer both similar and distinct processes in accomplishing goals similar to ours to inform how the design of these measures align with components and principles of FOI.

Frameworks for the Validation of Assessment Procedures

Drawing from both the implementation science and prevention research literature, Schoenwald and colleagues (2011) recommend that when developing an observational measure to assess FOI, researchers should refer to the Standards for Educational and Psychological Testing (*Standards*;

AERA, APA, and NCME, 2014), as they offer "a unifying element for any test development or evaluation efforts" (p. 36) by providing elaboration on the types of evidence relevant to the evaluation of the validity of an assessment procedure. In particular, the *Standards* discuss the value of five strands of validity evidence, based on (1) test content (e.g., expert reviews of how well the content of the assessment represents its intended purpose, and the relevance, clarity, and importance of each item on the assessment); (2) response processes (e.g., how raters collect and interpret data); (3) internal structure (including, for example, evaluation of the psychometric properties of individual items and the assessment procedure as a whole); (4) relations to other variables (e.g., correlational or experimental studies examining the extent to which scores obtained with an instrument accurately predict outcome variables); and (5) the consequences of testing (e.g., studies of whether anticipated benefits and/or unanticipated negative consequences of testing are realized). Studies that use researcher-developed observation tools to assess FOI typically give little evidence of validity beyond relations to specific external variables and/or statistics related to interrater reliability and internal consistency (e.g., Dane & Schneider, 1998), thereby limiting how the validation process described by scholars such as Kane (2006) and Wilson (2004) applies to fidelity measurement.

Contemporary argument-based frameworks for validation (e.g., Kane, 2006) emphasize the need to begin the validation process with a clear statement of the proposed uses and interpretations of test scores, and then to construct an evidence-based argument to defend the adequacy and appropriateness of the test for its intended uses. For example, in the present case, the claim is that scores on the IVC are interpreted as measurements of fidelity to the CSR instructional model and can be used in any research setting in which understanding FOI of CSR is of interest. Although the argument-based approach to validation articulated by Kane and codified in the *Standards* are perhaps most commonly associated with traditional educational testing, they may apply in principle to any situation in which an instrument (such as an observational protocol) is used to make claims that stretch beyond that which is immediately observed. Measures of fidelity such as the IVC-R use direct observational evidence to support inferences about a broader attribute of teachers and classrooms, and as such can (and, we believe, should) be vetted using the same rigorous standards as are found elsewhere in educational and psychological testing and measurement.

Applying such validation processes to our case study, we ask the following four research questions: Does the revised version of the IVC show evidence of validity based on (1) test content; (2) rater response processes; (3) internal structure; and (4) relations to other variables? Research questions related to the consequences of testing are not of primary interest in FOI research since whether or not an intervention is implemented as intended is typically not used to make consequential (e.g., promotional) decisions about individual teachers, such as with our case study.

Criteria for Assessing Fidelity of Implementation (FOI)

Fidelity of implementation is typically defined in terms of *dosage* (the frequency of program delivery), *adherence* (whether program components are delivered as prescribed), *quality of delivery* (how well the program material is implemented), *participant responsiveness* (how well the instruction is received or perceived), and/or *program differentiation* (the degree of contrast between treatment and control strategies and/or activities; Dane & Schneider, 1998; Mowbray, Holter, Teague, & Bybee, 2003). In classroom-based K–12 intervention studies, FOI is often considered in terms of instructional quality, commonly operationalized as the amount of improvement or change that occurs in a teacher's practice, though overall fidelity is often considered synonymous with adherence and integrity (O'Donnell, 2008). Initially, fidelity to CSR (Klingner et al., 2012) was assessed via the IVC (e.g., Boardman et al., 2016a, 2016b; Boardman, Klingner, Buckley, Annamma, & Lasser, 2015; Vaughn et al., 2013) designed to measure both procedural fidelity and quality of implementation, though little evidence was available for its validity. Our case study illustrates how the FOI tool was revised with a focus on *adherence* (i.e., implementation as inscribed) to the CSR model by following recommendations from the *Standards* (AERA, APA, and NCME, 2014) and applying Kane's (2006) contemporary argument-based framework for validation of an assessment procedure.

Difficulties of Measuring FOI

Though FOI is important to unpack because it is a complex phenomenon, it can be very difficult to measure. There is no perfect process for accurately measuring FOI (Schoenwald et al., 2011). Sound measurement practices informing the development and use of practical FOI observational tools, however, will ensure that an intervention's delivery is accurately assessed. The need to further understand FOI has been identified across several fields, including the case management (Drake & Resnick, 1998), healthcare (Greenhalgh, Robert, MacFarlane, Bate, & Kyriakidou, 2004), education (O'Donnell, 2008), and implementation science (Carroll et al., 2007) intervention literature. This gap in understanding, according to many scholars, encompasses how to (1) define the FOI concepts to be measured; and (2) develop empirically-validated measures that assess FOI for different interventions. FOI measures must also be user-friendly and appropriate for different contexts; when linked with outcomes, they become "an important tool in building evidence-based practices" (George & Childs, 2012, p. 197).

While there is a need to understand how instructional models are implemented in classrooms, claims about FOI based on observations of instruction can be problematic for a number of reasons. O'Donnell (2008) described how many difficult-to-measure features of instruction outside the prescribed intervention may influence student learning. Examples include the extent to which "good teaching" (in general) interacts with implementation of the (specific) instructional model under investigation (Shulman, 1990), and the impact of adaptations to the prescribed model or materials (Rogers, 2003). Given this challenge, Mowbray et al. (2003) noted the considerable effort it takes to develop protocols that result in consistent, accurate, and interpretable observations. Despite researchers' best efforts, results are commonly influenced by idiosyncratic rater variance "even if response scales are well anchored" (Mowbray et al., 2003, p. 330). In addition, measuring FOI involves translating observed behaviors into numeric form (Schoenwald et al., 2011). Two issues are therefore of critical importance: (1) accurately coding reported operations in alignment with the intervention components; and (2) effectively transforming the ordinal or categorical ratings into interval scales from which scores are derived to interpret FOI. Observational coding systems with trained raters have effectively been used in many efficacy trials because they have the potential to provide objective and highly specific information about a program's implementation (Mowbray et al., 2003). Developing methods for rating observations, however, is challenging given the substantial time and expense that goes into designing protocols, hiring and training raters, scoring observations, reviewing scores, and recording, analyzing and disseminating data. Throughout this process, ensuring adherence of raters to coding protocols and high interrater reliability is crucial, and scores must be appropriately analyzed and accurately reported (Schoenwald et al., 2011). The aforementioned difficulties may explain why the validation process for fidelity measures is generally overlooked or underemphasized in education intervention studies, and why clearly communicated methods and procedures are needed to help make this process more efficient, less costly, and thus more practical to adopt.

Process of FOI Validation in Related Fields

Though minimal research has evaluated ways to marry effective and efficient fidelity measurement (Schoenwald et al., 2011), there are some studies in the prevention science research base (which is tightly linked with the implementation science literature) that describe the process for developing a scientifically validated FOI measure. Below are two examples, each of which provides both similar and distinct processes to ours in accomplishing a common goal of improving the interpretation of program outcomes in the context of experimental studies.

School-Wide Positive Behavior Interventions and Support (SWPBIS) provides a systems approach to promoting a social culture with behavioral supports needed for students to experience social and academic success

(Lewis & Sugai, 1999). Research conducted over the past 30 years has shown SWPBIS to be effective in decreasing school-wide behavior problems, improving academic achievement, and creating a positive school climate (Bradshaw, Mitchell, & Leaf, 2010; Horner, Sugai, & Anderson, 2010). Two empirically validated FOI measures of SWPBIS include (1) School-Wide Evaluation Tool (SET; Horner et al., 2004) and (2) Benchmarks of Quality (BoQ; Cohen, Kincaid & Childs, 2007).

The SET is administered by a trained external evaluator and focuses on initial implementation activities of SWPBIS. As per Messick (1988), the measurement theorist who maintained that inferences generated from test scores often require different types of evidence but not different validities, researchers first created a conceptual logic to (1) guide the structure and intended use of the SET; and (2) provide a framework for the ongoing assessment of the validity of the instrument. The content, item format, and scoring of the SET took place over 3 years and involved the teachers and administrators of 150 elementary and middle schools. Trained observers conducted 1–2 hours of interviews at each school with administrators, teachers, staff members, and students. Raters also reviewed archival documents such as school policies, training curricula, and SWPBIS meeting minutes, and they examined systems used to collect and store SWPBIS data. Multiple analyses conducted to assess the psychometric properties of the SET show that SET scores demonstrate adequate central measures of tendency and variability for sensitivity at the item, subscale, and total levels. In addition, internal consistency and interrater observer agreement were both high. Findings also show the SET has adequate test-retest reliability, yields a valid index of SWPBIS as defined by Lewis and Sugai (1999), and can document change in implementation levels (Freeman et al., 2016).

The BoQ is a self-report FOI measure of SWPBIS (Childs, Kincaid, George, & Gage, 2016; Cohen et al., 2007). Similar to the iterative procedure for revising the IVC FOI measure of Collaborating Strategic Reading described in our case study and as per Messick (1988) who pointed out that instrument development and validation is an ongoing process, but specifically following guidelines described by McKennel (1974), the BoQ was developed in three stages: (1) a qualitative pilot to develop the instrument content; (2) another pilot to test the scale structure; and (3) development of the main survey derived from a conceptual network that includes assessing the reliability and validity of the instrument (Cohen et al., 2007). Items on the BoQ were developed from a training manual that is based on the critical elements of SWPBIS (Lewis & Sugai, 1999). The protocol for the scoring guide was generated from the implementation goals spelled out in the SWPBIS training manual. Once the items were generated, 20 observers (i.e., trainers from across several states who are experts in Positive Behavioral Support) rated the importance of each item to the PBS process on a scale from 1 (minimally important) to 3 (critically important). These ratings were then used to establish point values for each item (Cohen et al.,

2007). Next, cognitive interviews were conducted to investigate sources of response error in individual survey items (Schechter, Blair, & Hey, 1996). The BoQ was piloted in Florida with 10 SWPBS coaches and teams, and feedback was provided on unclear items or directions. Additional revisions to the instrument were made using these qualitative data (Cohen et al., 2007). Multiple studies validating the BoQ provide evidence of strong internal consistency, interrater reliability, and test-retest reliability (e.g., Cohen et al., 2007; Horner et al., 2004). In addition, Horner et al. (2004) showed moderate concurrent validity between the BoQ and the SET. Meanwhile, Cohen et al. (2007) conducted another assessment of concurrent validity using data from 720 schools completing both the SET and the BoQ with results showing a significant relationship.

Unlike the IVC described in our case study, research describing the BoQ does not specify which FOI construct (i.e., adherence, dosage, quality, participant responsiveness, or program differentiation) the instruments measure. Later studies (e.g., Bradshaw et al., 2010) claim the instruments measure implementation quality. The SET and BoQ have been used in several studies to assess the relationship between fidelity and outcomes (Childs et al., 2016; Freeman et al., 2016)—a chief rationale for validating the revised version of the IVC. Our case study therefore builds on studies that follow sound procedures for evaluating the reliability and validity of FOI measures (e.g., Kazdin & Kendall, 1998; Schoenwald et al., 2011). While we could find no education studies that provide much detail in validating FOI measures, we were able to draw ideas from a few (e.g., Hamre, Pianta, Mashburn, & Downer, 2007; Piburn & Sawada, 2000; Sawada et al., 2002) in following the guidelines offered by Schoenwald et al. (2011) and Kane (2006) to describe the iterative process for developing and validating a classroom observation tool that includes expert and trained raters and a standardized scoring system for assessing FOI.

Case Study: Collaborative Strategic Reading

Collaborative Strategic Reading (CSR; Klingner et al., 2012), the instructional model described in our case study, provides students with metacognitive knowledge and self-regulation skills needed to successfully read complex content-related texts. Before reading, students begin with the "Preview" strategy (teacher introduces text and students brainstorm and set a purpose for reading). During reading, students work together in small, heterogeneous, collaborative groups to "Click and Clunk" (monitor understanding by identifying and figuring out unknown words and ideas) and "Get the Gist" (determine main ideas of designated sections of texts). After reading, students engage in the "Question" (asking/answering questions about the reading) and "Review" strategies (summarizing and justifying key ideas). Finally, the teacher brings the class back together for a whole-class wrap-up.

Fidelity and CSR

In previous studies, CSR has benefitted a variety of learners (Boardman et al., 2015; Klingner, Vaughn, & Schumm, 1998; Vaughn et al., 2011) with especially beneficial results for struggling readers in mixed-ability classrooms (Boardman et al., 2016a, 2016b; Kim et al., 2006; Klingner, Vaughn, Arguelles, Hughes, & Leftwich, 2004). In several of these studies, fidelity was assessed the IVC (e.g., Boardman et al., 2015, 2016a, 2016b; Vaughn et al., 2013). This previous version of the IVC contained items scored on a five-point rating scale (e.g., not observed, low quality, mid-low, mid-high, very high quality), with each of these items combining teacher and student behaviors. Although the IVC exhibited acceptable levels of interrater agreement (around 90%; Boardman et al., 2015, 2016a, 2016b; Vaughn et al., 2013) and internal consistency (.80 –.91.; Boardman et al., 2016a), like many FOI assessments, items asked for holistic judgments and thus required a considerable amount of subjectivity. Additionally, there was little evidence of validity beyond the reliability checks referenced above. Finally, observers have noted forms of variation in the quality of CSR implementation, as well as features that also frequently occur in non-CSR classrooms (e.g., main idea strategies)— observations that helped clarify what is unique to CSR. For these reasons, a new version of the IVC was sought, with items specifically linked to concrete observable behaviors and with robust checks on the validity of the assessment. The following hypotheses were explored as assumptions of CSR that would be demonstrated through a validated IVC-R instrument: (1) Student and teacher behaviors embedded in the CSR model can be consistently observed across raters, classrooms, and schools; (2) CSR implementation will necessarily vary across teachers; (3) CSR lessons are distinct from business-as-usual lessons, even though some practices might be shared across lesson types (e.g., student collaboration); and (4) higher quality of CSR implementation will be associated with higher student reading outcomes.

Methods

Guidelines that emphasize the importance of examining fidelity (Mowbray et al., 2003; Nelson, Cordray, Hulleman, Darrow, & Sommer, 2012; O'Donnell, 2008) as well as work on developing classroom observation instruments (Fish & Dane, 2000; Hamre et al., 2007; Hill et al., 2012; Pianta & Hamre, 2009) were drawn from in developing the IVC-Revised (or IVC-R). Additionally, guidance was sought from the general literature on creating high-quality educational measures (e.g., Kane, 2006) and empirically validated FOI assessments (e.g., Cohen et al., 2007; Horner et al., 2004; Schoenwald et al., 2011). Roughly following the procedural guidelines established by the Berkeley Evaluation and Assessment Research (BEAR) Assessment System (Wilson, 2004), the steps for revising the IVC-R consisted of: (1) defining the constructs of fidelity to CSR

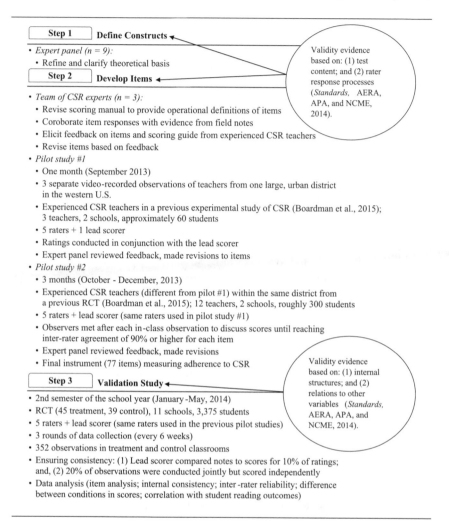

Figure 1. **Steps for validating the Implementation Validity Checklist-Revised (IVC-R).**

by drawing from prior work and through additional conceptual analysis; (2) designing new items and developing scoring guides though an iterative combination of team-based discussions and analysis of field notes collected by classroom observers; and (3) validating the IVC-R by evaluating the psychometric properties of the FOI measure. The first two of these steps generated validity evidence based on test content and on rater response processes, while the third step generated validity evidence based on internal structure and relations to other variables. Figure 1 illustrates this process.

Case Study Context

Data for the case study were drawn from a 5-year investigation of CSR implemented across 21 middle schools in one large urban school district in the western United States. Theory formation (i.e., defining constructs; step 1, Figure 1) and item development (step 2, Figure 1) occurred with middle school teachers who had previously participated in an experimental study of CSR (e.g., Boardman et al., 2015). The student population in this district is 20% white, 59% Hispanic, and 15% African American. Seventy-two percent of the students are eligible for the free or reduced-price lunch program and 35% are English language learners. A different group of teachers from the same district involved in a separate RCT investigating the efficacy of CSR was included in the validation study (step 3, Figure 1). For each experimental study, teachers who were assigned to the CSR condition received 2 days of up-front professional development, along with 6 hours of follow-up professional development throughout the school year. They were also offered individual coaching sessions approximately one time per month. Treatment teachers received lesson plans and student materials needed to implement the CSR model. Teachers in the control group did not receive professional development in CSR. The level of professional development ensured that teachers in the treatment group understood the CSR process and were supported in implementing CSR with fidelity. Inasmuch as teachers were well supported in their professional learning and implementation of CSR according to models of effective professional development (e.g., Garet, Porter, Desimone, Birman, & Yoon, 2001), CSR teachers were nevertheless subject to the common demands of teaching including time constraints, balancing multiple initiatives, and uneven commitment to implementation across schools.

Defining the Constructs of Fidelity to CSR

The CSR model was developed based on the extant literature in the domains of cognitive psychology (Flavell, 1979; Palincsar & Brown, 1984), evidence-based reading comprehension practices (Scammacca et al., 2007), and evidence-based pedagogical practices such as cooperative learning (e.g., Johnson & Johnson, 1999; Kagan, 1986). The original IVC captured the practices outlined in CSR. For the case study, an expert panel of reviewers helped refine and clarify the theoretical basis of the original IVC in developing the IVC-R. The expert panel consisted of nine individuals with diverse expertise and included the authors of this study, a developer of CSR, a measurement expert, a statistician, trained classroom observers, and former classroom teachers with extensive experience with CSR and reading instruction.

The expert panel defined the following two constructs underlying the IVC-R: (1) procedural fidelity, which refers to fidelity *across* the five CSR components, and (2) pedagogical fidelity, which refers to fidelity *within* each CSR component.

Procedural Fidelity

This construct represents the five components of the CSR model (Preview, Click and Clunk, Get the Gist, Questions, and Review), and items are specific to reading comprehension strategies observed in each CSR component. For example, a teacher implementing CSR with fidelity will engage in the observable behavior as inscribed by the following item: "Attends to quality of students' questions by discussing question types, asking questions related to correctness [of textual interpretations], or guiding students to re-read or re-work a question that isn't quite right," during the Questions portion of a lesson.

Pedagogical Fidelity

This construct represents teaching approaches embedded in the CSR process that incorporate discussion about texts into instruction as a means of increasing engagement and comprehension (Lawrence & Snow, 2010). It includes(1) fostering collaboration, in which teachers encourage students working in small collaborative groups to build upon one another's ideas in making sense of the reading; and (2) managing the learning environment, where teachers facilitate pacing and participation so that all students have opportunities to share and to hear ideas from others. These items are observable behaviors that may occur consistently throughout a lesson. For example, a teacher may "keep students engaged and participating" during each portion of the CSR lesson, so that item, which is part of the "managing the learning environment" domain, will be assessed within each CSR component. These items are not unique to CSR and may be observed in non-CSR lessons. However, because they are integral to the CSR model, they are included in the observation tool.

Item Development

Item development started with a team of CSR experts, including the principal investigator and two postdoctoral fellows with expertise in reading (each of whom were also members of the expert panel) drafting descriptions of specific observable teacher and student behaviors or actions that characterize high-quality CSR implementation. A list of possible items was presented to experienced CSR teachers (not involved in the pilot or validation studies, described further in the next section) and to CSR coaches for review. These teachers and coaches were then interviewed by the team of CSR experts about the relevance and clarity of items. Results were presented to the expert panel, which then revised and/or eliminated items as needed. Further revisions were made by iteratively examining field notes and videos collected by observers and receiving additional feedback from observers and other members of the design team.

Scoring Process

The nature of the identified behaviors informed the scoring system of the IVC-R; all teacher behavior items and most student behavior items are scored dichotomously, as observed (1)/not observed (0). Since collaboration and cooperative learning are key features of CSR and students work in groups of up to four as part of the learning process, taking note of the frequency of group participation was an important indicator of adherence to the CSR model. Therefore, for each of the general student behaviors (e.g., sharing gist statements with the group during reading), an additional set of items was designed to be scored as a percentage of students in a group engaged in the observable behavior. For example, if three out of the four students in the group "write their own main idea (gist) statements," the item is scored as .75. The scoring manual was adapted from the original IVC to reflect items from the IVC-R in providing operational definitions of the possible scores for every item on the IVC-R, a practice that has been used in other intervention studies examining the relationship between fidelity and outcomes using a rating scale (Childs et al., 2016; George & Childs, 2012). While conducting an observation, raters took field notes and used the manual to score items on the IVC-R by either checking a box if the item is observed or by entering a ratio of students engaged in the behavior.

Observing Student Groups

A process was needed for capturing a representative sample of student behaviors observed across the classroom at each phase of the CSR process. Since classes in the case study averaged more than 25 students each (with some class sizes as high as 35 students), the number of cooperative student groups per class ($n = 4$) typically ranged from six to eight. Because of the inherent variation in student participation in classroom activities, the difficultly of accurately capturing student behaviors across all student groups was a known weakness of the original IVC, however collecting data on every student's behavior in the classroom was impractical and inefficient. Devine, Rapp, Testa, Henrickson, & Schnerch (2011) suggest that accurately assessing students' behavior in a classroom setting requires that students be randomly selected for observation or that data be collected class-wide with the class considered as a single entity using recording methods such as time sampling. Examining discrete student behaviors in a classroom setting via a time-sampling method has been used in several observational studies (Flower, McKenna, Muething, Bryant, & Bryant, 2014; Guo, Connor, Yang, Roehrig, & Morrison, 2012; Tiger et al., 2013). For example, Cappella, Kim, Neal, & Jackson (2013) used time sampling in a series of systematic

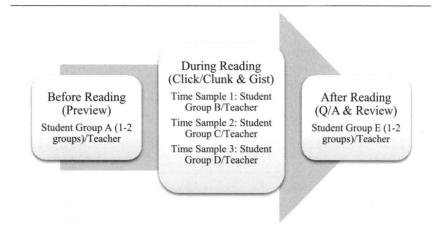

Figure 2: **Rotation schedule for observing cooperative/student groups using the IVC-R (for each rotation, a new student group is observed, for a total of up to 5 groups observed throughout a lesson). For classes with larger sizes, 1–2 groups (*n* = 4 per group) are observed for the "Before Reading" and "After Reading" portion of the CSR lesson.**
Note: IVC-R = Implementation Validity Checklist – Revised; CSR = Collaborative Strategic Reading; Q/A = Question and Answer.

classroom observations to assess behavioral engagement among second to fifth graders. Time sampling was also used by the National Institute of Child Health and Human Development Study of Early Child Care and Youth Development to successfully capture discrete behaviors and classroom conditions related to the social and academic development of students in grades 1–5 (Pianta & Hambre, 2009). As described further below, a plan was thus developed for rotating observations of students so that most or all cooperative groups are observed for some portion of the lesson (Figure 2).

Identifying groups to observe was done randomly with the rater moving to an unobserved group during each rotation. For the first rotation, the observer watches and scores 1–2 student groups and the teacher during the "Preview" portion of the lesson. The second rotation occurs in the "During reading" part of the process and includes three 10-minute time samples with the observer watching and scoring an additional three student groups that were not observed during "Preview," one for each time sample, while simultaneously watching and recording teacher behaviors throughout all three time samples. For the Questions and Review components ("After reading"), the observer watches and scores 1–2 additional previously unobserved student groups, while continuing to record teacher behaviors.

Rater Response Processes

The investigation of the response processes employed by raters in recording observations made visible the ways in which the IVC tool captured key instructional and learning moves within a CSR session. To the extent possible, item responses were corroborated with evidence from field notes. Conflicting evidence was resolved by discussing the notes with the rater and revising wording so that each item was clear to observers.

Pilot study. The IVC-R was field tested using five raters consisting of four CSR coaches with up to 3 years of experience supporting CSR implementation, and a former administrator in the school district who was also serving as a CSR coach. These raters also had expertise in literacy, something Hill & Grossman (2013) say is necessary in utilizing instruments designed to measure teacher evaluation systems aimed at improving instructional practice. All teachers in the study agreed to participate in data collection. Classroom observations were scheduled in advance, and teachers were told that observers would be taking field notes. Raters were assigned to observe classrooms according to schedules and availability, resulting in each rater observing teachers across schools and content areas.

The pilot included two phases. In the first phase, which occurred in the first month of the school year, a lead rater from the expert panel led joint scoring sessions with all raters that included watching 50-minute video-recorded CSR lessons of three teachers and approximately 60 students from two middle schools and discussing the scoring of the observation. The raters' scores were compared with the lead rater's scores. The lead scorer thus served as the "gold standard of reliability," a training process that has been used in other studies that report FOI results (Wanzek et al., 2014). Discrepancies were discussed and this process continued with each of the three video-recorded observations, allowing raters practice in rating using the lead scorer's input and guidance. The expert panel then reviewed and discussed all forms of feedback until consensus was reached for wording and scoring of each item (Cavanagh & Koehler, 2013).

In the second phase, the initial IVC was field tested over a 3-month period with 12 veteran CSR teachers and approximately 300 students from two middle schools. These teachers and their students were not included in the validation study (i.e., step 3, Figure 1). A classroom observation consisted of an observation of one session of CSR. In this way, observation length varied from 44 to 90 minutes according to class schedules and the amount of time teachers engaged in CSR instruction. This second round of pilot observations was conducted by the same team of five raters who observed each lesson together and then discussed scores as a group. Discrepancies were addressed until reaching an interrater agreement of 90% on all items and problematic items (i.e., those with consistently low reliability) were revised by the expert panel. This process identified 77 observable IVC items that comprise teacher and student behaviors representing adherence to the CSR model (Table 1). To ease with interpretation, scored responses were summed across all 77 IVC items (19 items scored as a percent of student behaviors observed in cooperative groups and 58 student and teacher items scored dichotomously as observed/not observed) and then the raw scores were standardized to have a mean of 100 and standard deviation of 15.

Validation study. The validation study (step 3, Figure 1) occurred in the context of a RCT in which teachers were randomly assigned to either implement CSR (treatment) or continue to use their business-as-usual instructional strategies (control). The study included 79 social studies, science and language arts teachers (45 in treatment and 34 in control) from 11 middle schools across a large urban district in the Western United States. Students received CSR in two separate classes (i.e., social studies and science or language arts). In addition, some teachers taught multiple subject areas and/or grade levels. Therefore, to ensure that teachers and students maintained condition (treatment or control), randomization occurred at the teacher, grade, or school level, depending on each school's structure. Thus, the nature of the "coin flip" of randomization resulted in unequal numbers of teachers in each condition. Because the study was designed so that CSR was implemented 1 day a week throughout the school year in social studies and 1 day a week in either science or language arts classes, each social studies class roster was paired with either a science class roster or a language arts class roster within each school to create one social studies/science teacher pair or one social studies/language arts teacher pair. Thus, the experimental unit included a possible combination of 78 teacher pairs of social studies, science and/or language arts teachers and the initial sample included 3,375 students (2,133 in treatment and 1,602 in control). Raters conducted three rounds of IVC-R observations per teacher, starting in winter and re-occurring every 6 weeks until the end of the school year, resulting in a total of 210 classroom observations conducted in CSR and non-CSR classes using the IVC-R instrument.

Raters were assigned to observations based on the availability of their schedules and upon the days in which teachers responded that an observation could occur. Thus, raters observed across school sites within the district. Raters for the experimental study consisted of the same raters for the pilot study. Though having raters blind to condition is ideal in experimental design studies, such objectivity is generally not possible in fidelity observations since the many models, by design, have distinct features that are unmistakable to an observer (e.g., unique student materials, names of specific strategy components). To increase objectivity, raters received extensive training in how to become reliable using the IVC in CSR classrooms and in classrooms without CSR. In addition, as mentioned previously, all raters held

Table 1

Items on the Implementation Validity Checklist – Revised (IVC-R)

Preview: teacher behaviors	Item	Preview: student behaviors	Item
Presents the topic;	1	Write what they already know about the topic;	6
Presents a brainstorm prompt;	2	Share their brainstorm with their group or partner;	7
Presents a purpose for the lesson;	3	Are on task and attentive, e.g., listen, contribute when prompted, participate.	8
Prompts use of specific student roles;	4		
Reminds students to share brainstorms in groups.	5		
Clunks/fix-up strategies: teacher behaviors		Clunks/fix-up strategies: student behaviors[a]	
Attends to the quality of definitions by asking questions related to correctness, guiding students to redefine an unknown word/phrase that isn't quite right, or providing information when needed;	51	Identify unknown words/phrases;	9, 23, 37
		Use fix-up strategies to define unknown words/phrases;	10, 24, 38
		Check definitions by returning to the text;	11, 25, 39
		Use CSR resources such as flipbooks, role cards;	12, 26, 40
Encourages students to collaborate/work together.	52	Discuss unknown words and definitions.	13, 27, 41
Gist: teacher behaviors		Gist: student behaviors[a]	
Attends to quality of students' main idea statements by asking questions related to correctness, or guiding students to re-read or re-work a statement that is not quite right;	53	Identify the most important who/what and the most important information about the who/what;	14, 28, 42
		Write their own main idea statements;	15, 29, 43
Encourages students to discuss the most important "who/what" and the most important information about the "who/what";	54	Share their main idea statements with their group;	16, 30, 44
		Refer back to the text when discussing ideas;	17, 31, 45
		Revise their main ideas after discussing with their group or with the teacher;	18, 32, 46
Encourages students to collaborate/work together in discussing content and/or offering feedback related to main idea statements;	55	Use CSR resources such as flipbooks, role cards;	19, 33, 47
		Discuss ideas about the main idea;	20, 34, 48
		Discuss content of and/or offer feedback on each other's main idea statements;	21, 35, 49
Prompts students to work in a timely manner during reading: keeps students engaged and participating.	56	Are on task and attentive.	22, 36, 50

(continued)

Table 1 (continued)

Preview: teacher behaviors	Item	Preview: student behaviors	Item
Questions: teacher behaviors	Item	Questions: student behaviors	Item
Attends to quality of questions by discussing question types, asking questions related to correctness, or guiding students to re-read or re-work a question that isn't quite right;	57	Write own leveled questions;	60
		Answer their own questions;	61
		Share one/more of their questions with their group;	62
	58	Answer each other's questions in their groups;	63
Encourages students to collaborate/work together in discussing content and/or offering feedback related to leveled questions;	59	Return to/reference the text to answer questions;	64
		Use CSR resources such as flipbooks, role cards;	65
Prompts students to work in a timely manner: Keeps students engaged and participating, e.g., students are not waiting for the teacher.		Discuss the answers to each other's questions and/or offer feedback to each other in writing leveled questions;	66
		Are on task and attentive.	67
Review: teacher behaviors	Item	Review: student behaviors	Item
Attends to quality of summary statements by discussing content, asking questions related to correctness, or guiding students to re-read or re-work a statement that isn't quite right;	68	Write one or two of the most important ideas from the entire passage;	72
		Share their summary with their group;	73
Brings whole class together for a brief review;	69	Provide evidence from the text to support why the ideas they included in their summary statement are important;	74
Encourages students to collaborate/work together in discussing content and/or offering feedback related to review;	70	Discuss ideas about the summary;	75
		Discuss content of each other's summary statements and/or offer feedback on the ideas presented;	76
Prompts students to work in a timely manner: Keeps students engaged and participating, e.g., students are not waiting for the teacher.	71	Are on task and attentive.	77

[a]These items appear three times in the IVC-R instrument because during a CSR lesson, a teacher selects a content-focused text and then divides the text into sections (usually three for one class period).

deep knowledge of evidence-based reading comprehension practices and effective instruction. While the purpose of the IVC-R scoring protocol was to assess CSR usage, it was also designed to capture similar evidence-based comprehension practices in comparison classrooms.

Observations consisted of the full length of the class period and ranged from 50 minutes across six school sites (n = 40 teachers) to 90 minutes across five school sites (n = 39 teachers). The number of sections taught by each teacher varied from one to five classes a day. A different class was observed for each teacher during each round of IVC-R data collection to maximize the sampled breadth of CSR instruction. As such, at least one class was observed more than once for those teachers who taught less than three sections (n = 5). Likewise, teachers with more than three sections had some classes that were not observed during any of the three IVC-R rounds of data collection (n = 37). The remaining 32 teachers taught three sections, so each of their classes were observed during one round of IVC-R data collection. Observations were scheduled to ensure that a CSR lesson would be observed with treatment teachers, or a typical day of instruction with control teachers.

The global CSR adherence score (i.e., the sum of the 77 items), averaged across the three observations, was used for analysis. For each observation, items in the "during reading" portion of the instrument are averaged across each section completed. Thus, if a group observed during the time samples completed all three sections of the text, the denominator is 3; if the group completed only 2 sections, the denominator is 2, etc.

Of the 210 observations, approximately 20% were conducted by two raters observing the same classroom together and scoring the observation independently to test whether student and teacher behaviors embedded in the CSR model could be consistently assessed across raters, classrooms, and schools. These double-scored observations were used to determine interrater reliability (estimated using intra-class correlations). IRR analysis was based on scores assigned to observations before any discussion occurred among raters and the lead scorer about reconciling differences in scores. The remaining 80% of observations were conducted independently, of which approximately 10% were randomly sampled by the lead scorer to check for accuracy. The lead rater used field notes to analyze scores by CSR component (Preview, Click and Clunk, Get the Gist, Questions, Review). Discrepancies between the recorded rating and the lead scorer's rating were discussed and scores were revised as needed so as to ensure all double-scored observations were reconciled and that one score for each teacher across each observation round was used in the final analyses.

Instrument Analysis

In contrast to many traditional tests (for example, of cognitive ability, academic proficiency, or personality characteristics), FOI measures such as the IVC are not hypothesized to measure an attribute of persons (or "construct") that exists and possess a particular dimensional structure independent of the measuring instrument. For example, the IVC-R described in our case study can be used to summarize and communicate information about fidelity to the CSR instructional model according to overall fidelity, procedural and pedagogical fidelity, and fidelity on specific CSR components. Further, the choice to summarize information in these ways, and more specific choices regarding which of these levels of focus are of interest in any given application, are based on the theoretical definition of CSR and on human judgment concerning which forms of information are most valuable and meaningful, rather than on a priori theories concerning the "true" structure of fidelity to the CSR instructional model. In other words, it is not hypothesized that variation in the attribute of fidelity to CSR (or more specific subattributes) causes variation in the specific items on the IVC; rather, "fidelity to CSR" can be thought of as an inductive summary of the behaviors observed on the IVC. As such, reflective latent variable models (e.g., confirmatory factor analysis) may not be appropriate in validating FOI measures, as with the investigation presented as our case study (Bollen & Lennox, 1991; Edwards & Bagozzi, 2000). Nevertheless, basic item and test analysis can be pragmatically utilized in the service of quality control when measuring FOI; here we focus on three statistics used in Classical Test Theory (CTT): (1) the p value, or item difficulty, estimated based on the frequency with which a specific behavior was observed; (2) the (corrected) item-total (or point-biserial) correlation coefficient, which estimates the correlation between each item and scores on the total instrument after omitting that item; and (3) Cronbach's alpha, which estimates the proportion of total score variance that is not due to measurement error.

Relations With Other Variables

The IVC-R is intended to provide an assessment of fidelity to the CSR instructional model (that is, whether or not CSR was used as intended in a classroom), as opposed to an assessment of the overall quality of classroom teaching. It would therefore be problematic if the IVC-R could not differentiate between high-quality classes taught using CSR methods and high-quality classes not taught using CSR methods. Thus, given that treatment teachers had professional development in the CSR model and control teachers did not, it was hypothesized that the CSR teachers would receive higher scores on the IVC-R compared with teachers in the control condition. To test whether the IVC-R was indeed sensitive to the features unique to CSR, multilevel models were employed using the Hierarchical Linear Modeling 7.0 software program (Raudenbush, Bryk & Congdon, 2010), thereby accounting for the clustering of observations between schools within teachers. IVC-R scores, entered as grand mean centered, were regressed on a treatment indicator variable (level 1), in which the reference group was typical instruction. Random intercepts for school (level 2) were included, thus treating teachers as randomly sampled from hypothetical distributions of possible schools and allowing each school to have its own mean on the response variable. Applying the notation of Raudenbush and Bryk (2002), model specifications are provided below.

Level 1 (teacher-pair level):

$$y_{ij} = \beta_{0j} + \beta_{1j} * \left(Treatment_{ij} \right) + r_{ij}$$

where:

y_{ij} is the outcome of interest (i.e., overall fidelity) for teacher-pair i in school j;

$Treatment_{ij}$ is a dummy variable for treatment (1 if teacher-pair i in school j is in the treatment group, 0 otherwise);

β_{0j} is the estimated adjusted mean of the outcome of interest;

β_{1j} is the estimated treatment effect; and

r_{ij} is the residual associated with teacher-pair i in school j (assumed to be normally distributed with a mean of zero and variance of σ_e^2);

Level 2 (school level):

$$\beta_{0j} = \gamma_{00} + u_{0j}$$

where:

γ_{00} is the estimated adjusted mean of the outcome of interest in comparison schools;

u_{0j} is the residual associated with school j (assumed to be normally distributed with a mean of zero and variance of σ^2 and uncorrelated with the teacher-pair-level residual).

Additionally, given the empirical link between instruction—as measured by classroom observation tools—and achievement (e.g., Abbott & Fouts, 2003; Belsky et al., 2005; Hamre et al., 2007; Sawada et al., 2002) along with the theoretical basis for the CSR instructional model, higher fidelity to CSR should, in principle, be associated with higher levels of reading comprehension among students. In the case study, the reading comprehension subtest of the Gates-MacGinitie Reading Test (GMRT), Fourth Edition (MacGinitie, MacGinitie, Maria, & Dreyer, 2000) was used, which is the outcome measure in several experimental studies of CSR (e.g., Boardman et al., 2015, 2016b; Vaughn et al., 2011). Two parallel forms were employed to permit pre- and posttesting. The GMRT (a timed, paper-and-pencil test) was group-administered to students in treatment and comparison classrooms by trained researchers blind to condition at the beginning and end of the school year. Estimates of internal consistency for the GMRT range from .91 to .93 and estimates of alternate-forms reliability range from .80 to .87.

Multilevel models were again employed, this time to investigate differences in GMRT scores at posttest as a function of IVC-R scores, controlling for GMRT pretest scores. For this analysis, three-level models were estimated in which students were treated as nested in teacher pairs and teacher pairs were treated as nested in schools. Given the interest in a treated-on-the-treated model assessing the relationship between fidelity to the CSR model and reading outcomes, the IVC-R overall fidelity score of the teacher pair (as opposed to a dichotomous variable for condition) was the primary treatment variable. Since prior research has found CSR to be particularly effective for struggling readers (Boardman et al., 2016a, 2016b; Kim et al., 2006; Klingner et al., 2004), an additional model was fit with an interaction term between pretest GMRT scores and IVC-R scores to examine the hypothesis that higher adherence to the CSR model is associated with greater gains in reading for students with a lower initial level of reading ability compared to those with a higher initial level of ability. IVC-R scores varied at level 2 because that is where the random assignment took place, and GMRT pretest scores were entered into the model as grand mean centered. The model took the following form:

Level 1 *(student level)*:

$$y_{ijk} = \pi_{0jk} + \pi_{1jk} * \left(Pretest_{ijk}\right) + e_{ijk}$$

where:

y_{ijk} is the outcome of interest (i.e., GMRT) for student i in teacher-pair j in school k;

$Pretest_{ijk}$ is the pretest score for student i in teacher-pair j in school k;

π_{0jk} is the estimated adjusted mean of the outcome of interest;

π_{1jk} is the total effect of pretest;

e_{ijk} is the residual associated with student i in teacher-pair j in school k;

Level 2 *(teacher-pair level)*:

$$\pi_{0jk} = \beta_{00k} + \beta_{01k} * \left(Overall\ fidelity_{jk}\right) + r_{0jk}$$

$$\pi_{1jk} = \beta_{10k} + \beta_{11k} * \left(Overall\ fidelity_{jk}\right)$$

where:

$Overall\ fidelity_{jk}$ = Overall fidelity score of teacher-pair j in school k;

β_{00k} is the estimated adjusted mean of the outcome of interest in comparison teacher pairs;

β_{01k} is the estimated main effect of fidelity;

β_{10k} is the estimated main effect of the pretest;

β_{11k} is the estimated interaction between fidelity and the pretest;

r_{0jk} is the residual associated with teacher-pair j in school k (assumed to be normally distributed with a mean of zero and variance of σ_e^2);

Level 3 (school level):

$$\beta_{00k} = \gamma_{000} + u_{00k}$$

where:

γ_{000} is the estimated adjusted mean of the outcome of interest in comparison schools;

u_{00k} is the residual associated with school k (assumed to be normally distributed with a mean of zero and variance of σ_u^2 and uncorrelated with the student- and teacher-pair-level error terms).

Results

Evidence of Validity Based on Response Processes

Evidence of validity based on response processes was established by including assurances that raters were consistent in their understanding and use of the IVC-R instrument, and that raters' intended interpretation of the scores was accurate (as described in the methods section). An analysis of how raters collected and interpreted data during data collection showed high interrater reliability (ICC = .972) for the 20% of observations (n = 42) that were conducted by two raters independently scoring the IVC-R.

Evidence of Validity Based on Internal Structure

Results of the item analysis are displayed in Table 2. This table includes the average score of all respondents (across both treatment and control groups) on each item (i.e., the p value, or estimated difficulty level), and lists results by the 49 procedural fidelity and 28 pedagogical fidelity items.

Item Difficulty

Approximately 65% of the items had p values between .25 and .75. Of the 58 dichotomously scored items, only five (less than 10 percent) had p values over .50 of the time. In contrast, 14 items (about 25%) had p values below .10. Overall, among the dichotomous items, strategies in the Preview component were observed the most and Review strategies were observed the least. While there are more items about student behaviors than teacher behaviors, teacher behaviors were on average observed more often than student behaviors. Among the continuous items, student behaviors related to being on task (i.e., management) were observed more than student behaviors demonstrating the use of strategies (i.e., collaboration). These patterns are in relation to the items listed and categorized in Table 2.

Table 2
Item Analysis Used to Tap Each of the IVC-R Domains

Item	M^a	ITC^b	Domain	Subdomain	CSR component
1[d]	0.81	0.388	Procedural fidelity	Strategies	Preview
2[d]	0.68	0.452	Procedural fidelity	Strategies	Preview
3[d]	0.67	0.414	Procedural fidelity	Strategies	Preview
4[d]	0.38	0.521	Procedural fidelity	Strategies	Preview
6[c]	0.52	0.559	Procedural fidelity	Strategies	Preview
9	0.51	0.554	Procedural fidelity	Strategies	Clunk, fix-up (time sample 1)
10	0.25	0.469	Procedural fidelity	Strategies	Clunk, fix-up (time sample 1)
11	0.14	0.408	Procedural fidelity	Strategies	Clunk, fix-up (time sample 1)
12	0.27	0.585	Procedural fidelity	Strategies	Clunk, fix-up (time sample 1)
14	0.42	0.520	Procedural fidelity	Strategies	Gist (time sample 1)
15[c]	0.31	0.596	Procedural fidelity	Strategies	Gist (time sample 1)
16[c]	0.15	0.501	Procedural fidelity	Strategies	Gist (time sample 1)
17	0.22	0.358	Procedural fidelity	Strategies	Gist (time sample 1)
18	0.08	0.224	Procedural fidelity	Strategies	Gist (time sample 1)
19	0.17	0.378	Procedural fidelity	Strategies	Gist (time sample 1)
23	0.40	0.566	Procedural fidelity	Strategies	Clunk, fix-up (time sample 2)
24	0.19	0.521	Procedural fidelity	Strategies	Clunk, fix-up (time sample 2)
25	0.11	0.292	Procedural fidelity	Strategies	Clunk, fix-up (time sample 2)
26	0.15	0.447	Procedural fidelity	Strategies	Clunk, fix-up (time sample 2)
28	0.40	0.506	Procedural fidelity	Strategies	Gist (time sample 2)
29[c]	0.41	0.718	Procedural fidelity	Strategies	Gist (time sample 2)
30[c]	0.24	0.594	Procedural fidelity	Strategies	Gist (time sample 2)
31	0.14	0.308	Procedural fidelity	Strategies	Gist (time sample 2)
32	0.07	0.320	Procedural fidelity	Strategies	Gist (time sample 2)
33	0.11	0.429	Procedural fidelity	Strategies	Gist (time sample 2)
37	0.32	0.571	Procedural fidelity	Strategies	Clunk, fix-up (time sample 3)
38	0.11	0.485	Procedural fidelity	Strategies	Clunk, fix-up (time sample 3)
39	0.08	0.437	Procedural fidelity	Strategies	Clunk, fix-up (time sample 3)
40	0.09	0.390	Procedural fidelity	Strategies	Clunk, fix-up (time sample 3)
42	0.33	0.472	Procedural fidelity	Strategies	Gist (time sample 3)
43[c]	0.33	0.679	Procedural fidelity	Strategies	Gist (time sample 3)
44[c]	0.19	0.569	Procedural fidelity	Strategies	Gist (time sample 3)
45	0.13	0.334	Procedural fidelity	Strategies	Gist (time sample 3)
46	0.05	0.333	Procedural fidelity	Strategies	Gist (time sample 3)
47	0.11	0.370	Procedural fidelity	Strategies	Gist (time sample 3)
51[d]	0.33	0.463	Procedural fidelity	Strategies	Clunk, Fix-up
53[d]	0.44	0.626	Procedural fidelity	Strategies	Gist
57[d]	0.26	0.511	Procedural fidelity	Strategies	Questions
60[c]	0.30	0.775	Procedural fidelity	Strategies	Questions
61[c]	0.30	0.802	Procedural fidelity	Strategies	Questions
62[c]	0.12	0.620	Procedural fidelity	Strategies	Questions

(continued)

Table 2 **(continued)**

Item	M^a	ITC^b	Domain	Subdomain	CSR component
63	0.12	0.459	Procedural fidelity	Strategies	Questions
64	0.04	0.257	Procedural fidelity	Strategies	Questions
65	0.23	0.644	Procedural fidelity	Strategies	Questions
68[d]	0.10	0.345	Procedural fidelity	Strategies	Review
69[d]	0.24	0.334	Procedural fidelity	Strategies	Review
72[c]	0.23	0.590	Procedural fidelity	Strategies	Review
73[c]	0.05	0.349	Procedural fidelity	Strategies	Review
74	0.08	0.177	Procedural fidelity	Strategies	Review
5[d]	0.30	0.490	Pedagogical fidelity	Collaboration	Preview
7[c]	0.22	0.525	Pedagogical fidelity	Collaboration	Preview
13	0.37	0.566	Pedagogical fidelity	Collaboration	Clunk, fix-up (time sample 1)
20	0.28	0.483	Pedagogical fidelity	Collaboration	Gist (time sample 1)
21	0.07	0.297	Pedagogical fidelity	Collaboration	Gist (time sample 1)
27	0.24	0.607	Pedagogical fidelity	Collaboration	Clunk, fix-up (time sample 2)
34	0.29	0.529	Pedagogical fidelity	Collaboration	Gist (time sample 2)
35	0.09	0.428	Pedagogical fidelity	Collaboration	Gist (time sample 2)
41	0.19	0.603	Pedagogical fidelity	Collaboration	Clunk, fix-up (time sample 3)
48	0.23	0.481	Pedagogical fidelity	Collaboration	Gist (time sample 3)
49	0.08	0.420	Pedagogical fidelity	Collaboration	Gist (time sample 3)
52[d]	0.24	0.360	Pedagogical fidelity	Collaboration	Clunk, fix-up
54[d]	0.39	0.329	Pedagogical fidelity	Collaboration	Gist
55[d]	0.28	0.477	Pedagogical fidelity	Collaboration	Gist
58[d]	0.09	0.189	Pedagogical fidelity	Collaboration	Questions
66	0.13	0.409	Pedagogical fidelity	Collaboration	Questions
70[d]	0.02	0.023	Pedagogical fidelity	Collaboration	Review
8[c]	0.86	0.241	Pedagogical fidelity	Management	Preview
22[c]	0.88	0.265	Pedagogical fidelity	Management	Gist (time sample 1)
36[c]	0.81	0.365	Pedagogical fidelity	Management	Gist (time sample 2)
50[c]	0.67	0.236	Pedagogical fidelity	Management	Gist (time sample 3)
56[d]	0.68	0.386	Pedagogical fidelity	Management	Gist
59[d]	0.39	0.662	Pedagogical fidelity	Management	Questions
67[c]	0.45	0.670	Pedagogical fidelity	Management	Questions
71[d]	0.34	0.428	Pedagogical fidelity	Management	Review
75	0.06	0.226	Pedagogical fidelity	Management	Review
76	0.02	0.105	Pedagogical fidelity	Management	Review
77[c]	0.43	0.327	Pedagogical fidelity	Management	Review

Note. IVC-R = Implementation Validity Checklist – Revised; [a]M = mean value (average score); [b]Item-to-Total Correlation (ITC) = Point-biserial correlation coefficient. [c]Items scored as a percentage demonstrating the behavior (the remaining items are scored dichotomously, with 1 = observed). [d]Item measuring a teacher behavior.

Table 3
**Fixed and Random Effects of Condition on Fidelity to
CSR, as Measured by the IVC-R**

Predictor	Fixed Effects			
	Estimate *(SE)*	*T* Ratio[a]	*p* value	Hedges' *g*
Intercept, β0				
Intercept, γ000	85.75 (1.59)	54.10	<.001	
Intercept, β10				
Condition[b], γ100	22.83 (2.11)	10.84	<.001	2.61

	Random Effects			
	Variance (SD)	*T* ratio[a]	*p* value	% of total variation
Level 1 (teacher)	74.80 (8.65)	8.65		97.1%
Level 2 (school)	2.28 (1.51)	1.51	.264	2.9%

Note. CSR = Collaborative Strategic Reading (CSR); IVC-R = Implementation Validity Checklist – Revised. IVC-R raw scores were transformed into z-scores and then standardized with a mean of 100 and standard deviation of 15. [a]The T ratio for fixed effects was determined by dividing the estimate by its standard error; for random effects, the T ratio was determined by dividing the variance component by its standard deviation. [b]Reference group is business-as-usual instruction (control group). Condition (CSR = 1, Control = 0).

Item-Total Correlations

For the majority of items, item-total correlations were in line with expectations; that is, high total scores on the IVC-R were associated with high scores on individual items, and vice versa. No items had an item-total correlation at or below zero. As presented in Table 3, however, 12 of the 77 items had marginal to low item-total correlations ($r < .30$). Six of these 12 items were targeted at strategies related to Questions and Review, components of the CSR model that were scored as "not observed" for the majority of lessons. Observation data indicate that teachers frequently did not get to these components, which are included as part of the "after reading" portion of the CSR lesson. Factors such as pacing, short class periods, and emphasizing other CSR strategies contributed to the low observation rate of these items.

Reliability

Cronbach's alpha was estimated at .951, suggesting an acceptable level of internal consistency.

Evidence of Validity Based on Relations to Other Variables

As described previously, we investigated the extent to which the IVC-R was sensitive to differences between classrooms taught by CSR-trained teachers and control classrooms. Descriptive statistics show the mean IVC-R score for the treatment group was 109.66 (SD = 14.49) for round 1, 107.12 (SD = 12.90) for round 2, and 109.92 (SD = 13.08) for round 3, and the mean IVC-R score for CSR teachers averaged across all three rounds was 109.73 (SD = 13.03). In contrast, the mean IVC-R score for the control group was 85.37 (SD = 5.90) for round 1, 85.46 (SD = 4.47) for round 2 and 87.75 (SD = 4.38) for round 3 with a mean averaged across all three rounds of 87.67 (SD = 4.77). The large standard deviation in the treatment group (compared with control), however, suggests varying levels of CSR implementation, a finding that was consistent across all three rounds of data collection. Results, presented in Table 3, show that the average IVC-R score was higher for teachers in treatment than for teachers in control (β = 22.83, SE = 2.11, p < .001). Thus, on average, CSR was implemented to a greater extent in the treatment group compared to the control group. This difference is equivalent to a bias-adjusted Hedges g effect size of 2.61. The interpretation of Hedge's g (like most effect size metrics), however, assumes that the standard deviations of the two groups are equal and are normally distributed. Since there is a floor effect in the control group (that is, most of the items on the IVC-R were marked as "not observed"), these assumptions are violated; therefore, we corroborated our finding with the observer field notes.

Adherence to the CSR model, as measured by the IVC-R, was positively associated with Gates-MacGinitie Reading Test scores at posttest, while controlling for pretest scores (β = 0.05, SE = 0.02, p < .05; Table 4). Contrary to expectations, there was a significant positive interaction effect between fidelity and pretest scores (β = 1.5^{-3}, SE = 5.0^{-4}, p < .05), indicating that higher IVC-R scores are associated with greater growth in reading for students with initially-higher scores. However, the magnitude of this difference in effects was very small.

Discussion

Assessing FOI is important for understanding treatment effectiveness (Nelson et al., 2012), offering insight into whether or not a program was implemented as planned (Dane & Schneider, 1998; O'Donnell, 2008), enhancing the validity of claims derived from studies of treatment effectiveness, and optimizing how findings can be used to inform practice (Cordray & Pion, 2006). Findings produced from valid measures of FOI can improve upon researchers' ability to attribute outcomes to the intervention and help practitioners feel more confident in implementing the chosen intervention as

Table 4

Fixed and Random Effects of Fidelity to CSR (as Measured by the IVC-R) and Pretest Scores on Posttest Scores

	Fixed Effects		
Predictor	Estimate *(SE)*	*T* ratio[a]	*p* value
Intercept, β0			
Intercept, γ000	96.59 (0.59)	162.68	<.001
Fidelity[b], γ010	0.05 (0.02)	2.10	.040
GMRT pretest, β10			
Intercept, γ100	0.70 (0.01)	60.54	<.001
Fidelity[b], γ110	0.002 (0.0001)	2.59	.010

	Random Effects			
	Variance (SD)	*T* ratio[a]	*p* value	% of total variation
Level 1 (individual)	71.24 (8.44)	8.44		90.15%
Level 2 (teacher)	5.97 (2.44)	2.44	<.001	7.55%
Level 3 (school)	1.82 (1.35)	1.35	.006	2.31%

Note. Pretest scores were entered into the model as grand mean centered. CSR = Collaborative Strategic Reading (CSR). IVC-R = Implementation Validity Checklist – Revised. GMRT = Gates MacGinitie Reading Test.
[a]The T-ratio for fixed effects was determined by dividing the estimate by its standard error; for random effects, the T-ratio was determined by dividing the variance component by its standard deviation.
[b]Fidelity = The sum of the 77 items on the IVC-R. IVC-R raw scores were transformed into z-scores and then standardized with a mean of 100 and standard deviation of 15.

it was intended. Yet, rigorous assessment of FOI observational tools is a complex endeavor that many intervention research studies do not undertake (Mowbray et al., 2003; Nelson, 2013; O'Donnell, 2008). Following Kane (2006), who argued that researchers should construct an evidence-based argument for defending the appropriateness of a test for its intended uses, and the guidelines of the Standards for Educational and Psychological Testing that provide types of evidence relevant to the evaluation of an argument for the validity of an assessment procedure (*Standards;* AERA, APA, & NCME, 2014), this study describes a process for the validation of FOI observational measures and applies this process to a case study involving the IVC-R. The IVC-R is a classroom observation tool designed to measure the extent to which teacher and student enactment adhere in practice to the CSR model. Findings from the multistep process of item writing, scoring calibration, piloting, and revisions suggests that the IVC-R is a valid instrument for measuring adherence to CSR.

Results of this study reveal important considerations for the field regarding how to measure and analyze FOI using observational tools in an effort to better understand the translation of evidence-based intervention results into actual practice. Lessons learned therefore fall into one of two categories related (1) specifically to the case study presented (i.e., CSR) from data collected via the IVC-R instrument and (2) to the field in general learned from the process of developing a valid classroom observational measure of fidelity. In terms of the former, based on the data constructed through the IVC-R observational tool, results reveal that CSR may best fit a class schedule that extends beyond a 50-minute period; as such, efforts to clarify methods for shortening sessions without compromising quality may be an important next step in the program's professional development process. Further, greater focus on fostering in-depth discussions and providing feedback through additional professional learning sessions may provide the needed support for teachers who struggle with such aspects of CSR. Finally, while the 77-item IVC-R can be used to assess fidelity in future CSR evaluations, the instrument also provides examples of items that have been shown to validly measure specific, observable teacher and student behaviors or actions that can be adapted and tested in assessing fidelity to other instructional models aimed at improving achievement among middle school populations.

We also learned several lessons about what it takes to develop a valid instrument for observing teachers in action. One most evident point was the need for following an iterative approach, as contended by Messick (1988) and Kane (2006). While this article discusses the measurement properties of a specific instrument, results highlight the rigorous and ongoing process necessary for measuring fidelity to a treatment in education intervention studies. As such, this article presents a model that addresses a gap in the literature on methods for supporting claims about the validity of a fidelity observational tool through various sources of evidence. While there is general consensus among researchers that FOI is important, limited time and financial resources is likely the driving force behind this dearth of literature. Our study is the first we are aware of that provides a comprehensive example of how researchers who investigate education interventions can provide the systematic decision making and transparency needed for better understanding the effects of a treatment. In adapting models on creating high-quality educational measures (e.g., Kane, 2006; Wilson, 2004) to the domain of fidelity, and reporting on the multistep process that required frequent revisions and empirical assessment of the IVC-R used to assess FOI to CSR, this article makes more visible what is neglected in efficacy studies. It also provides a model that researchers can use to develop their own observational fidelity tools without having to start from scratch, thereby streamlining the process for validating FOI measures.

Specific to our case study, future investigations should continue to involve multiple aspects of fidelity to determine the strength of CSR and the implications of variation across classrooms. Now that there is a process for validating the IVC-R, the most important items can be identified to develop a shortened, more practical version of the instrument for regular use by school district personnel. An interesting area for research might then be to examine the costs versus benefits of the IVC-R compared with a pared-down version of the same instrument. On a more global level, however, we argue that all such intervention research should support and elevate issues related to validity and instrument design of fidelity instruments, thus holding the field more accountable to higher standards. A stronger focus on the validity of fidelity observational assessments will add nuance and clarity to such investigations.

FOI measures that demonstrate validity through various sources of evidence, and that have practical application, will help the field in making data-based decisions at the local, district, state, and federal levels. Finding ways to expand uses of FOI data could help justify the time and effort required to develop such instruments as well as the ongoing FOI data collection and analysis. For example, information can be used to provide feedback and information about implementation to teachers and to inform improvements in professional development as well as teacher and student resources. Intervention delivery must therefore be evaluated for fidelity to content and process so that one can explain whether failure to replicate designed outcomes is a function of the intervention or of its application. This distinction between intervention and application variation is not unique to education or any one field. As demand increases for evidence-based programs and policies, so does the expectation that service providers and organizations be held accountable for their outcomes (Schoenwald et al., 2011). However, fidelity is just one aspect of a complex system and should be used as a starting point to explore the reasons that a particular intervention may be easier to implement well, encouraging the field to explore competing demands on teachers and schools, limitations in time and resources, and more personal factors such as teaching style and philosophy.

Limitations and Future Research

Measuring treatment adherence and quality of delivery is challenging for any intervention when some items are inconsistently or rarely observed. In the case study, few teachers achieved a very high level of adherence to the CSR model, which is a limitation of this research. For instance, while most teachers taught Preview components (which are implemented at the beginning of CSR lessons and are also features of overall quality literacy instruction emphasized in the district in which the study was conducted), the majority failed to consistently implement the Questions and Review components that occur toward the end of the model. Other items were observed infrequently because they were more difficult (e.g., discussing and providing feedback). Additional research will be needed to understand how rarely observed items related to a particular intervention influence learning (in the case of CSR) or outcomes in general.

A second limitation is that FOI provides information about adherence to the intended model. As we have argued, accurate measurement of FOI is needed to draw conclusions about a program's outcomes. Still, we are cognizant of Guttiérez and Penuel's (2014) caution that

> "Scientifically rigorous research on what works in education requires sustained, direct, and systematic documentation of what takes place inside programs to document not only 'what happens'... but also how students and teachers change and adapt interventions in interactions with each other in relation to their dynamic local contexts" (p. 19).

The IVC-R was designed to assess features of the CSR model and was therefore not sensitive to adaptations. Future research should continue to expand on rigorous methods for measuring fidelity in ways that also capture localized adaptations.

Finally, we recognize that significant shifts in research planning and allocation of resources may be needed to meet the standards for validation reported here. Yet, we argue that attention to validation of FOI instruments allows for more complex ways of understanding how new practices are taken up in classrooms, and may thus allow us to learn more from the studies we are able to undertake. For example, the research presented in the case study included significant collaboration between measurement experts, researchers, program developers, and practitioners to plan how best to develop and validate the IVC-R. Such collaborations can only benefit the field as those with different expertise build on each other's knowledge and experiences. The approach outlined in this article serves as an example of a way in which FOI can be better understood. Future research should continue to expand the uses of fidelity data to inform design, implementation, and evaluation of classroom-based instructional programs.

Notes

The authors would like to acknowledge the substantial intellectual contribution of Dr. Janette Klingner to the development and study of CSR. Dr. Klingner's legacy in special education, reading comprehension strategy instruction for culturally and linguistically diverse students, and enhancing the sustainability of evidence-based and culturally responsive instructional practices will inform teachers and researchers for years to come. Dr. Janette Klingner passed away in March, 2014. We would also like to acknowledge Dr. Sharon Vaughn and Dr. Greg Roberts and their team at the University of Texas at Austin for their contribution to the study of CSR fidelity and the development of the original CSR IVC.

This research was supported by grant U396B100143, from Investing in Innovation, U.S. Department of Education. The content is solely the responsibility of the authors and does not necessarily represent the official views of the U.S. Department of Education.

Underlying research materials related to this article can be accessed by contacting Dr. Pamela Buckley (Pamela.Buckley@colorado.edu).

References

Abbott, M. L., & Fouts, J. T. (2003). Constructivist teaching and student achievement: The results of a school-level classroom observation study in Washington. Lynnwood, WA: Washington School Research Center. Retrieved from: http://eri c.ed.gov/?id=ED481694

American Educational Research Association, American Psychological Association, & National Council on Measurement in Education. (2014). *Standards for educational and psychological testing*. Washington DC: American Educational Research Association.

Belsky, J., Booth-LaForce, C. L., Bradley, R., Brownell, C. A., Burchinal, M., Campbell, S. B., & Weinraub, M. (2005). A day in third grade: A large-scale study of classroom quality and teacher and student behavior. *Elementary School Journal, 105*(3), 305–323. doi:10.1086/428746.

Boardman, A. G., Buckley, P., Vaughn, S., Roberts, G., Scornavacco, K., & Klingner, J. (2016a). The relationship between implementation of Collaborative Strategic Reading and student outcomes for adolescents with disabilities. *Journal of Learning Disabilities, 49*(6), 644–657. doi:10.1177/0022219416640784.

Boardman, A. G., Klingner, J. K., Buckley, P., Annamma, S., & Lasser, C. J. (2015). Collaborative Strategic Reading in content classes: Results from year 1 of a randomized control trial. *Reading and Writing: An Interdisciplinary Journal, 28*(9), 1257–1283. doi:10.1007/s11145-015-9570-3.

Boardman, A. G., Vaughn, S., Buckley, P., Reutebuch, C., Roberts, G., & Klingner, J. (2016b). Efficacy of Collaborative Strategic Reading with upper elementary school students: Results of a randomized control trial. *Exceptional Children, 82*(4), 409–427. doi:10.1177/0014402915625067.

Bollen, K., & Lennox, R. (1991). Conventional wisdom on measurement: A structural equation perspective. *Psychological Bulletin, 110*, 305–314. doi:10.1037/0033-2909.110.2.305.

Bradshaw, C. P., Mitchell, M. M., & Leaf, P. J. (2010). Examining the effects of schoolwide positive behavioral interventions and supports on student outcomes: Results from a randomized controlled effectiveness trial in elementary schools. *Journal of Positive Behavioral Interventions, 12*, 161–179. doi:10.1177/1098300709334798.

Cappella, E., Kim, H.Y., Neal, J. W., & Jackson, D. R. (2013). Classroom peer relationships and behavioral engagement in elementary school: The role of social network equity. *American Journal of Community Psychology, 52*, 367–379. doi:10.1007/s10464-013-9603-5.

Carroll, C., Patterson, M., Wood, S., Booth, A., Risk, J., & Balain, S. (2007). A conceptual framework for implementation fidelity. *Implementation Science, 2*, 40. doi:10.1186/1748-5908-2-40

Cavanagh, R.F. & Koehler, M.J. (2013) A turn toward specifying validity criteria in the measurement of Technological Pedagogical Content Knowledge (TPACK). *Journal of Research on Technology in Education, 46*(2), 129–148. doi: 10.1080/15391523.2013.10782616.

Childs, K. E., Kincaid, D., George, H. P., & Gage, N. A. (2016). The relationship between school-wide implementation of positive behavior intervention and supports and student discipline outcomes. *Journal of Positive Behavior Interventions, 18*(2), 89–99. doi:10.1177/1098300715590398.

Cohen, R., Kincaid, D., & Childs, K. E. (2007). Measuring School-wide Positive Behavior Support implementation: Development and validation of the

Benchmarks of Quality. *Journal of Positive Behavior Interventions, 9*(4), 203–213. doi:10.1177/10983007070090040301.

Cordray, D. S., & Pion, G. M. (2006). Treatment strength and integrity: Models and methods. In R. R. Bootzin & P. E. McKnight (Eds.), *Strengthening research methodology: Psychological measurement and evaluation* (pp. 103–124). Washington, DC: American Psychological Association.

Crocker, L. M., & Algina, J. (1986). *Introduction to classical and modern test theory.* New York, NY: Holt, Rinehart, and Winston.

Dane, A. V., & Schneider, B. H. (1998). Program integrity in primary and early secondary prevention: Are implementation effects out of control? *Clinical Psychology Review, 18,* 23–45. doi:10.1016/S0272-7358(97)00043-3.

Devine, S. L., Rapp, J. T., Testa, J. R., Henrickson, M. L., & Schnerch, G. (2011). Detecting changes in simulated events using partial-interval recording and momentary time sampling III: Evaluating sensitivity as a function of session length. *Behavioral Interventions, 26,* 103–124. doi:10.1002/bin.328.

Drake, R. E., & Resnick, S. G. (1998). Models of community care for severe mental illness: A review of research on case management. *Schizophrenia Bulletin, 24,* 37–43. doi:https://doi.org/10.1093/oxfordjournals.schbul.a033314.

Edwards, J. R., & Bagozzi, R. P. (2000). On the nature and direction of relationships between constructs and measures. *Psychological Methods, 5,* 155–174. doi:10.1037/1082-989X.5.2.155.

Fish, M. C., & Dane, E. (2000). The classroom systems observation scale: Development of an instrument to assess classrooms using a systems perspective. *Learning Environments Research, 3,* 67–92. doi:10.1023/A:1009979122896.

Flavell, J. H. (1979). Metacognition and cognitive monitoring: A new area of cognitive-developmental inquiry. *American Psychologist, 34,* 906–911. doi:10.1037/0003-066X.34.10.906.

Flower, A., McKenna, J., Muething, C. S., Bryant, D. P., & Bryant, B. R. (2014). Effects of the good behavior game on classwide off-task behavior in a high school basic algebra resource classroom. *Behavior Modification, 38*(1), 45–68. doi:10.1177/0145445513507574.

Freeman, J., Simonsen, B., McCoach, D. B., Sugai, G., Lombardi, A., & Horner, R. (2016). Relationship between School-Wide Positive Behavior Interventions and Supports and academic, attendance, and behavior outcomes in high schools. *Journal of Positive Behavior Interventions, 18*(1), 41–51. doi:10.1177/1098300715580992.

Garet, M. S., Porter, A. C., Desimone, L., Birman, B. F., & Yoon, K. S. (2001). What makes professional development effective? Results from a national sample of teachers. *American Educational Research Journal, 38*(4), 915–945. doi:10.3102/00028312038004915.

George, H. P., & Childs, K. E. (2012). Evaluating implementation of schoolwide behavior support: Are we doing it well? *Preventing School Failure, 56,* 197–206. doi:10.1080/1045988X.2011.645909.

Greenhalgh, T., Robert, G., Macfarlane, F., Bate, P., & Kyriakidou, O. (2004). Diffusion of innovations in service organizations: systematic review and recommendations. *Milbank Quarterly, 82*(4), 581–629. doi:10.1111/j.0887-378X.2004.00325.x.

Gutiérrez, K. D., & Penuel, W. R. (2014). Relevance to practice as a criterion for rigor. *Educational Researcher, 43,* 19–23. doi:10.3102/0013189X13520289.

Guo, Y., Connor, C. M., Yang, Y, Roehrig, A. D., & Morrison, F. J. (2012). The effects of teacher qualification, teacher self-efficacy, and classroom practices on fifth graders' literacy outcomes, *The Elementary School Journal, 113*(1), 3–24. doi:10.1086/665816.

Hamre, B. K., Pianta, R. C., Mashburn, A. J., & Downer, J. T. (2007). Building a science of classrooms: Application of the CLASS framework in over 4,000 US early childhood and elementary classrooms. New York, NY: Foundation for Child Development. Retrieved from http://fcd-us.org/sites/default/files/BuildingA ScienceOfClassroomsPiantaHamre.pdf.

Heck, S., Steigelbauer, S. M., Hall, G. E., & Loucks, S. F. (1981). *Measuring innovation configurations: Procedures and applications.* Austin, TX. Research and Development Center for Teacher Education, University of Texas.

Hill, H. C., Charalambous, C. Y., & Kraft, M. A. (2012). When rater reliability is not enough: Teacher observation systems and a case for the generalizability study. *Educational Researcher, 41*, 56–64. doi:10.3102/0013189X12437203.

Hill, H. C., & Grossman, P. (2013). Learning from teacher observations: Challenges and opportunities posed by new teacher evaluation systems. *Harvard Educational Review, 83*(2), 371–384. doi:10.17763/haer.83.2.d11511403715u376.

Horner, R. H., Todd, A. W., Lewis-Palmer, T., Irvin, L. K., Sugai, G., & Boland, J. B. (2004). The School-wide Evaluation Tool (SET): A research instrument for assessing school-wide positive behavior support. *Journal of Positive Behavior Interventions, 6*(1), 3–12. doi:10.1177/10983007040060010201.

Horner, R. H., Sugai, G., & Anderson, C. M. (2010). Examining the evidence base for school-wide positive behavior support. *Focus on Exceptionality, 42*(8), 1–14.

Hulleman, C. S., & Cordray, D. S. (2009). Moving from the lab to the field: The role of fidelity and achieved relative intervention strength. *Journal of Research and Educational Effectiveness, 2*, 88–110. doi:10.1080/19345740802539325.

Johnson, D. W., & Johnson, R. T. (1999). Making cooperative learning work. *Theory into Practice, 38*(2), 67–73. doi:10.1080/00405849909543834.

Kagan, S. (1986). Cooperative learning and sociocultural factors in schooling. In Bilingual Education Office, California State Department of Education (Ed.), *Beyond language: Social and cultural factors in schooling language minority students.* Los Angeles, CA: Evaluation, Dissemination and Assessment Center, California State University.

Kane, M. T. (2006). Validation. In R. L. Brennan (Ed.), *Educational measurement* (4th ed., pp. 17–64). Santa Barbara, CA: Greenwood Publishing Group.

Kazdin, A. E., & Kendall, P. C. (1998). Current progress and future plans for developing effective treatments: Comment and perspectives. *Journal of Clinical Child Psychology, 60*, 733–747. doi:10.1207/s15374424jccp2702_8.

Kim, A. H., Vaughn, S., Klingner, J. K., Woodruff, A. L., Klein, C., & Kouzekanani, K. (2006). Improving the reading comprehension of middle school students with disabilities through Computer-Assisted Collaborative Strategic Reading (CACSR). *Remedial and Special Education, 27*, 235–248. doi:10.1177/0741932 5060270040401.

Klingner, J. K., Vaughn, S., Arguelles, M. E., Hughes, M. T., & Leftwich, S.A. (2004). Collaborative Strategic Reading: "Real world" lessons from classroom teachers. *Remedial and Special Education, 25*, 291–302. doi:10.1177/074193250402 50050301.

Klingner, J. K., Vaughn, S., Boardman, A. G., & Swanson, E. (2012). *Now we get it! Boosting comprehension with Collaborative Strategic Reading.* San Francisco, CA: Jossey Bass.

Klingner, J. K., Vaughn, S., & Schumm, J. S. (1998). Collaborative Strategic Reading during social studies in heterogeneous fourth-grade classrooms. *Elementary School Journal, 99*, 3–22. doi:http://dx.doi.org/10.1086/461914.

Lawrence, J. F., & Snow, C. (2010). Oral discourse and reading. In M. Kamil, P. D. Pearson, E. B. Moje, & P. Afflerbach (Eds.), *Handbook of reading research* (Vol. 4). Mahwah, NJ: Erlbaum.

Lewis, T. J., & Sugai, G. (1999). Effective behavior support: A systems approach to proactive schoolwide management. *Focus on Exceptional Children, 31*(6), 1.

MacGinitie, W. H., MacGinitie, R. K., Maria, K., & Dreyer, L. G. (2000). *Gates–MacGinitie Reading Tests* (4th ed.). Itasca, IL: Riverside.

McKennel, A. C. (1974). Surveying attitude structures. Amsterdam, the Netherlands: Elsevier

Messick, S. (1988). The once and future issues of validity: Assessing the meaning and consequences of measurement. In H. Wainer & H. Braun (Eds.), *Test validity* (pp. 33–48). Hillsdale, NJ: Erlbaum.

Mowbray, C., Holter, M. C., Teague, G. B., & Bybee, D. (2003). Fidelity criteria: Development, measurement, and validation. *American Journal of Evaluation, 24*, 315–340. doi:10.1177/109821400302400303.

Munter, C., Wilhelm, A. G., Cobb, P., & Cordray, D. S. (2014). Assessing fidelity of implementation of an unprescribed, diagnostic mathematics intervention, *Journal of Research on Educational Effectiveness, 7*(1), 83–113. doi:10.1080/19345747.2013.809177.

Nelson, M. C., Cordray, D. S., Hulleman, C. S., Darrow, C. L., & Sommer, E. C. (2012). A procedure for assessing intervention fidelity in experiments testing educational and behavioral interventions. *The Journal of Behavioral Health Services & Research, 39*(4), 374–396. doi:10.1007/s11414-012-9295-x.

Nelson, M. C. (2013). *New tools for intervention fidelity assessment* (Doctoral dissertation, Vanderbilt University). Retrieved from http://etd.library.vanderbilt.edu/available/etd-04032013-015440/unrestricted/mnelson.pdf.

O'Donnell, C. L. (2008). Defining, conceptualizing, and measuring fidelity of implementation and its relation to outcomes in K–12 curriculum intervention research. *Review of Educational Research, 78*, 33–84. doi:10.3102/0034654307313793.

Palincsar, A. S., & Brown, A. L. (1984). The reciprocal teaching of comprehension-fostering and comprehension-monitoring activities. *Cognition and Instruction, 1*, 117–175. doi:10.1207/s1532690xci0102_1.

Pianta, R. C., & Hamre, B. K. (2009). Conceptualization, measurement, and improvement of classroom processes: Standardized observation can leverage capacity. *Educational Researcher, 38*, 109–119. doi:10.3102/0013189X09332374.

Piburn, M., & Sawada, D. (2000). Reformed Teaching Observation Protocol (RTOP) reference manual. Retrieved from: http://files.eric.ed.gov/fulltext/ED447205.pdf.

Raudenbush, S. W., Bryk, T., & Congdon, R. (2010). HLM 7 hierarchical linear and nonlinear modeling. [Computer software]. Skokie, IL: Scientific Software International.

Raudenbush, S. W., & Bryk, T (2002). *Hierarchical linear models: Applications and data analysis methods.* Thousand Oaks, CA: Sage.

Rogers, E. (2003). *Diffusion of innovations.* New York, NY: Free Press.

Rosenbaum, P. R. (1995). *Observational Studies.* New York, NY: Springer-Verlag.

Sawada, D., Piburn, M. D., Judson, E., Turley, J., Falconer, K., Benford, R., & Bloom, I. (2002). Measuring reform practices in science and mathematics classrooms: The Reformed Teaching Observation Protocol. *Measuring Reform Practices, 10*(6), 245–253. doi:10.1111/j.1949-8594.2002.tb17883.x.

Scammacca, N., Roberts, G., Vaughn, S., Edmonds, M., Wexler, J., Reutebuch, C. K., & Torgesen, J. K. (2007). Reading interventions for adolescent struggling readers: A meta-analysis with implications for practice. Portsmouth, NH: RMC Research

Corporation, Center on Instruction. Retrieved from http://files.eric.ed.gov/full text/ED521837.pdf.

Schechter, S., Blair, J., & Hey, J. V. (1996). Conducting cognitive interviews to test self-administered and telephone surveys: Which methods should we use? In 1996 *Proceedings of the Section on Survey Research Methods* (pp. 10–17). Alexandria, VA: American Statistical Association.

Schoenwald, S. K., Garland, A. F., Chapman, J. E., Frazier, S. L., Sheidow, A. J., & Southam-Gerow, M. (2011). Toward the effect and efficient measurement of implementation fidelity. *Administration and Policy in Mental Health and Mental Health Services Research*, *38*(1): 32–43. doi:10.1007/s10488-010-0321-0.

Shulman, L. (1990). Foreword. In M. Ben-Peretz, *The teacher–curriculum encounter: Freeing teachers from the tyranny of texts*. Albany, NY: State University of New York Press.

Tiger, J. H., Miller, S. J., Mevers, J. L., Mintz, J., Scheithauer, M. C., & Alvarez, J. (2013). On the representativeness of behavior samples in classrooms. *Journal of Applied Behavior Analysis*, *46*, 424–435. doi:10.1002/jaba.39

Vaughn, S., Klingner, J., Swanson, E. A., Boardman, A. G., Roberts, G., Mohammed, S., & Stillman-Spisak, S. J. (2011). Efficacy of collaborative strategic reading with middle school students. *American Educational Research Journal*, *48*, 938–964. doi:10.3102/0002831211410305.

Vaughn, S., Roberts, G., Klingner, J., Swanson, E., Boardman, A., Stillman-Spisak, S.J., Mohammed, S., & Leroux, A. (2013). Collaborative strategic reading: Findings from experienced implementers. *Journal of Research on Educational Effectiveness*, *6*(2), 137–163. doi:10.1080/19345747.2012.741661.

Wanzek, J., Vaughn, S., Kent, S., Swanson, E. A., Roberts, G, Haynes, M., . . . Solis, M. (2014). The effects of team-based learning on social studies knowledge acquisition in high school. *Journal of Research on Educational Effectiveness*, *7*, 183–204. doi:doi:10.1080/19345747.2013.836765.

Wilson, M. (2004). *Constructing measures: An item response modeling approach*. New York, NY: Routledge.

Manuscript received January 28, 2016
Final revision received June 22, 2017
Accepted June 24, 2017

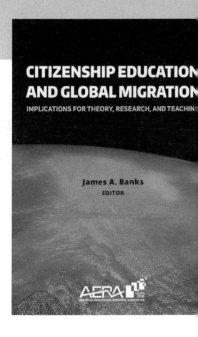

EDUCATION

From Chicago

The Testing Charade

Pretending to Make Schools Better

Daniel Koretz

Cloth $25.00

Educational Goods

Values, Evidence, and Decision-Making

Harry Brighouse, Helen F. Ladd, Susanna Loeb, and Adam Swift

Paper $27.50

What Do *You* Think, Mr. Ramirez?

The American Revolution in Education

Geoffrey Galt Harpham

Paper $25.00

American Academic Cultures

A History of Higher Education

Paul H. Mattingly

Paper $35.00

The University of Chicago Press

www.press.uchicago.edu